PHILOSOPHY OF GORAKHNATH

Philosophy of Gorakhnath

with

Goraksha-Vacana-Sangraha

AKSHAYA KUMAR BANERJEA

Prefatory Note by

MAHAMAHOPADHYAYA GOPINATH KAVIRAJ

Foreword by

C.P. RAMASWAMI AIYAR

MOTILAL BANARSIDASS PUBLISHERS
PRIVATE LIMITED • DELHI

First Edition: Gorakhpur, 1962
Reprint: Delhi, 1983, 1988, 1999

ISBN: 81-208-0534-8 (Cloth)
ISBN: 81-208-0535-6 (Paper)

Also available at:

MOTILAL BANARSIDASS

41 U.A. Bungalow Road, Jawahar Nagar, Delhi 110 007
8 Mahalaxmi Chamber, Warden Road, Mumbai 400 026
120 Royapettah High Road, Mylapore, Chennai 600 004
Sanas Plaza, 1302 Baji Rao Road, Pune 411 002
16 St. Mark's Road, Bangalore 560 001
8 Camac Street, Calcutta 700 017
Ashok Rajpath, Patna 800 004
Chowk, Varanasi 221 001

PRINTED IN INDIA
BY JAINENDRA PRAKASH JAIN AT SHRI JAINENDRA PRESS,
A-45 NARAINA, PHASE I, NEW DELHI 110 028
AND PUBLISHED BY NARENDRA PRAKASH JAIN FOR
MOTILAL BANARSIDASS PUBLISHERS PRIVATE LIMITED,
BUNGALOW ROAD, DELHI 110 007

Dedicated

To

Truth-Seekers of the World

PUBLISHER'S NOTE
TO THE SECOND EDITION

Numerous errors were detected in the first edition of this book. Most of the errors were due to the fact that the author's mother-tongue is Bengali which has only 'ब' for 'ब' and 'व' both and as a result in the Sanskrit words in which the letter 'व' occurs and their Romanization 'ब'/'b' was wrongly used in the first edition. Such errors have been corrected in this edition.

But it is regretted that because of a pressing public demand for the book, it was not possible to correct the errors of diacriticals such as 'jivanmukti', 'hathyoga', 'śunya', 'samasti', 'vyasti', 'varna', etc. which as a rule with complete diacritical marks should be written as jīvanmukti, haṭha-yoga, śūnya, samaṣṭi, vyaṣṭi, and varṇa respectively, since it would have meant re-composing the whole thing which would have proved to be a very time-consuming and costly affair.

FOREWORD

BY

Śrī C. P. Ramaswamī Aiyar

Dealing with the long chronicle of Indian Philosophy and thought, one cannot but realise that our country has been fortunate, from time to time, in having given birth to Sages and Yogis who have interpreted and re-interpreted the primeval message contained in the Vedas, the Puranas and the Prasthānatraya, and added to by successive Seers according to the needs and circumstances of the times.

This volume contains the essence of the writings and teachings of Mahayogi Gorakhnath. It is well pointed out that while the ultimate object of search is the same for a Yogi and a philosopher, their modes of approach are different, the latter's being intellectual and the former's intuitive and spiritual. The task of a Yogi does not require any subtle intellectual speculation or the framing of hypotheses and theories. The quest of the Yogi is direct spiritual experience of truth on a high plane of consciousness. The highest state of Samādhi attained by the Yogi is neither purely subjective nor objective. It transcends both categories and it is really an integrated experience beyond formal description. Such a transcendent state of consciousness is alone called Samādhi. This book analyses in detail the nature of Samādhi Experience. The term "Experience" is perhaps inaccurate, because in this state of Samādhi, there is no relation between subject and object, the experiencer and the experienced. It is the fulfilment of life as described in the Yogasutras. The Yogi who comes back from Samādhi may not have attained Kaivalya or Moksha, but he is illuminated by his experience. If he assumes the role of a teacher or preacher, he gives expression to his experience in such forms as may be easily intelligible to the people at large. Gorakhnath was a Mahā-Yogi. He did not indulge in controversial metaphysics. As pointed out in this book, the Sampradāya associated with the name of Gorakhnath is embodied in a great body of literature in Sanskrit and other languages. It is further stated that the Metaphysical doctrine which Gorakhnath preached and the discipline of his Yoga rested upon his experience which lay beyond the domain of mind and intellect.

Chapter II of the book deals with the sources of the Sage's philosophical views and this volume is mainly based upon the Siddha

Siddhānta Paddhati. This book is written partly in the form of Sutras or aphorisms and partly in the form of discourses and seeks to explain the philosophy and yoga-discipline of the Siddha Sampradāya. In the introductory verse, the name of Siva is invoked as the greatest of Yogis and Gorakhnath (also called by the names of Srinath and Nityanath) discusses various philosophical topics under several heads called Upadeśas or lessons. His theory is that the Supreme Spirit, though essentially above time and space, manifests itself as a diversified Universe in the form of countless orders of individual bodies and also as the Indwelling Soul. The various Yogic centres in the physical form and other aspects of the Yoga Philosophy are elucidated and it is shown how the human body can be spiritualised and obtain Kāya Siddhi. The discussion then proceeds to identify the individual body with the cosmic body and thereafter, the function of Sakti or the Supreme Spiritual Power is explained and expounded. The Unification of the individual body with the cosmic body and the process by which it is achieved is then dealt with and finally, the conduct, behaviour and outlook of the Avadhuta Yogi are recounted. The conception of Ultimate Reality is perfected by Super-conscious experience and a whole chapter is devoted to what is termed Parā-Sambit. A most suggestive account is given in this book of the manifestation of the power of the Supreme Spirit and the development of the cosmic system.

Chapter XI deals with the evolution of world systems, including in this expression, not only the world of animal bodies and manifestations, but the world of mind, the world of reason or Buddhi and the world of Dharma or moral order, which is described as a special manifestation in the moral consciousness. It is then explained how the Absolute Spirit seems to hide its essential character behind phenomenon. Through the Vimarśa Śakti of the Supreme Spirit, various forms of knowledge, wisdom, desire, actions and feelings emerge. In fact, the problems of the existence of evil can be solved only by a complete realisation of the Vedic maxim '*tatwamasi*'.

An outline of Lord Buddha's teachings as well as of the Sankhya system forms an important part of the book. Discussion then turns on the philosophy of action as compared and contrasted with the philosophy of renunciation (namely, Pravṛttimarga, Nivṛttimārga and Bhakti marga). Discussions on the Sankhya Darsana of Kapila, the doctrine of cycles and the explanation of the various Gunas form the subject of a complete chain of arguments. The significance of the Bhagavat Gitā, from the point of view above stated, is followed by a general disquisition on the works of Vyasa, Valmiki and the Puranakartas. The Siva-Sakti-Vāda and the

Brahma-Sakti-Vāda end up with the assertion that the Supreme Spirit may be conceived and represented in the form of a Divine Couple associated by union. In other words, Brahman is one in two and two in one, the dynamic aspect of the Absolute Spirit being represented by Sakti. The description of the Aspects of Nārāyana and Lakshmī, Krishna and Rādhā, Ram and Sitā and the process of worship of various names and forms of Siva and Sakti end up with a full discussion of the objectives and rationale of image worship.

The last Chapter of the book deals with Modern Hinduism and the impact on Modern India of Western culture and ideas. It is emphasised that a comprehensive synthesis of Karma, Jñāna, Yoga and Bhakti are essential, as well as the implementation of the harmony of religious faiths and the recognition of the spiritual efficacy of all modes of discipline following upon the discovery of the underlying unity of all forms of true faith.

This volume is the result of profound research and contains a closely-reasoned and logically-constructed analysis of Bhakti Yoga which is not irreconcilable and can be coordinated with the Yoga of wisdom or Jñāna.

C.P. Ramaswami Aiyar

29.10.1961

A PREFATORY NOTE

BY

Mahamahopadhyaya Gopinath Kaviraj, M. A., D., Litt.

An attempt has been made in the following pages to present a systematic and consistent account of the philosophical background of the spiritual culture associated with the names of Yogi Goraksha Nāth and other adepts of the Nātha Brotherhood. The account is mainly based on an original Sanskrit Text of the school attributed to Goraksha Nāth or Nitya Nāth. It is difficult to say how far this account reflects the actual teachings of Goraksha Nāth, but it is believed that it faithfully records some of the traditional views of the school. I congratulate the author on the great ability with which he has accomplished his self-imposed task,—a task which is difficult not only for the great depth of *Yogic* wisdom implied in the teachings, but also for the great paucity of necessary materials.

The writer has said almost everything worth knowing for a beginner in regard to the philosophical outlook of *Nāthism*. The Ultimate Reality —Brahman and Parā-Samvit; the inter-relation of Śiva and Śakti; the gradual unfoldment of the Supreme Śakti and the origin of the universe consisting of an infinite series of world-systems; the appearance of the individual souls and their relation to the Cosmic Purusha; the Supreme ideal of human life; the relation between macrocosm and microcosm; the Universe Body of the Transcendent;—these are some of the topics on which the learned author has tried to throw light. As Nāthism represents a particular aspect of Hindu spiritual life, the writer has done well in dealing at some length with the ideal of Hindu spirituality in general.

The Supreme Ideal of *Yoga-Sādhana* as conceived in this school seems to differ essentially from the conceptions of Patanjali, of the earlier and some later Buddhistic systems and even to a great extent of Śankara's Vedānta. Nevertheless we must observe that the Nātha ideal is analogous to what we find in the Āgamic systems of non-dualistic thought in ancient and medieval India.

This Ideal is described in one word as *Sāmarasya*, which implies obliteration of traces of all kinds of existing differences, not by a process of *transcendence* as in Sānkhya, or of *sublation* as in Vedāntic Māyāvāda, but by a positive process of what may be described as *mutual interpenetra-*

tion. This ideal underlies the principle of unification between *Purusha* and *Prakriti*, or between *Śiva* and *Śakti*. The attainment of this ideal is the Supreme Unity of *Parama Śiva*, where Śiva and Śakti are one undivided and indivisible Whole. It is called *Mahā·Śakti* in the language of the *Śaktas* and represents the Absolute of the Śākta Āgamas. It stands for the *Samatā* of the Avadhūta Yogins, which is really a unification from the logical point of view of *Tattwa* and *Tattwātīta*, i.e. the One and the Beyond.

A cursory glance at the ancient spiritual literature of India would reveal the fact that in almost all the systems associated with Āgamic culture we find a strong insistence on the ideal of *Sāmarasya* in some form or other. By way of illustration I may refer to the *Tāntric Buddhism* of the *Kālachakra* school, in which the union of *Prajñā* and *Upāya*, technically known as *Vajrayoga*, is strongly emphasized.

Thus the *Hevajra Tantra* says:—

समं तुल्यमित्युक्तं स्यात् तस्य चक्रे रसः स्मृतः ।
समरसं त्वेकभावमेतेनात्मनि भण्यते ॥

The *Vajrayoga* which is the ideal of *Kālachakra Buddhism* represents in fact the state of Supreme Oneness.

The *Vīra Śaivas* of the *Jangam* School also recognise this ideal in their own way. A brilliant exposition in the form of *Sāmarasya Bhakti* representing the self-luminous Unity of Delight realised after a course of continued *sādhana* is to be found in Māyideva's *Anubhava-Sutra* and in Prabhudeva's works.

The *Swacchanda-Tantra* which is one of the earliest Āgamas available to us furnishes a detailed account of the several stages in the process of the unification which ends in Supreme *Sāmarasya*. In this process seven grades are mentioned and described.

Swatantrānanda Nātha, the author of *Mātrikā Cakra Viveka*, was a brilliant exponent of the *Siddha* School. He explains this doctrine in his own inimitable manner. He says,—

मायाबलात् प्रथमभासि जडस्वभावम्
विद्योदयादथ विकस्वरचिन्मयत्वम् ।
सुप्त्याह्वयं किमपि विश्रमणं विभाति
चित्रक्रमं चिदचिदेकरसस्वभावम् ॥

Here in this context the *Sāmarasya* referred to is between *Cit* and

Acit, i. e. between Consciousness and Unconsciousness, which neutralise each other and appear as One. He illustrates this with an interesting example of a pictorial representation, which in reality is one, but which appears to one onlooker as representing an elephant and to another as representing a bull according to the view-point taken.

In the *yogic sādhana* of certain *Tāntric* schools, especially those affiliated to the *Ardhakālī* line, we are told that the two twelve-syllabled *Mantras* constituting the complete *Pādukā-Mantra* of *Śrī Gurudeva* represent *Unmanī* and *Samanī* aspects of the Absolute respectively. The former suggests the upward motion in the direction of the Supreme Purusha (ह) with the Supreme Prakriti (स). The latter suggests that the Supreme Prakriti (स) which descends from the glance (ईक्षण) of *Para-Brahma* or *Unmanī Śiva* floods with Delight the Supreme Purusha (ह) in the course of its descent. These symbolize in the undivided Absolute Consciousness (चित्) both the upward and downward movements of the Divine. Behind *Unmanā* and *Samanā* there is only one single Essence, for *Purusha* and *Prakriti* are ultimately one and the same *Brahman*, one symbolized by the triangle with its vertex upwards and the other by the triangle with its vertex downwards. The familiar diagram of *Shatkona* as an interlaced figure signifies this union which is represented (they say) by the twelve-petalled lotus above the pericarp of the *Sahasradala* Lotus. In fact the conception of *Guru-Pādukā* in its highest expression is the conception of *Sāmarasya* par excellence.

It is said,—

स्वप्रकाश शिवमूर्ति रेकिका
तद्विमर्श तनुरेकिका, तयोः ।
सामरस्य वपुरिष्यते परा
पादुका परशिवात्मनो गुरोः ॥

This indicates that the *Divine Guru* or *Para Śiva* has three *Pādukās*, two being lower and one higher. The two lower *Pādukās* symbolise Self-luminous *Śiva* on one hand and His Self-reflecting *Śakti* on the other. The higher *Pādukā* is the integration in the form of *Sāmarasya* of the two in the Supreme Unity.

It may be noted in passing that even the realisation of Christian Trinity is only a partial manifestation of the truth of *Sāmarasya*. The great Spanish saint Teressa through Divine Grace once realised this and tried to express it in her own language, in course of which she said that at first an illumination shining like a most dazzling cloud of Light appeared before her followed by the emergence of the three Persons of Trinity. She felt that the three Persons were all of one Substance, Power and Knowledge and were one God. This vision was not the result of the function of the bodily eye nor even of the eye of the soul. It was an intellectual vision of an intimate kind. Henry Suso, the disciple of the great German mystic Meister Eckhart referred to the union of the soul and God. She spoke of God as saying,— "I will kiss them (the suffering saints) affectionately and embrace them so lovingly that I shall be they and they shall be I and the two shall be united in one for ever". Elsewhere it is said,— "The essence of the soul is united with the essence of the Nothing and the powers of the one with the activities of the Nothing". (The Little Book of the Truth, edited by J. M. Clark, Page 196). This is exactly like the union *(Samyoga)* of *Linga* or *Paramātmā* with *Ātmā* of the *Vīra Saiva* School.

From what has been said above it is abundantly clear that in some form or other *Sāmarasya* is the ideal, not only of the Āgamic Culture, but also of many other spiritual *sādhanas*.

It now remains to be seen how the Nātha Yogins conceived this highest consummation of Oneness. It is said that the true process of *Sāmarasya* begins only when the Sadguru's grace has succeeded in effecting Mental Quiet (चित्त-विश्रान्ति). The real *sādhana* cannot commence until the mind is rendered quiet and free from disturbances incident on a sense of identity with the body. The mind being at rest, the Divine Bliss and an experience of Pure Infinite Glory dawn on the soul which is awakened from its age-long slumber. The sense of duality disappears in the serene Light of Undifferentiated Unity. This Light, unbounded and one, brings out the powers of Consciousness. The Universal Consciousness being once awakened produces in the *yogin* a perfect knowledge of his own Body, which results in the illumination and stabilization of the Body concerned (पिण्ड सिद्धि).

In other words this Body becomes immortal and immune from the ravaging effects of Time. The *Yogi* is now an adept (सिद्ध). This Luminous Form which is the essence of *Caitanya* has to be made, as a further step, one with the Universal Uncreated Light of *Paramapada* already revealed. This is done through a continuous process of investigation into the real nature of *Ātmā*. It is to be remembered that *Sāmarasya* should not be a momentary attainment, but a permanent possession, in the sense that no reversal (व्युत्थान) may ever occur. Before this state (निरुत्थान) is made permanent after *Sāmarasya* is once attained, some successive moments in the Supreme Experience are noted :

(I) The Transcendental Reality is revealed as the Universe. In other words, the difference between what is Formless and what has Form disappears for ever and it is co-eternal with the vision of the Universe in *Ātmā*.

(II) In the transitional stage there is a tendency in the Powers to move out. This has to be restrained and the Powers kept as contained within the *Ātmā*.

(III) The *Ātmā* is realised as a continuum of unbroken *Prakāśa* with Supreme Dynamism.

(IV) As a result of all this there is a unique Vision of Being which is unborn. This is the Supreme Integral Vision which marks the stage of *Nirutthāna*. It is a Vision of Eternity when infinite varieties are seen as an expression of the One and when the One reveals Itself in every point of the Infinite.

It seems true that the Nātha-Yogin's view of पिण्ड सिद्धि and Patanjali's idea of कायसंपत् are not exactly the same, though it is true that in each the control of the elements is the result The ideal of (वज्रदेह) was behind both and dominated the Tāntric Buddhist also. In 'Nāthism' the fact that पिण्ड सिद्धि results from a vision of *Paramapada* and is an antecedent of the unification of the two indicates that, though Patanjali's कायसंपत् aims at physical purification to its utmost extent, it can never be equated to the natural purity of ***Purusha*** and continues to remain an inalienable property of ***Prakriti***.

In this light it may be presumed that the criticism of Goraksha Nāth's ideal of पिण्ड सिद्धि by Prabhudeva, as found in legends current in some South Indian Śaiva- schools, has to be explained as the outcome of sheer sectarianism.*

The Nātha ideal is first to realise ***Jivanmukti*** through पिण्ड सिद्धि which secures an Immaculate Body of Light free from the influence of Time, i.e. a deathless undecaying spiritual body and then to realise ***Parā-Mukti*** or the Highest Perfection through the process of mutual integration (समरसीकरण). The Bengali Nātha work, entitled हाड़माला, a comparatively late work of the

---

* For *Deha-Siddhi* the reader is referred to the following :—

(1) The Doctrinal Culture and Tradition of the Siddhas, by V. V. Raman Sastri in the Cultural Heritage of India, Vol. II. Pages 303—319.

(2) M. M. Gopinath Kaviraj's Series of articles in Bengali on the *Process of effecting physical immortality*, published in the Bengali Weekly Paper, *Himadri*.

(3) M. M. Gopinath Kaviraj's article in Sanskrit on the subject, in the 'Saraswati Sushamā Journal' of the Varanasi Sanskrit University, 1961, Pages 63-87.

Nātha School of Bengal and published by Shri Prafulla Chandra Chakravarty in his book on *'Nātha Dharma and Sāhitya'*, also points out that the complete course of Nātha spiritual culture did not end with the attainment of *Siddha-Deha* through drinking of nectar after the completion of the process technically known as transcendence of the Moon ;—it was only a state of *Jivanmukti* as free from death. It is only a prelude to the realisation of the highest ideal of Perfection through the culture of *Oṁkāra*.

I have nothing more to add to this brief foreword. I have only to thank the revered author for the honour he has shown me in asking me to write a few lines by way of an introductory note to his work. I have tried even on my sickbed to comply with his request as briefly as possible. The learned author has laboured hard and long in a more or less untrodden field and as a result of his labours has presented us with a brilliant work on an important medieval school of philosophical thought. He is a pioneer worker in this field. I hope, however, that young scholars interested in the subject will follow him and try to utilise all the resources accessible to us in the different libraries of the country.

Gopinath Kaviraj.

INTRODUCTORY REMARKS

BY

Dr. Sampurnanand, Rajpal of Rajasthan

I welcome the publication of this book to which I have been invited to write a foreword. It is not for me to assess the worth of the labour and scholarship which the author has brought to bear upon his work. What is of more interest to me is that such a book has been brought out at all. The need has been felt for long by students of the religious and spiritual history of India.

It stands to reason that Goraksha,—Gorakhnath as he is popularly known,—had a most powerful personality which profoundly impressed those who came in contact with him. He probably travelled wide; in any case, his fame travelled wider. There are a number of places spread all over northern India associated with him and his disciples. There are legends, some of them of very doubtful historical authenticity, which have now become part of the traditional folk-lore of the people. Evidence of the place which Goraksha occupied in popular estimation comes from another and rather unexpected quarter. The followers of some of the Saints who followed him centuries later apparently felt that the reputation of their Master would not be placed at a sound footing unless he was shown to have been a greater man than Goraksha. Stories were, therefore, invented of disputations between Goraksha and the founder of their own school. The discussions were generally verbal, but they were not unoften accompanied by an overt or veiled display of occult power. Goraksha was, of course, invariably worsted in all such contests. There are many references to such contests in works attributed to Kabir and Nanak. Of course these great men had no hand in the authorship of these compositions, which are obviously the work of their followers, remarkable more for their devotion than commonsense. The contemptuous disregard of time which they display is breath-taking. The philosophical content of such compositions is elementary and their reference to Yogic experience not at all profound. But while they do not enhance the reputation of men like Kabir and Nanak, who, by the way, do not stand in need of such spurious support, they certainly indicate the esteem in which Goraksha's memory was held by the people several centuries after his disappearance; no one could easily be accepted as a great saint unless he was proved to be superior to Goraksha.

The story of the Nath School, of which Goraksha was such a

distinguished representative, is an important chapter in the history of India's spiritual development. The *Tantriks* were followed in course of time by the *Sādhs* (साध), the *Siddhas* (सिद्ध) and the *Nāths* (नाथ) and the succession was taken up later by the *Sant-mat* (संत मत). In a sense, none of these schools brought any absolutely new message. What they preached and practised were simply variations and derivatives of lessons which have been handed down from the most ancient times. There were apparently two schools of religion and spirituality in Vedic times which may roughly be called the orthodox and heterodox. The orthodox school, further, functioned in two forms which may be called the exoteric and the esoteric. *Karma Kanda*, the performance of Vedic sacrifices, was the concern of the former, while the latter concerned itself with *Yoga* and philosophy. There was no conflict between the two ; they complemented and supplemented each other. Those who belonged to the unorthodox school were called *Vrātyas.* They spurned ritual, did not follow many of the conventions of the Vedic society and were given to esoteric disciplines. All medieval and present-day Hindu religious and philosophical thought and spiritual discipline stemmed from these ancient schools.

The Veda declares "*Ekam Sat, Viprā bahudhā vadanti*",—The Absolute Reality is One, the wise call It by many names ; and "*Sarvam khulu idam Brahma*",—all this is verily Brahma. It is difficult for philosophy to go beyond Absolute Monism. The only possible alternative is Absolute Negation, and this pas posited by Buddhism. Almost all prominent schools of Hindu thought are variants of the theme of Monism. As for spiritual discipline, the ancient word is *Yoga,* and all the various forms of spiritual practice adopted at different times are really forms of *Yoga.* Even *Bhakti* which prides itself on being something utterly unique and different and claims to offer a straighter road to the ultimate goal of human existence is, in reality, to the extent that it is a genuine spiritual discipline, only *Yoga* with a new name.

The various schools to which I have referred,—the *Tantra*, *Sādha, Siddha*, *Nāth* and *Santmat*,—disown all connection with one another or with anything that historically preceded them. Such a position is untenable or is the product of ignorance and blind prejudice. Each new school has not received a new commission directly from God in one of His manifestations : each, in fact, learnt much from its predecessors and passed on the torch to its successors. The core of truth, which each cherishes, is *sanātana*, old as time itself. What is new is the expression of it which varies with place and time and circumstances, created by political and other external factors.

The founders of the *Nāth Sampradāya* did not propound a new system of philosophy. In this they were at one with the *Sādhs* and the *Siddhas* who had preceded them and the *Santmat* which may be considered to have succeeded them. The *Tantriks* had a philosophical doctrine worked out in great detail ; the others seem to me, from the study of their available literature, to have covered the whole gamut from the Absolute Monism of Shankaracharya to the Vishishtādvaita of Ramanuja with Shuddhādvaita of Vallabha, somewhere in between, according to personal taste and inclination. But while they did not bother themselves much about a clear exposition of philosophical theory and engage in hair-splitting discussion about subjects which really transcend reason, they paid the greatest attention to spiritual discipline, the practice of Yoga. Success in Yoga demands an unblemished character, continence and denial of all pleasures of flesh, withdrawal from the distractions of the world, and no one can deny that the fathers of the Nāth school practised these virtues to an extraordinary degree. They were recognised as great adepts in Yoga and credited with the development of those so-called occult powers which the practice of Yoga unfolds. They were objects of universal reverence coupled with awe. A school of this kind could command respect, but it could not become popular. Its doctrines and disciplines would naturally be confined to an elite ; the people at large could not be expected to live that life of austerity and self-denial which the practice of Yoga demands.

It would not be inopportune to say a few words here about Yoga. The Naths are generally reputed to be exponents of *Hatha-Yoga,* about which a good deal of misconception prevails. We hear to-day about different kinds of Yoga :—*Rāja-Yoga, Hath-Yoga, Jñāna-Yoga, Laya-Yoga, Bhakti-Yoga* and *Karma-Yoga.* These are all modern terms. They were not known to ancient Yogis and, if some of them occur at all in old literature, their use is purely incidental and not indicative of a separate and exclusive technique. The standard text-book on Yoga, Patanjali's *Yoga-Sutra,* makes no mention of them. Certain aspects of the practice of Yoga have been needlessly apotheosized and elevated to the false dignity of separate sciences, without paying heed to their inter-relations. The object of the practice of Yoga as defined by Patanjali is चित्त वृत्ति निरोधः (*Cittavritti-nirodha*) which automatically result in स्वरूपे अवस्थानम् (*Swarupe avasthanam*) of the द्रष्टा (*Drastā*). The Ego having realised itself becomes established in its own true nature, when the cessation of that ceaseless flux of stages of consciousness is brought about, which relates the 'I' to the 'not-I'. Any technique, any spiritual discipline, which aims at any other objective, is not Yoga, whatever else it may be. Goraksha or any of the other Naths did not posit any other objectives ; the whole aim of what they practised was *Moksha,* release from nescience, realisation by the Self of its true nature. This, they knew could come only by passing through the three highest stages of Yogic practice:—*Dhāranā, Dhyāna* and *Samādhi.* These are purely mental stages and after all it is the mind that has to be controlled. But they realised the absolute correctness of the procedure laid down by Patanjali. A healthy body is necessary, so is the control of the psychic and nervous currents and the emotions. Fidgettiness and hankering after the pleasures of the flesh are not conducive to concentration and mental peace. All these things classed by Patanjali under *Āsana* and *Prānāyāma* are generally associated with the modern term of *Hatha-Yoga.* As so understood, *Hatha-Yoga* is a necessary stage in Yoga, which leads directly to the higher stages of purely mental practice. It was not that he believed that the practice of bodily contortions or the control of bodily functions was the final goal of Yoga, nor was he under the delusion that such control of the body would, in and by itself, produce *Samādhi* and self-realisation. What he did, and quite rightly, was to emphasise the irrevocable necessity of going through the lower stages, which are apt to be neglected and ignored because they seem so difficult and, by a process of wishful thinking, so unnecessary.

I hope this book will succeed in stimulating attention in Goraksha and his school, which represents a notable chapter in our country's spiritual history. The works attributed to Goraksha are available in Sanskrit and Hindi. The Hindi contains some words of foreign origin here and there, indicating that the influence of the arrival of Muslims in India had already reached the part of the country in which he mostly lived. It would be interesting to study if any Sufi influence is traceable in his writings. Again, some of the technical terms he uses have been taken over by Kabir and the *nirguna* saints who came after him and are also to be found in the works of the *Sādhs.* It would be useful to find out when they first began to come into use and what the corresponding terms are in Sanskrit and Pali Yogic literature. There are so many other fields of possible research, to which a study of Nath literature would open the doors. I hope that such work will be earnestly taken up.

Mount Abu,
June 19, 1962.

SAMPURNANAND.

TABLE OF CONTENTS

Both a Yogi and a Philosopher are seekers of the Absolute Truth. But they differ in their modes of approach. A philosopher advances in the path of rational logic and wants to intellectually understand the Truth, whereas a Yogi advances in the path of moral and psychical self-discipline and aspires for spiritually realising the Truth. The conclusion of philosophical speculation cannot rise above the status of an intellectual theory (*Vāda*), whereas *yogic* spiritual discipline is expected to lead to direct supra-intellectual experience of the Truth. No theory can satisfy all truth-seekers and the history of the philosophical quest of the Absolute Truth is found to be a history of continuous intellectual warfare among different schools of philosophers. The Absolute is variously conceived by various thinkers and they refute each other's views. The Absolute Truth, which is the Soul of the universe and the Soul of every individual being, unveils its true character to the innermost illumined consciousness of a perfect Yogi in the deepest supra-intellectual transcendent state of *Samādhi*. This transcendent experience is distinct from normal or abnormal subjective experience as well as from phenomenal objective experience, but is not on that account a negation of experience. The exact nature of this experience cannot be intellectually conceived or defined; but it gives perfect satisfaction to the truth-seeking consciousness. When a Yogi returns from the illumined state of *Samādhi* to the normal plane of phenomenal experience, the deep impression of his Samādhi-experience exercises a wonderful enlightening influence upon his normal mind and intellect and behaviour. The enlightened Yogis become free from all kinds of dogmatism and bigotry and narrow outlook. They look upon all men and all affairs of the world from a spiritual point of view and live in the world as embodiments of the highest wisdom and universal love and compassion. All the highest moral and spiritual ideals of the human society originate from the enlightened Yogis. When any Yogi, out of love for humanity, assumes the role of a public teacher, he often finds it suitable to impart lessons to truth-seekers in the form of a philosophical system, which he regards as an effective mode of intellectual discipline.

CHAPTER I.—Gorakhnath—A Mahayogi. **Pages 23-25.**

Gorakhnath was an enlightened Mahāyogi, and not a philosopher in the commonly accepted meaning of the term. He did not attach any primary importance to metaphysical speculations and controversies as a means to the realisation of the Ultimate Truth. But he considered them valuable as modes of intellectual discipline and helpful in the path of search for Truth. He adopted philosophical reflection as a part of the comprehensive *yogic* self-discipline, which alone could lead to the perfect illumination of consciousness and the transcendent experience of the Absolute Truth. Gorakhnath and his Sampradāya have a vast literature, but books dealing purely with metaphysical problems are very few. All standard works are chiefly on various processes of *yoga*. Books on *yoga* incidentally discuss scientific and metaphysical topics. The ultimate basis of his philosophy was his and other enlightened yogis' supramental and supra-intellectual experience in the highest *samādhi* state. He, though mainly an illustrious teacher of *yoga*, preached along with it a system of philosophy which has a special place among the philosophical systems of India

CHAPTER II.—Literary Sources of his Philosophical Views. **Pages 26-28.**

Sanskrit works of Gorakhnath and his Guru Matsyendranath, *Upanishads* dealing specially with *yoga*, other authoritative treatises on *yoga*, and numerous old treatises in Bengali, Hindi, Rajasthani, Napalese, Tibetan, and other regional languages, based on the lives and teachings of Gorakhnath, Matsyendranath and other Mahāyogis of the Nāth-yogi sect, give informations about his views on the Absolute Truth and other philosophical topics. *Siddha-Siddhānta-Paddhati* is an important philosophical work of Gorakhnath. The present thesis is mainly based on this book.

CHAPTER III.—Contents of Siddha-Siddhanta-Paddhati. **Pages 29-32.**

The topics are discussed under six heads, called *Upadeśa* (lessons). The first lesson discusses *Pindôtpatti* (i.e. the origin of the bodies, cosmic as well as individual) of the Absolute Spirit. The second lesson is on *Pinda-Vicāra*, i.e. deeper contemplation on the constitution of the bodies. Nine *Cakras*, sixteen *Ādhāras*, three *Lakshyas* and five *Vyomas* are explained from *yogic* view-point. The third is on *Piṇḍa-saṃvitti*, i.e. true insight into the spiritual nature of the bodies. It shows the essential identity of individual bodies with Cosmic Body. The fourth is on *Pindādhāra*, i.e. Container and Sustainer of the bodies. It shows how all bodies are contained in and sustained by one Supreme Spiritual Power (*Śakti*) of the Absolute Spirit. The fifth deals with *Samarasa-Karana*, which is the supreme ideal of the life of a *yogi.* The sixth describes the character of an *Avadhuta*, i.e. a perfectly enlightened *yogi.*

CHAPTER IV.—Conception of the Ultimate Reality. Pages 33-37.

The basis of Gorakhnath's conception of the Ultimate Reality is direct transcendent experience in the highest state of Samādhi. Relation between direct experience and conception,—Conception is an affair of the intellect, necessitated for rational interpretation and understanding of the contents of direct experience. Being in the domain of theory, conception cannot reach the certitude of the direct experience of the Absolute Truth. An enlightened Mahāyogi does not require any conception for being sure of the validity of his transcendent experience. But he cannot but take the help of intellectual conception to explain his experience to others. Gorakhnath asserts that from the view-point of transcendent experience, in which the Absolute Truth reveals Itself in Its perfect self-shining nature and the individual consciousness is wholly identified with It, there is no question of the origination of the cosmic order with the plurality of individual existences, since they are all unified in Its transcendent nature. Still for the satisfaction of the rational demand of the people of the normal planes of phenomenal experience, this world-process must have to be accounted for from the nature of the Absolute Reality, and accordingly an adequate intellectual conception of the Absolute has to be formed. The transcendent experience of an enlightened Mahāyogi and the intellectual demand of a common man must be linked together. Gorakhnath conceives the Ultimate Reallty accordingly as *Parā-saṃvit* with *Nijā-Śakti*,—Absolute Consciousness or Absolute Spirit eternally possessed of infinite unique Power for self-expression in the form of a boundless phenomenal cosmic order evolving countless orders of finite and transitory existences in time and space and also harmonising them into one whole.

CHAPTER V.—Sat-Cit-Ananda Brahma. **Pages 38-55.**

The Ultimate Reality as realised in the transcendent state of consciousness is described by Mahāyogis as *Sat-Cid-Ānanda-Brahma,* i.e. the Absolute Spirit Whose character is pure and perfect Existence-Consciousness-Bliss. This conception is however considered not quite adequate by Gorakhnath and his school, in as much as the *dynamic* aspect or the aspect of Śakti of the Absolute Spirit is ignored in it. They conceive the Absolute Spirit as absolutely *perfect* and infinitely *dynamic* Existence-Consciousness-Bliss. The conception of Pure Existence is discussed. How the categories of *Sat* and *Asat*, *Śunya* and *Purna*, *Dwaita* and *Adwaita* can be reconciled in this conception is pointed out. The conception of Pure Consciousness is discussed. Doubts and misconceptions are removed. Pure Existence and Pure Consciousness are distinguished from phenomenal existence and phenomenal consciousness. Gorakhnath maintains that in all orders of phenomenal contingent derivative existences One self-existent self-illumined Transcendent Consciousness (*Parā-saṃvit* or *Cit*) reigns as their originator and sustainer and revealer and unifier, that in all of them it is this Consciousness that manifests Itself in manifold finite and changing objective forms and that in all kinds of mental experiences also it is the same Consciousness that reveals Itself in various subjective forms under various self-imposed limiting conditions. The conception of Pure Bliss (*Ānanda*) is discussed. Perfect Bliss which is the supreme ideal of our conscious life is the essential character of the self-existent self-illumined and absolutely free and self-manifesting Transcendent Consciousness. Objections are raised and refuted. *Ānanda* implies the absolute self-fulfilment of existence, life, knowledge, feeling and will, and this is characteristic of the Absolute Consciousness or Spirit, Who unconditionally enjoys His perfection in His transcendent nature and also enjoys His perfection under an infinite variety of conditions which He freely creates in the phenomenal cosmic system. The Absolute Spirit is beyond the scope of formal and empirical logic, but is realisable in Absolute Experience through the practice of *yoga*. Gorakhnath's philosophy is known as *Dwaitādwaita-vilakshana-vāda* and *Pakshapāta-vinirmukta-vāda*.

CHAPTER VI.—Para-Sambit with Unique Power. **Pages 56-61.**

Gorakhnath does not discard the phenomenal cosmic system as false or illusory or as having only subjective reality. The phenomenal existence of the whole system with the plurality of phenomenal subjects and phenomenal objects must be recognised as phenomenally real from the standpoint of our normal experience and a rational explanation of the system must be obtained from the essential nature of the Absolute Spirit realised in transcendent experience. Hence Gorakhnath and his school recognise the presence of the Unique Power for phenomenal diversified self-manifestation as pertaining to the essential character of the Absolute Spirit,—*Parā-Sambit, Brahma, Śiva. Power* is a reality which can be known only from its action (*kriyā*) or product (*kārya*). The power of a thing implies all the possibilities of its actions and self-expressions under all possible conditions. The possibilities cannot be truly known till they are actualised. The power is essentially identical with the nature of a thing and has also differentiated self-manifestations. Manifestations are gradual in time, but the power is constant in the essential nature of a thing. Gorakhnath and the yogi school hold that the gradually evolved diversities of phenomenal existences constituting the cosmic system are free self-manifestations, in time and space and in a related order, of the *Unique Power* of the Absolute Spirit, Whose essential character is Perfect *Sat-Cid-Ānanda*. Thus the Ultimate Reality has an eternal *transcendent* aspect and an eternal *dynamic* aspect. The transcendent aspect is revealed to the perfectly illumined *samādhi*-consciousness of the *yogi*, and the dynamic aspect is manifested in the normal planes of the consciousness. Gorakhnath describes the dynamic aspect or the Unique Power of the Absolute Spirit as of the nature of perfectly free Pure Will (*Icchā-mātra-dharmā*). This Will is distinguished from Desire of our normal mind. It is the immanent urge of Perfect Existence for self-expression as diverse orders of phenomenal existences, of Perfect Consciousness for self-revelation as diverse orders of phenomenal consciousnesses, of Perfect Bliss for self-enjoyment as diverse orders of joys. By virtue of this immanent urge the Absolute Spirit freely and delightfully manifests and enjoys Himself as infinitely various orders of phenomenal existences and consciousnesses and experiences, which constitute His Cosmic Body.

CHAPTER VII.—Siva and Sakti in Eternal Union **Pages 62-74.**

Since time immemorial in all the sacred literature of the *Yogi Sampradāya* the Absolute Spirit is designated as *Śiva* and His

Unique Power as *Śakti.* The same Absolute Reality viewed as the transcendent self-shining self-perfect differenceless and changeless Spirit is *Śiva,* and as revealing and enjoying Himself freely and eternally in an ever-changing diversified phenomenal cosmic order is *Śakti.* There is really no difference between *Śiva* and *Śakti.* In the ultimate *samādhi*-experience in which the cosmic plurality is merged in absolute unity He is realised in His transcendent aspect as *Śiva,* (His Ś*akti*-aspect being hidden in Him), and in the enlightened phenomenal experience in which the cosmic plurality appears as an objective reality He is realised in His self-manifesting dynamic aspect as *Śakti.* The two aspects are in eternal union. Hence *Śiva* and *Śakti* are popularly conceived as eternally wedded to and in loving embrace with each other. *Śiva* is conceived as *Śaktimān.* Accordingly *Śiva* is regarded as the Father and *Śakti* as the Mother of the universe, though there is no difference between the Father and the Mother and there is no question of *gender* in the nature of the Spirit. The Divine *Śakti,* as conceived by Gorakhnath and Siddha-yogis, is neither the non-spiritual non-self-conscious *Prakriti* of *Sankhya,* nor the illusion-producing inexplicable *Māyā* of *Adwaita-Vedanta,* nor the *Śakti* distinct from but possessed and governed by the Supreme Spirit, as conceived by many dualistic *bhakti* schools. She is *Sat-Cid-Ānanda-mayee Mahāśakti,* i.e. self-manifesting self-diversifying all-harmonising all-unifying ever-active Dynamic *Sat-Cid-Ānanda.* The cosmic system is conceived, not as *Cid-Vivarta,* but as *Cid-Vilāsa.* The *Śakti* is conceived, not as *āvarana-vikshepātmikā,* but as *Prakāśa-Vimarśātmikā.* Gorakhnath and his school teach the truth-seekers to appreciate the world as *Cid-Vilāsa,* as *Saundarya-lahari,* as *Ānanda-lahari,* and not to renounce it out of disgust or to think of it as an evil. Renunciation has to be practised for the purpose of the realisation of the Ideal of Absolute Śivahood in his Divine World.

CHAPTER VIII—Gradual Unfoldment of Sakti. Pages 75—87

Gorakhnath and his school are upholders of *Sat-Kārya-Vāda.* They accordingly hold that before creation the whole world of effects *exists* in an absolutely unmanifested and undifferentiated state in the nature of the Unique Power of Śiva and that destruction or dissolution consists in the merging of all the diversities in the absolute unity of the same Power (*Śakti*). Creation or origination of the cosmic system is thus regarded as the gradual unfoldment of Śiva's inherent Śakti, which is essentially non-different from Śiva. The temporal process of creation and dissolution, of evolution and involution, has no absolute beginning or end in time. The Ultimate Cause and Ground and Support of this temporally eternal process of creation and continuity and dissolution, constituting the cosmic order, must be some supra-temporal self-existent Reality having the Power for such self-expression in a temporal order, and this is the Absolute Spirit or Śiva with His Śakti. The unique causal relation between the supra-temporal changeless transcendent Spirit or Śiva and the temporal ever-changing phenomenal world-order is conceived by Gorakhnath and the Siddha-yogi Sampradāya as *Cid-Vilāsa* or *Śiva-Śakti-Vilāsa*, which means perfectly free and delightful sportive self-manifestation of the Transcendent Spirit in the phenomenal plane. This is of the nature of a free play and self-enjoyment of one self-fulfilled perfect Spirit in the forms of countless orders of imperfect phenomenal existences evolved from His own Śakti. Gorakhnath's *Śiva-Śakti-Vilāsa-Vāda* or *Cid-Vilāsa-Vāda* is distinguished from *Ārambha-Vāda*, *Parināma-Vāda* as well as *Vivarta-Vāda*. Vedanta's *Māyā* is given a more exalted position by Yogis, who conceive *Māyā* as *Mahā-Māyā* or *Yoga-Māyā* or real *Cit-Śakti* of Brahma or Śiva,—the real Mother of the real cosmic order,—and as such an Object of adoration to all individuals. The self-unfoldment of Divine Śakti is perfectly free and delightful. Śakti's self-unfoldment is described as through five stages,—*Nijā, Parā, Aparā, Sukshmā, Kundalinī*. Gorakhnath attempts to give an idea of each of these stages. *Kundalinī-Śakti* unfolds Herself as the glorious Mother of the unlimited spatio-temporal cosmic order and all kinds of individuals and classes within it. She is also present as the sleeping spiritual Power in every individual body.

CHAPTER IX—Self-Manifestation of Siva As Cosmic Purusha. Pages 88—99

The gradual self-unfoldment of *Śakti* within the spiritual transcendent nature of the Absolute Spirit, Śiva, gives birth to the Supreme Spiritual Body of Śiva, called *Parapinda* The birth of *Parapinda* means the self-manifestation of the Absolute Spirit as the Supreme Individual—*Parama Purusha*—with the full consciousness of all His eternal infinite glorious powers and attributes. The Supra-personal Spirit becomes a perfectly self-conscious Personality,—*Brahma* becomes *Iśwara*. Reference to the difference of Gorakhnath's view from Patanjali's view of Iśwara. The significance of the term *Pinda*. *Pinda* means an *organised whole*, a *unity of diversities*. Gorakhnath attaches special importance to the term, in order to show that all our conceptions of concrete realities in all the planes of our knowledge and thought involve the idea of unity of diversities. Accordingly even in the highest plane of Spiritual Reality he rejects *Pure Non-Dualism* of the *extreme Adwaita-Vādis* as well as *Pure Dualism* of *extreme Dwaita-Vādis* and *Pure-Pluralism* of *Vahu-Padārtha-Vādis*. In the lowest physical plane also he rejects the doctrine of the plurality of unrelated material units or *paramānus* integrated and disintegrated by external causes. The whole universe is conceived by him as one organism consisting of countless orders of organisms,—one *Samasti-Pinda* consisting of innumerable *Vyasti-Pindas*. This universe is the self-embodiment of the Absolute Spirit, Śiva, by virtue of the Gradual self-unfoldment of His Śakti.

Gorakhnath describes the *Para-Pinda* of Śiva as consisting of five forms of spiritual consciousness, all shining at the same time without overshadowing each other in His all-comprehensive Divine consciousness;—viz. *Aparamparam, Paramapadam, Śunyam, Niranjanam, Paramātmā*. These are explained in terms of psychological concepts. This *Para-Pinda* is also called *Anādi-Pinda* as well as *Ādi-Pinda*, implying that this Divine Individuality is without any origination and without any Higher Source of existence and that this is the Supreme Source of all other *Pindas* or individual existences. *Anādi-Pinda* is described as having the characters of *Paramānanda, Prabodha, Cid-udaya, Prakaśa, Sohambhāva*. Thus the Absolute Spirit, by virtue of the unfoldment of His immanent *Śakti* in the transcendental plane, reveals Himself as a magnificently glorified self-conscious self-active omnipotent omniscient playful Divine Personality embodied with an ideal universe. This *Ādi-Pinda* is the eternal link and meeting-ground between the transcendent and the phenomenal planes of existence,—between the Transcendent Spirit and His phenomenal cosmic self-manifestation.

CHAPTER X—Evolution Of The Cosmic Body Of Siva. Pages 100—114

Having described the nature of *Para-Pinda* or *Ādya-Pinda* in the supra-physical plane, Gorakhnath exposes the evolution of the physical world-system from this *Ādya-Pinda.* Śiva as *Ādya-Pinda*, the Cosmic Purusha, evolves from within Himself, through the further self-unfoldment of His Śakti, a Physical Cosmic Body, extending in space and changing in time, and makes it an integral part of His all-comprehending and all-enjoying Self-Consciousness. The universe, which was *ideally* real in the nature of *Ādya-Pinda,* becomes *physically* and *objectively* real as theCosmic Body of Śiva, and this Body is called *Mahā-Sākāra-Pinda.* Śiva with His infinite and eternal Mahā-Sakti is seen by a Mahāyogi as immanent in and revealing Himself through all the diversities of this physical order. A Mahāyogi looks upon and loves this world as the sacred Divine Body.

From *Ādya-Pinda* evolves *Mahā-Ākāśa,* from *Mahā-Ākāsā* evolves *Mahā-Vāyu,* from *Mahā-Vayu* evolves *Mahā Tejas,* from *Mahā-Tejas* evolves *Mahā-Salila,* from *Mahā-Salila Mahā-Prithwī.* These five *Tattwas* (Basic Elements) are gradual stages of self-unfoldment of the Divine *Śakti* in more and more complex physical forms and they are all organised by the same *Śakti* into an unlimited and ever-continuous physical embodiment of Śiva. The distinctive characteristics of each of these physical *Tattwas* (generally called *Mahā-Bhutas*) are described in details. General reflections are made with reference to the different schools of Indian philosophy on the relation of the basic physical elements of the universe of our experience to the Ultimate Reality or the Absolute Spirit. Acc. To Gorakhnath and the Siddha Yogis, this Physical Cosmic Body is the grossest and most complicated and diversified form of free self-manifestation of the Absolute Spirit through the gradual self-unfoldment of His infinite and eternal Spiritual Power, and hence it is essentially a spiritual entity. In relation to this Cosmic Order the Supreme Spirit reveals Himself principally in the forms of eight Divine Personalities, Which are called *Ashta-Murti* of *Mahā-Sākāra-Pinda* Śiva—*viz. Śiva, Bhairava, Śrikantha, Sadāśiva, Iśwara, Rudra, Vishnu* and *Brahmā.*

In the Cosmic Body of Śiva various *orders* of phenomenal existences are gradually evolved, and these are conceived as distinct interrelated worlds or *Lokas*. First, there is the world of material bodies and physical forces, governed by what are known as *natural laws*. This is *Jaḍa-Jagat*. Secondly, there is the world of Life and Vital Forces, governed by *biological laws*. This is *Prāna-Jagat*. Life and vital forces are embodied with and manifested through material bodies, but life transcends matter and exerts regulative influence upon its phenomena. Thirdly, there is the world of Mind,—*Mano-Jagat*. All phenomena of empirical consciousness are expressions of mind. Mental phenomena are manifested through living physical bodies, but Mind transcends Matter and Life and uses them as its instruments Mind and Body are found to act and react upon each other, but Mind does not occupy any special part of the physical body nor does it die with the death of the physical body. Mind has a higher order of reality than Matter and Life,—being a higher self-expression of the Supreme Spirit. Fourthly, there is the world of Reason or Intelligence,—*Buddhi*. *Buddhi* is higher than Mind, and it is manifested in the acts of discriminating between valid and invalid knowledge, correct and incorrect thought, and in the urge for the attainment of truth. *Buddhi* exercises a regulative and enlightening influence upon Mind. Cosmic *Buddhi* with Cosmic *Manas* and Cosmic *Prāna* is all-pervading. Fifthly, there is a still higher world,—the world of Moral Consciousness, the world of *Dharma*. *Dharma* is revealed in the form of some Ideal of goodness or righteousness or moral perfection, having the inherent claim to regulate and elevate all natural phenomena of matter and life and mind and reason towards the Ideal. *Dharma* governs the course of evolution in this Cosmic Body of Śiva. Though *Dharma* is all-pervading and underlies all spheres of phenomenal existences, it is specially manifested in the Moral Consciousness of man. Sixthly, there is the world of *Rasa*,—Aesthetic Order. This is specially revealed to the Aesthetic Consciousness of man, to which the whole universe is a universe of Beauty. Seventhly, there is the world of Bliss,—*Ānanda*. *Ānanda* is the real and eternal nature of the Supreme Spirit and it underlies all self-manifestations of the Spirit. To different orders of phenomenal consciousnesses different orders of existences are revealed. The infinite richness of *Mahā-Sākāra-Pinda* is unfathomable. Every *world* has *ādhyātmika*, *ādhidaivika* and *ādhibhoutika* aspects.

Recapitulation of the foregoing discourses, indicating the way of philosophical thinking of *Siddha-Yogis*. The conceptions of the eight Divine Cosmic Personalities further explained. With the evolution of the eight Divine Personalities and their respective planes of consciousnesses and existences, the constitution of *Mahā-Sākāra-Pinda* (Cosmic Body) of *Śiva-Śakti* is complete, so far as the Universal Cosmic Principles are concerned. The plane of *Brahmā* is the lowest and grossest of all and is most closely related to the gross world of our sensuous experience. Gorakhnath traces the evolution of the individual existences and consciousnesses of this world from the Conscious Will *(Avalokana)* of Brahmā. This Conscious Will is manifested in the form of *Prakriti-Pinda,* from which all individual bodies *(Vyasti-Pindas)* are evolved. Every individual body is a particularised manifestation of *Prakriti-Pinda* and ultimately of the Cosmic Body of Śiva. Gorakhnath is particularly interested in the study of the constitution of the individual *human* body. In the human body all the external and internal organs of an individual body are fully evolved, and also life and mind and reason and moral consciousness and aesthetic consciousness are fully manifested in individualised forms. The human body is realised as an epitome of the entire Cosmic Body of Śiva. It is in and through the human body that the Divine Śakti, Who in the process of cosmic self-manifestation comes down from the highest transcendent spiritual plane of absolute unity and bliss step by step to the lowest phenomenal material plane of endless diversities and imperfections, ascends again by means of self-conscious processes of *Yoga* and *Jñana* and *Bhakti* to the transcendent spiritual plane and becomes perfectly and blissfully united with the Supreme Spirit, Śiva. Man with his developed individuality can experience Śiva as his own true Soul as well as the true Soul of the universe

From the standpoint of *yogic* discipline, Gorakhnath conceives the human body as consisting of (1) the gross material body called *Bhuta-Pinda*(2)the mental body described as *Antah-karana-Pancaka,* (3) *Kula-pancaka,* (4) *Vyakti-pancaka,* (5) *Pratyaksha-*

karana-pancaka, (6) *Nādi-samsthāna*, and (7) *Daśa-Vāyu*. The *Bhuta-pinda* is constituted of the five gross physical elements, purposefully organised by the Creative Will of Brahmā with life-power and mind-power immanent in the organism and regulating teleologically the functions of its various organs. The conceptions of *wholes* and *parts* and their relations are discussed from the view-point of *yogic Sat-kārya-vada*. Gradual evolution of parts within parts from the Cosmic Whole leads to the organisation of the amazingly diverse parts of individual bodies of various orders and kinds. The individual minds are individualised self-manifestations of the Cosmic Mind in relation to and apparent dependence upon individual living bodies. The individual lives also are individualised self-manifestations of the Cosmic Life. Every individual human mind is manifested in five forms according to functions,—viz. *Manas*, *Buddhi*, *Ahankāra*, *Chitta* and *Caitanya*. The functions of each are explained. *Kula* is here interpreted by Gorakhnath as the forces which exercise their directive influence from behind the scene upon the psycho-physical phenomena and give special inclinations and aptitudes to them It is conceived as of five forms, viz. *Sattwa*, *Rajas*, *Tamas*, *Kāla* and *Jeeva*. These are explained. *Vyakti pancaka* refer to the five forms of self-expression of the individual mind and they are classified as *Icchā*, *Kriyā*, *Māyā*, *Prakriti* and *Vāk*. The various subdivisions of each are described. The forms of *Vāk*,—viz. *Parā*, *Paśyantī*, *Madhyamā*, *Vaikharī* and *Mātrikā*, are discussed. By *pratyaksha-Karana* Gorakhnath indicates the efficient and material causes which practically contribute to the maintenance and development and also renewal of the indvidual body. He enumerates then as, *Kāma*, *Karma*, *Candra*, *Surya* and *Agni*. Their characteristics and influences are discussed. The knowledge of *Nādi-Samsthāna* or the nervous system is of great importance to *yogis*. Of countless *Nādis*, ten are specially mentioned. Of these, three are highly important, viz. *Idā*, *Pingalā* and *Sushunmā*. *Sushumnā* is the most important from *yogic* view-point. *Vāyu-Samsthāna* also is of special importance from yogic view-point. *Vāyu* or *Prāna-śakti* is essentially one, but it is conceived as tenfold, acc. to different functions it performs in different parts of the living organism. Of the tenfold *Vayu*, *Prāna* and *Apāna* are of special importance for yogic discipline. In this connection the nature and inner significance of *breath* are discussed and *Ajapā-Gāyatrī* is explained.

CHAPTER XIV—The Esoteric Aspects Of The Body. Pages 169—194

For the purpose of attaining true enlightenment about the inner nature of the sacred human body, Gorakhnath regards it essential to acquire insight into nine *cakras*, sixteen *ādhāras*, three *lakshyas*, five *vyomans*. The nine *cakras* are conceived as different stations in the central *Sushumnā-Nādī*, which is called *Brahma-Mārga*. These are centres of psycho-vital forces and indicate different planes of esoteric experience in the path of *yogic* discipline. They are like wheels and whirls in the path of spiritual progress, and they act sometimes as hurdles and often as revolutionary steps in the path.

Cakras are enumerated by Gorakhnath somewhere as nine and somewhere as seven (including the highest, Sahasrāra). The special features of these *Cakras* are described at some length. The underlying conception is that, *Kundalini-Śakti*, the Supreme Divine Power, lies sleeping like a coiled serpent in the lowest *Mulādhāra Cakra* of every human body, becomes awakened with the awakenment of the spiritual consciousness of every individual, rises step by step through yogic discipline to higher and higher *Cakras* (higher and higher planes of spiritual illumination), blesses individual consciousness with various kinds of occult experiences and miraculous powers in the particular *Cakras*, and finally ascends to the highest *Cakra*, the plane of the perfect blissful union of *Śakti* with *Śiva* or *Brahma*, in which the individual consciousness becomes absolutely united with Universal Consciousness, the Absolute Sat-Cid-ananda.

After describing the *Cakras*, Gorakhnath describes what he calls *Ādhāras* and for the students of *Yoga* he enumerates them as sixteen. By *Ādhāras* he refers to the principal seats of the vital and psychical functions, which have to be brought under control and then transcended by means of appropriate methods of yogic discipline. Having given lessons on the sixteen *Ādhāras*, Gorakhnath imparts instruction on the three kinds of *Lakshyas*,— internal and external and non-located. *Lakshya* means an object upon which a yogi should fix his attention temporarily for practising concentration of psycho-vital energy with the ultimate view of elevating it to the highest spiritual plane. Lastly, Gorakhnath gives lessons on *Vyoma* or *Ākāśa* or *Sunya*, which, though really one, he enumerates as five for the sake of the practice of concentration.

CHAPTER XV—The Cosmos In The Individual Body. **Pages 195-205**

In the view of enlightened *yogis* there is no pure and simple matter, as conceived by scientists, anywhere in the universe. Even *Ākāśa,* which is the ultimate form of matter and which appears as pure contentless space or void, evolves from and is ensouled by the Supreme Spirit with infinite Power immanent in His nature. Through the Power's gradual self-unfoldment the other *Mahābhutas* with specific characteristics emerge from it and they are all ensouled by the Spirit. In the course of this evolution, individual material bodies with apparently distinctive existences and characteristics emerge in the Cosmic Body of the Spirit, and life and mind and intellect are found to be gradually evolved in individual forms in relation to individual physical bodies, in which the character of the Spirit is more and more brilliantly reflected. Every individual body with life, mind, etc. is thus a self-manifestation and self-embodiment of the Supreme Spirit, Śiva. All causal activities of all material things and all processes of evolution and emergence of apparently newer and newer and higher and higher orders of realities in the universe are governed by the free Creative Will-Power inherent in the essential nature of the Absolute Spirit. The Spirit is revealed as the material cosmic system.

As a *yogi* draws upward in a systematic way his psycho-vital energy to higher and higher *ādhāras* and *cakras* and concentrates his consciousness upon deeper truths unveiled therein, the individual body is gradually realised as liberated from the grossness and impurity and spatio-temporal limitations and imperfections of its normal material nature and hence as a true spiritual entity. When the consciousness is adequately refined and illumined, the whole is experienced in every part, the entire cosmic system is experienced in every individual body, *Mahā-Sākara-Pinda* is realised in *Vyasti-Pinda.* This realisation of the Cosmic Body in the individual body is called by Gorakhnath the true knowledge of the body (*Pinda-saṃvitti*). For training the intellect of truth-seekers Gorakhnath describes the location of all the worlds in the Cosmic Order within distinctive parts of the individual body.

CHAPTER XVI—Individual Souls. **Pages 206—223**

The individual soul and the individual body are both phenomenal self-manifestations of the transcendent Supreme Spirit. The soul is evidently a spiritual manifestation, and the body is a physical manifestation. The body appears as a finite changing composite material entity, while the soul appears as a simple self-luminous entity without any spatio-temporal characteristics and limitations and changes. The soul does not occupy any special portion of the body, but gives unity to the whole body and is realisable in every part of it. The soul is the master of the body, and all the operations of all the organs of the body revolve round the soul as their dynamic centre. The soul is distinguished not only from the physical body, but also from life, mind, ego, intellect, moral and aesthetic consciousness, and even spiritual consciousness. It is self-luminous witness to them, the innermost dynamic centre of all their operations, and it realises and enjoys itself in and through them. The individual soul is ultimately one with Śiva, the Supreme Spirit, Who in His phenomenal cosmic play freely enjoys Himself as the plurality of individual souls in relation to the various orders of individual bodies.

The souls are not really touched by the joys and sorrows and bondages and limitations and changes of the respective individual bodies. So long as *Avidyā* or Ignorance prevails over the phenomenal consciousness, these are falsely attributed to the souls. Discussion on the conception of *Vidyā* and *Avidyā* from the view point of Siddha-Yogis, *Vidyā* and *Avidyā* are two-fold aspects of the phenomenal manifestation of the *Swatantrā Nijā Śakti* (Free Unique Power) of Śiva (Absolute Spirit). Gorakhnath and the yogi school more often use the terms *Prakāśa* and *Vimarśa* in place of *Vidyā* and *Avidyā*. The significance of these terms is discussed. In this universe of phenomenal self-manifestations of the Absolute Spirit, His *Prakāśa-Śakti* and *Vimarśa-Śakti* are apparently conditioned and limited by each other, and the Soul as manifested in each individual body appears to be conditioned and limited by the nature and limitations of the body. It is the Supreme Spirit Who reveals Himself as individual souls. The Absolute, while manifesting and experiencing Himself freely and playfully under limitations of all kinds of forms, remains eternally in His own true Self as the One Transcendent Spirit.

The problems of Evil, Sorrow, Sin, Warfare, etc. are discussed and solved from this view-point.

From the earliest age of Hindu spiritual culture, *Moksha* or *Mukti* is generally accepted as the Supreme Ideal (*Parama Purushārtha*) of human life. It is commonly understood in the rather negative sense of perfect and absolute deliverance from the present earthly state of existence subject to sorrows and bondages and imperfections. Many schools of philosophers and spiritual aspirants lay special emphasis upon Sorrow which is the most universal and the most undesirable fact of human experience and conceive absolute cessation of sorrow as the ultimate Ideal of all human endeavours. The significance of Sorrow is discussed. All Hindu saints and sages proclaim the possibility of the absolute conquest of Sorrow, not by means of external contrivances and changes of physical conditions, but by means of internal self-discipline and self-enlightenment. Perfect self-enlightenment really consists in the elevation of empirical consciousness to the transcendent spiritual plane, and the experience of this plane can not be exactly and adequately described in terms of intellectual concepts. Attempts at such description lead to different religio-philosophical views about *Moksha*. The transcendent experience is often described negatively as absolute cessation of Sorrow and positively as the attainment of *Ānanda* or perfect Bliss. Discussion of Mahāyogi Buddha's conception of *Nirvāna*, and his doctrine of the suppression of all desires and universal sympathy as the means to it. Discussion on the conception of *Ātmā*, on which all Hindu schools of philosophy lay special stress. The realisation of *Ātmā* or the true Self is conceived as the real nature of transcendent experience and the essential nature of *Moksha*. Discussion on *Jīvanmukti* and *Videha-mukti*. The nature of *Ātmā* after absolute disembodiment is a puzzling problem, on which even the greatest saint-philosophers are found to differ. Views of Buddha, Kapila, Patanjali, Gautama, Kanāda, are briefly mentioned. Discussion of the Upanishadic and Vedantic view of the realisation of the identity of the individual *Ātmā* with the Absolute Spirit, Brahma, as the Ultimate Ideal. Gorakhnath agrees with this view, though he denies the illusoriness of the Cosmic Order and of the individual *Ātmā*. Reference to the *Bhakti* schools. Acc. to Gorakhnath, the perfect realisation of *Śivahood* or *Brahmahood* by the individual soul through *yoga* is the Supreme Ideal. Gorakhnath's grand conception of *Samarasa-karana* and his conception of the true character of a *Nātha* or *Avadhuta* are explained. A *Nātha* not only realises the identity of himself and all existences with Śiva or Brahma and experiences the whole universe within himself, but also becomes a complete master of all physical forces in the universe.

CHAPTER XVIII—The Evolution of Hindu Spiritual Culture. (I) **Pages 251—280**

Vedas the basis of Hindu spiritual thought. Some fundamental Vedic Truths,—that this world-order is essentially a spiritual and moral and aesthetic system, that all phenomena of all planes of existences are governed by Universal and Inviolable Moral and Aesthetic and Spiritual Principles, that the Cosmic System is not only an *ādhibhautika* but also an *ādhidaivika* and *ādhyātmika* system, that in the scheme of the universe *man* as a self-conscious intellectual and moral and spiritual being endowed with a highly developed physical body occupies a unique position. The Vedas unveiled the inner secrets of the order of the universe and human nature and showed the way to the solution of the most fundamental problems which are puzzling to the greatest intellectualists of all ages. The principal modes of discipline taught by Vedas for elevating man to higher planes of existence and consciousness till the highest spiritual plane is reached,—the cultivation of the spirit of *Yajña* in practical life, the cultivation of devotional sentiments and spirit of worship to the Supreme Spirit as revealed in this wonderful Cosmic System, the cultivation of Renunciation and *Tattwa-Jñāna* and *Yoga*. The wide-spread influence of Vedas upon the practical life of the Aryans. Controversies on the true interpretation of Vedic Texts,—interpretation from the view-point of *Karma*, from the view-point of *Jñāna* and *Yoga*, from the view-point of *Upāsana* or Devotion. In the period of progressive expansion and consolidation of the Aryan society people were naturally more interested in a *philosophy of action* than in a philosophy of renunciation or emotional devotion, and hence the interpretation from the view-point of *Karma* prevailed in the society. The view-point of *Jñāna* and *Yoga* and *Vairāgya* also steadily

pāyana Vyāsa and his disciples. He compiled and rearranged all the available Vedic Texts with their varied interpretations, preached the Upanishads as constituting the essence of the Vedas, composed the great national Epic, *Mahabhārata*, founded the school of *Vedānta-Darśana*, and initiated the composition and propagation of the *Purānas*. These together with the other great national Epic, Vālmīki's *Rāmāyaṇa*, exercised a powerful influence upon the development and popularisation of Hindu spiritual culture and the permanent unification of this vast sub-continent.

More than a thousand years after Śri Krishna and Vyāsa, Lord Buddha and Lord Mahāvīra, both of whom were *Mahāyogis* and followed practically the *Nivritti-Mārga* of the *Vedas*, initiated two powerful ethico-spiritual movements, which led to the creation of Buddhism and Jainism within the fold of Hinduism. They really preached the ancient *Yoga-Mārga* with special emphasis on renunciation, universal sympathy and compassion and purity of ethical conduct, and particularly on the principle of *Ahimsā*. Their special contributions to Hindu spiritual culture and the causes of their conflict with the orthodox Hindu community are briefly discussed.

A few centuries later, Kumārila, Śankara and Gorakhnath appeared as very powerful exponents of Vedic *Karma-Mārga*, *Jñāna-Mārga* and *Yoga-Mārga* respectively, and their contributions to the restoration and consolidation of the moral, spiritual and cultural unity of the vast country on the basis of the Vedic outlook on life and the world are most remarkable. The special features of their contributions are briefly expounded. While Kumārila strongly defended Vedic Hinduism against the attacks of Buddhism and Jainism, Śankara and Gorakhnath contributed greatly to their assimilation with Hinduism.

In the Middle Ages, while the different interrelated currents of Vedic spiritual culture continued to flow on, the *Bhakti-cult* or *Upāsana-Mārga* got a great impetus from the life and teachings of a good number of *Bhakta-saints* with high spiritual attainments and magnetic personal influences born in different provinces. A good many *Upāsaka Sampradāyas*,—*Śaiva*, *Śākta*, *Vaishnava*, *Rāmāyata*, etc.,—worshipping the same Supreme Spirit in different Divine Names, in different visible and tangible Forms and in different methods, developed at this age throughout the country. Image-worship and Pilgrimage became very popular. *Islam* came and made a permanent place for itself in India at this period.

Hinduism, as it took shape and form in the middle age, continues without much substantial change in the present age, though it had to meet the challenge of the invasion of the materialistic culture and civilisation of the West and had to adjust itself with new situations. The contributions of the modern saints, and particularly of Ramkrishna and Vivekananda, are most remarkable. These are briefly referred to.

INTRODUCTION

A YOGI AND A PHILOSOPHER

Both Have The Same End In View—The Absolute Truth

A Yogi and a Philosopher have the same ultimate end in view. They are inspired by the same inherent urge of the innermost consciousness of man. Both of them are seekers of the Absolute Truth. Both of them refuse to remain content with the knowledge of the finite transitory relative truths of the world of normal human experience. They feel within themselves a deep yearning for the discovery of the infinite eternal Absolute Reality behind and beyond them. They devote themselves to the quest of the ultimate root of all existence, the ultimate Cause and Ground of this world-order, the ultimate solution of all the problems of human knowledge and experience. The human consciousness is ordinarily imprisoned in the closed domain of space, time and relativity. It is as it were condemned to live and move under spatial and temporal limitations, to think and know in terms of relativity, causality and reciprocity. It is given opportunities to develop and expand and enrich itself within the compound of this prison; but it is not permitted to go beyond the walls of this prison. It seems that human knowledge and experience must necessarily be finite and relative, and the world of space, time and relativity must be all in all to the human mind.

The Yogi as well as the Philosopher revolts against this bondage of the human mind. Both of them aspire to break through the walls of this prison. They want to transcend the limitations, under which the ordinary human consciousness is placed by nature. For the satisfaction of the innermost craving of their souls, they attempt to penetrate into the innermost meaning of this cosmic order. However bewilderingly complex the constitution of the world of our normal experience may appear to be, it cannot be a meaningless and purposeless process, going on by chance or accident. The wonderful order and harmony perceptible in all the departments of this complicated system of the Universe point to some dynamic Centre or Soul of this system, some obviously inscrutable Governing Principle or Power regulating its intricate operations, some Supreme Ideal which is being realised in and through this continuous phenomenal process. A Yogi and a Philosopher are both inspired by some such faith, and both of them devote their energy to the discovery of that Centre or Soul of the Universe, that Governing Principle or Power, that Supreme Ideal, which may furnish a rational explanation of this world-order and give a meaning to it.

2

They Differ in their Modes of Approach

While the ultimate object of search is the same for a Yogi and a Philosopher, their modes of approach appear to be widely different. A Philosopher's approach is intellectual, and a Yogi's approach may be said to be spiritual. A Philosopher advances in the path of rational logic, a Yogi advances in the path of moral and psychical self-discipline. A Philosopher aims at a logically unassailable conception of the Absolute Truth, a Yogi aims at a direct spiritual experience of the Absolute Truth. A Philosopher's interest in the pursuit of the Truth is chiefly theoretical, he being chiefly concerned with the satisfaction of the demand of his intellect; a Yogi's interest is thoroughly practical, in as much as he is predominantly concerned with the satisfaction of the fundamental demand of his soul. A Philosopher does not cease to be a philosopher, even if his practical life is not in tune with his conception of the Truth, but a Yogi ceases to be a Yogi, if his entire life is not disciplined in strict accordance with his idea of the Truth. The knowledge which a Philosopher attains and can possibly attain by the most careful applications of the principles and rules of Logic is indirect or mediate knowledge (*Paroksha Jñāna*); while the knowledge which a Yogi seeks and expects to attain through the purification and refinement and illumination of his entire consciousness is direct or immediate knowledge (*Aparoksha Jñāna*). An earnest Philosopher makes serious attempts to purify and refine and enlighten his reason and to liberate it from all kinds of logical fallacies and imperfections, so that it may form the most valid and most comprehensive conception of the Absolute Truth. An earnest Yogi undergoes a systematic course of self-discipline for the purification of his body and senses and mind, for the suppression of his desires and passions and worldly tendencies, for the liberation of his thought from the bondage of all preconceived ideas and notions, for the concentration of his attention upon the unknown but yearned-for object of his search and for the elevation of his entire consciousness to higher spiritual planes, so that the self-luminous Absolute Truth may perfectly illumine this consciousness and directly reveal Itself to it. A Philosopher is an aspirant for *understanding* the Absolute Truth by making it an object of his refined logical conception, while a Yogi is an aspirant for *realising* the Truth by elevating his consciousness to the highest spiritual plane, in which the subject-object-relativity also vanishes and the consciousness becomes practically one with the Absolute Truth.

A Philosopher's Method

In his quest of the Absolute Truth, a Philosopher has to rely chiefly on speculation (*Yukti*). He has to form theories and hypotheses and to put them to logical tests. He has to keep one eye upon the facts of normal human experience, which are all finite and relative, and he has to be careful that the conjectural opinion he forms about the Absolute Reality may not be inconsistent with the established facts of this world of finitude and relativity and may on the other hand offer the most adequate rational explanation for all these facts. His consciousness habitually dwells in the plane of the finite, the temporal and the relative, and his intellect and imagination, led by some inner urge, jump or fly from the finite to the infinite, from the temporal to the eternal, from the relative to the absolute. The Infinite Eternal Absolute, *i.e.*, what he conceives to be the Ultimate Reality above and beyond the limitations of space, time and relativity, remains to his normal consciousness an unwarranted conjecture or undue assumption, until and unless it is logically demonstrated that the essential demand of the human intellect for a rational explanation of this world-order is not possible without the assumption of such an Absolute Reality and that the Reality as conceived by him is *alone* capable of supplying the most adequate rational explanation of the system of facts constituting this world. Thus a Philosopher has to take his stand on the phenomenal relative world of normal human experience, and the Absolute Truth he arrives at by the exercise of his imaginative insight and logical intellect is a *theory*, the validity of which is measured by its necessity and adequacy for the rational explanation of this world. The conclusion of philosophy, however well-reasoned, cannot rise above the status of a theory (*Vāda*).

Another serious difficulty which arises in the path of the philosophical quest of the Absolute Truth is, that for the purpose of the intellectual comprehension or apprehension of the Absolute, a Philosopher has to think of It and define It in terms of the *concepts of his understanding*, of which the legitimate scope of application is the relative phenomenal objective world. The logical principles and methods which he has to rely upon for the establishment of the validity of his conception about the Absolute Reality are also primarily meant for the proof of the relative truth of our empirical and discursive understanding. When these principles and categories are applied to the Absolute Truth, the Absolute is unconsciously brought down within the realm of the relative.

Existent and non-existent, conscious and unconscious, active and inactive, changeless and changing, unity and plurality, substance and attribute, cause and effect, simple and complex, dynamic and static, personal and impersonal—all such concepts are applied by our intellect in the field of our normal relative knowledge, and their generally accepted meanings have reference to the relative phenomena of this objective world. A Philosopher, while attempting to determine the nature of the Absolute Reality and to form an intellectual conception of it, cannot help making use of the same concepts. Confusion arises as a matter of course. He has not unoften to radically change the meanings of these fundamental concepts of our normal understanding. In spite of all his earnest efforts he cannot liberate his intellect from the bondage of the elementary concepts of his rational understanding, which are by their very nature concerned with the world of relativity. A Philosopher has sometimes to manufacture new terms and concepts, the exact significance of which becomes incomprehensible to the normal understanding of a common man. He thinks of 'transcendent existence' above and behind 'phenomenal existence,' 'transcendent activity' as distinguished from 'phenomenal activity', 'transcendent consciousness' above 'phenomenal consciousness', and so on. Sometimes he thinks of the Absolute Reality as neither existent nor non-existent or as above both existence and non-existence. Sometimes he thinks of It as neither conscious nor unconscious or as having an order of consciousness which is above consciousness and unconsciousness of our normal experience.

Sometimes Inexplicableness or Inscrutableness is used as a category of understanding. In this way, Philosophers find themselves compelled to introduce many conceptions which are inconceivable to the common logical intellect. When they try to expound and establish these metaphysical conceptions, they have necessarily to argue on the basis of generally accepted logical principles. They cannot defy the Principles of Identity, Contradiction and Excluded-Middle, which are fundamental principles of logical thought. They cannot disregard the Principles of Causation and Sufficient Ground, which rule over their intellect in its search for Truth in this world. But all these principles of our common empirical thought and understanding cannot help them to convincingly prove the validity of their supra-logical supra-intellectual metaphysical conceptions about the Absolute Truth. It seems that they try to prove by means of logic what is above the sphere of logic.

A War of Theories

The history of the philosophical quest of the Absolute Truth in the human race shows that there have been thousands and thousands of theories or intellectual conceptions about the nature of the Ultimate Reality, and there has not been a single one which could satisfy the intellect of all. The philosophical literature has been developing from the earliest times, and it is still progressing. No philosophical view has been found to be logically unassailable. The history of philosophy has become a history of a continuous warfare on the intellectual plane among the greatest and wisest rational truth-seekers of the world. A sincere and earnest Philosopher, even to satisfy himself that his conception truly represents the character of the Absolute Reality, has not only to be convinced that his theory is free from all possible logical fallacies and is capable of offering an adequate rational explanation for the world-order, but has also to be convinced that no other rival theory is or can possibly be so free from defects and can furnish such a satisfactory explanation. He therefore feels impelled to put to test not only his own conception, but also the conceptions arrived at by other philosophers. This leads him to seek and find defects in the arguments and conclusions of all other truth-seekers who differ from him and thereby to demonstrate the exclusive validity of the conception which he himself adopts. As Philosophers differ from one another in their modes of approach and the conclusions they intellectually arrive at, every system of philosophy becomes an object of attack from all sides, from the exponents of all other systems of philosophy. This intellectual warfare amongst the Philosophers, age after age, has been tremendously enriching the philosophical literature. But no philosopher can have the inner assurance and satisfaction that he has found out the Truth, that he has been blessed with the true knowledge of the Absolute Reality. Every Philosopher is afraid, unless he becomes dogmatic and arrogant, that the idea which he cherishes about the Supreme Object of his life-long search may not be the correct one and that it may be proved to be false by other philosophers. In fact, it is the fate of every philosophical theory that it is supported with logical arguments by philosophers of one school and refuted with counter-arguments by philosophers of many other schools.

The Absolute Truth has been conceived by illustrious philosophers in amazingly various ways, such as, Pure Void (*Śunya*), or Non-Being or Non-Existence (*Asat*), Pure Being or Existence (*Sat*). Pure Transcendent Consciousness (*Cit-mātra*), Pure Unconscious Matter (*Acit Prakriti*), Pure Primordial Energy or Power (*Mahā-śakti*), Pure Consciousness with Power (*Śaktimatcaitanya*), Creative Will, Absolute Idea, Absolute Spirit, Supreme Personality (*Parama Purusha*) with infinite Power and Wisdom, Morally and Aesthetically Perfect Personality (possessing not only infinite power and wisdom and bliss, but also the most lovable and adorable excellences), *Satya-Śiva-Sundara Purushottama—Premānandaghana Parameśwara,* and so on and so forth. The world of phenomenal diversities is conceived by some as an illusory appearance, by others as self-manifestation of the Ultimate Reality, by others again as created by the Ultimate Reality, by others again as the Sole Reality having no noumenal Reality behind it, and so on. The finite spirits are conceived by some as uncreated and eternal and by others as created and destructible, by some as atomic in nature, and by others as all-pervading, by some as different from the Ultimate Reality and by some as essentially non-different from the Ultimate Reality, by some as essentially pure and free and incorruptible and by others as subject to degradation and development, by some as essentially different from and independent of the physical bodies and by others as evolved out of them, and so on. The Ultimate Ideal of human life is also variously conceived by various philosophers. There seems to be no end of differences among the views of philosophers, (*Nāsau munir yasya matam na bhinnam*). Each view is splendidly supported by its exponents with strong and elaborate logical arguments, which carry conviction to certain classes of truth-seekers.

Every strongly supported view has given birth to a particular school of philosophy. But it seems that every strong logical argument has its weak points. Critics discover these weak points in the arguments of a philosophical school and lay special emphasis upon them to repudiate the whole system propounded by it. Thus every system of philosophy is ably supported by its advocates and most cruelly refuted by its opponents. If a particular view is found to be satisfactory to one class of truth-seekers, it is proved to be unacceptable by many classes of truth-seekers. Every apparently well-reasoned theory about the Ultimate Truth is thus reduced merely into a particular view-point from which the Truth is sought to be approached, and no theory can evidently reach It. The intellectual path adopted by a Philosopher fails to lead him to the *realisation* of the Absolute Truth, for which he feels within himself a persistent demand.

The Path of Yoga

A good many philosophers, having realised the inherent weakness of the method of logical reasoning and intellectual theorising as a means to the perfect satisfaction of the innermost demand of the soul for the attainment of the Absolute Truth, have turned towards the method of spiritual self-discipline. One great Western philosopher has said that "Learned ignorance is the end of philosophy and the beginning of religion". Religion here does not of course mean blind submission to any particular dogma or creed or performance of certain prescribed rites and ceremonies; but it means systematic discipline of the body, the senses, the mind, the intellect and the heart, under expert guidance, for the purification and refinement of the entire being of a man and the elevation of the empirical consciousness to higher and higher spiritual planes, so as ultimately to make it fit for being perfectly illumined by the light of the Absolute Truth. This is the path of *Yoga*. The most illustrious philosopher of ancient Greece, who was proclaimed by the Oracle of Delphi as the wisest man of the age, gravely said that his wisdom perhaps lay in the fact that "I know that I know nothing". This great *Guru* of many great philosophers frankly confessed that with all his philosophical reflections he could not reach the Ultimate Truth which his heart craved for.

The term *Philosophy* itself is very significant in this connection; it carries the sense of its own inherent limitation with it. It means love of wisdom, and not the perfect attainment of wisdom. It implies sincere and earnest pursuit of Truth, and not the direct realisation of Truth. A Philosopher, so long as he relies solely upon logical reasoning and intellectual argumentation, may continually advance towards the Truth with all the earnestness of his heart, but will never reach it. In his very attempt to make the Absolute Truth an *object* of his logical conception and intellectual comprehension, the Absolute Truth eludes his grasp. He always searches and misses. His Eternal Beloved never unveils Himself to his logical intellect. He has to transcend his logical intellect in order to be united with the Transcendent Truth. His consciousness has to rise above the domain of Space, Time and Relativity in order to be in the closest embrace of the Infinite Eternal Absolute Truth. This is the path of True Religion. This is the path of *Yoga*.

After a good deal of deep thinking, the *Upanishadic Rishi* also came to the conclusion that *Ātmā* is not attainable by means of philosophical dissertation (*pravacana*) or intellectual acumen (*medhā*) or extensive study (*bahuśruta*); It is attainable only by him to whom It reveals itself (*Yameva eṣa vṛṇute tena labhyaḥ*). A truth-seeker has however to make his consciousness fit for the self-relevation of *Ātmā*. It does not reveal itself to the consciousness of a person, howsoever intellectually gifted he may be, unless he is free from all vices and evil propensities, unless his mind is pure and steady and calm and tranquil, unless his entire consciousness is with intense longing directed towards the Divine Light. So long as the sense of *Ego* predominates in the consciousness of a person, so long as he thinks that by dint of his own intellectual power he will unveil the true nature of *Ātmā*, the veil will remain in the form of his egoistic vanity. For the attainment of fitness for the self-revelation of *Ātmā*, the consciousness must be freed from the sense of *Ego* as well as all egoistic desires and attachments and inclinations of the mind. It is upon moral and spiritual self-preparation of the truth-seeker that fitness for Truth-realisation depends. This means the systematic practice of *Yoga*. This is the conclusion at which the *Upanishadic Rishi* arrived.

It is to be noted that by the term *Ātmā* the *Rishi* meant the True Self of all existences—the True Self of every individual as well as of the Universe—*i.e.*, the Absolute Truth. The *Upanishadic Rishi* uses the term *Brahma* also in the same sense. Though the term *Ātmā* primarily means the True Self of an individual and the term *Brahma* means the *Supreme*, the *Greatest*, the *Infinite* and *Eternal*, *i.e.*, the *True Self of the Universe*, the essential identity of the True Self of the Individual and the True Self of the Universe was revealed to the illumined consciousness of the *Rishi*; hence

Ātmā and *Brahma* are often used synonymously in the *Upanishads*, meaning the Absolute Truth. The Seers of the *Upanishads* have sometimes described all the *Vedas* and *Vedāngas*, and as a matter of fact all intellectual knowledge, as *Avidyā* (Ignorance) or *Aparā Vidyā* (Lower knowledge). *Parā Vidyā* (True knowledge) is that by which the Absolute Truth is directly realised (*Yayā tad aksharam adhigamyate*). This *Parā-Vidyā* is *Yoga-Vidyā*—the spiritual approach to the Absolute Truth.

The Vedānta-Darśan, which is the most widely accepted philosophical system of India,—and in fact almost all the principal philosophical systems of India,—frankly confessed that the method of logical argumentation was incapable of independently leading a truth-seeker to the final Truth (*Tarka-apratisthānāt*). They all practically admitted that there could be no such logical argument as could not be refuted by counter-arguments. They therefore had to accept the spiritual experiences of enlightened seers (*Āgama* or *Āptavacana* or *Śrutis*) as much more reliable evidence with regard to the nature of the Ultimate Truth. Many great sages spoke of the Ultimate Truth as beyond the range of thought and speech (*Avāng-manasa-gocaram*), and they warned the truth-seekers against the application of logical categories for the ascertainment of the character of transcendental realities (*Acintyāh khalu ye bhāvā na tān tarkena yojayet*). They advised the earnest seekers of Truth to have faith in the spiritual experiences of enlightened saints and to practically follow their instructions for the personal realisation of the Same.

Philosophers, while expounding their particular views about the Ultimate Truth, often cite as evidence the spiritual experiences of universally adored saints and make them the bases of their logical argumentation. But, in doing so, they have necessarily to rely upon the verbal expressions given by the saints of their inner spiritual experiences, which are according to their own confessions beyond the scope of verbal expressions and logical argumentations. Naturally, the advocates of different systems of philosophy put different interpretations to these verbal expressions and try to strengthen their own views with their help. The Vedāntic System of Philosophy has been divided into a number of separate philosophical sub-systems, holding separate views with regard to the nature of the Ultimate Reality and strongly refuting each other's conceptions and arguments, though they are all based upon the sayings of the *Upanishads* and the *lBhagavadgītā*, which all of them believe to be the verbal embodiments of the Truth of the supra-intellectual spiritual plane. Each of them tries to establish logically that its own interpretation of the sayings is the only correct one and that the interpretations given by other schools are wrong. Similarly, the Buddhist philosophers became divided into different schools, though they all claimed to expound rationally the spiritual experiences of Lord Buddha, as expressed in his words. This has been the fate of all earnest attempts at the philosophical interpretations of the spiritual experiences of enlightened saints. Logical argumentations almost invariably lead to differences of views.

The path of Yoga does not require any such intellectual speculation. It does not necessitate the framing of hypotheses and theories and their testing by logical argumentations. A truth-seeker in this path is not involved in academic controversies with the advocates of divergent philosophical views. He is not interested in the logical establishment of any particular theory or dogma, and hence he does not feel impelled to refute the rival theories or dogmas upheld by other schools of thinkers. His aim is not to acquire an *objective* knowledge of the *Absolute Truth* and to form a logically valid intellectual *conception* of the supra-logical supra-intellectual Reality. He aims at the direct spiritual experience of the Truth on a supra-logical supra-intellectual plane of consciousness. He advances in his path with an indomitable faith in the possibility of such experience. He does not create confusion in his mind by an attempt at an intellectual ascertainment of the nature of such experience, which is expected to be attained in the supra-intellectual plane, or of the possibility of any such transcendent experience.

It is as a matter of course impossible to demonstrate in any lower plane of existence and consciousness what is or is not possible in the higher and higher planes of existence and consciousness. What may be quite natural in a higher plane of existence and consciousness would appear unnatural or supernatural or logically untenable in a lower plane. A child cannot form any idea of the aesthetic and emotional experiences which are most natural to young men and women, though the objects stimulating such experiences may be present before the eyes of the child. A person, whose artistic faculty is not sufficiently developed, fails to appreciate and enjoy the beauty of a sweet song or a nice poem or a fine picture, though these may be the spontaneous expressions of the inner sentiments of a musician or a poet or a painter. Similarly, the nature of the direct inner experiences of an enlightened Yogi cannot be an object of intellectual conception to any person, whose consciousness has not been sufficiently refined and has not ascended to the higher spiritual plane through the systematic practice of *Yoga.* Even an enlightened Yogi himself fails to give an accurate linguistic expression to his deeper spiritual experiences. He can guide a Truth-seeker in the path of advancement towards his truthful and blissful experiences, but he cannot give him a correct idea of his own experience of Truth by means of language or prove to him the possibility of such Truth-realisation by means of logical reasoning.

The Yogi's method of search for the Absolute Truth is based on the idea that though the Absolute Truth may not be an object of intellectual comprehension and logical reasoning, It unveils Itself to the human consciousness, when this consciousness is adequately purified and refined and concentrated and thus becomes perfectly free from the impediments in the way of the self-revelation of the Truth to it. A Yogi, therefore, instead of making futile attempts to form a perfect logical conception of the nature of the Absolute in the lower empirical planes of his consciousness, directs his attention and energy to the progressive purification, refinement and concentration of his empirical consciousness and its elevation to higher and higher spiritual planes, until the supreme transcendent plane is reached, in which the veil between the Ultimate Truth and the consciousness vanishes altogether and the consciousness is absolutely united with the Truth.

In the normal nature of a man, his empirical consciousness is related to and conditioned by his physical body, his senses and nervous system and brain, his mind and intellect and heart and his individual ego. All these together constitute the embodiment of his self-conscious soul. The soul appears to be imprisoned in this complex psycho-physical embodiment. A man's perceptions and inferences, imaginations and reasonings, feelings and sentiments, desires and aspirations, thoughts and ideas, are all conditioned and determined by the characters and limitations of this embodiment. Hence they are all confined within the world of finitude and relativity. A man, however, feels within his innermost consciousness, a persistent urge for transcending all limitations and bondages of this psycho-physical organism and attaining and enjoying the Absolute Truth, the Absolute Beauty, the Absolute Goodness, the Absolute Bliss—of which, under his normal conditions, he cannot even form any positive conception. It is this inner urge of his soul which does not allow him to get permanent satisfaction from any achievement, however glorious, in this world of finite transient relative phenomena, and always prompts him to seek for *more and more*. *Tatah kim, tatah kim*—what after this, what after this? It is this inherent spiritual urge of his innermost consciousness which assures him (though not in an argumentative way) of the possibility of the apparently natural limitations of his psycho-physical embodiment being transcended by him by means of some appropriate form of self-discipline, and of the Absolute Truth-Beauty-Goodness-Bliss, which his soul craves for, being directly realised.

With the ultimate object of the attainment of this supreme spiritual experience, a Yogi devotes himself to the practice of such courses of self-discipline as may free his consciousness from the limitations which the psycho-physical embodiment imposes upon it. He holds before himself as the practical object of his pursuit an ideal state of his own consciousness, perfectly free from all impurities and distractions and doubts and perplexities, perfectly free from all desires and attachments and passions and propensities, perfectly free from all argumentative thought and preconceived notions, perfectly free from the sense of individual ego and the sense of distinction between the subject and the object, the internal and the external, the self and the not-self. It is in such a perfectly pure and refined, calm and tranquil, desireless and thoughtless, egoless and subject-object-less, transcendent state of the consciousness that the Absolute Truth-Beauty-Goodness-Bliss is expected to unconditionally reveal Itself, not as an object of the consciousness, but as the true Soul or Essence of the consciousness. The consciousness is in that state perfectly illumined by this Soul, and no difference exists between the consciousness and the Absolute Soul of all existences and experiences. In that transcendent experience no time or space exists, no relativity or causality exists, no distinction between Truth and Beauty and Goodness and Bliss exists. It is one absolute integrated experience, which cannot be described in terms of the analytical and synthetical categories of our normal intellectual understanding. The experience carries its certitude within itself, and it does not require any extraneous proof. Logical reasoning can neither deny its possibility, nor furnish any proof of its validity. But a Yogi, who is blessed with this experience, is free from all doubts. His yearning for the Absolute is perfectly satisfied. An earnest aspirant for Truth-realisation advances in the path of *Yoga* under the guidance of such a Truth-realiser with faith and perseverance.

In the *Yoga-Śastras*, this transcendent state of the consciousness is called *Samādhi*. The whole course of self-discipline in the path of *Yoga* is directed towards the attainment of this *Samādhi*, in which alone the direct and perfect experience of the Absolute Reality is possible. *Samādhi* is a thoroughly practicable ideal. Every step of progress in the direction of the realisation of this ideal can be *practically* tested and verified. Hence *Yoga* is regarded as the most practical path to the realisation of the ultimate Ideal of human life. As Bhiśma says in the Mahābhārat—Direct experience is the basis of *Yoga* (*Pratyaksha-hetavo yogāh*). *Samādhi* is not a static condition of the consciousness. There are higher and higher stages of *Samādhi*, and in each higher stage there is a deeper realisation of Truth.

The Nature of Samadhi-Experience

The experience which is attained in the highest state of *Samādhi* cannot be regarded either as purely *subjective* experience or as *objective* experience or as *negation* of experience. It is not of the nature of subjective experience like that in the dream-state of consciousness or in the state of reverie or imagination or illusion or hallucination, in which the experiencing subject projects itself as the objects of experience under the influence of some internal or external stimulation. Such experiences are not accepted as forms of valid knowledge. They occur only in the impure and restless states of the empirical consciousness. In them, there is no correspondence between the objects of experience and the actual realities. In the *Samādhi* state, the consciousness is pure and calm and tranquil, free from the influences of all external and internal stimuli. In it there is no room for imagination or error or self-projection. In it there is no functioning of the mind or the intellect. The sense of the ego as the experiencing subject disappears, and hence this also does not condition the experience and make it an affair of a particular egoistic mind. In the deepest *Samādhi*, what is experienced does not appear as an *object* of experience, as distinct from and related to the experiencing *subject*. The individual consciousness ascends in that state to the transcendent universal plane, and the Reality as experienced in this plane cannot be merely a subjective reality—real to a particular individual and unreal to others. Every individual consciousness that rises to this plane should be blessed with the same transcendent experience. Hence the Reality as revealed in the highest state of *Samādhi* must be recognised as the Absolute Reality.

It is also clear that *Samādhi*-experience is not of the nature of *objective* experience like that of the normal waking-state of the consciousness, in which the experience is conditioned by the natural limitation of the psycho-physical embodiment, and in which the objects of experience are as a matter of course finite relative phenomenal realities. In the state of *Samādhi*, the consciousness, though not unrelated to the psycho-physical organism, transcends its limitations, rises above the plane of finite egohood and the relativity of subject and object and becomes perfectly pure and tranquil and refined and illumined. The Reality revealed in the experience of this transcendent consciousness does not appear as a phenomenal object, distinct from the experiencing subject, but as one with it.

It may be questioned whether there is any real experience at all in this *Samādhi*-state of the consciousness. From the standpoint of the plane of our normal objective and subjective experiences, the question is not irrelevant. How can there be any real experience in the state in which there is no distinction and mutual relation between the subject and the object, the experiencer and the experienced? Can it be called any real experience, if only pure consciousness exists and nothing is present before it as its object? No only that. It may also be questioned if consciousness can at all exist as consciousness, when there is neither any subjective experience nor any objective experience in it. How can consciousness exist without any functions or phenomena of consciousness? May not what is called *Samādhi*-state be really the suicide of the consciousness? Or, may it not be a state analogous to the state of deep sleep (*suṣupti*) or swoon (*moorchhā*), in which there is no real experience, in which the consciousness is in a state of absolute ignorance,—in which it is ignorant of the psycho-physical embodiment, ignorant of the objective world, and even ignorant of its own existence ? May not the *Samādhi* state be a state of absolute ignorance or an absolutely unconscious state?

Such doubts may naturally arise in the fickle minds and speculative intellects of those who had never got the beatific experience of the *Samādhi* state. The enlightened Yogi, whose consciousness has risen to the highest spiritual plane and had an actual taste of this state, is free from all such doubts. To him this state of *Samādhi* is not a vacant state, but a state of fulness, not a state of darkness, but a state of perfect illumination, which is never experienced by the mind in the normal conditions. In this state, the consciousness does not commit suicide, it is not reduced into a state of unconsciousness or absolute ignorance; but it elevates itself into a state of *absolute knowledge* (*purnagñāna* or *kevalagñāna*), in which the knower and the knowable become perfectly united with each other, in which no difference remains between the Reality and the Consciousness and nothing more remains to be known, in which the entire universe of the apparent plurality of existences unveils its essential spiritual unity to the consciousness as well as its identity with the consciousness itself. The all-unifying truth-revealing transcendent experience of the highest spiritual plane of the consciousness, though indescribable and even inconceivable in terms of the normal objective and subjective experiences, is to the Yogi the most real experience.

Normally, we live and move and have our being in a world of plurality—a world of differences and inter-relations. Differences among the various kinds of realities appear to be fundamental, and at the same time mutual relations among them also appear as inherent in their very nature. Spirit and matter are, so far as our normal experience goes, essentially different from each other; neither can be proved to be the cause or the effect of the other. But the inter-relation between them is so rooted in their nature, that we cannot even form any definite conception of the one except in relation to the other. In the world of living beings, matter constitutes the embodiment of the spirit and the spirit is the soul of the material body. We conceive matter as unconscious and inanimate and inert and it cannot by itself be conscious and living and moving; it is the conscious spirit which, entering into every particle of matter, converts it into a living and moving and self-organising conscious body, and it is this body which becomes the medium and instrument of all self-expressions of the spirit. What we experience as inorganic material things are also what they are as objects of experiences of the conscious spirit; apart from relation to the conscious subject, *i.e.* the spirit, they seem to have no characters—they are as good as nothing. The spirit also appears to be contentless and characterless, except in relation to the material body and material objects. Thus, in our normal experience. spirit and matter are essentially distinct as well as essentially related.

Again, in this world of plurality of our normal experience, spirits appear to be innumerable and essentially distinct from one another; different spirits are embodied in and conditioned by different psycho-physical organisms, having different kinds of experiences and different kinds of hopes and aspirations. But inter-communications and inter-dependences among them are also quite obvious. Similarly, the elementary material things which constitute the objective material world appear to be essentially different from one another; but they are all inter-related.

It is the plurality of inter-related phenomenal realities which constitute the contents of our normal experience and knowledge. Our empirical consciousness cannot transcend this plurality. But, there is always a feeling in the depth of our consciouness that this knowledge is not perfect. It mysteriously feels within itself that there must be some underlying Unity, holding together the plurality, harmonising and unifying all the phenomenal diversities, and that that Unity must be the real Truth of the plurality.

It is the inherent demand of the consciousness for the discovery of One Absolute Reality as the Ultimate Truth of the inter-related plurality of existences, that is at the root of all sciences and philosophy. Every science makes serious efforts through the methods of keen and careful observation and experiment as well as logical reasoning and theorising to discover some principle of Unity behind the plurality of phenomena within the scope of its investigation. The ambition of every philosophical system is to discover some Unity as the Truth of all existences. Since their methods of approach are inherently incapable of giving any sure knowledge of this Unity, they invariably fail to reach their goal. Whatever theories they may form, they can never grasp the Unity of Spirit and Matter, the unity of the conscious subject and the Objective Universe, the Unity of the knower and the knowable. The knowledge which is attainable through the scientific and philosophical methods is phenomenal and objective knowledge; while the Unity that underlies and unifies all kinds of phenomena of the past, the present and the future and is the Infinite and Eternal Ground of all cannot be a phenomenal reality and cannot therefore be an object of scientific or philosophical knowledge. The Reality, which is the Supreme Ground of the relations among all conscious subjects and all objects of consciousness, cannot itself appear as a particular object of the empirical consciousness of a particular knowing subject. Thus the Ultimate Unity of all existences, for which there is an inherent demand of the consciousness, remains beyond the reach of all scientific and philosophical knowledge.

The *Samādhi* experience of an enlightened Yogi at the highest spiritual plane of the consciousness is the direct knowledge of this Unity of all existences. It is distinct from all scientific and philosophical knowledge. It is distinct from knowledge of sense-perception and inference and logical reasoning. In it the consciousness transcends the difference between Spirit and Matter, the difference between the Subject and the Object, between the Internal and the External, between the One and the Many. In it the consciousness becomes perfectly one with the Truth of all existences. The inherent demand of the consciousness for the Absolute Truth is in this experience perfectly satisfied. It is *transcendent experience.*

A Yogi who is blessed with this spiritual experience in the state of *Samādhi* has not merely the intellectual satisfaction of having discovered the Ultimate Truth, but also attains the perfect satisfation of the fulfilment of life. He becomes free from all sorts of bondage and sorrow, from all kinds of weakness and infirmity, from all senses of imperfections and limitations. Having in the transcendent plane of his consciousness experienced the perfect character of his innermost Self and its identity with the Infinite Eternal Self of the Universe, he becomes free from all fears, all cares and anxieties, all attractions for and attachments to, as well as all disgusts against and repugnance to the finite and transitory things of the world. What he feels is so described by the illustrious commentator of the *Yoga Sutras:—*

Jñātam jñātavyam, prāptam prāpaniyam, kshināh kshetavyā kleśāh, karma-bandhanāni śithilāni.

What is worth knowing has been known, what is worth getting has been got, all the *Kleśas* (imperfections) which are fit to be destroyed have been destroyed, all the bondages of *Karma* (actions—virtues and vices) have become infructuous. The *Yoga-Sutras* enumerate five kinds of *Kleśas i.e.* fundamental imperfections and sources of sorrows and bondages, *viz., Avidyā* (ignorance or false knowledge), *Asmitā* (egohood—I-am-ness) *Rāga* (attachment), *Dvesha* (aversion) and *Abhiniveśa* (lust of life and the consequent fear of death). It is these which determine all our worldly activities, virtuous as well as vicious; and it is these which place us under subjection to the *Law of Karma* and compel us to reap the pleasurable and painful fruits of our actions in repeated births and in various forms of living existence. All these *Kleśas,* to which our consciousness is subject in the normal planes, and by which all our actions as well as enjoyments and sufferings in the worldly life are determined, are destroyed, when the consciousness is illumined by the Transcendent Experience. An enlightened Yogi thus attains perfect freedom from all bondages of individual life. This is called *Mukti* or *Moksha*. In his enlightened experience, he virtually ceases to be a finite individual and the world also ceases to exist as a reality external to him. The lamp of his life as a finite changing mortal individual is extinguished. This is therefore spoken of as *Nirvāna*. The individual then attains the character of the Absolute—the one without a second. He is therefore said to attain *Kaivalya*.

Enlightening Influence of Samadhi-Experience Upon Normal Life

The individual psycho-physical life of a Yogi does not however end with the experience of *Kaivalya* or *Nirvāna* or *Moksha*. The consciousness again comes down from the transcendent plane to the normal plane, from the state of *Samādhi* to the state of *Vyutthāna* (the normal waking state), from the perfectly illumined state to the state of conditioned knowledge. The enlightened Yogi again becomes conscious of himself as an embodied being, conscious of the objective world of plurality as external to himself. His knowledge of the world as well as of himself is again conditioned by his senses, mind, intellect and ego. He again apparently becomes one of innumerable finite individuals of the world.

Though outwardly he appears to become the same individual as he had been before the attainment of the Transcendent Experience of the *Samādhi*-state, yet inwardly this is not the case. The Truth-experience which illumines his consciousness in the supramental supra-intellectual supra-egoistic transcendent state exercises a great enlightening influence upon his normal mind and intellect and ego. His entire outlook on himself, his fellow-beings and the world of inter-related diversities undergoes a radical transformation as the result of that experience. Before he was blessed with that experience, the Spiritual Unity of all existences had been veiled from his empirical consciousness. He used to see the plurality as plurality, but he had not the eyes to see the Unity that shone in and through them. The Absolute One that manifests Itself in the diverse forms of relative plurality, that sustains their existence, regulates their movements, links them with one another and constitutes them into a magnificent cosmic order, had been concealed from his view, though he had felt a deep craving within his consciousness for having a glimpse of that Absolute One. Now, that Absolute One has revealed Itself to his consciousness; the veil has been removed; the consciousness has been illumined. This illumination is transmitted to the intellect, the ego and the mind and even to the senses. They do not now experience merely what they used to experience before the illumination descended upon them, but also the Absolute One along with and as the real essence of the objects of their normal experience. The ego now feels the Absolute One as its True Self and feels itself as an individualised self-expression of the Absolute One. The intellect now no longer theorises, but finds in the Absolute One the ultimate rational explanation of all the problems that may appear before it. All the thoughts, feelings and volitions of the illumined mind now revolve round the Absolute One as the centre. All the diverse kinds of objects of sense-perception are experiences as diversified appearances or manifestations of the One.

In the transcendent experience of the *Samādhi*-state, the objective world of plurality and the experiencing ego are both completely merged in one Absolute Consciousness (or Super-consciousness), which is the Absolute Truth or Reality of both; while in the enlightened experience of the Yogi in the normal plane of his empirical consciousness the ego and the objective world of plurality are both present, both appear as pervaded by the One, as having their being in the One, as the two-fold manifestations of the One. The One being the Truth of both, the Yogi sees himself in all and all in himself. He looks upon all the diversities from the standpoint of Unity; he sees the Infinite in the finite, the Eternal in the temporal, the Changeless in all changes, and the spirit in all material things. He thinks and feels all as essentially non-different from himself, and hence he loves all and hates and fears none.

In the *Samādhi*-experience, a Yogi transcends time and space. The beginningless and endless flow of time is in this ultimate Truth-experience merged in one changeless Eternity. The boundless space is also merged in one differenceless Infinity. In the enlightened normal experience, the Yogi sees the timeless Eternity manifested in the flow of time, the extensionless Infinity pervading all parts of space. In the *Samādhi*-state, his senses, mind and intellect are all functionless; they do not condition and diversify the experiences of the consciousness. He then does not perceive any external objects; he does not feel any pleasure or pain, any hunger or thirst, any affection or compassion, any duty or obligation; he has no process of thinking, no conception or judgment or reasoning; at that stage, he has no behaviour at all. His consciousness then shines in its unconditioned undifferentiated unveiled fulness, in which the Reality and the consciousness are one. When the Yogi comes down to the normal plane with the memory or illumination of his transcendent experience, his senses, mind and intellect perform their normal functions, but with some new enlightenment. His senses appear to perceive some super-sensuous Reality behind the ordinary objects of perception; his mind, even in course of its normal operations, seems to dwell in some supra-mental plane, and an attitude of unconcern and disinterestedness towards all affairs of the world prevails in his mind under all circumstances. He remains under all conditions free from cares and anxieties, desires and attachments, confusions and perplexities. All his intellectual thinking also appears to have as its centre the Truth of the super-intellectual experience.

An enlightened Yogi in his normal life lives and moves in the domain of the senses, the mind and the intellect, but has his inner being in the peaceful and blissful realm of the super-sensuous super-mental super-intellectual Reality. As the result of systematic discipline, his body, senses, mental functions and intellectual reflections are of course much more refined and tranquillized than those of ordinary men whose lives are almost wholly governed by worldly interests and worldly forces. Not only that. By means of appropriate Yogic practices, he often acquires such extraordinary powers and visions even with regard to the relative realities of the world as appear miraculous and superhuman to others. He acquires the powers of seeing and hearing things beyond the range of normal ocular and auditory perceptions and of seeing without eyes and hearing without ears. He acquires the powers of knowing the events of the past and the future just as those of the present. He acquires the powers of entering into the minds of others and reading their thoughts and feelings and often exercising control over them. He may acquire the power of making his gross material body lighter than air and rising high up in the air and moving to distant places by the aerial path. He can often make his body invisible to the people present before him and can make his way through thick walls. He can acquire the power of assuming many bodies at the same time, making himself visible to people of different places and performing different actions with the different bodies. He may acquire the power of exerting control over the forces of nature and of transforming one natural thing into another. He may acquire the power of creating new things by the mere exercise of his will and of changing the natural characters of things; and so on, and so forth. According to the *Yoga-Śāstras,* an enlightened Yogi may develop in himself even the power of creating a new world. Truly enlightened Yogis seldom make any display of their Yogic powers, which appear miraculous or superhuman to ordinary people. But, some Yogi teachers give occasional expressions of their minor occult powers, perhaps in order to demonstrate to the self-diffident people of the world what great powers lie hidden and dormant in them and to inspire them with the faith that they also can become masters of the forces of nature, if they undergo a systematic course of self-discipline under expert guidance in the path of *Yoga* and thereby become masters of themselves,

Although in the plane of transcendent spiritual experience no difference exists between one Yogi and another, nevertheless when enlightened Yogis come down to the normal planes of practical life, their behaviours are often found to be different. These differences are generally due to the natural differences of their psycho-physical embodiments, their habits and modes of training in the pre-enlightenment period, as well as their environmental conditions. Different Yogis are found to have temperamental differences. Some Yogis are found to cut off all connections with the affairs of the external world and to pass their time in solitude in a constantly meditative mood and in continuous enjoyment of the bliss of *Samādhi*-experience. They seldom allow their consciousness to come down to the lower planes. Other enlightened Yogis are moved by love and compassion for the people of the world, whom they see suffering various kinds of sorrows on account of their ignorance of the Eternal Truth and their hankering for and attachment to the petty transitory things of this earth. They come in close contact with these people and adopt various means to give them True Light and emancipate them from sorrows and bondages. Inwardly, they also dwell in the plane of the Infinite and Eternal; but outwardly love and compassion make them active. It is these Yogis who become *Gurus* or spiritual guides in the society. It is through them that spiritual light comes down to the people of the world and awakens in their consciousness the yearning for the Infinite Eternal Absolute Reality, which otherwise remains dormant in it.

The enlightened Yogis, who look upon all human beings and all the affairs of the world from the spiritual point of view and move among the people on account of their deep-seated love and compassion for them, have in all ages been the true teachers of humanity and the true leaders of culture and civilization. It is from their lives and teachings that the people living and moving normally in the physical, vital, sensuous, mental and intellectual planes, get glimpses of the Supreme Truth underlying and pervading and transcending the world of ordinary experience and some ideas about the Highest Ideal of their lives. It is these saints who present before their fellow-beings the noblest ideals of their intellectual pursuits and social activities, the highest standards of values, the deepest meanings of life and its aspirations, the innermost significance of the wonderful order and harmony in all the departments of this most complicated cosmic process. They are the permanent sources of inspiration to men and women of all grades of the society.

The ideas of Universal Brotherhood, Universal Love and Sympathy, Equality of all men, Sacredness of the lives of all creatures, Inherent Right to Liberty and Justice of all people, Respect for Truth for Truth's sake, Selfless and Disinterested Service to all fellow-beings, Unity of mankind and Unity of the world-order,—all such lofty ideas, which have been pushing mankind to higher and higher types of civilization, have been obtained from enlightened Yogis, who have been instilling these ideas into the minds and hearts of the people from time immemorial. All the noblest and most dynamic ideas, which have been progressively refining the human civilization, have been based upon the spiritual experiences of enlightened Saints, who have been preaching them in all parts of this earth for hundreds of years. It is from them that the people learn that the cultivation of their social virtues and their sense of duty and obligation should not be confined within certain territorial boundaries or within certain racial or communal or national limits. We learn from them that our morality does not become truly human morality, until and unless it transcends the narrow domestic and communal and racial and national limits and recognises the entire mankind as one grand and beautiful family, and that our religion does not become truly spiritual religion, until and unless it rises above all sectarian and communal exclusiveness and bigotry and dogmatism and fanaticism and inspires us to feel in our heart of hearts the unity of all men and all creatures. It is these saints who have taught the human society to value self-control as superior to self-gratification, self-sacrifice as superior to self-aggrandisement, self-conquest as superior to the conquest of other people, spiritual self-fulfilment as superior to materalistic advancement, all-embracing love as superior to all-vanquishing brute-force, renunciation of all earthly goods for the sake of the eternal good of the soul as superior to ambition for and attainment of even the greatest possible power and prosperity and pleasure in this physical world. The examples they set up through their own character and conduct and the precepts they preach by words of mouth elevate the sense of dignity of man to a higher spiritual level, awaken in man the consciousness of his inner spiritual possibilities and of the true seat of his glory as the crown of the creation, and practically lead him in the path of his perfect self-realisation. These Yogis are the true makers of civilization.

When a Yogi, out of deep sympathy and compassion for the ignorant and distressed people of the world, feels prompted to assume the role of a public teacher and preacher, he is required to give expression to his inner experiences in such intellectual and emotional forms as may be easily intelligible and appealing to those people of the lower planes. Knowing fully well that the truth of the higher planes of spiritual experience cannot be adequately expressed in the language and concepts of the lower planes, he takes the help of various kinds of figures of speech, poetic imageries, suggestive parables, imperfect analogies, mystic formulas, inspiring exhortations, etc., in order to awaken the deeper consciousness of the people and to raise their thoughts and imaginations forcefully to the higher planes. The instructions of an enlightened Yogi, coming out of his heart with the force of his inner experience, carry conviction to the hearts of the listeners and often bring about a radical change in their outlook and mode of thought. Sometimes a Yogi does not require any word of mouth or movement of limbs for the purpose of exercising his spiritual influence upon the minds and hearts of people; his presence is enough. His very presence as a living embodiment of Truth, Beauty, Goodness, Love and Bliss, exerts a mysterious influence upon the consciousness of those who come to learn from him, and even upon the cultural atmosphere of the society in which he lives.

But usually the enlightened Yogis, who compassionately undertake the work of bringing down spiritual light to the people of the Society suffering from ignorance and earthly desires and attachments, adopt the usual means of imparting true knowledge to them. Though inwardly dwelling in the supra-mental supra-intellecual spiritual plane, they practically adjust their modes of teaching and preaching to the mental and intellectual and even the social and physical needs of the people whom they want to serve. While in their teaching life, they primarily concern themselves with inspiring the people with spiritual ideas and ideals on the basis of their deeper experiences, they often attempt to bridge over the chasm between the practical experiences and intellectual conceptions of the ordinary people and their own spiritual realisations in the higher planes of consciousness, by means of suitable logical arguments and philosophical speculations which may appeal to the intellects and imaginations of those people. Thus the Yogis convert themselves into Philosophers to suit the purpose of their teaching.

Very few among the truly enlightened Yogi teachers built up any regular system of philosophy. They usually give suggestive hints with regard to the Ultimate Truth, which they have realised in the plane of transcendent consciousness and which they instruct the truth-seekers to realise themselves by means of proper self-discipline, and they teach them the path in which they should proceed. Systems of philosophy are generally built up by their disciples and admirers who dwell in the intellectual plane, on the basis of the inspiring formulas and aphorisms uttered by those adorable teachers. Even those enlightened Yogis who happen to present a system of philosophy to the intellectualist truth-seekers do not lay undue emphasis upon the *concepts* in terms of which they describe the Ultimate Truth and the logical arguments leading to these *concepts*. To them all such intellectual concepts are necessarily imperfect expressions of the Ultimate Truth realised in the supra-intellectual plane of the consciousness and no logical arguments can possibly lead to that Supreme Truth. Nevertheless they recognise the value of philosophy as a mode of search for the Truth and as a mode of discipline of the mind and the intellect. The mind and the intellect are greatly purified and refined and emancipated from irrational ideas and superstitious beliefs and earth-bound dispositions through a regular course of philosophical discipline. The systematic study of philosophy under the guidance of enlightened teachers can very well raise a sincere and earnest Truth-seeker from the physical, vital, sensuous and mental planes to the plane of refined intellect and lead him very near to the realisation of the Ultimate Truth. The enlightened Yogi-teachers therefore encourage their intellectualist disciples and truth-seekers to take to the systematic study of philosophy with an unbiassed mind as a very suitable method of self-discipline and self-enlightenment. They accordingly sometimes present before them a system of philosophy for the proper regulation of their reasoning faculty and their mode of approach to Truth. These Yogi-philosophers seldom entangle themselves in polemical controvesies with the advocates of other systems of philosophy. To these enlightened teachers every well-reasoned system of philosophy is a particular mode of intellectual approach to the same supra-intellectual Truth and a particular form of effective discipline of the intellect. When the intellect is properly disciplined and refined, it becomes much easier to transcend the domain of the intellect.

CHAPTER I

GORAKHNATH—A MAHAYOGI

Gorakhnath was a Mahāyogi. He was not essentially a philosopher in the commonly accepted meaning of the term. He did not seek for the Absolute Truth in the path of speculation and logical argumentation. He was not much interested in logically proving or disproving the existence of any Ultimate Noumenal Reality beyond or behind or immanent in the phenomenal world of our normal experience or intellectually ascertaining the nature of any such Reality. He never entangled himself seriously in controversial metaphysical discussions. He never made a display of his intellectual capacities as the upholder of any particular metaphysical theory in opposition to other rival theories. He knew that in the intellectual plane differences of views were inevitable, specially with regard to the Supreme Truth, which was beyond the realm of the normal intellect. He did not attach any primary importance to philosophical speculations and controversies as a means to the realisation of the Ultimate Truth. But he considered them valuable as modes of intellectual discipline and helpful in the path of search for Truth, provided that they were carried on with sincerity and earnestness and humility, and without any bigotry or arrogance or prejudice or blind partiality to particular schools of thought.

Unbiassed pursuit of Truth in the path of philosophical reflection was according to him a very effective way to the progressive refinement of the intellect and its elevation to the higher and higher planes, leading gradually to the emancipation of the consciousness from the bondage of all intellectual theories and sentimental attachments. Philosophical reflection (*Tattva-Vicāra*) was therefore regarded as a valuable part of *yogic* self-discipline. Its principal aim should be to make the individual phenomenal consciousness free from all kinds of bias and prejudice, all forms of narrowness and bigotry, all sorts of pre-conceived notions and emotional clingings, and to raise it to the pure supra-mental supra-intellectual spiritual plane, in which it may be blessed with the direct experience of the Absolute Truth by becoming perfectly united with it. It was with this object in view that Yogi Guru Gorakhnath taught what might be called a system of philosophy for the guidance of the truth-seekers in the path of intellectual self-discipline.

The *Sampradāya* associated with the name of Gorakhnath has a vast literature, in Sanskrit as well as in many of the provincial dialects of India. The authorship of a good many Sanskrit treatises is attributed to Gorakhnath himself. Numerous instructive and inspiring short poems in the oldest forms of some of the regional popular languages, such as Hindi and Rajasthani and Bengali, are directly connected with his name. Which of the books ascribed to him, or bearing his holy name, were really written by the Mahāyogi himself is however a matter of controversy. The region in which he was born and the regional language in which he usually spoke are as yet unascertained. Here we are to assume that the old sacred literature which passes in his name and which has long been recognised as authoritative or reliable by his long line of followers was either produced by him or based on his teachings and hence faithfully represents his views. We should attach greater value to the Sanskrit works, which are regarded as more authoritative by all sections of his *sampradāya* as well as by other earnest scholars.

Now, what is particularly noteworthy in connection with the subject-matter of our present discourse is that, though there are so many well-written Sanskrit works which are highly valued by the *sampradāya* and which are believed to embody the teachings of the Great Master, there is scarcely a single book available, which is exclusively or even principally devoted to metaphysical discussion. All the standard works are chiefly concerned with the exposition of the principles and practices of *Yoga*. *Yoga* is a method of systematic discipline of all the external and internal organs of the physical body, of all the senses and vital forces and nerves and muscles, of all the psychical functions and natural propensities and subtle desires and passions and of all the intellectual ideas and judgments and reasonings, with a view to the establishment of perfect control over and harmony among all of them and the refinement and spiritualisation of the entire psycho-physiological organism and with the ultimate object of the realisation of Absolute Truth in the most tranquil and integral and illumined state of consciousness. Hence the exposition of *Yoga* necessarily presupposes a profound knowledge of the structure and operations of the various parts of the organism and a clear conception of the Supreme Ideal towards which the whole course of discipline is to be directed. The *Art of Yoga* must have a scientific and philosophic background. Hence books on *Yoga* incidentally discuss relevant scientific and metaphysical topics.

The metaphysical doctrine, which Gorakhnath preached along with his instructions on *yogic* discipline, was not purely the result of any logical reasoning, nor did he attempt to put his doctrine in exact logical forms. The ultimate basis of his philosophy was his supra-mental and supra-intellectual experience in the *samādhi*-state of his consciousness. It was an intellectual expression of his transcendent experience, with due regard for the valid experiences of the normal life, and an attempt to link them together. He presented it as an enlightening way of thinking and meditation to the seekers of truth and peace and freedom from bondage and sorrow. He generally adopted the terminology and modes of linguistic expression which were current among the *Siddhà-Mahāyogis* for hundreds of years and which were commonly found in the old *Śaiva* and *Śākta Āgamas* and *Tantras*. He never dogmatically declared that all truth-seekers must adopt the same terminology in their methods of thinking or even the same way of thinking for the refinement of their thoughts. He would teach the people that Truth was the same, in whatever forms of language It might be expressed and in whatever paths the intellect might approach It. The mind must seek for the Truth with sincerity and earnestness and must not be led away by undue attachment to particular forms of language or particular methods of thinking.

It should be remembered that the Ultimate Truth reveals Itself in a plane of consciousness higher than those in which these speeches and thoughts move, and that the methods of philosophical thinking and the expressions of thoughts in appropriate linguistic forms are only means to the purification and enlightenment and concentration of the empirical consciousness and its elevation to the higher planes. Gorakhnath himself freely made use of the terminology and nomenclature current among other schools of philosophical thinking and religious discipline as well and pointed out that their inner significance and purpose were the same. He would often make use of poetic imageries, similes, metaphors and figures of speech and analogical arguments for giving expression to his inner thoughts and experiences, which really belonged to higher planes. Nevertheless, Gorakhnath preached a system of philosophy which has a special place among the philosophical systems of India and a special distinctive character and value of its own.

CHAPTER II

LITERARY SOURCES OF GORAKHNATH'S PHILOSOPHICAL VIEWS

It has already been noted that the authorship of a good many books in Sanskrit as well as in several old regional dialects is traditionally attributed to Mahāyogi Gorakhnath and that it is very difficult at the present age to ascertain definitely which of them were really written by the Mahāyogi himself. We may however mention here the names of several Sanskrit treatises which are traditionally believed to have been composed by Gorakhnath—*Goraksha Samhitā, Goraksha Śataka, Siddha Siddhānta Paddhati, Yoga Siddhānta Paddhati, Viveka Mārtanda, Yoga Mārtanda, Yoga Chintāmani, Jñānāmrita, Amanaska, Ātmabodha, Goraksha Sahasra Nāma, Yoga-bīja, Amaraugha Prabodha, Goraksha Pistika, Goraksha Gitā,* etc. etc. Many other books were current in his name. Gorakhnath's Guru Matsyendra Nath is said to have been the author of a good many treatises, such as, *Matsyendra Samhitā, Kaula Jñāna Nirnaya, Kulānanda Tantra, Jñāna Kārikā, Akula Vīra-Tantra,* etc. There is a number of later *Upanishads,* the names of whose authors are not available but which elaborately deal with the *yogic* concepts and *yogic* methods as taught by Matsyendranath, Gorakhnath and other *Siddha Yogi* teachers. For examples, *Nāda-Bindu Upanishad, Dhyāna-Bindu Upanishad, Tejo-Bindu Upanishad, Yoga-Tattwa Upanishad, Yoga-Chudāmani Upanishad, Yoga-Sīkhā Upanishad, Yoga-Kundalī Upanishad, Mandala-Brāhmana Upanishad; Śāndilya Upanishad, Jābāla Upanishad, etc.* There is one *Upanishad,* which is known as *Goraksha Upanishad. Nātha Sutra, Śiva Gitā, Avadhuta Gitā, Śiva Samhitā, Suta Samhitā, Dattātreya Samhitā, Śāvara Tantra, Gheranda Samhitā, Hatha-Yoga Pradīpika,* and many such Sanskrit treatises are definitely connected with the *Yogi Sampradāya* of Gorakhnath, and they are authoritative guide-books for spiritual aspirants in the path of *Yoga.* Most of these books give valuable informations about the philosophical concepts and principles, on which the *yogic* methods of discipline are based, but very few of them attach primary importance to philosophical discussions on controversial topics.

Many old poetical works have been discovered in Bengali, Hindi, Rajasthani and other regional languages of India, as well as of the bordering countries, like Nepal and Tibet, which were based on the lives and teachings of Matsyendranath, Gorakhnath and other illustrious saints of the Nāth-Yogi sect. The authorship of some of them is ascribed to those great founders of the sect. Matsyendranath is regarded as the earliest poet in the Bengali language. Many great *Nāth-Āchāryas* or *Siddha-Āchāryas* were writers of Bengali poems. The earliest poems in Hindi and Rajasthani were those, which are believed to have been composed by Gorakhnath. There were many poets among their followers also, who preached their ideas through literature. All these literary works are valuable sources of information about the Great Master's philosophical ideas.

Among these books, *Siddha Siddhānta Paddhati* occupies a special position. This Sanskrit treatise gives a systematic exposition in a rather abridged form of the metaphysical ideas and the way of thinking of the *Siddha-Yogi Sampradāya* as well as of the Supreme Ideal which the Yogis seek to realise in their life through the practice of *Yoga.* This book is cited as an authority in many other books of the *Sampradāya.* No other book of this *Sampradāya* has as yet been discovered, which presents to us such a clear account of the philosophy and religion of this great school. The book itself proclaims Gorakhnath as its author, though some modern scholars gravely doubt the genuineness of this declaration.

Like many other standard works of this *Sampradāya, Siddha Siddhānta Paddhati* had been in manuscript form for so many centuries and had been available for study only to the initiated members and specially inquisitive scholars of this *Sampradāya.* It was for the first time published in printed form from Hardwar by Yogindra Purnanāth with a Sanskrit commentary by Pundit Dravyeśa Jhā Śāstri and a Hindi commentary by Yogi Bhishmanath, in the year 1996 Vikram Sambat (1940 A. D.). Quite recently, Dr. (Mrs.) Kalyani Mullik, M. A., Ph. D., of the Calcutta University, has published another edition of this book with an English summary of her own.

There is a poetical work, named *Siddha Siddhānta Sangraha,* which is a summary in verse of *Siddha Siddhānta Paddhati.* This book was published in printed form in 1925 by Mahamahopadhyaya Gopinath Kaviraj. The date of the composition of this book also could not be ascertained. One verse in the book indicates that it was written by some person, named Balbhadra, at the bidding of Krishnaraja, in the sacred city of Kashi. It is certainly an old book and it ably summarises the contents of the original, often reproducing the language of the original. It was available to the general readers before the publication of the original work.

Goraksha Siddhānta Sangraha is another important Sanskrit treatise in prose, which briefly expounds the philosophical and religious views of

Gorakhnath. This book makes profuse quotations from the sayings of old Mahāyogis like Matsyendranath, Gorakhnath, Jālandharnath, Bhartrihari and others as well as from a good many older texts on *Yoga*. But *Siddha Siddhānta Paddhati* appears to be the main basis of this treatise. This book also was first edited and published with a short Prefatory Note by Mahamahopadhyaya Gopinath Kaviraj in 1925. The name of the author of this book is not definitely known, but he must have been a highly learned yogi-teacher of Gorakhnath's school a few centuries back. Another edition of the book was published from Hardwar.

The present discourse on the philosophy of Gorakhnath will be mainly based upon *Siddha Siddhānta Paddhati,* inasmuch as it is among all the works of the school discovered so far, the most systematic and comprehensive presentation of his philosophical doctrines and it claims to be and is generally accepted as a genuine work of the Master himself. Help will of course be taken from other authoritative works. The specific characteristic of this book is that it is purely a constructive work and does not enter into any logical disputation with other systems of philosophy and religion. It is written partly in the form of aphorisms (*Sutras*) and partly in the form of verses *(Ślokas).* It presents in a methodical way the *Siddha Sampradāya's* conception of the Ultimate Spiritual Ground of the Universe, the process of the evolution of the diversities of the world from One Absolute Dynamic Spirit, the true nature of the individual souls and their psycho-physical embodiments as well as their essential relation to the cosmic order, the highest ideal to be realised by the individual souls for their perfect self-fulfilment, the systematic course of discipline of the body and the senses and the vital forces and the mind and the intellect for the realisation of this Supreme Ideal, and other relevant problems. It emphasises that the systematic course of self-discipline for the attainment of perfect self-illumination and self-fulfilment must be learnt from a competent *Guru* or *Nātha* or *Avadhuta,* who has himself realised the supreme ideal and attained direct experience of the Absolute Truth in the transcendent *Samādhi*-state of his consciousness. Without the enlightened guidance of such a *Guru,* real progress in the path of spirituality can scarcely be expected.

CHAPTER III

CONTENTS OF SIDDHA SIDDHANTA PADDHATI

The book introduces itself to the truth-seekers thus :—

Ādināthaṃ namaskritya śaktiyuktam jagadgurum
Vakshye Gorakshanāthoham Siddha-Siddhānta-Paddhatim.

Having bowed down to Ādinātha (Śiva, the Supreme Spirit), Who is eternally possessed of Supreme Power and is the eternal *Guru* (Source of True Knowledge) of the world (*i.e.* all conscious beings of all times and all places), I, Gorakshanātha, will expound *Siddha Siddhānta Paddhati* (*i.e.* the way of thinking of the *Siddha-sampradāya* or the long time of enlightened *Yogis*). (S.S.P.I.1.).

This introduction (if its authenticity be not questioned) shows that Gorakhnath himself was the author of the book. There are other statements also within the book, which corroborate this introductory declaration. *Goraksha Siddhānta Sangraha*, while making quotations from this authoritative work, refers to the author sometimes as *Śri-Nātha* and sometimes (at least once) as *Nitya-Nātha.* In his discussions, this compiler of the philosophical and religious doctrines of Gorakshanath (*i.e.* the writer of this *Sangraha*) leaves no doubt that by *Śri-Nātha* and *Nitya-Nātha* he meant Goraksha-Nātha, whom he believed to be the Incarnation of Īśwara, *Ādi-Nātha, Mahā-Yogiśwara Śiva,* the eternal Master of all Yogis. There was however another great *yogi* of the name of Nityanātha who also was a celebrated author of many important works on *Yoga* and Medicine.

In *Hatha Yoga Pradīpikā* the name of one Nitya-Nātha is mentioned as one of the great *Mahāsiddha Yogis* who having conquered death moved freely in the world. The name of Nitya-Nātha is also found in other old Sanskrit treatises, particularly in treatises on the science of medicine. He is regarded as the author of the famous book, named *Rasa Ratnākara,* which bears the name of *Pārvati-putra* (son of Parvati), *Nitya-Nātha Siddha.* He was a great chemist. His name is mentioned with respect byVāgbhaṭa in his *Rasa Ratna Samuccaya.* Nitya-Nātha is also reputed to be the author of a book, named *Indra-jāla Tattwa* (science of magic). He is sometimes referred to as Nityānanda, Nitya-pāda and Dhyāni-Nātha. That Nitya-Nātha was a celebrated *Siddha-Yogi* and a great scientist and philosopher and author is beyond doubt. But there is no strong ground for attributing to him the authorship of *Siddha Siddhānta Paddhati.* The time of Nitya-Nātha also it is difficult to surmise. We may assume that Gorakhnath was the author of this most authoritative philosophical work of Gorakhnath's *sampradāya* or that it truly represents his views.

In *Siddha Siddhānta Paddhati,* the great *Āchārya* discusses various important topics under six principal heads, called *Upadeśa* (lessons). The first lesson is on *Pindotpatti* (*i.e.* origin of the body, cosmic as well as individual). In this lesson, he explains briefly the nature of the Absolute Reality and exhibits how and through what gradual stages the diversified cosmic system with the various orders of material organisms in it evolves out of the dynamic spiritual character of One Supreme Reality. He shows how the Supreme Spirit, though essentially above time and space and relativity and eternally differenceless and changeless in His transcendent nature, manifests Himself by virtue of His unique Power as a diversified universe (*Samasti-pinda* or *Brahmānda*) in time and space with countless orders of individual bodies (*Vyasti-pinda*) and as the Indwelling Soul in each of them. This is one of the fundamental metaphysical conceptions of the *Siddha Yogi Sampradāya.*

The second lesson is on *Pinda-Vicāra* (*i.e.* contemplation on the constitution of the body). In this lesson, the Āchārya gives instruction about some of the special conceptions of the school with regard to the inner constitution of the individual body, such as *Cakra, Ādhāra, Lakshya* and *Vyoma* or *Ākāśa.* Nine *Cakras,* sixteen *Ādhāras,* three *Lakshyas,* and five *Vyomas* are enumerated, their locations within the particular parts of the body are indicated and the methods of contemplation upon them are suggested. Such contemplations are of practical importance from the standpoint of self-discipline in this path and the elevation of the mind to the higher and higher planes and the progressive dematerialisation and spiritualisation of the physical body (*Kāya-siddhi*). Gorakhnath attached special value to the knowledge of these *Cakras,* etc., and contemplation on them in conformity with the instruction of the *Guru.* This is evident from his other treatises also, such as *Goraksha Śataka, Goraksha Samhitā, Viveka-Mārtanda, etc.*

The third lesson is on *Piṇḍa-saṃvitti* (*i.e.* true insight into the body). In this lesson, the Āchārya points out clearly the identity of the individual body with the Cosmic Body, the identity of the Microcosm with the Macrocosm. He shows in a detailed way that whatever exists in the vast world outside exists also within this individual body. The realisation of the identity of this apparently finite and mortal body with the beginningless and endless universe is a unique and magnificent ideal placed before the spiritual aspirants by Gorakhnath and his school. The yogi has to realise, not only the unity of the individual soul with the Cosmic Soul, but also the unity of the individual body with the Cosmic Body. The Yogi attains perfect freedom and bliss in the universe by becoming one with the universe.

The fourth lesson is on *Pindādhāra* (*i.e.* Container and Sustainer of the body). In this lesson, the Āchārya reveals that all the bodies are ultimately contained in and sustained and held together by one *Śakti*, or Supreme Spiritual Power, Who is in Her essential character identical with and non-different from *Śiva*, the Non-dual Supreme Spirit. All the bodies are the self-manifestations of one self-evolving Divine *Śakti*—One Supreme Spiritual Power; they are contained in and sustained by the same Power (*Śakti*); the same Power is immanent in and pervades them and regulates all their relations and changes; they have really no existence apart from the existence of that *Śakti*. This *Śakti*, again, is non-different from *Śiva*—the Power is identical with the Spirit. The same self-conscious self-enjoying non-dual Spirit, when conceived as existing in and by Himself in His transcendent character, is called *Śiva*, and when conceived as actively transforming Himself into a Cosmic Body and creating and developing and regulating and destroying innumerable finite bodies in time and space and revealing Himself in various forms and various ways, is called *Śakti*. The Absolute Reality in Its transcendent aspect is *Śiva* and in Its dynamic aspect is *Śakti*. When a *Siddha-Yogi* ascends to the plane of *Samādhi*, to him there is no difference between *Śiva* and *Śakti*, and he enjoys the bliss of the perfect union of *Śiva* and *Śakti*.

The fifth lesson is devoted to the discussion on the Supreme Ideal of *Samarasakaraṇa* (perfect unification) of the individual body with the Cosmic Body, of the bodies with the Supreme Power, and of the Power with the Absolute Spirit, as well as on the way of the realisation of this Ideal. When this Ideal of *Samarasa* is truly realised, the difference between Matter and Spirit vanishes, the difference between the Finite and the Infinite disappears, the difference between *Jeeva* and *Śiva* passes away, the difference between the Self and the World ceases to exist. The Yogi then sees the world within himself and himself in all the existences of the world. He sees *Śiva* in himself and all and sees himself and the whole world as unified in *Śiva*. In his experience, his own body is spiritualised and the whole universe is spiritualised. To his illumined consciousness, the Absolute Spirit, *Śiva*, alone exists in all these names and forms, and nothing but Him really exists. He sees and enjoys the most beautiful and blissful Unity in all apparent diversities.

The sixth lesson gives a fine description of the character and conduct of an *Avadhuta Yogi, i.e.* a Yogi who has perfectly realised the Ideal of *Samarasakaraṇa* as explained in the fifth lesson and attained perfect freedom from all ignorance and ego-consciousness, all bondage and narrowness of outlook, all desires and attachments, all cares and fears and sorrows, all sense of difference and plurality. An *Avadhuta Yogi* is one who has not only been blessed with the direct experience of the Absolute Truth in the state of *Samādhi*, but who has also been able to bring down the light of that transcendent experience to the intellectual and mental and vital planes of his consciousness and whose normal life is always illumined by that Divine Light. His state of *Samādhi* seems to continue undisturbed and unclouded even in the midst of his outer activities in relation to various sorts of people under various kinds of circumstances. It is such an *Avadhuta Yogi*, who is called a *Nātha* in the true sense of the term. He is a perfect master of himself, a perfect master of the circumstances in which he may dwell in his outer life. It is such a *Nātha* who is truly worthy of being *Sad-Guru*, because he is capable of destroying the darkness of ignorance which prevails in the minds of ordinary people and of awakening the spiritual wisdom and the spiritual power which normally lie asleep in the human consciousness.

Now, it is the experience of a perfect *Nātha* or *Avadhuta-Yogi*, which is the real basis of the philosophy of the *Yogi-Sampradāya*. Gorakhnath, himself a *Nātha* or *Avadhuta-Yogi*, proceeds with his philosophical discourses on the basis of his own spiritual experiences as well as those of the other *Avadhuta Yogis*, who preceded him in this path. His philosophy practically consists in the explanation of the facts of the lower planes of normal human experience in the light of the Truth realised by himself and the other *Siddha-Mahāyogis* in the perfectly illumined state of their consciousness as well as the relative occult truths experienced in the supernormal states of consciousness intermediate between the normal sensuous plane and the perfectly illumined state.

CHAPTER IV

CONCEPTION OF THE ULTIMATE REALITY

It has been observed that Mahāyogi Gorakhnath's conception of the Ultimate Reality is not merely the result of any process of logical reasoning from data supplied by normal sense-experience of ordinary people. It is not to him a theory or hypothesis conceived for the purpose of offering rational causal explanation of the world of common experience, as it is the case with purely intellectualist philosophers. The basis of his intellectual conception about the Ultimate Reality is super-sensuous super-mental super-intellectual direct experience in the state of *Samādhi*, *i.e.*, in the perfectly illumined and perfectly universalised and unconditioned state of the consciousness. Conception, however, is an affair of the intellect. In the field of direct experience, whether sensuous or super-sensuous, mental or super-mental, there is no room for conception. Conception comes in, when the necessity is felt for the rational interpretation and intellectual understanding of such experience. It is the function of the intellect (*buddhi*) to operate upon the direct experiences and to interpret them in terms of conceptions in order to constitute a system of valid knowledge out of them.

The necessity for such interpretation is inherent in the nature of sensuous experience, since the isolated sense-perceptions cannot by themselves constitute any real knowledge to the full satisfaction of the rational human mind. It is through the formation of conceptions that our knowledge of the phenomenal world of sensuous and mental experiences develops and expands, and with the development and expansion of knowledge the necessity for the formation of deeper and deeper, higher and higher, more and more comprehensive conceptions increases. Finally, the necessity is felt for the formation of an all-comprehending all-integrating all-illumining conception, which may fully satisfy the rational mind by furnishing an adequate explanation for the entire world of sensuous and mental experiences and may link together all experiences into one integral knowledge. Such a conception is regarded as the conception of the Absolute Ultimate Reality. Nevertheless, the conception is and will be in the domain of the intellect, in the domain of theory, and it can never amount to nor can it have the certitude of the direct experience of the Absolute Truth.

A Mahāyogi who attains the direct transcendental experience of the

Reality in the *Samādhi* state does not for his own satisfaction feel any necessity for the formation of any intellectual conception, since to him this experience is the most perfectly integrated knowledge of all possible existences in the universe and beyond it and this experience carries its certainty within itself. He enjoys the bliss of this experience, for herein he feels the fulfilment of his knowledge, the fulfilment of his life, the fulfilment of his mind and heart and intellect. Herein he becomes perfectly united with the Absolute Truth. But, when a *Mahāyogi* becomes a teacher and comes in contact with the truth-seeking people, living and moving in the sensuous and mental planes of experience and knowledge, he is required to give glimpses of his transcendental experience in terms of intellectual concepts and to demonstrate (as far as practicable) by means of logical reasoning that the Truth realised in that experience can furnish the most adequate rational explanation for all the phenomena of the sensuous and mental planes of human experience.

He has to show for the satisfaction of the intellectual demand of these people that the diversified objective world of phenomenal realities of the lower planes of human experience derives its existence from, is sustained and regulated and harmonised by and is again dissolved in the Absolute Reality, the true nature of which is revealed to the human consciousness in its perfectly purified and concentrated and illumined transcendent state. He has somehow to rationally account for the diversified self-expressions of the Absolute Reality in the form of the spatio-temporal cosmic order and again the unification of all these diversities in Its undifferentiated supra-temporal and supra-spatial spiritual nature. He has to explain how the plurality of material realities can originate from the one Supreme Spiritual Reality, how the Reality above time and space can manifest Itself in a temporal and spatial order, how the One can become many and remain One all the same. Many such questions arise in the minds of the intellectualist people, and the *Mahāyogi* Teacher has to offer answers to them for removing their doubts and bringing them to the path of Truth, though to his own enlightened consciousness all such questions and answers are of little value.

Mahāyogi Āchārya Gorakhnath begins his discourse on the philosophical conception of the Ultimate Reality with an important statement :—

Nāsti satya-vicāre smin nutpattis cānda-pindayoh
Tathāpi loka-vrittyartham vakshye sat-sampradāyatah.
(S. S. P. I. 2).

[From the standpoint of the Absolute Truth, there is really no origination of the cosmic order and the plurality of individual existences within it; nevertheless I shall explain (the origination, etc., of this world-system from the nature of the Ultimate Reality) in accordance with the way of thinking of the enlightened *Yogi-Sampradāya* with a view to the satisfaction of the normal rational demands of people in general.]

The view-point of the Absolute Truth is the view-point of transcendent experience in *Samādhi*, in which the Truth reveals itself in its perfect self-shining nature and in which the individual consciousness is fully identified with the Truth. This plane of experience is above time and space, above change and plurality, above causality and relativity. The world of space and time, the world of finite and changing and causally related existences, is in this plane of experience merged in one infinite eternal changeless differenceless self-luminous Existence. From the view-point of this plane of experience, there is no real origination of the diversified and changing world-order in space and time, and hence no real destruction or dissolution of it. What appears as such a world-order to individual consciousness in the lower planes of its experience reveals itself in the highest plane of its experience as nothing but the infinite eternal self-shining Supreme Spirit, in which its own individuality also is merged. Hence the question of its origination or destruction does not arise at all.

Origination means a temporal process of the coming into existence of something which did not previously exist as such. It also implies the pre-existence of a reality from which it comes into being and a temporal process of causation and change in that reality. Nothing can be originated without some cause and without some sort of temporal change or modification in the cause. Now, can we conceive of any time when the phenomenal world-order, whether in a gross or a subtle form, whether in a manifested or an unmanifested state, did not exist ? Time implies a change, a process, a succession, and every kind of change or process or succession must be within the phenomenal world-order. The changes or processes may be of the forms of gross transformations or subtle modifications, may be outwardly manifested or may remain outwardly unmanifested, but they are all included in the cosmic order. Thus the cosmic order cannot be conceived as having any temporal beginning or origination. Again, if there be any Reality behind or beyond this world-order, that Reality must be above time, free from all possible temporal changes or modifications, and cannot therefore be the cause of the production of this world-order in the phenomenal sense.

Thus, on the one hand, in the plane of transcendent experience, in which all temporal relations cease to exist and all plurality are unified in the nature of one infinite eternal Spiritual Reality, the question of the origination of the world-order as an entity separate from that Supreme Spirit does not arise at all; on the other hand, in the plane of normal phenomenal experience, this spatio-temporal order cannot be thought of as having had any absolute beginning in time or as produced by any causal process of modification or transformation of some Reality existing above time and space, and hence its origination at any point of time is unthinkable. Nevertheless, it is quite obvious that our normal intellect can neither deny or ignore the objective existence of this world-order, consisting of the plurality of phenomena in time and space perceived by our normal senses and minds, nor can it think of this spatio-temporal phenomenal world as a self-existent, self-revealing, self-evolving, self-regulating and self-harmonising Absolute Reality. The intellect demands an explanation in terms of the *a priori* categories of our rational understanding for this objective world of our sensuous and mental perception, in relation to the Absolute Reality Which unveils Its true nature in the transcendent experience and Which comprehends and unifies this world in Its transcendent non-duality.

The world of our normal experience is obviously of a derivative contingent relative conditional and composite nature, and our reason demands that it must have the ground and source and support of its existence and continuity and harmonious operations in some self-existent self-conditioned self-revealing dynamic and transcendent Absolute Reality, which is necessarily beyond the scope of our senses and mind, beyond the scope of the phenomenal conditioned and relative knowledge of our finite understanding. This Absolute Reality unveils Itself to our consciousness in its super-sensuous super-mental super-intellectual transcendent state, in which the subject-object relation vanishes and the consciousness realises itself as perfectly identified with the Absolute Reality. The Absolute Reality is thus experienced as the Absolute Consciousness, in which all time and space and all existences in time and space are merged in perfect unity, and the One Infinite Eternal Undifferentiated Changeless Self-Effulgent Consciousness shines as the Ultimate Reality. As this Absolute Consciousness is above the plane of the normal intellect, the intellect cannot form any true conception of It and cannot describe Its nature except in negative terms; but still it tries to conceive It in relation to and as the ground of this world-order.

Gorakhnath, in pursuance of the earlier *Siddha-Yogis,* designates this Absolute Consciousness as *Parā-Saṃvit*. This *Parā-saṃvit* is the Absolute Reality. This *Parā-saṃvit* is also spoken of by *Yogis* as the Perfect Union of *Śiva-Śakti.* From the view-point of the *Parā-saṃvit*, there is no world-order having any separate existence, and hence the question of Its origination does not arise. Nevertheless, as in the intellectual plane the phenomenal existence of the world-order is undeniable and as this world-order cannot be conceived as self-existent, its origin must be traced to the Absolute Consciousness, and the character of this Ultimate Reality also has to be relatively so conceived from the intellectual view-point that the evolution of this world of harmoniously related finite and transitory phenomenal realities may be adequately explained. Thus, Gorakhnath, in his philosophical system, makes the attempt to link together the transcendent experience of an enlightened *Mahāyogi* and the intellectual demand of a common man, with the practical purpose of refining and elevating the consciousness of the truth-seeking people and disciplining their thoughts in the proper direction.

Gorakhnath thus describes the pure character of the Ultimate Reality of transcendent experience :—

Yadā nāsti swayam kartā karanam na kulākulam
Avyaktam ca param brahma anāmā vidyate tadā.
(S. S. P. I. 4).

[When there is no active doer (creator), no causality (or process of causation), no distinction between power and reality (*i.e.*, the dynamic and the static aspects of the Spirit), when the Supreme Spirit is wholly without any self-manifestation (in finite and changing phenomenal forms), He then exists purely as the Nameless One.]

He adds :—

Anāmeti swayam anādisiddham ekam eva anādinidhanam
Siddha-siddhānta-prasiddham.
Tasya icchā-mātra-dharmā dharminī nijā śaktih prasiddhā.
(S. S. P. I. 5).

[That nameless (and formless and manifestationless) Supreme Spirit is eternally self-existent, absolutely one (*i.e.* differenceless), without any birth or death (or modification). This is the well-known conception (about Reality) of the *Siddhas* (enlightened seers). His unique Power, which is eternally inherent in His nature and one with Him and which is of the character of Pure Will (*i.e.* without any manifestation or any object of will or process of willing in the transcendent plane) is also well-known.]

Thus, according to the *Siddha-Mahāyogis*, the Ultimate Reality, though revealing Itself in the *Samādhi* state as pure changeless infinite eternal Consciousness, is not a static, but a dynamic Spirit with will. The Transcendent Spirit is eternally endowed with *Śakti*. Śiva with Śakti non-different from Him is the Reality.

CHAPTER V

SAT-CID-ANANDA BRAHMA

The Ultimate Reality as realised in the transcendent state of consciousness is described in this way by Mahāyogis:—

Na brahmā vishnu-rudrau na surapati-surāh naiva prithwī na cāpah
Naivāgnirnāpi vāyur na ca gaganatalam no diśo naiva kālah
No vedā naiva yajñā na ca ravi-śaśinau no vidhi'r naiva kalpah
Swa-jyotih satyam ekam jayati tava padam saccidānanda-murte.

(Quoted from *Siddha-Siddhanta-Paddhati* in *Goraksha-Siddhānta-Sangraha*)

No distinctive existence of Brahmā, Vishnu, Rudra and Indra and other Deities is there; nor is there any existence of earth or water or fire or air or sky; time and the directions (which imply space) do not exist; the *vedas* and the *yajñas*, the sun and the moon, the laws and the cyclic order are all absent; Your true Self alone shines as the sole self-luminous Absolute Reality, O You, who reveal Yourself as pure and perfect Existence-Consciousness-Bliss.

This is the Ultimate Reality according to the *Siddha-Yogi Sampradāya.* But the elightened Mahāyogis were conscious that this conception, based as it was on transcendent experience, did not fully represent the entire nature of the Absolute Reality and could not satisfy the rational demand of the empirical intellect. It may be noted that this conception of the Ultimate Reality appears to be in perfect agreement with the view of *Adwaita-Vedānta,* which also is based upon the transcendent experience of *Mahāyogis* as verbally expressed in the texts of the *Upanishads.* It is the conception of *Nirguṇa Brahma*, above time, space, relativity and causality, untouched by all kinds of differences external and internal, and devoid of any power or will or action. The Ultimate Reality is according to this view one timeless and spaceless, infinite and eternal, changeless, differenceless and processless, transcendent non-dual self-luminous Consciousness. It is described as pure Existence-Consciousness-Bliss.

Now, this conception of the Absolute cannot give perfect satisfaction to the rational intellect. First, it appears to be purely a negative and abstract idea, not giving any positive knowledge about the nature of the Absolute Reality. It merely informs us that the Absolute Reality is Something altogether of a different and distinct character from whatever we know and can possibly know, but fails to give us any intelligible positive idea as to what Its character truly is. Pure Existence-Consciousness-Bliss also does not appear to be an intelligible positive Reality. Secondly, the perfect nature of the Absolute Spirit must also have a dynamic element, which can furnish an adequate ground for the appearance or evolution of the cosmic system. This dynamic aspect of the Absolute Reality finds no mention in the above description.

(a) *Conception of Pure Existence:—*

It is contended by intellectualists that Pure *Existence* without *Something existent* cannot be rationally conceived as a *real entity.* It is as good as non-existence. It is meaningless to say that Existence exists. Existence is meaningful, when it is affirmed or denied of something. Something may exist or may not exist; affirmation of existence means the reality of a thing, and denial of existence means its unreality. The category of existence may be variously qualified. Something that exists may have self-existence or derivative existence, unconditional or conditional existence, eternal or temporary existence, infinite or finite existence, changeless or changeable existence, real existence or illusory existence, But in every case existence, in order to have an intelligible meaning, must be predicated of some *subject* or entity. Without some subject of which it is affirmed, existence is merely an abstract idea without any content and has therefore no real difference from non-existence. If, however, Pure Existence implies a *Reality* having eternal infinite changeless differenceless absolute self-existence, then of course the term acquires a distinctive meaning, rich in contents.

It is, in truth, in this sense that the *Mahāyogis* and the *Rishis* of the Upanishads use this term, and it certainly conveys some positive idea about the Absolute Reality. Pure Existence as the characteristic of the Ultimate Reality means Perfect Existence. It does not indicate merely the negation of non-existence, but also the negation of all forms of imperfect existence. This negation of imperfect existence, again, does not imply that there are numerous kinds of realities having different forms of imperfect existences, separate from the Ultimate Reality, and that the Ultimate Reality is distinguished from them by Its attribute of perfect existence; for in that case Perfect Existence would be *limited* and *relative* existence and therefore not perfect in the true sense. The Absolute Reality is characterised by Perfect Existence, in as much as It is the sole non-dual Reality and nothing exists in any form either within or beside Itself. Negation of imperfect existence implies that all kinds of temporal and spatial, derivative and conditional, mental and material existences, which are or may be objects of internal or external experience in the lower planes of consciousness, are absolutely merged in and unified with the Perfect Existence, and there is no plurality or duality therein. A *Mahāyogi* experiences this Perfect Existence by elevating his empirical consciousness to the super-empirical plane, the plane above duality and plurality, above time and space, above all empirical imperfect conditional existences.

Those who hold that existence necessarily means empirical existence of the normal planes of experience or that 'practical efficiency' is the sole criterion of existence, this Perfect Existence may appear to be as good as non-existence, the transcendent experience may seem to be negation of experience and annihilation of existence. They speak of what is above phenomenal experience as *Asat* (non-existent) or *Śunya* (Void), and the phenomenal reality as the only *Sat* (Existent) and phenomental experience as the one source of real knowledge. To them all real existences have origination and destruction. They cannot explain wherefrom they are originated and wherein they are lost. They ignore that empirical existences having origination and destruction necessarily imply some self-existent Reality, for the satisfaction of the reason's demand for a causal explanation of these existences.

In the *Yoga-Śāstras* the transcendent experience in the state of *nirvikalpa* or *asamprajñāta samādhi* is found to be described in terms of *śunya* (void or vacancy or negation of everything) as well as *purna* (fullness or perfection or unification of all). It is a state of—

Antah-śunyo bahiḥ-śūnyaḥ śunya-kumbha ivāmbare
Antah-purno bahiḥ-pūrṇaḥ purna-kumbha ivārnave.

—void within and void without, like an empty vessel in the sky; fulness within and fulness without, like a vessel full of water immersed in the ocean.

Since in that experience there is nothing which is experienced as its object, there is no subject-object relation and no *process* of experience, there is no consciousness of any inside and outside or any before and after, it may quite appropriately be spoken of as a state of absolute Void, (*śunya*), absolute negation of existence and consciousness in the empirical sense. On the other hand, as it is the state of the perfect fulfilment of all earnest and systematic endeavours for liberation from all limitations and realisation of the Absolute Truth, as it gives the sense of complete satisfaction to the human consciousness seeking for Truth and Freedom and thus results in perfect calmness and tranquility and bliss, as after the attainment of this blessed state nothing else appears to remain to be known and enjoyed, it is rightly described as the state of absolute fulness and perfection,—the state of the realisation of Perfect Existence, in which all orders of phenomenal existences are not simply negated, but realised as resolved into Absolute Unity. What appears to be *Śunya* or *Asat* (negation of all existences) from the empirical view-point is really the *Purna-Sat* (Perfect Existence), in which the ultimate character of all orders of existences is unveiled as One Self-luminous Differenceless Non-dual Spiritual Existence. This Perfect Existence is immanent in all empirical realities, which are only partial imperfect conditioned self-manifestations of It in the spatio-temporal order.

Gorakhnath and his school do not seem to be fanatically infatuated with any of such categories of intellectual understanding, as *Sat* or *Asat, Purna* or *Śunya*, Duality or Non-duality (*Dwaita* or *Adwaita*), etc., with regard to the Absolute Truth, since in their view the Absolute Truth is beyond the scope of such categories and directly realisable in absolute transcendent experience. Hence they refer to this Ultimate Reality as *Sat* in some contexts and *Asat* in others, *Purna* in some and *Śunya* in others, *Adwaita* in some and *Dwaita* in others, and often as above and beyond *Sat* and *Asat*, *Śunya* and *Aśunya*, *Dwaita* and *Adwaita*. *Hatha-Yoga-Pradipikā*, a standard work of this school, written by Swātmārāma Yogindra, writes,—

Śunya-aśunya-vilakshanam sphurati tat tattwam param śambhavam.

—That Ultimate Truth realised in the highest *Samādhi* through the practice of *Śāmbhavi-Mudrā* shines as distinct from *Śunya* and *Aśunya*. In the very next sentence it speaks of the bliss of the dissolution of the mind in *Śunya*, which is of the character of Consciousness-Bliss,—"*Bhavet citta-layānandah Śunye cit-sukha-rupini.*" *Śunya* and *Brahma* are often used synonymously.

(b) *Conception of Pure Consciousness:*—

Similar difficulties arise, when we try to form an intellectual conception of *Pure Consciousness* (*Cit* or *Cetana*). In the domain of our phenomenal knowledge we distinguish between conscious and unconscious beings, and consciousness appears to us as an attribute of the conscious beings, and not as a *being* or substance or reality by itself. Secondly, conscious beings also are not *always* found to be conscious, as in the state of deep sleep or swoon; in such cases though the psycho-physical organism exists and the mind may be supposed to be existent, there is no indication of the presence of any consciousness. Thirdly, there are many mental operations which seem to take place in the subconscious and the unconscious levels of the mind, and these are evident from our memories and dreams and other phenomena. Fourthly, we get no evidence of the existence of consciousness, except in relation to and as a quality of a living psycho-physical organism, and hence we cannot conceive of any unembodied Pure Consciousness existing by Itself. Fifthly, even in a psycho-physical organism consciousness does not appear to be a permanent inalienable changeless feature; but it seems to originate from and continue to exist under certain favourable conditions. It thus appears to be a temporal process, having origination, continuity, development, degradation and destruction, and not a permanent reality. Sixthly, consciousness in our normal experience invariably involves a subject-object relation. Even a subject having the capacity for consciousness remains unconscious, unless there is present before it an object of which it becomes conscious and unless there is a mental process establishing a relation between the subject and the object. The subject does not become conscious even of itself without relating itself to and distinguishing itself from its objects.

On account of all these conditions on which our normal consciousness depends, it becomes almost impossible for us to form an idea of *Pure Consciousness* as a self-existent and self-shining Reality-in-itself, transcending any subject-object relation or any temporal process, independent of any psycho-physical organism and without any origination and modification and destruction,—a timeless spaceless eternal infinite non-dual Absolute Reality. Standing on the plane of normal human experience, an ordinary intellectualist thinker may very well ask,—even if there be any such Absolute Reality beyond space and time and plurality and relativity, how can It be conceived as *conscious*, when there is no object of which It can be conscious and when It cannot even possibly make Itself an object of Its consciousness? In the absence of any other objective reality within or without Itself, Its self-shining or self-luminous character appears to be meaningless. It may have pure existence, but how can It be conceived as having a conscious or self-conscious existence?

Enlightened Yogis and philosophers point out that though it may be difficult to form a clear conception of Pure Transcendent Consciousness as a self-existent reality in the normal plane of experience, a deeper analysis of and reflection upon our phenomenal experience reveals the presence of this self-existent and self-shining, infinite and eternal, Pure Consciousness as the background of all our experience and knowledge.

First, when a distinction is known between conscious and unconscious beings, does it not imply that phenomenal consciousness and unconscionsness are both objects of the same Consciousness, that the affirmation and the negation of empirical consciousness are witnessed and asserted by one self-illumining subject lying behind both? Would there be any knowledge of the diverse kinds of conscious and unconscious beings, if there had not been One Consciousness witnessing them and distinguishing them from one another and at the same time distinguishing Itself from them? There must be one self-luminous Consciousness underlying and illumining consciousness as well as unconsciousness.

Secondly, what is the proof of the existence of the *objective world*, which is a magnificent organisation of countless diversities of finite and transitory phenomenal realities? Can there be any valid conception of such an objective world except with reference to One Universal Subiect-Consciousness, to Which it appears as such an object, by Which it is organised and illumined and experienced as a composite objective reality, Which without Itself undergoing any change and losing Its unity along with the various changes within this world links together all the temporal and spatial changes and harmonises and unifies them into one vast complex and continuous Cosmic System? In truth, we can think of this beginningless and endless, ever-changing and ever-complicated, ever-diversified and ever-unified system of the universe, only as existing to and by and for One Infinite Eternal Self-luminous and All-illumining Universal Consciousness. Otherwise what we call the world-order or the cosmic system would be altogether meaningless. Our individual empirical consciousnesses gain only partial and imperfect experiences of this world-order, in so far as they are illuminated by that Universal Consciousness, and they partially and imperfectly participate in Its infinite experience under the limiting psycho-physical conditions. Our individual experiences must be harmonised by some Universal Consciousness, otherwise they would have no objective validity. If and when the individual consciousness can get rid of these limiting conditions in *Nirvikalpa Samādhi*, it may be perfectly illumined by that Infinite Eternal Consciousness and may then be blessed with a perfect experience of the Cosmic System. In that experience, however, the Cosmic system will be merged in and unified with that Absolute Consciousness.

Thirdly, with regard to the unconscious states of the mind in deep sleep (*Sushupti*) and swoon (*murcchā*) and the mental functions in the unconscious and subconscious levels, it may be asked, who is witness to these unconscious states and the unconscious or subconscious operations of the mind? Do they not imply the presence of a consciousness of these unconscious states, distinct from the mental act of awareness? It is quite evident that if what is called the mind had been self-illumined, i.e., if self-consciousness had been its essential characteristic, it could not have any unconscious state. The mind, as it is experienced, passes through various states, such as waking, dream, sleep and swoon; in every state it passes through various modifications and changes, which are as a matter of course temporal processes; in the waking state it passes through various sensations and perceptions, thoughts and imaginations, feelings and emotions, passions and propensions, desires and wills; in the unconscious or subconscious state also it passes through various modifications and changes, the effects of which are experienced in the conscious state; in the mind numerous phenomena occur, of which it is not at all conscious at the time of occurrence, but which it becomes conscious of or recollects afterwards. The very existence of the mind appears to consist in its continuity in the midst of various modifications and changes.

Every act or process of the mind is a mental modification. Now, what is it that witnesses all these various states and changes and modifications of the mind, links them together, relates them with one another and maintains and reveals the unity and continuity of the mind in and through them? As the mind, which is sometimes conscious and sometimes unconscious and undergoes all these changes in time, cannot rationally be conceived as a conscious reality by its own essential nature, there must be some self-existent changeless Consciousness illumining and unifying all the states and processes of the mind in all the levels of its phenomenal existence and preserving and exhibiting its unity and continuity. Its conditions of awareness and unawareness, waking and dream and sleep, are equally revealed to and by that Consciousness. Without assuming the existence of such an underlying Witness-Consciousness (*Sākshi-Caitanya*), the phenomena of the conscious and sub-conscious and unconscious mind and what is called the empirical consciousness (*Vritti-Caitanya*) cannot be rationally accounted for. The Witness-Consciousness is a self-illumined reality and is witness to all the conscious and unconscious states of the empirical mind,—witness to all processes of knowledge and feeling and will as well as the negation of all such processes and operations of the mind and intellect. It may be regarded as a Changeless Mind behind as well as immanent in the changing mind, —a Super-empirical Mind illumining and unifying all the states and processes of the empirical mind. It is the Soul of the psycho-physical organism.

Fourthly, after awaking from deep sleep every person has a mental awareness of this sort,—'I slept soundly and in perfect peace, I did not know anything, I was unconscious'. This awareness is of the nature of remembrance. Now, how can there be such a remembrance, if there had been absolutely no experience in that state of deep sleep? It is reasonable to assume that the state of deep sleep is not a state of absolute negation of all experience, all consciousness. Though the empirical mind is then unconscious and ignorant and senseless and inactive, there must be some sort of non-mental or supermental experience and consciousness of that unconsciousness and ignorance and senselessness and inactivity of the mind; otherwise this remembrance would not have been possible. This is an evidence of the presence of one ever-awake ever-vigilant self-shining Witness-Consciousness, which is witness to all the changing states of the mind,—witness to our knowledge as well as ignorance, awareness as well as unawareness, all the functions of the waking and dreaming mind as well as the inactive senseless peaceful unconscious condition of the mind in deep sleep, and also the subtle operations and modifications of the mind in the subconscious and unconscious levels.

In the apparently unconscious state the mind remains unified with that Witness-Consciusness, without losing its *Sanskāras* (impressions of previous experiences). It is this Consciousness which is the real ground of the unity of our mental life and is the true Soul of our phenomenal existence. All the mental states and processes are like waves and ripples on the surface of the sea of Consciousness. Consciousness is immanent in them as their real substance and also transcends them as their disinterested Witness-Consciousness is truly the changeless selt-luminous *substance*, appearing in all the diverse forms of states and functions of the mind (including those of the intellect, the ego and the heart) and at the same time distinguishing itself from them as their *knower* or *seer*. When the empirical mind remains in an apparently functionless and unconscious and unmanifested state or when it functions in a subtle way below the levels of empirical consciousness, even then it exists as merged in and undifferentiated from the Witness-Consciousness and it is present to that Consciousness with all its dormant impressions (*sanskāra*) and individual characteristics, and it is from that state of unification with this Consciousness that it reappears to the levels of differentiated and conscious functions. The self-luminous permanent Consciousness is the unerring witness to empirical consciousness as well as empirical unconsciousness.

Fifthly, this Witness-Consciousness, underlying and witnessing all the conscious and semi-conscious and sub-conscious and unconscious states and processes of the empirical mind and illumining and unifying all its temporal changes and modifications, cannot reasonably be regarded as itself a temporal process, undergoing successive changes; for in that case our reason would demand the presence of another self-luminous and illuminating changeless Consciousness to illuminate and witness and unify these changes. Time itself has its existence only with reference to the changeless Witness-Consciousness. The past, the present and the future,—the *before* and the *after*,—the moments appearing to be related by way of succession,—must be equally present to the Consciousness, and must be linked with and distinguished from each other, in order that there may be idea of *time*. This implies that there must be a Consciousness, which without itself undergoing changes along with the succession of moments would witness this succession, which is the essence of time. The knower of time must transcend time. The Consciousness which witnesses all temporal processes and changes and sees them together as arranged in time cannot itself be regarded as one of the temporal processes. It must be conceived to be a supra-temporal experiencer of time, a changeless seer of changes. It must be regarded as a transcendent illuminer, and not an empirical process. Its knowledge or experience is not of the nature of mental modification, but of the nature of illumination from above or behind. It throws light on all temporal phenomena, without itself being subject to any temporal change.

Similarly, this Consciousness is the seer and knower, i.e. illuminer, of all the plurality in space and unifier of them into one harmonious system; but It is not itself a relative reality in space; It is not one of the plurality constituting the objective world-system; It does not occupy any portion of space either within the individual psycho-physical organism or outside. It is illuminer of the body and not a dweller within it: It is illuminer of space and not a occupier of it. It has neither any temporal nor any spatial limitation. Time and space have their continuous and boundless existence only for and to this all-immanent and all-transcendent and all-illumining Witness-Consciousness. It is this Witness-Consciousness that perfectly reveals Its true character to the empirical consciousness of a *Yogi* in the state of *Samādhi*, when this empirical consciousness becomes absolutely pure and calm and tranquil and liberated from the limiting conditions of the psycho-physical organism and the sense of ego.

Now, it is evident that *Pure Consciousness* and *Pure Existence* are the same. Pure Consciousness alone appears to be the sole-existent self-luminous infinite eternal absolute Reality. It is above and beyond and behind time, space, causality and relativity. It is necessarily implied in all derivative contingent conditional non-self-luminous phenomenal realities in the spatio-temporal cosmic order. They are what they are as revealed by and to this Consciousness. They may rationally be regarded as deriving their phenomenal existence from this self-existent Reality. They are manifested by the self-shining light of this self-luminous Reality. Space and time, co-existence and succession, causality and relativity, are real only so far as they are illuminated and revealed by this differenceless and changeless and limitationless self-shining Consciousness. All differences, all relations, all unities, are revealed by It. They are as it were the diversified forms in which this One Infinite Eternal Absolute Consciousness unfolds and manifests Itself to Itself in a spatial and temporal order. Nothing can be rationally conceived as having any existence and character without reference to this underlying Reality.

But it is quite obvious that in our normal experience we are conscious only of our empirical consciousness. Empirical consciousness is dependent upon mental modification. It involves a distinction of the self from its objects. It is of the nature of a temporal process. It is conditioned by time, space and relativity. Hence in the state of deep sleep, in which the mind is apparently inactive and there is no duality or plurality, no distinction between the knowing subject and the knowable objects and between one object and another, we seem to be devoid of empirical consciousness, though the vital functions go on continuously as in the waking state and the psycho-physical organism gets refreshed. Now, the highest state of *samādhi* is called *nirvikalpa,* i.e. devoid of any form of difference and change. Can there be any empirical consciousness in that state? The *Yoga-Śāstras* speak of this state as *asamprajñāta,* i.e. without any empirical knowledge or consciousness. It is a supra-mental state and in it there can obviously be no such knowledge or experience as arises from mental modification. If there had been in that state any such knowledge or experience, it would be relative and conditioned knowledge and in that case the realisation of the Absolute Truth would have been impossible. Hence it must be admitted that in the highest state of *Samādhi* the empirical consciousness with all its conditions and limitations is absent or is transcended. But on that account it must not be regarded as empirically an unconscious state. It is a state of the perfect unification of the empirical consciousness and its perfect identification with and illumination by the Absolute Existence-Consciousness. Hence it is a state of the perfect fulfilment of empirical consciousness and empirical individuality.

In the following Sloka Gorakhnath gives a beautiful and sublime description of *Parā-Saṃvit* (Pure consciousness), emphasising that It is the Reality of all realities, the Truth of all existences, the Illuminer and Unifier of all phenomenal experiences and the Builder of the Cosmic System.

Sattwe Sattwe Sakala-racanā rājate Saṃvid! ekā
Tattwe tattwe parama-mahimā Saṃvit evā-vabhāti
Bhāve bhāve bahula-taralā lampatā Saṃvid ekā
Bhāse bhāse bhajana-caturā brimhitā Saṃvid eva.

S. S. P. IV. 28.

In all orders of substances it is One *Saṃvit* that reigns as the unifier of their parts and attributes; in all orders of realities (the basic elements of substances) it is all-glorious *Saṃvit* alone that reveals itself; in all orders of phenomenal existences it is this One *Saṃvit* that manifests itself in finite changing and diversified objective forms; in all kinds of mental experiences it is this One *Saṃvit* that appears in manifold subjective forms and skilfully assumes various limiting characteristics.

(c) *Conception of Pure Bliss:—*

Thus One Differenceless Changeless Self-existent Self-luminous Consciousness or Spirit (*Saṃvit* or *cit*) is conceived by the Siddha-Yogis as the Ultimate Reality and the Sole Source and Soul and Sustainer of all orders of finite temporal relative phenomenal realities (conscious and unconscious, living and non-living, organic and inorganic, gross and subtle) constituting the cosmic system. Besides Perfect Existence and Perfect Consciousness, another idea is attached to the Absolute Reality, and this is the idea of Perfect Bliss (*Ānanda*). It is equally, if not more, difficult to form an adequate conception of Perfect Bliss as the Absolute Reality in the normal plane of our phenomenal experience. In our normal life we have experiences of pleasure or happiness, which is an agreeable state of the phenomenal body or vital organs or senses or mind, which is necessarily imperfect and limited and temporary and relative, and which is always conditional upon contacts with objects of enjoyment and other external and internal circumstances. Of unconditioned unlimited permanent absolute self-enjoyment we have no experience in our actual life, and we cannot even think of it. We are constitutionally incapable of thinking of any pleasure or happiness apart from relation to the objects (whether real or ideal, actual or imaginary, external or internal) which may produce or stimulate it. Pleasure or happiness does not appear to belong inherently to the nature of the empirical consciousness. It is occasionally produced and has generally to be attained through efforts. Sorrow rather seems to be a more permanent characteristic in our psycho-physical life, though sorrows also are produced from external and internal conditions. How can we conceive of Perfect Bliss, and that as an essential character of Pure Consciousness and Ultimate Reality ?

Perfect Bliss may however be conceived as the highest Ideal of our conscious life. By nature we seek for more and more happiness. In our normal life we aspire for more and more intense, more and more durable, more and more intoxicating, more and more qualitatively superior happiness. Ordinarily the happiness we enjoy is found to be alloyed with and to be preceded and followed by pain or sorrow. Even at the time of enjoyment our happiness is often marred by desires for greater happiness and other kinds of happiness and fears of losing what we have gained. Not to speak of the positive distresses and calamities which overwhelm most of us so often, no worldly man is at any time fortunate enough to enjoy unmixed happiness. Pure happiness, in which there is neither any alloy of actual sorrow nor any fear of possible sorrow nor any pain of want or craving for more nor any sense of imperfection or limitation, seems always to be an ideal, and never an actual fact in the normal planes of human experience. It is at every stage of human life something yearned for and hoped for, and never practically attained. The highest ideal of human life is generally conceived in terms of perfect happiness or bliss (*Ānanda*).

Perfect happiness accordingly implies the consciousness of the perfect fulfilment of human life, in which there should be no sense of imperfection in any respect, no sense of bondage or limitation, no want, no desire, no fear, no sense of dependence upon other forces or conditions for the enjoyment of fulness within. So long as there is any sense of imperfection in the empirical consciousness of man—whether imperfection of knowledge or imperfection of power or imperfection of goodness or beauty or imperfection of life (implying the possibility of death),—this ideal of perfect happiness or bliss cannot be realised. Nevertheless, the human consciousness can never abandon this ideal as altogether impracticable to be realised. The idea of the possibility of the realisation of this supreme perfection is inherent in the essential nature of our consciousness. The *Mahāyogis,* having reached the highest stage of their spiritual self-discipline, self-concentration and self-illumination, discovered that this supreme Happiness or Bliss *(Ānanda)*,—this ideal perfection of existence and life, knowledge and power, goodness and beauty,—eternally pertains to the essential character of the Pure Transcendent Consciousness, which is the Source and the True Self of the empirical consciousnesses as well as of the world of their subjective and objective experiences, and that every empirical consciousness is endowed with the inherent potentiality and capacity to realise this perfection and hence this *Ānanda,* by being identified with and illumined by the Transcendent Consciousness. What is the Supreme Ideal of our practical life is the Essential Character of our Soul, i.e. the Supreme Spirit. Hence Self-realisation means the attainment of perfect Bliss.

But to our logical intellect the question remains,—how can there be any positive *Ānanda* in the nature of Transcendent Consciousness, in which there can be no distinction and therefore no relation between the enjoyer and the enjoyable, no process of enjoyment, no feeling or emotion or sentiment, no psychological process whatsoever? We may no doubt speak of *Ānanda* in the sense of the complete absence of all actual and possible sorrows, absence of all feeling of bondage and limitation and imperfection. But in that negative sense *Ānanda* may be said to pertain to the nature of inanimate things as well, and every conscious being may be said to be in the enjoyment of *Ānanda* in the unconscious state, in the state of deep sleep or swoon. This certainly cannot be and ought not to be the supreme ideal of our conscious life. *Ānanda* can be thought of as the ideal of our conscious life, if it means not merely the absence of the consciousness of all sorrow, all imperfection and limitation, but also the presence of the consciousness of blissfulness, the presence of the feeling of perfection, infinity, immortality and sweetness within the self, the presence of positive and unrestricted self-enjoyment. But such positive and really meaningful *Ānanda* does not seem to be compatible with the character of differenceless modificationless subject-object-less Transcendent Consciousness.

Mahāyogins however assert with certainty on the strength of their supersensuous supermental superintellectual experience that *Ānanda* in the highest positive sense pertains to the character of Transcendent Consciousness, and that this is definitely realised when the empirical consciousness shakes off all its impurities and ficklenesses and relativities, rises above the spatio-temporal limitations imposed by the psycho-physical organism and becomes inwardly identified with Transcendent Consciousness. *Ānanda* is the fulfilment of the empirical consciousness and is the nature of Transcendent Consciousness, Which is the true Self of the empirical consciousness. The realisation of absolute *Ānanda* means the perfect Self-realisation of the empirical consciousness.

Perfect Existence, Perfect Consciousness and Perfect Bliss, which are in essence *one*, are the supreme Ideals immanent in the nature of all spatio-temporal existences, all conditioned individual consciousnesses, all imperfect living beings subject to joys and sorrows. These are all moved by an inherent urge for the realisation of those Ideals. In truth, the whole process of evolution in the cosmic system is governed from within by these Ideals. The reason is that these Ideals constitute the essential and ultimate nature of the true Self of all phenomonal existences, all phenomenal lives and consciousnesses, in this evolutionary cosmic order. It is the character of all to seek for self-realisation.

Our normal experience as well as our logical thought based upon it is confined to the phenomenal world. Here we have experience only of imperfect existence, imperfect life, imperfect consciousness, imperfect happiness. All these are subject to the conditions and limitations of time, space, relativity and causality. Here all existences are of a derivative conditional changing and destructible nature. Here life is found to be necessarily associated with a finite and mortal material body; and struggle for the preservation and development of the material body amidst favourable and hostile conditions and struggle for the adjustment of the empirical self with the environments appear to be the inalienable character of life. It is extremely difficult, if not impossible, for us to conceive of life without a material body, gross or subtle, or with an unborn undecayable infinite and eternal body, or free from any kind of effort for self-preservation i.e. struggle against death. This means that life which we experience and think of is always imperfect life, life shadowed by death. All progress of life is towards perfection. Perfect life may be the ultimate Ideal, the urge of which is at the root of all struggles in actual life. But when we try to conceive of Perfect Life,—i.e. Life which is infinite eternal absolute, which has no fear of decay or death and no scope or necessity for further development, in which there is no distinction between soul and body and there is perfect self-illumination and self-enjoyment, and in which therefore there is no struggle or effort or activity whatsoever,—we find no indication of *real* life in this Ideal Perfect Life. Thus our conception of Perfect Life appears to involve an obvious self-contradiction.

Similar is the case with our conceptions of Perfect Consciousness and Perfect Joy or Bliss. Consciousness which we experience and which we can actually conceive seems to necessarily involve a distinction between subject and object and a process of knowing or feeling or willing. But this is the imperfect manifestation of Consciousness under psycho-physical conditions. Again, we never experience and therefore can never think of consciousness except as associated with and dependent upon some psycho-physical embodiment. Under these conditions our empirical consciousness appears to be always restless. Our consciousness inwardly seeks for getting rid of the limitations imposed by the psycho-physical embodiment apparently different from itself. It aspires after transcending all relations of externality, assimilating all objects within itself and thus liberating itself from the subject-object distinction and the necessity of any process (i.e. effort) for bridging over the distinction. The ultimate Ideal which urges every individual consciousness from within for self-development, self-expansion, self-refinement and self-fulfilment, is Perfect Consciousness, Which transcends all spatio-temporal and subject-object relations, and Which is the true Soul of every individual phenomenal consciousness. But in the lower planes Perfect Consciousness without subject-object relation and process appears to involve obvious self-contradiction.

Similarly the idea of Perfect *Ānanda*, in which there is no distinction and relation between the enjoyer and any object of enjoyment and no psychological process, appears to be self-contradictory; but this is the ultimate Ideal of our joy-seeking life and we can never rest fully satisfied till this Ideal is realised.

Thus, we are unable to form a logically consistent conception of Perfect Existence, Perfect Life, Perfect Consciousness and Perfect Bliss on the basis of our imperfect experiences in the psycho-physical planes of our phenomenal existence, struggling life, empirical consciousness and sorrow-ridden pleasure; but still we cannot altogether deny the *ideal-reality* of such Perfect Existence—Life—Consciousness—Bliss and the possibility of Its being experienced, inasmuch as This is at the root of our phenomenal evolutionary conscious living existence and seems to irresistibly urge us on towards self-transcendence at every stage till perfection is reached.

Philosophical speculation of the intellectualist truth-seekers cannot reach any certainty with regard to the positive reality of this infinite eternal differenceless relationless supra-mental supra-intellectual Absolute Existence-Life-Consciousness-Bliss. They generally grope in the dark and arrive at various mutually-conflicting conclusions. Some become agnostic, holding that the Absolute must exist, but can never be known or even conceived. They even refuse to apply the concepts of life, consciousness and bliss to the Absolute Reality, since these are all borrowed from our phenomenal experience and necessarily imply relativity and limitation and change. Some even refuse to apply the category of existence to the Absolute, since the concepts of existence and non-existence also are mutually related and they also are borrowed from phenomenal experience. Hence the Absolute is negatively conceived by many acute thinkers as indefinable in terms of existence and non-existence, as above all intellectual conceptions, as beyond tbe possibility of all positive experience and mental imagination; but this absolutely indefinable and inconceivable Absolute is nevertheless presupposed necessarily as the background of all phenomenal existence, all empirical life and consciousness, all duality and plurality and relativity and causality, all our experience and thought. Living and moving and having our actual being in the phenomenal world-order, within which all our experiences and thoughts are as a matter of course confined, we can never say or know or even think what the character of the Absolute Reality is.

(*d*) *Above logical conception :—*

Enlightened *Mahāyogis* are not much interested in the question as to whether Absolute *Sat-Cid-Ānanda*—Perfect Existence-Consciousness-Bliss—is a logically self-consistent intellectual conception or not. They do not entangle themselves in any *tarka* or logical argumentation with other schools of philosophers with regard to the precise definition of the nature of the Absolute Reality. They readily admit that the Absolute Reality is beyond the scope of formal and empirical logic—beyond the range of our speech and thought. (*Yato Vāco nivartante aprāpya manasā saha*). They are fully aware that whenever people will try to form an intellectual idea about the nature of the Absolute Reality on the basis of their normal experience and logical reasoning and with the help of common language, they are sure to miss the Reality, arrive at mutually conflicting opinions and quarrel with one another. (*Anye bhedaratā vivāda-vikalā Sattatwato vancitāh*). They know that what is above space and time, above duality and relativity, above subject-object relation, cannot be a direct *object* of thought to any thinking *subject* and cannot therefore be truly described in terms of any qualifying attributes or distinguishing characteristics or any of the common concepts of the understanding.

While admitting the futility of our empirical thought and speech and logical understanding as means to the true knowledge of the Absolute Reality, the enlightened *Mahāyogis* do not accept the agnostic view,—the view of despair. They take their stand on *illumined experience,*—the direct experience of the transcendent plane. They speak with authority about the Absolute Reality on the strength of supersensuous supermental superintellectual super-empirical spiritual experience attained in the highest state of *Samādhi,* in which the character of the empirical consciousness is completely transformed, in which the empirical mind and intellect are perfectly purified and refined and unified and liberated from all the limitations of the psycho-physical organism, in which the whole being of the conscious subject transcends the empirical plane and becomes perfectly free from all spatio-temporal conditions, all subject-object relations, all duality and plurality and relativity. It is in this transcendent plane that the Absolute Reality is directly experienced, *not as object of experience,* but as perfectly *self-luminous Experience Itself.* The true Soul of all experience is unveiled in this *Absolute Experience.*

As the result of the all-round discipline and purification and refinement of the body, the senses, the vital forces, the mind and the intellect, and the continued practice of deep concentration and meditation, as well as the subtle operation of the Immanent Spiritual Ideal, the empirical consciousness gets rid of all limitations and rises to the plane of Absolute Experience and realises the Absolute Truth. But so long as the psycho-physical organism continues, the forces of the lower planes which are suppressed during the period of the practice of *Samādhi,* but are not totally destroyed or radically assimilated, bring the empirical consciousness down again and again to the mental and intellectual and sensuous planes, —the planes of time, space, causality, and relativity. From *Nirutthāna-daśā* the consciousness comes down to *Vyutthāna-daśā,* In these lower planes, however, the light of the Samādhi-Experiece is clouded, but not lost. The empirical consciousness, while descending to the plane of relativity, carries with it some sweet and blissful memory of the Absolute Experience and the spiritual enlightenment attained therein. As a consequence the enlightened Yogi's outlook on the world of objective experiences is thoroughly transformed. He looks upon everything, within and without, from the standpoint of the Truth of the Absolute Experience. He cannot of course give any accurate description of the Absolute Experience or the Absolute Truth realised in that transcendent plane, nor can he form any perfect mental or intellectual conception of that Experience or Truth. But still he is absolutely certain that that Experience is the all-comprehending all-uniting all-explaining perfect Experience and that the Truth realised therein is the Absolute Truth.

Enlightened Mahāyogis, while authoritatively asserting the Absolute Truth on the strength of their Experience (*Anubhava*), never try to dogmatise the Truth in terms of the categories of mental understanding or intellectual reflection. As it has been noted, they do not often attach much importance even to the most fundamental categories, such as *existence* and *unity*. The Absolute Truth is spoken of by Mahāyogis sometimes as *Sat*, sometimes as *Asat*, sometimes as *Śunya*, sometimes as neither *Sat* nor *Asat*. Sometimes they decry those who quarrel about *unity* and *duality* as ignorant.

Adwaitam kecid icchanti dwaitam icchanti cāpare
Param tattwam na bindanti dwaitā-dwaita-vilakṣaṇam
(Avadhuta—Gita)

—Some uphold *adwaita* (non-duality) and others uphold *dwaita* (duality); they do not realise the Ultimate Truth, Which is distinct from and transcends both *dwaita* and *adwaita*.

In the book *Amanaska* Gorakhnath says,

Bhāvā-bhāva-vinirmuktam nāśotpatti-vivarjitam
Sarva-samkalpanātītam para-brahma taducyate.

Gorakhnath says that the Absolute Truth Which is realised in the highest spiritual experience is above the concepts of *bhāva* (existence) and *abhāva* (negation of existence), absolutely devoid of origination and destruction, and beyond the reach of all speculations and imaginations, and That is called *Para-Brahma*. In the fourth verse of the first lesson of *Siddha-Siddhānta-Paddhati* (already quoted) the great *Yogācharya* has described *Para-Brahma* as without any name, without any form, without any ego, without any causality or activity, without any self-manifestation or any internal or external difference. Gorakhnath along with other enlightened saints asserts that Para-Brahma or the Absolute Spirit, though empirically indescribable, unknowable and even unthinkable, is perfectly realisable in the state of *Samādhi,* in which the empirical consciousness rises above all relativity and becomes one with Brahma. *Pakṣapāta-vinirmuktam Brahma sampadyate tadā,* -the enlightened Yogi then becomes perfectly identified with Brahma and free from all *paksha-pāta* (partisanship, meaning adherence to any particular intellectual view). He then ceases to be an exponent of any particular philosophical view-point in opposition to other rival view-points based on the experiences of the lower planes. Thus the philosophy of Gorakhnath and the *Siddha-Yogi-Sampradāya* came to be known as *Dwaitā-dwaita-vilakshana-vāda* and *Pakshapāta-vilakṣaṇam-vāda.*

For the guidance of truth-seekers however the adoption of intellectual concepts is inevitable. *Sat, Cit* and *Ānanda,* being the most fundamental concepts for indicating the nature of the Reality sought for by all truth-seekers, are adopted by the Mahāyogis, while imparting lessons to them. Though *Sat, Cit* and *Ānanda* are not experienced as distinct characteristics of the Absolute Reality (*Para-Brahma*) in the Absolute Experience; it is in these terms that the superempirical undifferentiated self-existent self-luminous self-fulfilled nature of the Absolute Reality can be most approximately indicated in the mental and intellectual planes. In the intellectual plane the concepts of *Sat, Cit* and *Ānanda* appear to be distinct from each other, indicating different aspects or qualifications of Reality; in our normal experience we find things which exist without *Caitanya* or *ānanda* and conscious beings without *ānanda;* but perfect existence involves perfect consciousness and bliss, and in the transcendent Experience there is really no distinction between *Sat, Cit* and *Ānanda.* The Yogi-Guru has beautifully addressed the Absolute Reality as *Sat-Cit-Ānanda-Murti,* i.e. One Who reveals Himself as *Sat, Cit* and *Ānanda.* He cautions the truth-seekers against misconceiving that Existence, Consciousness and Bliss are revealed in the transcendent state as separate and distinct glorious characteristics of the Supreme Spirit. The perfect Character of the Supreme Spirit, as transcendentally realised in the highest *Samādhi-experience,* is interpreted as Perfect Existence, Perfect Consciousness and Perfect Bliss, though there is no distinction among them in the nature of the Absolute Spirit. *Sat-Cit-Ānanda* is regarded as the highest *form* of self-manifestation of the Formless and Manifestationless One, as *Brahma, Śiva, Paramātmā,* Parameśwara, etc. are the holiest names of the Nameless One.

CHAPTER VI

PARA-SAMVIT WITH UNIQUE POWER

Thus the Absolute Reality is described by Gorakhnath and all *Siddha-Yogi philosophers* as the Absolute Union of Perfect Existence, Perfect Consciousness and Perfect Bliss (which also implies Perfect Purity, Perfect Beauty, Perfect Goodness and Perfect Love) above time, space, duality and relativity. This Reality is unveiled to the super-conscious transcendent Experience of a perfectly enlightened Mahāyogi in the highest state of *Samādhi,* in which there is no subject-object relation and the experiencing consciousness becomes absolutely united with the Reality. This Absolute Experience identified with Absolute Reality is *Parā Saṃvit.* To this Experience the phenomenal world-order of time, space, duality, plurality and relativity does not exist at all and hence the question of any causal and rational explanation for this world-system does not arise. But to our normal experience this cosmic system with all its diversities and complexities and changes and relations and all the phenomenal individualities and limitations within it does surely exist.

Gorakhnath and the *Siddha-Yogis* do not, like some metaphysical schools, discard the phenomenal cosmic system as *false* or *illusory,* or as having only subjective reality. *Illusion* or *error* necessarily pre-supposes the existence of imperfect and finite observing and knowing consciousnesses liable to malobservation and erroneous thinking. There is obviously no such imperfect consciousness outside the cosmic system, which may possibly be deluded by the false or illusory appearance of this world of plurality. Nor can we conceive of the existence of any such imperfect experiencing consciousness, either within or outside the Absolute Reality, to which this Absolute Reality may *falsely* or *illusorily* appear as a system of phenomenal realities in time and space or which may super-impose such a phenomenal cosmic order upon the Absolute Reality. All imperfect consciousnesses, capable of valid phenomenal knowledge as well as liable to error and illusion, are within this cosmic system, of which they are integral parts and apart from which they have no existence. It is therefore most unreasonable to think that the entire phenomenal cosmic order owes its origin to the imperfection and ignorance of the individual consciousnesses to which it appears as a system of objective realities. In fact, the cosmic system essentially consists of the plurality of phenomenal consciousnesses and the diverse orders of objective realities related to them. The phenomenal existence of the whole system,—including phenomenal subjects as well as phenomenal objects,—has to be recognised as such from the standpoint of our normal experience. A rational explanation for this cosmic system, which is real so far as our normal experience is concerned, must be obtained from the nature of the Absolute Reality.

Gorakhnath and the *Siddha-Yogi* school maintain that the Self-Existent Self-Shining Self-Perfect Infinite and Eternal Consciousness, which is the Absolute Reality above time-space-relativity, reveals Itself as a spatio-temporal cosmic system, wherein It originates and develops and sustains and destroys diverse orders of derivative and finite phenomenal existences with various kinds of forms and attributes, and a plurality of imperfect and changing phenomenal consciousnesses embodied in various kinds of physical and vital organisms and playing their parts in this cosmic system. While manifesting Itself in this phenomenal pluralistic cosmic system, the Absolute Reality never loses Its transcendent unity and perfection. It shines as the changeless self-luminous Soul of the whole system and of all individual realities within it. This process of self-manifestation of the Absolute Reality in the spatio-temporal order is without beginning and without end in time; but Its eternally transcendent non-dual character is in no way affected by this phenomenal self-manifestation.

But how is this possible? Gorakhnath and the enlightened *Yogis* reply that this is the Unique Power (*Nijā-Śakti*) of the Absolute Reality, the Supreme Consciousness or Spirit, *Brahma*. According to them, this Unique Power must be conceived as pertaining to the essential character of Perfect *Sat-Cid-Ānanda-Brahma,* since this is evident from the presence of the cosmic system to our normal phenomenal experience. Power (*Śakti*) is a reality which can be known only from its action (*kriyā*) or product (*kārya*). Even within the domain of our normal experience, the power of a thing remains non-differentiated from and therefore hidden in the essential nature of the thing until and unless it exhibits itself in the forms of actions or effects. Apparently the same thing may have a variety of powers which are manifested in the forms of different kinds of actions or effects under different conditions and in relation to different other things. But all these powers remain unknown and unknowable (at least to our common understanding) till their manifestations are observed. Their existence in the nature of the thing, even when unmanifested, must however be assumed, though by mere abstract analysis of the essential nature of the thing we may not discover them. Now, if we speak of *the power* of a thing, it ought to include all the possibilities of its actions and self-expressions under all possible conditions. This can obviously never be fully known. *The power* of a thing gradually reveals itself to us in course of the development of our experience about it. It is however clear that the power of a thing (including all possibilities) is essentially identical with the nature of the thing and has also differentiated self-manifestations. We cannot create any new *power* in a thing; we can however help the expressions of the power already existing in the nature of a thing, through the creation of suitable sets of circumstances.

Powers are indeed the most amazing and bewildering mysteries in the nature of things. Diverse kinds of material things, diverse orders of living organisms, diverse grades of minds and intellects,—all are repositories of wonderful *powers,* the presence of which could not even be dreamt of before they revealed themselves under special sets of circumstances. Modern sciences are engaged in the discovery of *powers,* which have been hidden in and identified with the nature of things since their creation. Different branches of physical and chemical sciences, sciences of heat, light, electricity and magnetism, biological sciences, medical sciences, psychological sciences and so on,—all are expanding the sphere of human knowledge and influence by progressively discovering and making use of the wonderful *powers,* which had been previously unknown and undreamt of, though present in the nature of things not unfamiliar to ordinary people. A good many great thinkers of the past and the present, of the east and the west, came to the conclusion, and not without reason, that a thing is nothing but *a seat or centre of powers,* and the entire world is constituted of *powers* (condensed into material forms), which are ultimately diversified manifestations of *One Supreme Power or Energy.*

Gorakhnath and the *Yogi* school hold the view that all the harmonised diversities of phenomenal existences constituting the cosmic system are the self-manifestations in time and space of the *Unique Power* of the Supreme Spirit, Brahma, Whose essential character is Perfect *Sat-Cid-Ānanda.* Apart from the phenomenal self-manifestations, the Power is absolutely identical with the Supreme Spirit, but the truth that the power is inherent in the transcendent nature of the Supreme Spirit is evident from the spatio-temporal cosmic system in which It is manifested. The *Power,* according to them, is the *eternal dynamic aspect* of the Supreme Spirit, Brahma. The Absolute Reality, i.e, the Supreme Spirit, has, in their philosophic view, an eternal *transcendent* aspect and an eternal *dynamic* aspect. In the transcendent aspect the Absolute Reality is eternally pure changeless *Sat-Cid-Ānanda,* and in the dynamic aspect It is eternally manifesting Itself in the ever-changing ever-old and ever-new spatio-temporal cosmic system. Or it may be said that by virtue of the dynamic aspect, i.e. the *Unique Power,* the super-temporal super-spatial super-personal Absolute Existence-Consciousness-Bliss freely and eternally comes down to the spatio-temporal plane and manifests and enjoys Itself as the Personal Creator and Governor and Destroyer of diverse kinds of phenomenal existences and phenomenal consciousnesses and endows Itself with one continuous cosmic body and innumerable individual bodies.

Thus according to the *Yogi-sampradāya* the Absolute Reality is eternally both a changeless differenceless transcendent super-personal *Sat-Cid-Ānanda* and an ever-self-evolving ever-self-differentiating ever-self-phenomenalising ever-self-embodying active personal *Sat-Cid-Ānanda.* In the highest state of *samādhi* the consciousness of the *Yogi* is perfectly illumined by and unified with the transcendent *Sat-Cid-Ānanda,* and the dynamic aspect of *Sat-Cid-Ānanda* with the cosmic system evolved out of it does not appear to exist in this subject-object-less experience. But when from that timeless spaceless egoless relationless transcendent plane of experience, the consciousness of the *Yogi,* illumined by that experience, descends to the plane of the ego and the mind and the senses and time and space and relativity, the cosmic system with its diversities and changes reappears before it; but the entire system with all orders of existences in it is revealed as pervaded and illuminated by *Sat-Cid-Ānanda;* all objects of phenomenal experience, though apparently diversified, appear to the enlightened consciousness of the *Yogi* as self-expressions of one self-existent self-enjoying Perfect Consciousness. He sees one Existence in all existences, one Consciousness in all consciousnesses, the play of the *Ānanda* amidst all joys and sorrows of the world.

Thus in the *Vyutthāna* (reawakened) state of the empirical consciousness after Samādhi-experience, the Power-aspect of the Supreme Spirit becomes revealed to the *Yogi* with all its glories and beauties and splendours. He finds expressions of the absolute Goodness of the Supreme Spirit in all the apparent evils of the world, expressions of Its transcendent Beauty in all the apparent deformities and horrors. Like other men he has sensuous perception of diverse kinds of worldly phenomena and his normal heart often responds to them in different ways, but at the same time he perceives with his enlightened insight one *Sat-Cid-Ānanda* immanent in and revealed through all of them and hence remains calm and tranquil under all apparently catastrophic changes of our circumstances. He sees with his inner eyes the Infinite in the finite, the Eternal in the temporal, the Absolute in the relative, the Perfect in the imperfect, the Blissful in the sorrowful, the Supreme Spirit in all material realities. Through the most intensive practice of *Yoga*, his empirical consciousness may be so refined and illumined that he may at the same time enjoy transcendent experience of *Samādhi* and the diversified experience of the normal plane. The *Yogi* philosophers do not speak of the varieties of sensuous and mental experiences as altogether false or illusory and the whole spatio-temporal order as metaphysically non-existent; but regard these as the evidences of the dynamic aspect of the Absolute,—the Unique Power (*Nijā-Śakti*) of the Supreme Spirit.

(*a*) *Conception of Pure Will:—*

With regard to the ultimate character of this Unique Power of the Supreme Spirit, Gorakhnath says, as it has been already mentioned, that this power is of the nature of Pure Will (*Icchā-mātra-dharmā*) and that this Will is eternally and essentially inherent in the nature of the Supreme Spirit, Brahma. It is through the operation of this inscrutable and omnipotent Will immanent in Its nature that transcendent *Sat-Cid-Ānanda*, while eternally existing and shining by Itself above time and space and relativity, eternally manifests Itself in time and space as a phenomenal order of existences and consciousnesses with various kinds of characteristics.

Now, what is meant by Pure Will, and how can Will be consistent with the nature of Perfect *Sat-Cid-Ānanda?* Ordinarily by will or *icchā* we mean desire, which is associated with the feelings of want and imperfection and dissatisfaction and sorrow. It implies a craving and effort for certain things or certain changes for the removal of felt wants and imperfections and sorrows and for the attainment of a sense of temporary satisfaction. How can Perfect *Sat-Cid-Ānanda* be conceived to have any such desire? Desires and efforts can pertain only to the nature of imperfect consciousnesses in this world of limitations and changes. How can there possibly be any desire or effort in the transcendent nature of the Supreme Spirit? What can possibly be the motive force impelling the timeless and spaceless Supreme Spirit to manifest Itself in a plurality of imperfect existences and imperfect consciousnesses in a world of time and space? How can there be any place for motive or intention in the transcendent character of Perfect Existence, Perfect Consciousness and Perfect Bliss? This appears to be obviously absurd.

The *Yogi* philosophers do not certainly attribute any want or desire or motive or intention in the empirical sense to the Supreme Spirit. They do not use the term *icchā* or will in this sense. *Icchā-mātra* or Pure Will means the *immanent urge for self-expression*, which is inherent in the perfect transcendent nature of the Supreme Spirit. Will in this sense is associated with perfection and not with imperfection, with consciousness of fulness and not with consciousness of want. Desires originate from sorrow, while Pure Will is inherent in *Ānanda*. Perfect Existence has an immanent urge for self-expression in diverse orders of existences; Perfect Consciousness has an immanent urge for self-expression in diverse orders of consciousnesses; Perfect *Ānanda* seeks self-expression in diverse kinds of joys. This is the dynamic character of Perfect *Existence-Consciousness-Bliss.* Self-expressions must inevitably be through the processes of evolution and involution, expansion and contraction, diversification and unification (*vikāśa and sankoca*). What is eternally unified in transcendent perfection is temporally manifested through diverse orders of empirical realities.

Mahāyogi Gorakhnath has given a very interesting account of the gradual manifestation of the Unique Power of the Supreme Spirit and the origination and development of the cosmic system and the diverse orders of material bodies and conscious beings within it. This will be discussed later on. But what he has specially emphasised in all his dissertations is that the entire spatio-temporal order and all kinds of empirical realities within it should be looked upon as the self-expressions of the Divine Power, Which is essentially identical with the Divine Spirit. He has paid equal homage to the transcendent and the dynamic aspects of the Absolute Reality. He has drawn pointed attention to the truth that the dynamic nature (*Śakti*) of the Supreme Spirit (*Brahma* or *Śiva*) is immanent in Its transcendent nature, and the transcendent nature also is immanent in the dynamic nature and all its spatio-temporal self-expressions. He has shown that as the Divine *Śakti* is non-different from the Divine *Spirit,* and as all the products or self-manifestations of *Śakti* are essentially non-different from *Śakti,* an enlightened person should learn to see and appreciate the Divinity of the world and all existences in it,—he should see God in all and all in God. In the *samādhi-experience* all the changing diversities of the world-order are merged in the changeless transcendent Unity of the Absolute Spirit, and in the enlightened waking experience the Unity of the Absolute Spirit is perceived as unfolded in various names and forms in the cosmic system.

The *Siddha-Yogi* teachers, while forming a philosophical conception of the Absolute Reality, do not base their conclusion purely on transcendent experience in the highest state of *Samādhi,* but also take due note of the phenomenal experiences in the normal planes of practical life. Thus they try to present before the truth-seekers a most comprehensive conception (as far as practicable) of the Absolute Reality. The Absolute Reality is conceived as the Supreme Spirit (*Adwaya Sat-Cid Ānanda*) realised in transcendent experience as well as the Spiritual Source of all relative realities of phenomenal experience,—Pure Spirit as well as Spirit revealed through Power. To the *Yogi* The Absolute Spirit is thus *Nirguna* as well as *Saguna, Niskriya* (actionless) as well as *Sakriya* (active), Impersonal as well as Personal, Transcendent as well as Immanent,

CHAPTER VII

SIVA AND SAKTI IN ETERNAL UNION

Since time immemorial in all the sacred literature of the *Yogi Sampradāya* the Supreme Spirit,—the Ultimate Spiritual Reality behind all phenomenal existences,—the Changeless Differenceless Nameless Formless Self-luminous Non-dual One,—has been designated as *Śiva*, and the Self-modifying Self-differentiating Self-multiplying Dynamic Source of all spatio-temporal relative phenomenal existences has been designated as *Śakti*. The world of diversities and changes is the self-manifestation of *Śakti*, and in our worldly experiences the true transcendent character of *Śiva* remains veiled from our view and we see only the multiform self-expressions (*vilāsa*) of *Śakti*. Even the true nature of *Śakti* is not revealed to us, since we do not actually experience all the forces and phenomena of the world as the self-expressions of One Self-unfolding *Śakti*. We neither perceive One Self-existent Self-shining Reality behind all derivative relative realities, nor do we perceive One Self-revealing Free Ultimate Power behind all changing phenomena and secondary forces. We live and move and have our being apparently in a world of plurality and changes, but we do not know how and wherefrom this world has come into being and how and by what power it is sustained and regulated and systematised and towards what goal it is ceaselessly moving on. But our rational consciousness is impelled by an inner urge to discover Unity behind all plurality, One Supreme Reality behind all realities of our experience, One Supreme Power originating, controlling and harmonising all forces and phenomena, and One Supreme Law behind all the laws of nature. All scientific and philosophical efforts are governed by this urge and aspiration immanent in the human consciousness.

The universally adored enlightened *Yogis* claim to have discovered some methods of spiritual self-discipline for the perfect satisfaction of this urge and aspiration. Through the most earnest practice of these processes of self-discipline they ultimately attain to a state of perfectly illumined consciousness, in which that One Reality behind all relative realities is directly experienced and the true character of the Ultimate Power behind all phenomena and forces is also fully unveiled. In the foregoing discourses we have sought to give a general idea of the nature of that Ultimate Experience, the nature of the Reality experienced therein and the nature of the Power pertaining to that Reality. The *Siddha-Yogi-Sampradāya*, to which Gorakhnath belonged and whose religious and philosophical terminology and nomenclature he usually adopted in his teachings, referred to that Supreme Transcendent Reality as *Śiva* and that Supreme all-originating all-embracing Power as *Śakti. Śiva* with *Śakti* eternally and essentially immanent in His nature, or *Śakti* in eternal union with *Śiva*, is, according to this *Sampradāya,* the Absolute Reality.

In *Siddha-Siddhānta-Paddhati* Yogi-Guru Gorakhnath has variously described this eternal and essential union between *Śiva* and *Śakti,*—the Supreme Transcendent Spirit and the Supreme All-originating Power. He says—

Śivasya abhyantare Śaktih Śakter abhyantare Śivah
Antaram naiva jānīyat candra-candrikayor iva.

Śakti is immanent in *Śiva,* and *Śiva* is immanent in *Śakti;* see no difference between the two, as between the moon and the moon-light. Here in the illustration the Mahāyogi conceives the moon as the serene light in the most concentrated form shining by itself and within itself, and the moon-light as the self-expression of the moon in the form of rays radiated in all directions round about the centre. Evidently in accordance with this conception of the moon there is no essential difference between the moon and the moon-light, just as between a flame of light and the light diffused from it (between *dīpa-śikhā* and *dīpāloka*). The moon-light has no existence apart from and independently of the moon, and the moon also, though (figuratively speaking) self-existing and self-shining has no self-manifestation except through the moon-light inherent in its nature.

In the same way, says Gorakhnath, Śiva is the eternal and infinite (above the plane of time and space) Soul and Seat of Śakti; He is, so to say, Śakti in the most concentrated self-centred self-conscious self-enjoying transcendent form without any self-expression or self-unfoldment in the shape of actions or phenomena; Śakti again is the infinite and eternal dynamic Power inherent in and pervading the transcendent nature of Śiva and She is the self-manifestation of Śiva in the form of the continuous evolution and involution of the cosmic system. Śiva may be described as the Spirit or Soul of Śakti, and Śakti as the Body of Śiva, there being essentially no difference between the Soul and the Body, since the Body is nothing but the self-expression of the Soul. Śiva may be spoken of as *Śakti in the transcendent plane,* and *Śakti as Śiva in the phenomenal plane.* Apart from and independently of Śiva, Śakti has no existence, and if Śakti is negated, Śiva has no self-expression, no manifold self-manifestation, and even no self-conscious personality. It is by virtue of His Śakti, that Śiva becomes conscious of Himself as omnipotent omniscient and perfectly blisssul Personal God, and as the Creator and Governor and

Enjoyer of the cosmic order. In His transcendent nature His Śakti is hidden (*avyakta*) in Him, and in the cosmic self-unfoldment of His Śakti, He is Indweller (*antaryāmi*) in His Śakti and in all Her diversified phenomenal self-manifestations and wonderful plays. In His cosmic self-expression Śiva appears to keep Himself concealed behind the sportive operations of His Śakti and to enjoy them as the Innermost Soul of a whole order, and in His supra-cosmic transcendent nature Śakti remains concealed in Him,—(*Antarlīna-Vimarśah*).

Gorakhnath says in clear terms,—
Śivopi Śakti-rahitah śaktah kartum na kincana
Swa-śaktyā sahitah Sopi Sarvasya Ābhāsako bhavet
(S.S.P.IV.13)

Śiva, bereft of His Power, is not able to do a single thing; but with His own Power He becomes the absolute revealer (creator and illuminer) of all orders of existences.

It is said that Śiva, the Supreme Spirit, does not even experience Himself as the Supreme Spirit without being reflected on His *Śakti,* Which serves as the spiritual mirror to His nature.

He continues,—

Ata eva parama-kāranam parameśwarah parātparah Śivah,
Swa-swarupatayā sarvatomukhah sarvākāratayā sphuritum śaknoti,
Ityatah Śaktimān.

By Himself Supreme above the Supreme (transcendent above the highest phenomenal realities and above time and space and action), Śiva, by virtue of the infinite Power inherent in His nature, becomes the Supreme Cause of all phenomenal existences and the Supreme Iśwara (Personal God), and with His essential self-luminous self-perfect character not in the least affected, becomes many-faced (paying attention to all directions) and manifests Himself in the forms of all kinds of phenomenal existences.

The unique capacity of Śiva (the Supreme Spirit) to remain eternally absorbed in the enjoyment of His changeless differenceless self-luminous transcendent existence and just the same to reveal and enjoy Himself as the Personal God creating and governing and destroying countless orders of conscious and unconscious phenomenal existences and pervading them all as their Indwelling Self, is, according to the *Siddha-Yogis,* the sure evidence of the Infinite Power inherent in His nature. *Iti atah śaktimān,*

—thus He must be possessed of Power,—asserts *Siddha-Yogi* Gorakhnath in an argumentative way. Further he makes the clear statement,—

Ata eva ekākārah ananta-śaktimān nijānandatayā avasthitah api nānākāratwena vilasan swa-pratisthām swayam eva bhajati iti vyavahāraḥ

Alupta-śaktimān nityam sarvākāratayā sphuran, punah swenaiva rupena eka eva avaśishyate.

(S.S.P.IV. 12)

Hence, Śiva, though essentially dwelling in His own perfectly blissful differenceless and changeless nature with His infinite Power immanent in Him, playfully (without any effort and out of the fulness of His nature) manifests and enjoys Himself in manifold forms (*nānākāratwena bilasan*), and thus practically appears in the *dual* aspects of the enjoyer and the enjoyable, the creator and the created, the supporter and the supported, the soul and the body, the self and its expressions, etc. He never abandons His Śakti and His Śakti is never alienated from Him (*alupta-śaktimān nityam*). Thus though by virtue of His Śakti He eternally (in time) manifests Himself in all kinds of forms, (*sarvākāratayā sphuran*), He in His own Self eternally (timelessly) exists as *one without a second* (*eka eva avaśishyate*),—as the changeless differenceless non-dual Reality—as *Nirguna Brahma*.

Gorakhnath, as a philosopher, takes a most comprehensive view of the Absolute Reality and attaches almost equal value to the transcendent experience of *Samādhi* and the enlightened phenomenal experience of the normal waking state. He equilibrates (*samarasa-karana*) the two planes of experience. He brings down the Light of the transcendent experience to the plane of the phenomenal experience, and raises up the contents of the phenomenal experience to the supra-phenomenal plane for the fullest conception of the Absolute Reality. In the transcendent experience of *Nirvikalpa Samādhi* there is no room for difference and change, no room for duality and relativity, no definite indication of any Power or the Dynamic Nature of the Supreme Spirit; in this experience time and space are concentrated in the supra-temporal supra-spatial absolute self-luminous unity of the Supreme Spirit, all duality and relativity are merged in non-dual Unity, the entire cosmic system is assimilated in one subject-object-less self-existent blissful supra-personal Consciousness. This might appear to be the experience of *Śiva Without Śakti,—Nirguna Brahma—Kevala Śiva,*—the Absolute Non-dual Spirit. There is no doubt that this is the Ultimate Truth, since this experience is the ultimate fulfilment of the truth-seeker's life-long search for Truth. It is in this Experience that the search for Truth reaches its goal.

But the world of phenomenal experiences, which is transcended and unified in this Experience, can not be disregarded as absolutely false; because in that case there would be no real individuality of the truth-seeker and the truth-seer, no real spiritual urge and spiritual discipline for the realisation of the Truth, no attainment of the transcendent experience, no ascertainment of the character of the Absolute Reality. The denial of the phenomenal world or the phenomenal experience would be a self-contradictory proposition. All affirmations and denials belong to the domain of phenomenal experience. The denial of duality and relativity would itself imply the existence of duality and relativity. The transcendent experience of the Mahāyogi being the final fulfilment of phenomenal experience, the absolute falsity of the latter would render the former meaningless.

On the other hand, this world of duality and relativity revealed to phenomenal experience cannot be conceived either as self-existent and self-revealing or as having some other independent source of existence and revelation; for in that case the intensive search for the Ultimate Truth of this world would not end in the discovery of Śiva, the changeless differenceless self-existent self-luminous non-dual Spirit, and the phenomenal consciousness would not have its ultimate self-fulfilment in the super-phenomenal subject-object-less Transcendent Experience. Śiva, therefore, must be the Ultimate Truth of this phenomenal world, and He must have in his nature the Ground and Source of this world,—the Dynamic Urge and Power for manifesting Himself phenomenally in a spatio-temporal order of ever-changing relative diversities and enjoying the infinity of His transcendent nature in infinite forms of phenomenal existences.

Accordingly the *Siddha-Yogis* proclaim that Śiva, the Supreme Spirit, has eternally a non-dual (*adwaita*) nature and a dual (*dwaita*) nature, a transcendent nature and a phenomenal nature, a self-absorbed nature and a self-active nature, a self-concentrated nature and a self-diversifying nature, an inwardly self-enjoying nature and an outwardly self-enjoying nature, a nameless formless changeless differenceless absolute nature and also a nature of perfectly free self-manifestation in innumerable names and forms and wonderful varieties of changes and differences constituting the cosmic system. Śiva is eternally above and beyond the world, untouched by the worldly activities and changes and diversities, and He also eternally manifests Himself as the world of ceaseless changes and endless diversities, as the omnipotent and omniscient Lord of this world, and as the innermost Soul of all the beings that are appearing in and disappearing from this world. He is transcendent of as well as immanent in the cosmos.

An enlightened *Mahā-Yogi* sees and recognises and makes self-offering to Śiva in both these aspects,—in both His transcendent and dynamic aspects, in His non-manifested and manifested aspects, and does not disown or disregard either of these eternal characteristics of the Divine Spirit. It is the dynamic aspect of the nature of Śiva, that is conceived and described as His Śakti,—His eternal infinite unique Power of revealing and enjoying Himself in infinitely diverse ways in a phenomenal world of plurality and changes. This Śakti is not conceived as any distinct *attribute* or *quality* or any special feature of the character of Śiva. Śiva's Śakti is no other than Śiva Himself. To the Yogis *Śiva is Śakti* and *Śakti is Śiva*. In His transcendent nature Śiva appears as if without Śakti, since Śakti has no outer expression in that state. But in reality Śakti is not then altogether absent. The dynamic aspect of Śiva is then perfectly identified with and indistinguishable from His transcendent aspect. In His phenomenal self-expression the dynamic aspect is more predominant; Śiva then reveals Himself as Śakti. He then appears as the Cosmic Player, the Cosmic Dancer. This dynamic self-manifestation in changeable diversified forms in the temporal plane does not however create any duality or plurality or transformation in His supra-temporal transcendent nature. Śakti exists in the nature of Śiva not as a second reality, but as one with Him. The manifold self-expressions of Śakti in the spatio-temporal order are also essentially non-different from Śakti and hence from Śiva. Thus, according to the *Siddha-Yogis*, Śiva, though always with Śakti and eternally manifesting Himself through His Śakti-aspect in the plurality of changing phenomenal forms, is eternally the One without a second,—the non-dual change-less self-shining self-enjoying Brahma,—the absolute Existence-Consciousness-Bliss. Though eternally playing various games and eternally dancing in various rhythms, Śiva is eternally in the state of perfect *Samādhi*. He is thus worshipped as *Mahā-yogīśwareśwara*, the eternal Guru and Ideal of all Mahāyogis.

Gorakhnath, in pursuance of the long line of enlightened *Siddha-Yogis*, explains the spiritual identity of Śiva and Śakti and describes Śakti as revealing the unity of the transcendent and phenomenal aspects of Śiva. He says,—

Saiva śaktir yadā sahajena swasmin unmīlinyām nirutthāna-daśāyām vartate, tadā śivah sa eva bhavati. Ata eva kula-akula-swarupā sāmarasya-nija-bhumikā nigadyate.

(S.S.P. IV. 1,2)

That same Śakti (Which is the Ground and Cause and Sustainer of the multitude of phenomenal forms), when existing in Her essential self-illumined transcendent character in Śiva, remains as absolutely Identical with Śiva. Hence She is described as equally of the nature of *Kula* and *Akula*,—as of phenomenal as well as transcendent nature,—and as revealing the perfect harmony and unity of both these aspects in the state of spiritual illumination.

Kula and *Akula* represent the two aspects of Reality. *Akula* implies *Eternal Being*, and *Kula* implies *Eternal Becoming*. *Akula* means the *noumenal essence* of Reality, and *Kula* means the *phenomenal self-expression* of Reality. *Akula* refers to the Infinite Eternal Absolute Self-existent One, and *Kula* refers to the self-manifestation of the One in the forms of finite temporal relative derivative existences. *Akula* points to Changeless Differenceless Transcendent Existence-Consciousness-Bliss (*Sat-Cid-Ānanda*), and *Kula* the self-revelation of this Transcendent Existence in various orders of phenomenal existences, the self-revelation of this Infinite Self-luminous Consciousness in diverse orders of finite conditioned phenomenal consciousnesses, the self-revelation of this perfect non-empirical limitless *Ānanda* in numerous forms of limited empirical enjoyments. *Kula* exhibits *Akula* under various kinds of limitations and makes these limitations also materials for the self-enjoyment of *Akula*. In the phenomenal self-manifestations of Transcendent *Sat-Cid-Ānanda*, all existences are limited by births and deaths and transformations, all consciousnesses are limited by ignorance and error and processes and subject-object-relations and psycho-physical conditions, all joys are limited by sorrows and wants and necessary objects and conditions for enjoyment. In the *Kula-aspect Akula* freely and delightfully manifests and realises and enjoys Himself in the phenomenal planes in and through various forms of self-imposed limitations, while in His *Akula*-aspect He eternally exists and shines in His blissful undifferentiated transcendent Self, above and untouched by all these phenomenal self-manifestations. This is the Unique Power (*Nijā-Śakti*) of Śiva. His *Śakti*, pervading His whole nature, eternally links together His transcendent and dynamic characters and is therefore called *Kula-Akula-Swarupā*.

It has been noted that in the state of *Nirutthāna* or *Samādhi*, Śakti is revealed as *Śiva*, and in the state of *Vyutthāna* or reawakenment from *Samādhi*, Śiva appears as Śakti, and that there is really no difference between the two aspects of the Absolute Reality. The empirical consciousness of the *Yogi*, when it transcends the conditioned phenomenal plane of experience and ascends to the transcendent plane, becomes transformed, as it were, into differenceless changeless effortless Transcendent Consciousness and wholly identified with the *Akula*-aspect of the Absolute Reality. When it descends back to the phenomenal plane with the illumination obtained in the higher plane, it experiences *Akula* as embodied in *Kula*, Śiva as manifested through Śakti, the Transcendent Existence-Consciousness-Bliss as assuming various forms of phenomenal existences, consciousnesses and imperfections and playing various parts in the ever-changing cosmic system. In the highest plane it experiences pure *Adwaita*,—Unity without difference and change,—and in the lower planes it experiences *Dwaita-Adwaita*,—Unity with differences and changes,—the Absolute playing freely and delightfully in the world of relativity. In the transcendent plane it becomes *Absolute Experience* without any distinction between the experiencer and the experienced Truth, and in the phenomenal planes it becomes the experiencer and the Reality appears to it as an objective Truth embodied in varieties of forms. In the super-empirical plane its sense of individuality is merged in the all-embracing all unifying all-transcending *Pure Experience,* and in the empirical planes its sense of individualistic ego is at the centre of all its experiences. An enlightened *Mahā-Yogi,* expert in the practice of *Samādhi,* easily passes from one plane of experience to the other by the concentration of his attention. He therefore feels an inner harmony and unity of both the planes of experiences. He feels the presence of the Dynamic Ground and Source of phenomenal experiences in the nature of the Reality of transcendent experience and feels the presence of the Reality of transcendent experience in the midst of his phenomenal experiences. Thus he feels the presence of Śakti in the transcendent non-dual nature of Śiva, and the presence of *Sat-Cid-Ānanda Śiva* in all the evolutions of Śakti,—he feels the presence of *Kula* in *Akula* and *Akula* in *Kula. Kula* and *Akula* are in the closest and most delightful embrace with each other in the spiritual experience of a *Mahā-Yogi.* He sees the infinite in the finite and the finite in the infinite,—Spirit in Matter and Matter in Spirit.

Akulam kulam ādhatte kulam cākulam icchati
jala-budbuda-bat nyāyāt ekākārah Parah Śivah

(S.S.P.IV. 11)

Akula embraces *Kula*, and *Kula* yearns for *Akula.* The relation is analogous to that between water and water-bubbles. In reality *Para-Śiva* (Supreme Spirit) is absolutely One.

The idea is that it is the inherent nature of *Akula* (non-dual Spirit) to manifest and enjoy Himself in the form of *Kula* (the system of phenomenal dualities), and that it is the inherent nature of all dualities to seek for union with the Non-dual Spirit, since they are in truth one and the same. To illustrate the relation between the *Adwaita* and the *Dwaita,* Gorakhnath takes the example of *water* and *bubbles.* Water remains in its essential character as water and at the same time appears in the forms of bubbles. Outwardly the bubbles appear to be different things, born from water, dancing on the surface of water, playing distinct parts and holding distinct relations with one another, and again being destroyed or losing their identity in the mass of water. Water becomes bubbles and bubbles become water. We witness these phenomena. We can not deny them as false. But still when we deeply look into the phenomena, we are convinced that even in the forms of bubbles water does not become anything other than water. In the changing multiplicity of bubbles water remains the same water all along, it does not really undergo any change and does not really become many. Similar is the case with the relation between *Akula* and *Kula*,—between the Transcendent One Śiva and the varieties of His phenomenal self-manifestations in the spatio-temporal order through the operation of His Dynamic Power, Śakti. The varieties appear to come into particularised existence from the Universal Existence of Śiva, play particular parts in this phenomenal cosmic system, hold different relations with one another and the whole system, and in the end lose their differentiated existences in the undifferentiated existence of Akula Śiva. But even in these spatio-temporal self-manifestations Śiva does not become some reality or realities other than Himself, does not substantially transform Himself intosomething distinct from Himself, does not lose His Universal Existence in the particularised existences; His *akhanda-sattā* remains eternally the same in and through the appearance and disappearance of all forms of *khanda-sattā.* Hence amidst all cosmic manifestations a *Mahā-Yogi* experiences *Ekākārah-Parah-Śivah,*—the One undifferentiated self-shining Supreme Spirit. He sees *Akula* in *Kula, Adwaita* in *Dwaita*, the Changeless Infinite in all changing finites, the perfect *Sat-Cid-Ānanda* in all phenomena of nature. There is perfect *sāmarasya* of the Transcendent and the Dynamic in his experience.

Thus the essential identity of Śiva and Śakti is an important truth in the philosophy of the *Siddha-Yogi* school. Śakti is no other than Śiva Himself, viewed as mainfesting and enjoying Himself in the spatio-temporal cosmic system. The Supreme Spirit, Śiva, is Himself the Efficient-cum-Material Cause of the universe, and in this aspect He is called Śakti. This Śakti, i.e. Śiva in this aspect is eternally devoted to the service of Śiva in His transcendent aspect. Thus Śiva and Śakti.—i.e. the Supreme Spirit as the transcendentally infinite and eternal self-existent self-luminous self-enjoying Soul and the same Spirit as the phenomenally infinite and eternal self-active self-evolving self-multiplying Power,—are as it were eternally *wedded* to each other, eternally in loving embrace with each other, eternally in inseparable union with each other. Śiva eternally illumines and spiritualises Śakti and all Her evolutions in the phenomenal system, and Śakti eternally reveals the infinite existence and consciousness and beauty and goodness of Śiva in an infinite variety of phenomenal names and forms and contributes to the eternal enjoyment of Śiva. Transcendent Śiva is the Soul of the cosmic system and of all the diverse orders of existences within it; Dynamic Śiva, i.e. Śakti, constitutes the body of the system and all individual bodies within it.

Śiva is looked upon as the Father, and Śakti as the Mother of the universe, though there is essentially no distinction between the Father and the Mother, and there is no question of *gender* in the sensuous sense in that plane. Śiva as the transcendent efficient Cause of all phenomenal realities is conceived as the Father, and Śakti as the dynamic material Cause actively assuming diverse forms and sustaining and nursing them and again assimilating them within Herself is conceived as the Mother. Śiva shines and reigns as the Soul in all, and Śakti builds up the body and the life and the mind and the intellect for Him and contributes to His self-expression and self-enjoyment through their various functions in various stages of their developments. In this phenomenal order of self-manifestation, Śakti has a diversifying tendency (*prasārana*) as well as a unifying tendency (*Sankocana*). She diversifies the One and unifies the many. She creates many existences out of One Existence, and again unveils the essential Unity of all existences through a process of illumination. She materialises the Spirit and again spiritualises matter. She furnishes the Spirit with various kinds of physical and vital and mental bodies and fields of self-expression and self-enjoyment, and reveals the essential spiritual character of all these bodies and the entire cosmic play-field. She finitises the Infinite and again exhibits the One Changeless Infinite in all changing finites. This two-fold play of Śakti is ceaselessly going on.

It is evident that the *Siddha-Yogi* school does not conceive of the Ultimate Cause of the phenomenal cosmic system as one non-spiritual non-conscious Primordial Matter or Energy, called *Prakriti*, eternally associated with an infinite number of inactive self-luminous spiritual souls, called *Purusha*, and spontaneously modifying itself according to a process of evolution into this world of diverse orders of existences, as the Sankhya school of Kapila does. Nor does it conceive of this Ultimate Dynamic Source of phenomenal existences as of the nature of some inscrutable Cosmic Ignorance or some inexplicable neither-real-nor-unreal Principle or Power (called *Māyā*) *somehow* veiling the essential transcendent *Sat-Cid-Ānanda* character of the Absolute Spirit (Brahma) and creating (with Brahma as the changeless differenceless self-luminous Substratum) an *illusory* world of bewildering diversities, as the orthodox *Adwaita* school of Śankara does. Nor does it support the view of those advocates of *Dwaita-vāda*, who hold that the Material Cause of the world of plurality is of the nature of a non-spiritual Reality or a Power or Energy, which is eternally and existentially different from the Supreme Spirit, but is eternally associated with, related to and dependent upon the Supreme Spirit, and which transforms itself into and sustains the world of phenomenal diversities under the supervision and direction and governance of the Supreme Spirit. Nor does it agree that this Power is merely an attribute or quality of the Supreme Spirit and is related to the Spirit just as an abstract quality to a substance.

According to the *Siddha-Yogis*, the Source of this world is not a material substance, but a Spiritual Reality, not an *Acit-Śakti*, but a *Cit-Śakti*, not of the nature of *Avidyā* or *Māyā* (an illusion-producing inexplicable Ignorance), but of the nature of *Vidyā* or *Saṃvit* (knowledge or Consciousness), not essentially *āvarana-vikshepātmikā* (of the character of a Power for veiling the Truth and falsely superimposing illusory diversities upon It), but *prakāśa-vimarśātmikā* (of the character of a Divine Power for revealing the Supreme Spirit and bringing out in a variety of forms the infinite glories and beauties of His transcendent nature). Gorakhnath describes the Power thus,—"*Parāpara-Vimarśa-rupinī Saṃvit nānā-śakti-rupena nikhila-pindādhāratwena vartate iti siddhāntah.*"—One Dynamic Consciousness-Power, whose character is to unfold in various higher and lower (collective and individual) forms the nature of the Absolute Spirit, manifests Herself in the forms of diverse kinds of forces and countless species of *pindas* (bodies) and holds them together in Herself by the living unity of Her all-pervading spiritual existence. She is conceived as self-manifesting self-diversifying all-harmonising all-unifying ever-active Dynamic *Sat-Cid-Ānanda*. The Supreme Power, the Divine Mother and Nurse of the universe, is *Sat-Cid-Ānanda-mayee* i.e. of the nature of perfect Existence-Consciousness-Bliss.

The view of the *Siddha-Yogi* school with regard to the Dynamic Source of the cosmic system is found to be generally akin to that of the *Tāntrik* school. According to both the schools, the Power (Śakti) from Which this phenomenal world of our normal experience is originated and by Which it is sustained and regulated and in Which it is ultimately merged and unified, is the Divine Power, the self-conscious and self-active Power of the Supreme Spirit (*Cit-Śakti*), the Power Whose essential nature is self-unfolding self-multiplying self-delighting Perfect Existence- Consciousness-Bliss (*Ātma-vilāsinī Sat-Cid-Ānanda-Swarupinī Śivānī-Śakti*) and Which is inwardly in eternal union with and non-different from Śiva, the Supreme Spirit, the Transcendent Existence-Consciousness-Bliss. Both the schools maintain that this sublime and beautiful cosmic order (in which we as finite conscious beings play our allotted parts and obtain scope for self-enlightenment and elevation to the super-empirical plane of Absolute Experience) is the product, not of a Power of Darkness, but of a Power of Light, not of a Power of Evil, but of a Power of Supreme Goodness, not of a Power that veils and distorts the Face of Truth, but of a Power that reveals in a spatio-temporal order the infinite Goodness and Richness and Bliss inherent in the nature of Truth, not of a Power antagonistic to the Transcendent Supreme Spirit, but of a Power delightfully devoted to the loving service of the Spirit and participating in His infinite joy. The enlightened persons of both the schools see the Transcendent Spirit revealed in the Power, see in the cosmic play of *Śakti* the play of *Cit*, see in all the waves of the world the reflections of Brahma.

The cosmic system with all its apparently bewildering complexities and catastrophes is often described by them as *Cid-Vilāsa,* i.e. the luxuries as it were of the Spirit, the delightful self-expressions of the transcendent perfection of the Spirit. Matter also is looked upon as a form of self-expression of the Spirit. They see the play of the Spirit in all material phenomena. To them matter, life, mind, intellect,—all these appear as forms in which the Supreme Spirit is playing various delightful games through the medium of His unique *Śakti,* His Power of diversified self-manifestation, Which is non-different from Himself. Thus they look upon the whole world as Spiritual, they look upon their own bodies also as spiritual, they enjoy all phenomena of mundane experiences as the joyful play of *Śiva-Śakti.*

It is generally known that from time immemorial the *Siddha-Yogis* have been upholders of the Path of Renunciation (*Nivṛtti-Mārga*) and the Ideal of Perfect Self-Illumination in *Samādhi,*—the Ideal of *Kaivalya* or *Moksha* or *Nirvāna,* - the Ideal of Absolute Śivahood. The enlightened teachers of this *Sampradāya* have always scrupulously practised and preached abstinence, calmness and tranquillity, mastery over the body, the senses, the vital forces and the mind, freedom from all worldly desires and passions and attachments, unconcernedness with all outer affairs of the world and deeper and deeper concentration into the innermost spiritual self-shining nature of the Soul. But nevertheless they did not entertain or preach any pessimistic view about the cosmic order or phenomenal existence. They never taught the spiritual aspirants or seekers for liberation from worldly sorrows and bondages to cultivate the feeling that all (mundane existence) is sorrow, all is evil, all is ugly and repulsive in this phenomenal world, that this world had its origin in some sort of Ignorance or Illusion or some sort of Deceptive Power veiling and distorting the nature of Truth, that the existing order of things is devilish or the whole plan of the world is satanic, or that the world is the chance-product of some blind Material Energy and man in his conscious life has always and inevitably to struggle against the forces of the world, which are by nature hostile to the aspirations of the human consciousness. Many religio-philosophical schools, advocating the Ideal of *Moksha* or *Nirvāna* or Perfect Liberation and the Path of Renunciation and Deep Meditation, deliberately teach their followers to cultivate such views and feelings about the world and the worldly life. Such views and feelings, whatever may be their practical values in the path of spiritual self-discipline, appear to be repugnant to the spiritual philosophy of the *Siddha-Yogi* school, to which Gorakhnath belonged.

According to this school, this world originated not from Ignorance, but from Fullness of Knowledge which is characteristic of Śiva-Śakti, not from any Deceptive Power veiling transcendent nature of the Supreme Spirit, but from the *Nijā-Śakti* of the Supreme Spirit, through Which the Spirit reveals His transcendent *Sat-Cid-Ānanda* character in various forms of phenomenal existences, consciousnesses, activities, beauties and enjoyments under various kinds of freely self-imposed spatio-temporal limitations. The enlightened saints of this school teach the truth-seekers to see in this world-order not the sorrows and evils and repulsive scenes created by any hostile Satanic Force, but the delightful plays of One Supremely Loving Motherly Power, Who is eternally full of affection and mercy for Her children, Who is leading Her children (Her own self-expressions) in this cosmic system through various stages and various circumstances towards perfect illumination and realisation of Śiva in themselves. They teach us to appreciate and enjoy the world as *Cid-Vilāsa,* as *saundarya-lahari,* as *ānanda-lahari,*—as the Spirit in various playful garbs, as the waves of the Ocean of Beauty and Bliss.

CHAPTER VIII

GRADUAL UNFOLDMENT OF SAKTI

The first chapter of Gorakhnath's *Siddha-Siddhānta-Paddhati* is devoted to the exposition of the gradual self-unfoldment of *Śakti,* immanent in the transcendent nature of Śiva, the Supreme Spirit, leading step by step to the manifestation of the magnificent Cosmic Body of Śiva and the diverse orders of individual bodies within it.

From our foregoing discussions it must have been evident that Gorakhnath and his school are supporters of what is generally called *Satkārya-vāda.* They maintain that the world of effects exists before its actual production in an unmanifested (*avyakta*) state in its Material Cause (*Upādāna-Kārana*), and they hold that the Spiritual Power of Śiva or the Supreme Spirit in His dynamic aspect is the Material Cause (as well as the Efficient Cause) of this cosmic system, which appears to our phenomenal experience as a vast material world. From the view-point of *Sat-Kārya-Vāda* they assert that all the diverse orders of realities of this material world exist, before their manifestation in the effect-forms, as undifferentiated from one another and hence altogether unified in the nature of their ultimate Material Cause, viz. the Divine Power, Which also being then actionless exists as perfectly identified with the Supreme Spirit, Śiva. Śiva-Śakti has then no outer self-manifestation. Śiva does not in that state even experience Himself as the Owner of Śakti or as a Dynamic Personality. Śiva, with Śakti absolutely immanent in and identified with Him, exists as differenceless and changeless *Parā-saṃvit* or Pure *Sat-Cid-Ānanda.* From the metaphysical stand-point this is conceived as the eternal transcendent nature of the Ultimate Reality, the Supreme Spirit, and from the phenomenal empirical or temporal stand-point this is conceived as the pre-creational (*Sristeh prāk*) state or the state of *Mahā-Pralaya* (absolute dissolution) of the cosmic order. Creation and Dissolution have reference to the phenomenal world of diversities; 'before' and 'after' have reference to time and change. Before creation and after dissolution of the phenomenal world, only the Ultimate Reality, i.e. the Supreme Spirit, exists in His own self, in His transcendent nature. Nothing else exists. There is no evidence of even space and time. But the facts of creation and dissolution indicate that the *bīja* (seed) of this world must exist in the nature of that Non-dual Spirit even before creation and after dissolution and that this *bīja* must exist in the form of the *Power* of the Spirit,—the Power Which has no self-expression in that state and is therefore absolutely identical with the Spirit.

Now, when we look at the relation between the Cause and the series of effects from the phenomenal or temporal view-point, we find that what remains folded in the cause becomes unfolded in the effects, what is potentially existent in the cause becomes actually existent in the effects through the causal operations, what is involved in the cause is gradually evolved in time in the forms of the effects. From this point of view the process of causation or evolution or *becoming* apparently shows some *progress* or *advance* from unity to plurality, from simplicity to complexity, from homogeneity to heterogeneity, from potentiality to actuality, from an unmanifested state to more and more manifested states; and the process of dissolution or destruction again shows a *regress* or *backward movement* from plurality to unity, from complexity to simplicity, from heterogeneity to homogeneity, from actuality to potentiality, from the gross manifested states to some subtle unmanifested state. The pre-creational state of being and the state of being after total destruction or dissolution appear to be exactly similar or the same. Temporally the state of being before the beginning of the actual cosmic process and after the end of the actual cosmic process must be conceived as a state of being which is as good as non-being,—an absolutely unmanifested state of being (*avyakta*), a state of absolute void (*śunya*). From the view-point of the temporal process there is nothing improper in the statement that the cosmic system starts from *Śunya* and ends in *Śunya*, or that it starts from *Avyakta* and ends in *Avyakta*, or even that it starts from *Nothing* and ends in *Nothing*.

But it must be remembered that this temporal process cannot have any absolute beginning or absolute end, since Time cannot have any beginning in time or end in time. The state of Dissolution preceding the beginning of the current creative process must itself have been preceded by a state of Creation, and the state of Dissolution which will follow the present state of Creation will again be followed by another order of Creation, and so on. From the phenomenal view-point there is a continuous cycle of Dissolution followed by Creation and Creation followed by Dissolution without any absolute starting point or absolute termination. Every Dissolution, though apparently a state of Void, contains in undifferentiated unity the seed or the material cause of the future Creation, and every Creation also contains in its nature the ground of its destruction and goes ahead inevitably in course of time towards Dissolution. This *Sristi-sthiti-pralaya-cakra* is temporally an eternal order, and this is the Cosmic System. Gorakhnath and *Siddha-Yogis* also accept this view from the phenomenal standpoint.

From the metaphysical view-point the Cause is not to be conceived as temporally antecedent to the effects or as being transformed into the effects through any process of change. The Ultimate Cause of the world of plurality and change must be conceived as above time and space and as having no spatio-temporal relation with the cosmic system which is Its effect. It cannot be thought of as passing through any spatio-temporal process in order to produce this effect. All spatio-temporal processes and relations are within this cosmic system. which originates from the Ultimate Cause. The origination of the cosmic system from the differenceless changeless self-existent self-luminous Supreme Spirit (with infinite Power immanent in His nature) cannot be compared to the origination of the tree from the seed or to the origination of milk-products from milk or to the origination of cloth from thread or to the origination of earthen vessels from earth or to any other case of real origination within the world of our experience. In all such cases the cause and the effect belong to the same plane of experience, they are equally subject to spatio-temporal conditions, they are similarly governed by forces and laws of nature, and some changes take place in the cause for the production of the effect. No such case can possibly bear comparison with the causal relation, in which the Cause belongs to the supra-temporal supra-spatial supra-phenomenal spiritual plane and the Effect consists of all existences in the temporal spatial phenomenal plane, in which the Cause is One Infinite Eternal Unconditioned Non-dual Spirit and the Effect comprises all possible differences and diversities and changes and conditions, in which the Cause is absolutely free, perfectly self-fulfilled, infinitely good and beautiful and blissful in His transcendent nature, and the Effect consists of various kinds of creatures suffering from bondages and sorrows, natural and moral evils, deformities and imperfections, etc. The Cause is unique and the Effect also is unique. The beginningless and endless cycle of Creations and Continuities and Dissolutions is within the phenomenal Cosmic Order and as such is related to the all-transcending Supreme Spirit as His effect. The Supreme Spirit must be conceived as the Absolute Cause of this beginningless and endless order, without any change or modification or Transformation in His transcendent nature and without any effort on His part. What can be nature of this unique causal relation?

It has already been noticed that *Siddha-Yogi* philosophers conceive of this unique causal relation as *Cid-vilāsa* or *Śiva-Śakti-vilāsa*, which means perfectly free and delightful sportive self-manifestation of the Transcendent Spirit in the phenomenal plane. This view implies that in the nature of the Spirit there is immanent some unique Power or *Śakti*, by virtue of which the Spirit (*Caitanya*) without any change or modification in His transcendent spiritual character and without any desire or effort, manifests and enjoys the infinite glory of His nature in the phenomenal plane,—in the plane of time and space and relativity,—in the plane of succession and co-existence and varieties of relations and limitations,—in the forms of numerous conscious and unconscious, living and non-living, mental and material, finite and changing phenomenal realities. This is what is called the free unfoldment of His *Śakti*. It is not unfoldment in the same plane, like the unfoldment of a bud into a flower or a fruit or that of a seed into a plant or that of an embryo into an animal-body. In the super-temporal super-spatial super-relative transcendent plane of pure Existence-Consciousness-Bliss there is no question of folding and unfolding, no question of contraction and expansion, no question of involution and evolution. All these conceptions pertain to the phenomenal plane.

According to the view of the enlightened *Mahā-Yogis*, the Truth that is absolutely realised in Itself above time, space and relativity in the transcendent plane, is always in the process of realisation under conditions of time, space and relativity in the phenomenal plane. It is a sort of progressive realisation of the perfect One as imperfect many, of the unconditioned absolute One as the conditioned relative many, of the changeless noumenal One as the changing phenomenal many, of the spiritual One as psycho-physical many. This is of the nature of the free play and self-enjoyment of one self-fulfilled Spirit in many names and forms under a variety of self-imposed conditions and limitations in time and space. It is the delightful self-expression of a Reality of a higher plane in the forms of many realities in a lower plane and enjoyment in innumerable instalments as it were of the infinite riches of Its nature enjoyed as one undifferentiated whole in the higher plane. This is described as *Cid-Vilāsa* and self-unfoldment of the Power of the Absolute Spirit.

The Vedantists of Sankara's school describe this self-manifestation of the transcendent Absolute Spirit in the phenomenal plane as *Cid-Vivarta* and hence they are called *Vivarta-Vādi*. *Vivarta* is distinguished from *Parināma*, since the latter implies a kind of *transformation* of a Cause (partly or wholly) into effects of the same order of reality as the Cause, while the former means the *appearance* of a Cause in the forms of effects of a lower order of reality without involving any change or modification in the Cause. *Vivarta-Vadis* hold that as the Supreme Spirit is above all changes and modifications, He cannot be regarded as a real cause of a real world-order, but only an illusory cause of an illusory world-order. He falsely *appears* as the world of plurality. For the illustration of such illusory causal relation, i.e. the false appearance of a cause in the form of an effect which it *neither becomes nor actually produces*, they often cite the examples of a rope appearing as a snake, an oyster appearing as a piece of silver, the appearance of mirage in the desert, and so on. These are generally examples of invalid or defective perception,—the perception of some object as something which it is not (*adhyāsa*), under certain conditions, on account of the imperfections in the powers of the senses and the mind of the perceiver. When the true knowledge of the object is attained by the perceiver through more careful observation under better conditions, the illusion disappears and it becomes evident that the thing as wrongly perceived was never produced at all. These are regarded as cases of *Vivarta*, and on the analogy of such examples all cases of *Vivarta* are regarded as cases of illusion (*adhyāsa*) by the aforesaid *Vivarta-Vādis*. Accordingly they come to the conclusion that the phenomenal world of plurality and change is nothing but an illusory appearance of the Supreme Spirit to the people suffering from positive Ignorance (*avidyā*) or erroneous knowledge, and that when the true knowledge of the Supreme Spirit is attained by them it becomes evident that the world was never created and never really exists as such. The orthodox Vedantists of Sankara's school take great pains to prove the illusory character of the phenomenal world, and in order to make this illusory appearance logically compatible with the non-dual character of the Supreme Spirit they have conceived the idea of one mysterious *Māyā*, which they do not regard as the real unique Power of the Supreme Spirit, but which they conceive as a neither-real-nor-unreal positive entity somehow mysteriously existing with Him and revealing Him eternally in illusory names and forms in an illusory world.

The *Yogis* agree with the Vedantists in holding that the Supreme Spirit is the One Changeless Non-dual Reality and that this beginningless and endless phenomenal cosmic order is neither a product of His wishful creation (*Ārambha-vāda*) nor a product of His self-modification or self-transformation (*Parināma-Vāda*). The *Vivarta-Vāda* of the Vedantists is not unacceptable to the Yogis, if *Vivarta* means the self-manifestation of a Reality of a higher order in the forms of realities of a lower order,—i.e. the self-manifestation of One Transcendent Spirit in the forms of a plurality of phenomenal existences. But the enlightened *Yogis* find no reason why such self-manifestation should be regarded as illusory appearance, nor do they see any necessity for recognising such an inexplicable extraneous entity or power, called *Māyā*, essentially unrelated to the Supreme Spirit, for explaining this self-manifestation of the Supreme Spirit in the forms of phenomenal realities. What the Vedantists conceive as *Māyā* is given a much more exalted position by the Yogis, who regard this *Māyā* as the *Cit-Śakti* (the unique and inscrutable, eternal and infinite Power of the Spirit for free self-expression in infinite ways), immanent in the essential nature of the Supreme Spirit, Who by virtue of this Power freely and delightfully manifests the transcendent glory of His nature in the forms of manifold phenomenal realities. This *Māyā* is adored by them as

Mahāmāyā or *Yogamāyā*. They do not accept the analogy of rope-snake, oyster-silver, mirage, etc. for explaining this wonderful world-order, since such analogy would irrationally pre-suppose the existence of imperfect observers before the appearance of this phenomenal system. *Māyā*, if conceived as the Mother of the Cosmic order, must be regarded as the real Power of Brahma.

Yogi-Guru Gorakhnath, in his *Siddha-Siddhānta-Paddhati*, gives an interesting account of the gradual self-unfoldment of the Divine *Śakti*—*Mahāmāyā* or *Yogamāyā*, towards the creation of the phenomenal cosmic system. The exposition starts from the conception of the Absolute One,—the Transcendent *Sat-Cit-Ānanda*,—in Whom the Power is absolutely unmanifested and undifferentiated from the essential nature of the Spirit. The Power is then of the nature of Pure Will (*Icchā-mātra-Dharmā*)—a Will which wills nothing and as such is altogether indistinguishable from the Willer (*Dharmin*). The Will is immanent in the Non-dual Spirit, but it has no manner of manifestation, not even a subtle impulse to manifest itself in duality or plurality. The presence of the Absolute Will-Power in the transcendent nature of the Absolute Spirit indicates His absolute freedom of self-manifestation and self-enjoyment in all planes of existences. There is no second Power to limit His freedom or to offer any resistance to His Will-Power, and there is again no necessity or determining force for His self-manifestation in any particular form at any particular time. By recognising the presence of the absolute *Will-Power* in the transcendent nature of the Absolute Spirit, the Yogi school gives recognition to the *perfect-freedom* of the Spirit to reveal and enjoy His infinite and eternal Existence-Consciousness-Bliss in the forms of various orders of existences and consciousnesses in diverse planes at all times. The unfoldment of His Śakti is perfectly free and is therefore appropriately described as the expression of His infinite joy (*ānanda-vilāsa*).

In his exposition of the gradual self-unfoldment of the Divine *Śakti*, Gorakhnath first describes five stages of Her progressive self-manifestation and characterises each of the stages in terms of five attributes (*guna*). The *Nijā-Śakti*,—i.e. the Divine Power in Her original form, in which She is f the nature of Pure Will and is wholly indistinguishable from the transcendent character of the Supreme Spirit,—is mentioned as the first stage and is described as possessing these five attributes, viz., *Nityatā, Niranjannatā, Nishpandatā, Nirābhāsatā*, and *Nirutthānatā*. (I. 10). *Nytatā* means eternity, which implies that this *Śakti* is eternally and inalienably present in the nature of the Spirit. *Niranjanatā* means stainlessness, which implies that She is absolutely pure and participates in the perfect self-luminosity of the Spirit. *Nishpandatā* means vibrationlessness, which implies that there is as yet no internal change nor even any positive urge for change in Her nature. She is perfectly calm and tranquil and enjoying sound sleep as it were within the bosom of Śiva. *Nirābhāsatā* means unreflectingness, which implies that as the existence of Śakti is not yet distinguishable from that of Śiva, the character of Śiva is not reflected upon Her. Lastly, *Nirutthānatā* means unawakenedness of Her own character as distinct from the transcendent character of Śiva. At this stage Śiva is Śakti and Śakti is Śiva. This is pure *Parā-saṃvit* .

At the second stage there arises within the self-radiant Divine Will *(Nijā-Śakti)* a very subtle impulse or tendency *(unmukhatwa)* to activate Herself, to unfold Her dynamic character. The apparently sleeping Will becomes as it were characterised by an inner awakening about Her infinite phenomenal possibilities together with an inner urge for their gradual realisation in the phenomenal plane. The Power Which was wholly unmanifested in and identified with the transcendent spiritual nature of Śiva is now slightly manifested as a distinct aspect within His nature. Śiva appears to be dimly conscious of Himself as the Possessor of this infinite *Śakti* and to experience Her as His own dynamic nature. Some sort of distinction without difference arises between Śiva as the changeless differenceless self-existent self-luminous self-enjoying Supreme Spirit and His Infinite Power of self-manifestation. The Power seems to become an Object of delightful experience to Him within Himself. *Śakti* then exists no longer perfectly *as Śiva,* but *in and for Śiva* At this stage *Śakti* is spoken of as *Parā-Śakti.* Says Gorakhnath,—

Tasya unmukhatwa-mātrena Parā-Śakti rutthitā. (I. I. 6).

This *Parā-Śakti* is the first slightly unfolded form of the eternal *Nijā-Śakti* of the Absolute Spirit, Brahma or Śiva. She is the Supreme Mother of all Powers, all orders of existences, all orders of individualised consciousnesses, the whole phenomenal universe. There is as yet no actual movement or action in Her. From *Nirutthāna-daśā* this is the first *utthāna-daśā* of *Śakti.* Gorakhnath describes this *Parā-Śakti* also in terms of five attributes *(Panca Gunāh),* viz., *Astitā, Aprameyatā, Abhinnatā, Anantatā, Avyaktatā.* (I. I. 11). The first attribute predicable of *Parā-Śakti* is spoken of as *Astitā,* which means the quality of *existing.* The intention obviously is that prior to the self-unfoldment of *Śakti* as *Parā-Śakti,* even *existence* as an attribute could not be predicated of Her, in as much as *Nijā-Śakti* was absolutely identified with Pure Existence-Consciousness-Bliss and could not be said to have the quality of existence of Her own. *Pure Existence* conceived as the character of the Supreme Spirit should not also be confused with the *quality of existing,* there being no subject-predicate or substance-quality relation in His essential transcendent character.

The second quality by which *Parā-Śakti* is characterised Is *Aprameyatā*, which means immeasurableness. Being free from all kinds of determinations or limitations,—being the Supreme Mother or Originator of all kinds of determinations and limitations, spatial, temporal, etc.,—Her nature is evidently incapable of being measured, i.e. spatially or temporally, quantitatively or qualitatively, or in any other way determined or limited.

The third attribute is *Abhinnatā,* which means undifferentiatedness. There is nothing, whether outside or within Herself, from which She can be differentiated as a separate entity, nor is She differentiated from the Supreme Spirit, in and for Whom She exists.

The fourth attribute is *Anantatā,* which means infinitude or inexhaustibleness. *Parā-Śakti,* though as yet undifferentiated from the transcendent nature of Śiva, contains within Herself infinite contents, which are inexhaustible in temporal, spatial and phenomenal manifestations. She may continue to manifest Herself in infinite ways through eternity, but Her possibilities will never be exhausted; there will continue to be ever-new creation from within Herself. The richness which is immanent in the transcendent dynamic nature of the Supreme Spirit can never be exhausted through manifestation in the phenomenal plane, in the plane of time, space and relativity.

The fifth attribute is *Avyaktatā,* which means unmanifestedness. This implies that all the inexhaustible richness of Her nature, though present eternally, is up to this stage wholly unmanifested.

Parā-Śakti has within Herself infinite wisdom, infinite beauty, infinite goodness, infinite splendour, infinite power, infinite life, infinite love, infinite happiness,—She has within Herself all the supreme ideals of conscious existence perfectly realised,—but all these remain unmanifested, undifferentiated, unified in Her supra-temporal supra-spatial supra-phenomenal nature. The dynamic aspect of the essential nature of the Supreme Spirit is at this stage at the junction, as it were, of the transcendent and the phenomenal planes,—the plane of absolute Existence-Consciousness-Bliss and the plane of His relative spatio-temporal self-expressions. Śiva, qualified by this infinitely rich and powerful Creative Will, as yet unmanifested, but tending towards manifestation, seems to advance one step in the direction of revealing and enjoying Himself as a self-conscious self-determining Creative Personality.

The self-unfoldment of the immanent Divine Power as *Parā-Śakti,* as expounded by Gorakhnath, may remind one of the Upanishadic conception, *"Tad aikshata, bahusyām,, prajāyeya"*,—That (Non-dual Brahman) *witnessed*, I will become many, I will become phenomenally born. The absolutely indeterminate Being *(Sat)*—the One without a second *(Ekam eva adwitīyam)*,— *willed* to be born in the plane of time and space as determinate many, to manifest Himself as a cosmic system and as Indwelling Spirit of this system. It should be noted that to the Transcendent Spirit *willing* and *witnessing* are the same, and this involves no change in His perfectly calm and tranquil self-luminous nature. It may also remind one of the *mantra* of *Nāsadiya-Sukta*,—*"Kāmas tad agre samavartatādhi"*,—*Will* to create first came into existence, and this *will* was the first seed of mind,—*(manaso retah prathamam yad āsīt*.

At the third stage some sort of vibration *(spandana)* or internal agitation arises in the infinite spiritual bosom of this *Parā-Śakti*. The Divine Will is then characterised by some internal *push* for external self-manifestation, though not by any outward transformation. *Śakti* somewhat activated by such *spandana* within Herself is designated as *Aparā-Śakti*. *Tasya spandana-mātrena Aparā-Śakti rutthitā*. (I. I. 7).

The five attributes of *Aparā-Śakti* are,—*Sphuratā, Sphutatā, Sphāratā, Sphotatā* and *Sphurtitā*. (I. I. 12). It is difficult to bring out the exact significance of each of these attributes. *Sphuratā* seems to imply that *Śakti* at this stage has not merely the quality of existence, but somewhat agitated existence,—existence agitated with an inner movement for self-revelation. *Sphutatā* seems to imply that *Śakti* has now a more manifested presence in and before the consciousness of Śiva,—a more explicit presence in His self-experience. *Sphāratā* seems to mean that this *Śakti* has a tendency for further self-unfoldment or self-expansion,—that there is in Her an incessant pull for progressive self-manifestation or self-externalisation. *Sphotatā* seems to indicate that the realities which remain ideally present, but actually unmanifested, in Her nature, are seeking for realisation in the phenomenal plane. *Sphurtitā* seems to imply that there is an inner delight and enthusiasm in Her nature for the gradual unfoldment of Her inner glories in the phenomenal plane. Thus what is called *Aparā-Śakti* is one step forward towards the outward self-manifestation in the spatio-temporal plane of the transcendent glories of the Divine nature. The dynamic aspect of the character of the Supreme Spirit is somewhat more explicitly manifested at this stage. Brahma or Śiva as the sole Owner, Illuminer, Seer, Enjoyer and Soul of the Creative Will appears at this stage somewhat like an active Self-revealer through His dynamic nature, though He in Himself transcends all forms of actions and dwells in the realm above time, space and relativity.

Here again we should keep in remembrance that the phenomenal world of plurality and succession has not yet come into existence. There is no earth or water or fire or air or ether ; no sun or moon or star ; no day or night, no light or darkness, no heat or cold ; no knowing subject, no knowable object or event. Śiva or Brahma alone exists, without any *in* and *out*, without even any ego-consciousness. He has, as it were, just been awakened from the state of *Nirvikalpa-Samādhi* and become conscious of Himself as possessed of infinite power or energy and also of a sort of pulsation and thrill within Himself for some indefinable creative self-expression. His consciousness is still inwardly immersed in the transcendent blissful experience of the perfectly changeless and differenceless state, but along with that His consciousness seems to have become somewhat dynamic and agitated for outer self-expression.

Then comes the fourth stage, in which one pure *I-ness* or Egohood evolves within the dynamic consciousness of Śiva or Brahma. His consciousness then takes the form of "I am conscious of myself", though there is no differentiation between 'I' as the conscious subject and 'myself' as the object of consciousness. One pure *I-ness* pervades the entire subtly-agitated dynamic consciousness. The Divine Śakti is at this stage called ***Sukshmā-Śakti***. Gorakhnath says,—

Tatah Ahamtā-mātrena Sukshmā-Śaktih utpannā. (I.I.8)

At this stage of the self-unfoldment of *Śakti* in the direction of phenomenal self-manifestation, Śiva appears to be revealed as the sole self-conscious self-determining dynamic Personality. Before this stage Śiva had been an Impersonal or Superpersonal Spirit,—He had been as it were so immersed in Himself as not to be fully conscious of the infinite glory of His self-existent self-conscious omnipotent dynamic nature. Now He becomes a Personal God. But even now He is the One without a second. Even now there is no differentiation or relativity in His self-consciousness. He is conscious of Himself as One Integral Personality, without any parts, without any psychophysical embodiment, without any differentiated self-expressions, without any distinction between *in* and *out*. The *Mahā-Yogi* Philosopher in his usual manner describes the nature of this *Sukshmā-Śakti* in terms of five attributes :—Viz, *Niramśatā, Nirantaratā, Niscalatā, Niscayatā, Nirvikalpatā*. (I.I. 13)

Niramśatā implies that this Divine I-consciousness does not involve any duality or plurality or relativity within itself. *Nirantaratā* implies that there is no discontinuity or any temporal or spatial gap in this I-consciousness. *Niscalatā* implies that there is no fickleness or no expansion and contraction or no increase and decrease of intensity in this consciousness.

Niscayatā means perfect certitude or fulness of self-knowledge. It implies that here there is no room for any doubt or error or any element of uncertainty, which usually pertains to empirical and conceptual knowledge. *Nirvikalpatā* implies that this Divine Self-knowledge is not of the nature of such knowledge as involves any empirical process or any abstract conception or any speculation or theorisation ; there is not even any phenomenal subject-object relation in it. This is pure omniscience ; the Supreme Spirit with His Śakti being all that really exists, His self-knowledge is truly all-knowledge.

Thus though Śiva has now the delightful self-experience as the absolute Divine Personality, absence of any distinct duality or plurality, absence of any temporal sequence or spatial co-existence, absence of any empirical process of cognition or volition or emotion, absence of the sense of any limitation or imperfection or unrealised ideal, absence of any doubt or uncertainty or incompleteness with regard to the eyperience, are the characteristics of His perfectly calm and tranquil and all-comprehending self-consciousness. He now *perceives* His non-duality, His omnipotence and omniscience, His infinite and perfect existence, but there is no process or effort or relativity in this act of perception. What is called the *Vimarśa-Śakti* of the Spirit,—the inherent Power of Self-reflection and Self-experience of Śiva,—is revealed at this stage.

It is quite evident that this *I-consciousness* of Śiva or Brahma or the Supreme Spirit is altogether of a distinct character from the ego-consciousness of individual persons of the phenomenal world. It is for this reason that Gorakhnath has studiously mentioned the absence of the characteristics of the ego-consciousness of finite individuals in the perfectly illumined Self-consciousness of the Supreme Spirit. By virtue of this perfectly illumined I-consciousness the Supreme Spirit experiences Himself as the absolutely perfect Spiritual Personality. The self-consciousness of a man of the world, however empirically enlightened, is under the influence of *Avidyā* and therefore involves duality and plurality, process and change, limitation and imperfection. etc. The I-consciousness of the Supreme Spirit is spoken of as the manifestation of His *Suddha-Vidyā* (pure self-illumination), which is characteristic of His *Śakti*.

This I-consciousness of the Supreme Spirit is referred to in the Upanishad in the conception of "*Aham Brahma asmi*" (I am Brahma). A Yogi can, through the intensive practice of spiritual knowledge and deep meditation, get his empirical consciousness perfectly illumined and participate in this I-consciousness of the Supreme Spirit, when all the limitations and dualities and relativities of his individual ego-consciousness vanish and he experiences his oneness with the Supreme Spirit. This elevation of the

Yogi's consciousness to the enlightened spiritual plane is also a form of the self-expression of the Divine Śakti, and this will be dealt with later on. Here we are discussing the downward or outward progress of the Divine Consciousness for diversified self-expression in the phenomenal plane, in the plane of space and time, plurality and change. It is the perfect dynamic Self-consciousness of the Supreme Spirit that freely and delightfully unfolds Itself in this phenomenal cosmic order.

At the fifth stage within the self-conscious spiritual Personality of Śiva His Śakti unfolds Herself as a distinct Psychic Power,—a Power characterised by the processes of knowing, feeling and willing,—though as yet no objects of knowledge, feeling and will as externally related to the Power have evolved. This Śakti is called *Kundalinī-Śakti*. "*Tato vedana-śīlā Kundalinī-Śakti rudgatā.*" (I.I.9). Gorakhnath in his usual way speaks of this *Kundalinī-Śakti* as characterised by five attributes,—viz., *Purnatā, Pratibimbatā, Prabalatā, Proccalatā, Pratyagmukhatā.* (I.I.14).

Purnatā means perfect character. It may also imply infinite possibilities of self-manifestation, self-diversification, self-transformation. She is the material cause of the amazingly complicated phenomenal universe. She contains within Herself in a potential form (in a *coiled* form as it were) the entire spatio-temporal order. She is spoken of as the Seed (*bīja*) of the cosmic process, which is the phenomenal uncoiling of this Śakti. *Pratibimbatā* implies that She operates as a sort of mirror, upon which the self-luminous spiritual character of Śiva is capable of being reflected in an infinite variety of forms, material, vital, mental, intellectual. *Prabalatā* means omnipotence, infinite capability, unlimited power for creating from within Herself various orders of existences and sustaining and regulating them harmoniously and again assimilating them within Herself. *Proccalatā* implies Her inherent self-transforming, self-expanding, self-multiplying and also self-harmonising and self-unifying character. She is quite free or self-determined in Her internal and external movements and She is the controller of the movements of finite and temporal beings born of Her and nourished in her lap. *Pratyagmukhatā* implies that even while unfolding Herself in the direction of phenomenal creation or self-diversification and maintenance and destruction of diversities, Her face is always directed towards the Supreme Spirit, Śiva, Who is Her Soul and Lord, Her Illuminer and Inspirer, the Sole Being of Her being and becoming, in Whom, By Whom and for Whom, She eternally exists and moves and to contribute to Whose infinite delight She plays Her part. As the playful Śakti has Her face invariably towards Śiva, the Supreme Spririt, all the children of Śakti, all Her phenomenal self-manifestations, also have an inherent yearning for conscious union with Śiva,—all consciously or unconsciously move towards blissful union with Him. His Śakti creates out of Herself every individual body as a specialised seat for the self-expression and self-enjoyment of Śiva,—Śiva is, truly speaking, the Soul in every individual body as well as of the cosmic body.

CHAPTER IX

SELF-MANIFESTATION OF SIVA AS COSMIC PURUSHA

Having thus expounded the gradual self-unfoldment of *Śakti* within the spiritual transcendent nature of Śiva, Gorakhnath concludes that in this way the Supreme Spiritual Body of Śiva is born, in which all the qualities of all the five stages of Śakti's internal self-unfoldment are harmoniously manifested and organised as it were in His Self-Consciousness. This Supreme Spiritual Body of the Absolute Spirit is called by the Siddha-Yogis *Para-Pinda.* "*Evam ca Śakti-tattwe panca-panca-guna-yogāt Parapindotpattih.*" (I.I. 15). Gorakhnath summarises his statement by quoting an earlier authority. He says,—"*Uktam ca,—Nijā-Parā-Aparā-Sukshmā-Kundalinī āsu pancadhā, Śakti-tattwa-kramena-uttho jātah Pindah Parah Śivah.*"—It has been said (by recognised enlightened Mahā-Yogis) that Śiva was born (*jāta*) as it were as *Para-Pinda* (Supreme Body) through the progressive evolution of *Śakti-Tattwa* within His nature in the five forms of *Niiā, Parā, Aparā, Sukshmā* and *Kundalinī* with their characteristic attributes.

It is to be carefully remembered that though on account of the natural limitations of our power of thinking as well as of our power of giving verbal expression to our thoughts we have to describe the so-called progressive self-unfoldment of the eternally inherent *Śakti* of the Absolute Spirit in the language of temporal succession and development; the time-factor in our empirical sense does not really exist there in the spiritual plane and does not condition the self-unfoldment and self-awakening of *Śakti* in the nature of Śiva. Every stage of the self-unfoldment of *Śakti* and Śiva's *vilāsa* (self-enjoyment) in it is eternal. Śiva's birth as *Para-Pinda* is also not a temporal phenomenon. What is described in our exposition as a succeeding stage does not come into being by superseding the preceding stages and destroying their characteristics. Our intellectual conception of the gradualness of the self-unfoldment of *Śakti* in the nature of Śiva is not to be construed as anything more than a mere mental analysis and reconstruction of the various phases of the superglorious character of the Divine Spiritual Power in the spatio-temporal form of our empirical knowledge. Śiva is in truth eternally endowed with and glorified by all the phases of self-unfoldment of His Śakti, and all the characteristic features of all the stages are wonderfully adjusted and assimilated in the all-comprehending all-assimilating all-enjoying spiritual consciousness of Śiva. The attributes of the different stages of *Śakti*, as described, may from our plane of experience often appear contradictory to one another. But Śiva's Consciousness is the meeting-ground of all contradictory qualities (*Sarva-virodhi-gunāśraya*). He enjoys *nirvikalpa samādhi* along with the active waking state.

The birth of *Para-Pinda* means the self-manifestation of the Supreme Spirit as the Supreme Individual (*Parama-Purusha*) with all His eternal and infinite glorious powers and attributes and with full consciousness of all these powers and attributes, while retaining the perfect calmness and tranquillity of His self-luminous transcendent nature. In the language of Yogācārya Patanjali's *Yoga-Sutra*, He is perfectly free from any touch of *Kleśa*, *Karma*, *Vipāka*, and *Āśaya*, but all the same He is *Purusha-Viśesha*. *Kleśa*, according to Patanjali, means *Avidyā* (Ignorance), *Asmitā* (Egohood), *Rāga* (Attachment), *Dwesha* (Aversion), *Abhiniveśa* (Lust of life or Fear of death). *Karma* means actions which are voluntary and born of desires with a view to the attainment of certain desired consequences or the realisation of some unrealised ideals. *Vipāka* means the fruits of such actions, which have to be reaped (enjoyed or suffered) by the performers in accordance with the Law of Karma. *Āśaya* means the impressions which remain deep-seated in the sub-conscious mind on account of such *kleśa*, *karma* and *vipāka* and originate new *karma*, new *kleśa* and new *vipāka*. These are the general characteristics associated with the conception of phenomenal individuality.

But the Divine Individual is eternally free from the bondage of such characteristics, but is still a *Purusha-Viśesha*,—a perfectly self-conscious Personality. He has absolutely no imperfection in His nature, either in respect of existence, or in respect of power, or in respect of knowledge and wisdom, or in respect of moral and aesthetic excellence, or in respect of spiritual illumination. He is perfectly active and perfectly inactive. He perfectly enjoys the bliss of His transcendent nature within Himself, and nevertheless there is in Him an urge for His manifesting and enjoying Himself in diversities of names and forms in a spatio-temporal cosmic order. He is absolutely calm and tranquil, but still He feels within Himself a tremendous upheaval, as it were, for creative action, for self-diversification. He is absolutely indifferent to the cosmic affairs and is in eternal *samādhi* within Himself, and at the same time He is the Indwelling Spirit in all these affairs, the Inspirer and Regulator of all processes, the Soul of the whole phenomenal order. He sees the entire spatio-temporal system within Himself and Himself in every part of it, and yet there is absolutely no perturbation in the unity of His consciousness. He dwells in the phenomenal and the transcendent planes at the same time.

It may be remarked in this connection that though Patanjali's *Yoga-Sutra* is a highly admirable exposition of the main philosophical doctrines as well as of the ideals and methods of self-discipline of the *Yogi-Sampradāya*, His conception of Iśwara (or Śiva) does not appear to be exactly the same as the conception of Śiva or the Supreme *Purusha* of Gorakhnath and the *Siddha-Yogi* school. Patanjali mostly adopted the metaphysical view of the *Sānkhya* school of Kapila, who was universally adored as the *Ādi-Vidwān* (probably meaning the First Philosopher) among the *Siddha-Yogis*. In the *Bhagavat-Gītā* Kapila is specially mentioned as a glorious self-manifestation (*Vibhuti*) of God in the community of Siddhas:— "*Siddhānām Kapilo Munih*". But Kapila had no place for God or Eternal Iśwara in his philosophy, as promulgated in the direct line of his followers. According to his metaphysical reasoning, the Ultimate Material Cause of the world-order is one non-spiritual self-modifying Entity, called *Mulā-Prakriti*, with which innumerable inactive pure *spirits* (essentially of the nature of changeless self-luminous consciousness), called *purusha*, are somehow eternally associated (by way of *aviveka* or indiscrimination). *Prakriti* and *Purushas* are eternally of opposite characters. All orders of phenomenal existences gradually evolve from *Prakriti*, and *purushas*, though pure and changeless, are *somehow* associated with them as their *souls*. All individual bodies, together with all senses, minds, egos and intellects, are the products of the non-spiritual non-conscious *Prakriti*, while the souls are mere witness-consciousnesses. But the souls are somehow through *Avidyā* falsely identified with psycho-physical bodies and hence they become apparently subject to sufferings. They are in course of time blessed with True Knowledge and released from this false self-identification with the products of *Prakriti* and are restored to their own essential spiritual character.

In Kapila's philosophy no self-existent self-conscious infinite and eternal Absolute Spirit is provable by logical reasoning based on our normal experience,—(*Iśwarā-siddheh pramānābhāvāt*),—nor is it necessary to admit the existence of such Absolute Spirit to account for this cosmic system. His philosophical system is very strongly argumentative. From very ancient times many truth-seekers followed his path from the philosophical view-point. Maharshi Patanjali also mainly adopted his metaphysical view, while expounding the Yoga-system of discipline. He however seems to have somewhat differed from him in recognising the eternal self-existence of Iśwara as the perfectly enlightened *Purusha-Viśesha*. He recognised Him as the Supreme Ideal for all *Yogis* as well as the Supreme Source of all spiritual illumination. According to him, perfect omniscience is eternally and essentially present in Him, and He is the eternal *Guru* (Giver of Divine Light) of all truth-seekers of all ages. He proclaimed that deep meditation on *Iśwara* was one of the most effective means to the speedy attainment of *Samādhi* and experience of the Ultimate Truth. But he did not admit Him as the Sole and Supreme Cause of the cosmic order,—as the One Who manifests and enjoys Himself as the changing plurality of the world.

In agreement with all *Siddha-Yogis* Patanjali holds that Iśwara or Śiva is eternally *Mahā-Yogīśwara, Mahā-Jñānīśwara, Mahā-Tyāgīśwara*, that all *yogis, jñānis* and *tyāgis* of all ages look up to Him and contemplate on Him as the Supreme Personality in Whom the highest ideals of *yoga, Jñāna* and *Tyāga* are eternally and absolutely realised and Who is the perpetual fountain of inspiration, hope and strength in their path of self-discipline, self-elevation and self-enlightenment. Patanjali maintains that He is the Supreme Lord of *Prakriti* in the sense that He by virtue of His perfect Self-knowledge eternally transcends *Prakriti* and Her cosmic processes and that Prakriti can never bring Him under any sort of bondage. Patanjali further admits His mercy and compassion upon the souls (*purushas*) under the bondage of *Prakriti* and the power of this mercy and compassion in delivering them from apparent bondage and sorrow through the bestowal of true spiritual enlightenment upon them. But he does not seem to admit that this Divine *Purusha-Viśesha* is Master of *Prakriti* in the sense that He governs the course of Her evolution and rules over all the affairs of the world, or in the sense that *Prakriti* depends upon Him for Her existence and self-unfoldment.

To Patanjali as well as to Kapila, *Prakriti* is a self-existent and self-evolving non-spiritual reality and does not depend for Her existence and evolution upon Iśwara. Gorakhnath and the true *Siddha-Yogi* school fundamentally differ from this view. According to their conception, *Prakriti* is one aspect of the inherent *Śakti* of the Supreme *Purusha*,—Śiva or Iśwara or Brahma,—and has no existence apart from the existence of the *Purusha*. Evolution of Prakriti is nothing but the self-unfoldment of the Divine Power. The cosmic system is in their view the self-manifestation of Iśwara. He is therefore the Absolute Master of *Prakriti* in every sense. *Prakriti* is accordingly not a non-spiritual independent reality, but essentially a spiritual reality, being an integral aspect of the nature of the Supreme Spirit. The plurality of *Purushas* or individual souls also are individualised spiritual self-manifestations of the One Non-dual Supreme Spirit ; each of them is essentially *Śiva* in a particular psycho-physical embodiment. Thus the conception of Iśwara as given in *Yoga-Sutra* represents only a partial aspect of Śiva or Iśwara as conceived by Gorakhnath and the Siddha-Yogi School. Again, according to Kapila and Patanjali, every *purusha* or *jeeva* (individual spirit), in the state of *Moksha* or *Kaivalya*, becomes perfectly dissociated from *Prakriti*, but retains its individuality and exists eternally as pure *Cit* (pure transcendent Consciousness), distinct from all other liberated *purushas* as well as from *Iśwara* (of Patanjali's system); while according to Gorakhnath and the Siddha-yogi school every such liberated *purusha* realises its identity with *Iśwara* or *Śiva* and thus attains *Śivahood* and experiences *Prakriti* or *Śakti* as non-different from itself.

Gorakhnath and the Siddha-Yogi school have used the term *Para-Pinda* to signify the Supreme Personality of the Absolute Spirit with His gradually self-unfolding *Śakti*, the Mother of the phenomenal cosmic system. The term *Pinda* means an *organised whole*, a living unity of many parts, a one consisting of and unifying a plurality. In it the whole exists in every part, the one pervades and enlivens and harmonises each of the plurality of parts, though the constituent parts may have their distinctive qualities or characteristics. Again, all the parts exist in and for the whole, the fulfilment of their distinctive characteristics and the final purposes of their existences also lie in the whole. The parts may be more and more multiplied, they themselves may be organised wholes of still smaller parts, they may undergo changes and transformations; but all their self-multiplications and self-divisions and self-transformations take place within the whole and they all participate in the unity of the life of the whole. The parts with all their changes contribute to the life-history of the whole, and the life-power of the whole determines the course of the changes of the parts. The parts are parts only in relation to the whole, and the whole is whole only in relation to the parts. They are interrelated. The primary point to be noted is that unity pervades the diversities.

Gorakhnath seems to attach some special importance to the term *Pinda*, and uses the term very often in various contexts. His intention appears to be to emphasise the truth of the unity of diversities in all planes of existence,—from the highest spiritual plane to the lowest physical plane. He teaches the truth-seekers to carefully observe that all our conceptions of concrete realities in all the planes of our knowledge and thought involve the idea of unity of diversities. All diversities in every sphere of our knowledge and thought involve unity underlying them, unifying them as parts or organs of one whole; and all unities also are found through deeper analysis to be wholes consisting of parts,—subtler and subtler constituents. Accordingly even in the highest plane of Spiritual Reality Gorakhnath rejects pure Non-dualism of the extreme Vedantists as well as pure Dualism of the *Dwaita-Vādis* and pure Pluralism of *Bahupadārtha-vādīs*. On the other hand in the lowest physical plane also he rejects the doctrine of the plurality of unrelated material units or *paramānus* integrated and dis-integrated by external causes. The Non-dual Spirit is to him embodied with His own Śakti, which is non-different from Him. The Absolute Reality is therefore neither purely non-dual nor purely dual nor plural. He applies this principle everywhere. The idea appears to be confirmed by our experience of *living organisms*,—from those that are infinitely small (e.g. bacilli) to those that are majestically great. The whole universe is conceived as one organism, comprising countless orders of organisms,—one *Samasti Pinda* comprising innumerable orders of *Vyasti-Pindas.*

The Absolute Spirit conscious of Himself as one infinite and eternal self-perfect Individual through the awakening of the *Śakti* immanent in His nature has been called *Para-Pinda* (Supreme Organism).. Gorakhnath describes this *Para-Pinda* of Śiva,—the self-conscious spiritual individuality of the Absolute Spirit,—as consisting of five forms of spiritual consciousness, all shining at the same time without overshadowing each other in His all-comprehensive Divine Self-consciousness. These five forms are,—

Aparamparam Paramapadam Śunyam Niranjanam Paramātmeti. (S.S.P.I. 17). The Mahā-Yogi has attempted to make the character of each of them intelligible or at least conceivable to ordinary truth-seekers by describing each in terms of psychological concepts, though he was himself quite conscious of the inadequacy of such descriptions. *Aparamparam*, he says, implies *sphuratā-mātram.* It gives us the idea of one changeless and differenceless self-effulgent transcendent consciousness, in which there is no trace of even any subtle distinction between the Spirit and His *Śakti.* This refers to the pure consciousness of the Absolute Spirit in relation to His *Nija-Śakti*, when She is completely hidden in His transcendent nature, i.e. when the dynamic aspect of the Spirit is wholly unmanifested. In the Personal Self-consciousness of *Para-Pinda Śiva* this pure self-less consciousness shines as the chief constituent factor.

Parama-Padam, he says, implies *bhāvanā-mātram.* This refers to the subtle unfoldment of the dynamic aspect of the Spirit as *Parā-Śakti*, when in the Divine Consciousness there is subtle form of *reflection* upon Her. The Spirit then becomes as it were Witness to His Śakti and by this mere act of *witnessing* (which is truly speaking no act at all) inspires Her with a creative urge. The Divine Consciousness in this form of a pure disinterested Witness of His Creative Power, it may be noted, is often meditated upon by the Yogis as the Supreme Ideal (*Parama-Pada*) to be realised by them through their *sādhanā* within their own consciousness.

Śunya, according to Gorakhnath, implies *Swa-sattāmātram*, i.e. pure self-existence. The Divine Consciousness is here in the form of a pure empty background or substratum of His self-vibrating *Śakti* rich with infinite potentialities. This refers to the stage of the unfoldment of His *Śakti* as *Aparā-Śakti*, in which Śakti appears to be vibrating for phenomenal self-expression, and Śiva appears to hide Himself behind the scene altogether and become a Void as it were from the phenomenal view-point, though illuminating and enthusing Śakti from within as Her Soul and Lord. Many Yogis meditate on and worship Śiva, the Absolute Spirit, as *Śunya*, in order to be absolutely liberated from the sense of *Me* and *Mine*. They seem to practise what may be called self-annihilation for the purpose of the attainment of absolute liberation from all kinds of bondage and sorrow.

Niranjana is explained by Gorakhnath as *Swa-sākshātkāra-mātram*,—i.e. the Absolute Spirit experiencing Himself as pure *I*,—as the true Self, distinguished from and transcending His own Śakti. He is in this form of His consciousness conscious of Himself as the Seer (*Sākshī*) of His own self-evolving Power. His self-consciousness involves a duality within His non-dual nature,—some sort of *Dwaita-adwaita* relationship,—the consciousness of a subtle distinction between Himself as the eternally changeless witnessing Spirit and Himself as the eternally self-evolving *Śakti*. He feels within Himself the pulsations of His dynamic nature and at the same time feels Himself as absolutely unmoved and untouched and unaffected by these pulsations. This refers to the unfoldment of His dynamic character as *Sukshmā-Śakti*, in which the manifestation of the I-ness in the transcendent nature of the Absolute Spirit is the important feature. This form of consciousness represents the realisation of perfectly pure *I-consciousness* transcending all kinds of limitations and impurities and bondages. Many Yogis meditate on the Supreme Spirit as *Niranjana* with a view to the realisation of this perfectly pure and free and blissful *I-consciousness* within themselves.

The fifth form of the all-comprehensive consciousness of Śiva is the consciousness of Himself as *Paramātmā*, meaning the Universal Soul,—the Soul and Lord of the Divine Mother of the universe, *Kundalinī-Śakti*. He feels Himself as possessed of infinite power, infinite wealth, infinite goodness, infinite beauty, infinite wisdom, infinite love, etc., and He feels within Himself an impulse of delight to play with all these through His unique *Śakti* in an infinite variety of forms in a phenomenal cosmic system of time and space and relativity. As *Paramātmā* the Absolute Spirit is conscious of Himself with His *Śakti* as the most perfect Spiritual Personality, eternally enjoying the infinite richness of His self-existent nature in His transcendent self-consciousness as well as in His phenomenal self-manifestations,

Gorakhnath describes the character of each of these forms of Divine Consciousness according to his usual practice by means of enumerating five *gunas* and then concludes that the character of Śiva as *Para-Pinda* is a perfect harmony of all the twenty-five *gunas* of all of them. Within the Self-consciousness of *Para-Pinda* all forms and all stages of consciousness are most wonderfully harmonised and unified. He is the Supreme Divinity comprising all Divinities. With the self-unfoldment of His *Śakti* His self-conscious Personality is glorified.

This *Para-Pinda* is also called by the *Siddha-Yogis Anādi-Pinda* as well as *Ādi-Pinda*, meaning that this Divine Individuality is without any beginning or origination, without any Cause or Higher Sourcc of existence, and that this is the *Ādi* or the Supreme Source of all other *pindas* or individualised existences.

This *Anādi-Pinda* or the Uncreated and All-creating Divine Personality is further explained as unfolding Himself into five glorious self-revelations, viz., *Paramānanda*, *Prabodha*, *Cid-udaya*, *Prakāśa* and *Soham-bhāva*. *Paramānanda* implies that there is an upheaval of emotional delight in His tranquil nature. This is characterised by *Spanda* (some sort of agitation in the consciousness), *Harsha* (some thrilling sensation), *Utsāha* (some sort of enthusiasm in the being), and at the same time *Nishpanda* (perfect calmness) and *Nitya-sukhatwam* (unemotional enjoyment of eternal bliss within). Thus a great wave of emotional *ānanda* seems to activate His nature without disturbing the inner current of tranquil self-enjoyment, which is the essential character of His self-consciousness.

Prabodha implies that there is as it were a new phenomenal *awakenment* in His transcendent self-conscious nature. He is as it were newly awakened from a state of deep sleep, which is truly speaking a state of *Samādhi*. The light of His self-illumined consciousness now falls upon and illuminates all the aspects of His glorious nature seeking for phenomenal self-expression. This is explained as characterised by such attributes, as, *Udaya* (the rising of the consciousness above the horizon of the perfectly tranquil non-differentiated state), *Ullāsa* (some sort of upheaval in the essentially tranquil nature for objective self-manifestation), *Avabhāsa* (experience of the spiritual contents of His own nature as objective realities), *Vikāsa* (experience of the self-evolution of His *Śakti*), and *Prabhā* (shedding lustre upon all the aspects of His all-pervading existence.)

By *Cid-udaya* Gorakhnath means the self-manifestation of the Transcendent Consciousness as the self-knowing and all-knowing, self-reflecting and all-reflecting, self-determining and all-determining, Conscious Subject. He characterises this aspect of the Divine Personality by such attributes, as, *Sadbhāva* (the Spirit's clear knowledge of Himself as the sole Reality), *Vicāra* (His reflection upon Himself as the Source and Centre of all possible phenomenal realities), *Kartritwa* (His consciousness of Himself as the Source of all possible actions), *Jñātritwa* (His consciousness of Himself as the Knower of objects), and *Swatantratwa* (His consciousness of Himself as perfectly free or governed by his own Laws).

By *Prakāśa* Gorakhnath emphasises that in spite of the appearance of the various forms of upheavals in the self-conscious nature of the Divine Personality on account of the urge of His dynamic character (*Śakti*), He is inwardly untouched and unmoved by them, and His transcendent consciousness always dwells in the supra-phenomenal plane amidst all kinds of phenomenal self-manifestations. *Prakāśa* is explained as characterised by *Nirvikāratva* (freedom from all kinds of changes), *Nishkalatwa* (freedom from any sense of partition within Himself), *Nirvikalpatwa* (freedom from any sense of doubt or uncertainty in knowledge), *Samatā* (perfect harmony, calmness and unity in His consciousness), and *Viśrānti* (perfect rest). Thus while on the one hand the dynamic aspect of the Divine Personality is developing and becoming more and more conspicuous, the transcendent aspect of His Consciousness is on the other hand wholly undisturbed and unshadowed.

Lastly Gorakhnath mentions the unfoldment of *So-hambhāva* (He-I-am-ness) in the self-consciousness of the *Anādi-Pinda*. He explains it as consisting in the following attributes:—*Ahamtā, Akhand-aiśwarya, Swātmatā, Viśwānubhava-sāmarthya* and *Sarvajñatwa*. *Ahamtā* means all-comprehending Egohood. The whole cosmic order is *ideally* manifested in His consciousness and becomes objectively an integral part of His Self. His Ego is expanded as it were into all and the inherent richness of His nature becomes objectified within His self-consciousness. Hence he feels within Himself *akhanda aiśwarya,* i.e. undivided and unlimited power and prosperity. The whole universe which is manifested to His consciousness being His own self-expression, He feels absolute sovereignty (*Iśwaratwa*) over it. Then, *Swātmatā* implies that he feels all His *aiśwarya* as non-different from Himself. His consciousness of the universe never overshadows the consciousness that He is Himself the universe. His Self-consciousness (*Swātmānubhava*) appears to be evolved into *Viśwānubhava,* i.e. the consciousness of the entire spatio-temporal order, without any disturbance to its essential unity of undivided self-luminous character. Thus space and time, plurality and change, diversity and relativity, which are inalienably associated with His phenomenal self-manifestation, arise within His self-consciousness. His Self pervades them and also transcends them and thus plays as one and manifold, changeless and changing, transcendent and phenomenal, at the same time without any disharmony. In His Own Self-Knowledge He becomes All-Knowing, Omniscient, *Sarvajña*. He knows all within Himself and Himself in all. In this way the *Mahāyogi* traces the self-unfoldment of the Supreme Spirit (with His *Śakti* immanent in Him) into a Universal Soul with an ideal Cosmic Body, which he gives the glorious name of *Ādya-Pinda* (S.S.P.I. 25-30).

Thus it is conceived that on account of the internal urge of the Divine *Śakti* for phenomenal self-expression and self-enjoyment there is some sort of awakening and activation and development (which is often described as *Tapas* in the Vedas, e.g. *ritam ca satyam cābhiddhāt tapasah adhyajāyata*) in the transcendent nature of the Absolute Spirit (Brahma or Śiva or by whatever name the Transcendent Spirit may be designated), and He reveals Himself as a magnificently glorified self-conscious self-active omnipotent omniscient and playful Divine Personality embodied with an ideal universe. This ideal universe is the phenomenal manifestation of the eternal and infinite glories involved and unified in the transcendent nature of the Spirit. His awakened self-consciousness means the consciousness of Himself as possessed of all the glories and the cosmic body.

This conception of *Ādya-Pinda* of the *Siddha-Yogi* school appears to correspond to the conception of *Hiranya-Garbha* of the Veda. It is proclaimed in the *Rig-Veda*,—"*Hiranyagarbhah samavartata agre, bhutasya jātah Patir eka āsīt.*" It means that the Divine Personality with the entire cosmic order *in an ideal form in His womb* manifested Himself first of all and He became by nature the sole Lord of all existences (which would gradually evolve out of His being in the spatio-temporal system). It is also said,—"*Sa vai śarīrī prathamah, Sa vai Purusha uccyate.*" This means that He is the First Embodied Being, and He is called the Person (i.e. the Divine Personality). He is spoken of as *Saguna Brahma* and often as *Kārya-Brahma* in the Vedanta philosophy.

Most of the schools of thought, which conceive the Ultimate Reality as one differenceless changeless attributeless impersonal Transcendent Spirit, appear to find themselves under the rational and spiritual necessity to conceive of a perfectly self-conscious, perfectly self-illumined, gloriously and excellently qualified, omniscient and omnipotent Divine Personality, as the most appropriate and effective link and meeting-ground between the transcendent and the phenomenal planes of existence and thought, between the Absolute Spirit above time and space and relativity and His diversified and changing phenomenal self-manifestation in the domain of time and space and relativity. Between the One and the many, the Infinite and the finite, the Changeless and the changing, the Eternal and the temporal, there must be a self-conscious Personality, Who is One and at the same time unifies many within His own existence, Who is conscious of Himself as Infinite and Changeless and is also conscious of the possibility of infinite varieties of finite and changing existences within and as part and parcel of His all-pervading and all-comprehending existence, Who experiences Himself as manifested in all orders and forms of phenomenal existences and at the same time continuously experiences Himself as the Soul and Lord of them all and also as one absolutely disinterested transcendent Witness-Consciousness. The Divine Personality dwells inwardly in the transcendent plane and outwardly in the phenomenal plane and there is a wonderful harmony of the two planes in His self-conscious nature. The Yogis conceive this Divine Person as eternal *Mahā Yogīśwara* and as the perfect embodiment of the Yogic Ideal which they all seek for realising. He is to them *Ādi-Nātha, Ādi-Guru, Ādi-Siddha.* The phenomenal and the transcendent planes of experience are eternally harmonised in the spiritual self-realisation of this perfectly enlightened *Mahā-Yogi.* He experiences himself in all existences of the universe, experiences the universe within himself, and also transcends the universe as Pure Consciousness. He enjoys absolutely blissful changeless existence within and also enjoys the manifold self-expressions of the Spirit in the cosmic order. This is *Ādya-Pinda* or *Cosmic Purusha* of the *Siddha-yogi Sampradaya.*

The process of creation of the cosmic system is, according to the Siddha-Yogi school, the progressive descent of the Transcendent Divine Consciousness into more and more manifested and differentiated self-expressions of His Dynamic Nature. This may on the one hand be viewed as the gradual self-veiling, self-limiting, self-conditioning, self-finitising and self-despiritualising of the eternal, infinite, absolute, impersonal, self-luminous transcendent character of the Supreme Spirit ; and on the other hand it may be viewed as the progressive self-expanding, self-diversifying, self-magnifying, self-glorifying and self-delighting of the Spirit through the phenomenal self-unfolding of the Unique Power eternally innate in and identified with His Transcendent Nature. It may be imagined as One Infinite Light projecting out of itself shades of various characters, which, while offering resistance to it, add to its brilliance and exhibit it in various colours ; or as One Infinite Ocean creating big and small waves upon its bosom, which while disturbing its calmness and tranquillity greatly magnify its grandeur and magnificence. Infinite and Undifferentiated Self-perfect Knowledge without any process and subject-object distinction in it divides itself into numberless subjects in different planes of experience and thought and numberless objects of various forms and characters appearing to them in various relations, and thereby manifests and enjoys in all possible details in the phenomenal order the Absolute Truth that shines undivided in its transcendent state. Infinite Impersonal Bliss multiplies itself into diverse kinds of enjoyers and enjoyables and realises itself through numerous orders of finite enjoyments in different planes of experience in the beginningless and endless time and space. Thus the Transcendent seems to take delight as it were in manifesting Himself as the Phenomenal. This is the root of creation,—the cosmic self-expression of the Spirit.

The Divine Existence, the Divine Knowledge, the Divine Power, the Divine Bliss, the Divine Beauty, the Divine Magnificence, the Divine Love and Magnanimity,—all these are perfectly unified in the transcendent impersonal Divine Nature, and they are phenomenally manifested in diverse forms and under different conditions and limitations in the cosmic system. The Divine Spirit, as the Ground, Support, Soul, Lord, Witness and Illuminer of them all, assumes in relation to them various kinds of glorifying epithets and enjoys Himself in them. The Spirit, Who is transcendentally one differenceless attributeless self-luminous Being, is in His phenomenal self-manifestation the Omnipotent Omniscient Magnificent Perfect Personal God. The *Śakti* unfolded becomes His manifested Body, and the more is the Power diversified, the more magnificent does the Divine Body appear to be. As the one all-illumining Soul of the cosmic body, Śiva pervades the entire universe and enjoys Himself in it.

CHAPTER X

EVOLUTION OF THE COSMIC BODY OF SIVA

Having given a brilliant account of the nature of *Ādya-Pinda* in the ideal supra-physical plane, Mahāyogi Gorakhnath proceeds to the exposition of the evolution of the physical world system from the nature of this *Ādya-Pinda*. Śiva as *Ādya-Pinda,* the Cosmic Purusha, evolves from within Himself, through the further unfoldment of His Śakti, a physical cosmic body, extending in space and changing in time, and makes it an integral part and parcel of His all-comprehending and all-enjoying Self-Consciousness. The universe, which was *ideally real* in the nature of *Ādya-Pinda,* becomes *physically and objectively real* as the Cosmic Body of Śiva, and this Body is designated by Gorakhnath as *Mahā-Sākāra-Pinda*. Śiva Himself reveals and enjoys Himself as this *Mahā-Sākāra-Pinda*. this magnificent world-organism, this splendid spatio-temporal order, this physical universe full of apparently bewildering complications and catastrophic changes: It is one of the forms of self-manifestation of the *Mahā-Śakti* of Śiva. Śiva with His infinite and eternal *Mahā-Śakti* is immanent in all the diversities of this physical order, is regulating and harmonising all its phenomena, and is manifesting and enjoying the glories of His transcendent nature in and through various kinds of limitations and complications pertaining to this physical organism subject to temporal and spatial conditions.

An enlightened *Yogi* sees the delightful self-expression of *Mahā-Śakti-Vilāsī* Śiva in all the variegated affairs of this physical universe. He sees and loves this world as the Divine Body, that can be actually perceived with the physical senses, that offers opportunities for the appreciation and enjoyment of the beauties and sublimities and excellences of the Divine nature in particularised forms and for practical participation in the Divine play through the loving performance of good works in His world for His sake in a desireless sportive spirit. The *Yogi* feels that he lives and moves and has his being in the Divine Body, that he is never alienated from Him, that in the waking or dreaming or sleeping state he never loses direct contact with Him. All phenomena of the world, all orders of existences, all pleasant and unpleasant circumstances, appear to be sacred to him, because they pertain to the Divine Body, because they all form parts of the playful self-expressions of Śiva-Śakti. The conception of the physical universe as the Cosmic Body of Śiva is a most magnificent idea of the philosophy of *Siddha-Yogis.*

Gorakhnath traces the evolution of this *Mahā-Sākāra-Pinda* thus:—

Ādyān Mahākāśo, Mahākāśan Mahāvāyuh, Mahāvāyor Mahatejo, Mahātejasó Mahāsalilām Mahāsalilān Mahāprithwī.

(S.S.P.I. 31).

From *Ādya-Pinda* evolves *Mahā-Ākāśa* (Great Ether), from *Mahā-Ākāśa* evolves *Mahā-Vāyu* (Great Air), from *Mahā Vāyu Mahā-Tejas* (Great Fire), from *Mahā-Tejas Mahā-Salila* (Great Water), from *Mahā-Salila Mahā-Prithwī* (Great Earth). The English equivalents given here in pursuance of common practice are of course inaccurate.

It has been previously shown that the entire cosmic system is in a subtle or ideal form revealed in the perfectly self-conscious nature of Śiva as *Ādya-Pinda* or First Cosmic Personality. Now through a further process of the self-unfoldment of His *Śakti,* this cosmic system is manifested in grosser and grosser physical forms and endows *Ādya-Pinda* with a great physical embodiment infinite in space and ever-continuous in time. In agreement with all the important systems of Indian philosophy Gorakhnath and the Siddha-Yogis conceive this physical universe as constituted of five Great Elements which are called *Mahā-Bhutas* (otherwise called *Mahā tattwas*), namely, *Ākāśa, Vāyu, Tejas* (*Agni*), *Salila* (or *Ap* or *Jala*), and *Prithwī* (or *Kshiti*). The physical universe, including all suns and stars and nebulae, all kinds of material things, all forms of physical bodies of all species of living and conscious beings, is a most wonderful organisation of these five Great Elements.

Ākāśa is the finest and subtlest of these physical elements and evolves directly from the dynamic psycho-spiritual Cosmic Body of Śiva, called *Ādya-Pinda. Vāyu* has a grosser and more complex nature and it evolves from *Ākāśa. Tejas* is endowed with a still more gross and complex character and it evolves from *Vāyu. Salila* is still grosser and more complex than Tejas and is conceived as evolving out of *Tejas. Prithwī* is the grossest and most complex and hence most physical of all the great elements and is conceived as evolving out of *Salila. Ākāśa* pervades *Vāyu; Vāyu* with *Ākāśa* pervades *Tejas; Tejas* along with *Ākāśa* and *Vāyu* pervades *Salila,* and together with *Ākāśa, Vāyu,* and *Tejas Salila* pervades *Prithwī. Ādya-Pinda* inwardly pervades and enlivens and harmonises and organises them all and constitutes out of them this gross physical Nature (*sthūla pārthiva jagat*) with all apparently inorganic material objects and organic physical bodies within it. This physical world is called *Pañcabhautika-Jagat* (the gross world constituted of five original elements) or simply *Pārthiva Jagat* (the world made of Prithwī, since *Prithwī* comprises all the physical elements). This is conceived by *Yogis* as *Mahā-Sākāra-Pinda* of Śiva-Śakti.

In his usual manner Gorakhnath describes each of these five *Mahābhutas* or five physical *Mahā-tattwas* (as he also designates them) as possessed of five attributes (*guna*).

Avakāśah acchidram aspriśatwam nīlavarnatwam śabdatwam iti panca-gunah ākāśah.

(S.S.P.I. 32)

Avakāśa means vacuum or emptiness or penetrability. Though it occupies all space, it has room for all grosser realities evolving and existing and freely moving within it and playing their parts without any resistance in its bosom. It is a non-resisting reality. When all other physical realities disappear from any portion of space, *Ākāśa* remains there, and when other visible or tangible things are perceived to occupy any portion of space, there also *Ākāśa* is present. The second attribute is *acchidra*, which means gaplessness or perfect continuity. It is not divisible into distinct parts, it cannot be cut into pieces. It is all-pervading. Whatever contents may evolve within it, in whatever other physical forms the Divine Energy may manifest Herself within its bosom, it pervades all of them and its continuity is never broken. The third attribute is *aspriśatwa*, which means untouchability. It has no tangible properties. Though it is the container of all other physical realities which evolve from and within it, it is not touched by them, it is unaffected by the changes which take place in them. Though permeating all things,—solid, liquid and gaseous, heat, light, electricity and magnetism, etc.—it remains behind them and is not physically touched by them. The fourth attribute is described as *nīla-varnatwa*, which literally means blue-colouredness. We ordinarily speak of the blue sky (*nīla-ākāśa*). But truly it means colourlessness. *Ākāśa* has really no visible property. Colours are particularised appearances of light, and light evolves from *Ākāśa* and cannot show *Ākāśa* in any particular colour. *Ākāśa* always remains at the background of, but never becomes an object of ocular perception.

The fifth attribute of *Ākāśa* is mentioned as *śabdatwa* (the quality of sound). In all Indian systems of philosophy *Śabda* (sound) is regarded as the essential quality (*guna*) of *Ākāśa*. This of course does not mean any particularised form of sound, but the possibility of all sounds. It does not imply that *Ākāśa* is audible or has any auditory property. Indian systems in general, and *Yoga-Śāstras* in particular, recognise four stages of the evolution of Sound, viz., *Parā*, *Paśyanti*, *Madhyamā* and *Vaikhari*. Of these *Vaikhari* is the grossest form of sound, and this alone is audible to the sense of hearing. *Madhyamā*, *Paśyanti* and *Parā* are gradually subtler and subtler forms of Sound. Subtler forms of Sound are not perceptible to the normal sense of hearing until and unless they are manifested in the grossest forms through particular physical processes. Sound in the subtlest form, as one unproduced unbroken continuous *Mahā-Nāda*, the origin of all particularised sounds, pertains to the essential nature of *Ākāśa*, and it has the potentiality of producing or appearing as the grosser forms of sound in relation to the other grosser elements. There will be occasions to discuss this topic in other contexts.

Pure *Mahākāśa*, infinite in space, without any grosser physical contents, without any sensible characteristics, without any waves or movements, perfectly calm and tranquil, may be called the *Etherial Body* (*Vyoma-Pinda*) of Śiva-Śakti. This is the first self-manifestation of Śiva-Śakti in the spatio-temporal cosmic order. From this Body evolves *Mahā-Vāyu*, which represents the second stage of Śiva-Śakti's physical self-manifestation in this cosmic order. *Mahā-Vāyu* also is described in terms of five attributes.

Sancārah sancālanam sparśanam śoshanam dhumra-varnatwam itipanca-guno Mahā-Vāyuh. (S.S.P.I. 33).

The first primary quality of *Vāyu* is *sancāra* or motion. This not only implies passing from one portion of space to another, but all forms of agitation and vibration and wave and upheaval. When motion appears on the perfectly calm and tranquil bosom of *Mahākāśa*, it indicates a new development, the birth of a new physical element, and this element is called *Mahā-Vāyu*. It has not only the quality of movement, but also the quality of causing movement (*sancālana*). It is endowed with the property of acting as a force for causing movement in apparently inert bodies. All movements, all waves and upheavals, all physical and chemical and electrical and biological changes, all integrations and disintegrations of matter, which we experience in nature, are explained in *Yoga-Śāstras* as well as in other Indian systems as originating from the operation of this great active element, *Mahā-Vāyu*, which evolves from and within *Mahākāśa*.

It is quite obvious that the great Indian thinkers do not use the term *Vāyu* in this context in the sense of ordinary air or wind, which is a composite thing,—a *Pañcabhautika padārtha* in Indian terminology,—and in which *Vāyu*, the *Mahābhuta*, of course plays its game and is one of the primary constituents.

The third quality mentioned is *Sparśa*, which means that it is perceptible to the sense of touch or that it stimulates the sense of touch. This tactual property of *Mahā-Vāyu* does not of course imply that this original element is by itself capable of being touched by our gross sense of touch.

Our special senses are endowed with the capacity of perceiving only particular properties of particular gross material objects, which are the specialised manifestations of the combination or organisation of all the five original elements (*bhutas* or *tattwas*). No one of the original elements is directly perceptible to them. But each of these original elements has special reference to particular primary senses. *Vāyu* has special reference to the sense of touch, and our tactual sensations are regarded as concerned with the particularised manifestations of *Vāyu* in the composite bodies. According to many schools,—especially those which conceive the ultimate physical elements in terms of rudimentary sensuous experiences,—*Sparśa-guna* is the most primary attribute of *Vāyu.*

The fourth quality of *Vāyu* is *Śoshana*, which means absorption of the particles or qualities of other grosser elements evolved from it,—such as *Agni, Salila* and *Prithwī*,—into itself. Thus it absorbs the heat of *Agni*, the coldness of *Salila*, the scent of *Prithwī*, etc., into its nature without destroying or dissolving them, and becomes thereby endowed with those qualities. Otherwise *Vāyu* by itself has neither any heat nor any coldness nor any odour. The fifth quality is described as *Dhumra-varnatwa*, which literally means smoke-coloured-ness. It is to be noted that like *Ākāśa Vāyu* also is not an object of ocular perception,—it has no visible colour. But perhaps in some special sense Mahāyogi Gorakhnath has mentioned *nīla-varnatwa* and *dhumra-varnatwa* as *gunas* of *Ākāśa* and *Vāyu* respectively. He might have had in his mind the idea that whatever is *sākāra* (possessed of form), i.e. whatever is of the nature of a physical substance, must have some sort of colour, whether visible or invisible to our gross sense of sight. Since *Ākāśa* and *Vāyu* are the first two primary constituents of the *Mahā-sākāra-pinda*, i.e. the objective physical universe, they ought to be conceived of as possessing certain *rupa* or *varna* or colours, though not yet manifested in such gross physical forms as to be objects of gross ocular experience. Grosser visible colours are supposed to evolve out of those subtle invisible colours. On account of the imperfection of verbal expression, those invisible colours have to be described in terms conveying senses of gross visible colours. It is to be remembered that these two subtle physical elements, *Ākāśa* and *Vāyu*, represent the first two stages of the self-unfoldment of the Divine Energy in objective physical forms, in which even light and heat and sound, as we normally experience them,—not to speak of the suns and stars and planets and satellites and the various orders of material things and living organisms,—have not as yet evolved.

Mahākāśa, pervading the entire space, without any particularised contents,without any motion or agitation or transformation, has been described as the ***Etherial Cosmic Body of Śiva.*** Yogis often concentrate their attention upon this infinite tranquil *Mahākāśa-Rupa* of *Śiva-Śakti* and merge their individuality in It. When Motion is evolved, Force is manifested, Changes appear, in this Etherial Cosmic Body, Śiva-Śakti is revealed with an infinite *Aerial Body,—Mahā-Vāyu-Rupa. Mahā-Vāyu* (of course ensouled with Śiva-Śakti) is conceived as the source of all forces of nature. The vital forces operating within our physical bodies are also conceived as expressions of *Mahā-Vāyu*, and they are designated *Prāna-Vāyu. Vāyu* is the principal dynamic element in the cosmic system. *Vāyu* appears to be surcharged with life-power, which energises all other elements.

From *Mahā-Vāyu* evolves *Mahā-Tejas* in the Cosmic Body of *Śiva-Śakti. Mahā-Tejas* also is described as possessing five essential attributes, viz., *Dāhakatwa, Pācakatwa, Ushnatwa, Prakāśatwa*, and *Rakta-varnatwa. Dāhakatwa* means the quality of burning or combustion, which tends to destroy the cohesion among the constituents of grosser material bodies and to reduce them into their ingredient elements. *Pācakatwa* means the quality of assimilation or transformation of material things, so as to bring out apparently new characteristics in them. It is through the operation of *Tejas* or *Agni* in the living bodies that they digest their food and convert the material objects they consume into live tissues and vital forces. It is *Tejas* or *Agnī* present in living plants that brings about transformations in the colours, tastes, etc., of leaves and flowers and fruits and so on. *Tejas* applied to clay vessels changes their colours. All such facts are cited as illustrations of *Pācakatwa-guna* of *Agni. Ushnatwa* means heat and *Prakāśatwa* means light. These are the two fundamental attributes of *Tejas*, just as *Sancāra* and *Sancālana* (motion and causing motion) are the fundamental attributes of *Vāyu*, from which *Tejas* evolves.

Like *Mahākāśa* and *Mahā-Vāyu, Mahā-Tejas* also is all-pervading. Suns and stars and blazing fires are special manifestations of *Mahā-Tejas*, and so also are the lightning sparks. Movements in them are the expressions of *Mahā-Vāyu* Heat, light, burning, transforming, etc., which are phenomenal expressions of *Mahā-Tejas*, are all evolved from motion or vibration, which is the chief characteristic of *Mahā-Vāyu.* They are all manifested in the bosom of *Mahākāśa.* Sound, which in its subtlest form of calm and tranquil *Mahā-Nāda*, is characteristic of *Mahākāśa*, is also manifested in grosser and grosser forms through the operations of *Mahā-Vāyu* and *Mahā-Tejas. Mahā-Tejas* is further described as possessing *Rakta-Varna*, which means red colour. This of course is not intended to be literally understood on the basis of our normal sense-experience. *Mahā-Tejas* by itself has no particular visible colour. All colours evolve from it, and even the sense of vision evolves from it. But in Indian systems of thought invisible realities also are often described as possessing particular colours. Thus *Sānkhya-darśan* describes *Sattwa*, *Rajas* and *Tamas* as characterised by white, red and black colours respectively. Śruti says that red colour pertains to *Tejas*, white pertains to *Ap* or *Salila*, and black to *Prithwī* or *Anna*. Generally speaking, the five primary colours of our common visual experience are conceived as pertaining to the nature of the five ultimate physical realities,—*Panca Mahā-Bhutas*,—in subtle forms, from which the gross forms are evolved. All-pervading *Mahā-Tejas* is the *Jyotir-maya* or *Tejomaya-Rupa* (*Fiery Body*) of *Śiva-Śakti* and is meditated upon as such by *Yogis*.

From *Mahā-Tejas* evolves *Mahā-Salila* in the Cosmic Body of Śiva. The five *gunas* of *Mahā-Salila* are described as *Pravāha*, *Āpyāyana*, *Drava*, *Rasa*, and *Śweta-varnatwa*. *Pravāha* means current or continuous flow. *Āpyāyana* means fertilizing or fecundating quality. *Drava* means fluidity. *Rasa* means palatableness, *Śweta-varnatwa* means white-coloured-ness. *Mahā-Tejas* appears to be conceived as cooling down partially into the form of *Mahā-Salila* endowed with softer qualities in the process of evolution in the cosmic physical embodiment of *Śiva-Śakti*, so as to make it suitable for the growth of various orders of finite individual living bodies (*Vyasti-Pindas*) within it. *Mahā-Salila* should not of course be confused with the gross water of our common experience. *Mahā-Salila* is the cool soothing *Drava-Rupa* (Fluid Body) of *Śiva-Śakti*.

Last of all in this process of the self-manifestation of *Śiva-Śakti* as a cosmic organism, evolves *Mahā Prithwī* out of *Mahā-Salila*. *Mahā-Prithwī* is endowed with five *gunas*; viz, *Sthulatā*, *Nānākāratā*, *Kāthinya*, *Gandha* and *Pīta-varnatwa*. *Sthulatā* means grossness. This is the grossest and most condensed form of physical self-manifestation of *Śiva-Śakti*, the other four being comparatively subtler than this. *Nānākāratā* means multiformity,—the quality of assuming various shapes and sizes. *Kāthinya* means solidity. *Gandha* means odour,—the quality of being an object of the sense of smell. *Pīta-Varnatwa* means yellow-coloured-ness. These are regarded as the special characteristics of this grossest of the five ultimate constituents of the physical universe, which is conceived as the *Mahā Sākāra-Pinda* of *Śiva-Śakti*. This is the *Sthula-Murti* of *Śiva-Śakti*.

Since all these *Mahā-Bhutas* (which are also called *Mahā-Tattwas*) evolve from the dynamic nature of the super-physical *Ādya-Pinda* of *Śiva-Śakti* and are organically united for constituting the Cosmic Physical Body of *Śiva-Śakti*, the qualities of each interpenetrate all in various ways and make this phenomenal material universe a bewilderingly complex and nevertheless a wonderfully harmonised system. Gorakhnath describes this

Mahā-Sākāra-Pinda as characterised by the above-mentioned twenty-five *gunas* of the five constituent elements. Embodied with the *Mahā-Sākāra-Pinda,*—this phenomenal cosmic order,—*Śiva* with His unique *Śakti* comes down to the gross sensible physical plane and reveals Himself as the Supreme Omnipotent Omniscient Omnipresent Active Deity manifested in various forms and freely and delightfully playing various cosmic games in the spatio-temporal system. *Śiva-Śakti* is everywhere in this world and immanent in every part of it as well as in the whole.

There is a general agreement among all the systems of Indian philosophical thought with regard to the conception of *Ākāśa, Vāyu, Tejas* (or *Agni*), *Salila* (or *Jala* or *Ap*), and *Prithwī* (or *Bhumi* or *Kshiti*), as the five ultimate material elements (*panca Mahā-Bhutas*), of which the physical universe is constituted. The basic reason for this conception is also the same. It is a universally recognised fact that our sense-experience is the sole evidence to us for the existence of the objective physical world in space and time and the primary source of our knowledge of the nature of this world. We are endowed with five special senses of knowledge (*panca jñānendriya*),—viz., the sense of hearing, the sense of touch, the sense of sight, the sense of taste, and the sense of smell(*śravana-indriya, sparśa indriya, darśana-indriya, rasana-indriya* and *ghrāna-indriya*). These *Indriyas* (special powers of perception) have special organs in the physical body, through which they operate and form contact with particular classes of objects in the external world. *Śabda* (sound), *Sparśa* (touch), *Rupa* (colour), *Rasa* (taste), and *Gandha* (odour) are respectively the special objects of perception of these special senses. We are so constituted that we in our normal life naturally perceive and conceive this world in terms of these sensible properties of the objects of our experience, viz., *Śabda, Sparśa, Rupa, Rasa* and *Gandha.* Hence it is concluded that this objective physical world must ultimately be constituted of five subtle physical elements, which are endowed with these five primary sensible properties as their essential characteristics. Thus, *Ākāśa* is conceived as essentially characterised by *Śabda-guna, Vāyu* by *Sparśa-guna, Tejas* by *Rupa-guna, Salila* or *Ap* by *Rasa-guna,* and *Prithwī* by *Gandha-guna.* Among these ultimate physical realities constituting the sensible world, each succeeding one is regarded as comparatively grosser and more complex in nature than the preceding one. Thus *Vāyu* is conceived as endowed with *Śabda-guna* of *Ākāśa* along with its own *Sparśa-guna.* *Śabda* and *Sparśa* enter into *Tejas* and co-exist with *Rupa* in its nature. Accordingly, *Salila* possesses *Śabda, Sparśa, Rupa* and *Rasa*, and *Prithwī* is characterised by all the five ultimate sensible properties,—*Śabda, Sparśa, Rupa, Rasa,* and *Gandha.* Some sort of evolution among these ultimate constituents of physical nature is also generally recognised. Sometimes the process is described as the process of *Pancika-*

rana, by which the character of each of the five partially enters into all of them. Besides the generally recognised essential sensible qualities, Gorakhnath mentions, as it has been already shown, several other characteristics of each of them. He seems to attach more primary importance to such attributes, as vacuity of *Ākāśā*, Motion of *Vāyu*, Heat of *Tejas*, *Fluidity* of *Salila* and Solidity of *Prithwī*.

While there is a general agreement among the Indian philosophical schools about the *Panca-Mahābhutas* being the ultimate material constituents (*jada upādāna*) of the physical world, there are fundamental differences among them with regard to the question of the origin of this wonderfully harmonious cosmic system (with various orders of living and conscious beings within it) out of them. There are materialist schools (e.g. *Lokāyata* or *Cārvāka*) which stubbornly maintain that they are the ultimate realities out of which this cosmic system with all its law and order and all its living and conscious and rational beings has gradually come into existence in course of time through various processes of integration and disintegration by nature (*swabhāva*) or by chance (*Yadricchā* or *niyati*) and into which all the bodies, whether inanimate or animate, unconscious or conscious,—are dissolved in course of time. They hold that *Caitanya* (spirit or consciousness) is nothing but a quality or attribute of certain classes of organised material bodies constituted of the five,—(according to some, four, leaving out Ākāśa as no physical reality),—material elements and never exists apart from and independently of these gross material bodies. It is needless to say that they feel no rational or spiritual necessity for admitting the existence of God or Supreme Spirit to explain this Cosmic Order.

There are strongly argumentative schools (such as *Nyāya* and *Vaiśeshika*) which like the former maintain that these *Panca-Mahābhutas* are *nitya dravya* (eternal substances) eternally existing by themselves in inert atomic (*paramānu*) forms, but unlike the former hold that these ultimate material elements being essentially inert cannot by themselves move and combine together and arrange and organise themselves in a planned manner so as to produce such a wonderful cosmic system and that they being *jada* can never originate *Caitanya* (consciousness) through any kind of organisation in themselves. *Ātmā* (Spirit) and *Manas* (instrument of empirical consciousness) are also recognised by them as eternal substances. They recognise the eternal existence of innumerable individual souls (*jīvātmā*) and of one Supreme Spirit (*Paramātmā*), Who is *Iśwara* (God). They hold that *Iśwara*, by the exercise of His innate infinite wisdom and power, creates in a planned manner this cosmic order out of the five kinds of material atoms, which are however not created by Him. According to them, the *Panca-*

Mahābhutas are the material cause and *Iśwara* is the efficient cause of this objective world, and *Iśwara* is also the Supreme Ruler of all the phenomena of this world. The world is not however any *part* or *self-manifestation* or *body* of the Supreme Spirit, and the individual souls also are not spiritual parts or self-manifestations of the Supreme Spirit. The *Naiyāyika* philosophers adduce many logical and moral and cosmological arguments to prove the existence of *Iśwara* as the Efficient Cause of the cosmic system and the Moral Governor of all individual souls. It is through His Grace that individual souls devoted to His worship can attain *Mukti* or *Apavarga.* In *mukti* these souls are not only released from all bondage and sorrow, but also from phenomenal consciousness, which cannot remain without the soul's contact with *Manas.*

According to the Sānkhya system, *Panca-Mahābhutas* are evolved from *Panca-Tanmātras*, which are the same *Mahābhutas* in their pure and subtle states (*apancikrita sukshma mahābhuta*) and characterised by the purest and simplest sensible qualities : these *Tanmātras* are evolved from *Aham-tattwa* (One Ego-Principle), which is also the source of the empirical mind (*manas*), the five senses of knowledge (*iñānendriya*) and the five senses of action (*karmendriya*). Thus, according to this view, the ultimate constituents of the objective physical world (including our individual physical bodies) and the primary instruments of our knowledge of and action upon this objective world originate from or are the mutually related manifestations of one higher reality (*tattwa*), viz , *Ego-Principle*, which is conceived as the meeting-ground or the ground of union of the subjective and the objective aspects of our experience,—of the instruments of knowledge and action and all objects of knowledge and action. The *Ego-Principle* is therefore also called *Bhutādi*, the Source of the *Bhutas* and of the whole world of physical realities. The *Ego-Principle* is however not an individual ego, which is always manifested in relation to the individual mind and senses and the objective realities. It is a principle, a reality, a *tattwa*, which is manifested in the two-fold ways of the plurality of individual subjects with the individual minds and senses on the one side and the diversified objective physical world constituted of material elements on the other. This *Ego-Principle* again is conceived as evolved from *Mahat-tattwa*, which is the first manifestation (*vyakta-rūpa*) of *Mulā-Prakriti* or *Avyakta-tattwa*—the Ultimate Material Cause of the subjective-objective phenomenal world in space and time. The Sānkhya system does not however hold that the plurality of individual souls or spirits are evolved from *Prakriti.* It asserts that an infinite number of souls or spirits (called *Purusha*), the essential character of which is pure changeless transcendent consciousness, are eternally associated (*Saṃyukta*) with *Prakriti* and all its evolutes and only apparently or illusorily participate in their qualities and functions and limitations. When it is perfectly realised by any individual soul, through the refinement and illumination of the mind and intelligence related to it, that it is essentially pure and changeless and limitationless *Caitanya* and in no way *really* connected with the affairs of *Prakriti* and the cosmic order, it becomes emancipated from the apparent bondage of this phenomenal world and exists in its transcendent character. Thus the *Mahābhutas*, according to *Sānkhya*. are not ultimate realities, though they are the ultimate material constituents of the objective world. This objective world is not conceived as created by or evolved from any Supreme Spirit or Iśwara, but as evolved from *Mulā-Prakriti*, from which all phenomenal knowledge and action and all instruments of knowledge and action also are evolved, without any supervision and control of any eternal Supreme Lord of this *Prakriti*.

The Upanishadic thinkers, like the *Siddha Yogi Sampradāya*, trace the origin of the *Panca-Mahābhutas* from the Supreme Spirit,—*Brahma* or *Ātmā*. The *Rishi* of the *Brahmānanda-Valli* of *Taittiriya Upanishad* proclaims,--

Tasmād vā etasmād ātmana ākāśah sambhutah. ākāśād vāyuh, vāyor agnih, agner āpah, adbhyah prithivī.

From that Supreme Spirit (Brahma, the changeless transcendent *Satyam Jñānam Anantam*) Who is also *Ātmā* or the True Self of every being, *Ākāśa* is born. From *Ākāśa Vāyu* is evolved, from *Vāyu Agni*, from *Agni Ap*, and from *Ap Prithivī*.

This view is supported by other *Rishis*. All the *Upanishads* hold the view that one changeless differenceless transcendent Supreme Spirit (*Brahma, Ātmā, Śiva*) with infinite power and intelligence inherent in His nature is the Sole Cause (Material and Efficient as well as Final Cause) of the entire Spatio-temporal Cosmic Order. Brahma is described as *a-śabda a-sparśa a-rupa a-rasa a-gandha* (without sound, without touch, without form, without taste, without scent) and at the same time *Bhuta-Yoni* (the Origin of all the *bhutas*). He is *a-prāna a-manah* (without life and mind in the empirical sense) and at the same time the Sole Source of all life and mind,—all vital and mental phenomena,—in the Cosmic System, and the Indwelling Spirit (*Antaryāmi Ātmā*) in them all. The Upanishads clearly proclaim that from Brahma all these *Bhutas* are born, by Brahma all of them are sustained and enlivened, towards Brahma they are all moving on, and into Brahma again they enter and merge and lose their differences. This is exactly the view of the *Mahā-Yogis*.

The Vedantic schools of philosophy base their speculations on the authoritative texts of the *Upanishads*. But some of them are so much under the influence of the idea of the fundamental difference between Spirit and Matter,—between Pure Changeless Transcendent Consciousness above all spatio-temporal relations and the diverse orders of ever-changing physical phenomena in the world of time and space,—that they fail to logically conceive how the latter can *really* originate from or be a *real* self-manifestation of the former. Hence they regard the world of *Mahā-bhutas* as having only an *illusory* existence born of some inexplicable mysterious Power, called *Māyā* or *Avidyā*, and the Supreme Spirit, Brahma, as nothing but a substratum (*adhiṣṭhāna*) of this illusion. Of the vedantist philosophers Ramanuja and Śrikantha and some others follow the *Mahā-Yogis* in interpreting the cosmic system or the phenomenal world of *Mahābhutas* as a self-manifestation and embodiment of the Supreme Spirit, by virtue of the real Power (*Śakti*) inherent in the Spirit.

Origination of Matter from Spirit and dissolution of Matter in Spirit,—origination of spatio-temporal phenomenal realities from one infinite eternal changeless Transcendent Consciousness and absolute unification of the former in the Latter,—free playful self-manifestation of one non-dual *Cit* in the complex relative multiplicity of *Jaḍa* and merging of this multiplicity in the perfect blissful unity of *Cit*, do not present insurmountable conceptual difficulties to the enlightened *Mahāyogis*, because through the systematic discipline and refinement of their body and mind and intellect and the practice of deep meditation they easily pass from one plane of experience to another,—from the plane of phenomenal Matter to the plane of Transcendent Spirit and back from the latter to the former, from the plane of changing diversities to the plane of absolute unity and back from the latter to the former,—and the transition becomes quite natural to them. They directly experience the Transcendent as well as Dynamic character of the Non-dual Spirit. Matter also is experienced by them as ultimately a spiritual entity.

In *Śwetāśwatara Upanishad* and also in other *Upanishads* there is eloquent testimony to such spiritual experiences of enlightened *Mahāyogis*. It is said in the Upanishad,—*Te dhyāna-yogānugatā apaśyan devātma-śaktim swagunair nigudhām:*—They (the enlightened *Mahāyogis*) through the most intensive practice of *dhyāna-yoga* saw the Supreme Spirit's own *Śakti*, Whose essential character is concealed by Her own self-manifestations. They see this *Śakti* (Which is essentially non-different from the Supreme Spirit) manifested in various phenomenal forms in various planes of experience. *Jñāna* (knowledge), *bala* (force) and *Kriyā* (action) are quite natural self-expressions of this *Parā-Śakti* of the Supreme Spirit,—*Parāsya Śaktir Vividhaiva śruyate svābhāviki jñāna-bala-kriyā ca.* All expressions of intelligence, all expressions of power or force, all expressions of activity,—

creation and destruction, evolution and involution, expansion and contraction, organisation and disorganisation, etc.,—are diverse forms of self-manifestation of the Supreme *Śakti* of the Supreme Spirit (Who may be designated as Brahma or Śiva or by any other name) and they all together constitute the Cosmic Body of the Supreme Spirit. He is in all of them, and all are in Him, by Him and for Him. The *Mahāyogis* actually experience this great Truth. To them the whole universe is the embodiment and free delightful self-manifestation of *Śiva-Śakti.*

Having described the constitution and character of the Cosmic Body (*Mahā-Sākāra-Pinda*) of Śiva, Mahāyogi Gorakhnath emphatically says,—*Sa eva Śivah,*—He (the *Mahā-Sākāra-Pinda*) is veritably Śiva Himself. (S.S.P.I.37). The Body is not to be conceived as separate from the Soul. The Cosmic Body of Śiva is not to be conceived as separate from Śiva Himself, Who is the Soul of this Cosmic Body. It is quite true that the Soul transcends space and time and the Body is in space and time, that the Soul is transcendent Spirit and the Body is phenomenal matter, that the Soul is the absolutely changeless One and the Body is in a continuous process of change and diversification ; but still it is evident that the Body has no separate existence apart from the Soul, that the Body exists by and for the Soul, that the Soul manifests Himself in and through the Body and all the phenomena pertaining to the Body. The Soul transcends the Body and is also immanent in the Body,—in the whole Body as well as in every part of the Body. When an intelligent person sees the Body, he sees the Soul also manifested in it. When an enlightened *Yogi* sees the physical world, he also sees Śiva manifested through His Śakti in this world. To the spiritual insight of a *Yogi* the physical world also is Śiva, because it is the Body of Śiva and Śiva manifests Himself in and through it. Being the self-expression of the Supreme Spirit, this physical world is revealed to his enlightened eyes as a spiritual entity. Śiva with His Spatio-temporal Cosmic Body being conceived as Śiva Himself, the Oneness of Śiva is never hidden from view. The One comprehending the many is One all the same.

It is to be noted that in every stage of the self-unfoldment of His Unique Power,—His Own Dynamic Nature,—the Absolute Spirit manifests Himself in newer and newer forms with newer and newer attributes and embodiments and newer and newer expressions of His glories. The physical Cosmic Body is the grossest (*sthulatama*) form of His self-manifestation. In this Body His infinite Wisdom and Power, His infinite Goodness and Beauty, His infinite Purity and Bliss, His infinite Love and Compassion, are manifested in an infinite variety of finite forms, and He in His serene and tranquil self-consciousness enjoys them all.

Having expounded his doctrine of the evolution of the Cosmic System from the dynamic nature of Śiva, Mahāyogi Gorakhnath says that in relation to this Cosmic Order the Supreme Spirit Śiva manifests Himself principally in the forms of eight Divine Personalities,—eight Cosmic Deities,—Who are called *Ashta-Murti* of *Mahā-Sākāra-Pinda Śiva.*

Sivād Bhairavo, Bhairavāt Śrikanthah, Śrikanthāt Sadāśivah, Sadāśivāt Iśwarah, Iśwarād Rudrah, Rudrād Vishnuh, Vishnor Brahmā,
Iti Mahā-Sākāra-Pindasya Murtyashtakam. (S.S.P.I. 37).

First Śiva Himself, second Bhairava, third Śrikantha, fourth Sadāśiva, fifth Iśwara, sixth Rudra, seventh Vishnu, and eighth Brahmā. These are spoken of as *Ashta-Murti* (eight special Divine Self-manifestations) of *Mahā-Sākāra-Pinda Śiva* (Śiva embodied in the Cosmic System).

Through these special Divine Self-revelations Śiva appears to perform different cosmic functions,—to perform and regulate and harmonise the works of creation, preservation, destruction, etc., to maintain law and order in this diversified and ever-changing cosmic system, to establish the reign of justice in the world of living beings and to distribute equitably happinesses and miseries among them, to confer blessings upon them and set before them high and noble ideals of Truth, Beauty, Goodness, Love and Absolute Transcendent Unity, and provide opportunities to them for the realisation of these ideals, and so on and so forth. They are all non-different from Śiva. The Same Divine Power operates in all of them. It is in the light of the different kinds of self-manifestation of the one *Śakti* of Śiva in the cosmic system that different glorious names are given to Śiva and different glorious powers and qualities and functions are associated with these names. In the Hindu scriptures the name of Brahmā, Vishnu and Rudra are most widely known and they are associated with the cosmic functions of Creation, Preservation and Destruction, which are equally important for the continuity and ever-newness of this spatio-temporal order. Brahmā is conceived as the God of Creation. He is the Creator of diverse orders of individual bodies,—animate and inanimate, conscious and unconscious, rational and non-rational, big and small,—endowed with diverse kinds of qualities and powers and tendencies, within the Cosmic Body of Śiva. Vishnu is the God of Preservation. He preserves harmonious relationships among all these diverse orders of individual bodies and rules over their behaviours and destinies in accordance with the universal principles of *Dharma* immanent in this cosmic system. He is the Divine Administrator of this system. Rudra is conceived as the God of Destruction. He destroys these individual bodies in due course and resolves them into their constituent elements. Creation is the process of diversification and destruction is the process of unification. All these processes are continuous in the Cosmic Body of Śiva.

CHAPTER XI

EVOLUTION OF A SYSTEM OF WORLDS IN THE COSMIC BODY

In this Cosmic System,—in this magnificent *Mahā-Sākāra-Pinda* of the Supreme Spirit,—we experience various orders of phenomenal existences, which may be described as different *worlds* (*loka*), though they are all interrelated and harmoniously organised in this Cosmic Body. In relation to each of these worlds there is a specialised Divine Self-manifestation of Śiva. First, there is the world of material bodies and physical forces (including mechanical, chemical, thermal, electrical and other forces), in which there is no distinct manifestation of life and mind and spirit, which is governed by *natural laws* (not obviously indicating any reign of morality and spirituality or any design and purpose in their operations), in which the processes of creation and preservation and destruction, in smaller and bigger scales, are going on in natural course in all periods of time and all regions of space. This is called the Material World (*Jada-Jagat*).

Secondly, there is the *world* of life and vital forces which is governed by biological laws or laws of *Prāna*. This is the ***Prāna-Jagat***. Life is always found in our ordinary experience as related to material bodies,—e.g. plants, insects, birds, beasts, men, etc. It is difficult for us even to conceive of life or *Prāna* apart from relation to such bodies. But that life is distinct from matter as such admits of no doubt. The presence of life gives distinctive characteristics to the material bodies which it organises and enlivens. How life appears in the material world and becomes so closely related to material bodies is a puzzling problem. Life pervades the individual body which it animates and organises and whose functions it regulates for the realisation of some ideal immanent in it. The phenomena of living bodies are teleogically governed. The body may be in the form of a small seed or it may grow into a big tree with branches and leaves and flowers and fruits;—the body may be of the nature of some minute semen or it may develop into a full-grown multi-limbed animal body or human body;—the same life which makes it grow and develop pervades the whole and every part of it at every stage of its growth and development. Though the material bodies are governed by natural laws of matter, in the cases of living organisms the biological laws or laws of life rule over these natural laws and prove themselves more powerful than the latter. When in any living body the vital force becomes weaker than the natural forces, it faces death, which implies that it is reduced into the state of a pure material body.

Living bodies have birth and growth and decay and death, but Life has not. Life transcends the bodies, through which it may manifest itself for any period of time. Life is embodied in matter, but is not material. In the Cosmic Body the world of life is intrinsically superior to the world of lifeless matter, because the Divine *Śakti* is more manifested in and reflected upon Life than lifeless Matter. ***Prāna*** is superior to *śarīra*. *Śarīra* is a seat and an instrument of the manifestation of ***Prāna***. ***Prāna*** or Life seems to come down from a higher plane into material bodies which it pulls up partially to its own plane. It is the power of ***Prāna*** in the world of matter, that transforms the processes of constructive and destructive metabolism in the living organisms, brings about in the material bodies many such wonderful changes as would not be possible by means of any mechanical powers. The power of ***Prāna*** over ***Matter*** is visible in every department of nature. *Prāna* represents a higher plane of existence than pure Matter.

Thirdly, there is the world of Mind (*Mano-jagat*). Empirical consciousness pertains to the nature of Mind. Mind manifests itself in various kinds of phenomena, such as, sensation, perception, instinct, impulse, feeling (pleasure, pain, etc.), desire, emotion, volition, knowledge, doubt, imagination, memory, dream, illusion, hallucination, thinking, designing, etc. The states of waking, dream and sound sleep belong to the mind. Love and hatred, mercy and cruelty, sympathy and selfishness, courage and cowardice, jealousy and fear, lust, anger, avarice, ambition, generosity, charity, forgiveness, etc. etc.,—all these are phenomena of the *world* of Mind. The phenomena of Mind are normally experienced as related to the more developed and more complex living physical bodies, and particularly to the nervous system and the brain, which are the finest parts evolved in a living body. As in our normal experience mental phenomena are invariably found in relation to individual living bodies, it is difficult for us to imagine even the existence of mind apart from connection with the material body.

Ordinarily it is found that Mind and Body act and react upon each other, and that each is conditioned by the other. But Mind does not occupy any special part of the Body, because unlike a material body it does not require to occupy any particular portion of space for its existence and functioning. Nor does Mind die with the death of the gross physical organism. Mind, though related to Life and Body, transcends them. Mind is not mortal, in the sense in which a living body is mortal. Mind uses the living physical organism to which it may be temporarily related as an instrument (*karana*) for its self-expression in the physical world. But, as it is believed by all the important schools of Indian philosophy and religion, the same Mind may cut off its connection with one physical organism (when the latter is disorganised and is dissolved in its constituent elements, may remain in a disembodied state (i.e. without any gross physical body), and may again take a new birth in (i.e. form connection with) a new physical body, which it then adopts as the new instrument for its self-expression. In this way the same individual mind may pass through numerous physical bodies one after another, till it is finally merged in the Cosmic Mind of Śiva or in the nature of the Absolute Spirit.

It may be noted, by the way, that the super-ordinary Mind of a *Master-Yogi* may create, by the exercise of its will-power, any number of gross physical bodies at the same time, and may make use of them as instruments of its self-expression in diverse forms. It must be remembered that all the phenomena of the *world* of Mind, whether ordinary or extra-ordinary, are evolved in the Cosmic Body,—*Mahā-Sākāra-Pinda*,—of Śiva-Śakti, and that they are all essentially of the nature of *Cid-Vilāsa*,—sportive self-manifestations of the Supreme Spirit. In this Cosmic System Mind has a higher order of reality than Matter and Life and is therefore capable of exercising a controlling influence over them.

Fourthly, we experience in this Cosmic Body of Śiva-Śakti the evolution of a world of Reason or Intelligence (*Buddhi*), which may be called Higher Mind. It is principally manifested in the form of the ascertainment of Truth (*adhyavasāya* or *satya-niscaya*). *Buddhi* discriminates between valid knowledge and invalid knowledge, correct thought and incorrect thought, true perception and false perception or illusion, right judgment and wrong judgment, etc., and seeks to regulate the natural functions of the mind towards the attainment of the *ideal of Truth*. The urge for the attainment of Truth in the human mind is due to the influence of *Buddhi* upon it. *Buddhi* sits in judgment upon the normal operations of the mind with its standard of Truth, condemns many of them as erroneous and exercises its power and influence upon the mind to rectify them and to search for Truth. It is on account of the regulative and enlightening influence of *Buddhi* that discrimination between Truth and untruth arises in the mind and the mind feels an urge to seek for Truth and avoid untruth. *Buddhi* appears to have an inherent right to rule over the phenomena of the mind in the cosmic process.

In our normal experience we find definite expressions of *Buddhi* in relation to highly developed minds embodied in superior orders of living physical organisms,—particularly human. In the lives of the lower animals, though there are various kinds of expressions of the mind, there is very little evidence of the regulating and enlightening operation of *Buddhi* in them. *Buddhi* seems to be, relatively speaking, unmanifested (*avyakta*) in the subhuman creatures, though there are different orders mental and vital and physical developments in them. Empirical philosophers generally speak of man as a rational animal and all other animals as non-rational,—reason being evolved in the former (the highest of all animals) and unevolved in all the rest. Indian philosophers in general maintain that *Buddhi* is present in all creatures,—in all living bodies, along with the mind, but as its manifestation is conditioned by the suitability of the physical organism and the development of the mind, it is not distinctly manifested as *individual reason* in the lower species of creatures. It manifests itself as individual reason with a distinct consciousness of *ego* or *self* in the human psycho-physical organism. The Cosmic *Buddhi* with the Cosmic Mind and the Cosmic Life is of course all-pervading,—pervading even all apparently inorganic matter. It is the Cosmic Body of Śiva-Śakti that is manifested in all these forms. Though in our common experience *Buddhi* (Reason or Intelligence) is invariably found to be associated with physical body and life and mind, it essentially transcends them. *Śuddha-Buddhi* (pure and enlightened Reason) can, according to *yogis*, rise above the limitations of these physical, vital and mental embodiments and be united with the Supreme Truth. The world of *Buddhi* (*Vijñāna-Jagat*) is higher than the *Mano-Jagat*.

Fifthly, in this Cosmic Body of Śiva we experience a world of *Dharma*, which essentially means a *Moral Order*. Morality chiefly consists in the distinction between good and evil, right and wrong, virtue and vice, ideal and actual, ought and ought-not, superior and inferior, higher and lower. It implies a judgment of *intrinsic value* upon the actual phenomena by reference to some Ideal having inherent authority to rule over the actual and judge their merits. It is on account of the evolution of *Dharma* in this cosmic self-manifestation of Śiva-Śakti that many phenomena (whether physical or vital or mental), which appear in the natural course and play their parts in this diversified universe, but do not conform to the Ideal, are condemned as evil and wrong, while others which conform to the Ideal are appreciated as good and right. *Dharma* presents itself in the form of some Ideal of goodness or righteousness with the inherent claim that the actual should be guided and controlled by it or be checked and superseded by it.

It is *Dharma* which governs the process of natural evolution in the world of our experience, and hence we find that higher and higher orders of existences evolve from lower and lower orders in spite of forces of resistance, and a wonderful harmony is maintained by putting down the forces of disharmony in all the stages. It is *Dharma* which proclaims that forces of union and harmony are superior to the forces of disunion and disharmony, that forces of love and compassion are superior to the forces of hatred and cruelty, that forces of peace and non-violence are superior to the forces of war and violence, that forces of creation and preservation are superior to the forces of destruction and disorganisation, —though all of them make their appearance on the cosmic stage in natural course from the dynamic nature of the Absolute Spirit and play the roles allotted to them. It is the power of *Dharma* in the Cosmic System that makes the higher and superior forces victorious in it. It is among the diverse orders of cosmic self-manifestations of *Śiva-Śakti* that Dharma, which also is a glorious self-expression of the same Śiva-Śakti, makes such distinctions of good and evil, right and wrong, ought and ought-not, superior and inferior, higher and lower, and claims the right of good and right to prevail over evil and wrong, the right of the superior and higher to supersede the inferior and lower, the right of what ought to exist to destroy and survive what ought not to exist in this cosmic system. Thus *Dharma,* having evolved in the *Mahā-Sākāra-Pinda* of *Śiva-Śakti,* plays an exceptionally brilliant and sublime role in this Divine Body. *Dharma* appears to convert, so to say, the spatio-temporal psycho-physical Body of the Spirit into a *Moral Body,*—a Moral Order. *Dharma* is the originator of all sorts of Moral Dualism in this world.

Dharma has its special manifestation in the Moral Consciousness associated with the rational nature of Man and has its special application to man's voluntary activities,—external as well as internal, physical and vital as well as mental and intellectual. Man as a rational being,—as a rational self-manifestation of Śiva-Śakti,—is endowed with a relative and conditioned *freedom* in this Cosmic Order,—freedom of will, freedom of action, freedom of thought, freedom to control and regulate the phenomena of his physical body and senses and life and mind and intellect and also freedom to exercise a considerable amount of influence upon his environments. He with his sense of ego (*aham*) feels that he is or can be the master of himself,—the master of his psycho-physical embodiment,— and even the master of the circumstances in which he may find himself. Though he experiences various kinds of limitations imposed upon his freedom and self-mastery and mastery over the external circumstances, he feels within himself that he has the power and right and duty to remove or rise above these limitations,—if not wholly, at least to a great extent, —by dint of his own voluntary efforts. Man in his inner consciousness feels that freedom is his birth-right and that he can immensely develop this freedom through the wisely regulated exercise of the limited freedom which he actually possesses. Man is endowed with this relative and dynamic freedom in the *Mahā-Sākāra-Pinda* of *Śiva-Śakti*, and this freedom and the concomitant moral consciousness and consciousness of duties and responsibilities form a glorious aspect of the cosmic self-expression of the Divinity.

It may be noted that perfect freedom pertains to the essential character of the Spirit, and that in the cosmic self-expression of the Spirit there are various grades of the manifestation of this freedom. In the world of Matter this freedom appears to be practically unmanifested; in the world of Life it is very slightly manifested, the *consciousness* of freedom being absent there. In the world of non-rational (animal) Mind there is greater manifestation of freedom than in the world of Life, but here also there is no distinct consciousness of freedom and hence no moral consciousness. It is in the world of Reason or Rational Mind that the consciousness of freedom is distinctly manifested (though under limitations). This consciousness of partial conditioned relative freedom is associated with Moral Consciousness or the Consciousness of *Dharma*, and the phenomenal expressions of this consciousness of relative freedom are tbe special objects of Moral Judgment or Judgment of *Dharma*. Though *Dharma* is all-pervading and underlies all the spheres of phenomenal existences in this Cosmic System, the sphere of conscious relative freedom constitutes the special sphere of *Dharma* in this system. Here moral discrimination is prominently manifested.

The Moral Consciousness of man, which is alienably associated with the Consciousness of Limited Freedom, has an inherent faith in the reign of *Dharma* in this objective universe in which he lives and moves and finds ample scope for the exercise of this freedom. He believes that in this cosmic system virtue is rewarded with happiness as well as with favourable conditions for the progress and elevation of life and mind and intellect, and vice is punished with misery as well as with unfavourable and undesirable conditions. He believes that according to the Law of *Dharma* in the cosmic system every individual enjoys and suffers the sweet and bitter fruits of his own good and evil deeds,—of the proper and improper use of his partial freedom,—in the physical and the mental planes. His moral consciousness creates in him the confidence that every individual is the builder of his own destiny, that the cosmic order returns in due course to every individual just what he *deserves* on account of the merits and demerits of his own actions. This is called the *Law of Karma* by Indian philosophers. It implies the reign of *Dharma* in the cosmic process,—the Law of Moral Justice ruling over even the apparently physical and non-moral phenomena in this cosmic system, at least in so far as they affect the enjoyments and sufferings of the relatively free living beings and present to them favourable or unfavourable conditions for their self-expression and self-development. This faith in the reign of *Dharma* in the cosmic process awakens in the human mind a sense of moral dignity and a dynamic sense of duty and responsibility in practical life.

Just as man's intellectual consciousness manifested in his valid perception and inference and reasoning is the guarantee for the objective reality of the natural order in the cosmic system, so his moral consciousness stands as the guarantee for the objective reality of *Dharma* or the *moral order* in this system. The Cosmic Body of *Śiva-Śakti* reveals itself to the intellectual consciousness as a *natural order* and to the moral consciousness as a *moral order*,—as a world of *Dharma*.

It is this strong faith in the reign of *Dharma* in the cosmic order, which is at the basis of the doctrine of *Rebirth*,—birth after birth and assumption of newer and newer physical embodiments under newer and newer circumstances according to moral deserts,—which is accepted practically by all schools of Indian philosophy. In every birth an individual ego enjoys and suffers the sweet and bitter fruits of the good and evil deeds of previous births and gets fresh opportunities for the fulfilment of the demands of his moral consciousness. This continues till the individual rises to a higher plane of consciousness and transcends the domain of *Dharma*. A yogi with his refined Moral and Intellectual Consciousness can recollect a number of his past births and can also know the past births of other persons through the concentration of his attention in that direction.

Sixthly, in this Cosmic Body of Śiva-Śakti there is a world of *Rasa* (Aesthetic Order). This is specially revealed to the refined Aesthetic Consciousness of man. *Rasa* pervades the entire Cosmic Body. It makes the whole universe a magnificently *beautiful order*. All forms and all grades of realities in this infinitely diversified universe are elements of Beauty, and they all participate in and contribute to the Beauty of the entire cosmic system. The wonderfully interrelated and intermingled worlds of Matter, Life, Mind and Reason are all impregnated with the Beauty of the whole system, and they all play their allotted parts wonderfully for giving expression to the Beauty inherent in the nature of the sportive delightful self-manifestation of Śiva-Śakti in this Cosmic Organism. All the moral distinctions appearing in the world of *Dharma* are merged and beautified in the world of *Rasa*. All good and evil, all virtue and vice, all right and wrong, that are evolved in the cosmic process and particularly in the human nature, are appreciated and enjoyed as elements of Beauty by the refined Aesthetic Consciousness, which experiences the *Rasa* manifested in and through all such moral dualisms of the world of *Dharma*.

The refined Aesthetic Consciousness that habitually dwells in the world of *Rasa* finds as much beauty in destruction as in creation, as much beauty in the violent and furious forces of nature as in the benign and beneficent forces, as much beauty in the distresses and agonies in the world of living creatures as in their happinesses and prosperities. It appreciates and enjoys the beauty and sublimity of the whole Cosmic Body of the Supreme Spirit and experiences the whole reflected in every part, in every particularised manifestation of the whole. A man whose enlightened Aesthetic Consciousness prevails over his mental intellectual and moral consciousness has the delightful experience that he really lives and moves and has his being in a world of *Rasa,* in a world of all-harmonising and all-sweetening Beauty, whatever may be the outer appearances of the phenomena occurring around him. Accordingly he feels a deep love and admiration for this Cosmic System,—a love and admiration for all that play their allotted parts in this beautiful order and contribute to the infinite grandeur and magnificence and variety of this beautiful self-expression of the Supreme Spirit.

To the Aesthetic Consciousness of man, the *Rasa* pervading the Cosmic System manifests itself in a variety of phenomenal forms, which excite different kinds of feelings and emotions and sentiments in the mind, but are all the same appreciated and enjoyed as beautiful and delightful. Philosophers reflecting upon *Rasa-tattwa* (the nature of *Rasa*) enumerate various forms of its manifestation, such as,—*Madhura* (sweet or lovable, exciting the feeling of joy), *Karuna* (pathetic or tragic, exciting the feeling of compassion or sadness), *Vīra* (heroic or courageous, exciting the feeling of admiration), *Rudra* (majestic, exciting the feeling of awe), *Bhīshana* (furious or dreadful, exciting the feeling of fear), *Hāsya* (comic or amusing, exciting laughter or light pleasure), *Adbhuta* (strange, exciting the feeling of surprise or astonishment), *Śānta* (calm and serene, exciting the feeling of calmness and tranquillity), *Bibhatsa* (loathsome or odious, exciting the feeling of disgust or repulsion), and so on. In fact the various forms of manifestation of *Rasa* cannot be exhaustively enumerated, and the various kinds of feelings excited by them cannot also be adequately described. What is remarkable is that what appears as *Bibhatsa* or *Bhīsana* or *Karuna* in our normal experience, - whether in the physical world or in the animal world or in the human world,—and excites in our minds the feeling of repulsion or dread or sadness, is also a form of manifestation of *Rasa* or the Beauty immanent in this Cosmic Order and is appreciated and enjoyed as such by refined and enlightened Aesthetic Consciousness. We fail to appreciate and enjoy the beauty of many phenomena of our ordinary experience, because our mind and senses are not properly disciplined and illumined to see them in their true perspective, to view them in relation to the whole of which they are parts, to recognise their true places and functions in this beautiful cosmic order. Persons with well-developed Aesthetic Consciousness often describe this universe with all the diverse kinds of beings and phenomena in it as a Great Work of Art, in which everything is in its most appropriate place and in which all parts (whatever may be their apparent divergences and antagonisms when viewed in isolation from one another) contribute to and participate in the sublime beauty of the whole. Sometimes they describe this universe as one ever-continuous flow of the finest and richest Music and enjoy all phenomena as the modes and modulations and rhythms of the same eternal and infinite Music. Sometimes it is described as a great Epic Poem or a great Drama. A Mahāyogi enjoys the beauty and sublimity of all forms of phenomenal self-expressions of Śiva-Śakti and describes them as *Cid-Vilāsa*.

Seventhly, this *Mahā-Sākāra-Pinda of Śiva-Śakti* is a world of *Ānanda* (Spiritual Bliss). This *ānandamaya* aspect of the cosmic order is revealed to and enjoyed by the Illumined Spiritual Consciousness of man, —the consciousness of *Mahāyogis, Mahājñānis, Mahābhaktas.* All joys and sorrows of our common experiences are to this consciousness elements of *Ānanda* and are enjoyed as such. Phenomenally speaking, *Ānanda* implies the perfect fulfilment of existence, fulfilment of life and power, fulfilment of mind and reason, fulfilment of morality and religion, fulfilment of goodness and beauty. The perfect fulfilment of all the aspects of this cosmic self-expression of Śiva-Śakti is unveiled to the empirical consciousness, which is perfectly illumined by the Spiritual Light of the ultimate character of Śiva-Śakti,—i.e. the transcendent and dynamic, self-luminous and self-revealing, nature of the one non dual Supreme Spirit.

Truly speaking, this *Ānanda* is the real and eternal nature of the Supreme Spirit,—Śiva in eternal and perfect union with His Śakti,—and all the grades and all the forms of self-manifestation of the Supreme Spirit are the manifold expressions of His *Ānanda.* Accordingly the *Mahā-Sākāra-Pinda* or the Cosmic Body of the Supreme Spirit is also a variegated spatio-temporal expression of the *Ānanda* of the Spirit. All the constituent elements of the physical universe, called *Mahābhutas* or *Mahātattwas* by the *Yogis,* are self-embodiments of *Ānanda.* All Matter and Life and Mind and Reason, which are evolved in this Cosmic Body, are forms of self expression of this *Ānanda*. All the dualities of the world of mind and senses and the world of *Dharma*, all the varieties of aesthetic enjoyments in the world of *Rasa*,—all these evolve from and are pervaded by the *Ānanda* of the Supreme Spirit; *Ānanda* is immanent in them all. All the apparent imperfections and evils and vices and miseries, which we ordinarily experience in this world, have got *Ānanda* as the Reality behind and within them. In truth, there is no reality save and except *Ānanda* in this universe. Hence it is proclaimed in the Upanishad that all the phenomenal realities of this universe are born from *Ānanda*, they are all sustained by *Ānanda*, they all move towards the full realisation of *Ānanda*, and they are all ultimately merged in *Ānanda*. The universe is nothing but *Ānanda* in a variety of forms in time and space. The true knowledge of this universe is the realisation of it as the diversified manifestation of *Ānanda*, which is the essential nature of the Supreme Spirit. *Mahāyogis*, *Mahājñānis* and *Mahābhaktas* realise themselves as well as the universe as *Ānandamaya*.

It is pointed out by the yogi-philosophers that such classification and gradation of different worlds or different orders of existences and experiences in the Cosmic Body of Śiva-Śakti can never be complete or exhaustive or certain. From different view-points different principles of classification and gradation may be adopted, and accordingly classification and gradation would assume different forms. To different orders of phenomenal consciousnesses, different worlds or orders of existences are revealed, and these consciousnesses also are evolved in this Cosmic Body. Moreover, all such classifications and gradations are based on human experience and speculation, and who can certify that human experience and thought can reach all the aspects of the Cosmic System,—all the modes of cosmic self-expression of the Supreme Spirit,—or that human experience and thought must be recognised as the sole and sure ascertainer of the true and entire nature of the Cosmic Order?

The human consciousness may, through the intensive practice of the appropriate *yogic* methods of self-concentration and self-enlightenment, be capable of rising above the limitations of phenomenal knowledge, transcending the Cosmic Order, and becoming perfectly united with the Supreme Spirit, Who is the Soul of the Cosmic Order, the Soul of all phenomenal existences. But that does not necessarily mean that such enlightened human consciousness can attain perfect and thorough knowledge of the entire phenomenal Cosmic Body of the Supreme Spirit,—of all the infinitely diversified spatio-temporal self-manifestations of Śiva-Śakti. The phenomenal experience and knowledge of even a perfectly enlightened Mahāyogi can not be expected to be all-comprehensive. What is called *sarvajñatā* (omniscience) of a *Mahāyogi* does not mean the phenomenal knowledge of all the details of this Cosmic System, but the intuitive or spiritual knowledge of the Ultimate Truth of all existences.

The infinite richness of the various aspects of the *Mahā-Sākāra-Pinda* of Śiva-Śakti is unfathomable even to the highest order of human intelligence,—even to the most spiritually illumined empirical consciousness of a *Mahāyogi, Mahājñāni, Mahābhakta.* Hence the Scriptures speak of innumerable *Brahmāndas* (worlds) of different kinds in this Cosmic Body of the Supreme Spirit. The human experience and knowledge are confined only within one *Brahmānda,* which also is too rich in contents to be fully comprehended. Many scriptures have enumerated fourteen *Lokas* or *Bhuvanas* in this *Brahmānda.* These are mentioned by Gorakhnath also. We are dwellers of *Bhuh.* Above this *Bhuh* there are *Bhuvah, Swah, Mahah, Jana, Tapah, Satya,* which are gradually higher and higher worlds, inhabited by higher and higher orders of beings, each being presided over by Divine Personalities. There are lower worlds also, such as *Atala, vitala, Sutala, Mahātala, Talātala, Rasātala, Pātāla,* (S.S.P. III. 2-4). Various orders of *Swarga* and *Naraka* also have been enumerated. All these point to the inconceivable greatness of the Cosmic Body of Śiva-Śakti. This Body is ever-new, ever-fresh, ever-young, through the processes of creation and transformation and destruction, and has no beginning or end either in time or in space and no limit to the varieties within its unity.

In *Siddha-Siddhānta-Paddhati* Mahāyogi Gorakhnath makes mention of various worlds,—various orders of existences and experiences,—in the Cosmic Body of Śiva-Śakti, and, as it will be seen hereafter, he shows how all these worlds can be experienced by a *Yogi* within the individual body, which he describes as the epitome of the Cosmic Body. Besides the seven lower worlds and the seven higher worlds named above, he also specifies a number of still higher worlds,—such as, *Vishnu-loka, Rudra-loka, Iśwara-loka, Nilakantha-loka, Śiva-loka, Bhairava-loka, Anādi-loka, Kula-loka, Akula-loka, Para-Brahma-loka, Parāpara-loka, Śakti-loka.* As it has been remarked before, the Mahāyogi never presumes that such enumeration is or can be exhaustive. It is rather suggestive. It suggests how the infinite greatness of the Cosmic Body of the Supreme Spirit should be contemplated upon. The *yoga-system* which he preaches teaches every spiritual aspirant not only to contemplate upon the infinite expanse, infinite complexity, infinite grandeur, infinite beauty, infinite goodness, infinite richness, perfect order and harmony, perfect inner unity amidst the most bewildering outer diversities, of the cosmic self-expression of the Supreme Spirit, but also to realise through the most intensive contemplation and meditation the infinite greatness and sacredness of his own individual body and its essential identity with the Cosmic Body.

Samarasakaraṇa of the *Vyasti-pinda* (individual body) with the *Samasti-pinda* (Cosmic Body),—the realisation of the same *rasa* or the same spiritual infinity and beauty and bliss within the self and the universe—is the grand ideal preached by the Siddha-Yogi school. This ideal of *Samarasakaraṇa* of the Yogi-school differs, as we shall see more clearly later on, from the ideal of *Brahmātma-jñāna* of the *Adwaita-Vedānta* school, which preaches the illusoriness of the Cosmic System and all individual existences and consciousnesses within it and the metaphysical identity of *Brahma* (as free from the *upādhi* of this illusory cosmic order) and the individual *Ātmā* (as liberated from the *upādhi* of the false individual body, individual consciousness and individual existence). The Yogi-school preaches the spiritual ideal of *Samarasakaraṇa* of *Brahma* (together with all His cosmic self-manifestations) and the individual *Ātmā* (with his individual consciousness perfectly illumined by Brahma-consciousness and his individual psycho-physical organism reflecting the glories of the Cosmic Body of Brahma). The Yogi teachers accordingly present to us a glorious conception of the phenomenal universe, which is a real manifestation of the infinite glory of the Unique *Śakti* of Brahma or Śiva, and want to awaken in us the consciousness that we are also real participators in the glory of this *Mahāśakti* and that what are manifested in the Cosmos are manifested in us as well.

The Siddha-Yogi school, in general agreement with most other important Indian schools of philosophy and religion, maintains the view that every *world* in this phenomenal Cosmic System has got three essentially interrelated aspects; called *ādhyātmika*, *ādhibhautika* and *ādhidaivika*. The *ādhyātmika* aspect implies a certain plane of phenomenal consciousness and a certain order of phenomenal experiences, with an appropriate system of instruments (*indriya* or *karana*) of knowledge and feeling and action for the differentiated self-expressions of this consciousness and for giving definite particularised forms to its experiences. The *ādhibhautika* aspect implies a certain order of objective realities revealed to this consciousness through such instruments. These objective realities constitute the embodiment of this consciousness, the external region in which it finds scope for self-expression in manifold forms of knowledge and feeling and desire and action, as well as the varieties of objects which appear and disappear in this region and are perceived as real in this plane of consciousness.

The *ādhyātmika* and the *ādhibhautika* aspects may be regarded as the subjective and the objective—or as the psychical and the physical,—

manifestations of the realities of the same order, and neither has any evidence of its existence except as related to the other. E.G., the *ādhibhautika jagat* (objective world) in which we now actually live has the proof of its existence and its special nature in our sensuous experiences;—this world so extensive in space and so continuous in time with all the varieties of sounds and colours and tastes and smells and shapes and sizes, with all the phenomena of heat, light, electricity, etc., with all the history of its evolution and the emergence of various species of beings within it, is a real world *only* in relation to our specially constituted senses of perception and minds and intellects. This system of specially constituted senses and minds and intellects is the *ādhyātmika* or subjective aspect of our world, and the evidence of the reality of these senses and minds and intellects lies in their revelation of those objects. The eyes are the proof of the existence of colours and the perception of colours is the proof of the existence of the eyes. They are so interrelated that they are legitimately supposed to have a common source of existence. That is the case with all the rest. Every order of phenomenal existence has an *ādhyātmika* and an *ādhibhautika* aspect, each contributing to the revelation of the realitiy of the other. It is held that in every world there is a distinctive *ādhyātmika* system for experiencing objective realities and a distinctive *ādhibhautika* order of realities capable of being objects of experience to that psychical system.

The *ādhidaivika* aspect of a world implies that every particular world in the Cosmic Body of Śiva-Śakti is a well-designed well-ordered system, governed by a Divine Spiritual Agency, i.e. a glorious Spiritual Manifestation of Śiva-Śakti, a great *Devatā*, Who governs and harmonises all the affairs of this world and maintains its unity and continuity amidst all its varieties and changes, Who is revealed as the Special Indwelling Spirit of this particular world and Who stands as the guarantee for the correspondence and correlativity of its *ādhyātmika* and *ādhibhautika* aspects. Each world has its own *Adhisthātrī Devatā* or Presiding Deity, Who keeps up its organic unity and shines as its Life and Soul, and every such Deity is a Special Spiritual Self-Revelation of Śiva-Śakti. In each world the Presiding or Central Deity again manifests himself as a number of Minor Deities, who are often called *Anga-Devatā* (meaning that they are like limbs or organs of the Central Deity), and who appear as active Spiritual Agencies governing and harmonising particular departments of the *ādhyātmika* and *ādhibhautika* aspects of the world. Thus the Scriptures speak of numerous *Devatās* with varieties of characters and powers and functions in relation to the same world. They are all specialised Spiritual Self-Revelations of Śiva-Śakti in this infinite and eternal Cosmic Body, and as such are non-different from Śiva-Śakti. These *Devatās* have phenomenal realities of a higher order than ourselves and the objects of our normal experience. All the various orders of worlds with their *ādhyātmika, ādhibhautika* and *ādhidaivika* aspects are perfectly organised and harmonised and unified by the spiritual immanence of the Supreme *Devatā,—Paramātmā, Para-Brahma, Śiva,* with His infinite Divine *Śakti*. The entire Cosmic System, comprising all orders of worlds, is thus a magnificent self-manifestation of the Absolute Spirit and is therefore rightly conceived as essentially a spiritual system. This is *Mahā-Sākāra-Pinda* of the Absolute Spirit, according to Gorakhnath and the school of enlightened yogis.

CHAPTER XII

THE EVOLUTION OF INDIVIDUAL BODIES IN THE COSMIC BODY

Recapitulation:— It has been observed that in the view of Gorakhnath and the Siddha-Yogi Sampradāya the Ultimate Reality is One, Who is above time and space, above duality and relativity, above substantiality and causality, above quality and number, above all activity and change, above all phenomenal existence and phenomenal consciousness. He transcends all differences between spirit and matter, the knower and the knowable, the conscious and the unconscious, the living and the non-living, the doer and the deed, the cause and the effect, the creator and the created, etc. He is absolutely differenceless and changeless and attributeless and actionless and formless and nameless. He is first referred to as the Nameless One.

But the Ultimate Reality must be conceived as the Absolute Source and Sustainer of all existences, all consciousnesses, all orders of phenomena in this universe of our actual and possible experiences. Hence for the purpose of our conception the Ultimate Reality is described as pure and perfect and absolute Existence (*Sat*), pure and perfect and absolute Consciousness (*Cit*), and as such, also pure and perfect and absolute Bliss (*Ānanda*). Existence and Consciousness and Bliss are not of course conceived in the abstract sense, but as the essential nature of the Ultimate Reality, the all-transcending Nameless One, in Whom the difference between the abstract and the concrete,—the qualities and the owner of the qualities,—does not exist. The Ultimate Reality so conceived is spoken of by the Siddha-Yogi school as *Parā-Saṃvit*. This *Parā-Saṃvit* is referred to in common discussions as *Śiva* or *Brahma* or *Paramātmā* or *Ādinātha* or by any other generally accepted Divine Name, conveying the idea of the Supreme Spirit. The Name Śiva has special sanctity in this school in as much as this school adopts the Śiva-Cult for the purpose of religious and spiritual discipline. Accordingly in this Sampradāya Śiva is the Ultimate Reality, the Absolute Truth. He is *Parā-Saṃvit*, pure and perfect *Sat-Cid-Ānanda*, the Absolute Source of all orders of existences and consciousnesses and experiences in the universe.

Now, Śiva or Brahma or *Parā-Saṃvit* is on the one hand self-existent self-luminous self-perfect differenceless and changeless non-dual transcendent Consciousness or Spirit above time and space and relativity, and on the other the absolute Ground and Source and Sustainer of all temporal and spatial and relative phenomenal realities,—of the bewilderingly diversified and changeful and wonderfully harmonious and organised cosmic system and all orders of individual existences in it. This necessarily implies that the Absolute Reality must have a *transcendent* as well as a *dynamic* aspect,—an aspect of changeless undifferentiated self-perfect Consciousness and an aspect of self-modifying self-differentiating self-revealing self-multiplying Creative Power. The Yogi-school accordingly holds that the Absolute Reality is *Śiva* with infinite *Śakti* immanent in and non-different from Him,—the Transcendent Spirit with Unique Power for phenomenal self-manifestation. Without Śakti, Śiva would have no phenomenal self-expression and He would not be the Ground of this Cosmic order, and without Śiva Śakti would have no existence at all. Śakti eternally exists in and by and for Śiva, the self-existent and self-luminous Spirit. Śiva and Śakti have no separate existence. Śakti is Śiva in His dynamic aspect. On account of the immanent presence of Śakti in the transcendent nature of Śiva or the Supreme Spirit, Śiva is eternally *Being* and eternally *Becoming*, is eternally the changeless One and is eternally manifesting and enjoying Himself as Many, is eternally dwelling in His supra-phenomenal Self and eternally revealing Himself in various relations in the phenomenal universe.

It is through the gradual self-unfoldment of His Śakti that Śiva reveals Himself in more and more manifested (*vyakta*) forms, in more and more qualified (*Saguna*) characters, in more and more concrete embodiments (*Pinda-rupa*), though in His transcendent nature He remains eternally changeless. Initially His Śakti is identical with Him and is called His *Nijā-Śakti*. This Śakti is of the character of *Pure Will* or Will that wills nothing and is therefore undistinguishable from Pure Consciousness. This Śakti gradually unfolds Herself into *Parā-Śakti, Aparā-Śakti, Sukshmā-Śakti* and *Kundalini-Śakti*. These may be conceived as the pre-cosmic stages of the self-unfoldment of the Divine Śakti. Through these stages Śiva is said to be equipped with a subtly qualified and embodied state, which is named *Para-Pinda*. Thus Śiva becomes *Para-Pinda*. In relation to each of the stages Śiva is said to acquire a new Name with new qualifying attributes, such as, *Aparamparam, Paramapadam, Śunyam, Niranjanam, Paramātmā*. With all these names and qualities Śiva becomes known as *Anādi-Pinda*. In this way while His *upādhis* (epithets) go on developing through the free and delightful play of His own *Śakti*, Śiva the Soul and Master of all these *upādhis*, always transcends them and enjoys in Himself the bliss of His eternal perfection.

Through further self-revealing of the Divine Śakti, five more *tattwas* (realities) with their special characteristics are evolved in the nature of

Anādi-Pinda. These are named *Paramānanda, Prabodha, Cidudaya, Prakāśa* and *Ahambhāva.* They with their attributes further qualify the nature of Śiva, the Supreme Spirit, and constitute what is called *Ādya-Pinda. Ādya-Pinda* is conceived as the Causal Body with reference to the phenomenal spatio-temporal Cosmic Order, which has not as yet been evolved, but the seed or the potentiality of which is manifested in an *ideal* form in this Causal Body of Śiva. Śakti is ever-active in the nature of Śiva, continues revealing and objectifying ever-new qualifications in His nature and creating more and more complex *bodies* for Him. Śiva shines as the Indwelling Spirit in all of them, as their Soul and Lord, as their Illuminer and Unifier and Enjoyer. They all appear as His *Vilāsa-rupa.*

Thus there is further self-unfolding activity of Śakti in the nature of *Ādya-Pinda* or the Causal Body of Śiva, and the Spatio-temporal Cosmic Body is gradually evolved, which is called *Mahā-Sākāra-Pinda.* This *Mahā-Sākāra-Pinda* of Śiva consists of *Mahākāśa, Mahāvāyu, Mahātejas, Mahsalila* and *Mahāprithwī,* which with their specific characteristics are in a gradual process evolved from the nature of *Ādya-Pinda.* Various worlds, various orders of existences and experiences, various grades of phenomenal consciousnesses and phenomenal realities revealed to them, various kinds of forces and their actions, various forms of relations and complications, are evolved in this magnificent *Mahā-Sākāra-Pinda,* and they are all most wonderfully and beautifully organised and harmonised and unified in this Cosmic Body of Śiva. Creations and Preservations and Destructions are going on continuously within this Cosmic Body, and through them this Cosmic Body is ever-new, ever-fresh, ever-living, ever-beautiful. Śiva Himself becomes this Cosmic Body through the self-revealing activity of His Śakti. This universe is thus conceived by Gorakhnath and the Siddha-Yogis as the magnificent and beautiful Divine Body,—as Śiva or Brahma Himself present in this form of the universe. All the varieties of the universe are to them variegated self-manifestations of Śiva and are thus essentially spiritual and enjoyable.

Then Gorakhnath says that Śiva having manifested Himself as the *Mahā-Sākāra-Pinda* further reveals Himself in relation to it as Eight Cosmic Divine Personalities, Who are called *Ashta-Murti* of this *Mahā-Sākāra-Pinda.* These Cosmic Deities are Śiva (Himself), Bhairava, Śrikantha, Sadāśiva, Iśwara, Rudra, Vishnu and Brahmā. These majestic Gods are of course no other than Śiva Himself, the Supreme Spirit, the Indwelling Soul and Lord of the entire universe and all orders of worlds within it. But they appear to be specially glorious self-revelations of the Supreme Spirit in the forms of eight orders of Cosmic Consciousnesses related to, immanent in and ruling over the Cosmic System and the seven orders of worlds evolved within it.

Śiva Himself is conceived as the First *Murti*, the Supreme Cosmic Personality, Whose self-luminous consciousness is all-transcending and all-comprehending, all-illumining and all-unifying, and Who reigns over and determines the courses of all orders of worlds,—all planes of existences and experiences,—in His Cosmic Body. From Him and within Him is evolved Bhairava, the Second *Murti*, the Second Cosmic Deity, Whose consciousness is perfectly spiritual, Who dwells in the realm of perfect spirituality and blissfulness, in Whose perception the whole Cosmic System,—the Cosmic Body of Śiva,—is full of *Ānanda* and *Caitanya*, wherein there is no imperfection and limitation, no bondage and sorrow, no veil upon the Supreme Spirit. Bhairava is therefore often worshipped as the perfect Ideal of *yoga* and *jñāna*. The aim of a spiritual aspirant is to attain the plane of consciousness which Bhairava represents. Gorakhnath often refers to Bhairava as the Ideal of a *yogi*. The Third Cosmic Deity is Śrikantha, evolved from Bhairava. He seems to represent the perfection of Aesthetic Consciousness. He always dwells in the world of Beauty or *Rasa*. To Him the Cosmic Body is *rasamaya*, a perfectly beautiful order, every part of which is in sweet harmony with and contributes to the beauty of the whole. He is the most perfect Musician, the most perfect Poet, the most perfect Painter, the most perfect Artist in all respects, and to Him the whole cosmic self-manifestation of the Supreme Spirit is a perfect flow of Music, a perfect Poem, a perfect Picture, a perfect Artistic Product, a perfect Dance. The all-pervading Beauty of Śiva's Cosmic Body is always unveiled to and enjoyed by His Consciousness, and He reigns and shines in this world of Beauty. He is worshipped and meditated upon by the yogis as the Supreme Ideal of *artistic sādhanā*, for the realisation of the immanent Beauty of the Cosmic Order. He is conceived as *Raseśwara*, the Lord of Beauty. With Him as the Ideal, a *yogi* undergoes systematic courses of self-discipline for the perfect harmonisation and beautification of his entire self-conscious being and for putting himself in perfect tune with the beautiful universe.

Sadāśiva is mentioned by Gorakhnath as the Fourth Cosmic Deity. He is evolved from Śrikantha. He appears to represent the perfection of Moral Consciousness. He is the Indwelling and all-regulating Spirit of the world of *Dharma*. To Him the Cosmic System is a perfect Moral Order, in which the Ideal of Goodness or perfect moral excellence is the immanent regulative principle and in which this Ideal is being progressively realised in and through all moral dualisms and apparent antagonisms. To His consciousness all apparent evils and vices, all hatreds and furies and catastrophies and agonies, etc., are so well designed and regulated and harmonised that they all contribute to the realisation of Perfect Goodness in the Cosmic System. He therefore looks upon all such seeming aberrations in a sportive mood and is kind and compassionate and forgiving to all. He is worshipped by all people living in the domain of *Dharma* or moral dualisms for receiving inspiration and strength for the cultivation of purity and goodness and moral excellences and for getting ready forgiveness for occasional deviations from the righteous path. He is meditated upon as the Ideal of perfect Goodness,—the Ideal of perfect *Dharma*.

Iśwara is named as the Fifth Divine *Murti* in the Cosmic Body of Śiva. He is described as evolved from Sadāśiva. In this context Iśwara seems to represent the fullness of Rational or Intellectual Consciousness. He is the Indwelling Spirit and the Supreme Lord of the world of *Buddhi* (Reason). To Him the Cosmic System is a magnificent Rational Order, in which the Ideal of Truth is being progressively revealed and realised in and through the diversities of phenomenal realities in time and space. In His consciousness Truth is perfectly realised, and He is the Supreme Ideal to those who seek for Truth in the world-order. He is the Source of inspiration to all truth-seekers and the omniscient *Guru* of all at all times. He awakens the urge for Truth in all minds and leads them from ignorance and error to Truth. Through the worship of Iśwara and by His Grace the *Buddhi* of a truth-seeker is enlightened and he realises the whole world-system as a rational order and perceives the revelation of Truth in all mental, vital and material phenomena. It is by the Grace of Iśwara that all branches of human knowledge,—all sciences and philosophies, all languages and literatures,—are developed in this human society.

The Sixth Divine Personality in the Cosmic System is Rudra, Who is described as evolved from Iśwara. In this context Rudra may be viewed as representing the Cosmic Mind. He is the Indweller and Ruler of the world of Mind. He manifests Himself in all kinds of mental powers and mental phenomena in the Cosmic Body of Śiva, exercises control over them and preserves harmony and unity among them. He is conceived as all-powerful and all-knowing and as bestowing power and knowledge and greatness and brilliance upon all minds that seek for them. But He does not appear to be directly concerned with the Ideals of Truth and Goodness and Beauty and Spiritual Bliss, which are represented by Iśwara, Sadāśiva, Śrikantha and Bhairava. Rudra (conceived in this way) is worshipped chiefly for the development of the mind-power, for the gratification of desires and ambitions, for the expansion of the frontiers of knowledge and for the favourableness of the mental atmosphere.

In this hierarchy of Cosmic Divine Self-Revelations of the Supreme Spirit the Seventh Position is occupied by Vishnu, Who is described as evolved from Rudra. Vishnu here appears to stand for the Cosmic Life (*Viśwa-Prāna*). He is the all-pervading Life-Power in the universe. He is the Soul and Lord of the world of Life. He manifests Himself in all kinds of vital forces and vital phenomena in the Cosmic Body of Śiva, controls and regulates them and maintains harmony and unity among them. According to this conception, Vishnu also is not directly connected with the higher intellectual, moral, aesthetic and spiritual Ideals immanent in this Cosmic Order. But He is the Indwelling Spirit ruling over the world of Life, upon the harmonious development of which the development of the world of Mind and the realisation of those Ideals in the Cosmic System greatly depends. He is therefore to be worshipped for the development and elevation of the life-power in the worshippers and for peace and harmony and unity in the vital atmosphere.

It may be remarked by the way that to the followers of the Rudra-Cult Rudra is the name for the Supreme Spirit (with His perfect consciousness and infinite power), to the followers of the Vishnu-Cult or the Nārāyana-Cult Vishnu or Nārāyana is the name for the same Supreme Spirit, and similarly to the followers of the Krishna-cult or the Rāma-cult Krishna or Rāma is the name for the same Supreme Spirit. The followers of different religious cults give different sacred names to the same Ultimate Reality,—the Nameless One,—the perfect *Sat-Cid-Ānanda*—the Spiritual Ground and Source of all existences. True *Yogis* and *Jñānis* and *Bhaktas* never quarrel about these names. The significance of each name is to be understood in the light of the conception attached to it by the respective sects.

The Eighth Divine *Murti* in the Cosmic Body of Śiva, according to Gorakhnath's conception, is Brahmā, Who is described as evolved from Vishnu. Brahmā is conceived as Soul and Lord of the gross physical or material world. He manifests Himself in and through all kinds of material bodies, material forces, and material phenomena, and controls and regulates and harmonises them and gives a unity to this material universe. He is regarded as the Dynamic Source—the actual Designer and Creator—of all the diverse forms of gross individual existences with gross material bodies within the Cosmic Body of the Supreme Spirit. He may be said to supply the plurality of material embodiments to Life and Mind and Reason as well as to Moral Consciousness and Aesthetic Consciousness and Spiritual Consciousness. It is through Him that Śiva with His Śakti comes down to and manifests Himself in the grossest and lowest material and sensuous plane of existence and experience. Accordingly Brahmā is conceived as the Creator of the world of material diversities of our normal sensuous experience. As physically embodied individual beings, we are born from the existence and conscious will (*avalokana*) of Brahmā in His material world and are governed by His law, and hence we are bound to pay our homage to Him and offer worship to Him.

Thus though Gorakhnath conceives in a general way the entire universe,—the entire Cosmic Body (*Mahā-Sākāra-Pinda*) of Śiva, as *Pañca-bhautika*, i.e. constituted of five *mahā-bhutas* evolved from His *Ādi-pinda*, he indicates the development of various planes of Cosmic Realities and Cosmic Consciousnesses in this spatio-temporal Cosmic Order. It is to be noted that the course of development as traced by him does not imply a process of *ascent* from lower planes to higher planes, but rather a process of *descent* from the highest plane of Spiritual Consciousness and Spiritual Existence to gradually lower and lower planes of Consciousness and Existence, till the lowest sensuous plane of consciousness and material plane of existence is reached. Since the Uitimate Reality is eternally in the highest transcendent plane, His cosmic self-manifestation must be in the direction of lower and lower phenomenal planes. The infinite richness of His nature which is perfectly unified in the transcendent plane is unfolded in more and more diversified forms in lower and lower planes. But in all such planes the urge for *return* to the highest plane of infinite bliss remains in the innermost nature of phenomenal realities and acts as the immanent Ideal. Hence there is a downward process as well as an upward process,—a tendency towards variety as well as a tendency towards unity,—in the cosmic system.

Another important feature of this system of philosophy is remarkable. In it the evolution of the Cosmic Body and the Cosmic Principles (*Tattwa*) within it is followed by the evolution of the diverse orders of individual phenomenal realities and individual phenomenal consciousnesses. The *Samasti-Pinda* (the Collective Organism) as one whole is manifested first from the supra-cosmic nature of Śiva-Śakti with all the universal Powers and Principles involved in it, and then the *Vyaṣṭi-Piṇḍas* (individual organisms) are gradually in due course evolved within it in temporal succession and spatial co-existence to give the *Samaṣṭi-piṇḍa* more and more diversified appearance. The *absolute* Unity of the Supreme Spirit becomes through the gradual unfoldment of His infinite *Śakti* more and more *diversified* and *variegated* Unity in His Cosmic Self-expression.

With the evolution of the Eight Divine Personalities and their respective planes of Consciousnesses and existences, the constitution of the *Mahā-Sākāra-Pinda* or *Samaṣṭi-piṇḍa* of Śiva-Śakti is complete, so far as the Universal Cosmic Principles are concerned. The plane of Brahmā is the lowest and grossest of all and is most closely related to the gross world (*sthula-jagat*) of our sensuous experience. Hence Gorakhnath traces the evolution of the individual existences and consciousnesses of this world from the Conscious Will (*Avalokana*) of Brahmā. This Conscious Will is manifested in the form of what he calls *Prakriti-Pinda*, from which all individual bodies (*Vyasti-Pindas*) are evolved. Thus says Gorakhnath :—

Tad Brahmanah sakāśād avalokanena nara-nārī-rupah Prakriti-Pindah samutpanna stacca panca-pancātmakam śarīram. (S. S. P. I. 38)

He describes *Prakriti-Pinda* as of the nature of a union between a male and a female principle (*nara-nārī-rupa*). It seems that according to his view all individual living bodies are born of a union between a paternal and a maternal principle and as such involve male and female elements in their constitution. Every individual body is a particularised manifestation of *Prakriti-Pinda*, in which both the principles are in union by the will of Brahmā, the Creator of individual bodies in this physical universe. Innumerable species of individual bodies are evolved with various characteristics, various kinds of physical features and qualities and potentialities, from *Prakriti-Pinda* in the world of Brahmā. They are all ultimately individualised manifestations of the Cosmic Body of Śiva and as such essentially non-different from Him.

Yogi-Guru Gorakhnath is particularly interested in the constitution of the individual human body. First, it is in the human body that all the external and internal organs of an individual body (*Vyasti-Pinda*) are evolved in the fully manifested forms. There are lower orders of individual bodies, in which many of these organs are not perceptibly manifested, but remain only in potential forms. It is often stated in the scriptural texts that there are eighty-four lakhs of species of living bodies, and the human body is the most developed, most complex, most organised and most harmonised of all. In the human body the finest and subtlest organs are clearly manifested and they are wonderfully adjusted to the grossest organs. In it the physical organs, the vital organs, the psychical organs, the intellectual organs,—all these are proportionately developed and they nicely cooperate with one another. In it Life and Mind and Reason are prominently manifested in individualised forms and find relatively free scope for their self-expressions. Moral consciousness, aesthetic consciousness and spiritual consciousness also find ample facility for being brilliantly manifested and developed in the human body.

Hence man as an individual has on account of his fine bodily constitution an exceptional opportunity for dwelling in all the various orders of *worlds* and participating in the various orders of existences and experiences. An, individual man with his individual phenomenal consciousness can, through appropriate methods of self-discipline and self-refinement, acquire the power to pass easily from one world of existence and experience to another. Thus the individual human body occupies a very important position in the evolutionary process of the cosmic system—in the process of the phenomenal self-manifestation of Śiva-Śakti in the spatio-temporal cosmic order. Gorakhnath accordingly dilates in a rather elaborate manner upon the psycho-physiological constitution of the human body, which is evolved from the *Prakriti-Pinda* of Brahmā, Who is conceived as the immediate Divine Source of the world of individual existences in the physical plane.

Secondly, Gorakhnath and the Siddha-Yogi school conceive the individual human body as an epitome of the Cosmic Body of Śiva-Śakti. A Yogi can, through the intensive practice of contemplation and meditation, realise the whole universe within himself and identify himself with the whole universe. All worlds in the Cosmic System, all orders of existences, all planes of experiences, are in some mysterious way represented within the fully developed human body. Though apparently occupying a small portion of space, though living for a short period of time on the gross earthly plane, the human body is a fine mirror of the *Mahā Sākāra-Pinda* of Śiva-Śakti. It reflects in an apparently miniature scale the entire Cosmic Order with all its complications and diversifications and all its beauty and grandeur. When a man's phenomenal consciousness, through its progressive self-refinement and higher self-discipline, becomes liberated from the limitations and imperfections of the lower planes and enlightened about the infinite richness of this apparently small bodily structure, he is blessed with a highly glorified self-consciousness and feels himself free from all bondages and sorrows. He then perceives all in himself and himself in all, and to him there is nothing which restricts his freedom and becomes a source of annoyance and misery for him. This possibility of the experience of the whole Cosmic Order within the human body infinitely enhances the value and importance of this body, and hence Gorakhnath particularly deals with the nature of the human body.

Thirdly, it is in and through the human organism that the Divine Śakti, Who in the process of cosmic self-manifestation comes down from the highest transcendent spiritual plane of absolute unity and bliss step by step to the lowest phenomenal material plane of endless diversities and imperfections, ascends again by means of the self-conscious processes of *Yoga* and *Jñanā* and *Bhakti* to the transcendent spiritual plane and becomes perfectly and blissfully united with the Supreme Spirit, Śiva. The descending and self-diversifying manifestation of Śakti is illustrated in the creative and regulative and destructive phenomena of the Cosmic Order, while the ascending and self-unifying manifestation of *Śakti* is most brilliantly illustrated in the spiritual urge in the phenomenal consciousness of man and the systematic spiritual self-discipline and self-elevation and self-enlightenment of the human individual. Man with his developed individuality can experience Śiva, the Supreme Spirit, as his own true Soul as well as the true Soul of the universe. Hence the human body is conceived as having a very important place and function in the cosmic self-expression of Śiva-Śakti.

CHAPTER XIII

THE CONSTITUTION OF INDIVIDUAL BODY

Gorakhnath takes a comprehensive view of the nature of human individuality and analyses its constitution from the yogic standpoint. He conceives the human organism as consisting of (1) the material body called *Bhuta-pinda*, (2) the mental body, described as *Antahkarana-pancaka* or five-fold *antahkarana*, (3) *Kula-pancaka* or five-fold *Kula*, (4) *Vyakti-pancaka* or five-fold *Vyakti*, (5) *Pratyaksha-karana-pancaka* or five-fold perceptible determinant causes, (6) *Nāḍī-samsthāna* or the system of the *Nāḍīs*, (7) *Daśa-Vāyu* or ten *Prāna-Vāyu* or vital forces, forming the vital body.

(1) *The gross material body :—*

The *Bhuta pinda* (or *Bhautika-pinda*), i.e. the material body, is constituted of the five gross material elements, purposefully organised by the Creative Will of Brahmā with the Life-power and the Mind-power immanent in the organism. In different parts of the organism, however, different elements appear in more conspicuous proportions. In bones (*asthi*), flesh (*māmsa*), skin (*twak*), tissues (*Nādī*) and hair (*roma*)—i.e. in all the solid parts,—the element of *Bhumi* or *Prithwī* appears predominantly, and Gorakhnath speaks of them as the *five gunas* (perhaps in the sense of special manifestations) of *Bhumi.* In the liquid substances of the body,— such as, saliva (*lālā*), urine (*mutra*), semen (*sukra*), blood (*śonita*) and sweat (*sweda*),—the element of *Ap* or *Salila* appears more conspicuously, and they are called the five *gunas* of *Ap*. Hunger (*kṣudhā*), thirst (*triṣnā*), sleep (*nidrā*), lustre (*kānti*) and sloth (*ālasya*) are conceived by Gorakhnath as physical phenomena, in which there are special manifestations of the element of *Tejas.* According to him, these phenomena occur on account of the varying functions and influences of *Tejas* or *Agni* in different parts of the living body. Movement (*dhāvana*), fidgeting (*bhramana*), expansion (*prasārana*), contraction (*ākuncana*) and suppression (*nirodhana*) are bodily phenomena, which are chiefly determined by the element of *Vāyu* and are therefore called *Gunas* of *Vāyu.* The phenomena of physical attraction (*rāga*), repulsion (*dwesha*), fear (*bhaya*), shame (*lajjā*) and callousness (*moha*) are regarded as the special manifestations of the element of *Ākāśa* and are accordingly described as the five *Gunas* of *Ākāśa.* Thus the Mahāyogi describes the gross physical body as constituted of the five gross *bhutas* and as possessing twenty-five *gunas* mentioned above. (S.S.P.I. 39-43).

It is noticeable that in enumerating the special contributions of the ultimate material elements (*mahābhutas*) to the physical body, the Mahāyogi has mentioned some phenomena which are obviously expressions of our vital or psychical nature. But they are mostly due to our changing physical conditions. Many of them can be properly regulated through the appropriate treatment and discipline of the physical body. They are therefore traced to the ultimate ingredients of this body. It is undeniable that the gross physical body (*bhautika-śarīra*) exercises a great influence upon our life and mind, upon our temperaments and habits, upon our impulses and dispositions. Hence *Yogis* attach great importance to the constitution of this body and the regulation and control of the physical functions for moral and spiritual upliftment.

(2) *Antahkarana-pancaka* or *the mental body :—*

Gorakhnath then proceeds to the analysis of the nature of Mind or the mental body of a human individual. In order to understand the philosophy of Gorakhnath, it has at every stage to be remembered that the whole is essentially prior to the parts, which are its self-manifestations. The whole is really *one* and it manifests itself in the forms of *many*, and in relation to these manifestations it is called the whole. Ultimately Śiva (the Supreme Spirit) with His Śakti immanent in and identified with Him is One Reality, and through many stages of self-unfoldment and self-diversification of His Śakti, He becomes the Cosmic Soul with the Cosmic Body, Which is one Whole with numerous self-manifestations organically interrelated and united within It. Again, Śiva as the Cosmic Soul with the Cosmic Body is One Reality, and He manifests Himself as a number of Cosmic Deities and inter-related *worlds* of existences and experiences with Himself as their Soul and Centre and Ruler and Unifier. Thus He seems to become one greater and more magnificent Whole, revealing far more numerous diversities organised and united within Himself. Again, as this greatly complicated Cosmic Personality, He through further self-diversification of His Śakti manifests Himself in the forms of innumerable kinds of individual bodies, individual consciousnesses and individual souls, variously conditioned by the limitations of time and space and causality and relativity. But in all of them it is Śiva Who reveals and enjoys Himself, and in all of them Śiva is the innermost Soul and all-governing and all-harmonising Lord. In relation to them Śiva appears to become a still more complicated and glorified Whole. Further, each of the individual bodies imbued with the Divine Soul is one whole, with all its possibilities inherent in it, and it becomes a more and more complex whole through the manifestation of its parts and limbs and organs and powers and qualities which had remained unmanifested in its nature in the initial stages. The more they are manifested in diversified forms, the more are they organised and unified in the nature of the individual body and the more does the body become a complex whole. Thus at every stage the whole originates the parts, and the parts contribute to the richness of the whole; every living part again functions as a whole giving birth to parts which enrich it. In this way evolution goes on, and the Ultimate Reality becomes a greater and greater whole through the origination of parts within parts, all of which had been initially present in an unmanifested state in that ultimate Cause and are in the manifested states also essentially one with it. This is the *Sat-kārya-vāda* of Gorakhnath and his school. The cause becomes the effects and is enriched by them. The Whole becomes the parts and becomes a more and more complex whole with them. Nothing absolutely new is added to the ultimate Reality, the ultimate Cause.

In our actual experience we find that the individual mind is evolved from and within the individual living body gradually, when the body is adequately developed and equipped with diverse organs or instruments through which the mental phenomena are manifested. With the very birth of the physical (*bhautika*) body in the form of the minutest germ, life is associated with it and infuses into it the capacity for growth, which implies progressive self-diversification and spontaneous organisation of the diversities evolved. The vital forces appear to operate actively in the physical body and determine its growth, long before the mind is manifested in it. Of course, the vitality also becomes more and more manifested with the evolution of the vital organs in the body. The manifestation of the mind is found to be definitely conditional upon the development of the suitable organs,—such as the sense-organs, the nervous system and the brain, etc., in the body by the life-power innate in it. But according to the *yogic* view this does not mean that before the development of the organs the mind does not exist at all, that it is the product of the organism and is newly created or produced after the development of the instruments. The mind really exists in the unmanifested state even in the nature of the living germ or protoplasm, but only its outer phenomenal self-expression is dependent upon the development of the organs. Even in the unmanifested state the mind exercises its determining influence upon the courses of development of the physical organs, and it is for this reason that the organs are so developed as to become suitable vehicles for the self-expressions of the mind.

The *Yogis* see in the individual minds the individualised self-manifestations of the Cosmic Mind in relation to and apparent dependence upon the individual living bodies. In the individual lives also they see the individualised self-manifestations of the Cosmic Life in relation to and apparent dependence upon the individual physical bodies. It has been noticed that the Cosmic Mind and the Cosmic Life are evolved from and within the *Mahā-Sākāra-Murti* or Cosmic Body of Śiva-Śakti. Hence every individual being is looked upon as an incarnation of Śiva-Śakti. One point is to be specially noted. In the cosmic process of evolution, Mind is prior to Life, and Life is prior to the Material Body, while in the process of the evolution of individual existences, the material body appears first, and it is followed by the appearance of life and thereafter by the appearance of the mind. The higher and higher orders of existences and experiences appear later and later. What is first in the Cosmic Order is revealed last in the process of the evolution of individual existences.

Now, the Mind gradually manifests itself in the individual living body. Though there are various orders of manifestations of the mind in the diverse species of animal bodies, we are here specially concerned with the human body, in which the bodily organs (which are progressively developed) are suited to the fullest manifestation of the mind. In course of its gradual self-manifestation the mind naturally diversifies itself, makes itself more and more complex in its phenomenal character and at the same time organises all its manifestations so as to constitute a single whole. Gorakhnath (consistently with the sanctity which he attaches all along to the number five) classifies all phenomenal manifestations of the mind under five names,—viz., *Manas*, *Buddhi*, *Ahamkāra*, *citta* and *caitanya*, and he calls them *Antah-karana-pancaka* (i e. fivefold internal instrument or empirical mind). (S.S.P.I 44). According to him *Antahkarana* or the Mind is essentially one, but it appears in five different forms in accordance with its five distinct kinds of functions or phenomenal expressions.

In his usual manner Gorakhnath discribes each of these divisions of the Mind as possessing five characteristics or as expressed in five kinds of psychological phenomena. *Manas* or undisciplined empirical mind is manifested in such phenomena as, (1) *Samkalpa* (desire and will), (2) *Vikalpa* (doubt and hesitancy), (3) *Murcchā* (swoon or temporary senselessness), (4) *Jaḍatā* (idiocy or confused thinking), and (5) *Manana* (reflective thinking). *Buddhi* (intellect or reason or disciplined mind) is described as manifested in such phenomena, as *Viveka* (discrimination of truth from untruth, right from wrong, good from evil, valuable from valueless, beauty from ugliness, etc.), (2) *Vairāgya* (voluntary restraint of desires and attachments, or turning away of the mind from what is conceived as untrue, unreal, wrong, evil, ugly, useless, etc.), (3) *Śānti* (cultivation of calmness and tranquillity of the mind, or peacefulness of character), (4) *Santosha* (cultivation of contentment), and (5) *Kshamā* (cultivation of the spirit of forgiveness in relation to others). *Buddhi* is the higher mind which regulates *Manas* or the lower mind.

Ahamkāra is expressed in such phenomena, as, (1) *Abhimāna* (sense of I-ness or ego), (2) *Madīyam* (sense of mine-ness, or the consciousness of the body, senses, mental and intellectual functions, etc., as one's own), (3) *Mama-sukham* (brooding over and planning for one's own happiness), (4) *Mama duhkham* (brooding over and struggling against one's own sorrow), and (5) *Mama-idam* (the sense of 'this-is-mine' i.e. the sense of possession and monopoly). *Ahamkāra* plays the most important role in the constitution of an individual, inasmuch as it really gives him the sense of individuality and the sense of unity and permanence amidst all the varieties and changes in the physical body and the vital and mental functions. It is *Ahamkāra* which ascribes all the bodily and vital and mental phenomena to one ego or 'I' and regards the 'I' or ego as their owner and master as well as the owner and master of properties and environments. *Buddhi* and *Ahamkāra* are actually found to be involved in comparatively higher stages of the development of individual minds.

The phenomena which are conceived as expressions of *Citta* are,— (1) *Mati* (disposition or instinctive and habitual tendencies), (2) *Dhriti* (power of conservation of energy and experience), (3) *Smriti* (memory or power of recollecting and reproducing past experiences), (4) *Tyāga* (the capacity for renunciation or sacrifice or forgetting), and (5) *Swīkāra* (the capacity for assimilation or appropriation or making one's own what is obtained from external sources). It appears that *Citta* is manifested chiefly in the retention and revival of old *sanskāras* and in the sub-conscious operations of the mind. The phenomena which are specially attributed to *Caitanya* are, (1) *Vimarśa* (rational reflection), (2) *Śīlana* (systematic self-discipline), (3) *Dhairya* (patience or self-control), (4) *Cintana* (contemplation and meditation), (5) *Niḥspṛhatva* (cultivated desirelessness). (S.S.P.I. 44-49).

In this way Gorakhnath enumerates twentyfive forms of manifestation of Mind in the individual body. The individual mind so characterised is called *Antahkarana* or the inner instrument for the self-expression of the individual Soul or Spirit in this phenomenal world, the *Bahihkarana* or the outer instrument being the physical body with the diverse sense-organs, the nervous system, the vital mechanisms, etc. The physical body is known as *Sthula-śarīra* (gross body) and *Antahkarana* with the psychical and vital forces is designated as *Sukshma-Śarīra* (subtle body) of the Individual Soul, i.e. the individualised spiritual self-manifestation of the Supreme Spirit, Śiva. The individualisation of the Soul, according to the Yogi-school, consists in its *apparent* self-identification with these phenomenal embodiments. Essentially the Soul is no other than Śiva Himself.

In this connection it may be noted that some schools of Indian philosophy (such as Sānkhya and others) recognise three fundamental divisions of *Antahkarana*,—viz., *Manas*, *Buddhi* and *Ahamkāra*,—while some other schools (such as Vedānta) recognise four divisions,—viz, *Manas*, *Buddhi*, *Ahamkāra*, and *Citta*. Gorakhnath adds one more, which he calls *Caitanya*. In the enumeration of the phenomena under each division he does not exactly follow the principle adopted by the other schools. His point of view is more *yogic* than purely psychological. *Manas* seems to be chiefly concerned with the phenomena of the animal mind and the lower orders of the human mind, which a *yogi* has to control and transcend. *Buddhi* is concerned with the phenomena of the higher orders of the human mind, including the phenomena of the elevated moral, aesthetic and spiritual consciousness. *Ahamkāra* is concerned with the egoistic consciousness, which also has to be progressively enlightened and transcended. *Citta* principally refers to the subconscious mind which also has to be brought under control and purified and ennobled. *Caitanya* chiefly refers to the higher orders of human consciousness which have to be further enlightened and concentrated for the direct experience of the Supreme Spirit in itself.

(3) *Kula-pancaka:*—

Having dealt with the evolution of the physical body (*bhautika pinda*) and the mental body (*antahkarana-pancaka*), Gorakhnath deals with what he calls *Kula-pancaka*. *Kula* is one of the most technical and most puzzling terms of the philosophy as well as *sādhanā* of the *Yogis* and the *Tāntrikas*. It is defined in a variety of ways and is used in different senses in different contexts. We have elsewhere discussed the meanings of the terms *Kula* and *Akula*. In the present context the term *Kula* appears to convey a somewhat different idea. Gorakhnath explains *Kula* here as manifested in five ways, viz, *Sattwa*, *Rajas*, *Tamas*, *Kāla* and *Jeeva*. (S.S.P.I. 50). All of them exercise their directive influence upon the psycho-physical phenomena from behind the scene and give special inclinations and aptitudes to them.

The influence of *Sattwa* is manifested in such mental phenomena, as, *Dayā* (kindness or compassion), *Dharma* (righteousness), *Kriyā* (pious habits or willingness to perform good and noble deeds), *Bhakti* (reverence or devotion), and *Sraddhā* (faith). It is the influence of *Sattwa*, which inspires the human mind with higher moral and spiritual ideals, elevates it to higher planes of consciousness, urges it to control the natural passions and propensities and desires and ambitions, and directs its thoughts and emotions and wishes towards the realisation of perfect truth and beauty and goodness and freedom.

The influence of *Rajas* is manifested in such phenomena, as, *Dāna* (making of gifts or charities with an egotistic sense of one's own superiority, and not with a spirit of humility and disinterested service), *Bhoga* (hankering for more and more sensuous and mental enjoyment), *Śringāra* (love for decoration and ornamentation and artististic luxuries), *Vastu-grahana* (love for the appropriation of more and more property), and *Swārtha-sangrahana* (acquisition and accumulation of things for selfish purposes). It is the influence of *Rajas* in the nature of man, that makes him active and energetic and enterprising and moves him in the direction of self-aggrandisement, selfish interests, worldly ambitions, acquisition of power and prosperity and pleasure, artistic enjoyments, etc. In men of *Āsuri prakriti Rajas* is predominant, while in men of *Daivi-prakriti Sattwa* is predominant.

The influence of *Tamas* leads to propensities for, *Vivāda* (useless controversies), *Kalaha* (quarrelsomeness), *Śoka* (lamentation or melancholia), *Vadha* (killing) and *Vancana* (deception). What are called evil or ignoble or wicked propensities are regarded as due to the influence of *Tamas* in the human nature.

The influence of *Kāla* is manifested in—*Kalanā* (calculation of numbers and periods with regard to objects and events and perception of the relations of coexistence and succession among them), *Kalpanā* (the appreciation of regular temporal orders in the production and transformation of natural phenomena), *Bhrānti* (confusion of thoughts at particular times), *Pramāda* (periodical insanity), *Anartha* (facing accidental misfortunes). Time exercises a considerable influence upon us. Courses of evolution and development of bodies, fruition of actions, favourable and unfavourable conditions of life,—all these are greatly influenced by *Kāla* (Time).

What is called *Jeeva* in this connection is conceived as manifested in the changes of states (*avasthā*) of the empirical consciousness, and the sustenance of the unity and identity of the individual existence and consciousness amidst all these changes. These states are,—*Jāgrat* (the waking state, in which the mind comes in direct contact with external realities through the instrumentality of the sense-organs of perception and action), *Swapna* (the state of dream, in which in spite of the absence of direct contact between the mind and the objective realities through the senses the mind has various experiences within itself due to its operations in the subconscious level), *Sushupti* (the state of deep sleep in which the mind exists in the unconscious level without any objective or subjective experiences and is in complete rest and peace), *Turiya* (the fourth state, the state of the perfect concentration of the mind upon the transcendent character of the Spirit or Soul, the blissful state of the illumination of the phenomenal consciousness by the self-luminous transcendent Spirit), and lastly *Turyātīta* (a state even beyond this fourth state, in which the state of perfect concentration is elevated to the state of absolute union or identification, in which the individual mind realises itself as absolutely one with the Transcendent Spirit, Śiva).

The possibility of the same individual mind passing through all these widely different states without losing its individuailty indicates, according to Gorakhnath, a higher power and reality immanent in it and determining and witnessing these changes of states, and this he gives the name of *Jeeva. Sattwa, Rajas, Tamas, Kāla* and *Jeeva* are regarded as invisible determining forces, which operating together in various ways give the direction to the evolution of the character of an individual mind in an individual body and make the nature of an individual so very complex and at the same time harmonious. They seem to be immanent in the nature of every individual even from his embryonic state and exert their influence during all the stages of his development. They are given by Gorakhnath the generic name of *Kulapancaka*. This *Kula* appears to evolve from the Divine *Śakti* for determining the courses of the evolution of the individual bodies and minds in this cosmic order and leading them stage by stage towards their highest fulfilment according to the cosmic design. They all play their allotted parts in the Cosmic Body of Śiva-Śakti.

(S.S.P.I. 50-55)

(4) *Vyakti-pancaka :—*

Thereafter Gorakhnath deals with what he calls *Vyakti-pancaka*, which means five forms of self-expression (*Vyakti*) of the individual mind. He classifies them as *Icchā* (volition), *Kriyā* (action), *Māyā* (which may to some extent be expressed by the term pretension), *Prakriti* (which may in this context be translated as temperament), and *Vāk* (speech). Each of these is expressed in five forms. *Icchā* is expressed in the forms of *Unmāda* (mad unbalanced uncontrolled impulses and excitements, such as are found in children, in insane and intoxicated persons and in persons lost in reverie), *Vāsanā* (deep-rooted desires, which may be due to instincts or past habits), *Vānchā* (desires for particular alluring or covetable objects. such as wealth and power and pleasure), *Cintā* (voluntary thinking and planning about desirable objects and ways and means to attain them), and *Cestā* (mental efforts or strong resolutions for the attainment of desirable objects or for the accomplishment of any cherished purpose). These are the fivefold manifestations of *Icchā*.

Icchā is followed by *Kriyā*. According to Gorakhnath, *Kriyā* is manifested in five forms, viz, *Smarana* (active remembrance of and contemplation upon the desirable object to be attained or purpose to be accomplished), *Udyoga* (making necessary preparations for the active pursuit of a desired object or a chosen purpose), *Kārya* (active pursuit of an object or ideal), *Niscaya* (pursuit of an object or ideal with strong determination and tireless perseverance), and *Swakulācara* (performance of duties and virtuous deeds in conformity to the customs and rules and expectations of the family and the society, even at the sacrifice of personal desires and inclinations). In the constitution of the nature of every individual, *Dharma* and *Adharma,*—good and evil traits,—dispositions towards higher moral and spiritual ideals and those in the opposite direction,—are both evolved in the normal course according to the cosmic plan. With the development of the individual consciousness a man is required to voluntarily and deliberately and actively put down the forces of *Adharma*, get rid of the evil propensities and dispositions and elevate his nature to the higher planes of morality and spirituality.

Icchā and *Kriyā* and the other forms of *Vyakti* are generally influenced by the predominance of one or the other of the determinant causes in the nature of an individnal,—such as, *Sattwa*, *Rajas*, *Tamas*, *Kāla* and *Jeeva*,—at any particular period. Hence desires and actions of different individuals are found to be directed towards different kinds of objects, good or bad, and even in the case of the same individual they take different directions at different times or at different stages of the development of his life.

Gorakhnath regards *Māyā* as a form of expression of the human individuality. It appears to consist in giving undue importance to one's own individual self and its interests and for that reason dealing falsely with others. It is one of the bad traits of the human nature, which have to be controlled and transcended by means of voluntary self-discipline and self-enlightenment, which are higher forms of self-expression. *Māyā* is described as having five forms. First, *Mada*, which means intoxication with a sense of pride or vanity and the desires and actions originating from it. Second, *Mātsarya*, which means an attitude of intolerance and envy and malice towards the happiness and prosperity and even the good qualities of others and the tendencies and actions originating from it. Third, *Dambha*, which implies the self-conceited expression of one's own superiority in the presence of others, overvaluing one's own deeds and achievements and powers and under-valuing those of others. Fourth, *Kritrimatwa*, which implies artificiality and duplicity in behaviour, an attempt to appear as what one is not, so as to create false impressions upon the minds of others. Fifth, *Asatya*, which implies having recourse to untruth or falsehood in speech and action and gestures for one's own self-aggrandisement. These are called by Gorakhnath the five forms of expression of *Māyā* in the active nature of man. They show the predominance of *Rajas* and *Tamas* in the nature of a man. They play their parts in the growth of the individuality of a man in the lower planes; but they are there to be conquered and transcended by aspirants for ascending to the higher planes of human personality.

The fourth kind of *Vyakti* (expression of individuality) is called by Gorakhnath *Prakriti*. *Prakriti* also is described as manifested in five forms. First, *Āśā*, which means hope for future prospects, which induces an individual to make efforts for achieving them. Second, *Trishnā*, which implies thirst for more and more. Third, *Sprihā*, which means desire for the attainment and appropriation of particular enjoyable objects. Fourth, *Kānkshā*, which implies ambition for greatness. Fifth, *Mithyā*, which in this context implies dreaming of the achievement of things beyond one's reach,—false hopes and aspirations. These are indications of the temperament of an individual, from which they evolve. They may be directed towards earthly things or towards higher ideals. They are self-expressions of the individual mind and contribute to its development.

The fifth form of *Vyakti* is *Vāk*. *Vāk* or speech has, according to Gorakhnath, five stages, viz, *Parā*, *Paśyanti*, *Madhyamā*, *Vaikhari* and *Mātrikā*. At the stage of *Parā*, *Vāk* or speech is wholly identified with consciousness. It is present in the consciousness in the form of an urge or will for self-expression, without any manifestation even in the form of a subtle sound or even in the form of an idea. This *Parā Vāk* is often described in the scriptures as *Śabda-Brahma*. In it *Śabda* or sound, being wholly unmanifested in any specialised form, is conceived as absolutely unified with its ultimate origin, Brahma or the Supreme Consciousness, the Soul of the individual as well as of the cosmic system. It is there in the form of Śakti or power immanent in the Consciousness. All the diverse forms of speech,—nay, all the various kinds of sounds,—have their origin in *Parā-Vāk*, and they are all perfectly unified therein. This *Parā-Vāk* is regarded as the ultimate self-shining form of *Pranava* (*OM*), which is the Sound of all sounds, the true Essence of all sounds, the Ground of Unity of all orders of sounds and speeches. In this *Parā-Vāk* there is no differentiation of *Vāk* from *Cit*, which is its ultimate seat and source.

At the stage of *Paśyanti*, *Vāk* is manifested in the form of subtle ideas, which the consciousness directly sees or perceives. *Vāk* is at this stage differentiated from the pure consciousness and becomes the object of its inner perception, and the consciousness finds itself expressed and objectified in the flow of ideas. This is the *ideal* form of *Vāk*, which though differentiated from the consciousness exists in and for the consciousness and has no manifestation in the gross physical organism. It is not manifested in any articulate sound-form, *Vāk* is here manifested in the mental plane, but not in the physical or the vital plane. But the urge or the will for self-expression in these grosser planes powerfully acts upon the physiological embodiment.

At the stage of *Madhyamā*, *Vāk* is manifested in the form of some upheaval in the physiological system, some organised vibrations in the vital and physical instruments whose coordinated activity is necessary for the vocal expression of the mental ideas, some spontaneously regulated movements in the vocal organs for expressing the ideas and feelings in the gross forms of uttered speech. *Madhyamā-Vāk* stands midway between the ideal form of speech and the articulate sound-form of speech, between mental speech and vocal speech. At this stage certain subtle sounds are produced within the physiological system in course of the internal effort to give outer expression to inner speech. *Vāk* is still within the body and has no outer manifestation in the forms of words and sentences.

At the stage of *Vaikhari*, *Vāk* comes out through the co-operative efforts of the vocal organs in the form of articulate speech or uttered words audible to the sense of hearing of others. It is through *Vaikhari Vāk* that an individual can communicate his mental ideas to other individuals and enable others to know and share his thoughts and feelings and desires. It is through a very complex physiological process that *Vaikhari Vāk* is produced, but due to the most wonderful organisation of the vital and physical instruments in the human body and as a result of learning and habit this process becomes almost spontaneous in well-developed individual bodies. In the absence of the proper development of the organs of speech as well as in the absence of proper learning and habit, the capacity for *Vaikhari Vāk* can not be properly developed. In case of the diseased condition of the organs or of the physiological system *Vaikhari Vāk* is adversely affected and sometimes wholly obstructed. *Vaikhari Vāk* is the most highly valuable and potent means of self-expression to the human individual. In its absence there would be no culture, no civilization, no society, no possibility of enlightenment, no possibility of self-realisation, in the human species. It is through the medium of *Vaikhari Vāk* that all kinds of development and progress have been possible. All human languages are the embodiments of *Vaikhari Vāk*.

According to Gorakhnath, the fifth stage of *Vāk* is *Mātrikā*. *Mātrikā* refers to the ultimate phonetic constituents of *Vaikhari Vāk*. All words (*pada*) and sentences (*vākya*, consisting of words or *padas* related to one another), in the forms of which *Vaikhari Vāk* of all human beings of all races and countries and epochs and climates may be expressed, are found on analysis and reflection to be constituted of a certain number of ultimate verbal sounds, which are represented by *varna* or *akshara* (letters). These are the units of vocal speech. They cannot be further analysed or divided. They are regarded by many schools of philosophers as *nitya* (eternal) in the cosmic order, while words and sentences composed of them are *anitya* (non-eternal) and as such are produced and destroyed. They are the seeds (*bīja*) of all languages, of all forms of articulate speech. They are accordingly called *Mātrikā*, from which all kinds of words and sentences of the apparently diverse forms of languages in the world are evolved. Though they are the roots of all vocal speech, they usually appear as uncognizably intermingled with words and sentences evolved from them. Their essential characters and deeper significance are discovered by enlightened persons after a good deal of reflection and contemplation. Later on, when linguistic study is developed in the society, students may begin with the study of letters and then proceed to the study of the formation of words and sentences out of them.

It may be noted here that according to the *Siddha-Yogi* and the *Tāntrika* schools the root-letters (*Mātrikā-Varna*) are not merely the ultimate constituents of articulate speech (*Vaikhari-Vāk*) or of words and sentences. They have by dint of the deepest reflection and meditation entered into the inner spirit of these letters and discovered that each letter is a particularised sound-embodiment of Śiva-Śakti and is associated with and manifested from a particular centre within the living physical body. Each letter is accordingly surcharged with a vital force and a spiritual meaning. In order to exhibit distinctly the Śiva-aspect and the Śakti aspect in these root-letters, each letter is pronounced with a *Bindu* (which sounds like *m* in utterance) attached to it. It is said.—

Bindu Śivātmako Bīja Śaktir Nādas tayor mithah
Samavāya iti khyātah sarvāgama-viśāradaih.

Bindu denotes *Śiva* and *Bīja* denotes *Śakti*. *Nāda* evolves from the mutual communion between them. This is well-known to those who are versed in all the *Āgamas*.

Thus the adepts in *Yoga* perceive the communion of Śiva and Śakti in every elementary sound (*Nāda*) and in every letter representing it. Śiva is the common unchanged Soul of all sounds and letters, and this is indicated by the *Bindu* attached to every letter. Śakti assumes the diversified forms of sounds and letters *(Nāda* and *Varna)*. All forms of articulate speech, all forms of verbal expressions of mental ideas, all kinds of words and sentences uttered apparently by human tongues (and recorded in various written forms), are complex manifestations of original *Nāda* and *Varna*. Yogis therefore perceive the self-manifestations of Śiva-Śakti in all of them.

The Yogis have traced the location of the root-letters and root-sounds in particular vital centres of the body, which are called *Cakra*. Details about this need not be discussed here. In the *Mantra-Yoga* practised by the Yogis these root-letters and root-sounds are developed into *Mantra*, having deep spiritual significance. *Mantras* are not mere symbols conveying some spiritual concepts, but they are charged with great potency. Repetition of the *Mantras* according to prescribed methods reveals the powers inherent in them, and it leads to the development of various psychical and spiritual capacities in the *sādhakas* as well as the attainment of many occult experiences. An adept can work wonders and perform miracles by activating the mysterious powers of the *Bīja-Mantras*. Among all *Bīja-Mantras, OM (Pranava)* is universally regarded as having a unique position. It is the perfect embodiment of Śiva-*S*akti. (S. S. P. I. 56-61).

(5) *Pratyaksha-Karana-Pancaka*:—

Gorakhnath then mentions some other subsidiary efficient and material causes which practically contribute to the maintenance and development and also renewal of the Individual body and which also require to be duly controlled and regulated for the realisation of the ultimate ideal of human life. These he calls *Pratyaksha-Karana-Pancaka*. He enumerates them as, *Karma*, *Kāma*, *Candra*, *Surya* and *Agni*. The influence of these upon the bodily life of an individual are quite perceptible (*pratyaksha*), though they often operate in subtle ways.

Karma means action or deed. Right and wrong actions, performed by an individual through his bodily limbs and sense-organs and mental thoughts and desires, exert direct beneficial and injurious influences upon his life, and their psychological and moral effects greatly determine the course of his future life and even future birth. Gorakhnath in his usual manner enumerates fivefold characters of *Karma*, viz, *Śubha* (good actions, bringing beneficial consequences to the doer) *Aśubha* (bad actions, bringing evil consequences to the doer), *Yaśah* (actions which are approved and praised by others and bring temporary or lasting fame to the doer), *Apakīrti* (actions which are blamed and condemned by others and which therefore create bad reputation or notoriety for the doer), and *Adrista-*

phala-sādhanā (righteous and unrighteous deeds which produce moral and religious merits (*punya*) and demerits (*pāpa*) for the doer and which thereby *invisibly* become the causes of happiness or misery and favourable or unfavourable conditions in future life in the present body as well as in bodies to which he may pass after the death of the present body.

Every action performed by an individual is believed to produce three kinds of *phala* or effects. The first is called *drista-phala*, which literally means *visible* effects, i.e. effects whose causal relation with the action can be directly perceived and established by means of our senses. These are the outer results of our actions. Taking nutritious food satisfies our hunger and helps the nourishment of the body. When one man does any injury to another out of any selfish motive, the injured man suffers and the injurer gains. All such cases are cases of *drista-phala*. We actually experience such effects of our actions in our worldly life. Some actions bring to us pleasure and prosperity and others become sources of pain and poverty, some actions make us objects of praise and honour and others objects of condemnation and dishonour. Our actions affect the interests of others, and others, actions affect our interests. All these are instances of *drista-phala*. Secondly, our actions produce corresponding *samskāra* (impressions) in our mind, which become the causes of our dispositions and tendencies and desires and attachments and aversions and thus influence our future actions. It is by our actions that our habits and characters are moulded. As we act, so we become. This is called the psychological effect (*samskāra-phala*) of our actions.

According to the *yogi* school, and in fact according to all the important systems of Indian thought, the psychological effects of our actions are very far-reaching. Many of our actions produce such deep-rooted *samskāras* in the mind that they are not destroyed even by our physical death. The psychical organism does not die with the physical organism. The physical organism becomes disorganised in course of time and its constituents are dissolved in the *Panca-Mahābhutas*. But the psychical organism retains its individuality even after this death and carries with it the *samskāras* which are produced by the actions of the life-time. The psychical organism, carrying the *samskāras* which become part and parcel of its nature, may exist in a subtle embodiment (*liṅga-śarīra*) for a certain period, and may after that be associated with a new physical organism (*bhautika-piṇḍa*) for its further course of self-expression and self-fulfilment. In this new body also the old *samskāras* produced by the actions performed in the previous embodied life exercise great influence in the forms of instinctive tendencies and propensities and capacities for adjustments with the new circumstances. Thus our nature in the current embodied life has to a great extent been constituted by the psychological effects of our deeds of the past embodied life or lives, and the nature of our future embodied life also will be similarly moulded by the *samskāras* which are being produced by our deeds in the present life. It is to be noted that in the human life there is ample scope for the exercise of freedom in all the fields of our active self-expression for the destruction of the old evil *Samskāras* and the development of new good *samskāras* through the voluntary performance of righteous actions and thus for a considerable transformation of our psychological nature and advancement towards higher and higher orders of life.

Thirdly, our saints and philosophers aver that every action,—and particularly every voluntary and deliberate action,—produces some *adrista-phala* in the forms of moral and religious merits and demerits (*punya* and *pāpa*, *dharma* and *adharma*), which are rewarded and punished in due course in accordance with the law of the cosmic order, the rewards being in the forms of happinesses or greater opportunities in life or higher levels of existence, and the punishments being in the forms of sufferings or unfavourable conditions of life or lower levels of existence. Virtuous deeds produce good *adrista* and vicious deeds bad *adrista. Adrista* is also called *apurva*, and it greatly determines the future destinies of individuals. Often this *apurva* or *adrista-phala* of actions is designated as *Karma* in scriptures. Like the psychological effect, this moral effect also is not generally exhausted in the same bodily life. It becomes the cause of happinesses and miseries, favourable and unfavourable conditions, developed or degraded levels of existence, in the disembodied life after death and in the future bodily life as well. Cultivation of virtue and avoidance of vice is of prime importance for progressive and enjoyable life. The constitution of our physical body also is greatly influenced by these three kinds of effects of our actions. What is generally known as the *Law of Karma* refers specially to the *adrista-phala* of actions, which indicates the principle of moral justice in the cosmic order.

Yogiguru Gorakhnath mentions *Kāma* as the second *Pratyaksha-karana* for the birth and growth of living individual organisms in the cosmic system. Here the term *Kāma* appears to be used by him in the restricted sense of sexual instinct, which is universally present in the nature of living beings and which plays an essential part in the multiplication of living creatures in the world. It is one of the fundamental laws of the cosmic play of Śiva-Śakti that living creatures in general are born through a process of sexual intercourse between a male and a female and they are themselves divided into males and females. This is more prominently manifested in the cases of *jarāyuja* animals (animals that are first born in the wombs of mothers and all whose limbs and organs are differentiated and manifested therein before coming out to the earth) and *andaja* animals (those that come out from their mothers in the forms of eggs and whose organs are evolved out of the eggs thereafter). Men are the highest among the *jarāyuja* animals. The birth of other living bodies also is somehow or other governed by the same rule of sexual intercourse. Through sexual connection *Bindu* or *Bīja* or *Śukra* (semen) is excreted from the paternal body and infused into the womb of the maternal body, where it is combined with *Rajas* or *Śonita* or *Rakta* (blood) secreted from the latter. The combination of these two gives birth to a new individual living body, with the dynamic potentiality to develop gradually under favourable conditions the physical features and other internal characteristics of the parents and the species. Thus by the Divine plan *Kāma* plays a very essential role in the evolution of various orders of living beings in the Cosmic Body of Śiva-Śakti. In the nature of diverse orders of living beings (*jeeva*), *Kāma* also is found to play its part in diverse ways.

According to Gorakhnath, in the nature of the higher orders of animals, and specially in the nature of the human species, five characteristics of *Kāma* appear prominently,—viz, *Rati, Prīti, Krīdā, Kāmanā* and *Āturatā*. *Rati* means sexual attachment or infatuation between a male and a female. *Prīti* means pleasure or happiness which is enjoyed by both in their mutual companionship and which develops their mutual attachment and love. *Krīdā* means sports or games which gratify their sexual passions. *Kāmanā* means desire for more and more enjoyment, more and more intimate companionship, more and more gratification of lust. *Āturatā* means exhaustion or loss of strength and enthusiasm as the result of excessive gratification of the lustful desires and hence a temporary reaction against it. However, the importance of *Kāma* in the scheme of creation is undeniable and easily demonstrable. It is through the operation of *Kāma* that men are born. *Kāma* is instrumental also in the development of many of their physical and vital organs as well as many of their mental attributes.

Gorakhnath mentions *Candra*. *Surya* and *Agni* (Moon, Sun and Fire) as the other three *Pratyaksha-Karana*, exercising their influence upon the evolution of life in this world. The physical effects of the Sun, the Moon and Fire and their bearings on our life and the lives of all creatures are evident to all thinking people. Without them life would have been impossible on earth. Days and nights, fortnightly changes, changes of seasons, changes of temperatures and climatic conditions, distribution of rain, changes in the atmospheric conditions, tides in the seas, fertility of the soil, etc., upon which life greatly depends, are due to the apparent movements of the Sun and the Moon round the Earth and Heat within her bosom. In the Veda the Sun has often been described as the Soul of all earthly existences, living as well as non-living (*Surya ātmā jagatas tasthushas ca*). It is also said that 'rain comes from the Sun, food comes from rain, and food sustains the life of all that are born (*Ādityād jāyate vṛṣṭiḥ vṛṣṭer · annam tatah prajāh*). The Sun raises vapour from the seas and rivers to the skies, this vapour being condensed comes down in the form of rain and is distributed upon the land-surfaces of the earth and makes them fit for the growth of food-materials, upon which living creatures depend for their sustenance and development. The Moon with its cool and soothing rays contributes a good deal to the development of life. In the Scriptures *Candra* is conceived as *Soma* full of life-giving juice (*rasa*). In the Gītā Bhagawān Śrikrishna says, 'I manifest myself as *Soma* or *Candra* full of life-giving juice and thereby nourish all kinds of plants (*pushnāmi coushadhih sarvāḥ somo bhutwā rasātmakah*). The importance of Fire for the nourishment of life is quite obvious to all. The Heat conserved in the bosom of the Earth plays a significant part in keeping its surface fit for the habitation of living beings. Heat is a sign of a living body; when it is deprived of heat, it is known to be dead and its decomposition begins. The utility and necessity of Fire for the preservation and development of our physical existence cannot be overemphasised. Thus, *Candra, Surya* and *Agni*, in their physical senses, are aptly regarded as perceptible instrumental causes of life.

But to the Yogis *Candra, Surya* and *Agni* have some deeper meanings, which are not obvious to ordinary people. They see *Candra, Surya* and *Agni* within the living body and find that it is upon the properly regulated and harmonious operations of these three elements or forces in the body that the healthy preservation and development of life depends. The living body is primarily built up by food (*anna*) and its proper assimilation and transformation into the various forms of live tissues and organs. The physical body is accordingly called *annamaya-kosha* (body made of food). Food, which is generally taken in from the outside world, is first converted into *rasa* (a fluid substance), and this *rasa* is gradually transformed into *rakta* (blood), *meda* (lumps of flesh), *māmsa* (muscles), *asthi* (bones), *majjā* (nerve-substance) and *sukra* (semen). These are called *sapta-dhātu* (seven ingredients of the living body) in the *Ayurveda*. Out of them all the organs are formed in accordance with the nature of the species to which the individuals belong, by some Divine plan. Heredity is found to play a leading part in the formation of the structure of the body and even of the mind. All these formations are ultimately dependent upon food and its assimilation and metabolic transformation.

Now, according to yogic terminology, *Candra* (Moon) represents that power within the living organism which makes food (*anna*) capable of being so assimilated and metabolized as to build up the diverse parts and tissues and organs of the body in accordance with the specific potentiality of the organism or the ideal immanent in the essential character of the organism. It thus supplies the materials for the building up of the body. It is often referred to as *Soma* and as the source of all *Rasa* (which is the essence of all food-materials). It is described as the source of all nourishment, the source of delight and vivacity, and as constituting the *bhogya* (materials capable of being consumed and absorbed into the system) in every living body. *Surya* (Sun) and *Agni* (Fire) are conceived as powers (within the living organism), which assimilate and metabolize the food, which absorb the food-materials into the system and convert them into the necessary ingredients and tissues and organs for fuller growth of the organism. They also contribute to the development of vital and mental strength and vigour and alertness and brilliance and even to the development of intellectual and moral and spiritual powers by drawing forth materials for these higher orders of phenomenal realities from the digested and transformed physical food. *Surya* and *Agni* are accordingly spoken of *Bhoktā* (consumer). Every living organism is conceived as *Bhoktri-Bhogyātmaka* (consisting of the consumer and the consumable, the eater and the eatable, the power to absorb aud objects to be absorbed). It is the unification of these two aspects that constitutes the indivinual living body. In this sense it is also spoken of as *agni-somātmaka* (consisting of *agni* and *soma*). Here *agni* represents both *surya* and *agni*. Sometimes the whole world is described as "*Agni-Somātmakam Jagat*", implying that the whole phenomenal world is evolved through the union of the duality of *Bhoktā-Bhogya*.

Candra, *Surya* and *Agni* are thus conceived as cosmic forces as well as biological forces in individual living bodies. There is constant interaction between the biological forces and the cosmic forces. In truth, the biological forces are the particularised manifestation of the cosmic forces. The growth of individual life is entirely dependent upon the favourable operations of the cosmic forces. The wonderful interactions among the forces of heat and light and wind and water and earth, the gravitational, the magnetic, the chemical, the electrical and the mechanical forces, and all other forces that are playing their parts in the physical cosmic body of Śiva-Śakti, exercise their influence upon the growth of individual life on this earth and upon the biological phenomena occurring within the individual body. The forces within the living body have to adjust themselves suitably with the external forces and to develop the body through their cooperative functions. All these external and internal forces are, according to the Yogi school, diversified self-manifestations of the Divine *Śakti*. Yogis perceive the cosmic system mirrored and operative in every bodily system. They see *Kāma* and *Karma* also as the expressions of cosmic life in individual life.

Gorakhnath describes *Candra* as having 17 *kalās, Surya* as having 13 *kalās,* and *Agni* as having 11 *kalās. Kalās* appear to mean the diverse kinds of forces (*śakti*) which enmanate from them and perform their functions in distinctive ways for the preservation and development of the individual living bodies as well as for the maintenance of harmony and order and freshness and beauty and grandeur of the cosmic system. 16 *kalās* of *Candra,* 12 *kalās* of *Surya* and 10 *kalās* of *Agni* are said to be actively operative in the individual bodies and the cosmic body, while each of them has one essential *kalā,* which keeps it in direct spiritual touch with the Supreme Spirit, by virtue of which its innermost nature is always illumined and blissful and in respect of which there is fundamental unity of all the three. In truth, *Candra, Surya* and *Agni* are manifestations of the same *Mahā-Śakti* of *Śiva* and hence they are essentially non-different from one another. Ultimately, *Bhoktā* and *Bhogya* (the consumers and the materials for their consumption) are one, and in their ultimate nature all *bhoktā-bhogya* relations vanish. In the enlightened view of the *Yogis, Karma, Kāma, Candra, Surya* and *Agni* are all ultimately playful self-manifestations of *Śiva-Śakti,* appearing in diverse forms.

The 16 active *kalās* of *Candra* are named, *Ullolā, Kallolinī, Uccalantī, Unmādinī, Taramginī, Śoshinī, Lampatā, Pravṛtti, Lahari, Lolā, Lelihānā, Prasarantī, Pravāhā, Saumyā, Prasannatā* and *Plavantī.* The names (in Sanskrit) give some vague ideas about their distinctive characters and functions. It would be futile to attempt to translate these terms and to explain the distinctive functions of these *kalās* in the living body or the world-order. No clear conception can be expected therefrom. The 17th or the essential *kalā* of *Candra* is called *Nivṛtti* , which has no active phenomenal function in the building up of the living body, but which is conceived to be the ultimate *bhogya,* the ultimate essence of all food-materials and all objects of enjoyment, which being attained, there should be cessation (*nivṛtti*) of all struggles for the preservation of life, and life should attain immortality (*amritatwa*). This is therefore also named *Amṛta-kalā.* The aim of a Yogi is to tranecend the domain of all the other phenomenally active 16 *kalās* and to enjoy the bliss of the

17th *Amrita-kalā*, through the practice of the deepest concentration of energy.

The 12 active *Kalās* of *Surya* are named, *Tāpinī*, *Grāsikā*, *Ugrā*, *Ākuncanī*. *Śoshinī*, *Prabodhanī*, *Smarā*, *Ākarshinī*, *tuṣṭivardhinī*,. *Urmirekhā*, *Kiranavatī*, and *Prabhāvatī*. These powers of *Surya* perform distinctive functions in the various transformations of the earthly phenomena as well as in the various transformations of the food-materials within the individual bodies. The 13th *kalā*, which is called its *Nijā-kalā* and which does not take any direct part either in the cosmic or in the bodily operations, is *Swaprakāśatā* (self-luminosity). In respect of this *Nijā-kalā* or essential character, *Surya* appears as identified with the Supreme Spirit, Who is the ultimate *Bhoktā* or Consumer and Enjoyer of all diversities, which are nothing but His own delightful self-expressions.

The 10 active *kalās* of *Agni* are named, *Dipikā*, *Rajikā*, *Jwālini*, *Visphulinginī*, *Pracandā*, *Pācika*, *Roudrī*, *Dāhikā*, *Rāginī*, *Śikhāvatī*. The 11th *kalā*, which is its own transcendent *kalā*, is named *Jyoti* (pure light), which is in direct union with the Supreme Spirit, the Illuminer and Life-giver and consumer of all. In Vedic texts *Surya*, *Agni* and *Candra* are often glorified as *Brahma*.

Thus it appears that *Candra*, *Surya* and *Agni* have not only their individual and cosmic aspects, but also their transcendent aspects. They not only play their important parts in the building up of individual living bodies and in the maintenance of the cosmic process, but also in revealing the transcendent self-luminous self-brilliant blissful character of Śiva-Śakti. Yogis, concentrating their attention upon the essential characters of *Candra*, *Surya* and *Agni* within themselves and in the cosmic system, find out that they are ultimately non-different from one another and that Śiva is manifest in them in glorious forms.

(S.S.P.I. 62-67).

(6) *Nāḍi Samsthāna or the Nervous System.*

The Yogi school attaches great importance to the knowledge of the nervous system for the understanding of the constitution of the individual body, and particularly the human body. The nervous system wonderfully organises all the parts of the body with one another and plays the most effective role in demonstrating the oneness of the entire body. The nerves (*Nāḍi*) are the finest and most sensitive substances evolved within the individual living body in course of its growth. In the higher and higher orders of living beings they are more and more diversified and more and more organised. In the adult human body the nervous system is most complex, most organised, most sensitive and active. The nerves are said to be infinite in number, they pervade all parts of the body, they are interconnected, and all together constitute one system.

The nerves are the chief instruments through which the active propensities of the mind are carried to each and every limb and organ of the body, the impressions produced upon the organs and limbs are carried to the mind, the mind and the body as a whole respond to react upon the diverse kinds of affections of the different parts of the body, and so on. Different nerves are directly connected with different parts of the body, and they extend even to the extremeties of the hair and the nails. Different kinds of nerves perform different kinds of functions. Some are afferent nerves and some are efferent nerves. Some contribute specially to sensation and perception and knowledge, some specially to passions and emotions and excitements, some specially to movements and exertions and actions, some to respiration, some to metabolism, some to distribution of energy, and so on. But they all have a common centre, a common source, a common purpose. They all play their parts for maintaining the harmony and unity of the psycho-physiological organism and adjusting it properly with its environments and the cosmic order. The nerves appear to serve as the links between the mind and the physical body.

The Yogi teachers, while recognising that the *Nāḍis* are countless, mention that there are at least seventytwo thousand *Nāḍis* throughout the body. They also assert that all of them have their common source in what they call *Mula-Kanda. Mula-Kanda* is said to be the most vital part of the body, located in some spot above the origin of the generating organ and below the centre of the navel, within the spinal column. It is from this vital centre that all the *nāḍis* are evolved, and they spread in all directions over the whole body, in upward, downward, sideward, straight and zigzag courses. The brain and the spinal column play the most important role in the nervous system. The brain, which is called *Sahasrāra-Cakra* (a wheel of a thousand spokes or a thousand-petalled Lotus), is the chief instrument through which Reason and Moral Consciousness and Enlightened Mind reveal themselves and exercise their influence upon the whole organism. This is the supreme part of the nervous system. The Spinal Cord standing in the middle of the body keeps up the balance of the whole organism. Other nerves are joined to the Spinal Cord. The Spinal Cord is often called *Brahma-danda* or *Meru-danda.*

In this wonderful network of *Nāḍis* issuing from the *Mula-kanda* and interlinking all parts of the body, seventytwo are regarded by the yogis as prominent and conspicuous. Of these seventytwo again, ten are considered to be specially important, in as much as they are connected with the important outer organs, through which the individual body perceptibly interacts with the outer world. They also exercise considerable influence upon the other nerves. They are specially named by Gorakhnath in *Siddha-Siddhanta-Paddhati* as, *Sushumnā*, *Iḍā, Pingalā, Saraswati, Pushā, Alambushā, Gāndhāri, Hasti-jihvikā, Kuhu*, and *Śamkhinī*.

Of these again, *Sushumnā* is the most important *Nāḍi* from the *yogic* point of view. It is often called *Brahma-Nāḍi*. Arising from *Mulakanda*, *Sushumnā* passes from *Mulādhāra* through *Brahma danda* (spinal cord) up to *Brahma-randhra* in the *Sahasrāra* (cerebrum). *Sushumnā* as the central *Nāḍi* plays the most significant role in the development of our intellectual and moral and spiritual life. It is the path in which our vital and mental energy moves upward for the realisation of the supreme ideal in the highest plane of experience. It is the fine path through which *Kundalinī Śakti*, which normally lies asleep as it were in *Mulādhāra*, rises up when awakened for being consciously united with Śiva in *Sahasrāra*, which is often called the capital-city of Śiva. When all energy is concentrated in *Sushumnā* and ascends through it to the highest plane in *Sahasrāra*, the individual consciousness is spiritually illumined by the transcendent self-luminosity of Śiva. But this is not the place for the elaboration of this topic. Suffice it to say here, that *Sushumnā* is the most central and most important *Nāḍi* in the whole system.

Next in importance to *Sushumnā* are *Iḍā* and *Pingalā*. They also issue out from the same common centre, and flowing by either side of *Sushumnā* they are said to be connected with the two nostrils and to be united in a vital centre just between the two visual organs. They are conceived as in the service of all the respiratory organs. As respiration occupies a very important position in the preservation and harmonisation and development of the individual life and as through the control and regulation of the process of respiration most of the vital organs can be brought under voluntary control and their operations regulated according to will and purpose, the importance of *Iḍā* and *Pingalā* cannot from the *yogic* point of view be overestimated. The Yogis speak of *Iḍā* as *Candra-Nāḍi* and *Pingalā* as *Surya-Nāḍī*, the former being connected with the left nostril and latter with the right nostril. They are regarded as on the two sides of *Sushumnā*. Their pulsations are vitally interconnected with movements of *Prāna-Vāyu*. Our vital energy is normally restless, and it moves round and round through *Iḍā* and *Pingalā* with every breath, and through them passes on to other *Nāḍīs* and vitalises the different organs.

With the restlessness of the vital energy our mental energy also moves on restlessly. They are very closely related. A *yogi* through the systematic practice of breath-control can bring the restless movements of the vital and mental energy under his voluntary control and can even bring them to a state of perfect rest. Control of breath and control of the movements of *Iḍā* and *Pingalā* play a very important part in this yogic discipline. *Iḍā* and *Pingalā* can be unified in *Sushumnā* and thereby the whole energy may be concentrated for truth-realisation.

Saraswatī-Nāḍī is connected with the mouth, the organ of speech. It thus connects the vocal instruments with the rest of the body and with the brain and makes them duly responsive to will and thought and sensations and emotions. *Pushā* and *Alambushā* are two *Nāḍīs,* which are conceived as connected with the two retinas and eye-balls, the organs of sight. They in cooperation with the other minor *nāḍis* carry the ocular sensations to the brain, the chief instrument of the mind. Similarly, *Gāndhārī* and *Hastijihvikā* are the names of two *nāḍīs* connected with the two ears, and all auditory sensations are conveyed by them. *Kuhu* is a *nāḍī* connected with the anus or the organ for excreting the waste and refuse materials from the body. *Śamkhinī* is the *nāḍī* which is specially connected with the generating organ.

These ten are mentioned by Yogiguru Gorakhnath as the principal *nāḍīs* (*mukhyā-nāḍī*) connected with the principal organs of perception and action and respiration. But, as it has been noted, according to him and his yogi school the *Nāḍīs* are innumerable and they form a network pervading all the parts of the physiological organism. They are inter-linked and they are said to be always in a flowing condition (*vahati*). They carry energy from every part of the body to every other part of the body, and thus unify the whole system. They originate from one common centre of energy and flow on in diverse courses to all the parts and enliven and energize them and unite them with the centre. Some other details about the *Nāḍī-Mandal* and *Nāḍī-Cakra* will have to be discussed in the sequel from the specially *yogic* point of view.

It has been occasionally remarked that the viewpoint of the yogi school is primarily practical and only secondarily theoretical. The analysis of the constitution of the individual body is also made primarily with the practical purpose of yogic discipline. It would be futile to attempt any empirical verification of the details of the physiological findings of the Yogis by the experimental methods generally adopted by modern sciences. We need not compare the discoveries of the enlightened *yogi* teachers with those of the modern scientists in all cases, particularly because their view-points and methods and purposes are fundamentally different. Now, the practical purpose of a *Yogi* is to become a perfect master of his body and mind and therefore to bring the entire physiological organism (including of course the nervous system) under the control of his reason and will by dint of appropriate *yogic* discipline. He analyses the bodily constitution with that end in view. The significance of this analysis will be more clearly understood, when its application to *sādhanā* is elaborately discussed. That Gorakhnath himself was not very serious about the naming and location of these *nāḍīs* is evident from his description of them in other treatises. In *Viveka-Mārtanda* he says that *Gāndhārī* is connected with the left eye and *Hasti-jihvā* with the right eye, Pushā with the left ear and *Yaśaswini* with the right ear, *Alambushā* is connected with the mouth, *Kuhu* with the sexual organ and *Śamkhinī* with the anus. Here he does not mention *Saraswatī*, but mentions *Yaśaswini* instead.

(7) *Vāyu-Sansthāna*

Having briefly dealt with the important functions of the *Nādīs* in the living body, Gorakhnath discusses the operations of *Vāyu* in the system. It is *Vāyu* which principally activates and moves all the internal organs of the body and helps the proper functioning of all its parts. *Vāyu* constantly draws materials from the outer atmosphere for the continuous refreshment of the bodily organs, it helps the assimilation of food and drink and their distribution in all parts of the body, it maintains the circulation of blood and helps the processes of secretion in the different organs, it keeps the living organism internally and externally active at all times during the periods of waking and dreaming and sleeping. It serves all the *nādīs*, it serves *Candra*, *Surya* and *Agni*, in the due performance of their functions, it moves throughout all parts of the body to keep them active and fresh. In relation to the living body *Vāyu* is conceived as the vital energy and is accordingly called *Prāna-Śakti*.

Though *Vāyu* or *Prāna-Śakti* is essentially one in the whole body, it is conceived as tenfold and given ten distinct names in accordance with the different functions *(vritti)* it performs in different parts of the living organism. One *Vāyu* operates as ten *Vāyus*. They are called, *Prāna*, *Apāna*, *Samāna*, *Udāna*, *Vyāna*, *Nāga*, *Kurma*, *Krikara (Krikala)*, *Devadatta* and *Dhananjaya*. Of these the first five are regarded as primary and the last five as secondary. The first one, *Prāna*, is given the place of honour. Its seat or centre is said to be in the *Hridaya* (heart, though this heart should not be identified with the heart of modern physiology). It is specially concerned with the process of respiration and as such with the main *nādis*,

Idā and *Pingalā*. It energises and activates all the organs connected with and affected by the vital functions of breathing-in and breathing-out. It is obvious to everybody, to every living creature,—that the normal operations of all the organs within the bodily system are dependent upon the regular and unimpeded continuity of the breathing process. The complete stoppage of the breathing process means death. It is not a gross exaggeration to say that breath is life (of course, imperfect phenomenal life). Through the successful control of the breathing process, Yogis acquire control over the whole bodily organism. The breathing process appears to be the main channel through which there is continuous interaction between the vital energy in the individual body and the inexhaustible storehouse of vital energy in the cosmic system.

The second important *Vāyu* is named *Apāna*. Its seat or centre of activity is said to be located near about the anus (*guda*). It energises and activates all the organs of the lower parts of the main body. It helps the organs in clearing out all the impurities and unnecessary materials which may be produced and accumulated within and around them in various forms. Its functions are closely connected with and complementary to those of *Prāna*. *Prāna* constantly introduces into the body fresh air and fresh energy and activates the organs to assimilate and metabolize food-materials and transform them into living parts of the organism; and *Apāna* constantly works for moving out the used-up air and energy and driving away the surplus and useless and injurious materials that are often produced and accumulated in course of the process of metabolism and the operations of the different organs. *Prāna* and *Apāna*, in cooperation with *Candra* and *Surya* and *Agni* (in the *yogic* sense) and also with *Candra-Nāḍi* (*Iḍā*) and *Surya-Nāḍi* (*Pingalā*), are regarded by the Yogi school as playing very essential roles in the wonderful organisation of the bodily system. We may in this connection recollect the beautiful words of Lord Śri Krishna in the *Gītā*,—

Aham Vaiśwānaro bhutwa prāninām deham āśritah
Prānāpāna-samāyuktah pacāmyannam caturvidham.

I (God Himself) having become *Vaiśwānara-Agni* (all-consuming fire within the abdomen) manifest Myself within the bodies of creatures and being united with *Prāna* and *Apāna* digest the four kinds of food-materials. The purport of these Divine words is that even the most natural bodily function of the digestion of food is, truly speaking, performed by God Himself; the power of assimilation of food and drink, the power of respiration, the power of excretion of unnecessary and harmful materials from the body, the power of transformation of nutritious food into living tissues and diverse complicated organs.—all these are really the manifestations of the Divine Power, the self-expressions of Śiva-Śakti. That is also the real import of all these dissertations of Gorakhnath about the apparently most complicated bodily system and the various kinds of powers manifested in it.

Samāna-Vāyu is regarded as having its seat and centre in the region of the navel and its chief function is considered to be to enkindle (*deepana*) the fire (*agni*) in the stomach and the intestines and thereby to increase the power of assimilation (*pacana*). *Vyāna-Vāyu* is conceived as moving about in all parts of the body, infusing fresh energy and agility into all the nerves and organs and making equitable distribution of nourishment among them. It greatly helps in keeping up the balance among different parts of this complicated mechanism. *Udāna-Vāyu* is conceived as located in the region of the throat (*kantha*). It activates the organs for easily swallowing food and drink and also for vomiting out what is rejected by the system. It also helps in the spontaneous movements of the organs of speech.

Among the other five *Vāyus*, *Nāga* is conceived as pervading the entire body and as contributing to the stoutness and strength and balanced movements of the body. *Kurma-Vāyu* is said to be the chief cause of the involuntary shaking of the body or its particular parts on particular occasions, and also of the spontaneous closing and opening of the eyelids, and the movements of the eyeballs. It thus helps the spontaneous adjustment of the delicate organs with unexpected circumstances. *Krikala* (or *Krikara*) is said to serve two purposes. It pushes out unassimilated gasses from the region of the stomach through the throat and the mouth and thus helps the restoration of the normal condition within the body. It also generates or intensifies hunger. *Devadatta* gives relief to the body from occasional abnormal conditions by means of certain spontaneous outbursts expressed through the mouth and other channels. Lastly, *Dhananjaya* is conceived as the *Vāyu* which pervades the whole organism and produces within the organism a continuous sound or a series of sounds (*nāda*) as an accompaniment of the operations and interactions of the various organs and various forces constantly going on for its preservation and development. It would not be an exaggeration to describe this living body as a field of continuous warfare, continuous constructive and destructive and reconstructive operations, continuous explosions and their wonderful assimilations. Various kinds of sounds, various kinds of smells, various kinds of tastes, various kinds of colours, various kinds of waves and upheavals, are being constantly produced within it. But all the operations are so miraculously designed and regulated that one harmonious system is the product.

Yogiguru Gorakhnath has presented to us a highly instructive and inspiring spiritual interpretation of the natural process of breathing of every individual living being. It is generally known that every single breath consists of three factors, viz. breathing-in (*puraka*), breathing-out (*recaka*) and a little suspension of breath (*kumbhaka*) in between the two. In normal respiration the suspension is practically imperceptible, but still in the transition between in-breathing and out-breathing there is a momentary suspension. By the exercise of our will and effort, however, we can considerably lengthen the period of suspension, and we can also lengthen the periods of in-breathing and out-breathing. In the normal course of healthy human life every single process of breathing (comprising the three factors) is completed in four seconds. Accordingly, throughout the day and night we normally breathe in and breathe out twenty one thousand and six hundred (21600) times. The calculation may not be quite accurate in all cases, since the normal breathing may be disturbed by various circumstances. Under certain conditions our respiration may be quicker and under others slower. Under diseased conditions of the body respiration may be variously affected. During waking hours and during sleeping hours, during the periods of physical exertions and during the periods of rest, at the times of mental excitement and at the times of peace and tranquillity, respiration does not continue with the same uniform speed and force. Nevertheless it is assumed that normally we breathe 21600 times during 24 hours.

Now, Gorakhnath teaches us that every time we breathe out, air passes out from within with the sound *Ham*, and every time we breathe in, air from outside passes into our body with the sound *Sah*. This we can easily perceive, if we pay close attention to our breath. This means that every creature,—and particularly every man,—is naturally and unconsciously repeating the Mantra '*Ham-sah*' '*Ham-sah*' with every breath day and night during waking as well as sleeping periods. This is a Divine design. Gorakhnath enlightens us about the deeper spiritual significance of this design. The sound *Ham* implies *Aham*, i.e. I or the individual self, and the sound *Sah* implies 'He' or the Cosmic Self,—*Brahma, Paramātmā, Śiva*. Thus with every out-breathing the individual self (*jeeva*) frees itself from the bodily limitations and goes forth to the Cosmos and identifies itself with the Soul of the Cosmic Body (*Śiva*); and with every in-breathing He,—the Soul of the Cosmos, Śiva,—enters into the body and reveals Himself as *Aham* or the individual soul. If in every breath *recaka* is supposed to precede *puraka*, the *mantra* is *Hamsah*; and if in the opposite way *puraka* is supposed to precede *recaka*, it becomes *Soham*. Both mean the same, i.e. identity of *jeeva* with *Śiva*.

Says Gorakhnath,—

Ham-kārena bahir yāti Sah-kārena viśet punah
Hamsah So'ham imam mantram jeevo japati sarvadā.

Every *jeeva* goes out with *Ham*-sound and enters again with *Sah*-sound; and thus every *jeeva* continually repeats this Mantra,—*Hamsah-So'ham.* This is called *Ajapā-Gāyatrī* and the best form of *Gāyatrī-mantra.* One is not required to repeat this *mantra* orally or with any volition and effort. *Gāyatrī* means a sacred song, by the singing of which one is delivered from all bondage. By the wonderful Divine design this great *mantra* pregnant with the highest spiritual truth is being constantly sung by every *jeeva* with every breath day and night without any effort. A *sādhaka* has only to pay deep attention to the inner meaning of his natural breath, in order to realise the identity of the individual self and the Cosmic Self and attain liberation.

Yogiguru proclaims in clear terms,—

Shat-śatāni divā-rātrau sahasrān yeka-vinśatih
Etat samkhyānwitam mantram jeevo japati sarvadā.
Ajapā nāma gāyatrī yoginām moksha-dāyini
Asyāh samkalpa-mātrena narah pāpaih vimucyate.

[*Viveka-Mārtanda*].

All through the day and the night a *jeeva* repeats the *mantra* (signifying the identity of the individual soul with the Cosmic Soul) 21600 times. This *Gāyatrī* named *Ajapā* is the giver of *moksha* (liberation from bondage) to the *Yogis* (who concentrate their attention upon this natural *japa*). By mere concentration of attention upon this *Ajapā-Gāyatrī* a man becomes liberated from all kinds of sins.

He sings the glory of this *Ajapā-Gāyatrī* in various ways and instructs all spiritual aspirants to make the best use of this natural device for their spiritual self-realisation. He says,—

Kundalinyām samudbhutā gāyatrī prāna-dhārini
Prāna-vidyā mahāvidyā yas tām vetti sa yogavit.
Anayā sadriśi vidyā anayā sadriśo japah
Anayā sadriśam jñānam na bhutam na bhavishyati.

This natural *Gāyatrī-mantra* has its origin in *Kundalinī Śakti* and is the sustainer of the vital system. The knowledge of this is called *Prāna-vidyā* (true insight into the vital system), and it is *Mahāvidyā* (great wisdom). He who attains the knowledge of this *Ajapā-Gāyatrī* is truly the knower of Yoga. Wisdom equal to this, *japa* equal to this, knowledge equal to this, have never been and will never be.

This is a magnificent conception of our natural breathing process. The highest enlightenment is associated with it. The cultivation of this conception and constant remembrance of the essential identity of the individual soul and the Soul of the universe with every breath occupies a very important position in Gorakhnath's system of *yogasādhanā*. It is known as *Ajapā-Yoga.*

Another yogic conception also may be noted in this connection. When calmness and tranquillity reigns in the body and the mind, when there is no disorder or disequilibrium in any of the nerves or organs, the breath naturally becomes very mild and gentle and slow, and quite rhythmical and almost soundless. It then appears to cease to produce the sound *Ham* while going out and the sound *Sah* while coming in. The *mantra Hamsah* or *So'ham* is then resolved into a continuous waveless monotonous sound *OM*, which is called *Pranava*. This sound *OM* signifies the complete unification of *Aham* and *Sah*, of the individual self and the Universal Self, of *Jeeva* and *Śiva*. In *Kumbhaka* (suspension of breath) no sound remains except this non-produced *OM*. This pure monosyllabic sound *OM* is conceived as the eternal sacred Name of the Nameless One, the Absolute Spirit, Brahma or Śiva. Patanjali In his *Yogasutra* says, *Tasya vācakah pranavah,*—*Pranava*, i.e. *OM* is the Name for Him (*Iśwara*). Śri Krishna in the *Gītā* describes *OM* as *Ekākshara Brahma* (i.e. Brahma revealed in one letter). According to *Māndukya Upanishad*, *OM* stands for All-Existence, the past and the present and the future and what is above and beyond time,—*Om* is *Brahma*, *Ātmā*, the whole universe and the Supreme Spirit transcending the universe. All the authoritative Scriptures identify *OM* with Brahma.

Gorakhnath and the Siddha-Yogi school further describe this *Pranava* as *Anāhata-Nāda* (Eternal Sound, not produced from any friction, not produced from any collision or upheaval, not broken into pieces or a number of distinct sounds, but one beginningless and endless natural monotonous integral Sound), which is the original self-expression of the Supreme Spirit in the form of Sound. This *Pranava*, *OM*, pervades the *Mahākāśa* and is immanent in the *Pañca-bhautika* universe. All particular sounds are evolved from this *OM* and are again ultimately merged in it. It is the essence of all the *Vedas* and *Vedāntas*, which only expound and interpret it in various forms of words and concepts. It is this *OM*, this *Anāhata-Nāda*, this *Śabda-Brahma*, this infinite eternal subtle Sound-Body of the Supreme Spirit, which naturally shines within the heart of every *jeeva.* This Mahā-mantra *OM* underlies the *Ajapā-Gāyatri, Ham-sah So'-ham.* In the perfectly calm and tranquil and concentrated state of the physical and mental and vital energy, when there is perfect equilibrium of in-breathing and out-breathing, when *Prāna* and *Apāna* are united in the heart without any tension, when *Candra-Nādī* and *Surya-Nādī* (*Idā* and *Pingalā*) are in thorough union with *Brahma-Nādī* (*Sushumnā*), every person can internally hear this *Pranavo*, this *Anāhata-Nāda*, this *Brahma-in-Sound-form*, within himself, and can realise this as the essence of his being. Mahāyogis thus point out how the Ultimate Reality and the Ultimate Ideal of our life presents Himself every moment in the constitution of our body and is within our easy reach. We can realise Him in ourselves through mere concentration of our attention.

CHAPTER XIV

THE ESOTERIC ASPECTS OF THE BODY

Having given a general description of the constitution of the Cosmic Body and of the individual bodies as the phenomenal self-manifestations of Śiva-Śakti (the Dynamic Supreme Spirit), Mahāyogi Gorakhnath teaches the truth-seekers to make a still deeper reflection (*vicāra*) on the inner structure of this bodily system in the light of the experience of the enlightened Siddha-Yogis. He calls it *Pinda-Vicāra.* Here he presents a doctrine which is rather esoteric and meant for those who are or wish to be initiated into the path of *yogic* discipline and which an ordinary intellectualist student of philosophy or physiology or psychology would naturally find it difficult to comprehend and appreciate. It is not based on ordinary observation and experiment, but on *yogic* introspection and meditation. But the spiritual influence of the *yogi* school upon the general culture of the vast country was so wide-spread and so deeply inspiring that many of these esoteric ideas are found to be familiar even to common religiously minded people of all parts of Bhāratavarsha.

Gorakhnath says that for the purpose of attaining true enlightenment about the inner nature of this sacred body which is a wonderful self-manifestation of Śiva-Śakti, familiarity with these concepts and deep contemplation in this line are essential. He says,—

Nava-cakram kalā-dhāram tri-lakshyam vyoma-pancakam
Samyag etat na jānātl sa yogi nāma-dhārakah.

(S.S.P.II.31)

If a yogi is not perfectly acquainted with the nine *cakras,* sixteen (*kalā*) *ādhāras,* three *lakshyas,* and five *vyomas,* he is only a bearer of the name of a *yogi* (but not a *yogi* in a true sense).

A. *Nine Cakras:—*

The nine *cakıas* are conceived (or perceived by the *yogis*) as different stations in the central *Sushumnā-Nāḍī,* which has been called the *Brahma-mārga* (the path for the realisation of the Supreme Spirit within the body or for the realisation of the perfect Existence-Consciousness-Bliss in one's own self). They are really different planes of esoteric experience through which a sincere and earnest seeker of perfect self-realisation in the path of *yogic* self-discipline passes in course of his systematic endeavour for ascending to the highest plane of spiritual experience and enjoying therein the blissful absolute unity of Śiva and Śakti and his own self.

As it has been mentioned in course of the discussion on the nervous system, the *Sushumnā-Nāḍī* is the finest and most brilliant and sensitive nerve which passes through the spinal column and links the lowest centre of vital and psychical energy (*mulādhāra*) with the highest (*sahasrāra*). Though it is evolved in and forms a part of the individual physical body, it is conceived as the most efficient channel for the continuous flow of the vital and psychical energy between the lowest and the highest planes. It appears to be of the nature of an ever-flowing current (having in normal life both an upward and a downward direction), which carries the energy upward and downward. When viewed in a gross way, the *Nāḍī* seems to be almost straight and the current practically smooth and even. But to deeper insight it is revealed that there are certain divisions and turning points in the current and at certain centres there are wheels or whirls which are called by the yogis *Cakras*. These *Cakras* exercise considerable influence upon the velocity as well as the direction of the flow of energy in the inner life of an individual. Sometimes they create revolutions in the vital propensities and mental dispositions of individuals.

They act sometimes as hurdles and sometimes as steps in the path of spiritual progress. Spiritual aspirants have to be acquainted with them and their specific characteristics in order to cross through the hurdles and also to make the best use of them for ascending to higher and higher steps of spiritual power and enlightenment. These *Cakras* also represent particular planes of spiritual experience. When a person's vital and mental energy moves in the domain of a lower *Cakra,* he looks upon things from a lower point of view,—from a sensuous or materialstic point of view or from the view point of his lustful or desireful mind. As his energy ascends to the domains of higher and higher *Cakras,* his outlook becomes more and more refined and enlightened, his interests become more and more spiritualised, he learns to appreciate more and more deeply the spiritual and divine character of his own self and of the cosmic system. According to the *yogis*, spiritual progress essentially consists in piercing through all the lower *Cakras* (*Cakra-bheda*) and ascending to the highest *Cakra* for being ultimately united with the transcendent character of Śiva-Śakti. When the *Cakras* are crossed, the *Sushumnā*-current becomes straightened, and the *yogi* can easily rise from the normal state of empirical consciousness to *Samādhi*,—to the state of perfect spiritual illumination and liberation from all bondage and limitation.

The spiritual urge is inherent in the nature of every individual living being, in as much as every individual is a self-manifestation of the Supreme Spirit and he is immanently meant for passing through various planes of conditioned and variegated mundane experiences to the ultimate blissful supra-mundane experience of perfect unity with the Supreme Spirit. The fulfilment of individual existence lies in the attainment of this ultimate experience and deliverance from the sense of individuality and its limitations. This ultimate ideal is immanent in the inner nature of all individuals and imperceptibly determines the most intricate courses of their development. In the lives of the lower (i.e. sub-human) orders of living beings, this spiritual urge never rises to the surface of distinct empirical consciousness, though it is present in their inner nature. Their psycho-physical organism is unfit for their actually feeling this urge. But they also are unknowingly inspired by it and the development of their nature is inwardly determined by it.

The human life too passes through many stages of development, man's psycho-physical embodiment too is developed in a gradual process. In the lower stages of development there is no actual feeling of the immanent spiritual urge. Even when a man rises to comparatively higher stages of physical, vital and mental development, and even when his moral and intellectual consciousness is considerably developed and refined, he may not have a clear perception of the spiritual urge immanent in his inner nature. In the normal course this spiritual urge rises upon the surface of the empirical consciousness of a man through contact with spiritually enlightened persons whose empirical consciousness had already been awakened to and inspired by this spiritual urge. Before this spiritual awakenment of the empirical consciousness the inherent spiritual urge appears to remain in what may be regarded as a *sleeping condition* and to exert its influence upon the course of development of the life of the individual from below the threshold of the empirical consciousness. When this awakenment comes, the individual consciously feels that he is essentially a spiritual being and that the fulfilment of his life lies in the realisation of the ultimate spiritual ideal. He then directs consciously and voluntarily and enthusiastically all his vital and mental energy towards the blissful experience of the identity of the individual soul with Śiva, the Supreme Spirit, as well as the eternal union of the *Mahā-Śakti* manifested in this cosmic order with the same spirit.

This awakenment of dynamic spiritual consciousness in the individual mind is described by Gorakhnath and the yogi school as the awakenment of the apparently sleeping Divine Power in man,—the awakenment (*bodhana* or *jāgarana*) of *Kundalinī-Śakti.* This Divine Power with infinite potentiality is conceived to be existing in every individual, but in a sleeping or dormant state, as if in the form of a coiled serpent, closely embracing the lowest or the most initial centre of physical, vital and psychical energy. This Śakti is present as the immanent power even in the most subtle and minute body which is first born in the mother's womb in the form of a *Bindu,* and it is the primal energy from which all forms of energy are evolved, all powers and capacities are developed, all tissues and organs and limbs are produced, mind and intellect also are manifested. It is essentially a Conscious Power (*Cinmayee Śakti*), Pure Consciousness or Śiva being the Soul of this *Śakti.* But it does not reveal itself as such a Conscious Power till the time of the spiritual awakenment, referred to above.

This sleeping Divine Power is imagined as existing in the form of a *sleeping serpent* coiling itself thrice round one *Śiva-linga* and deeply embracing it in the lowest centre of psycho-vital energy. In some texts eight coils also are mentioned. When this Divine Power is awakened in a man, his spiritual yearning becomes intense; his vital and mental energy is easily and almost spontaneously concentrated in the central *Sushumnā-Nāḍī* and strives to rise above in this spiritual path. The vital impulses and the mental inclinations which in normal life are diverted towards outward and downward directions come easily under the control of the spiritual urge and the disciplined will, the power of determination is therefore immensely increased, the internal and external obstacles in the path of spiritual progress are easily conquered, and there is steady and rapid ascent of the psycho-vital energy in the *Sushumnā-Mārga* towards the Supreme Ideal. This is often described as the sacred *Yātrā* (journey) of awakened *Kundalinī-Śakti* for the most blissful union with Her eternal Beloved, Śiva, in the highest region of spiritual experience, *Sahasrāra-Cakra.* In course of this gradual ascent of the psycho-vital energy along the path of *Sushumnā*, *yogis* meet with a number of subtle *Cakras*, at particular stages and particular centres, in which they are required to perform particular forms of meditation for particular *yogic* achievements, and which they have to pierce through in order to reach the highest plane of transcendent spiritual experience.

Yogiguru Gorakhnath mentions (in *Siddha-Siddhānta-Paddhati*) nine such *Cakras. Yoga-śāstras* and *Tantra-śāstras* are however not dogmatic with regard to the number of *Cakras. Cakras* are enumerated generally as six, and sometimes as seven or eight or nine. This perhaps indicates that no undue importance need be attached to the exact number. Experiences of *yogis* may sometimes differ on such minor points. *Yogigurus,* while imparting lessons to their disciples and guiding their methods of contemplation and meditation, are often found to voluntarily omit certain steps and lay stress upon others. However, older yogic literature often speaks of nine *Cakras.* It is said,—"*Nava-cakramayam vapuh*" (the body consists of nine *cakras*). Gorakhnath also says,—*Pinde nava cakrāni* (there are nine *cakras* in the body).

The first, according to *Siddha-Siddhānta-Paddhati,* is *Brahma Cakra* in *Mulādhāra.* *Mulādhāra* is defined thus:—

"*Bindu-rūpā-kundalinī—śakteh, prathamā-virbhāva-sthānam Mulā-dhārah,*— *Mulādhāra* is the seat of the first self-manifestation of *Kundalinī-Śakti* (the self-concealing Divine Power) in the form of *Bindu.* This *Kundalinī-Śakti* in the form of the *Bindu.* may be called the material as well as efficient cause of the individual body. When the body with its diversified parts and its complex structure is formed, the *Śakti* is revealed as the source of all psycho vital energy and has its primary seat in a dynamic centre of the body located in an intermediate position between the region of the rectum and the region of the generating organ. This is the point of the lowest termination of the Spinal Cord and of the *Sushumnā-Nāḍī.* Near about it is located what has been called the *Mula-kanda,* from which all the *nādīs* spread out in all directions. This is the primary seat of the psycho-vital energy, from which the living body originates and by which it is supported and sustained. Hence it is named *Mulādhāra.* Herein *Kundalinī-Śakti* lies in a spiritually sleeping condition and herein She is first awakened and pushes the psycho-vital energy (*manha-prāna-śakti*) upward in the path of *Sushumnā* (*Brahma-mārga*). In this *Mulādhāra* a yogi meets with the first *Cakra* which is called by Gorakhnath *Brahma-Cakra* (*Ādhāre Brahma-Cakram*).

Gorakhnath describes this *Brahma-Cakra* in *Mulādhāra* as conical in shape with the apex downward and as having three coils with the *Bindu* at the centre. It is to be remembered that neither the *Bindu* nor the *Cakra* is physically visible even with a powerful microscope. It is open only to *yogic* perception. From the view-point of gross sensible physical reality it would appear only as a knotty centre, and the description would appear to be figurative. But a *yogi* with his internal vision actually perceives it. The *Cakra* with its conical and coiled shape is a phenomenal manifestation of the *Bindu.* The three aspects of a phenomenal reality which remain unified in the *Bindu.* (it being of the size and shape of a mere point) become manifested in the form of the three sides of a triangle. These three aspects may be designated in general terms as Subject (*vishayī*), Object (*vishaya*) and the Process relating them to each other (*sambandha*). This triangularity of evolving and revolving phenomenal realities assumes various forms, such as, *jñātā* (knower), *jñeya* (knowable) and *jñāna* (process of knowing), *kartā* (doer), *kārya* (deed) and *karma* (the process of doing), *bhoktā* (enjoyer), *bhogya* (enjoyable) and *bhoga* (the process of enjoyment), and so on. All evolutions occur in such a triangular way and all phenomenal realities are accordingly relative and triangular in nature. What is called a cone is a conglomeration of numerous triangles with a common apex.

Brahma-Cakra in the *Mulādhāra* is conçeived as of such a conical shape, and it appears to be the dynamic source of all triangular developments in the psycho-physical organism. It has three coils, because *Śakti*, of which it is a manifestation, is *trigunamayee*, i.e. a complex of three *gunas*, viz, *Sattwa*, *Rajas* and *Tamas*. But this *Śakti* also transcends the three *gunas*, since in its essential nature it is identical with Śiva, the Supreme Spirit. The coils are therefore often described as three and a half, the half pointing to its transcendent aspect. It is sometimes described as having eight coils, which probably refer to eightfold evolutions (unified here) of *Prakriti*,—viz, five *Mahābhutas* and *Manas*, *Buddhi*, *Ahankāra*. When there is spiritual awakenment, this Divine Power is perceived in this *Cakra* to be shining very brilliantly like a blazing fire (*pāvakākāra*) or like a steady flash of lightning (*vidyut-vilāsa-vapuh*),—self-luminous and all-illumining. This is also described as the place of the mutual union of Śiva as *Kāmeśwara* (the Lord of all desires) and *Kāmeśwaree* (the *Devee* fulfilling all desires). It is therefore spoken of as *Kāmarupa-pitha*. When a *sādhaka's* psycho-vital energy is concentrated in this *Cakra* and he meditates on Śiva-Śakti in this aspect, whatever desires arise in his mind are fulfilled (*sarva-kāma-prada*). Hence in order to ascend to the higher spiritual planes, a *yogi* has to be very cautious in this plane, so that no worldly desires may arise in his mind and retard his progress.

The conception of *Śakti* in this *Cakra* is beautifully expressed in this Śloka:—

Vidyud-vilāsa-vapushah śriyam āvahanteem
Yānteem swa-vāsa-bhavanāt Śiva-rājadhāneem
Saushumna-mārge kamalāni vikāsayanteem
Deveem bhajed hridi parāmrita-sikta-gātrām.

A yogi should worship at heart the self-shining Goddess (awakened *Kundalinī-Śakti*), Whose entire body is saturated with spiritual nectar and displays the brilliant beauty of a steady flash of lightning, Who is on her delightful journey from her own home (at *Mulādhāra*) to the capital-city of her eternal Beloved, Śiva, (at *Sahasrāra*), and Who on her way through *Sushumnā* unfolds upwards the *lotuses* at the different centres of this spiritual path. (In normal worldly life the *lotuses* in the different *cakras* are described as blooming downward; in spiritually awakened life these lotuses bloom upward.)

An aspirant for greater and greater spiritual enlightenment in the higher and higher planes has to cultivate a deeply devotional attitude towards the Divine *Śakti* and to pray for Her mercy for conquering all the temptations of worldly power and prosperity and enjoyment, which may present themselves to him at this early stage of spiritual progress in the *yogic* path. It is *Śakti* that offers these temptations, it is *Śakti* that fulfils all the desires which may arise in the mind of the *yogi*, and it is *Śakti* again that delivers him mercifully from all such temptations and desires if he has an earnest spiritual aspiration and a humble and worshipful attitude of mind. If he is addicted to and infatuated with the powers and prosperities and enjoyments which may come to him (sometimes even without his wishing and seeking for them), the path of his ascent to higher spiritual planes is likely to be blocked for the time being, and even a downfall from this position is possible. He may however be rescued again, if he gets the help and guidance of a merciful enlightened *Guru* and is again actuated by the spirit of renunciation and earnest aspiration for Truth-realisation.

Thus, the *Cakra* at *Mulādhāra* is the starting station of *Kundalinī* in her sacred journey to the abode of Śiva in *Sahasrāra* and likewise the starting station of the concentrated psycho-vital energy of a *yogi* in its spiritual ascent in the path of *Sushumnā* towards the same goal.

The second *Cakra* mentioned by Gorakhnath, is called *Swādhisthāna-Cakra*. It is located within the *Sushumnā-naḍī* at a centre close to the origin of the generating organ. Within this *Cakra* there is, as the *yogis* experience with their penetrating vision, a very fine and bright red-coloured *Śiva-linga* facing towards the back (*pascimābhimukha*). *Kundalinī-Śakti* in Her upward journey, having first crossed through the *Mulādhāra-Cakra*, ascends to the *Swādhisthāna-Cakra* and is united with her Beloved Śiva, the Supreme Spirit, in this special form. This special form of manifestation of the union of *Śakti* with *Śiva* is so very beautiful and fascinating that it is revealed as the source of attraction to all phenomenal existences of the universe. A *yogi*, practised in the art of concentration and deep meditation, having renounced all worldly desires and conquered all worldly temptations and having thus crossed the hurdle of *Mulādhāra-Cakra*, raises his psycho-vital energy to this plane of *Swādhisthāna-Cakra*. When his energy is concentrated upon and charmed by this fascinating expression of the union of Śiva and Śakti, he himself becomes thereby a most attractive personality and the whole world seems to be attracted towards him (*Jagad-ākarshanam bhavati*).

Though he may not have any attraction for the honour and adoration and affection of the people of the world, the beauty and splendour of his *yogic* attainments and the Divine Power manifested in and through him naturally attract them towards him. This is also a great hindrance in the way of higher spiritual progress. Moreover, besides his personality becoming unusually attractive, his aesthetic ideas and artistic and creative faculties also are often extraordinarily developed at this stage. A *yogi* must not remain contented with these attainments. He must exert himself to ascend to higher planes of spiritual experience. For this purpose he should with a prayerful attitude deeply meditate upon Śiva with His Śakti united with Him, and pray to Śiva-Śakti for revealing to his consciousness higher and higher manifestations of Their holy union. He should never be elated with joy and pride at the charming experiences he has already gained. He should never cherish any sense of *ego* and never attribute the credit for these experiences to his individual self. He should value them as the merciful self-revelations of Śiva-Śakti, but should never be intoxicated with them. He should earnestly seek for and pray for higher orders of experience. In this way he should cross the whirl of the *Swādhisthāna-Cakra*.

The third *Cakra* is called by Gorakhnath *Nābhi-Cakra,* because it is experienced within the *Sushumnā-Nāḍi* at a centre in the region of the navel. It is generally known as *Manipura-Cakra.* The concentrated and upward-driving psycho-vital energy of an earnest and prayerful *yogi,* having crossed *Mulādhāra-Cakra* and *Swādhisthāna-Cakra,* arrives at this *Manipura-Cakra,* which is a dynamic centre of various kinds of *Yogic Siddhis* or miraculous powers. This *Cakra* is described as having five fold whirls (*pancā-varta*) and appearing in the form of a five-times-coiled serpent (*sarpa-vat kundalākārā*). Within this *Cakra, Kundalinī-Śakti* reveals Herself with the brilliance of a crore of morning suns (*bālārka-koti-sadriśee*) and enjoys a special bliss of union with Śiva. This is a higher plane of spiritual union between Śiva and Śakti than *Mulādhāra* and *Swādhisthāna.*

The difference between the nature and the degree of the spiritual enjoyment of one plane and those of another can not of course be understood by any person living and moving and having his being in the normal physical and sensuous plane of experience by means of any amount of subtle intellectual reasoning or any stretch of imagination. *Yogis* who attain experiences of those higher planes can not also make them intelligible to the men of the lower planes by means of verbal descriptions. Nevertheless, many yogi-teachers have, with the help of various kinds of similes and metaphors and poetic imageries, made some attempts to give vague and inadequate ideas about their inner experiences for the benefit of earnest truth-seekers, who might in the light of these descriptions feel the urge to advance in this path and subject themselves to the necessary discipline under proper guidance with the purpose of being blessed with similar experiences.

Kundalinī-Śakti as revealed in *Manipura-Cakra* is also named by Gorakhnath as *Madhyamā-Śakti*, indicating that this also is only an intermediate stage of the self-revelation of the essential character of *Śiva-Śaktī*. But even at this *madhyamā*-stage, *Kundalinī-Śakti* confers all kinds of supernatural powers (*sarva-siddhidā bhavati*) upon the devoted *yogi*, whose psycho-vital energy is concentrated upon Her in this plane. The *yogi* then acquires the power of changing his physical body into any form at his pleasure, of transforming one material thing into another, of making his existing body lighter than air or heavier than a mountain or invisible to others' eyes or capable of passing from one place to another on the aerial path by the mere exercise of his will, and so on. But the acquisition of such supernatural powers is not the ideal of *yoga*. It is only a passing stage. A *yogi* must transcend this stage and ascend to higher planes. Intoxication with such powers is a formidable hindrance in the way of further progress to higher stages of enlightenment.

The fourth *Cakra* is *Hridaya-Cakra*, also called *Anāhata-Cakra*. Like the other *Cakras*, it is also located in the *Sushumnā naḍī* within the spinal column and it is experienced near about the region of the heart. Within this *Cakra* there is, says Gorakhnath, a fine lustrous lotus with eight petals facing downward (*asta-dala- kamalam adhomukham*). In the middle of this lotus *Śakti* reveals Herself as shining in the form of an extraordinarily brilliant and beautiful and steady light (*jyoti-rupa*) of the shape of a *Śiva-Linga* (*lingā kāra*). *Kundalinī-Śakti* appearing in this self-luminous form, almost identified with *Śiva* and deeply enjoying the bliss of union with Him, is named *Hamsa-Kalā*. This *Hamsa-Kalā* is also spoken of as *Śree-Śakti*. When a *yogi* attains the ability to concentrate his refined and purified psycho-vital energy in this *Cakra*, he becomes the master of all his senses (*sarven-driyāni vaśyāni bhavanti*). His senses being perfectly under his control, and his mind being free from all worldly desires, free from the egoistic sense of his own superiority and also free from attachment even to his supernatural powers and grandeurs, he becomes an embodiment of calmness and tranquillity even in the normal state of his existence.

Through deep meditation on the pure self-luminous *jyoti* in this *Cakra*, the *yogi* not only experiences the unity of *Śakti* and *Śiva*, but also experiences the identity of his own self with *Śiva-Śakti*. *Śakti* in this plane unveils to his individual empirical consciousness that *kalā* (aspect) of herself, by the light of which his *aham* (self) is so iliumined that it is experienced as non-different (*abhinna*) from *Sa* (He, Śiva). It is in this

Cakra that true spiritual enlightenment of a *yogi* really begins. But there are still higher and higher stages of enlightenment, which a *yogi* has to attain through deeper and deeper reflection and meditation.

It may be noted in this connection that *Samādhi*, which is the most concentrated state of the empirical consciousness,—a state in which all differences apparently vanish,—may be attained in every plane of the consciousness, specially in each of the *Cakras* mentioned by the enlightened *yogis*. But the results of the *Samādhi* in the different planes,—in the different *Cakras*,—are not the same. The *samādhi*-state of the consciousness may superficially appear to be similar in every case; but the realisations depend upon the nature of the planes and the nature of the objects or ideals upon which the mind is concentrated. *Samādhi* in every plane and upon every object of meditation does not lead to spiritual illumination. The psycho-vital energy has to be purified and refined and raised to higher and higher planes for higher and higher orders of spiritual experience; perfect illumination is attainable in the highest plane, -in the highest *Cakra*.

The fifth *Cakra* is called *Kantha-Cakra*. It is also known as *Viśuddha-Cakra*. It is located in the *Sushumnā* in the region of the throat (*Kantha*). Here the *Sushumnā-nāḍī* shines most distinctly and brilliantly and beautifully with the *Candra-nāḍī* (*Iḍā*) on its left and the *Surya-nāḍī* (*Pingalā*) on its right. The *Sushumnā* as so revealed in this *Cakra* is conceived as the *Anāhata-Kalā* of the *Kundalinī-Śakti*, Who here deeply enjoys the bliss of union with Śiva. The psycho-vital energy of the *Yogi*, having passed through the *Hridaya Cakra* and become fully refined and profoundly concentrated, ascends to this *Cakra* and identifies itself with this *Anāhata-Kalā* for the most profound and steady enjoyment of *Śiva-Śakti-union*. The *yogi* is at this stage blessed with a spiritual realisation which Gorakhnath calls *Anāhata-Siddhi*. He then transcends all the forces of the world. No worldly forces (which are also manifestations of the same Divine Power, but in lower planes) can strike him or bring him under their subjection. *Anāhata-Siddhi* may also mean that he perfectly realises the all-pervading *Anāhata-Nāda* (the eternal unbroken undifferentiated unuttered Sound-*OM*), which is the first self-expression of *Śiva-Śakti* in the form of *Nāda* or Sound and which underlies all kinds of sound-waves in the phenomenal universe. The *yogi* at this stage transcends the domain of the plurality of produced sounds, becomes absorbed with the undisturbed experience of the unity and sweetness of the Eternal Sound and realises the oneness of this Sound with *Śiva-Śakti*.

The sixth *Cakra* is described by Gorakhnath as located at the root of the palate (*tālu-mula*) and is called *Tālu-Cakra.* In this *Cakra* there is a continuous flow of ambrosia (*amrita-dhārā-pravāha*) from the *Sahasrāra-Cakra.* The *yogi* can become absorbed with the taste of this *amrita* through the appropriate process of concentration of his psycho-vital energy in this *Cakra* and can thereby become perfectly free from hunger and thirst and attain even physical immortality. But Gorakhnath instructs the earnest spiritual aspirant to concentrate the attention on *Śunya* or absolute void in this *Cakra,* so that he may attain the state of *Citta-laya* (the dissolution of the empirical consciousness). *Citta-laya* is a very important step to perfect spiritual illumination and ascent to the plane of transcendent consciousness. Gorakhnath says that in the *tālu-mula* there is a *ghantikā-linga,* at the root of which there is a very small hole, a perfect vacuum, which is called *Śankhinī-vivara* and also *Daśama-dwāra* (tenth door). It is within this vacuum that the attention should be concentrated and *Śunya* should be deeply meditated on. As the result of this meditation, *Citta* will lose itself. Unlike the commonly known nine doors of the body open towards objects of mundane experience, here lies the tenth door open towards the realisation and enjoyment of spiritual truth and here the empirical consciousness should die, as it were, to be perfectly illumined by Transcendent Light.

The seventh *Cakra* is located at a nerve-centre between the two eyebrows and is called by Gorakhnath *Bhru-Cakra.* Here the *Sushumnā* takes the form of a steadily burning lamp-light (*deepa-śikhā-kāra*) of the size of a thumb (*amgustha-mātra*). This is called *Jñāna-netra,*—the eye of enlightenment. This is really an inner light which illumines the consciousness of a *yogi* whose whole attention is concentrated upon it. Through deep concentration the *yogi* becomes one with the light. When he comes down from this plane to the normal plane of experience, he looks upon all worldly objects and events with the illumined outlook. Besides, says Gorakhnath, he attains *Vāk-Siddhi;* whatever he speaks turns out to be true. His whole being becomes full of Truth and his utterances also spontaneously reflect Truth.

The eighth *Cakra* is called by Gorakhnath *Nirvāna-Cakra,* and it is located in *Brahma-randhra* within a part of *Sahasrāra.* This is the finest centre for the realisation of the Infinite and Eternal Spirit (*Brahma*) by the individual consciousness. The individual consciousness is in this plane merged in the Transcendent Existence-Consciousness-Bliss. *Kundalinī-Śakti* is here perfectly united with *Śiva,* the Supreme Spirit. In this plane the difference between light and darkness, between motion and rest, between finite and infinite, between phenomena and noumenon, vanishes altogether. *Yogis* often give it the poetic name of *Jālandhara-Pitha,* because this is the place of the perfect self-revelation (*pitha*) of the Supreme Holder of the magnificent net-work of the phenomenal cosmic order (*Jālandhara*),—the Supreme Spirit from Whom this cosmic net (*jāla*) originates, by Whom this net is sustained and governed and harmonised, of Whom it is the playful self-manifestation and Who is its infinite and eternal self luminous and all-illumining Soul. An individual remains *jāla-baddha* (bound in and suffering from this *jāla* or net), so long as he does not realise *Jālandhara* (the Supreme Net-holder) in himself and the cosmic system. When he perfectly realises his oneness with *Jālandhara*, he feels full freedom in this very world, he becomes free from all sense of bondage and limitation and sorrow. He attains *Moksha* or *Nirvāna*.

Above the *Nirvāna-Cakra* in the *Brahma-randhra*, which is the seat of the attainment of *Moksha* (liberation from all possible bondage and sorrow), Gorakhnath mentions the existence of the ninth *Cakra*, which he names *Ākāśa-Cakra*. This last *Cakra* is located at the highest point of *Sahasrāra*. It is described as of the nature of a fine self-luminous lotus with sixteen petals, facing upward. At the centre of this lotus the *trikutākārā* (manifested in a threefold form,—in the form of a self-luminous Experience holding within itself the experiencer and the experienced and the process of experience) *Sat-Cid-Ānanda-mayee Mahā-Śakti* in perfect union with the Supreme Spirit, Śiva, has Her highest and most glorious self-manifestation and self-realisation. This centre of experience is further described as *Purna-Giri-Pitha* (i. e. the seat of the highest mountain of Absolute Experience). Here the phenomenal consciousness is perfectly transformed into and fully realises itself as all-absorbing all-unifying all-transcending Absolute Consciousness. The holy journey of *Kundalinī-Śakti* from *Mulādhāra-Cakra* for the most blissful re-union with Her most beloved Soul and Lord, *Śiva*, reaches here its most successful end.

Śakti had separated Herself, as it were, from *Śiva* in course of Her world-ward journey, had put on veils over veils and concealed Her *Sat-Cid-Ānanda-mayee Swarupa-Prakriti* in course of Her cosmic journey to lower and lower planes of phenomenal existence and consciousness and enjoyment, and with Her face outward and downward had seemed to see Her Lord and Soul only as reflected upon Her diversified and ever-changing cosmic self-manifestations. Though never out of touch with Śiva, She seemed to have been bearing at heart a painful feeling of the want of direct and perfect spiritual union with Him, which meant the want of self-realisation on Her part. She appeared to have gone to a long distance from Śiva, i.e. Her own true Self, in the material plane. In course of Her phenomenal self-manifestation, She created the human body as the most suitable channel for Her return-journey to Her beloved Lord, i.e. Her own true Spiritual Self. This return-journey is completed, when *Śaki* reaches what has been called *Ākāśa-Cakra* in the human body, and She appears to become one with Śiva again. The *yogi* attains perfect self-fulfilment, when he can firmly establish himself in this plane of existence and consciousness and blissfulness. This is the plane of *Parā-Saṃvit*. Gorakhnath also calls it *Parama Śunyā*, because all objectivity and individuality vanish in this Experience, and there remains only one infinite eternal differenceless changeless Absolute Experience. *Śunya* does not mean absence of existence, but perfect subject-object-less space-time-less unconditioned Existence.*

---

*The above exposition of the *Nine Cakras* is like that of other topics in this book chiefly based on *Siddha-Siddhānta-Paddhati*. In *Goraksha-Śataka*, which also is regarded as an authentic work of Yogiraj Gorakhnath, the *Cakras* are enumerated as six. He says—

Shat-cakram shoḍaśādhāram tri-lakshyam vyoma-pancakam
Swa-dehe ye na jānanti katham sidhyanti yoginah.

Six *Cakras*, sixteen *Adhāras*, three *Lakshyas* and five *Vyomas*,—how can those *yogis*, who do not know these in their own body, attain perfection? (G. S. 13)

He adds—

Eka-stambham nava-dwāram griham pancādhidaivatam
Swadeham ye na jānanti katham sidhyanti yoginah. (G S. 14)

A house with one pillar, nine doors, and presided over by five Deities,—how can yogis, who do not know their own body as such a house, attain perfection?

Caturdalam syād ādhārah swādhisthānam ca shad-dalam
Nābhau daśa-dalam padmam sūrya-samkhya-dalam hṛdi.
Kanthe syāt shodaśa-dalam bhru-madhye dwidalam tathā
Sahasra-dalam-ākhyātam brahma-randhre mahā-patne. (G. S. 15-16)

The first *Cakra* is *Mulādhāra* which has in it a lotus of four petals; the second is *Swādhisthāna* with a lotus of six petals; the third is in the navel with a lotus of ten petals; the fourth is in the heart with a lotus of twelve petals; the fifth is in the region of the throat with a lotus of sixteen petals; and the sixth is in between the two eyebrows with a lotus of two petals. Above all these six *Cakras* there is in *Brahmarandhra*, the supreme path, the highest *Cokra* which is a lotus of a thousand petals.

Here as well as in all other authoritative texts, *Shat-Cakro* mean six *cakras* in the *Sushumnā*, exclusive of *Sahasrāra*. These six have to be transcended (*Cakra-bheda*), and the ultimate ideal has to be realised through the deepest concentration of the psycho-vital energy in the seventh and highest *Cakra*, viz. *Sahasrāra*. In S. S. P. Gorakhnath speaks of two *Cakras* in *Sahasrāra*, viz. *Nirvāna-Cakra* and *Ākāśā-Cakra*. Moreover he speaks of another *Cakra*, viz. *Talu-Cakra*, at the root of the palate. Thus the total number becomes nine. Further, in S. S. P. he does not make special mention of the lotuses with definite numbers of petals in the different *cakras*, except in the cases of *Hridaya-Cakra* and *Ākāśa-Cakra*; in the former he mentions the presence of a downward-looking eight-petalled lotus and in the latter an upward-looking sixteen-petalled lotus. In G. S. however he speaks of a twelve-petalled lotus in *Hridaya-Cakra*, and *Ākāśa-cakra* is not mentioned at all.

In *Goraksha-Śataka* as well as in many other books Gorakhnath instructs every truth-seeker to contemplate his own body as a house (*griha*) in which *Śiva* dwells as the individual soul (*jeeva*). This house is said to stand on one pillar. The pillar obviously refers to the spinal column (containing *Sushumnā* with its *Cakras* and supporting the whole bodily system) with *Sahasrāra* as its roof. The nine doors of this house indicate the two eyes, two ears, two nostrils, one mouth, one generating organ and one excretive organ, which are linked with the centre of vitality by the nine principal *Nādīs* (excluding *Sushumnā*) and which are the openings of this bodily house for contact with the outer world, A tenth door (*daśama dwāra*) is mentioned at the root of the palate (in *tālu-cakra*), which is an opening to the higher spiritual region. The five presiding Deities may mean according to the yogic view-point *Brahmā, Vishnu, Rudra, Iśwara*

(*Continued on next page*)

B. *Sixteen Ādhāras:—*

Having given lessons on the *Nine-Cakras*, Gorakhnath indicates the locations of the *Sixteen Ādhāras*, and gives some general hints as to how they should be utilized in the practice of *yoga*. *Ādhāra* literally means 'that which holds or contains.' Probably by the enumeration of the *Ādhāras* Gorakhnath refers to the principal seats of the vital and psychic functions, which have to be brought under voluntary control and then transcended by means of appropriate methods of *yogic* discipline.

The first *Ādhāra* he mentions is *Pādāmgusthādhāra*, i. e. the seat of the vital functions in each of the big toes. Gorakhnath instructs the aspirant for *yoga* to imagine this *ādhāra* at the extremity of the toe as a luminous (*tejomaya*) circle and fix his eyes steadily upon it. This practice is of great help for the concentration of the eyesight and the steadiness of attention. It is believed that there is a vital connection between the tissues in the big toes and the optical nerves.

The second is *Mulādhāra*. This is the primary seat of *Kundalinī Śakti* and the starting point of *Sushumnā-Nāḍī*. It is at this *ādhāra* that the psycho-vital energy should be first concentrated and then pushed upward in the path of *Sushumnā*. Gorakhnath instructs that a practitioner in *yoga* should deeply press the *mulādhāra-sutra* with the ankle of the left foot and sit erect in a steady posture *(āsana)*, so that the energy may not move downward. Through this practice there is, says Gorakhnath, a kindling of

---

Foot-note: (*Continued*)

and *Sadāśiv*, who are special spiritual self-manifestations of *Śiva-Śakti* for governing different planes of the Cosmic System as well as of the individual bodies. A *yogi* is to realise these Cosmic Divine Personalities within his own body as the glorious self-manifestations of his own true Soul, i. e. Śiva.

In yoga-literature this body is sometimes described as a seven-storied building, each of the seven *Cakras* (including *Sahasrāra*) being imagined as representing a storey or a plane of existence and experience under the supervision and governance of a Divine Personality. From *Mulādhāra* to *Kantha* the five storeys are governed by the five Divinities mentioned above, while *Ājñā* and *Sahasrāra* are under *Śri-Kantha* and *Bhairava*. *Śiva* is the Soul of them all. A perfectly enlightened *yogi*, having realised the identity of his individual soul with *Śiva*, the Supreme Spirit and Universal Soul, attains the power to move freely in all the storeys—to ascend from *Mulādhāra* to *Sahasrāra* and to descend from *Sahasrāra* to *Mulādhāra* and to enjoy the experiences of any of the planes, as he pleases, and to identify himself occasionally with any of the Deities. Through the mere concentration of his will, he can participate in the delightful play of Śiva-Śakti in all the planes of existence and experience in this very embodied state. He may at his sweet will take leave of this house and embrace death, which is as good as immortality to him, and thereby absolutely merge his individuality in the perfect Existence-Consciousness-Bliss of *Śiva*. Or he may retain this physical body as long as he likes, since his body is inwardly spiritualised and liberated from the bondage of the physical and the moral laws, to which the ordinary living bodies are subject. He conquers nature by the power of his *yogic* discipline and by his self-identification with Śiva.

fire (*agni-deepana*) there, which pushes the energy upward in the spiritual path.

The third is called *Gudādhāra* in the rectum. This is the passage through which the *Apāna-Vāyu* clears out the impurities and the rejected materials from the abdomen. A *yogi* is instructed to practise in a methodical way the expansion and contraction (*vikāsa-samkocana*) of this *gudā-dhāra*, and thereby to regulate and steady the function of *Apāna*. This contributes to the union of *Apāna* with *Prāna*, which is very important in the practice of *yoga*. It considerably helps the cure of all the diseases of the abdomen, which are great obstacles in the way of the successful practice of *Yoga*.

The fourth is called *Medhrādhāra*, located at the root of the sex-organ. This is evidently a very important seat of vital functions. This is the passage through which the most substantial elements of the physical body, viz. *Bindu* or *Vīrya*, passes out at the time of sexual intercourse and sometimes even involuntarily due to sexual excitement. *Bindu* or *Vīrya* is and the most vital substance in the body. It is saturated with *Prāna-Śakti* hence the source of vital strength. The development of mental powers also greatly depends upon the preservation and assimilation of *Bindu* within the body. Without preservation and assimilation of *Bindu*, no body can attain success in the practice of *yoga*. But any kind of indulgence to lustful propensities, any form of sexual excitement (even in dreams) dislocates it from its proper place in the bodily system and tends to drive it out through the channel of the sexual organ. Preservation of *Bindu* is spoken of as life, and loss of it as death. '*Maranam bindu-pātena jīvanam Bindu-dhāranāt.*' Hence not only *yogis*, but all decent men with moral and spiritual aspirations and even men with earnest yearning for physical and mental and intellectual development, attach the utmost importance to the preservation and assimilation of *Bindu*.

It has already been noticed that *Medhrādhāra* is generally known as *Swādhisthāna*. This means that it is regarded as the *adhisthāna* or the dwelling place of *Swa* (i. e. the self). *Swa* here denotes *Prāna* or the vital self. *Prānaśakti* is conserved here, and if it is not well-protected, it is lost also through this channel. *Prāna-śakti* principally lies in *Bindu* or *Vīrya*, also called *Retas*, and in *Medhrādhāra* strict guard has to be kept against its waste. It is incumbent on every spiritual aspirant, not only to carefully refrain from gratifying the sexual appetites and lustful propensities, but also to exercise the utmost control over the sexual organ and the nerves connected with it. For the purpose of bringing the sexual organ under control and suppressing all excitements of the sexual nerves, Gorakhnath instructs the *sādhakas* to learn the art of shrinking the sexual organ (*linga-sankocana*), which is a kind of effective *yogic mudrā*. Through the successful practice of this *mudrā* the outward or downward passage of *Bindu* is blocked and its inward or upward passage is opened. By this process the waste of vital energy (*bindu-kṣaraṇa*) is stopped and the conservation of vital energy (*bindu-stambhana*) is accomplished. Gradually the vital energy transcends the three knots (*granthi*), which are called *Brahma-granthi, Vishnu granthi* and *Rudra granthi*, and rises upward and contributes to the strength and vigour and brilliance and beauty of the whole system. *Yogis* speak of the presence of a *bhramara-guhā* (literally, bee-cave) somewhere at the uppermost end of the spinal column and in the lower region of *Sahasrāra*. Gorakhnath says that *Bindu* being successfully drawn upward goes to this *guhā* and thereafter becomes perfectly assimilated and makes the body invincible. *Bhramara-guhā* is regarded as the true seat of *vīrya* (*vīrya-sthāna*). Being dislocated from there, it comes down and is accumulated in *Meddhra*. This dislocation has to be stopped.

The fifth *ādhāra* mentioned by Gorakhnath is *Uddyāna* and it is located in an intermediate position between *linga-mula* and *nābhi-mula*. Gorakhnath says that by means of appropriate practice this *ādhāra* also can be brought under control. Its direct result is that the *yogi* can exercise control over the intestines and the urinary organs and there is diminution of the quantity of faeces and urine as well as cure of the intestinal and urinary ailments. The control of these is of great help in the purification of the body and in raising the vital energy to higher planes.

The sixth is called *Nābhyādhāra*, located at the root of *Nābhi* (navel). This is, as it has been already observed, the seat of *Nābhi-Cakra* or *Manipura-Cakra*. It is regarded as a very important centre of the vital functions, Gorakhnath specially refers to the manifestation of subtle *Nāda* (sound) in this *Ādhāra*. *Nāda* (Sound) is conceived by *yogis* as ultimately identical with *Brahma*, the Supreme Spirit of Whom it is a glorious self-expression. As *Yoga-Śikha-Upanished* says,—

Aksharam paramo nādah śabda-brahmeṭi kathyate.

—*Nāda* in its ultimate essence is *Akshara* or Brahma, —i.e. the Changeless Transcendent Supreme Consciousness. It is called *Śabda-Brahma*. It is manifested as *Nāda* in a very subtle form in *Mulādhāra*, but there it is non-distinguishable from *Śakti*. Thereafter it appears as identified with *Bindu* or *Bija*, which is the undifferentiated essence of the psycho-physical body as well as of sound,—of form (rupa) as well as name (*nāma*). *Yoga-Śikha-Upanishad* says,—

Mulādhāra-gatā śaktih swādhārā bindu-rūpiṇī
Tasyām utpadyate nādah sukshma-vijād ivānkurah.

In *Mulādhāra Nāda* is identified with *Śakti*, in *Swādhisthāna* it is identified with *Bindu* or *Bija*, and in *Manipura* or *Nābhi-ādhāra* it is revealed as the first subtle continuous Sound, which is perceptible to the refined sense of a *yogi*. This is called *Pranava*,—the sweet and undiversified and ceaseless sound of *OM*. In *Anāhata* or *Hridaya-ādhāra* this *Nāda* becomes quite distinct, but still monotonous and unbroken. Thereafter in and through the vocal organs *Nāda* becomes diversified into innumerable sounds. Here Gorakhnath instructs a practitioner in *yoga* to withdraw his attention from the diversities of sounds and concentrate it upon pure *Nāda* in *Nabhi-ādhāra*. This concentration may be practised by a novice with the prolonged utterance of *OM* with the mouth and the closing of ears. As a result of continued practice, the mind is merged in *Nāda*. (This is called *Nāda-laya*). In this way this important vital centre may be controlled and spiritualised.

The seventh is *Hridaya-ādhāra*. This is also a very important centre of vital functions. This is the seat of *Anāhata-Cakra*, where, according to *Siddha-Siddhānta-Paddhati*, there is the eight-petalled lotus, and according to the general view, there is the twelve-petalled lotus. It is the centre of the union between *Prāna* and *Apāna*. It is here that the *Anāhata-Nāda* can be most distinctly perceived, if attention is withdrawn from all produced sounds and concentrated in it. Gorakhnath instructs those who are under training in *yoga* to practise the concentration of *Prāna* at this centre by means of *Kumbhaka* (suppression of breath) and says that as the result of this concentration the petals of the lotus are opened upwards. This implies that the psycho-vital energy is not then dragged downward or world ward, but spontaneously moves upward in the spiritual path for self-fulfilment in the higher planes. A *yogi* is thereafter blessed with an enlighttened spiritual outlook.

The eighth is called *Kanthādhāra*. This contains the *Viśuddha-Cakra*, and according to the general view a bright sixteen-petalled lotus. Here Gorakhnath instructs a trainee to practise what is called *Jālandhara-Bandha*, in which *Kantha* (throat) has to be very cautiously contracted and the chin has to be placed on the chest. Through the systematic practice of *Jālandhara-Bandha* a *yogi* can bring under control the movement of *Prāna-Vāyu* in *Iḍā* and *Pingalā* and push the psycho-vital energy upward through *Sushumnā*.

It may be noted here by the way that each of the *yogic* processes, of which Gorakhnath has made only a passing mention in connection with the different *ādhāras* in *Siddha-Siddhānta-Paddhati*, has far-reaching importance for giving deeper and deeper knowledge of the bodily system and bringing the entire bodily system under the voluntary control of the *yogi*. The processes and their results are dealt with more elaborately in other books by Gorakhnath and other teachers. But everywhere they have emphasised that without the guidance of competent *Gurus* it is very difficult and often unsafe to venture to practise these *yogic* methods merely in reliance upon the study of books. Gorakhnath has mentioned here several processes of *Bandha* and their consequences,—such as *Mulabandha, Uddyānabandha*, and *Jālandharabandha*,—in the simplest possible forms. But they have very far-reaching consequences in the acquisition of mastery over the psycho-physical organism and the attainment of spiritual perfection. This is not the place for discussing them, because we are here mainly concerned with the enumeration of *ādhāras*. Gorakhnath has in a general way made mention of some forms of *Mudrā* and *Bandha* and *Dhyāna* in connection with his emumeration of *Nāḍīs, Cakras* and *Ādhāras* within the body, because it is by means of these methods that a truth-seeker can penetrate into the true nature of them and can be firmly convinced of their existence in the organism. True knowledge leads to the establishment of mastery over them.

The ninth is called *Ghantikādhāra*, which is located at the root of the soft palate. Within it there is a minute channel through which nectar (*amrita-kalā*) flows gently from what is called *Candra-mandala* in *Sahasrāra*. Normally it is not perceptible and it is wasted, because it passes down to the lower regions through the channels of Iḍā-Pinglā. Gorakhnath instructs the trainee to turn the tip of the tongue inward and to put it carefully in touch with this channel in this *Ghantikādhāra*, so that *amrita* may not pass down untasted and undetected. This process enables the *yogi* to enjoy the most delightful taste of the *amrita*, which cures him of many of the bodily evils and attracts his attention inward for the enjoyment of spiritual bliss. It demonstrates that the real source of joy is in the higher regions and not in the lower regions,—in the higher planes of life and not in the lower sensuous planes.

The tenth is called *Tālu-ādhāra*, which is in a still deeper region of the palate. It is inwardly connected with *Ājñā-Cakra* and *Sahasrāra*. Here a *yogi* is instructed to practise what is called *Khecari-Mudrā*, which is greatly efficacious for the attainment of *Samādhi*, (though this *Samādhi* does not mean the highest state of spiritual experience). The process is apparently simple, though practically not so very easy. The tongue has to be methodically softened and drawn out and lengthened, and then it has to be turned and gently pushed inward. Then the tip of the tongue has to be led into the small hole within the soft root of the palate and gently pushed into the innermost aperture. If the practice is quite successful, the *yogi* becomes free from all fickleness, all movement and all outer consciousness and appears like a piece of wood (*kāsthī bhavati*). This is often called *Jaḍa-Samādhi.* His innermost consciousness, however, is full of joy and intoxicated with the nectar which is absorbed by the tip of the tongue. All *yoga-śāstras* testify to the most wonderful and far-reaching consequences of this *Khecari-Mudrā.*—*Tālu-ādhāra* has also been pointed out as the seat of *Tālu-cakra,* of *Daśama-dwāra* and *Śankhinī-vivara* and *Amrita-dhāra-pravāha,* as noted already.

The eleventh is called *Jihvādhāra,* which is at the root of the tongue. A trainee is instructed to fix the tip of the tongue at this root. If this practice is methodically undergone, a person may be relieved from various kinds of diseases.

The twelfth in called *Bhru-madhyādhāra,*—inside at the meeting place of the two eye-brows. Here the trainee has to focus his vision and contemplate on the luminous disc of the moon emitting pure white and cool and tranquil rays. By this practice his entire body is made cool and calm and peaceful. The process is very helpful in steadying the attention and cooling down all kinds of excitements in the body and the mind. Here an extraordinarily bright and cool *Joyti* is experienced, which illumines the consciousness. It is the seat of *Ājñā-Cakra* or *Bhru-Cakra.*

The thirteenth is called *Nāsādhāra,* which is in the nose. The nose is an important centre of vital functions. The trainee is advised to focus his vision on the tip of the nose and concentrate his attention upon this one point. If this practice is continued for some time, the mind becomes free from restlessness and fit for deep meditation.

The fourteenth is called *Kapātādhāra,* which is at the root of the nose (*nāsa-mula*). At this point also the trainee is instructed to practise focussing his vision and attention. Gorakhnath says that the systematic practice of this mode of concentration of vision and attention for a period of six months results in the actual seeing of a mass of serene and soothing light (*jyotih-punja*) illumining the mental atmosphere. It is evidently very close to *Ājñā-Cakra* or *Bhru-Cakra.*

The fifteenth is called *Lalātādhāra,* which is at the centre of the forehead. The trainee has to fix his attention upon this *ādhāra* and deeply contemplate on a mass of self-shining light (*jyōtih-punja*) therein. The practice of contemplation of *Joyti* at this centre ·immensely develops the vital and mental strength of the practitioner and adds to the brightness and vigour of his bodily system (*Tejaswi bhavati*).

The sixteenth,—the last and highest,—*ādhāra* is *Brahma-randhra*, which is the seat of *Ākāśa-Cakra*. It is here that perfect spiritual self-fulfilment is to be experienced. Gorakhnath suggests that a *yogi*, having through the practice of higher and higher and deeper and deeper forms of meditation raised his purified and refined psycho vital energy to this highest plane of *Ākāśa-Cakra* in *Brahma-randhra* should meditate on and realise the lotus-feet of *Śree-Guru* (*Śree-Guru-Caranāmbuja-dvayam sadā avalokayet*). Thereby he should become perfect like *Ākāśa* (*Ākāśavat purno bhavati*). By *Śree-Guru* he evidently implies the Holy Spiritual Personality in whom the *yogi* has found the Union of *Śiva* and *Śakti*.—the Supreme Spirit and His Power of self-manifestation in countless orders of phenomenal existences and phenomenal consciousnesses,—perfectly realised, and who has been the source of his inspiration and wisdom and strength all along in the difficult path of his spiritual elevation and enlightenment. In the eyes of an earnest disciple *Śree-Guru* is identical with *Śiva-Śakti*, and meditation on *Śree-Guru* signifies the full concentration of the psycho vital energy upon the union of the Supreme Spirit and His Infinite Power in the most concrete personal form. The depth of this meditation culminates in the highest spiritual *Samādhi* and the illumination of the whole being, in which the *yogi* realises himself and the whole universe as identical with *Guru* and *Śiva-Śakti*. He becomes infinite and eternal, differenceless and changeless, perfectly illumined and spiritualised, perfectly calm and tranquil, like *Ākāśa*. It has been found that Gorakhnath has spoken of this *Ākāśa-Cakra* as *Purna-giri-pitha* (the realm of the most perfect spiritual self-fulfilment) and has instructed the *yogi* to be absorbed in the meditation of *Parama-Śunya*, i.e. the Absolute Differenceless Changeless One,—the unity of *Śiva* and *Śakti* and *Śādhaka*.

C. *Three Lakshyas:—*

By *Lakshya* Gorakhnath obviously means the objects upon which attention should be temporarily fixed for the purpose of practising the concentration of psycho-vital energy with the ultimate view of raising it to the highest spiritual plane and realising the Supreme Spirit (with His unique Power) everywhere within the individual body and the cosmic order. *Lakshya* literally means that which specially deserves to be attended to. The *Lakshyas* mentioned by Gorakhnath have no special importance for giving any knowledge of the internal or external features of the individual body or of the functions of any of the organs or centres of the psycho-physical organism. But they have their practical value from the standpoint of *yogic* discipline.

Though Gorakhnath speaks of *Tri-lakshya* or *Lakshya-traya* (literally meaning three *lakshyas*), he does not specifically mention only three particular objects of concentrated attention. He mentions three kinds of *lakshyas*,—some inside the body, some outside the body, and some in a general way without any special reference to the body. In accordance with the locations of the chosen objects of meditation, the *lakshyas* are classified into three,—viz. *Antar-lakshya, Bahir-lakṣya* and *Madhya-lakshya.*

(1) *Antar-lakshya*:—Gorakhnath gives directions about several processes of contemplation and meditation upon internal objects. He attaches primary importance to the concentration of attention upon *Kundalinī-Śakti* in *Sushumnā*. *Sushumnā-Nāḍī*, as it has been already described, is the finest and brightest nerve passing from *Mulakanda* (the source of all the *nāḍīs*) in *Mulādhāra*, the place of *Kundalinī*, to *Brahma-randhra* in *Sahasrāra*, the place of *Śiva*, and is the royal passage for *Kundalinī's* spiritual journey upward to be united with Her beloved Soul and Lord, Śiva, in *Śiva-sthāna* (*Sahasrāra*). A *yogi*, having by the power of his determination withdrawn his attention from all other things, should concentrate it upon this *Mahā-Śakti Kundalinī* rising in the path of *Sushumnā* with Her subtle self-luminous and all-illumining spiritual body. It is this *Mahā-Śakti Kundalinī* Who reveals Herself in the forms of *Maheśwarī, Mahā-Kālī, Mahā-Lakshmī* and *Mahā-Saraswatī* and in other effulgent forms to the *yogi* in course of his deeper and deeper meditation and bestows various kinds of spiritual and earthly blessings upon him, till She is absolutely identified with *Śiva* in *Sahasrāra*, i.e. in the state of perfect *Samādhi* and perfect illumination, in which the *yogi* loses his consciousness of individuality in the enjoyment of the bliss of the perfect union of *Śakti* with *Śiva*. The return-journey of *Śakti* to *Śiva* ultimately means the return of the individual soul to his own true Self, i.e. the infinite eternal absolute Spirit. Gorakhnath says that *Śakti* so meditated upon becomes to the *yogi* *Sarva-siddhi-dā*, i.e. the bestower of all kinds of perfection. *Śiva-Śakti* is the true essence or self not only of an individual's life and mind, but also of what appears as his material body. The material body is as much a playful self-revelation of the Supreme Spirit (with *Śakti*) as life and mind and has no really separate non-spiritual existence. The body is perceived as a non-spiritual reality, so long as the mind is concentrated upon its material spatio-temporal character. When the mind is concentrated upon the Spirit within it, not only the mind, but the body also is spiritualised, i.e. its spiritual nature is unveiled.

Gorakhnath points to several other centres within the head for the practice of the concentration of attention upon the deeper spiritual aspect of the body by a spiritual aspirant. A disciple under the guidance of a competent *Guru* may choose any one of them, as may be suited to his taste and capacity, and fix his attention thereon. Gorakhnath mentions a centre which he calls *Gollāta-mandapa.* It is just above the forehead (*lalāta-urdhe*) and in the front-part of *Sahasrāra.* Within it a steady and brilliant light is burning. A *yogi*, having driven out all other thoughts and desires from his mind and being seated in a suitable posture (*āsana*), should imagine the presence of the light there and concentrate his whole attention upon it. He should try to forget all his environments and even his own body and to be wholly absorbed with the light. Light is the most important symbol of the manifestation of the self-luminous Spirit. As the result of continued practice, his consciousness will be illumined by the Divine Light. Long practice of concentration upon this serene light greatly helps the spiritualisation of the whole being of the *yogi.*

Secondly, Gorakhnath speaks of *Bhramara-guhā*, which has been already mentioned. It is above the spinal cord and in a rather back-part of *Sahasrāra. Yogis* conceive of it as *Vīryya-sthāna* (the seat of *Vīryya* or *Bindu* or Vital Energy), and adopt such effective means that *Vīryya* may not be dislodged from this centre and cause excitements in the lower nerves and move downward towards the sexual organ. They adopt suitable methods for drawing even dislodged *Vīryya* also upward and restoring it to its source, so that the energy immanent in it may contribute to the well-being of the whole system and be re-transformed into spiritual energy. For this purpose special care must of course be taken for keeping the mind and the body free from all forms of sensual excitements. Mastery over the sexual appetites and conservation of *Vīryya* is of utmost importance, according to *yogis*, for advancement in the spiritual path and spiritualisation of the body and mind. Gorakhnath accordingly draws special attention to *Bhramara-guhā* for the practice of deep concentration upon it. Life-power is to be imagined as existing at this centre in the form of a red-coloured bee (*ārakta-bhramarā-kāra*) and attention is to be fixed upon it. This life-power is to be conceived as representing *Śiva-Śakti.* In comparison with the pure tranquil ecstatic joy felt in this form of meditation, all pleasures of sense-gratification would appear to be insipid and trifling, and sheer waste of physical and vital and psychical energy. Thus the mind would have contempt for all kinds of sensuous enjoyments and the whole energy would be devoted to the enjoyment of spiritual bliss within. *Bindu-stambhana* (perfect preservation and assimilation of the vital energy) and *Brahmacaryya* (perfect self-control) become almost natural with a *yogi* who becomes an adept in this practice. Through perfect conservation and spiritualisation of *Bindu* or *Vīryya* a yogi attains immortality and realises unity with *Śiva-Śakti.* Waste of energy gives momentary pleasure, while conservation of energy is the source of permanent joy and strength.

Thirdly, Gorakhnath instructs a *yogi* to practise concentration upon what he calls *Dhum-dhum-kāra Nāda* within the head (*śiro-madhye*). For the practice of listening to this internal sound, he advises the *yogi* in the initial stage to close firmly both the ears with the fore-fingers, so that no external sound may distract the attention. He would then hear a continuous sound like *dhum-dhum* within some centre of his brain. He should fix his attention upon this internal sound and become absorbed with it. The sound would gradually take the monotonous form of *OM*. His mind will then be filled with ecstatic joy and he would not like to attend to the various kinds of sounds outside. When concentration will be sufficiently deep, there will be realisation of the Spirit in the *Nāda*. It has already been mentioned that *Nāda* is the pure self-revelation of *Śiva-Śakti* in Sound-form.

Fourthly, Gorakhnath advises a *yogi* to concentrate his attention upon *Nīla-Jyoti* (blue self-luminous light) at the inner centre of the eyes. Deep concentration of the whole consciousness upon this *Jyoti* would gradually lead to the spiritual illumination of the consciousness and spiritualisation of his being.

(*2*) *Bahir-lakṣya* :—

Gorakhnath then makes mention of several outer objects for the practice of concentration of attention. A trainee may imagine the presence of a red bright light in front of his eyes at a distance of only two fingers (1½ inches) from the tip of his nose and fix his attention steadily on that light. Or he may think of a white sheet of water at a distance of ten fingers (7½ inches) from his nose and concentrate his attention thereon. Or he may imagine the presence of a yellow metal at a distance of twelve fingers (9 inches) from his nose and practise concentration on it. Or he may with steady eyes look towards any part of the blue and tranquil sky and be absorbed with the exclusive thought of this pure sky. Or looking upward he may fix his attention upon some intermediate position between himself and the sky and see there steadily a mass of brilliant rays. Or wherever the eyes may fall and whatever objects may be there, big or small, animate or inanimate, moving or motionless, the yogi may turn away his attention from all those objects and see nothing but *ākāśa* or empty space or *śunya* therein. Thus even with open eyes he may make his mind free from all the diversities of the objective world and by the power of his abstraction and concentration may see only one differenceless sky before his eyes. Similarly, with open ears he may withdraw his attention from all particular sounds and listen to one differenceless *Nāda* or perfect stillness in this noisy world. Or he may extend his look to the furthest limit of his eyesight and see there a vast expanse of land of bright golden colour. There are various such processes of concentration of perception and thought, with attention directed outward. (*Anekabidham bahirlakṣyam*). The sun, the moon, any particular star or planet, any burning lamp or blazing fire, any Divine image or the holy figure of an adorable person,—any such thing may be chosen for the practice of concentration. Fixing his attention upon any particular outer object, a *yogi* should try to see the manifestation of the Supreme Spirit or *Śiva-Śakti* in that form. The ultimate purpose should be to see the Supreme Spirit manifested in all forms.

(3) *Madhyama-lakshya:—*

By *Madhyama-lakshya* Gorakhnath obviously means any object of special attention, which is not to be conceived as either within the body or outside the body, upon which the mind is to be concentrated without any direct reference to any particular location (*sthāna-varjitam*). The idea of a particular object has to be formed in the mind and the whole attention has to be concentrated upon it. The choice of the object entirely lies with the *sādhaka*. He should choose it as he likes (*yatheṣṭam*), as it may suit his taste or disposition. The purpose should be the practice of concentration,—the development of the power of withdrawing attention from all other objects and fixing it exclusively upon the one object of his choice,—so that he may gradually become the perfect master of his attention and overcome all the internal and external forces which may draw his attention even against his will to different directions and make his mind fickle and unbalanced and restless.

The object chosen for the practice of concentration for the time being may be real or imaginary, material or ideal, very small or very big, dazzlingly bright or soothingly cool, of any colour or shape or size, of any form or without any form. Gorakhnath says that this *lakshya* may be of white or red or black colour, it may be of the form of a flame of fire or of the form of a bright light or of the form of a flash of lightning or of the form of the solar corona or of the form of the crescent moon or of any form which the *sādhaka* may choose (*yathesta*, *yathābhimata*, *yathāruci*). Hence *Madhyama-Lakshya* also may be of various forms (*anekavidham madhyamam lakshyam*). The fundamental point is that whatever object may be chosen, the mind should be wholly occupied with it during the period of practice. The *sādhaka* has to forget his body, forget his environments, forget even his ego, he has to keep under suppression all other thoughts and desires and passions and emotions and memories, he has to keep his body motionless in a definite posture and all his senses in a state of perfect rest, and he has to keep his mind fully occupied with one thing or one idea, whatever it may be. By the strength of his determination he has to be, as it were, fast asleep with regard to all other objects within and outside himself and wide awake with regard to the one particular object (real or imaginary) which he chooses for developing his power of concentration. When by such means his power of concentration is considerably developed, he can easily raise his concentrated mind to higher and higher planes of spiritual experience and enjoy higher and higher orders of self-expression of the union of Śiva-Śakti. In course of the practice of concentration the psychical and vital powers of a *yogi* are immensely developed in many directions and they appear to be supernatural. But the *yogi* must not be intoxicated with them, for then further progress would be obstructed. It is quite natural that the more the power of concentration is developed in the mind, the more refined and powerful it becomes. But a *yogi* should never forget the ideal that he has to realise and enjoy the perfect blissful union of *Śiva* and His *Śakti* in his own being as well as in all orders of phenomenal existences in the cosmic system.

D. *Five Vyomas:—*

According to Gorakhnath and the *yogi-sampradāya,* the concentration of the mind upon *Vyoma* or *Ākāśa* or what may be called *Śunya* or Void or empty space is a very effective method for the purification and refinement of the individual empirical consciousness and its liberation from unsteadiness and restlessness and the bondage of spatio-temporal limitations. It makes the mind fit for ascending to the higher and higher planes of spiritual experience, for being illumined by the Divine Light and for realising the ultimate Truth of the individual organism and the cosmic system, i.e. the eternal union of *Śiva* and His *Śakti*. *Vyoma* or *Ākāśa* is really one, pervading and underlying all diversities of physical existences,—all sounds and touches and visions and tastes and smells, all objects of sensuous experiences and imaginations. Attention has to be withdrawn from all the diversities, all the particulars and their names and forms and specific features and limitations, and to be directed to and fixed upon the all-pervading and all-underlying, infinite and undifferentiated space. It is the *Ādhāra* of all *ādhāras*. The individual consciousness which is fully concentrated upon such *Ākāśa* or *Vyoma* is elevated and transformed into pure and refined Universal Consciousness (*vyoma-sadriśo bhavati*).

Though *Vyoma* is essentially one, for the sake of the convenience and effectiveness of meditation it is conceived in five different ways and designated by five different names,—*Ākaśa*, *Parākāśa*, *Mahākāśa*, *Tattwākāśa*, and *Suryyākāśa*. *Ākāśa* is conceived as one perfectly pure (*atyanta-nirmala*) and formless (*nirākāra*) empty space pervading and unifying the outer and the inner worlds. *Parākāśa* is conceived as one absolute undifferentiated darkness (*atyanta-andhakāra-nibha*) pervading the inner and the outer worlds and obliterating all diversities. *Mahākāśa* is to be conceived as one infinite contentless fiery space like that in *Pralaya* or total cosmic destruction (*kālānala-samkāśam*). *Suryyākāsa* is to be conceived as one infinite all-absorbing sun shining perfectly alone with the brilliance of a crore of suns (*suryya-koti-nibham*). *Tattwākāśa*, which is also known as *Cidākaśa* or *Ātmākāśa*, is to be conceived as one infinite eternal differenceless changeless self luminous Soul or Spirit or Witness-Consciousness. In this meditation the meditator himself becomes one with the Object of meditation; he himself becomes this *Ākāśa*. The ultimate stage of each meditation is *Samādhi*, in which the individual consciousness is wholly absorbed in and identified with the object of meditation. But each *Samādhi* does not lead to the spiritual goal. In every *Samādhi* the empirical consciousness is not blessed with perfect spiritual illumination. The fruit of meditation greatly depends upon the chosen object of meditation. When the empirical consciousness attains *samādhi* in the Absolute Consciousness or the Supreme Spirit, then only there is perfect illumination and absolute bliss. All other forms of meditation are prescribed for making the mind fit for this. If there is any *upādhi* (conditioned character) in the object of meditation, the individual consciousness cannot attain the *nirupādhika* (unconditioned) Transcendent state.

CHAPTER XV

THE COSMOS IN THE INDIVIDUAL BODY

In the foregoing discourses it has been found that Yogi-Guru Gorakhnath regards a thorough knowledge of the *Cakras*, the *Ādhāras*, the *Lakshyas*, the *Vyomas*, or *Ākaśas*, as well as of the *Nāḍis* and the *Vāyus*, as essential for all-round success in the path of *yogic* discipline and the attainment of perfect freedom from all forms of apparent bondage and limitation and sorrow and perfect mastery over all the phenomenal forces governing the individual body and the cosmic system. He instructs the truth-seekers in the path of *yoga* to discover these within their own bodies, to concentrate their attention upon them and to practise particular forms of discipline in relation to them, with the ultimate view of realising the self-revelation of *Śiva* and His *Śakti* in each and all of them. But it is quite evident from the mode of his instruction that he does not conceive them as merely physical or even vital parts of the physical body. They are not to him purely physiological concepts based on what are ordinarily recognised as scientific proofs. He is not here concerned with the science of physiology, but with the science and philosophy of *yoga*. The individual body is not conceived by him as a purely material body (as physiological sciences ordinarily conceive it), but as a spiritual entity revealed in a material form, and as capable of being liberated from its material limitations.

These materialistic sciences cannot rationally account for the appearance of life and mind and reason in this material body, nor can they properly explain the nature of the relation of the material body with life and mind and reason which are empirically found to evolve from it and then to exercise a regulative and controlling influence upon its phenomena. Assuming matter as some reality essentially distinct from and independent of life and mind and spirit, these physical and physiological sciences can discover no rational ground, consistently with their conception of matter, for the production or emergence or evolution of life, mind, intellect, moral consciousness, aesthetic consciousness, spiritual consciousness, etc. from the nature of pure matter. On the basis of the manifold data supplied by sensuous observation (however marvellously the powers of observation may be magnified by the invention of fine scientific instruments), the sciences try to trace the history of the growth of this cosmic order and they find that the appearance of lifeless inorganic matter in this world precedes the appearance of living beings and that mind, intellect, etc., appear in gradual courses long afterwards. Hence they are led to infer that matter is an original substance and that life, mind, etc., are products of matter. Matter is earlier in appearance in the world-process than life, mind, etc.; therefore, they argue, matter must be the sole cause of them. But they fail to explain how these higher orders of realities (or even phenomena) can originate from lifeless inert insensate matter, unless there is in the inner nature of matter some active conscious living Principle, which gradually unfolds itself by transforming matter and realises itself as the higher orders of realities.

In the view of the enlightened *yogis* there is no pure and simple matter (as conceived by the scientists) anywhere in the universe. Even *Ākāśa*, which is the ultimate form of matter and which appears as pure *void* or as *contentless space*, has evolved from and exists as an embodiment of *Śiva-Śakti* (the Absolute Spirit with infinite Power immanent in His nature). *Ākāśa*, being ensouled by *Śiva-Śakti*, is not absolutely lifeless and inert matter, but is charged with a creative urge and filled with immense possibilities. Hence from *Ākāśa* evolves *Vāyu*, which also is ensouled by *Śiva-Śakti* and is similarly charged with a creative urge for further diversified self-manifestation of *Śiva-Śakti*, and so the process of the evolution of newer and newer *tattwas* (realities) continues. Every material element, as known to the scientists, is a particular form of the product of the combination of the five *mahābhutas* and a particular form of the embodiment of *Śiva-Śakti*. Though there is no manifestation of life, mind, etc., in these material elements or their compounds, *Śiva-Śakti*, the Source of all life, mind, etc., is present in every one of them as its Soul and inspires every one of them with a creative urge from within for further evolution.

All causal activities of all material things and all processes of evolution and emergence of apparently newer and newer orders of things in the universe are thus governed by the free Creative Will or the Will for phenomenal self-manifestation and self-diversification and self-enjoyment, in an infinite variety of forms, of the eternal and infinite Spiritual Power of the Absolute Spirit, Who is essentially transcendent of time and space and is also the indwelling Soul of all orders of self-expressions of His Power in time and space. It is on account of the immanent presence of the Supreme Spirit with His Supreme Power (*Śiva* with His *Śakti*) in all matter that life (which represents a higher order of the Spirit's phenomenal self-manifestation than matter) is found in the process of spatio-temporal evolution to emerge from matter and to vitalize matter as its body. It is for the same reason that mind with empirical consciousness, which represents a still higher order of *Śiva-Śakti's* phenomenal self-manifestation than life or purely living matter, is found to emerge from life in living organisms. In the same way and due to the same immanent presence of *Śiva-Śakti* there is in phenomenal nature the gradual elevation of mind into intellect or rational mind and there is the emergence of moral consciousness and aesthetic consciousness in the rational mind. The process of evolution in the spatio-tempora order reaches its final stage when the spiritual consciousness is awakened in the individual bodies and minds and enlightened and illumined by the transcendent self-luminosity of *Śiva-Śakti*. The process of the phenomenal self-manifestation of *Śiva-Śakti* in cosmic and individual forms ends with the appearance of the blissful spiritual consciousness in individuals of the unity and spirituality of all orders of existences, and this is accomplished in the lives of enlightened *yogis*.

Accordingly, to the enlightened spiritual experience of a *yogi*, the difference between the living and the non-living, the conscious and the unconscious, the rational and the non-rational, are not fundamental and insurmountable. They are only different grades of phenomenal self-manifestation of the Supreme Spirit with His Supreme Power. The different orders of existences are only different forms of phenomenal embodiments of the same Spirit. The same Spirit appears in and plays through all these varieties of forms by virtue of His infinite Spiritual Power. He is the Soul of them all, the Mover of them all, the Knower of them all, the Enjoyer of them all, and He transcends them all. The Soul and the embodiments are also not essentially different realities. The bodies are not distinct from the Soul. All His embodiments are His own phenomenal self-manifestations. He, as the Soul and Lord of these phenomenal bodies, is transcendent. All forms of embodiments, in which He manifests and enjoys Himself in His cosmic play, are apparently subject to limitations in quality and power, relations in space and the modifications and transformations in time, while He, the Soul of them, transcends all limitations and relations, all modifications and transformations. The enlightened *yogi*, with his illumined spiritual consciousness, experiences in all orders of existences the One Spirit as embodied in the plurality of forms, the One Transcendent as manifested in a plurality of phenomena, the One Supreme Being above time and space as assuming various phenomenal appearances in time and space. To him time and space have reality only in relation to the phenomenal self-manifestations of the Supreme Spirit, the Spirit Himself being timeless and spaceless. He sees the Timeless in time, the Spaceless in space, the Changeless in all changes, the Infinite in all finites.

Hence to a *yogi* the evolution of life from apparently lifeless matter, the evolution of mind from life, the emergence of higher and higher types of existences from apparently lower types, in this world of sensuous experience, are no miraculous or inexplicable phenomena. What reveals Itself in Its ultimate character in our highest supersensuous and supermental plane of experience is immanent as the Soul or Indwelling Spirit in all levels of phenomenal existences and raises them to higher and higher levels for more and more adequate phenomenal self-expression through them. The self-conscious self-luminous Spirit with His self-active Power is phenomenally more expressed in life than in matter, more expressed in animal-mind than in plant-life, still more expressed in human mind and intellect, and He has still higher self-expressions in man's moral and aesthetic and religious consciousness. In this phenomenal cosmic order, that level of existence is regarded as relatively higher, in which the essential nature of the Spirit is comparatively more unveiled. What is known by the name of evolution in the present age follows the course of the urge (immanent in the nature of all orders of existences) for more and more unveiling of the Spirit in the world of His phenomenal self manifestations. But both self-veiling and self-unveiling are equally prominent aspects of His cosmic play.

It is the aim of a truth-seeker in the path of *yogic* discipline to regulate most methodically and efficiently the relative and limited freedom of thought and will and action which has been developed in him in course of the natural (or rather divine) process of evolution, so as to penetrate through the veils of forms or embodiments in every level of the phenomenal self-manifestations of the Supreme Spirit (with His *Śakti*) and thereby to experience directly the delightful play of *Śiva-Śakti* in all orders of phenomenal existences,—material, vital, mental, intellectual, etc. The veils also are not externally superimposed upon the Spirit by any foreign power. The forms or embodiments which appear to conceal the essential nature of the Soul within them are not produced from any foreign element (any Primordial *Matter* or *Prakriti* or *Māyā,* distinct from the Spirit) somehow associated with the Spirit and conditioning His existence. Nor can they be reasonably conceived as mere illusory appearances to finite human minds, which are themselves their products and therefore presuppose them. Since the Spirit is the sole Ultimate Reality, all forms or embodiments of the Spirit in all levels of phenomenal existences,—all kinds of veils within which He appears to have concealed Himself in this cosmic system,—must be His own free self-manifestations, and hence they are also essentially spiritual. Hence to an enlightened person matter, life, mind, etc.,—all orders of phenomenal realities,—are essentially spiritual realities. The bodies are essentially no less spiritual than the Soul. The *yogi* aims at seeing the One Spirit in all kinds of bodies, and realising the essentially spiritual nature of all phenomenal realities. This is regarded as the *true knowledge* of the bodies, the phenomenal realities and the cosmic system.

The living human body with adequately developed external and internal organs and mental and intellectual faculties being from the empirical view-point the highest product of phenomenal evolution, a *yogi* first tries to discover the Supreme Spirit (with His Divine Power) within his own body. He undergoes a systematic course of moral and spiritual discipline for the enlightenment of his empirical consciousness and the experience of *Śiva-Śakti* in his whole being. He tries to realise his psycho-physical body as a spiritual body,—to realise the distinctive functions of his diverse physical and vital and psychical organs as particular forms of self-revelation and self enjoyment of *Śiva-Śakti* in different planes of experience. The physical and physiological and psychical concepts are gradually transformed in his consciousness into spiritual concepts; the different centres of the bodily organism are revealed as dynamic centres of diverse orders of spiritual experience and spiritual enjoyment. Through special forms of meditation in special centres he acquires newer acquaintance of more and more marvellous powers and glories normally hidden and dormant in his body and mind. Wonderful knowledge and insight, wonderful powers and capacities, are developed in him as the result of the dynamisation and spiritual unfolding of particular vital and psychic centres. The spiritual character of the body is revealed.

A *yogi* teacher, accordingly, while giving lessons to the learners on the constitution and the important physiological centres of the body, draws special attention to their significance from the spiritual point of view and takes special care to teach how the greatest spiritual benefits can be derived from their discipline and control and concentrated attention upon their spiritual aspects. The learners are instructed to be closely and practically acquainted with the nature of *Cakras, Ādhāras, Nāḍīs, Vāyus*, etc., within the body, not only as centres of physical and vital functions, but also as centres of psychical and spiritual experiences. They are described in the *yogic* scriptures from the physiological, psychical as well as spiritual view-points. Greater emphasis is laid upon the ways and means, by which they can be brought under voluntary control and converted into efficient instruments for the development of higher psychical powers, for the attainment of supernormal knowledge and wisdom, for ascending to higher and higher planes of spiritual consciousness and enjoyment of the blessings of more and more enlightened spiritual experiences.

Just as expert scientists invent various kinds of fine instruments and adopt various kinds of experimental methods for closer study of the inner structure and constitution of material bodies, plant-bodies, animal-bodies, human bodies, etc., and for deeper acquaintance with normally imperceptible physical, chemical, electrical, biological and other phenomena of the objective world, so the expert *yogis* of different ages adopted experimentally various kinds of technical devices and invented various processes of *Āsana*, *Prāṇāyāma*, *Mudrā*, *Bandha*, *Bedha*, *Neti*, *Dhouti*, etc., and also various modes of *Pratyāhāra*, *Dhāraṇā*, *Dhyāna* and *Samādhi*, for the most intimate acquaintance with the subtle operations of the various factors within their own bodies and the establishment of control over all of them. The knowledge, which is acquired through the intensive application of these methods of *yoga*, of the inner structure of the bodily organism and of the deeper potentialities of its different parts as well as of the significance of each vital centre in relation to the whole organism and particularly in relation to the spiritual energy and the spiritual ideal immanent in it, can not be expected to be attained by any other scientific method. The science of *yoga* is a special science, based on special types of observation and experiment. It enables a truth-seeker to penetrate into the innermost secrets of the living human body and to attain perfect mastery over all the parts of the body. It demonstrates such capabilities of the organs of this body, as are normally regarded as supernatural. It destroys the deep-seated notion about the fundamental difference between spirit and matter and shows how spirit is materialised and matter is spiritualised. It enables a man to realise the infinite in the finite body.

As a *yogi-scientist* draws upward in a systematic way his psycho-vital energy to higher and higher *ādhāras* and *cakras* and concentrates his consciousness upon higher and higher spiritual truths revealed therein, the individual body appears to his elevated and refined consciousness as being gradually liberated from the grossness and impurity and spatio-temporal limitations of its normal material nature and unveiling more and more brilliantly its inner spiritual character. Just as the modern physical science, having split up material atoms, has practically dematerialised matter and proved it to be a form of Energy, so this old *yogic* science enabled a spiritual aspirant to dematerialise his material body and to transform it so to say into a spiritual body,—a seat of infinite powers and spiritual glories.

In our normal experience conditioned by spatio-temporal relations, differences between parts and the whole, between distinct parts of the same whole, between the small finite individual body and the infinitely vast cosmic system and among the innumerable individual bodies within this system, are quite natural and inevitable. The differences among matter, life, mind and spirit also appear to be insurmountable. In our sensuous experience and sense-ridden thought we can never transcend these differences. But as our experience and thought ascend to higher and higher planes, these differences gradually lose their importance and their essential identity becomes more and more clearly unveiled. When the empirical consciousness is sufficiently refined and illumined, the whole is experienced in every part, the entire cosmic system is experienced in every individual body, the essential unity of all individual bodies is clearly revealed.

This experience is attained as the result of the systematic *yogic* discipline of the body, the senses, the mind and the intellect and the deepest concentration of attention upon the Supreme Spirit (with His *Śakti*) Who manifests Himself in the Cosmic Body and all forms of phenomenal existences within it. Differences among matter, life, mind and spirit also appear to be differences only in outer forms of phenomenal self-manifestation of the Supreme Spirit. The unity of the One Spirit pervades perceptibly all the diverse forms of derivative contingent impermanent phenomenal existences. The One becomes visible in all. In and through all kinds of limitations, the Infinite and Eternal is distinctly experienced by the Yogi with his enlightened spiritual consciousness. His vision does not turn back from the surface of things, as is the case with all normal experiences, (including scientific observations and experiments), but enters into the spirit of all things. The differences on the surfaces do not obstruct his vision of the unity of the reality.

Gorakhnath says,—

Pinda-madhye carācaram yo jānāti, sa yogī piṇḍa-saṃvittir bhavati.

—The yogi who experiences the whole cosmic system (comprising all animate and inanimate existences) within the individual body is the perfect knower (truth-realiser) of the body (*pinda*). Thus the complete and perfect knowledge of the individual body consists in rising above the spatial and temporal limitations of this body and identifying it with the whole universe, which is boundless in space and time and which comprises all the diversities in space and time. The complete truth of the individual body lies in or is revealed in the whole universe,—in the infinitely diversified and organised Cosmic Body of Śiva,— and the real glory of the human body (endowed with the most developed psycho-vital organism) lies in the possibility of realising the presence of this whole universe in it. The phenomenally infinite and eternal Cosmic Order is realisable in this obviously finite and transient body, the macrocosm is realisable in the microcosm. When the *yogic* vision is attained, the individual feels himself as *Viśwarupa* or *Virāt-Purusha* (Cosmic Personality) and sees all the worlds and all orders of phenomenal realities as comprehended within this all-pervading existence and as illumined by his universal consciousness Just as a person in the lower planes of experience feels all the internal and external phenomena of his individual psycho-physical organism as the multiform expressions of his own personal self, so a *yogi* in the higher and higher spiritual planes of experience feels all the phenomena of the Cosmic system,—those which are apparently magnificent and beneficent as well as those which are apparently terrible and cataclysmic or loathsome, those which are apparently indicative of forces of creation and preservation and harmonious development as well as those which are apparently indicative of forces of discord and disintegration and destruction,—as the variegated expressions of his own Cosmic Self. There is not only perfect *adjustment* of the individual body with the Cosmic System, but perfect spiritual *identification* of the one with the other.

As *Yogeśwara* Śri Krishna proclaims in the *Gītā*,
Ātmānam sarva-bhuteshu sarva-bhutāni cātmani
Ikshate yoga-yuktātmā sarvatra sama-darśanah.

A person who has attained true *yogic* experience sees himself in all beings and all beings in himself and thus becomes a true seer of perfect unity in all diversities.

In *Śiva-Samhitā*, which is an authoritative treatise on *Yoga*, Yogīśwara Śiva gives to Mother Pārvati a brilliant discourse on the cosmic character of the individual body. He describes that an enlightened *yogi* can experience *within his own body* the presence of all the *Lokas* (all the planes of phenomenal existences), all the suns and stars and planets and satellites, all the *Devas* and *Asuras* and *Yakshas* and *Rākshasas*, all *Rishis* and *Munis* and *Siddhas* and *Gandharvas*, all men and beasts and birds and reptiles, all seas and mountains and rivers and forests, i.e. whatever exist in the Cosmic Body of the Cosmic Purusha.

Siddha-Siddhānta-Paddhati, in its discourse on *Piṇḍa-Saṃvitti*, describes the presence of the entire *Brahmānda* in the *Pinda* in an elaborate manner. *Kurma*, Who is a special self-manifestation of *Śiva-Śakti* and is conceived as lying beneath and supporting the Cosmic Body, is perceived by the enlightened yogi as lying under his feet and supporting his body. The seven lower worlds,—namely, *Pātāla, Talātala, Mahātala, Rasātala, Sutala, Vitala* and *Atala*,—are perceived as constituting the lower parts of the body, from the toes of the feet up to the thighs. It is added that *Rudra* is the Presiding Deity and Governing Power of the seven lower worlds (*Sapta-Pātāla*). He is a special self-manifestation of the Soul of the whole Cosmic Body, i.e. Śiva with His infinite Power. He is also known as *Kālāgni-Rudra*. It is this *Rudra* that dwells within the individual body in the form of *Krodha* (wrath or violent indignation).

The three worlds (*Triloka*)—namely *Bhuh, Bhuvah* and *Swah*,—are located respectively in *Guhya-sthāna, Linga-sthāna* and *Nābhi-sthāna* (regions of *Mulādhāra, Swādhisthāna* and *Manipura*). *Indra,* Who is another glorious self-manifestation of Śiva with Śakti, is conceived as ruling over these three worlds, and this Indra is also conceived as dwelling in the individual body and ruling over all the senses (*indriyas*).

Similarly, the four higher worlds,—namely, *Mahah, Jana, Tapah* and *Satya,*—are conceived as located in the higher and deeper regions of the spinal cord within the individual body. As a man rises to higher and higher stages of contemplation and enters more and more deeply into the inner and inner essence of the body, he experiences these higher and higher *lokas* (finer and finer, subtler and subtler worlds) within himself. *Brahmā* and other majestic and glorious Deities, Who are all adorable self-manifestations of Śiva with Śakti and Who dwell in and govern these worlds, are also perceived as in-dwellers and rulers in the individual body.

Besides, Gorakhnath mentions *Vishnuloka* with *Vishnu* as its Deity, *Rudra-lokā* with *Rudra* as its Deity, *Iśwara-loka* with *Iśwara* as its Deity, *Nilakantha-loka* with *Nilakantha* as its Deity, *Śiva-loka* with *Śiva* as its Deity, *Bhairava-loka* with *Bhairava* as its Deity, *Anādi-loka* with *Anādi* as its Deity, *Kula-loka* with *Kuleśwara* as its Deity, *Akula-loka* with *Akuleśwara* as the Deity, *Para-Brahma-loka* with *Para-Brahma* as the Deity, *Parāpara-loka* with *Parameśwara* as the Deity, *Śakti loka* with *Para-Sakti* as the Deity. All these *lokas* are conceived as different planes of phenomenal existences within the Cosmic Body of the Supreme Spirit. These higher *lokas* are above the regions of normal and even supernormal sense-experiences, and some of them are even above the range of our ordinary mental and intellectual conceptions. But when the individual phenomenal consciousness is enlightened and the capacity for *yogic* experience is adequately developed through appropriate concentrated meditation in pursuance of the teachings of competent *Gurus,* the consciousness can inwardly rise to those planes and vividly experience the truths pertaining to them within the body.

The Deities are experienced as the Lords and Souls of these lokas with special spiritual characteristics and recognised by the enlightened *Yogis* as self-revelations of the Supreme Spirit, Śiva, the Soul of the Cosmic Body, enjoying Himself in the special ways in relation to these special realms of His Cosmic Body. In one plane He appears as perfectly calm and tranquil without any activity and without any joy or sorrow and without any compassion or sternness; in another *loka,* He appears as ever-active with waves of activities manifested all round Him; in another He appears as a stern God dispensing justice with stern hands; in still another He appears as an ever-joyful Deity radiating joys in all directions; in one plane He may appear as a pure abstract Principle, and in another as a perfectly good and beautiful and majestic Personality; in one plane He may appear as pure *Śunya* and in another as perfectly *Purna*; and so on. He reveals Himself in quite a variety of ways to the contemplative *Yogi* in different planes of his *yogic* experience, and the enlightened *Yogi* accepts all His glorious self-revelations as phenomenally real and enjoys Him in all these forms in his contemplation and meditation. The *Yogi* actually experiences all these *lokas* and all these *Devatās* within himself. He transcends the spatio-temporal limitations of his normal self and sees and enjoys the whole cosmos with all the apparently bewildering varieties in it within his own body.

Gorakhnath further elaborates his experience of the all-pervading all-comprehending character of every individual. Ultimately there is no essential difference between the individual and the cosmos. An enlightened *Yogi* experiences all men and women and children of all classes and castes and races and tribes within himself or as diversified manifestations of himself. He is therefore completely free from hatred and fear, competition and rivalry, selfishness and hostility, casteism and communalism and racialism and nationalism. In his practical behaviour he becomes an embodiment of love and sympathy to all. He experiences that all the seven divisions of the earth (*sapta-dwipa*), all the seven oceans (*sapta-samudra*, viz. *Kshāra-samudra, Kshīra-samudra, Dadhi-samudra, Ghrita-samudra, Madhu-samudra, Ikshu-samudra* and *Amrita-samudra*), all the nine regions (*nava-khanda,* viz., *Bhārata*-khanda, etc.), all the eight great mountains (*Kula-parvata*) and the numerous small hills (*upaparvata*), all the nine big rivers and their tributaries and branches, are within his body, that they constitute the different parts of his own body. Likewise, the twenty-seven *Nakshatras* (constellations of stars), the twelve *Rāśis* (signs of the zodiac), nine *Grahas* (planets), the fifteen *tithis* (lunar days), the thirty-three crores of *Devatās*, all *Dānavas, Yakshas, Piśācas, Bhutas* and *Pretas*, all *Gandharvas, Kinnaras, Kimpurushas* and *Apsaras*, all trees, plants, creepers, grasses and bushes, etc. etc.—all these are experienced by an enlightened *Yogi* as within himself, and not as external to him. Heaven and hell, bondage and salvation,—all these are enjoyed by him as conditions of his own experience.

Evam sarva-deheshu Viśwa-rupah Parameśwarah Paramātmā akhanda-swabhāvena ghate ghate Cit-swarupī tisthati.

Thus *Parameśwara Paramātmā,* Who is essentially pure Spirit (*Cit*) and Who manifests Himself as Cosmic Purusha (*Viśwarupa*), resides in every individual body with His whole nature (*akhanda-swabhāvena*). It is this *Viśwarupa* of *Paramātmā* that *Yogeśwara* Śri Krishna revealed to His

Bhakta Arjuna in His own body by giving him *yogic* vision (*divya-cakshu*). *Mahāyogi* Gorakhnath says that this *Viśwarupa* really exists in every individual body (*ghate ghate*), and a perfectly enlightened *Yogi* can see this *Viśwarupa* not only in the body of an exceptionally Divine Purusha like Śri Krishna, but also in his own body as well as in every other individual body. The Cosmic Whole pervaded by One Spirit is manifested in every individual form, and the difference between the Whole and the numberless parts is non-essential. So long as the individual consciousness moves in the material sensuous planes and cannot pierce through the veils created in them, the differences appear to be predominant, the Whole remains concealed behind the parts or is conceived merely as an abstract Principle underlying the concrete particulars. To spiritual insight the Whole is vividly visible in every part, the Infinite in every finite manifestation.

CHAPTER XVI

INDIVIDUAL SOULS

It has been found from the foregoing discourses that in the spiritual realisation and metaphysical reflection of Mahāyogi Gorakhnath and other enlightened saints of the Siddha-yogi school, it is the one non-dual transcendent Absolute Spirit, Śiva, Who, by virtue of the infinite Spiritual Power of the nature of absolutely free Will immanent in and non-different from His essential character, eternally reveals and enjoys Himself as an infinitely diversified and wonderfully harmonised Cosmic Body and also as the sole Indwelling Spirit and Absolute Lord of this phenomenal Cosmic Body. It has also been found that the same Supreme Spirit, by virtue of the same unique Power, has created within His Cosmic Body numerous orders of worlds,—i.e. numerous planes of phenomenal existences,—and has revealed Himself as numerous Deities or Divine Personalities functioning as their Indwelling Spirits and Governors and Harmonisers. It is the same Śiva, Who plays all these parts in all these forms as the World-Souls and the World-Bodies, as the Spiritual Rulers and their Phenomenal Regions, as the Deities and their domains of self-expressions. Thirdly, it has further been found that it is the same Supreme Spirit again, Who by virtue of the same unique Power reveals Himself as various orders of finite and transitory, simple and complex, individual bodies, and dwells in them and plays various roles in relation to them as their individual souls.

Thus, in the view of the enlightened Mahāyogis, whatever exists or may possibly exist in this spatio-temporal system or even above it is and must necessarily be a self-manifestation of the Absolute Spirit, Śiva, with His unique *Śakti*, freely active and essentially non-different from Him. The Mahāyogis do not even admit any fundamental difference of matter from spirit. Matter or body is no less a form of self-manifestation of the Supreme Spirit than spirit or soul. The entire universe with all that is or may be in it is spiritual in essence. A Mahāyogi with his illumined consciousnesss actually experiences it. Accordingly from the view-point of the enlightened experience of Mahāyogis, it is Śiva Himself Who dwells in every individual body as the individual soul, *Jeevātmā*. All psycho-physical organisms are His particularised bodily self-manifestations, and He plays the part of an individual soul with particular differentiating characteristics in each of them. Śiva is really the Soul of all creatures.

Though the soul and the body are both phenomenal self-manifestations of the transcendent Supreme Spirit and as such ultimately non-different from each other; nevertheless there is from the empirical viewpoint a good deal of difference between the two. The soul is evidently a spiritual manifestation of the Supreme Spirit, while the body is a physical manifestation. The body appears as a finite composite material entity, occupying a portion of space and undergoing various changes and transformations in time; the soul appears as a single simple self-luminous spiritual entity without any spatial characteristics and without any temporal modifications. The individual soul, though closely related to an individual body, does not specially occupy any particular portion of the body, but its presence can be realised in every part of the body; it is associated with the whole body and with every part of the body, amidst all changes that the body or particular parts of the body may pass through, without itself undergoing any such change. It is the unity and identity of the self-luminous soul that gives relative unity and continuity and identity to the composite body, which passes through various changes and transformations, integrations and disintegrations, organisations and disorganisations. From the state of the minutest seed (*bīja*) to the state of the fully developed and amazingly complicated organism, it is the same soul that reigns and shines in the body, exercises regulative influence upon all the functions of all elements of the body and maintains its harmony and unity and individual identity.

The soul is the master of the body, and all the operations of all the organs of the composite bodily organism revolve round the soul as their dynamic centre and by way of service to the soul. All the bodily functions appear to be immanently directed towards the fuller and fuller self-realisation of the soul, which is the spiritual owner of the body. The fuller and fuller self-realisation of the soul does not certainly imply any spatio-temporal change or modification of the soul, but it only implies the gradual self-emancipation of the soul from the veils and shades upon its essential spiritual and divine nature and from the conditions and limitations imposed upon its self experience by its phenomenal connection with the body and its environments. As the soul has no real spatial characteristics, no size or shape or magnitude, the Yogis consider it useless and beside the point to discuss whether it is of atomic size (*anu-parimāna*) or of the size of a thumb (*angustha-parimāna*) or of the size of the body (*madhyama-parimāna*) or of an all-pervading size (*vibhu-parimāṇa*),. Being essentially sizeless and shapeless and magnitudeless (though related to an individual body of any size or shape or magnitude), the soul may be conceived in any suitable way for the practice of meditation and contemplation or for the purpose of practical behaviour.

The soul is not only distinguished from the gross physical body, in its simplest and most homogeneous as well as most complex and heterogeneous form. But it is also distinguished from life, mind, ego and intellect, (*Prāna, Manas, Ahamkāra* and *Buddhi*). They all constitute its embodiments and instruments of self-expression and self-realisation in the phenomenal cosmic system. The soul is the centre and support and master of them and is the unifier and harmoniser of all their functions. The soul being of the nature of pure spirit (though apparently individualised in its phenomenal manifestation), transcends them all and is also immanent in and associated with them. All the phenomena of life, mind, ego and intelligence take place for the sake of the soul, and the soul is the sleepless and unfailing witness and illuminator and controller of them.

It may be remembered that Life, Mind, Ego and Intelligence have their existence and functions in the Cosmic Order as a whole, in the phenomenal Cosmic Body of Śiva-Śakti. The entire Cosmic System is pervaded by Life, Mind, Ego and Intelligence, and the enlightened yogis and philosophers find expressions of them everywhere in the universe. In the Cosmic System they are related to and are the instruments of phenomenal cosmic self-revelations of the Cosmic Soul, the Universal Spirit, Śiva. In relation to individual souls they have their particularised functions as instruments of self-expression and self-realisation of the respective souls. Though all of them are phenomenal self-manifestations of Śiva-Śakti and as such are spiritual in their essence, they are subordinate and subservient to the soul, in which the character of the pure spirit is substantially retained (although under limiting conditions) and in which there is the inherent possibility of the realisation and enjoyment of the perfectly and unconditionally self-illumined and blissful character of the Supreme Spirit, Śiva.

Thus the individual soul, in spite of its phenomenally individualised character, occupies a unique position and is essentially superior to and master of, not only the gross physical body, but also life, mind, ego and intelligence, which have their respective importance in this world-order. The soul is moreover to be distinguished from Moral Consciousness, from Aesthetic Consciousness and even from Spiritual Consciousness, though in and through them the soul has its noblest and most glorious forms of phenomenal self-expression. They also are forms of phenomenal consciousness, however refined and elevated and illumined they may be, and hence are subservient to the soul. It is in the state of perfect illumination of the Spiritual Consciousness that the soul realises its absolutely blissful identity with the Supreme Spirit, Śiva.

Though the soul is essentially distinct from the physical body and life and mind and intelligence and all forms of empirical consciousness, it normally identifies itself with them and ascribes their characteristics and changing conditions to itself. It is essentially free from all kinds of physical, vital, mental and intellectual limitations, free from origination and destruction, growth and decay, hunger and thirst, wants and sorrows, diseases and infirmities, passions and propensions, desires and emotions attachments and aversions, virtues and vices, ambitions and disappointments, errors and delusions, cares and anxieties, etc. They are all revealed and experienced in the individual bodies and lives and minds and intellects by the self-luminosity of the individual souls related to them; but the souls are not really affected by them, their essential nature is in no way contaminated by them. But in this phenomenal cosmic play of Śiva-Śakti, they are normally attributed to the individual souls, which are therefore regarded as subject to them. This is ordinarily spoken of as *Avidyā* (Ignorance) by philosophers of many schools.

According to the Yogi School, *Avidyā* is not to be conceived as an inscrutable or mysterious power, extraneous to the Absolute Spirit and inexplicably putting a veil upon the pure transcendent character of the Spirit, so as to make it illusorily appear as a plurality of finite and changing individual souls related to illusory bodies and lives and minds and intelligences in an illusory phenomenal cosmic system consisting of infinitely diverse orders of illusory phenomenal existences and experiences. Thus it does not accept the extreme Vedantist view of inexplicable *Avidyā* or *Māyā* for explaining the nature of the phenomenal cosmic order and the individual souls in it. Nor does it accept the Buddhist interpretation of *Avidyā*, assumed (unwarrantedly) as the first Principle in a cyclic chain of causation to account for the world of normal human experience,— an interpretation which leads to the illusoriness of the objective world and the permanent individual souls as well as to the denial of the Supreme Spirit as the Ground of this phenomenal order. The cosmic importance given to *Avidyā* by some of the Buddhist schools leads to the *Sarva-vainaśika Siddhānta* (all destroying conclusion) that this magnificent and harmonious world-order with all its wonderful laws and regularities and adjustments is a constantly changing illusory appearance without any real substratum or ground or permanent cause behind it. This view is unacceptable to the Sidddha-yogi school. The Sānkhya view of *Avidyā* as some unaccountable cause of non-discrimination (*aviveka*) between two such independent realities, as Spirit and Matter, *Purusha* and *Prakriti*, Pure Consciousness and the non-Conscious, does not also satisfy it. But nevertheless it accepts *Avidyā* as a real phenomenon in this phenomenal world of cosmic and individual self-expression of Śiva-Śakti.

In the view of the Siddha-Yogi, *Avidyā* is as much an essential element as *Vidyā* in the delightful phenomenal self-manifestation of the absolutely free (*Swatantra*) Will-Power (*Icchā-Śakti*) inherent in and non-different from the nature of the Absolute Spirit,—Śiva or Brahma. As it has been already explained, the Absolute Reality, though by itself eternally transcendent above time and space and causality and relativity and essentially of the nature of Absolute Existence, Absolute Consciousness and Absolute Bliss, has in Itself the unique free Will-Power of manifesting Itself in the forms of innumerable orders of phenomenal existences, innumerable orders of phenomenal consciousnesses and innumerable orders of phenomenal joys (shadowed by sorrows), under the conditions and limitations of time, space, causality and relativity. In the view of the Yogi School, the very notion of Absolute Existence, Absolute Consciousness and Absolute Bliss implies this Freedom and Power. The Absolute and Transcendent does not imply negation of or opposition to or incompatibleness with the relative and phenomenal. On the contrary, it indicates the perfect assimilation (*Samarasa*) and unification (*Ekatwa*) and identification (*Abhinnatwa*) of all relative and phenomenal realities within Itself. It implies Its absolute freedom to manifest from within Itself all kinds of phenomenal and relative realities, to experience and enjoy them in all levels of phenomenal experience, to reveal Itself as immanent in and as the Indwelling Spirit and Ruler of them all, and to merge all of them again in Its transcendent non-dual nature.

Without this freedom and power to reveal Itself in the phenomenal planes and without this freedom and power to link together and unify the transcendent and the phenomenal planes of existence and experience, the Absolute would not be really transcendent. The Infinite that excludes the finites and even the possibility of the finites can not be reasonably conceived as the real Infinite. The Eternal that excludes all temporal beings and becomings or that means only beginningless and endless continuity in time, is not the real Eternal in the metaphysical sense. The true Infinite and Eternal, while transcending space and time, must have the freedom and power to be revealed and manifested as all orders of spatial and temporal realities and to be immanent in them. Hence the true and adequate conception of the Absolute Spirit should be that It is transcendent as well as dynamic, eternally enjoying Itself above time and space and relativity as well as eternally revealing and enjoying Itself in infinite orders of finite and temporary phenomenal self-expressions.

Now, the phenomenal self-manifestation and self enjoyment of the non-dual transcendent and dynamic Absolute Spirit in the plurality of forms (*nānākāratayā vilāsah*) implies partial revelation and partial concealment (*āpekshika prakāśa tathā āpekshika āvarana*) of Its transcendent self-luminous non-dual character. Without partial self-concealment and self-imposed self-limitation there cannot possibly be any phenomenal self-manifestation and self-dualisation and self-diversification of the Absolute Spirit. It is only through various grades of self-concealment that there may be various forms of self-revelation, self-realisation, self-experience and self-enjoyment. The absolutely free Power (*Swatantra Śakti*), immanent in the nature of the Absolute Spirit, for Its phenomenal self-expression and self-enjoyment in infinitely diversified forms, must accordingly be conceived as a Power of illumination (*Prakāśa*) as well as as a Power of shadowing or darkening or obstruction of the light (*Āvarana-Śakti*), a Power of revelation as well as a Power of concealment, a Power of self-experience as the Unity of subject and object above all limitations and conditions as well as a Power of self-experience in the forms of diversities of subjects and objects in various planes under various conditions and limitations. It has to be conceived as a Power of expansion (*Prasāra*) of the Spirit to realise Itself as innumerable souls or subjects of experience and innumerable bodies or objects of experience, and it has also to be conceived as a Power of contraction (*sankoca* or *Samhāra*) of the Spirit to realise Itself as the Unity of existences and consciousnesses.

Thus the *Swatantrā Nijā Śakti* of Śiva is conceived as having eternally two-fold aspects in Her phenomenal manifestation, and these two aspects may be called *Vidyā*, and *Avidyā*. The free Divine *Śakti* in Her aspect of *Prakāśa* or illumination or revelation of the transcendent blissful nature of the Supreme Spirit in this phenomenal cosmic system is spoken of and adored as *Vidyā-Śakti*, and in Her aspect of *Āvarana* and *Vikshepa*, i.e. concealment or overshadowing of the transcendent nature of the Supreme Spirit and manifestation of the Spirit in diversities of phenomenal forms is spoken of and looked upon as *Avidyā-Śakti*. *Vidyā* and *Avidyā* are both real aspects of the nature of the *Śakti* immanent in and non-different from the nature of the Absolute Spirit, the Ultimate Reality. Without either of them the phenomenal self-manifestation and self-experience of the Ultimate Reality would have been impossible, the realisation and enjoyment by the Absolute Spirit of the infinite greatness and goodness and beauty and magnificence unified in Its transcendent nature would have been impossible.

Gorakhnath and the yogi school more often use the terms *Prakāsa* and *Vimarśa* in place of *Vidyā* and *Avidyā* to indicate the two-fold aspects of the inherent *Śakti* of *Śiva*, the unique Power of the Absolute Spirit. The term *Vimarśa* generally means reflection or detailed thinking. The Absolute Spirit is as it were reflecting upon the infinite contents of His eternally perfect transcendent nature. He is objectifying them to His own Consciousness. He may be said to be in the process of discovering Himself by thinking about Himself in a detailed way. This is the phenomenal aspect of His nature. In the transcendent aspect of His nature He is absolutely One; herein there is no differentiation between His Consciousness and His perfect Existence, there is no duality and relativity in His nature; herein He is in the state of what has been described as Absolute Experience, in which there is no distinction even between Himself as the Knowing Subject and Himself as the Known or Knowable Object. In this aspect the Absolute Spirit cannot even be said to be self-conscious, since self-consciousness in the sense in which we understand it involves a subject-object relation within itself. In Absolute *Prakāśa* (illumination) there can be no such relativity of consciousness, and hence no self-consciousness in the phenomenal sense.

The *Vimarśa* aspect of His *Śakti* makes the Absolute Spirit phenomenally self-conscious. The *Vimarsa-Śakti* is therefore interpreted as His Power of Self-consciousness or Self-reflection or the Power of His revelation of Himself to Himself. By virtue of this Power the Absolute Spirit comes down as it were from the plane of transcendent non-duality of Absolute Consciousness and divides Himself phenomenally into the duality of Subject and Object, so as to reflect upon and to become conscious of His own Self objectively. It is this objective self-consciousness or self-reflection of the Absolute Spirit, which appears as His Creation or phenomenal self-manifestation or realisation and enjoyment of Himself in the forms of diverse orders of experiencing subjects and experienceable objects. The whole universe,—the universe of time, space, causality and relativity,—the universe of finite changing existences, joy and sorrows, love and hatred, successes and failures, friendships and hostilities, etc.,—is nothing but the Absolute Spirit objectively reflecting upon and experiencing and enjoying His infinite spiritual nature in all possible forms in all levels of experience. His objective self-reflection is creation, sustenance and destruction of diverse orders of phenomenal realities in the spatio-temporal system. His *Vimarśa-Śakti* thus appears as His Power of self-diversification and is therefore called His *Māyā-Śakti.*

In the fourth lesson of *Siddha-Siddhānta-Paddhati,* having discussed the nature of the *Prakāśa-Śakti* and the *Vimarśa Śakti* of the Absolute Spirit or Absolute Consciousness, Śiva, Mahāyogi Gorakhnath says in conclusion:—

"*Kim uktam bhavati? Parā-para-vimarśa-rupinī Saṃvit nānā-śakti-rupena nikhila-pindā-dhāratwena vartate.*" What has been said so far? It is the One Self-luminous *saṃvit* (Absolute Consciousness) That reveals Itself as *Para-Vimarśa-Śakti* and *Apara-Vimarśa-Śakti* (Power of Collective Self-reflection and Power of Differentiated Self-reflection) and manifests itself.

(in the phenomenal cosmic system) in the forms of various orders and kinds of phenomenal *Śakti* (powers) and in and through them exists as the sole *Ādhāra* (upholder) of all the numberless *Pindas* (bodies, individual as well as collective) in the universe.

It has been noticed that in the phenomenal self-manifestation of the Absolute Spirit, Gorakhnath has mentioned the evolution of various orders of *Pindas* (bodies), beginning from the *Para-pinda* and ending with the diverse kinds of *Vyasti-pindas* (individual bodies). He has shown that in all these innumerable forms of *Pindas*, the Absolute Spirit, Śiva, is the One Soul, the One Upholder, Illuminer, Experiencer, Governor and Self-realiser. By virtue of His *Vimarsa-Śakti* He manifests all these infinite varieties of *Pindas* from within Himself, from the transcendent unity of His Absolute Existence-Consciousness-Bliss, and by virtue of His *Prakāśa-Śakti* He exists in all of them as their illumining souls and phenomenally experiences and enjoys the diversities of His own self-expressions under various kinds of conditions and limitations and in various planes of existence and consciousness and enjoyment. Śiva is as much the Soul of *Para-pinda*, *Anādi-pinda*, *Mahā-sākāra-pinda*, as of the bodies of individual gods and men and beasts and birds and insects, and even of the material bodies which outwardly appear to be lifeless and soulless. Every phenomenal reality is a manifestation of His Existence and is ensouled by Him. In this universe of His phenomenal self-manifestation and self-enjoyment, His *Prakāśa-Śakti* and *Vimarśa-Śakti* are apparently conditioned and limited by each other. Accordingly, the Soul, as manifested in each individual body, appears to be conditioned and limited by the nature and limitations of the body. All kinds of limitations and imperfections which are actually found in an individual soul are due to the bodily organism, through which it realises and expresses itself. Inwardly every soul transcends the bodily organism with all its instruments of knowledge and action and enjoyment, in as much as it is essentially of the nature of *Prakāśa* (illumination or pure consciousness).

At the close of the third lesson of *Siddha-Siddhānta-Paddhati*, after the exposition of the essential identity of each individual body with the Cosmic Body, Gorakhnath has asserted,—

"Evam sarva-deheshu Viśwarupah Parameśwarah Paramātmā akhanda-swabhāvena ghate ghate Cit-swarupī tisthati."

Thus *Paramātmā* (the Supreme Spirit), Who is *Parameśwara* (the Supreme Lord of all phenomenal existences) and Who reveals Himself as *Viśwarupa* (the Cosmic *Purusha* with the Cosmic Body) in all the individual bodies, exists in His unparticularised nature as pure Spirit (*Cit-swarupī*) in every finite individual body (*ghate-ghate*).

Thus in the view of the enlightened yogis, it is the Supreme Spirit Himself, Who exists in His pure spiritual nature (*śuddha-caitanya*) as individual souls (*jeevātmā*) in individual bodies. Accordingly in its essential character no individual soul is ever particularised or finitised or transformed or polluted or suffers from any bondage or sorrow or desire or aversion or fear. Every individual soul in its true nature participates in the pure existence and pure consciousness and pure bliss of the Supreme Spirit.

But from the phenomenal view-point the individual souls are found to be subject to *Avidyā* (ignorance or false knowledge or illusion) and consequent *Asmitā* (particularised egohood or self-consciousness), ***Rāga*** (desire and attachment), ***Dwesha*** (aversion and hostility), ***Abhiniveśa*** (lust for the present form of existence and fear of death or destruction). They also appear to be under the bondage of *Karma* (actions,—physical, mental and intellectual,—virtuous and vicious) and their consequences (pleasant and unpleasant, elevating and degrading). They, it is believed, have to pass through numerous births and deaths in numerous individual bodies and also through the experiences of heavens and hells for reaping the fruits of their various kinds of *Karma*. They have to struggle hard and to undergo systematic courses of self-discipline for the elevation and refinement and purification of their character and for the attainment of liberation from the oppressive and sorrowful conditions of existence in the individual bodies. How can all these be consistent with the view that the Supreme Spirit in His pure and unparticularised (akhanda) nature exists as individual souls in all individual bodies? How can the Supreme Spirit place Himself under subjection to all those bondages and limitations and sufferings and under the necessity of struggling for self-emancipation from all such undesirable conditions?

The reply to these questions from the view-point of the enlightened Mahāyogis has already been indicated. The Absolute Spirit, Śiva, by virtue of His infinite eternal free Will-Power in its *Vimarśa*-aspect, reflects upon and experiences and enjoys Himself in His absolute perfection as well as under all sorts of limitations,—limitations of existence and consciousness, limitations of knowledge and power, limitations of time and space, limitations of qualities and relations, etc. He experiences and enjoys Himself as the greatest of the great (*mahato-mahīyān*) and the minutest of the minute (*anor anīyān*) and in all conceivable intermediate forms. He experiences and enjoys Himself as *Paramātmā Viśwātmā Lokātmā*, *Jeevātmā*, as well as in the forms of all orders of *Pindas* in all planes of existence. It is the One Absolute Spirit Who is the true Soul in all of them, Who exists in all—

in the innermost heart of all,—in His *akhanda-swarupa* and takes delight as it were in experiencing Himself under all sorts of conditions and limitations. As Gorakhnath says,—

Alupta-śaktimān nityam sarvākāratayā sphuran
Punah swenaiva rupena eka evā vaśishyate.

Eternally possessed of infinite Power, the Absolute Spirit, while experiencing Himself in all kinds of forms, remains in His own self as the One without a second.

Avidyā or the phenomenal Ignorance of the essential infinite eternal self-luminous character of the Absolute Spirit is nothing but a form of self-imposed limitation, which His own *Vimarśa-Śakti* creates for His self-experience and self-enjoyment in the forms of the plurality of individual souls. As the result of this *Avidyā*, particularised and conditioned egohood is manifested, so that one individual soul may distinguish itself from other individual souls and may have a particular career in association with an individual psycho-physical embodiment. It is the One Absolute Spirit, Who quite freely embraces (i.e. reveals within Himself) relative Ignorance and Egohood by virtue of His immanent *Vimarśa-Śakti* for His phenomenal self-experience and self-enjoyment as a plurality of finite individual souls under various conditions and limitations. *Rāga, Dwesha, Abhiniveśa*, etc., actions and their consequences, births and deaths, joys and sorrows,—all these are concomitants of the sense of finite individuality. They all pertain to the phenomenal consciousnesses. The Soul behind the individual phenomenal consciousnesses is the same Supreme Spirit, Who is the ultimate Experiencer and Enjoyer of them all.

Take the case of a good wise happy man of the world, who, inspired by some lofty idealism, freely and voluntarily practises severe austerities, undergoes privations and hardships, abandons all domestic and social happiness, subjects himself to all sorts of trials and tribulations and even embraces torture and death. However outwardly terrible his sufferings may appear to be, he inwardly enjoys them, since he has freely and voluntarily adopted this path for the sake of his ideal and his whole heart is concentrated upon the cherished ideal. There is enjoyment in such freely courted sufferings, and there is true glory in them. In the human history those who suffered most for great ideas are universally adored. There is no reasonable ground for holding that the apparent limitations and imperfections and miseries from which individual creatures suffer in this phenomenal world are inconsistent with the essential Divinity of their Soul. The Divine Self of all has freely and voluntarily put Himself in all possible kinds of finite and imperfect individual bodies and enjoys the various kindse of partial experiences of Himself through them. He enjoys the various kinds of bondages and sorrows which He freely creates for experiencing Himself in all planes of existence and under all limiting conditions, and He likewise enjoys all kinds of struggle and self-discipline on the part of individuals for liberation from them.

Or think of the case of a wealthy talented person, who composes dramas and organises dramatic performances. All the characters and all the incidents in them are the products of his mind. He allots different parts to different players and exercises absolute control over them. He himself takes any part he freely chooses. He enjoys equal delight in playing the part of a slave or of a king, of a saint or of a sinner, of an oppressor or of a miserable victim of oppression, of a man rolling in luxuries or of a man suffering from want of food and shelter. He enjoys the most horrible incidents as much as the most amusing incidents. He takes delight in creating all kinds of *rasa* (aesthetic beauties),– not only those which rouse the feelings of pleasure or laughter or admiration or love or reverence, but also those which rouse the feelings of disgust or horror or hatred. He shows himself freely and joyfully in all these forms. They are all matertals for his self-expression and self-enjoyment as well as for giving joy to others. In the light of the variegated self-expression and self-enjoyment of a great artist we may form some idea of the perfectly free and delightful phenomenal self-manifestation and self-enjoyment of Śiva in the forms of various orders of finite and sorrowful individual creatures.

From this point of view the yogi philosophers easily solve what is called the *Problem of Evil,* which is a puzzling problem to all philosophical schools, and particularly the theistic schools. There is in the world of our normal experience the apparent prevalence of natural and moral evils, which we can not deny. There are natural catastrophes in the outer world, which are sources of sufferings to all sentient creatures. Sorrows and agonies prevail in the world of sentient living beings. Vices of various kinds are found in all strata of the human race. Philosophers are at a loss to explain these evils consistently with the infinite power, the infinite wisdom and infinite goodness of the Divine Creator. Various suggestions are offered by great philosophers to account for the presence of such evils in the Divine Creation, and every explanation is found by critics to be inadequate. Some schools of thinkers find the necessity of admitting the existence of a Second Power,—such as Satan or Ahriman,—as the sources of evil, for acquitting God of the responsibility for the creation of evil. This is obviously incompatible with the absolute creatorship of God. If God or the Supreme Spirit is accepted as the Ultimate Reality,—as the One without a second,—He must be regarded as the sole ultimate Cause of whatever may be experienced in this phenomenal world, and no second independent source of any phenomenon in this universe can be reasonably assumed. Nor can God be supposed to be compelled by any other cause,—whether material or efficient or final or formal,—to originate or to keep room for evils in the universe of His phenomenal self-manifestation.

The yogi philosophers not only accept the Supreme Spirit as the non-dual Ultimate Reality, but also regard the phenomenal universe with all orders of phenomenal realities appearing and disappearing in it as His *free* self-expression by virtue of His *Vimarśa-Śakti.* What we in our normal life experience or consider as natural and moral evils are also modes of His free self-revelations and as such are objects of His phenomenal enjoyment. Natural evils, i.e. pains and miseries, exist only for the empirical consciousness of sentient individual bodies, and moral evils exist only for the moral consciousness of rational human beings. Pleasures and pains, happinesses and miseries, are mutually related; they are modes of experience of the individual bodies in the sentient and psychical planes of their existence, desirse and efforts for getting rid of pains and miseries and attaining more pleasures and happinesses are associated with them and contribute to their development and elevation to higher planes; they play important parts in the cosmic design; and the Supreme Spirit as the individual souls witnesses them, regulates and harmonises and unifies them, and enjoys them. Pains and miseries are no more evils and play no less significant roles than pleasures and happinesses. As free self-expressions under self-imposed limitations they are equally enjoyable to the self-luminous soul.

There are really no catastrophes and disasters in inanimate nature. In the material world there are only various kinds of phenomenal changes, modifications and transformations, there are various forms of manifestations of physical and chemical and electrical and other forces leading to integrations and disintegrations and reorganisations of the material constituents of the cosmic system. The *Vimarśa-Śakti* of the Absolute Spirit is magnificently manifested in all these. The Absolute Spirit, though immanent in all of them as their *Ātmā* (true Self), seems to completely hide His essential spiritual character behind those phenomena, but must be supposed to enjoy them (or rather enjoy Himself in them), since they are His free self-expressions. These changes in the apparently inanimate nature are instrumental in preparing the ground for the evolution of life and mind and other higher orders of phenomenal self-manifestations and self-enjoyments of the free Divine Power. Some of these changes are interpreted as catastrophic and disastrous and evil by sentient thinking beings in accordance with their particular likes and dislikes and standards of values.

In the planes of living and conscious existences there are various grades of self-revelation and self-concealment of the Spirit, and hence various stages of development and limitation of life and consciousness. The various forms of pains and miseries, wants and pangs, diseases and deaths, cares and anxieties, disappointments and bereavements, etc., are only indications of the limitations and imperfections of life and consciousness in the individual bodies. The Supreme Spirit, in Whom life and consciousness are in eternal perfection, and Whose essential nature is *Ānanda*, takes delight in enjoying Himself under all possible limitations and imperfections by the exercise of His perfectly free *Vimarśa-Śakti,* and hence appears to embrace voluntarily all kinds of sorrows and disabilities in His individual self-expressions within His Cosmic Body. The necessary implication of all experiences of sorrows and sufferings is that they are sought to be transcended, that life and consciousness attempt to get rid of these limitations and imperfections and ascend to higher stages of development and perfection free from such sorrows. Hence sorrows stimulate efforts in the individual bodies for self-elevation to higher and higher planes of phenomenal experience, until they reach the plane of *Ānanda.* Sorrow is from this point of view nothing but *Ānanda* overshadowed by limitations created by the Divine Power and is instrumental in the progressive phenomenal realisation of *Ānanda* in the individual bodies. The Supreme Spirit as the individual souls in the individual bodies witnesses all these sorrows as well as the efforts and processes of liberation from them.

Again, the distinctions of virtue and vice, right and wrong, good and evil, justice and injustice, mercy and cruelty, partiality and impartiality, duty and crime, piety and sin, etc., belong to the moral plane of phenomenal consciousness. But for the evolution of moral consciousness in individual bodies, these notions would not arise, no such distinctions among phenomena would be drawn, and there would be no problem of moral evil to the philosophical thinkers. These virtues and vices, etc., are not of the nature of actual facts of phenomenal experience, but are of the nature of *judgments upon* facts by reference to some ideal or standard of value. It is in the moral plane of phenomenal consciousness that such judgments arise and certain kinds of phenomena are looked upon from the standpoint of some ideals. In the natural order of the phenomenal self-manifestation of the Supreme Spirit, just as various kinds of physical phenomena are manifested, so various kinds of vital and psychical phenomena are evolved.

The *Vimarśa-Śakti* of the Supreme Spirit with Her infinite freedom and infinite possibilities manifests Herself in various forms of vital tendencies, psychical dispositions, intellectual powers, etc., in various forms of knowledge and wisdom, desires and actions, feelings and emotions, etc. The same Divine *Śakti* manifests Herself in the evolution of Moral Consciousness, Aesthetic Consciousness and Spiritual Consciousness in relation to individual bodies. The Moral Consciousness, imbued with the Ideal of *Dharma* within itself, looks upon all phenomena from the standpoint of that Ideal and passes judgments of moral values upon them. Thus distinctions of virtue and vice, right and wrong, etc., arise. Some kinds of thoughts, feelings, dispositions, desires, actions, behaviours, etc., are regarded as good and virtuous and worthy of being cultivated and developed, and others are regarded as bad and vicious and fit to be abandoned or suppressed.

But those which are judged to be bad and vicious and which have to be abandoned or conquered or suppressed have their importance in the scheme of the elevation of life and mind and intelligence to higher and better and more enlightened planes. They also are modes of self-experience and self-enjoyment of the Supreme Spirit under various orders of self-imposed phenomenal conditions and limitations. He takes delight in freely creating these conditions and limitations and in progressively transcending or destroying them in the individual bodies for phenomenal self-experience and self-enjoyment in the higher and more illumined planes and ultimately raising the individual phenomenal consciousness to the transcendent plane. Just as sorrows are only His self-imposed veils and limitations upon His infinite bliss, so the vices are His self-imposed veils and limitations upon His infinite goodness and purity. In His phenomenal cosmic self-manifestation He freely imposes shadows and limitations upon His transcendent good and blissful nature and freely removes these shadows and transcends these limitations in gradual stages and enjoys all these processes as their all-illumining witness.

Just as the evolution of sensibility in the individual bodies is accompanied by the experiences of various kinds and degrees of pleasures and pains and the evolution of moral consciousness in them is accompanied by various forms of moral experiences of good and evil, *dharma* and *adharma*, so the evolution of aesthetic consciousness is accompanied by various forms of aesthetic experiences,—experiences of beauty and ugliness,—experiences of diverse kinds of *Rasa* from the sweetest (*madhura*) to the most loathsome (*bibhatsa*). These aesthetic experiences also are of the nature of judgments upon facts and involve reference to some conception of *ideal beauty*. What appears as relatively ugly or loathsome is, in the view of the enlightened *yogis*, really nothing but beauty experienced under various forms of limitations and distortions. Anything that may appear ugly in one set of conditions or in one state of the mental disposition may be appreciated and enjoyed as beautiful in a different set of conditions or in a differcnt state of the mental disposition. There is nothing absolutely ugly or abominable in the world-system, just as there is nothing which is absolutely evil or absolutely sorrowful. All phenomenal experiences are relative, and all our judgments of good and evil and beauty and ugliness are also relative. There may be a standpoint, viewed from which all phenomenal realities may be appreciated and enjoyed as good and beautiful and pleasant. Each of them has its proper place and function in the world-order,—in the cosmic system as well as in the individual organisms. They are all free and delightful self-manifestations in an infinite variety of conditioned and limited forms of One Who is infinitely good and beautiful and blissful. In the domain of the free play of the *Vimarśa-Śakti* of the Absolute Spirit, all possible forms of phenomenal relative existences and experiences are represented in the most suitable manners,—from the apparently most permanent to the apparently most momentary, from the apparently most beautiful to the apparently most ugly, from the apparently grossest to the apparently most subtle and fine, from the apparently best and most glorious to the apparently worst and most inglorious, from the apparently most happy and pleasant to the apparently most unhappy and unpleasant. We cannot, truly speaking, conceive of any form of existence and experience, which is not evolved in this spatio-temporal self-manifestation of the Infinite Power of the Supreme Spirit. This is the amazing and bewildering glory of *Mahā Śakti* of Śiva.

People living and moving and thinking in the plane of ignorance and egoism and wants and sorrows and desires and aversions and fears are often found to murmur that what is play to God is death to His creatures. They often charge Him with cruelty and partiality and injustice in His dealings with His creatures,—in moulding their characters and powers and propensities and environments and determining their fortunes and misfortunes, happinesses and miseries, elevations and degradations. To them the Law of *Karma* is no satisfactory ultimate explanation for the bewildering differences of the destinies of creatures, since desires and tendencies and actions of all creatures in all their births or embodied existences are no less governed by the Divine Will than their immediate or remote consequences. God must be as much responsible for the various kinds of deeds of all His creatures from the earliest stages of their individualised existence as for what are regarded as the happy and miserable fruits of those deeds. Sometimes failing to discover any satisfactory explanation for the wide differences experienced in the world of living beings consistently with their conception of the infinite power and wisdom and goodness of the Supreme Creator, many such people lose faith in God and the Divine Order of the world and think of the world-system as a chance-product of some blind

Force or orces operating without any wisdom or design or law or purpose.

In the enlightened view of Mahāyogis the questions of cruelty, partiality, injustice, etc., vanish, because the creatures of God are not other than or separate from God Himself. God or the Supreme Spirit is the Creator as well as the created. He reveals and experiences Himself in the phenomenal world in the forms of diverse orders of creatures, apparently happy as well as apparently miserable, relatively high as well as relatively low. There are of course cases of cruelty, injustice, oppression., in the world of His infinitely multiform self-manifestations. But as He is the individual soul in every body, He is the perpetrator of cruelty and injustice and He is the victim of cruelty and injustice, in every warfare He fights against Himself and He is both the victor and the vanquished, everywhere He is the master and the slave, the parents and the children, the teachers and the pupils, He is the wise and the foolish, the strong and the weak, the fortunate and the unfortunate and so on. By virtue of His infinite *Vimarśa-Śakti* He puts Himself in an infinite variety of situations in an infinite number of individual bodies, and as a plurality of individual souls He experiences and enjoys Himself in all these situations.

According to the Siddha-Yogis all differences are phenomenally real; but they lie in the bodily manifestations of the Spirit, and not in their Soul or *Ātmā.* All physical and vital differences, all sensuous and psychical differences, all intellectual and moral differences, all aesthetic and so-called spiritual differences, pertain to the bodies, but the Soul is in all cases essentially untouched by them. The Soul is their experiencer and illuminer and enjoyer, but is not really affected and qualified and conditioned by them. Smallness and greatness, sorrow and happiness, ignorance and knowledge, vice and virtue, and even bondage and liberation, are experienced in the bodies, and not in the Soul or Spirit, Which reveals them. All spiritual exercises and advancements also essentially consist in the elevation and refinement and purification of the bodies so as to raise them to higher and higher planes of spiritual experience and to make them more and more illumined and spiritualised. Bodies, it should be remembered, refer not only to the physical organisms, but also to vital, mental, intellectual embodiments of the Spirit and all forms of phenomenal consciousness in all planes. The Soul is ever-pure blissful consciousness in all forms of phenomenal embodiments, experiencing and revealing their differences and limitations and changes, but without being really affected and conditioned by them. As phenomenally reflected upon the finite and changing bodies, the Soul appears to be many and different in different bodies, but in truth It is one and the same in all bodies. In experiencing the diverse conditions and limitations and changes of the individual bodies, the Soul phenomenally identifies Itself as a matter of course with these bodies and hence appears to be individualised and diversely conditioned and qualified, but in reality It never loses Its essential transcendent character. Though phenomenally associated with and immanent in the finite bodies and the empirical consciousness, the Soul always inwardly transcends them. Hence though phenomenally playing the role of a finite individual and participating in the ups and downs of the individual bodily existence, the Soul is in Its essential character only the impartial witness to and enjoyer of them all. What is called *Moksha* is not essentially the liberation of the Soul from bondage and sorrow, but the liberation of the individual empirical consciousness from ignorance and impurity and limitations and bondages and sorrows, and the realisation in it of the essential purity and goodness and infinity and blissful character of the Soul, i.e. the identity of the Soul with the Supreme Spirit.

It is sometimes contemplated that the Absolute Spirit, having by virtue of His inherent *Mahā-Śakti* manifested Himself as the infinitely diversified phenomenal Cosmic Body, experiences and enjoys it and plays with it principally from three stand-points,—viz., *Paramātmā, Ātmā* and *Jeevātmā*. As the One Soul and Lord, Illuminer and Experiencer and Enjoyer, of His free self-evolving eternal and infinlte *Mahā-Śakti*, He is conceived as *Paramātmā*. As the Soul pervading the entire Cosmic Body and as the Indwelling Spirit of all orders of existences in it, He is conceived as *Ātmā*. As the plurality of Individual Souls of the individual bodies, He is conceived as *Jeevātmā*. These distinctions of *Paramātmā*, *Ātmā* and *Jeevātmā* lie only in the *upādhis*,—only in consideration of His phenomenal relation to His *Prakāśa-Vimarśā-tmikā Śakti* that is the dynamic source and cause of all phenomenal existences and consciousnesses, secondly in consideration of His immanent presence as the Soul of all orders of phenomenal self-manifestations of His *Śakti*, and thirdly in consideration of His playing the part of the individual soul in every individual body. Such conceptual distinctions, however, imply no real difference or change or modification in the true nature of the Spirit. He always transcends the parts He plays, transcends the situations which he creates for Himself, transcends the relations in terms of which He is characterised and His nature is defined. He experiences and illumines and enjoys all with His transcendent self-luminous nature wholly unaffected. The spiritual enlightenment of the empirical consciousness consists in the realisation of the oneness of *Jeevātmā, Ātmā* and *Paramātmā*,—in seeing the same Absolute Spirit, Śiva, as the souls of individual bodies and as the all-pervading changeless self-luminous Soul and Truth of all phenomenal existences as well as the all-transcending Soul and Lord of the Supreme Power, Which freely unfolds Herself into the phenomenal universe.

Gorakhnath says,—

Ātmeti Paramātmeti Jeevātmeti vicārane
Trayānām aikya-sambhutir ādeśa iti kīrtitah.

In our phenomenal reflection we distinguish between *Ātmā, Paramātmā* and *Jeevātmā.* The unity of the three is the truth, and the realisation of this truth is called *Ādeśā.* In view of this, whenever Yogis greet one another, they utter the words *Ādeśā Ādeśā.* By this form of salutation Yogis constantly remind one another of the identity of every individual soul with the Cosmic Soul and the Transcendent Spirit.

CHAPTER XVII

THE SUPREME IDEAL OF LIFE

From the earliest age of Hindu spiritual culture, ***Moksha*** or ***Mukti*** has been generally accepted as the supreme end of human life. ***Moksha*** or ***Mukti*** literally means freedom or liberation or emancipation or deliverance. As commonly understood, it is rather a negative term. It implies some state of existence, from which freedom or liberation or emancipation or deliverance is sought for, but gives no positive ideal of what will actually be attained, when this freedom or liberation from the present state of existence is achieved. It is in this apparently negative sense that it is universally accepted as the most desirable end of human life by almost all systems of religion and philosophy.

What is the state of existence from which deliverance is urgently sought for by all human beings,—nay, by all sensitive living beings? Perhaps it is obvious to all that *Sorrow* is the most universal fact of experience, not only to human beings, but also to all living beings having sensibility, and that all such beings naturally seek for getting rid of the sorrowful state of existence. Sorrow appears to be occasioned by various causes, external as well as internal. From birth to death the causes of sorrows are practically always present. Life seems to consist in continuous struggle with sorrows and their causes. Besides the causes of sorrows present in all orders of animal life, in human life the mental and intellectual and moral imperfections are additional sources of sorrows. Goaded by the natural urge for getting rid of sorrows, a man has throughout his life to struggle against all these causes of sorrows. Temporary successes in these struggles lead to temporary cessations of sorrows and temporary enjoyments of relief and pleasure. But causes of sorrows are never rooted out and hence permanent happiness appears to be unattainable in this life. Even physical death, which is itself attended with sorrow, cannot lead to permanent relief from sorrow, since the Law of Moral Justice,—the Law of Karma,—prevailing in the world-order assures continuity of life in a subtle body in the other worlds and also rebirth in fresh gross bodies for reaping the fruits of right and wrong actions and thus leads to the continuity of sorrows and struggles in the new bodies.

Truly speaking, Sorrow is at the basis of all human culture and civilization. It is the stimulating force behind all creative and destructive activities and all progress and development in the human world. Sorrows create desires and stimulate actions for getting rid of these sorrows.

The desires and actions, though giving temporary relief from particular sorrows, cannot destroy them, but rather become sources of fresh sorrows, which again originate fresh desires and fresh actions, and so on, perhaps *ad infinitum.* The human mind never becomes free from sorrows, from the sense of want and dissatisfaction and discontent, from the uneasy sense of imperfection and limitation and bondage, and hence never free from desires and struggles. In course of the struggle for attaining liberation from Sorrow, which constantly appears in newer and newer forms and creates newer and newer desires, the powers and qualities which are dormant in human nature are awakened and activated, the mind and the heart and the intellect become more and more developed and refined and enlightened, the fields of knowledge and activities are gradually expanded, men acquire greater and greater control over the forces of external nature and over other animals, sciences and arts and technologies are progressively developed, social and political and military and religious organisations are evolved and acquire more and more powers and influences, the human life becomes more and more complicated. The goading power of Sorrow is at the root of all these developments.

Thus Sorrow plays a very important part in the scheme of the world of living beings, and specially in the human world. From the beginning to the end, the human history is a continuous fight against Sorrow. It is this fight which has bestowed all glories upon man. But Sorrow has never acknowledged defeat. In the most civilized state of human existence Sorrow does not seem to be in any way less powerful than in any less civilized state. With the increase of the sources of pleasure and happiness, with the discoveries and inventions of finer and finer instruments of pleasure and happiness, there seems to be a corresponding increase of the sources of sorrows. All human efforts for the conquest of Sorrow by means of the improvements of the external conditions of physical existence appear to have utterly failed. Should we then conclude that human beings are born to suffer from sorrows and to struggle against them and never to conquer them or to attain liberation from them? This would be a pessimistic view of human life. This pessimism would itself be another source of sorrow. The highest and the most illumined human minds have not accepted this view.

All the greatest saints of India and all the major philosophical systems are unanimous in proclaiming that Sorrow can be absolutely conquered and that the absolute conquest of Sorrow is the ultimate ideal of human life. They also add that Sorrow cannot be absolutely conquered by means of any kind of improvements of the physical conditions or by means of developments of empirical knowledge and worldly powers.

or by means of acquisition of vast wealth and materials for earthly enjoyments, or by means of various kinds of organisations and scientific and technological achievements. In order to attain perfect freedom from all actual and possible sorrows, in order to destroy the root of all sorrows, man has to direct all his energy and wisdom inward, he has to concentrate all his attention upon the innermost essence of his being. This inward turning of the human energy and wisdom and their concentration upon the innermost essence of being is called *Yoga*, and this is the essence of Religion. It is by the attainment of perfect success in this religious self-discipline that man can root out the possibility of all sorrows. It is not through any kind of outward endeavours, individual or collective, but through inward concentration of energy, that man can rise above the domain of Sorrow.

It is universally proclaimed by the most enlightened saints and philosophers that the innermost essence of being,—the ultimate essence of the being of the individual as well as of the universe,—is untouched by Sorrow, is above the domain of sorrows and desires and struggles, is perfectly calm and tranquil and blissful. Sorrow rules over the lives and minds, to which the ultimate essence of being is veiled. When the mind is illumined by the experience of the essential Truth of its own being and of the being of the universe, there is no sorrow for it, no sense of limitation and bondage, no desire and struggle. For the absolute conquest of Sorrow, this illumination of the empirical mind, this experience of the ultimate Truth of the self and the universe, is regarded as the essential condition. This is evidently a positive Ideal of conscious life. According to most of the religio-philosophical systems of India, the Supreme Ideal of human life, which is negatively indicated as *Mukti* or perfect liberation from all actual and possible sorrows, essentially consists in the realisation or direct experience of the ultimate Truth of the being of the self and the universe,—*Tattva-sākṣātkāra*.

What is the exact nature of the ultimate essence of the self and the universe and what is the state of being that is attained through the realisation of this ultimate essence,—through what is called *Tattwa-Sākshātkāra*,—cannot however be precisely defined in terms of the categories of phenomenal understanding, because it is above the range of empirical thought and speech. Such definition is possible only in cases of the contingent and relative objects of the empirical mind. The Absolute Reality is indefinable and the ultimate realisation also is indefinable. As the Absolute Reality, i.e. the ultimate essence of the self and the universe, is above the subject-object relation and thus above the range of the empirical mind, so in the ultimate Truth-realisation the subject-object difference is wholly merged in the unity of one Absolute Experience, the empirical mind is either transcended or merged in the unity of the Spirit, and It is not known as an object of phenomenal understanding. Thus our phenomenal understanding can neither intellectually conceive nor verbally define either the Absolute Reality or the Absolute Truth-realisation.

But the enlightened *Gurus*, having descended from the plane of Absolute Experience to the normal plane of the phenomenal consciousness, from the plane of the indefinable Absolute Unity to the normal plane of relativity and contingency, find it necessary to give the truth-seekers and spiritual aspirants some positive idea, however vague, of the Ultimate Truth and the Ultimate Ideal of human life. So long as they explain their supra-phenomenal experience in negative terms, no appreciable difference arises in their teachings. But when they try to give to their disciples some positive ideas in terms of relative phenomenal understanding of the Absolute Truth and the Absolute Ideal, they are found to use expressions which convey different meanings to the truth-seekers living and moving and thinking habitually in the domain of empirical consciousness, in the domain of relativity and contingency. The effect upon the minds of the ordinary truth-seekers is the impression that the great saints and sages, the illustrious *Gurus*, all of whom are generally believed to have realised the Absolute Truth and the Ultimate Ideal of life, differ from one another in their knowledge or conception of the Truth and the Ideal. The followers of different *Gurus* are divided into different philosophical schools and different religious sects, and often fight with one another with their logical weapons for the substantiation of the teachings of their respective *Gurus* and the refutation of those of others. The disputes are never settled, because they are not soluble on the intellectual plane, the plane of phenomenal understanding.

The term *Moksha* or *Mukti* is a very convenient term and is almost universally accepted by all classes of religious teachers and philosophical thinkers in India to signify the ultimate Ideal of human life. As it has already been pointed out, this term has primarily a negative meaning, but all the same it holds before the normal human intellect a highly glorious view of the Supreme Ideal in terms of the actual facts of our general experience. When the significance of the term is deeply reflected upon and comprehended, it appears that though it is seemingly negative, the ideal is full of rich positive contents and its realisation would mean the perfect satisfaction of all the fundamental demands of self-conscious human life.

It has been mentioned that *Moksha* has primarily been interpreted by most teachers as the attainment of perfect freedom from all possible sorrows. This itself is revealed, on deeper reflection, as a supreme positive Ideal, when it is realised that absolute sorrowlessness means to a self-conscious mind perfect *Ānanda,* perfect self enjoyment, a perfectly blissful state of being, perfect fullness of existence. No self-conscious person in his normal state aspires after reducing himself into insensate lifeless matter or to annihilate himself in order to get rid of all actual and possible sorrows. It is assumed by all that life and mind are superior to lifeless and mindless matter, that life is preferable to death, though life and mind may be full of sorrows throughout the normal state of existence. Absolute sorrowlessness as the Ideal of life and mind must refer to the perfect fulfilment of life and mind, and not the annihilation of life and mind. A living and conscious being must develop and refine and elevate the life and mind to the state of absolute sorrowlessness, and must not go down to the state of stocks and stones to be released from sorrows nor commit suicide for this purpose. The state of the perfect fulfilment of life and mind may be incognisably unlike the present normal imperfect empirical state. In that supreme state life and mind may transcend their normal phenomenal conditions. But the full realisation of their possibilities in the normal phenomenal states is attained in that supreme state of sorrowlessness. This is the state of *Ānanda,* which every person inwardly aspires after, though the aspiration may not always appear on the surface of the empirical consciousness. This is certainly not a negative ideal, but the most inspiring positive ideal of life.

Now, why is it that we fail to realise the state of perfect and uninterrupted *Ānanda* or self-fulfilment in the normal plane of our conscious life? The general answer to this question is, as Lord Buddha said, that this is because we have desires and these desires are never satisfied. All sources of sorrows are sought to be accounted for in terms of desires, which appear to be insatiable in our actual life. But when we deeply reflect upon the nature of sorrows and desires, it becomes difficult to decide definitely which are the causes of which. In conscious life desires are found to be necessary accompaniments of sorrows. When sorrows are felt, the urge to remove the sorrows arises. Thus desires are ordinarily experienced as arising out of sorrows in our practical life. How can we definitely assert that desires are the real causes of sorrows on the basis of our normal experience? Do our desires create our hunger and thirst, our diseases and physical pains, our old age and infirmities, our adverse climatic conditions, the cruelties of the natural forces and the ferocious animals, our bereavements and pangs of death, etc.? Our desires for food and drink, health and comfort, clothing and shelter, wealth and security, etc., follow the sorrows naturally produced from those causes.

Desires are followed by actions for fighting against those causes. How can those causes of sorrows be regarded as the effects of desires? There may of course be many artificial desires or ambitions and their non-fulfilments, which may be causes of further sorrows, and these generally evolve in the conscious minds in their comparatively more developed stages. How on the basis of our normal experience can we conclude that Desire is the root of all sorrows? Desire may be said to be the first step in the struggles against sorrows, but not its invariable antecedent or cause.

It may be argued that if we accept ungrudgingly these sorrows which arise in natural course in our normal conscious life, if we do not desire to get rid of and to struggle against them, that is to say, if we can become practically dead to these sorrows, the sorrows will lose their stings and will not remain sorrows in our consciousness. Even if this were possible, it would not prove that Desire is the cause of Sorrow. It would rather mean abject self-surrender to Sorrow and helpless contentment under the reign of Sorrow. To live a totally desireless and actionless life in the domain of Sorrow by becoming wholly indifferent to Sorrow would not certainly be a life of *Ānanda* or perfect self-fulfilment. It would amount to the reduction of life into lifelessness, and the degradation of consciousness to the unconscious plane. Mere liberation from the distinction between the desirable and the undesirable without the realisation of a perfectly desirable and blissful state of consciousness is no inspiring ideal of human life.

To the ordinary people of commonsense suffering from various kinds of sorrows in their practical life, Mahāyogi Buddha preached that all existence is sorrow and that in order to get rid of sorrows and all possibilities of sorrows one must get rid of existence and all possibilities of future existences. By existence he meant phenomenal existence, existence under spatio-temporal conditions, existence in which everything is of impermanent and momentary nature and in which there is no stability and no security. It is only with such existence that all self-conscious minds are acquainted within themselves as well as outside themselves in this world of their experience. Accordingly he taught that desires for and attachments to such unstable impermanent momentary objects of the world and hankerings for the permanence of this life and the permanence of the objects of enjoyment herein make life sorrowful. If the consciousness of the unstable impermanent momentary nature of all objects of experience within and without becomes deeply rooted in the mind and all desires and attachments are driven out from it, there would be no feeling of sorrow, or at least the mind would not be perturbed by any changes in the physical and physiological conditions, since change is their nature.

In the absence of desires and attachments the mind illumined by the light of the consciousness of the momentary character of all existences would transcend the distinctions of desirable and undesirable, pleasant and unpleasant, good and evil, virtue and vice, and hence would transcend all sorrows. The Law of Karma would have no influence upon such an illumined mind, and hence it would have no rebirth. It would be free from the sense of the permanent ego, the sense of individuality. This illumined and perfectly sorrowless and calm and tranquil state of the mind is what Buddha designates as *Nirvāna*, which is synonymous with *Moksha* or *Mukti.*

But what will then happen to this illumined mind free from the sense of ego or individuality? Will it exist or cease to exist? That it will continue to have phenomenal existence so long as the bodily life continues does not admit of doubt. But what after that? As in Lord Buddha's terminology existence means impermanent ever-changing sorrowful phenomenal existence, the illumined mind must be verbally said to pass into the state of *non-existence*. But from Buddha's teachings it becomes evident that by this non-existence (*mahā-parinirvāna*) he did not imply absolute negation of existence, but he pointed to the indefinable *transcendent existence*, which is perfectly calm and tranquil, absolutely above the limitations of time and space, absolutely peaceful and blissful. It is liberation from phenomenal existence and the attainment of transcendent existence, which Buddha taught as the supreme ideal of human life.

But what is it that attains this state of infinite eternal peaceful and tranquil transcendent existence? Can the phenomenal mind be reasonably conceived as transcending the phenomenal plane of existence and ascending to the transcendent plane? The phenomenal mind, according to Buddhist philosophy, is not one permanent identical reality, but a temporary continuity of momentary units. How can it transcend time? How can it possibly exist by being free from its essential transient nature? If that which sustains its continuity is destroyed, it must as a matter of course cease to exist, and there would be no entity to attain *Nirvāna* and enjoy its peace and tranquillity. Lord Buddha generally kept silent on this problem, because he wanted to avoid the puzzling questions of metaphysics and to guide the seekers of liberation from sorrow in the practical path of physical and mental self-discipline and of the cultivation of desirelessness and non-attachment and selflessness together with universal sympathy. He could not openly and clearly give to the truth-seekers any positive idea of *Nirvāna* or *Moksha,* because, it seems, he was determined to observe absolute silence about the *Ātmā* or Soul behind the phenomenal mind. He often used the term *Ātmā* in the sense of phenomenal mind or the ego or the empirical self-consciousness and hence spoke of its nature as subject to change and sorrow and destruction.

All great Hindu saints and philosophers attached the utmost importance to the idea of the *Ātmā* or Soul existing permanently behind the phenomenal mind (i.e. behind *Mana, Buddhi* and *Ahamkāra*) as the changeless indestructible self-luminous centre of the being and becoming of every individual creature. According to all of them, *Ātmā* in its essential character is untouched by all kinds of sorrows, unaffected by all kinds of vicissitudes to which the individual *mana* and *buddhi* and *ahamkāra* and *prāna* and *śarira* are subject. Pure consciousness is its essential nature. Though related to particular psycho-physical organisms, its essential nature is free from the phenomenal conditions and limitations and bondages of these organisms. It is the self-luminous centre of the organism; all the physical and vital and mental organs perform their functions and undergo changes and modifications round about it; it witnesses all their operations and variations and furnishes the bond of union among them; it illumines all their activities and modifications; but it is in its essential nature transcendent of all of them.

This *Ātmā* is the true self of man. It is the self-luminous changeless self underlying his phenomenal ego-self. It alone has consciousness by its essential nature, while the consciousness of the phenomenal ego or self is derivative. The phenomenal self or ego is illumined by the self-luminous *Ātmā*; it becomes conscious by the innate consciousness of the *Ātmā* and experiences and knows itself and its objects by means of this reflected consciousness. *Ātmā* is accordingly the real seer or knower or experiencer of the ego and the mind and all objects of phenomenal experience or knowledge, though it itself undergoes no modification or change in this seeing or knowing or experiencing. It is pure witness to all phenomena, all changes and modifications. It is witness to the *knowledge* as well as the *ignorance* of the phenomenal mind or ego. It is witness to all processes of knowledge and feeling and volition and active endeavours and passive sufferings of the mind or ego; it reveals them all to the phenomenal consciousness; but it is not in any way disturbed or agitated or moved or modified by these processes.

In all phenomenal circumstances, *Ātmā*, i.e. the innermost self, is in its essential nature perfectly calm and tranquil, perfectly self-conscious and self-enjoying, perfectly in the supra-mental supra-temporal supra-spatial supra-phenomenal transcendent state of existence. Though appearing to be individual in relation to an individual psycho-physical organism, *Ātmā* is in itself free from the sense of individuality, as it does not participate in the conditions and limitations, the enjoyments and sufferings, the imperfections and hankerings, the achievements and failures, of any such organism. Though apparently individual, every *Ātmā* is really universal and limitless. Though revealing itself in and through a particular complex phenomenal embodiment, in its essential nature it is transcendent. All sorrows and imperfections and bondages and all longings and aspirations for liberation from them pertain to phenomenal ego, while *Ātmā* which lies behind it and is the ground of its existence and consciousness is essentially untouched by all these. This is the conception of *Ātmā* according to most of the greatest philosophers and religious teachers of India. Accordingly they hold that the attainment of the perfectly sorrowless state of existence really means the realisation by the phenomenal ego of the essential character of the *Ātmā*, which is its supra-phenomenal ground and of which it is a phenomenal self-manifestation. Thus *Self-realisation* is conceived to be the supreme Ideal of human life, the Self evidently meaning the true transcendent Self or *Ātmā*. *Ātmā* is the supra-phenomenal ground and dynamic centre and the ultimate goal of the phenomenal self.

All the principal Hindu religio-philosophical systems are based on this glorious and inspiring conception of *Ātmā* or the true Self of every living being. They proclaim to every man and woman and child,—You are not this physical body subject to birth and growth and disease and decay and death, you are not the vital system which is disorganised and devitalised in course of time, you are not the mind subject to pleasure and pain and various kinds of desires and emotions and imaginations and dreams and hallucinations and thoughts and cares and anxieties, you are not the intellect subject to doubts and errors and imperfections, nor are you the organised unity or totality of all or some of them; you are in your essential nature above them all; though you are apparently associated with them and you apparently participate in their phenomenal activities and struggles and sufferings and enjoyments as the dynamic centre of them all, you in the essential character of your true Self transcend them all and are untouched by their limitations and changes, developments and degradations, joys and sorrows.

They make the bold assertion that the true Self of an individual has no limitation or imperfection, no birth or growth or decay or death, no degradation or development, no want or desire or struggle or sorrow. The phenomena of the body and the senses and the vital organs and the mind and the intellect, the imperfections and limitations pertaining to them and the joys and sorrows experienced in relation to them, are falsely attributed to the essential Self due to the Ignorance of the transcendent character of this Self. When a person gets rid of this deeply rooted Ignorance and attains true knowledge of the Self or *Ātmā*, he becomes perfectly free from all sorrows and all possibilities of sorrows. The knowledge has of course to be attained by the phenomenal self or ego through the purification and refinement and enlightenment of the phenomenal instruments of knowledge and through the deepest concentration of the purified and refined mind and intellect upon the transcendent character of the true Self or *Ātmā;* the phenomenal self or ego has to be perfectly absorbed with and merged in the concentrated thought of the true Self. When in this way the phenomenal ego becomes fully identified with the transcendent Self, when the phenomenal consciousness is fully illumined by the self-luminous transcendent Self, there is perfect Self-knowledge or Self-realisation and there is perfect liberation or freedom from all sorrows and bondages and imperfections. The phenomenal ego, having perfectly purified and refined itself and having consciously identified itself with the *Ātmā* or transcendent Self, realises that it is essentially and eternally untouched by Sorrow.

Know thy Self, be thy Self, realise the essentially transcendent sorrowless character of the true Self in thy empirical consciousness and thereby be free from all impurities and weaknesses and wants and imperfections—this is the Ideal placed before man by all the Hindu religio-philosophical systems since the time of the revelation of the Vedas. So long as the Soul is embodied in a phenomenal psycho-physical organism, you should of course be physically and mentally active, but you should act with the enlightened consciousness of the infinite and eternal transcendent character of your true Self and hence wlthout any desire and attachment, without any care and anxiety, without any affection or aversion, and without any sense of difference between man and man and even between man and other creatures. This is spoken of as the state of *Jivanmukti* (*Mukti* or *Moksha* as realised in the living embodied condition).

Such an enlightened and liberated man, though outwardly living and moving and acting in the phenomenal world under psycho-physical conditions and limitations, is inwardly free from all bondages and limitations, all wants and sorrows, all good and evil, all virtues and vices. Though in the world, he is in his inner consciousness always above the world. Though apparently living a finite and changeful life, he is inwardly conscious that his Soul transcends all finitude and change and that he is essentially one with all. Amidst all apparent vicissitudes of mundane existence, he is inwardly always in the enjoyment of fulness and bliss. His actions are normally actuated by universal love and compassion and they contribute to the happiness and moral and spiritual welfare of the distressed people of the world, but inwardly he is conscious that he neither acts nor is acted upon, that he is neither the cause of any good nor the cause of any evil, that he neither removes the sufferings of the people nor inflicts sufferings upon them. He has no sense of ego, no sense of *me* and *mine.* Moreover, even while outwardly acting, he sees the same sorrowless and free transcendent Soul or Spirit in everybody and feels the essential identity of himself with everybody in respect of the Soul or Spirit. The life of a *Jivanmukta* is a life of inaction in action, a life of the enjoyment of infinity and changelessness amidst finite and changing environments, a life of unperturbed tranquillity and blissfulness in the world of sorrows and troubles, a life of universal love and sympathy and fellow-feeling in this world of struggle for existence and pleasure and consequent mutual rivalry and hatred. This is a great Ideal of life.

But what happens to the Soul, when it is perfectly released from its apparent association with the phenomenal psycho-physical organism? In physical death ordinarily the gross physical body (*sthula-deha*) only perishes, but the Soul remains associated with the subtle psychical body (*sukshma-deha*), which does not die with the death of the physical body; that is to say, the individual ego consciousness with subtle desires (*vāsana* or *trishnā*) and impressions of all past phenomenal experiences (*sanskāras*) as well as merits and demerits arising from past virtuous and vicious deeds remains attached to the Soul, and this becomes the cause of the assumption of fresh physical bodies and fresh courses of actions and struggles and enjoyments and sufferings in the physical world. But when physical death occurs after the attainment of perfect experience in the deepest *Samādhi* of the infinite and eternal transcendent character of the Soul and the perfect spiritual illumination of the phenomenal consciousness through that experience, the individual ego-consciousness with all its concomitants also dies out and the Soul is absolutely emancipated from its apparent association with all its phenomenal embodiments and hence from all possible sorrows and limitations. Then there remains no cause for fresh birth either on this earth or in any other world (*loka*) and for fresh subjection to transitory and conditioned joys and sorrows.

So far there is little difference of views among the greatest teachers of religion and philosophy in India. But how does the Soul exist after its absolute dissociation from all phenomenal embodiments? This is obviously not so much a matter of direct spiritual experience as of metaphysical speculation. On this question the greatest teachers appear to differ in accordance with their philosophical view-points. Though the Soul is generally recognised as the self-luminous centre and ground of all our individual phenomenal consciousnesses and experiences, the Soul absolutely disembodied and dissociated from the phenomenal psychical organism can not be said to have any consciousness or experience in the sense in which we can possibly understand it. The phenomenal consciousness obviously ceases to exist as such, when the Soul absolutely cuts off its connection with it. Even if the phenomenal consciousness could possibly exist without the transcendent Soul, it would not be possible for it to make the dissociated Soul an object of its experience or knowledge. Hence the problem of the nature of the Soul after absolute disembodiment appears to be insoluble.

It has been found that Lord Buddha, perhaps with a view to keeping his universal moral and religious teachings free from and unprejudiced by all metaphysical speculations, refused to commit himself to any definite doctrine in regard to the nature of the perfectly enlightened Soul in the state of absolute liberation from the empirical bodily existence. He refused to describe it either as existent or as non-existent, either as conscious or as unconscious, since all such terms have their phenomenal implications and are used in the field of our phenomenal experience. The enlightened Jaina saints preached that the disembodied Soul, liberated from the bondage of the body and subjection to *Karma* and *Vāsanā*, ascends to higher and higher planes of transcendent spiritual existence for the ultimate realisation of absolute *Kaivalaya* (absoluteness). They seem to have given to the spiritual aspirants an Ideal of infinite progress in the inward direction of spiritual illumination and self-enjoyment, in the realm of perfect freedom.

Mahā-Siddha Kapila, the founder of the *Sānkhya* system of philosophy, proclaimed that the individual Soul or Spirit (*Purusha*), when it is perfectly liberated and dissociated from the psycho-physical embodiment evolved from *Prakriti* and thus when its beginningless connection with *Prakriti* is entirely cut off, apparently *becomes* what it essentially and eternally *is*; i.e., it apparently returns to its esssential transcendent state as pure changeless infinite self-luminous noumenal consciousness, absolutely free from joys and sorrows and from all knowledge and emotion and will and effort. According to his metaphysical view, the Souls or Spirits (*Purushas*) are many and innumerable even in their essential character, though each of them, being above space and time, is transcendentally infinite and eternal. Hence in the perfectly liberated and disembodied state also, the Souls remain many and separate from one another, though without any sense of individuality and relativity. Each exists in the Absolute State (*Kaivalya*). The whole cosmic order becomes as good as non-existent to the liberated Souls, though it continues as a real world to all non-liberated Souls.

Yogācarya Patanjali, the author of the *Yoga-Sutras* (but not of course the founder of the *Yoga* system), subscribed to the metaphysical view of Kapila, and accordingly the conception he preached about the disembodied transcendent nature of the liberated Soul is essentially the same as that which Kapila preached. After the attainment of perfect intuition by the pure and refined and concentrated phenomenal consciousness as to the true supra-phenomenal character of the Soul, the Soul, i.e. the true Seer (*draṣṭā*), behind the phenomenal consciousness, is established in its essential transcendent character, and when it is entirely liberated from its connection with the phenomenal psycho-physical embodiment and its source, viz. *Prakriti*, it exists eternally in that infinite self-luminous transcendent state. This is the Supreme Ideal, for the realisation of which the systematic practice of *Yoga* culminating in *Samprajñāta* and *Asamprajñāta Samādhi* is urgently necessary.

The *Nyāya* system of Gautama and the *Vaiśeshika* system of Kanāda expound a different metaphysical view. According to them, the material world originates from innumerable material atoms (*paramānus*) which are eternal and without magnitude and of four different kinds. Ether, space and time are also eternally real entities. There are also countless minds of atomic nature, countless souls (each of infinite character) and one Supreme Spirit (*Paramātmā*) or *Iśwara* (Personal God) having inherent controlling power over all of them. *Iśwara* has created this cosmic system with all kinds of individual bodies in space and time intelligently and voluntarily and quite freely out of the material atoms and associated the souls and minds appropriately with the individual organised bodies in accordance with His plan and design. According to these *darśanas*, though the Souls are the real seats of consciousness and knowledge and will and effort, which are their qualities (*gunas*), they can not have any actual empirical consciousness and knowledge and will and effort without being connected with minds and senses. When this empirical consciousness is thoroughly purified and refined through appropriate processes of devotion and contemplation and meditation and rises by Divine Grace to the plane of spiritual illumination, the connection of the individual Soul with the individual mind and the senses is cut off and the Soul is liberated from the sorrowful bondage of the psychophysical embodiment. It has then no knowledge, no will, no effort, and even no consciousness. This is its infinite and transcendent character, and it exists eternally in that supra-spatial supra-temporal non-conscious transcendent state absolutely free from all sorrows as well as joys and all limitations.

The *Upanishads* and the *Vedānta-Darśan* made the most inspiring declaration of the essential identity of the individual Soul (free from the illusory bondage of the psycho-physical embodiment) with *Brahma*, the Absolute Spirit, the Transcendent Soul and Ground and Substratum of the phenomenal universe. It may be noted that *Brahma* or the Absolute

Spirit, as conceived in the *Upanishads* and the *Vedānta Darśan*, had no place in the religio-philosophical systems of Buddha and Jina; and in the *Sānkhya* system *Brahma* was nothing but a common name for the plurality of individual Souls (*Purusha*) free from association with *Prakriti* and hence from the sense of individuality and limitation. *Iśwara*, Whom Patanjali advises the aspirants for *Samādhi* to devotedly worship and to deeply contemplate upon, is not the *Brahma* of the *Upanishads* and the *Vedānta*, but a particular individual Soul (*Purusha viśesha*) eternally self-illuminated and free from all kinds of bondage and eternally the Supreme Ideal and Inspirer of all *Yogis*. The individual Souls that attain perfect liberation as the result of the most intensive practice of *Yoga* or *Samādhi* become perfectly of like character with Him, but do not become identical with Him.

Iśwara of the *Naiyāyika* school is the Creator or Designer and Artificer or the Efficient Cause of the Cosmic Order, but not its Material Cause, not its Substratum and Ground; He is the Supreme Lord of the phenomenal universe, but not its noumenal Soul; He rules over all the individual souls, dispenses justice to them, bestows blessings and mercy upon them, gives them by the exercise of His merciful discretion perfect enlightenment and thereby complete liberation from bondage and sorrow; but He is not the Soul of these souls, these souls are not His own spiritual self-manifestations or spiritual parts; these souls, even when absolutely liberated, do not become merged in or identified with Him.

The conception of *Brahma* or the Absolute Spirit, the infinite and eternal and perfect *Sat Cid Ānanda* above individuality and personality and causality and relativity, as the sole self-existent Reality, as the One-without a-second,—the conception of the phenomenal universe of endless diversities and complications and changes and discords and harmonies as an appearance or expression of this *Brahma* in time and space without involving any real modification or transformation in the essential transcendent character of *Brahma*,—and the conception of the individual souls as essentially one and identical with Brahma,—these are grand and beautiful conceptions preached by the Upanishads and the Vedānta. According to this view, an individual soul, when perfectly enlightened and liberated from the illusory bondage of the phenomenal psycho-physical embodiment and the phenomenal world, realises its essential identity with Brahma, the Absolute Spirit, and becomes one with Him,

The true Self of every person being, according to this view, God or the Absolute Spirit, Who is the true Self of the entire universe and of all creatures born and brought up and decaying and dying within it, Self-realisation (*Ātma-sākshātkāra*) truly means God-realisation (*Iśwara-sākshātkāra* or *Brahma-sākshātkāra*), i.e. the realisation of the identity of one's own Self with the Self of the universe and the Self of every man, every beast and bird and insect, every plant and creeper, and everything that appears to have temporary existence and then to pass out of existence. It implies the realisation of the essential unity and spirituality and Divinity of all existences. To a man of such realisation, the plurality is illusory, all differences are illusory, all births and deaths and joys and sorrows are illusory, and even time and space and causality and relativity are illusory. Illusions owe their apparent existence to Ignorance and imperfect knowledge of the Real Truth. As the whole cosmic system consists of such illusions, it is conceived as a product of Ignorance (*Māyā*). Self-realisation, which is the same as Brahma-realisation, is the realisation or direct experience of the Absolute Truth or Reality, the Spiritual Substratum of this illusory cosmic system.

To a man of such ultimate Truth-realisation, the Cosmic Illusion vanishes, and *Ātmā* or *Brahma* or the Absolute Spirit alone exists as the sole non-dual Reality. This is the real nature of *Mukti* or *Moksha*, from the Vedantic view-point. It is evident that the realisation is to be attained through *Yoga* and *Jñāña* in the embodied state of *Ātmā*; when after that realisation the psycho-physical embodiment perishes in due course, the individuality of *Ātmā* absolutely vanishes and Absolute *Ātmā* or *Brahma* shines unveiled in His non-dual existence. The inner self-enjoyment of an individual in the consciousness of the non-dual blissful character of the Self during the post-realisation period of embodied phenomenal existence is called *Jivanmukti*, in which the enlightened individual inwardly feels himself and the world as non-different from *Brahma* or the Absolute Spirit, while outwardly dwelling in the phenomenal world as a phenomenal individual without any desire or attachment or fickleness or sadness or fear or aversion or anxiety. When his physical body perishes, his mental body also perishes along with it, his illusory phenomenal existence comes to an end, and he exists as one with Brahman. This is called *Videha-mukti.*

There are a good many religio-philosophical schools in India, which are partly dualistic and partly non dualistic. They recognise the authority of the *Upanishads*, the *Bhagavad-Geeta* and the *Brahma-Sutras*, which are regarded as the three-fold expressions of the Vedānta, but they do not accept the extreme non dualistic interpretations of them as offered by Ācāryya Śankara and his famous school. They agree that *Brahma* or the Absolute Spirit is the sole Ultimate Reality, but they deny that *Brahma* is merely a changeless attributeless differenceless spiritual Substratum of an illusory cosmic order born of some Inexplicable Ignorance or *Māyā*. They maintain that the phenomenal cosmic system is a real creation or self-manifestation of a Real (though inscrutable) Power (*Śakti*) inherent in and forming part-and-parcel of the eternal nature of *Brahma*. As the *Power* has no existence apart from and independent of the Owner of the Power, Brahma, this cosmic order also, which is a magnificent production or self-expression of the Power in time and space, can not be said to have any independent separate existence outside of *Brahma*, Who is above time and space and on that account the all-pervading and all-indwelling and changeless Soul of this phenomenal universe.

Logically, the Power is conceived by some schools as different from, though dependent upon, Brahma, and by others as non-different from Brahma, (since it has no separate existence), and by others still as both-different-and-non-different from Brahma; the cosmic system also is correspondingly conceived and described in relation to Brahma by different schools in different logical terms. That Brahma is the Sole Ultimate Spiritual Reality and is the sole Ground and Cause and Lord and Soul of the universe is practically admitted by all.

Again, they deny that the individual souls are only *illusorily* individual and plural, but *really* one and absolutely identical with Brahma. They hold that the individual souls are, not only phenomenally, but also transcendentally individual and innumerable, that they are of *atomic* constitution and exist eternally as such even after liberation, that they are eternal spiritual parts (*amśa*) or sparks (*jyoti-kana*) of Brahma, that though having distinct real existence they exist eternally in and for Brahma. Accordingly, the enlightened and perfect Self-realisation of an individual soul, in which *Moksha* or *Mukti* consists, does not mean the realisation of its *absolute* oneness or identity with Brahma, but the realisation of its essentially pure blissful and transcendent spiritual character (free from all worldly bondage and sorrow, free from all desires and attachments and struggles and restlessnesses) *in* Brahma. In *Mukti* the soul does not lose its individuality and is not merged in Brahma, but is emancipated from the imperfections of its phenomenal individuality and enjoys the most loving communion with Brahma.

The religio-philosophical schools referred to above are chiefly exponents of the cult of Devotion (*Bhakti*) and they strongly advocate the Personality or Super-Personality of the Absolute Spirit, Brahma. They conceive Him as the Supreme Person above all temporal and spatial limitations, eternally possessing infinite knowledge and wisdom, infinite majesty and prosperity, infinite strength and prowess, infinite beauty and sweetness, infinite love and mercy, infinite detachment and calmness, infinite goodness and moral and spiritual excellence, infinite activity and tranquillity and self-enjoyment. He is eternally perfect in and by Himself and He eternally manifests Himself in a *playful* manner in the creation and regulation and destruction of countless orders of phenomenal existences and puts Himself in various sorts of relations with them. The devotees give Him various holy Personal Names and feel various love-inspiring relationships with Him. They cultivate with deeper concentration some intimate spiritual relationship with Him and become completely absorbed in His thought in *Samādhi.* Brahma in His infinite mercy and love bestows spiritual illumination upon the consciousness of the earnest devotee and releases his soul from the bondage of the limitations and imperfections of the psycho-physical embodiment and thus from all possible sorrows of the phenomenal worldly life.

The enlightened devotees of these schools believe that after being released from the embodied state in the gross phenomenal world, the liberated individual soul enters into the blissful *spiritual realm* of Brahma with its illumined individual consciousness in tact and enjoys perfectly its eternal spiritual relationship with Brahma. They often enumerate different forms of *Mukti* enjoyed by different emancipated and disembodied souls in the transcendent spiritual realm in accordance with their *sādhanā* in the embodied state; such as, *Sārsti* (i.e. blissfully dwelling in the kingdom of Brahma), *Sālokya* (enjoying the proximity of Brahma), *Sārupya* (enjoying the likeness of Brahma), *Sāyujya* (becoming consciously united with Brahma), and fifthly *Ekatwa* (attainment of perfect identity with Brahma). Some classes of earnest love-intoxicated devotees spurn the idea of every form of *Mukti* and cherish the hope that their illumined souls should eternally be in the loving and selfless service of the Lord, Brahma, in the transcendent blissful spiritual plane. It is also believed that in the transcendent spiritual realm the emancipated loving souls may be blissfully devoted to Brahma in the manner of a loving wife to her husband, or of an affectionate mother to her child, or of an intimate friend to his or her friend, or of a deeply devoted servant to his beloved master, and so on, just as in this phenomenal world, but without its limitations and imperfections.

The conception of these various forms of *Mukti* is not, however, inconsistent with the fundamental principles of non-dualistic Vedānta. Nor is Vedānta averse to the conception of *Personal Brahma. Māyā* may quite easily be conceived as the eternal Power (*Śakti*) of *Brahma. Brahma* conceived as *with Māyā* or eternal infinite *Śakti*, is *Personal Brahma* or *Iśwara*; but *Māyā* or *Śakti* being, as generally agreed to, essentially non-different from *Brahma*, *Brahma* is not essentially conditioned by the related existence of *Māyā* or *Śakti* and may therefore be quite reasonably thought of as *Impersonal* in His ultimate transcendent character. When it is contemplated that there is nothing which really exists as different or separate from

Brahma, whether independent of or dependent upon Him, He is conceived as *One without a second* and as such *Impersonal*; when again He is contemplated as the Supreme Self-shining Spirit endowed with Supreme Power (*Māyā*), He is conceived as *Personal*.

Evidently He is eternally both, because *in time* Power or *Māyā* (though essentially non-different from the Supreme Spirit) eternally reveals itself in some form or other (outwardly manifested or unmainfested) as *somehow* distinct from and belonging to the Spirit. The non-dualistic interpretation of Vedānta attaches far greater importance to the aspect of essential non-difference and applies the category of *Reality* or *Real-Existence* solely to the Supreme Spirit in His transcendent character without any kind of difference, and logically regards His Personal Character as endowed with Power (*Śakti* or *Māyā*) distinct from His essential spiritual character as purely phenomenal or apparent or illusory. The *Bhakti* schools on the other hand regard this *Personal Character* as the essential spiritual nature of the Supreme Spirit, and His Impersonal transcendent character as truly speaking a logical abstraction.

For practical religious self-discipline the Personal character of Brahma with Supreme Power and infinite glorious attributes is admitted by all. In relation to *Personal Brahma* the individual souls must be regarded as His eternal spiritual *parts* or self-manifestations, though, conceived in abstraction from the individuality of the souls and the all-comprehending Personality of Brahma, the souls in their strictly spiritual character may be regarded as identical with Brahma. The souls, having attained *Mukti* from the gross psycho-physical embodiment through spiritual illumination, may enjoy various forms and stages of *Mukti* in the higher spiritual planes; but they are, according to Vedānta, all within the realm of *Māyā* or the Supreme Power of Brahma and hence do not imply absolute liberation (*ātyantika mukti*) from the bondage of the world of *Māyā* or the phenomenal self-manifestation of Brahma. They of course enjoy higher lives in the higher worlds of Māyā. Absolute liberation lies in absolute self-identification with *Brahma*.

Vedānta as well as a good many other systems admit two forms of *Mukti*, viz. Immediate *Mukti* (*Sadyo-Mukti*), i.e. absolute liberation or union with the Absolute Spirit (Brahma) *immediately* after the dissolution of the physical body, and secondly *Mukti* in gradual stages (called *Krama-mukti*), i.e. ascent to higher and higher *worlds* or higher and higher planes of existence and experience in more and more refined and illumined supra-physical bodies, till the absolute liberation or union with the Absolute Spirit is realised. *Sadyo-mukti* is attained by those individual souls, whose empirical consciousness in the present physical body is perfectly illumined and purified and hence liberated from the veil of Root-Ignorance and the sense of ego or individuality as distinct from Brahma. But other individual souls, whose empirical consciousness does not attain in this body this glorious state of perfect spiritual illumination and freedom from the sense of individuality and direct experience of identity with Brahma, but is considerably refined and purified and freed from all earthly desires and attachments and the gross sense of ego, gradually rise to higher and higher spiritual planes of existence and experience in subtler and subtler non-material embodiments and after a long course of spiritual progress become ultimately merged in the Absolute Spirit.

The Cosmic Order, born of *Māyā* or the Infinite Inscrutable Power of the Absolute Spirit (in whatever way the Dynamic Source of this Order may be conceived), is generally conceived as divided into fourteen *Lokas* or worlds, i.e. fourteen planes of existence and experience. Seven are sub-human, and it would be irrelevant to enumerate them in details in the present context. One is our human world, which is called *Bhuh*, in which we live and move and make all our endeavours, economic, social, moral, spiritual, etc. There are six worlds or planes of existence and experience above this *Bhuh-loka*;—viz, *Bhuvah*, *Swah*, *Mahah*, *Jana*, *Tapah*, *Satya*, in order of superiority. *Bhuh*, *Bhuvah* and Swah, are considered as a group of three (*Tri-lokee* or *Trai-lokya*) closely related to one another. All departed souls with their subtle psycho-vital bodies pass on to *Bhuvah-loka* and are subjected to various pleasurable and painful experiences according to their good and evil deeds in the different regions of this *loka*. After a period determined by their *Karma*, many of them may be born again in this *Bhuh-loka* with gross physical bodies. Those that have performed highly meritorious acts and deserve higher orders of happiness for very long periods on that account ascend to *Swah-loka* and enjoy the rewards of their actions. After reaping the sweet fruits of their virtuous deeds, they also have to be born here. Those that can transcend this *Swah-loka* by dint of their superior spiritual merits enter into the realm of *Mukti* and progressively enjoy the spiritually gainful experiences of the higher *lokas* till they attain absolute *Mukti*. They have not to be born again.

Mahāyogi Gorakhnath agrees with the other Indian religio-philosophical systems in holding that *Moksha* or *Mukti* is the ultimate goal of human life and that *Moksha* or *Mukti* lies in the realisation of the essential transcendent character of the Self or Soul. As it has been found in the preceding chapters, he agrees with the Upanishads and the Vedānta in holding that *Śiva* or *Brahma* is the true Self or Soul in every individual body, though not accepting the interpretation that the *Jeevahood* or Selfhood of *Śiva* or *Brahma* is merely an illusion born of some mysterious inexplicable Ignorance or *Māyā*. He maintains that the Absolute Spirit,—Śiva or Brahma or by whatever other name He may be designated,—by virtue of His innate Power (*Nijā Śakti*), really manifests Himself as the phenomenal Cosmic System with innumerable individual bodies of various orders within it and also as the Cosmic Soul and Lord as well as an infinite number of individual souls related to the individual bodies. He with his *yogic* illumined insight saw that Śiva or Brahma, having *playfully* manifested Himself as individual souls and identified Himself with limited and conditioned and ever-changing individual psycho-physical embodiments, passes through and enjoys various kinds of experiences under various kinds of limitations and bondages in this infinitely complex and heterogeneous cosmic system, which is also His *playful* self-manifestation. In all kinds of phenomena in all the *worlds* (or planes of existence and experience) within this cosmic system, Mahāyogi Gorakhnath saw *Śiva-Śakti-Vilasa* (playful and free self-manifestation of the Absolute Spirit with His own infinite Spiritual Power).

Now, in this cosmic play of Śiva-Śakti, every individual soul or finite spirit, being in its essential character a spiritual self-manifestation of Śiva Himself, has in its inner nature a potentiality and an urge to realise its oneness with Śiva, and with that ultimate end in view to get rid of all actual limitations and bondages and imperfections of phenomenally embodied existence. Sorrow has a very great spiritual value as a moving force, impelling the finite spirit to struggle against all kinds of limitations and bondages and to advance progressively towards the ultimate realisation of its essential *Śivahood*. Every individual soul, having passed through various kinds of conditioned and sorrow-ridden experiences in various bodies, has ultimately to regain the perfect and blissful *Śiva-consciousness* and to realise absolute oneness with Śiva or Brahma. This is a wonderful design in the heart of this cosmic system. Śiva seems to play the game of losing Himself, then seeking Himself and finally finding Himself out.

Thus the perfect realisation of *Śivahood* or *Brahmahood* by the individual soul through the adequate purification and refinement and concentration and illumination of the empirical consciousness (with which it is related, by which it is conditioned, and through which it expresses and progressively realises itself in the state of its individual existence) is, according to Gorakhnath and his school, the Supreme Ideal of human life. This realisation is *Yoga* in the true sense of the term. Gorakhnath uses the term *Yoga* in the sense of both the end and the means. He defines *Yoga* as:—"*Samyogo yoga ityāhuh kshetrajña paramātmanoh*", i.e. by the term Yoga the enlightened Yogis mean the union of the soul of the body and the Soul of the whole cosmic system,—the union of *Jeeva* and *Śiva*, of *Aham* and *Brahma*. This is *Yoga* as the end. The systematic discipline of the physical body, the senses, the vital forces, the mental functions, the intellectual judgments, etc., for the purification and refinement and enlightenment of the phenomenal consciousness and its final elevation to the plane of transcendent Śiva-Consciousness, is *Yoga* as the means.

The system of discipline taught by Gorakhnath is essentially the same Eightfold Path (*astāngika-yogamārga*) as expounded by Patanjali in his *Yoga-Sutras* and by other ancient yogi-teachers; but he and his *sampradāya* considerably elaborated the system by the addition of various forms of *Āsana, Prānāyāma, Mudrā, Bandha, Vedha, Dhāranā, Dhyāna, Ajapā, Nādānusandhāna, Kundalinī Śakti-Jāgarana*, etc., *Yama* and *Niyama*, the universal moral principles meant for all human beings (whether systematically practising *Yoga* or not), were also amplified by them. This is not the place for explaining the processes of *Yoga-Sādhanā*. What is important in the present context is to note that according to both Patanjali's school and Gorakhnath school, *Samādhi* is the fulfilment of *Yoga*, and on that account the term *Yoga* is often used in the sense of *Samādhi*. *Samādhi* is accordingly presented by all yoga-schools as the Ideal of all human endeavours for self-fulfilment and liberation from all bondages and sorrows. In the interpretation of *Samādhi*, Patanjali appears to lay greater emphasis upon the perfect *suppression* of all mental functions (*citta-vritti-nirodha*), though it is pointed out that the transcendent character of the Soul is certainly revealed in that state. Gorakhnath appears to lay greater emphasis upon the perfect *mastery* over all the mental functions and the cosmic forces and the perfect *illumination* of the phenomenal consciousness in the state of *Samādhi*. The individual consciousness is then elevated to Universal Consciousness, the veiled *jeeva-consciousness* is elevated to illumined *Śiva-consciousness*, the mind transcends itself and realises itself as *Supermind* (*Unmani*).

The enlightened *Yogi*-teachers of all the Indian religio-philosophical schools (including Buddhism and Jainism) have described various forms and stages of *Samādhi*. The suppression (complete or partial) of the vagaries of the mind, at least for the time being, is the common factor in all forms of *Samādhi*. But mere suppression of the mental functions, even if complete, does not necessarily lead to the spiritual illumination of the phenomenal consciousness and the realisation of the transcendent character of the Self. For the purpose of spiritual illumination and Truth-realisation, *Samādhi*, together with the contributory *yogic* processes, has to be methodically practised under the expert guidance of an enlightened *Guru*, who can save the disciple from the possible dangers and misunderstandings and wrong estimates of successes. The necessity of placing oneself under the guidance of a competent *Guru* for perfect success in the attainment of the spiritual goal is stressed by every religious teacher of every school. Gorakhnath says,—

Durlabho vishaya-tyāgo durlabham tattwa-darśanam
Durlabhā sahajāvasthā Sad-Guroh karunām vinā.

It is extremely difficult for an ordinary spiritual aspirant to attain true success in the renunciation of all objects of sensuous and mental desires and enjoyments (which are really sources of sorrows and bondages), in the realisation of the Absolute Truth, and in the establishment of himself in the state of absolute freedom and peace, without the merciful help of an enlightened *Guru*.

Samādhi, in the sense of the temporary suppression of the mental functions, may be attained even in the lower planes of phenomenal consciousness. But the perfect Divine Light illumines this consciousness and liberates it from all possible sorrows and bondages and limitations and unveils to it the true transcendent Divine character of the Soul, when this consciousness fully purifies and refines itself and elevates itself to the highest spiritual plane and attains *Samādhi* or perfect self-absorption *in that plane*. Even in that plane there may be different stages of *Samādhi* and concomitantly different stages of Truth-realisation or Self-realisation. It is only in the highest stage of *Samādhi* that there is a complete transfiguration of the phenomenal consciousness into what has been called *Śiva-consciousness* or *Brahma-consciousness*. But according to Gorakhnath and his school, the supreme Ideal of human life is not fully realised, even if the *Śiva-consciousness* is attained and enjoyed in the deepest state of *Samādhi*. So long as the bodily existence continues, this *Śiva-consciousness* has to be brought down to all the lower planes,—the mental and vital and even the material planes,—of the empirical consciousness.

Let me quote here a few stanzas from Gorakhnath's *Viveka-Mārtanda* to indicate his view as to the true nature of *Samādhi*.—

Yat samatwam dwayoratra jeevātma-paramātmanoh,
Samasta-nasta-samkalpah samādhih sobhidhīyate.
Ambu-saindhavayo raikyam yathā bhavati yogatah,
Tathātma-manaso raikyam samādhir abhidhīyate.
Yadā samlīyate jeevo mānasam ca vilīyate,
Tadā samarasatwam hi samādhir abhidhīyate.

In the first stanza he says,—*Samādhi* is the name of that state of phenomenal consciousness, in which there is the perfect realisation of the absolute unity of the two, viz. the individual soul and the Universal Soul, and in which there is the perfect dissolution of all the mental processes (cognitive, emotional and volitional). In the second stanza he says,—Just as a perfect union of salt and water is achieved through the process of *yoga* (amalgamation or unification), so when the mind or the phenomenal consciousness is absolutely unified or identified with the Soul through the process of the deepest concentration (*Yoga*), this is called the state of *Samādhi*. In the third stanza he says,—When the individuality of the individual soul is absolutely merged in the self-luminous transcendent unity of the Absolute Spirit (Śiva or Brahma), and the phenomenal consciousness also is wholly dissolved in the Eternal Infinite Transcendent Consciousness, then perfect *Samarasatwa* (the essential unity of all existences) is realised, and this is called *Samādhi*.

In *Siddha-Siddhānta-Paddhati* Gorakhnath defines *Samādhi* thus:—"*Sarva-tattwānām samāvasthā nirudyamatwam anāyāsa-sthitimattwam iti Samādhi-lakshanam.*" The realisation of the spiritual unity of all orders of existences, the perfectly effortless state of consciousness, and living a life of perfect ease and equanimity and tranquillity and self-fulfilment,—this is the nature of *Samādhi*.

Gorakhnath's *Samarasakaraṇa* is a grand Ideal and he seems to assign to it a position superior even to that of *Samādhi*. *Samādhi* is of course a condition precedent to the realisation of *Samarasa*. *Samarasakarana* does not consist in merely rising above all kinds of differences of normal phenomenal consciousness and experiencing the absolute unity of transcendent consciousness (involving the perfect identity of the individual soul and the Cosmic Soul and the perfect dissolution of all diversities in transcendent Unity) in the deepest and most concentrated state of meditation, as in *Samādhi*. *Samarasakaraṇa* implies the enjoyment, with equal relish and joy and with perfect equanimity and tranquillity, in the normal waking state of phenomenal consciousness, of all orders and forms of phenomenal self-manifestations of the Absolute Spirit. It implies a permanent illumined spiritual state of the individual phenomenal consciousness, in which the consciousness does not withdraw itself from the experiences of the diversities of the phenomenal world (as in deep meditation), nor does it ever forget that all these diversities are variegated phenomenal self-revelations of Śiva or Brahma or the Absolute Spirit and as such are spiritual in essence and non-different from the Spirit, nor does it ever lose sight of the essential identity of the individual souls with the Absolute Spirit and the essential unity of all diversities.

An enlightened *Yogi*, who attains the stage of *Samarasa*, sees and enjoys the differences and at the same time sees and enjoys the internal unity of the differences; he consciously deals with the plurality of finite material things, and at the same time sees the One Infinite Eternal Spirit in them; he experiences the particular objects of various kinds in the phenomenal world, and at the same time experiences himself and Śiva or Brahma as manifested in all of them; he outwardly participates in the joys and sorrows of the people, and at the same time inwardly enjoys supreme bliss amidst all these particular and transitory enjoyments and sufferings. While living and moving amidst diversities and changes, he always inwardly dwells in the realm of blissful changeless spiritual Unity. He sees and enjoys himself in all and all in himself. Gorakhnath calls it *Sahaja-Samādhi* and also *Jāgrat-Samādhi*, i.e. *Samādhi* in the normal waking state. This is the true character of a Nātha or Avadhuta. Every *Yogi* aspires for attaining this perfectly enlightened state in his embodied life.

In *Goraksha-Siddhānta-Samgraha Moksha* or *Mukti* is defined as "*Nātha-swarupena avasthiti*", i.e. the perfect realisation of *Nāthahood*, which ultimately means the same thing as the realisation of *Śivahood* or the attainment of Śiva-consciousness. This is also described as the attainment of the state of *Avadhuta*.

The character of *Nātha* is indicated in this way:—

Nirgunam vāma-bhāge ca savya-bhāge adbhutā nijā
Madhya-bhāge swayam purnas tasmai Nāthāya te namah.
Muktāh stuvanti pādāgre nakhāgre jeeva-jātayah
Muktāmukta-gater muktah sarvatra ramate sthirah.
Vāma-bhāge sthitah Śambhuh savye Vishnuh tathaiva ca
Madhye Nāthah param jyotih tad jyotir mat-tamo-haram.

In His left part (i.e. in His transcendent consciousness) lies *Nirguna* (i.e. the infinite eternal changeless differenceless attributelesss transcendent aspect of the Absolute Spirit), and in His right part (i.e. in His refined and enlightened phenomenal consciousness) lies the unique and inscrutable Supreme Power innate in the nature of the Absolute Spirit (i.e. the infinite eternal self-revealing self-phenomenalising self-diversifying and all-harmonising and all-enjoying playful dynamic aspect of the Absolute Spirit). In the middle (i.e. combining both the aspects of the Absolute Spirit in His all-comprehending consciousness) shines *Nātha* Himself in His complete perfection. I (a spiritual aspirant) bow down to this *Nātha* (and aspire for realising His character in myself).

All orders of living beings (which are in the domain of ignorance and bondage and sorrow and are struggling to get rid of them) are offering their hearts' prayers (consciously or unconsciously) at the nails of Nātha's feet (i.e. to them also the attainment of the perfectly free and enlightened, all-seeing and all-enjoying, supramental consciousness is the highest object of aspiration and the ultimate end of evolution). Those who have emancipated themselves from the sorrows and bondages of this sensuous world and ascended to higher worlds of freedom and joy, are also dwelling with a prayerful attitude at the feet of *Nātha* (i.e. they also make spiritual efforts in those higher planes of existence and experience to attain perfect self-fulfilment by rising to the supreme plane of *Nātha* consciousness). *Nātha* dwells in a plane of consciousness which is above the planes of the *baddha* (non-liberated) as well as of the *mukta*. He enjoys Himself with perfect tranquillity and illumined outlook in all the planes and regions of phenomenal experience.

In the third stanza it is said :—On His left side is *Śambhu* (the Supreme Spirit in His all-transcending self-absorbed aspect), and on His right side is *Vishnu* (the Supreme Spirit in His all-immanent all-pervading aspect). In the middle (uniting the two aspects in His all-comprehending illumined consciousness) *Nātha* shines as the perfect Divine Light (enjoying Himself equally as *Śambhu* and *Vishnu*). May that Divine Light destroy the darkness of my ignorance.

In *Siddha-Siddhānta-Paddhati* a *Siddha-Yogi* (i.e. a perfectly enlightened *Yogi*) is characterised in this way :—

Prasaram bhāsate Śaktih samkocam bhāsate Śivah
Tayor yogasya kartā yah sa bhavet Siddha-yogirāt.
Viśwātitam yathā viśwam ekam eva virājate
Samyogena sadā yas tu Siddha-Yogī bhavet tu sah.
Paripurna-prasannātmā sarvāsarva-padoditah
Viśuddho nirbharānandah sa bhavet Siddha-yogirat.

The first stanza means :—*Śakti* (Power) is manifested in the expansion of the phenomenal cosmic order, and *Śiva* (the Supreme Spirit) is manifested in the contraction (harmonisation and unification and ultimate absorption) of this diversified phenomenal system. He who realises the identity of *Śiva* and *Śakti* (i.e. sees *Śiva* in every expression of *Śakti* and sees *Śakti* as immanent in and non-different from *Śiva*) in his perfectly illumined consciousness, is a perfect *Yogi*. Here the direct experience of the unity of *Śiva* and *Śakti* is spoken of as the Supreme Ideal of life.

The second stanza means :—The Supra-cosmic Spirit and the Cosmic Order,—the timeless and spaceless Unity of Absolute Experience (*Nirvikalpa Samādhi*) and the spatio-temporal system of changing diversities of normal relative experiences,—are essentially one and the same. (They do not contradict each other.) He who by virtue of the perfection of his *yogic* self-discipline (*samyak-yoga*) realises this oneness in the supra-mental supra-logical all-comprehensive consciousness is true ***Siddha-Yogi***. Such a ***Siddha-Yogi*** always sees that Time is ceaselessly moving on the breast of the Timeless, Plurality is dancing on the bosom of Unity, Matter is playing in the heart of Spirit, *Mahā-Kāli* is eternally marching onward and playing various parts of creation and preservation and destruction and revealing various kinds of *Rasa* on the eternally unmoved and calm and tranquil and self-enjoying breast of the Supreme Spirit, Mahā-Kāla, Śiva. He sees that the Absolute Spirit is eternally motionless as well as variously moving, eternally transcendent as well as self-revealing in infinite phenomenal modes and forms.

The third stanza means:— He whose consciousness is always in a perfectly peaceful and tranquil state, who identifies himself with all and at the same time transcends all, who is absolutely pure and who always dwells in the realm of unconditioned joy and self-fulfilment, is a true *Siddha-Yogi*. He sees all in himself and himself in all, he participates in the joys and sorrows of all, he feels deep compassion and sympathy and love for all; but all the same he always dwells above all, he always inwardly lives in a state of perfect peace and tranquillity and unity and undisturbed self-enjoyment. Though in his bodily life living in a world which is generally regarded as a world of sorrows and struggles, he by virtue of his perfectly pure and refined and illumined consciousness remains untouched by all kinds of sorrows and struggles and disturbances and always feels freedom and serenity and fullness within himself.

Thus a perfectly enlightened *siddha-yogi* lives in the embodied state amidst all kinds of mundane circumstances with undimmed and undisturbed *Śiva-consciousness,* and enjoys in this world of bondages and sorrows and struggles perfect freedom from bondages and sorrows and struggles. To him this world is, empirically speaking, transformed into a perfectly beautiful and blissful spiritual world. This is the state of *Jeevan-mukti*. In the disembodied state he becomes perfectly identified with *Śiva,* because every individual soul is nothing but an individualised self-expression of *Śiva*.

According to Gorakhnath and his school, the perfectly successful practice of *Yoga* is attended with various other glorious attainments. First, a perfect *Yogi* or *Nātha* becomes a complete Master of his physical body as well as of the physical forces of the world of normal experience. He acquires the power to transform his gross physical body, whenever he pleases, into an invisible atom or into an enormously big colossus, to make it lighter than air or heavier than a mountain without changing its size or form, to make it impregnable to deadly weapons and to deadly forces of nature, to create as many physical bodies as he likes at the same time and to perform different kinds of actions or enjoy different kinds of pleasures through them, to exercise hypnotic influence upon the minds of others and even to enter into the bodies of others, to convert one physical thing into another physical thing by mere wish, to perceive objects beyond the scope of senses, and even to immensely elongate the span of this physical life and to conquer death.

To Gorakhnath and the Siddha-Yogi school, the difference between Spirit and Matter is only relative and apparent, in as much as Matter is nothing but self-manifestation, self-embodiment and self-objectification of Spirit. The physical body, the subtle body, the life, the mind, the intellect, the forces and the phenomena of the world,—all these are free playful expressions of Spirit. According to the *Yogis,* man has within himself the power and possibility not only to experience Spirit in all of them, but also practically to convert the physical body into a vital or mental body or to produce from one mental body one or numerous physical bodies or to spiritualise the physical body or to transform one material thing into another, and to perform many other deeds which may appear miraculous to the people in general. All these can be done through the development or unfoldment of the spiritual power which is present in man, but which in normal life remains dormant or inactive. This power can be adequately developed through the systematic and intensive practice of *Yoga*. The rational Will in man can be so strengthened as to appear all-powerful in this phenomenal world. The aim of *Yoga* is not merely to perfectly enlighten the *cognitive aspect* of the phenomenal consciousness, but also likewise to perfectly realise all the potentialities of the *volitional* and *dynamic* aspect of the consciousness,—not merely to attain perfect experience of the Absolute Spirit, but also to participate in the Supreme Power of the Absolute Spirit.

CHAPTER XVIII

THE EVOLUTION OF HINDU SPIRITUAL CULTURE (I)

1. Vedas the basis of Hindu Spiritual Thought

For several thousands of years the *Vedas* have been universally accepted as the starting point and the solid foundation of the spiritual culture of Bhāratvarsha. The time when the Vedic *Mantras* and the lofty and sublime spiritual ideas embodied in them were first revealed to the Aryan Seers (*Rishis*) could never be even approximately ascertained. It was a matter of controversy among the most eminent intellectualists of the country even three thousand years ago. The modern truth-seekers of the West and the East, having started their speculations from different kinds of data, have arrived at hypotheses, which often differ from one another, not merely by centuries, but by millenniums. Some recent archaeological discoveries in several parts of India have led many thinkers to suppose that they indicate the existence of a pre-Vedic civilisation and culture in ancient India. But the grounds on which they base their theory that the Indus-Valley civilisation was prior to the revelation of the Vedas are regarded by other equally eminent scholars as altogether inadequate. There are however no substantial differences of views with regard to the conclusion that the Vedic Texts are the earliest available literary records of the highly spiritual and intellectual achievements of the Aryan race as well as of the entire human race and that all the ethical and spiritual thought-currents and life-currents of the Indian people have for so many thousands of years continually flown down from them and have been inspired and regulated and controlled by them. The Hindus in general regard the Vedas as the self-revealed linguistic embodiments of the eternal supra-mental and supra-intellectual Truth and Law (*Satyam* and *Ritam*) underlying the phenomenal universe, and they bow down to them as the supreme authority with regard to all moral and spiritual problems of human life, all the fundamental supra-mundane interests and ideals immanent in the human nature as well as all the ultimate questions of the human intellect.

It is obvious to any impartial scholar that more than three thousand years back the most influential saints and sages and thought-leaders of India, whose sacred memories are cherished with the deepest respect by all classes of people even to the present day, accepted the Vedas as infallible guides in the domain of super-sensuous moral and spiritual truths, which were considered beyond the range of normal human experience and even ordinary logical reasoning, but which were felt to be essential for the proper discipline and refinement of man's higher intellectual and emotional and practical life and its elevation to still higher and higher planes of existence and experience. They with their highly developed intelligence were led to believe that the loftiest and sublimest ideas and ideals and sentiments, which were expressed in the *Vedic Mantras,* could not possibly be the products of mere reflection and speculation and imagination even of the greatest intellectual geniuses and poets and must therefore have been *revealed* to the innermost consciousness of the pure-minded and pure-hearted *Rishis* from some unerring super-intellectual spiritual Source.

Those ancient thinkers also could not fix any time for the first revelation of the Vedic Truths to the human society. They got them through a long line of preceptors and disciples. The *Rishis,* with whose holy names particular *Vedic Mantras* are remembered as associated, were never regarded as their *composers,* but they were revered as the specially selected *recipients* of special aspects of the self-revealing Eternal Truths in the most concentrated and illumined states of their consciousness. They were the mediums, through whom the Truths came down from the super-intellectual spiritual plane to the planes of the human intellect and emotion and verbal expression. The linguistic forms, in which those super-intellectual Eternal Truths came out spontaneously from the mouths of those exceptionally inspired holy personalities, were so charming and so dynamic and forceful and were regarded by truth-seekers as so sacred and glorious, that they were remembered and reproduced with the utmost care and accuracy with their rhythms and accents and musical notes. They continued to pass on from generation to generation for centuries and millenniums.

II. Some Fundamental Vedic Truths

Some of the most fundamental Truths, revealed through the Vedas and accepted as well as verified by the most enlightened saints and sages of all times, may be briefly mentioned here.

First, the Vedas revealed that this magnificent world-order, of which neither the absolute temporal beginning nor the absolute temporal end we can rationally conceive, is not merely a physical and mechanical system, but essentially a *spiritual* and *moral* and *aesthetic* system. They unveiled the truth that this apparently material and pluralistic universe of our normal sensuous experience is essentially the spatio-temporal phenomenal self-manifestation of One Self-existent Self-luminous Self-revealing Infinite Eternal Transcendent Spirit. It is proclaimed that all the diverse orders of finite and changing realities of the phenomenal cosmic system are ultimately born of as well as sustained and governed and pervaded by the Spirit, that their courses of origination and destruction, evolution and involution, integration and disintegration, are all wonderfully regulated by the Supreme Law of phenomenal self-expression of the Spirit, that what appear to our sensuous knowledge as lifeless material objects are also particular embodiments of the Spirit and as such full of inner life and light.

The empirical consciousness of man is normally deluded by the outer physical properties of objective realities appearing to our outer senses; the Vedic *Mantras* teach this consciousness to see in them the shining presence of the Spirit. They open the inner eyes of men to see the Spirit in Earth and Water and Fire and Air and Ether, in Suns and Moons and Stars and Planets, in Mountains and Seas and Rivers and Forests, in all physical and mental and vital and social and political forces. They proclaim that the same infinite and eternal self-shining Spirit is the Indwelling Soul of all and that He is spoken of in different Divine Names (*Devatā*) in relation to different kinds of phenomenal embodiments and different kinds of powers and actions and striking features manifested through them. The One Spirit reveals Himself as a plurality of Spirits with a variety of phenomenal embodiments. Thus the Vedas give a magnificent spiritual conception of the universe, which is a basic conception of Hindu culture.

Secondly, it was revealed through the Vedas that all the phenomena of all the amazingly diverse orders and planes of existences in this spatially and temporally boundless Cosmic System are governed and regulated by Universal and Inviolable Laws or Principles, and that these Laws are not merely natural or physical or mechanical or biological Laws, but also Mental and Moral and Aesthetic and Spiritual Laws. Though this world outwardly appears to our normal understanding to be a scene of dreadful catastrophes and cataclysms and accidents, a scene of violent disruptions and upheavals and unforeseeable occurrences in nature, a scene of constant hostilities and struggles among the multifarious forces in all the spheres of our experience and a scene of unbearable sufferings and agonies in all species of living creatures ; nevertheless, behind all these outer appearances there are in this Cosmic Order eternal Principles of Harmony and Unification, Co-operation and Service and Sacrifice, Justice and Benevolence and Mercy, the Principle of the Triumph of order over disorder, virtue over vice, good over evil, love over hatred, beauty over ugliness, joy over sorrow, and the Principle of the gradual evolution and progressive realisation of the Ultimate Truth, the Highest Good, the Supreme Beauty, the Perfect Bliss and the Absolute Fulfilment Of Life.

Virtue which contributes to this realisation is in this Moral and Spiritual Government of the world invariably rewarded with happiness and favourable conditions of life, which supply impetus to the elevation of life to higher and higher planes. Vice is punished with sorrow, which stimulates desires and struggles for transcending the lower levels of existence. What appear as anti-moral anti-spiritual anti-evolutionary forces in the world are only meant for adding to the glories and splendours and beauties of the moral and spiritual and evolutionary forces which reign supreme in the system. The Vedas present to man a highly noble and dignified, lovable and attractive, magnificent and adorable picture of the Cosmic Order as a whole, without ignoring the presence of the apparently terrible and repulsive aspects of the phenomena in nature and the animal and human worlds, which, they assert, are subordinate and auxiliary features of this Great System and magnify its grandeur as the phenomenal self-manifestation of the Infinite and Eternal Absolute Spirit.

The Vedas taught the Hindus to cultivate an *ādhidaivika* and *ādhyātmika*(implying moral and spiritual) outlook on this world-order, instead of a merely *ādhibhautika* (or materialistic) outlook, in as much as all the affairs of this apparently material world are governed by Moral and Spiritual Powers in accordance with eternal Moral and Spiritual Principles, and ultimately by One Supreme Spirit. Man lives and moves and has his being in a magnificent moral and spiritual world, and as a self-conscious and self-determining participator in its ethico-spiritual scheme, man has to adjust himself with and fulfil his mission of life in this great world through free and voluntary self-discipline, and progressive development of his intellectual knowledge, moral character and spiritual enlightenment. This is a grand message of the Vedas for the Humanity and this has been the outlook of the Hindus for so many millenniums.

Thirdly, the Vedas emphasised that in the scheme of the universe *man* occupies a unique position, because he is endowed with a highly developed physical body in which the spirit can with comparative freedom and ease play its part and realise itself and the phenomenal consciousness is capable of being intellectually, morally, aesthetically and spiritually refined and enlightened and perfected. His intellectual power enables him to pierce through the veils of the outer appearances of this phenomenal self-manifestation of the Spirit and to be in direct communion with the Spirit, Who is the Ultimate Truth of all phenomena. The Vedas present before the human intellect the lofty ideal that the fulfilment of its capacity of knowledge lies, not merely in the discovery of the natural forces and laws which harmonise and organise the world into a *natural order*, but chiefly in the comprehension and appreciation of the moral and spiritual forces and laws which govern all classes of phenomena and develop the world as a *moral and aesthetic and spiritual order*, and ultimatety in the illumined experience of the Infinite Eternal Absolute Self-shining and Self-enjoying Spirit, Who freely and joyfully manifests Himself in the diverse forms of existences in this Cosmic System.

Again, by virtue of his moral consciousness, man develops within himself a sense of freedom and responsibility, duty and obligation, *dharma* and *adharma*, and a moral attitude towards his own actions and the affairs round about him. This moral consciousness greatly raises the intrinsic dignity of man in the scheme of the world and it distinguishes him from other creatures perhaps more prominently than his intellectual consciousness.

The concepts of good and evil, right and wrong, piety and impiety, *dharma* and *adharma,* intrinsic values of right actions and thoughts, intrinsic merits of *dharma* and demerits of *adharma,* rewards for virtue and punishments for vice, *deserts* for happiness and misery arising from righteous and unrighteous deeds, etc.,—all these concepts, which are universally accepted as the glories of human nature, have their origin in the inherent moral consciousness of man. Just as his *intellectual consciousness* assures him of the objective reality of the world of his actual and possible experience and knowledge and the validity of the laws and principles he discovers therein by the exercise of his thought, so his *moral consciousness* assures him that he has real freedom for self-development in this world, that here he is not merely a creature of the natural circumstances, but a real builder of his own destinies, that here he has a real right and power and duty to exercise effective control over and to make the best use of the natural environments and forces and materials, amidst which he may live, and thereby to realise the ideals, by which he is prompted or inspired from within.

The moral consciousness, which adds such great dignity to human nature and assigns to man such a unique position in the world, creates also many complications and puzzles to his intellect and life. Even the most highly developed intellect is perplexed to rationally conceive how there can be scope for real freedom and responsibility of man and for his building up his own destinies in a world, which is governed by inviolable and universal natural laws or by some Omnipotent Omniscient Divine Power. Moreover constant conflicts between the inner demands and commands of the Moral Consciousness on the one hand and the natural desires and propensities of the psycho-physical organism as well as the natural ambitions for happiness and prosperity (*kāma* and *artha*) on the other, do also create difficulties and perplexities which often baffle solution in practical life. Again, what is it that the Moral Consciousness ultimately demands ? What is the ultimate Ideal which the Moral Consciousness aspires after and prompts man to achieve by dint of his free well-regulated efforts in this life ? What is the essential nature of the Highest Good, the Absolute Right, the Perfect Moral Excellence ? What is the ultimate and supreme character of *Dharma* ? All such questions are puzzling even to the highly developed human intellect.

III. VEDAS UNVEILED THE INNER SECRETS OF THE ORDER OF THE UNIVERSE.

Long ages past the *Vedas* supplied the key to the solution of these problems by unveiling the inner secrets of the order of the universe to the illumined consciousness of the *Rishis* or the *Mahāyogis*. They saw with their inner eyes that this spatio-temporal phenomenal universe is the free self-manifestation, in various stages and grades, in various levels of existences, under various temporal and spatial limitations, of One Eternal Infinite Self-existent Self-shining Perfect Spiritual Super-Personality, in Whose transcendent nature Absolute Knowledge, Absolute Goodness, Absolute Beauty and Absolute Happiness, are eternally realised, together with the Absolute Freedom and Power of Diversified Self-expression. He is not only the Absolute Source and Sustainer of all orders of existences, but also the Supreme Ideal immanently operative in and regulating all processes of evolution and involution, creation and destruction, in all grades of His phenomenal self-expressions. The Absolute Cause is also the Supreme Ideal of Goodness and Beauty, Wisdom and Knowledge, Happiness and Prosperity, Power and Freedom, Peace and Tranquillity, which man's intellectual and moral and aesthetic and sensuous and spiritual consciousness seeks for realising by dint of voluntary efforts.

All orders of existences have come down from the Supreme Spirit, live and move in the Supreme Spirit, are inspired by the Ideal of realising the Supreme Spirit in themselves, are going ahead step by step towards perfect union with the Supreme Spirit through the processes of evolution and involution, and are ultimately merged in the unity of the Supreme Spirit. The world-order, being the free self-expression of the Supreme Moral and Spiritual Super-Personality, offers ample scope within itself for free self-expression and self-development to the individual spirits (*jeevas*), which are finite *spiritual* self-manifestations of the same Supreme Spirit. The innumerable spirits or souls, apparently conditioned by various orders of material and vital and psychical embodiments and playing various roles in this cosmic system under those conditions and limitations, essentially participate in the transcendent spiritual character of the Supreme Spirit and as such *inwardly* transcend their phenomenal embodiments and are impelled by a mysterious inner urge to *practically* get rid of all bondages by appropriate means and realise their True Self.

In inorganic material bodies the individual spirits or souls appear to be completely veiled, but they are not really non-existent therein, and it is the spiritual urge inherent in the souls of the material bodies that impreceptibly operate in and govern the course of evolution in physical nature. It is the imperceptible propulsion of the spiritual character of the souls of the material bodies that leads to the evolution of life within material bodies. In plant bodies the spirits or souls are only rudimentarily manifested. In them the biological factors, the organising functions of the vital forces, sensibility to impressions, the control and harmonisation of the operations of all parts of a massive body from a common centre and for some common purpose, etc.—all these are manifestations in them of the spirits or souls seeking to transcend the limitations and to realise their inner spiritual characteristics. It is on account of the presence of the spirits or souls actuated by the urge for realising their higher spiritual characteristics within living bodies, that there is in the warld-order the evolution of higher and higher orders of living beings endowed with different grades of minds and empirical consciousnesses and also different grades of freedom of movements and actions.

In the wonderful moral and spiritual scheme of this cosmic self-manifestation of the Absolute Spirit, the evolution of the human species is a phenomenon of great importance, in as much as in the human life the individual spirit or soul is embodied with the most suitable physical, vital and mental instruments, efficiently organised with one another and capable of infinite developments, for the progressive realisation of the highest Ideals eternally realised and unified in the transcendent character of the Absolute Spirit. The human embodiment of an individual spirit also passes through various stages of development, and in each higher stage the physical body with its nervous system and brain and other inner instruments is more efficiently organised and refined, its vital powers are more effectively strengthened and regulated, its mental capacities are more developed and expanded and liberated and coordinated, and they are gradually elevated to higher and higher planes; powers for freely thinking, freely speaking, freely moving and acting, freely cultivating various kinds of emotions and sentiments and thoughts and giving free expressions to them, are gradually developed in the human mind. At each higher stage of development the individual ego (which is the phenomenal self-expression of the individual spirit) becomes more self-conscious, more self-assertive, more self-determining, more self-reliant, more self-expansive, more consciously and voluntarily and rightfully exercising its controlling authority over the body and the senses and the vital forces and the mental functions, and more ambitious to realise its inner possibilities and to elevate itself to still higher planes. The intellectual consciousness, the moral consciousness, the aesthetic consciousness, the spiritual consciousness,—all these are more and more prominently and powerfully manifested at the higher and higher grades of development of the human embodiment of the individual spirit.

At the highly refined and enlightened stages of development of the intellectual, moral, aesthetic and spiritual nature of man, the *laws of necessity* are revealed to be subordinate to the higher *laws of freedom*, the *laws of physical nature* are revealed to be subordinate to the superior *moral and spiritual laws*, all the diversities of nature are experienced as a harmonious and beautiful and sublime system of free and joyful selfexpressions of one Infinite and Eternal Spirit. All the diverse orders of laws regulating and systematising the lower orders of phenomenal self-manifestations of the Spirit, though appearing to be inexorable in their respective planes, have provisions for the individual spirits' transcending them and ascending to higher planes of self-expression and self-realisation. The phenomenal universe itself is not a wholly closed system, but has *openings* for the individual spirits' rising above it and realising perfect identity with the Absolute Spirit, through the development and elevation and refinement of their intellectual and moral and aesthetic and spiritual consciousness within this universe and within their phenomenal embodiments.

The individual spirits are no other than the Absolute Spirit Himself, manifesting and enjoying Himself as a plurality of finite spirits or souls within finite and changing phenomenal embodiments and playfully seeking for the realisation of His own perfectly blissful transcendent character in and through them. The Absolute Spirit seems to have freely and voluntarily sacrificed Himself,—i. e. His Transcendent Unity and Perfection—in a great *Cosmic Sacrifice*, and became many imperfect spirits within this Cosmic Order, in order as it were to enjoy Himself in infinite ways and forms. These Vedic revelations supplied the key to the solution of all the puzzling problems of the normal planes of our intellectual and moral and aesthetic consciousness.

IV The Principal Modes of Discipline Taught by Vedas

(a) The cultivation of the spirit of Yajña in practical life.

In accordance with this glorious conception of man and the universe, the *Vedas* placed before man certain principles and ways of life for the proper discipline and development of his freedom and the final fulfilment of the inherent demand of his soul. One of them is the ideal of progressive self-elevation and self-expansion and self-fulfilment in the path of *Karma* or *pravṛtti* (action), sublimated by the spirit of *Yajña* (sacrifice) and gradually refined and promoted to higher and higher planes. The spirit of *Yajña* implies the sacrifice of the lower sensuous desires and hankerings of individuals for the sake of the fulfilment of the higher and nobler moral and spiritual aspirations, the sacrifice of smaller and transitory interests of the physical life for the sake of the wider and more abiding well-being of the inner life, the sacrifice of individual pleasures and possessions for contributing to the happiness and permanent welfare of the whole society, the sacrifice of the enjoyments of the lower planes of life for the fulfilment of the innermost urge of the soul.

The *Vedas* laid down the principle that Sacrifice *(Yajña* and *Tyāga)* is in the moral scheme of the universe the only sure and effective means for becoming worthy of the higher achievements of life. It is only through the sacrifice for common good of what one has got in one's possession that one deserves to possess more and to ascend to higher and higher planes of existence and self-fulfilment. It is only through perfect self-sacrifice i. e. by giving away all one's possessions for universal good, that one can rise to the most enlightened state of perfect self-realisation. The way of human life ought to be the way of free and voluntary self-sacrifice in progressive stages, with higher and higher ends in view. Our domestic and social life and its obligations always demand the voluntary sacrifice of our petty individual interests for common welfare, and we as individuals reap the true benefits of such sacrifices in the progressive ennoblement and elevation of our moral and spiritual character. According to the *Vedas*, all the earthly materials that we may possess, including all our physical and intellectual capacities and all our social and political and economic powers and privileges, ought to be regarded as materials Divinely given to us for the performance of *sacrifices (Yajñas)* and should be humbly and appropriately utilized for such sacrificial deeds contributing to general welfare, with a view to our inward self-elevation and self-realisation and eternal bliss. The true purpose of the unique status of man in the world-scheme is best served through free and voluntary acts of *sacrifices*, to which he ought to devote himself. *Yajña* as the principle of active life is a highly noble practical message of the *Vedas*.

The celebrated interpreters of the *Vedas* formulated various types of sacrificial works,—domestic, social, religious, political, etc.,—in accordance with various grades of physical, intellectual and moral calibre and various kinds of domestic, social, political and environmental conditions of the people,—for the elevation of their practical life to higher and higher planes and the advancement of their moral *deserts* for superior kinds of happiness and more favourable conditions of life. The *Vedas* instructed all people to perform all such *sacrifices* and all the duties of life with an attitude of devotion and worship to the Gods and with purity and humility of hearts, so that the entire practical life may be spiritualised and refined and elevated to higher and higher spiritual planes. The *Vedas* placed before man the inspiring ideal that the whole human life from birth to death, with all the variety of its natural demands and interests and duties and obligations and all the variety of circumstances which it may have to face, should be lived as a *religious life*, and all its affairs should be freely and voluntarily conducted with the moral and spiritual end in view, so that it may be in perfect tune with the moral and spiritual scheme of the universe. Through a series of *sacrifices* the human life should steadily and freely advance towards eternal life, eternal happiness, eternal goodness and eternal beauty.

(b) *Aspiration for attaining higher worlds through Yajña.*

The *Vedas* placed before man the idea of a hierarchy of *lokas* (worlds) or planes of existence and experience, both above and below this *Bhuh-loka,* the plane of normal human existence and experience. Above *Bhuh-loka,* there are *Bhuvah, Swah, Mahah, Jana, Tapah* and *Satya,* and below this *Bhuh-loka* seven planes of *Pātāla* are spoken of. Men, the dwellers of *Bhuh-loka*, through the voluntary and well-planned performance of higher and higher forms of *sacrifices* and through the development and purification and refinement of their moral and intellectual and emotional life on this earth, can acquire the *desert* to ascend to the higher and higher *lokas,* which are more and more free from the limitations and bondages and wants and sorrows of this material world and this sense-ridden plane of existence and experience. All the higher worlds are sometimes designated by the general name of *Swarga* (Heavens). Abuse of the powers and privileges and opportunities of human life on Earth results in the degradation of the human soul to the lower and lower worlds.

The *Vedas* exhort all morally and intellectually awakened human beings on Earth to free themselves from all sensuous desires and passions and all earthly ambitions for power and prosperity and to live a life of all-round *sacrifice* and altruistic service, with a view to acquire *deserts* for ascent to the Heavens or the Higher Worlds (*Swarga-kāmo yajeta*) and thereby for attainment of a higher and fuller and happier immortal life. They keep before their eyes also a terrible picture of the lower worlds, to which they should be degraded, if they abuse their freedom and opportunities by the transgression of the moral laws in practical life and thereby make themselves liable to dire punishment in lower forms of existence and experience. This is the moral scheme of the Cosmic System.

The *Vedas* further assert that if a man's practical life is governed by earthly desires and propensities, he must undergo repeated births and deaths in this human world, and the favourable and unfavourable conditions as well as the enjoyments and sufferings of each succeeding life are principally determined by the moral effects of the righteous and unrighteous deeds of the previous lives. It is an inviolable moral law of the world-order that an individual reaps what he sows,—that he enjoys and suffers what he earns as the result of his own past deeds,—while in this human life he is endowed with a relative freedom to further develop or degrade himself through the voluntary performance of fresh good or bad actions.

The physical death, it is authoritatively proclaimed, is no cessation of existence for an individnal; while the gross material organism is disorganised and ceases to exist as an individual body, neither the individual soul nor its subtle psycho-vital embodiment ceases to exist or loses its individuality along with the physical body. The individual soul, equipped with its subtle psycho-vital embodiment, with its moral *deserts* and psychical tendencies and with its spiritual yearnings and achievements, passes on to or adopts and develops and organises a new suitable physical body, for reaping the pleasant and unpleasant fruits of the virtuous and vicious deeds, for fulfilling the unfulfilled desires and aspirations and for getting and utilising further opportunities towards the satisfaction of the deeper urge of the inner consciousness for self-elevation and self-perfection. Thus an individual soul may pass through innumerable physical births and deaths; till it is finally released from the bondage of *Karma* and attains a perfect moral and spiritual life in the realm of Bliss.

(*c*) *Cultivation of devotional sentiments and spirit of worship.*

Again, the *Vedas* opened before man another path for the fulfilment of his self-conscious, moral and spiritual life. This is the path of the cultivation of the sentiments of wonder and admiration, reverence and devotion, love and self-offering, towards the plurality of magnificent and beautiful, awe-striking and bountiful, loving and merciful, delightful and playful, *Divine Powers* (*Devatās*) manifesting themselves in and regulating and harmonising the various orders of phenomena in Nature. Ultimately all these religious sentiments have to be directed towards the One Infinite Eternal Absolute Spirit,—the Supreme *Devatā* of all *Devatās,*— Who is the Non-dual Source of all orders of existences and powers and phenomena, Who reveals Himself by virtue of His inscrutable Power in and through all Names and Forms and embodies Himself in this phenomenal Cosmic System.

The *Vedic Hymns* teach man to appreciate deeply and widely the beauty and sublimity and the inner significance of the manifold self-manifestations of the Spirit in the infinitely diverse planes of phenomenal existences and consciousnesses, to bow down to them with humility and a worshipful attitude and to develop a relation of loving kinship and familiarity with them. The development of this spirit of cordial appreciation of the free and delightful Divine plays in the phenomena of Nature liberates man progressively from the superficial sensuous and materialistic outlook on the world and unites him with the Absolute Spirit. Just as Self-sacrifice in practical life is one pathway to spiritual self-realisation, so Self-surrender through love and devotion to the Supreme Spirit is another pathway, according to the Vedic teachings, to spiritual self-realisation.

The devotional approach to the Supreme Spirit through the cultivation of religious emotions towards Him and His Superordinary Spiritual Self-Revelations (*vibhūtis*) in the Cosmic Order has during all these thousands of years exercised a great influence upon the minds and hearts of all classes of people in India and upon the development of her moral and spiritual culture. The literary and artistic culture of India,—her poetry and drama, her epics and lyrics, her music and painting and sculpture and architecture, have in all ages been inspired principally by devotional sentiments. The millions of temples and images of Gods and Goddesses throughout the vast country are visible and tangible representations of the devotional spirit of the Indian people. All these have developed out of the teachings of the *Vedas*.

In India, even ordinary domestic and social functions are performed with religious ceremonies and with a spirit of worship to Gods and Goddesses:— the land is ploughed with a devotional attitude after worshipping ceremoniously the Goddess of Earth and other Deities, a new harvest is to be brought home with similar religious ceremonies; laying the foundation of a new building, first entrance into a new house, new admission of a child into an educational institution, the marriage of a young boy or girl, the funeral of a deceased member of a family, and so on and so forth,—all these are regarded as religious duties and performed with a devotional attitude and with due worship of Gods and Goddesses, which always involves acts of sacrifice. Indian culture has so developed ever since those ancient times that all men and women of this land are born with religion, grow in religion, perform their normal duties as religious worship, accept the enjoyments and sufferings of life with a religious disposition, breathe their last with the Name of the Supreme Spirit in the mouth and with the devotional sentiment of final self-offering to the Supreme Spirit.

From the viewpoint of Indian culture, the whole life is a life of religion,—a spiritual life,—and has to be freely and consciously and deliberately lived as such, with the ultimate Spiritual Ideal of life in view. Such a life of religion must as a matter of course demand on the one hand a constant control over all selfish earthly desires and propensities and ficklenesses of the mind and on the other hand a series of sacrifices (*yajñas*) in all fields of life. *Actions should be sacrificial* and *the attitude of mind should be devotional*. The life should be dedicated to the devotional worship (though in a variety of outer forms) of the Supreme Spirit, of Whom all Gods and Goddesses are superordinary spiritual self-revelations (*Bibhutis*) and the individual spirits (*Jeevas*) endowed with human embodiments are also specially privileged spiritual self-manifestations capable of realising unity with Him. The Ideal of such a life was presented by the *Vedas* for practical realisation by men, and it has inspired the Indian culture all along. These twofold pathways to spiritual self-realisation are generally known as *Karma-Kānda* (or *Yajña-Kānda*) and *Upāsanā-Kānda* (which is also spoken of as *Bhakti-Kānda*) of the *Vedas;* but they are not dissociated in real religious life, in which *Yajña* and *Upāsanā* always go together. Difference lies in emphasis. *Yajña* lays stress on the performance of right and good actions involving sacrifice of the lower interests of life, but it also enjoins that the actions should be performed with an attitude of worship and devotional sacrifice to the Supreme Spirit, Who is the Lord of all *Jajñas* (*Sarva-jajñeśwara*). *Upāsanā* lays greater stress upon the aspect of devotional sentiments, which inwardly unite the spiritual aspirants with the Supreme Spirit.

(*d*) *The path of Yoga Jñāna and Vairāgya.*

Lastly, the *Vedas* prescribed for man's spiritual perfection a third path,—viz. Austerity, Asceticism, Deep Meditation, Intensive Reflection and Perfect Absorption with the thought of the Absolute Spirit. This is an extraordinary way of life, which demands, as the direct means to spiritual self-fulfilment at the final stage, abandonment of domestic and social duties and obligations, abandonment of all individual and domestic and social prosperity and happiness, abandonment of even sacrificial works and works of public utility, complete restraint of all normal desires and worldly as well as other-worldly ambitions, perfect mastery over the body and the senses and the mind, and exclusive concentration of the energy upon the realisation of the identity of the individual soul with the Supreme Spirit. This is the path of *Yoga, Jñāna, Vairāgya* and *Sannyāsa*. This is the path leading directly to the realisation of the blissful transcendent character of the Soul and its absolute liberation (*Moksha*) from all possible bondages and limitations and sorrows, from which it apparently suffers in the planes of phenomenal embodied existences. This is the Supreme Ideal (*Parama-Purushārtha*) of human life, and men of exceptional moral and spiritual merits devote their whole time and energy to the pursuit of this Ideal, giving up the pursuit of the worldly Ideals, namely *Kāma* (happiness) and *Artha* (prosperity and power), and even the other-worldly Ideal of *Swarga* (heavenly blessedness), through the well-planned performance of sacrificial actions and domestic and social duties. The *Vedas* indicated and set proper values upon all the *Purushārthas* of human life, enjoined upon men the pursuit of these ideals and the performance of appropriate duties in accordance with their *adhikāras* (capacities and merits and positions), and showed the way to the progressive fulfilment of all orders of human life.

(*e*) *An ideal Language.*

Besides all these, the *Vedas* gave the human race an ideal language, which is unique in its beauty and sublimity, inexhaustible in its vocabulary, most scientific in its *varnas, mātrās,* roots and their derivations, conjunctions and disjunctions of letters, varieties of *swaras, chandas,* modulations of accents, etc., most refined and forceful in its expression. This language itself has been the bond of unity of all Indian people for thousands of years and has been the mother and nurse of all the popular dialects (*prākrita bhāshā*) in all parts of the country. This language is revered as *Deva-bhāṣhā* (a divine language), and Classical Sanskrit is a later form of it. The Vedic teachers advised men to learn this sacred language in order to get continuous inspiration and guidance in the path of the cultivation of the enlightened spiritual outlook on life and the world and their sure and steady advancement towards spiritual self-fulfilment.

V. The Influence Of Vedas Upon The Practical Life Of The Aryans

The great Indo-Aryan people, among whom the Vedic Truths and Ideals revealed themselves through the medium of the superordinary truth-seeking *Rishis*, were not only a virile and adventurous race, but also a highly intellectual and imaginative and withal a deeply moral and religious race. While the few inwardly illumined minds received by the Divine Grace the eternal moral and spiritual Truths of the *Vedas*, which came out through them in a Divine literary language, the people in general were not of course on the same plane of thought and imagination and realisation. They, with the gifts of their bodies and minds and hearts, were widely interested in pleasure and prosperity, in establishing their homes and organising their society on a sound and solid basis, in producing food, in domesticating useful animals, in protecting themselves and their food and animals, in expanding their dominions and spheres of influence, in all sorts of works necessary for secular development of a people. Those who were endowed with greater powers were naturally led by higher political and economic and social ambitions. The most highly talented poets and thinkers had aspirations for penetrating into the mysteries of nature and life, for discovering the ultimate origin and the final destiny of creation, for solving in general terms the intricate and puzzling problems of the ever-expansive social and political life of the people.

Thus, while the interests of the early Aryan people were in all directions, the highest and noblest ideals of their life were set up by the *Vedic* revelations. The secular ambitions of their individual and collective life were governed and kept under proper limitations by the moral and spiritual ideals with which the *Vedas* inspired them. Their desires for earthly happiness and prosperity and power and self-aggrandisement were checked and regulated by their higher aspirations for moral self-elevation and spiritual self-fulfilment. They earned *Artha* and *Kāma* with all earnestness and diligence, but with a view to *sacrifice* them for the sake of *Dharma* and *Moksha*. They performed their domestic and social duties faithfully and honestly, but with the consciousness that these were not ends in themselves, but only means to the attainment of higher and better and happier eternal life above all earthly relations and limitations. They cared more for the unearthly moral and spiritual fruits of their actions than the immediate earthly fruits. Their worldly life also was governed by an other-worldly attitude. This was the influence of the *Vedas* upon the practical life of the people at large.

VI. Controversies On The True Interpretation Of Vedic Texts

Now, even in the very early period of the development and expansion and consolidation of the Aryan society there were serious controversies among the pre-eminent intellectualist thought-leaders of the age with regard to the true interpretation of the *Vedic Texts* which were revealed through the mouths of the inspired *Rishis* and remembered *verbatim* by their intelligent disciples. In the systematic efforts for the correct interpretation, correct recitation and correct application of the *Vedic Texts*, various sciences and arts came into being. *Śikshā*, *Kalpa*, *Vyākarana*, *Nirukta*, *Chanda* and *Jyotisha* were the products of such efforts, and they were found to be so essential for the proper understanding of the *Vedas* that they came to be known as *Vedāngas* (limbs of the *Vedas*). The *Brāhmanas* and the *Āranyakas* largely elaborated and illustrated the teachings of the Vedic *Mantras* and brought them much nearer to the common understanding and the practical life of the people. They also were regarded as parts of the Vedic literature. Lastly, the *Upanishads* unveiled the deeper significance of the metaphysical and spiritual revelations of the *Vedas* and came to be known as *Vedānta*.

While the original *Vedic Texts* were almost universally believed to have been Divinely revealed, the greatest thinkers and thought-leaders of that early Aryan society appear to have had differences among themselves, not only in their interpretations, but sometimes even in regard to the words of the Texts. Accordingly, the Vedic literature was divided into a number of branches (*Śākhā*) and sub-branches. All of them were, however, respected as authoritative, by common thinkers and scholars. Attempts were not wanting for bringing about reconciliation among the various versions. The sacredness of all of them was not questioned. The entire Vedic literature was generally accepted as the basis of the domestic and social, moral and religious, aesthetic and philosophical culture of the Indo-Aryan race.

(a) *Interpretation from the viewpoint of Karma.*

Even among the earliest interpreters of the Vedic teachings, we find, broadly speaking, *three* main schools of thought. One school laid special emphasis upon the practical aspect of the teachings of the Vedas and held that all the Vedic revelations were chiefly concerned with the regulation of the practical behaviour of men in the path of righteousness (*Dharma*). According to this school every Vedic instruction enjoins upon men either to do something right or to refrain from doing something wrong. From the view-point of this school, all devotional utterances, all metaphysical statements, all descriptions of realities and narrations of events, which are found in the Vedic Texts and which have no direct reference to injunctions and prohibitions, are also to be interpreted as somehow connected with the practical instructions and the practical ideals given in other related Texts or as explanatory of the implications of those Texts which convey direct admonitions. Purely factual or theoretical statements of Truths, whether of the sensuous plane or of the higher supersensuous planes, whether empirical or transcendental, merely for the sake of right knowledge or the satisfaction of intellectual curiosity, have, according to this view, no place in the Vedic Revelations.

Man is essentially an active being, and the highest possibilities of his nature can be realised mainly through the faithful performance of higher and higher orders of righteous actions which are enjoined by the Vedas,—actions involving self-development and self-expansion and self-restraint and self-purification and the sacrifice of lower pleasures and narrower interests for the attainment of higher orders of happiness in this life and still higher orders of existence in after-life. Attainment of right knowledge and cultivation of the spirit of devotion are of course necessary and essential for the fulfilment of human life, but their utility lies principally in the progressive ennoblement and elevation of the *practical life*, so as to make it worthy of higher planes of free and blissful existence in the Heavens (*Swarga*), as indicated in the *Vedas*. Man's destiny is determined by his *karma* (action), and not by his mere knowledge of Truth or by his mere devotion to the Gods or the God of all Gods.

This school was not much interested in what the *Jñānis* and *Yogis* and the Upanishadic sages called *Moksha* or *Kaivalya* or *Amritatwa* or *Nirvāna* and what was regarded by them as the Supreme Spiritual Ideal of Human Life, but incapable of being attained through the performance of righteous actions even of the highest order. To this school *Moksha* meant the Perfect Fulness of Life in the highest *Swarga*, and this was attainable through the performance of the highest order of righteous actions at the sacrifice of all finite and transitory interests and ideals of this world and the other worlds. Thus this school stoutly advocated the *Karma-Kānda* of the Vedas and regarded *Jñāna* and *Yoga* and *Upāsanā* as subsidiary to *Karma*.

(*b*) *Interpretation from the viewpoint of Jñāna and Yoga*

Another school attached the utmost importance to the metaphysical and transcendental Truths revealed in the *Vedas*, and regarded all other principles and ideals, all injunctions and prohibitions, all rules and laws for the regulation and elevation of practical life, as well as all glorifications of Deities and exhortations for the cultivation of devotional sentiments and practices, as of subordinate and auxiliary values. The *Vedas* revealed that one self-existent self-luminous infinite eternal all-transcending Supreme Spirit is the Absolute Reality, that the whole universe of diverse orders of existences and experiences is a self-manifestation in spatio-temporal forms of that One Spirit, that the plurality of Deities are nothing but specially glorified self-expressions of the same Absolute Spirit and, though designated in different Names and adored in different forms, They are ultimately one and the same, that all individual souls also are essentially non-different from that Supreme Spirit and that the ultimate fulfilment of the worldly phenomenal life of every individual soul lies in the perfeet realisation of its identity with that one non-dual Spirit. Perfect Knowledge of these Truths, as revealed in the *Vedas,* is, from the view-point of this school, the end in itself for the self-conscious human life, and not merely a means to the proper regulation and ennoblement of its practical deeds for the sake of some happier state of individual existence.

Moksha (perfect liberation from all possible sorrows and bondages), which is the Supreme Ideal of man's life, lies in the attainment of this Perfect Knowledge. Since the individual soul is essentially a self-expression of and as such identical with the absolutely blissful and free Supreme Spirit, perfect knowledge of this identity is nothing less than *becoming* one with the Supreme Spirit or at least realising in the individual consciousness the perfectly free and blissful, infinite and eternal character of the Supreme Spirit. This Knowledge also involves the blissful experience of one's own true Self (which is nothing other than the Supreme Spirit) as revealed and manifested in and through all the diversities of the cosmic order. The attainment of this Knowledge cannot be the effect of any *Karma*, however noble and virtuous ; but the body and the mind and the intellect and the ego have to be disciplined and purified and refined and illumined in a systematic way so that the ultimate transcendent character of the Self or the Spirit may be unveiled to the calm and tranquil consciousness.

This school strongly advocated the ascetic view of life and interpreted the significance of the Vedic teachings from that view-point. The teachers of this school held that renunciation of all worldly concerns, repudiation of all domestic and social obligations, effective restraint and control of all sensuous appetites and propensities and all mental desires and ambitions, and exclusive self-application under the guidance of competent *Gurus* to deep reflection and contemplation and meditation, are essential for the realisation of the ultimate transcendent spiritual nature of the Self and the attainment of absolute liberation from all kinds of bondage and sorrow. According to them, the due performance of sacrificial duties, the cultivation of the spirit of sacrifice and service in domestic and social life, the expansion and elevation and refinement of desires and aspirations, as enjoined in the *Karma-Kanda* of the *Vedas*, are meant to be preparatory for complete renunciation.

They held that all fruits of *Karma*, whether in this world or in higher heavenly worlds, are originated in time and must be exhausted in time, and that *eternal Moksha*, which our innermost consciousness yearns for and of which also the *Vedas* speak, can not be the product of any *Karma*, however noble and great. *Eternal Moksha* is practically realisable, because it is the essential transcendent character of *Ātmā* or the innermost Spirit of every individual being, and this realisation means nothing but true intimate knowledge and experience of this ultimate Truth This true Self-knowledge can not be the effect of any pious *Karma*, but is attainable through getting rid of all *Karma* and its effects—through the experience of the eternally actionless sorrowless changeless relationless blissful nature of the Self. To be worthy of this self-knowledge, renunciation of the active domestic and social life, adoption of an ascetic mode of life, suppression of all passions and desires and attachments, systematic practice of concentrated reflection and meditation, etc., are regarded as essentially necessary.

This school of thought, again, was gradually divided into two sections. One section attached greater importance to metaphysical reflection and intellectual refinement, and the other to the practical discipline of the body, the senses, the vital system, and the mind, and regular practice of concentration and deep meditation. The former was known as *Jñāni* and the latter as *Yogi.* Both the sections were alike in their austere habits and indifference to worldly affairs and in their advocacy of the ***Nivṛtti-Mārga*** and ***Jñāna-Kānda*** of the *Vedas*. Their face was not towards *Kāma*, ***Artha*** and *Dharma*, but exclusively towards *Moksha*. '*Ātmānam viddhi*' is the motto of life to both the schools. This is according to them the Supreme Ideal taught by the *Vedas*.

(*c*) ***Interpretation from the viewpoint ofDevotion.***

The third school of thought was charmed by the exquisitely beautiful and inspiring aesthetic and devotional utterances of the *Vedas* and was led to regard the cultivation of the finest emotions and sentiments and an attitude of reverential and loving self-surrender towards the Supreme Spirit and His glorious and brilliant self-manifestations in the Cosmic Order as the essence of the *Vedic* teachings. The thinkers of this school did not hold the scrupulous discharge of domestic and social duties and the faithful performance of sacrificial rites and ceremonies as enough for the attainment of the Supreme Ideal of human life, nor did they hold the Supreme Ideal as attainable solely through renunciation and austerity or through abstract speculation and meditation. According to them, the Supreme Ideal of *Moksha* and *Tattwa-Jñāna* (Absolute Liberation and Truth-realisation) is a gift of Divine Mercy and the highest reward for whole-hearted devotion to the Supreme Spirit. Such whole-hearted devotion to the Supreme Spirit demands necessarily the purification of the body and the senses, the elevation of the mind and the heart to higher and higher planes, the enlightenment of the moral and aesthetic consciousness, the illumination of the intellect and the spiritual consciousness. All the teachings of the *Vedas* with regard to duties in domestic and social life, ritualistic sacrifices and services, as well as renunciation and austerities and contemplative life, are of course greatly useful, for the development of the true devotional spirit in the human heart. But the teaching of devotion is, according to this view, the centre of all Vedic revelations.

These three lines of thought and ethico-spiritual discipline and these three modes of interpretation of the Vedic Texts were evolved in the Aryan society in the very early period of its social develoment. They seem to have given rise to various kinds of controversies. But each of these three currents of thought gradually developed and expanded and exercised its influence upon the life and culture of the Society. Even in the present day these three main currents prevail in the domain of religious thought in Hinduism, which broadly means the ethico-spiritual culture of India.

VIII. Interpretation From The Viewpoint Of Karma Prevailed In The Society

In the period of progressive expansion and consolidation of the vigorous and enterprising Aryan race, people in general were naturally much more interested in a *philosophy of action* than in a *philosophy of renunciation* or *emotional devotion*,—in *Pravritti-Mārga* than in *Nivritti-Mārga* or *Bhakti-Mārga*—in the Ideal of *Abhyudaya* than in the Ideal of *Nihśreyasa* or *Moksha* or *Nirvāna*,—in a zealous and optimistic view of life (life here as well as life after physical death in higher and happier worlds) than in an indifferent and pessimistic view of earthly life implied in the cult of renunciation. The great exponents of *Karma-Kānda* or *Pravritti-Mārga* were accordingly acclaimed in the society as the true interpreters of the Vedic revelations, and the cult of *Yajña* (meaning well-planned actions involving service and sacrifice) was accepted as the best way of virtuous life for the achievement of all-round progress of the society as well as fulness of individual life here and hereafter.

The wise and active sages of this school, inspired by the ideal of individual and social welfare, wonderfully elaborated and systematised the principles and practices of Vedic *Karma-Kānda*, composed independent works on a rational basis for organising the economic and political and domestic and communal life of all sections of the society in accordance with the lofty ideals set up by the *Vedas*, and adopted all possible measures for popularising the cult of *sacrifice* and mutual service among all sections of people. They composed a good many *Smritis* or *Dharma-Śāstras*, for determining the sacred duties and responsibilities of each and every section of the people and attaching penalties to the violations of the laws. Of these Manu's *Smriti*, also known as *Mānava-Dharma-Śāstra*, was recognised as most authoritative. They composed a good many *Śrauta-*

Sutras and *Grihya-Sutras* and other works of various patterns for giving practical guidance to the people for religiously regulating all the departments of their life's interests and activities and for keeping them awake to the moral and spiritual ideals of human life. They introduced various kinds of elaborate and complicated rites and ceremonies into all grades of the society in accordance with their intellectual and moral calibre and economic resources with the same object in view. They founded a well-reasoned system of philosophy, based upon *Karma-Kānda* of the *Vedas,* and this was known as *Mimāmsā-darśana,* which steadily developed. They devised *Varnāśrama* as the best social system. Maharshi Jaimini was in ancient times the greatest exponent of *Mimāmsā Darśana,* and Manu was the most illustrious expounder of *Varnāśrama Dharma.*

So widely and deeply effective were the cultural and organisational works of the exponents of *Karma-Kānda* or *Pravritti-Mārga* of the *Vedas,* that they were generally regarded as the true interpreters of the essential teachings of the Vedic Revelations and the *Dharma* of the *Pravritti-Mārga* was accepted in the Aryan society as the true *Vedic Dharma.* While the Aryan society with its ethico-spiritual culture expanded in all parts of the Indian sub-continent and spread its influence over all the non Aryan races, it had naturally to face many complicated social, political, economic, moral and cultural problems; but it carried the banners of its *Vedic Dharma* everywhere with wonderful success. This *Vedic Dharma* claimed to be *Sanātana-Dharma,* —the eternal and universal religion for the humanity.

VIII. Development of the Viewpoint of Jnana and Yoga

The school of *Nivritti-Mārga,* with its cult of *Jñāna* and *Yoga* and *Vairāgya* and *Tapasyā,* developed, silently but steadily, more outside the social environments than within them. The most earnest advocates of this path of spiritual discipline usually bade farewell to their domestic and social duties and retired to hills and forests early in life for the speedy attainment of Self-Knowledge and perfect Liberation (*Ātma-Jñāna* and *Moksha*). The growth of this view-point was generally resisted by the powerful leaders of the society, who apprehended that the popularisation of this interpretation of the *Vedic Dharma* might lead the brilliant young men of the society away from the path of social well-being and harmonious development of individual life. But in spite of their life of retirement and exclusive devotion to the practice of *Yoga* and *Jñāna,* they were not altogether out of touch with the society, and the spiritual appeal of their calm and simple and care-free and peaceful life and their message of perfect purity and goodness and non-violence and universal love and absolute bliss was irresistible. Their literature, elaborating and systematising their philosophical views as well as their modes of ethical and psychical and spiritual discipline,—their works on *Jñāna* and *Yoga*,—greatly developed. Their literature, though the product of the deepest wisdom and innermost experience of the truth-seeking *Yogis* and *Jñānis*, was not however recognised in the prevailing society as Vedic literature. It came to be known as *Āgama* and *Tantra*.

The exponents of *Nivritti-Mārga* were, as it has been noted, divided into *Yogis* (saints) and *Jñānis* (philosophers). The *Āgama* literature developed principally through the teachings of the *Yogis* of the highest order of spiritual excellence, who were chiefly concerned with the practical methods of liberation from all bondages of the world, from ignorance of the Ultimate Truth and attachment to transitory and unsubstantial things of this world and the other worlds and from all forms of sorrow and restlessness arising from such ignorance and attachment. The origin of the *Āgamas* was traced to one Personal God, Who was *Mahā-Yogīśwara*, in Whose consciousness the Absolute Spirit was eternally realised and Who was eternally untouched by ignorance and egoism and attachment and aversion and restlessness and sorrow and bondage, but Who was full of love and mercy for all creatures and was the Source of all true knowledge as well as of the innerment urge in man for Truth, Beauty, Goodness, Freedom and Bliss. He was regarded as the *Guru* of all *Gurus*, the First Guru of *Jñāna* and *Yoga*, the First Author of *Āgama-Śāstras* He was variously named as *Iśwara, Maheśwara, Rudra, Hiranya-Garbha, Śiva, Ādi-Nātha*, etc. In course of time the original *Āgama-Śastras* were lost (perhaps due to the hostile attitude of the exponents of *Karma-Kānda*), but the school of *Yoga* and *Jñāna* continued to grow through the teachings and exemplary lives of earnest *Yogis* and *Jñānis* generations after generations, and its intellectual, moral and spiritual influence upon the thought and life of earnest and sincere truth-seekers even within the Vedic society continued to increase. The teachings of *Nivritti* and *Jñāna* and *Yoga* appeared to many intelligent and important members of the society as of a superior order than the teachings of *Pravritti* and *Yajña* and *Swarga*, which prevailed in the society. It is obvious that the great teachers of the *Upanishads*, which were accepted as the final portions of the *Vedas*, got their inspiration mainly, if not wholly, from the all-renouncing saints and philosophers who spent their lives in spiritual self-discipline and deep meditation in mountain-caves and forest-āśramas.

Kapila, the reputed founder of the *Sānkhya* school of philosophy, was probably the first philosopher who gave a complete system of philosophy on the strength of independent rational speculation and arrived at definite conclusions with regard to the origin of the world-order, the ultimate nature of the soul as transcendent self-luminous spirit, the true meaning of *Moksha* and the true way to realise it. He accepted the authority of the *Vedas*, but he was a staunch supporter of *Nivritti-Mārga*. To explain the origin of the cosmic system, however, he did not require to postulate the existence one *Iśwara* or creative Supreme Spirit. Kapila's *Sānkhya Darśana* exercised a great influence upon the subsequent evolution of Hindu spiritual thought. Patañjali developed his *Yoga*-system on the basis of the metaphysics of Kapila and the practical teachings of earlier *Mahāyogis*.

IX. The Sankhya-Darsana Of Kapila

Through profoundly thoughtful reflection upon the general nature of all subjective and objective phenomenal realities,—all orders of psychological and biological and material facts, gross as well as subtle,—*Mahāsiddha-Yogi* Kapila discovered that all of them appear in a manifested state from an unmanifested state and pass again from the manifested state to the unmanifested state in a cyclic process. The former is popularly known as creation or origination, and the latter as destruction or dissolution. Before production and after destruction, a thing is not absolutely non-existent, but it exists in an undifferentiated inexperienceable unmanifested state, with the potentiality for being manifested in some differentiated and experienceable form. This is logically known as *Sat-Kārya-Vāda*. Causation means, not the new origination of any effect previously non-existent, but the process of the actual manifestation of an effect from the state of its unmanifested and undifferentiated existence in the nature of its cause. Destruction also does not mean annihilation, but only dissolution of an effect in the nature of its cause and its existence therein in an unmanifested state. An activity is as a matter of course involved in the process of passing from one state to another; but deep reflection reveals that some subtle form of activity exists in the nature of a phenomenal reality, even when it is apparently at rest, whether in the manifested state or in the unmanifested state.

Thus Kapila points out that Potentiality, Actuality and Activity,—an unmanifested state, a manifested state and a state of unrest for passing from one state to another,—constitute ultimately the very nature of all phenomenal realities, i.e. the entire cosmic system. These three moments or constituents of phenomenal existence are called by him *Tamas*, *Sattwa* and *Rajas*, and they are designated as *Gunas*. They are however not to be conceived as attributes or qualities of any substance or reality, nor as substances or realities possessing other attributes or qualities, but as the ultimate characteristics of all phenomenal existences. Kapila conceives of a state of existence, in which *Sattwa*, *Rajas* and *Tamas* are in absolute equillibrium and hence there is no manifestation of any phenomenal reality or any process or change or action. It is a state of absolute non-manifestation (*Avyakta*) of all phenomenal existence. This is the state of existence of phenomenal reality before what is commonly known as Creation and after what is known as wholesale Dissolution. The ultimate phenomenal Reality in this state of absolute non-manifestation is called *Mulā-Prakriti*, and this is the ultimate Material Cause of the universe. From this Cause all orders of phenomenal existences in the manifested universe gradually evolve and in It they ultimately merge.

Kapila gave a wonderful conception of this subjective-objective phenomenal cosmic system in terms of his famous twenty-four realities (*Caturvimśati tattwas*). *Prakriti*, the absolutely unmanifested and undifferentiated state of existence of all phenomenal realities, and as such the ultimate Material Cause of the whole universe, is a self-modifying and self-evolving non-spiritual (but certainly not material or physical) Reality, with *Sattwa, Rajas* and *Tamas* as its constituents. The existence of *Prakriti* is proved by the evolution of this diversified order of the universe in gradual stages, since this evolution implies the ultimate Material Cause. *Prakriti* can never be an object of perception or direct experience, since all instruments of perception and experience evolve from it and are dissolved in it. But still its existence is indisputable. This is the first Reality, the Causal Reality, all manifested phenomenal existences being its effects. *Time* plays an important part in the course of the evolution of the universe from it. *Prakriti* cannot be conceived as *Matter* or *Energy*, since Matter as well as Energy evolves from it in course of its self-modification.

Prakriti, the Ultimate Cause, manifests itself first in the form of what is called *Mahat-tattwa* (the Great Reality),—also spoken of as *Buddhi-tattwa* (Intelligence-Reality),—which may be conceived as one universal cosmic phenomenal Intelligence or Consciousness without differentiation of subject and object and without any manifest active process. This is the Second Reality, being the first effect of *Prakriti*; it is the Material Cause of all the subsequent stages of evolution, and the whole universe exists in an unmanifested and undifferentiated state in its nature. Here *Sattwa* predominates over *Rajas* and *Tamas*, though of course they are present in it and stimulate further evolution.

The Third Reality is called *Aham-tattwa* or *Ahamkāra* (Ego-reality) which evolves from *Mahat-tattwa* and becomes the Cause of all subsequent subjective and objective phenomenal diversities. It may be conceived as one universal phenomenal active Ego-Principle, implying the presence of phenomenal intelligence or consciousness in its nature, but with the predominance of the active causal process (*Rajas*). From *Aham-tattwa* evolve the instruments of knowledge and action on the one hand and the objects of knowledge and action on the other, in differentiation from and also in inseparable relation to one another. The five special senses of perception and the five special senses of action, with the *Manas* or mind presiding over them all, are enumerated as the eleven subjective Realities, evolving from *Ahamkāra*. The five subtle objective Realities with the essential attributes of Sound, Touch, Visibility, Taste and Smell, are called five *Tanmātras* and are regarded as the constituents of the material world. They also evolve from *Ahamkāra* and are conceivable only in terms of the senses of perception. The five gross material elements evolve from those *Tanmātras*.

Thus *Prakriti*, *Mahat-tattwa*, *Aham-tattwa*, *Manas*, five senses of perception, five senses of action, five *Tanmātras* or *Subtle Bhutas* and five *Mahābhutas* or gross elements are the 24 *Tattwas* or realities, by means of which Kapila explains the evolutionary system of the universe. All kinds of objective material things are only different forms of combinations of the five *Mahābhutas*, and their characters are ascertained necessarily in terms of their perceptible qualities or attributes. Instruments of perception and all possible objects of perception must have a common source of existence, from which they evolve, and that source is discovered in the original Ego-Consciousness (*Ahamkāra*), in which both are united and in which both exist before differentiated manifestation. In the living organisms (including human bodies), all mental and intellectual phenomena as well as all physical and vital phenomena, all sensuous and super-sensuous experience as well as all objects of such experiences, originate or evolve from the same source, *Ahamkāra*; and this *Ahamkāra* again originates or evolves from one ego-less Phenomenal Consciousness, *Mahat-tattwa*, in which the entire universe of mental and material, subjective and objective, phenomenal realities, originally exist in an undifferentiated unmanifested state. *Mahat-tattwa*, as it has been found, is the first manifested state of *Prakriti*, which is the ultimate unity and potentiality of all phenomenal existences.

Just as all orders of existences gradually emerge from *Prakriti*, so they gradually merge in *Prakriti* in course of time in an involutionary process. The whole universe is a temporal order, in which the evolutionary and the involutionary processes,—the creative and the destructive processes,—are going on in eternal continuity; it had never any absolute beginning and will never have any absolute end. The entire manifested cosmic system may at one time pass into the unmanifested state, i. e. the state of *Prakriti*, but therefrom it again in course of time comes to the manifested state in the evolutionary order. There is no necessity for the active participation of any omnipotent and omniscient Supreme Spirit, Iśwara or Brahma, in this eternally temporal process of evolution and involution. Accordingly in Kapila's view *Prakriti* is a non-spiritual Reality having an eternal independent existence. But it is not conceived as a material entity or blind insentient energy or anything of this sort, because such terms apply only to particular forms of manifested realities or objects or phenomenal experience.

Kapila proclaims the eternal existence of an infinite number Spirits or Souls, called by him *Purusha*, which are of the nature of pure transcendent consciousness, without any change or modification, without any joy or sorrow, without any will or action, without any name or form, without any direct causal relation with any of the phenomena of the cosmic order and without any real bondage or limitation or imperfection. They are essentially above time and space and unaffected by the occurrences of this spatio-temporal and psycho-physical system evolved from *Prakriti*. They are, however, eternally associated with *Prakriti* in a mysterious way and are as it were forgetful of their essential transcendent self-luminous character. Somehow there is a relation of non-discrimination *(aviveka)* between these changeless *Purushas* and the ever-self-modifying *Prakriti*, and the changes in the domain of *Prakriti* are falsely attributed to the *Purushas*. It is however admitted that the self-luminous *Purushas*, by their mere actionless self-luminons presence, stimulate and illumine the activities of *Prakriti* and enable non-spiritual *Prakriti* to evolve from within itself phenomenal consciousness, phenomenal intelligence, phenomenal ego and the phenomena implying the manifestation of consciousness. But for the illumining presence of the spirits or souls, *Prakriti* could never have evolved consciousness from within itself, and without the evolution of consciousness there would be no real evolution at all,—no experience and no object of experience,—no knowledge and no knowable world,—and hence no cosmic system.

Thus though the changeless self-luminous spirits or souls do not directly participate in the evolutionary and involutionary processes of the cosmic order and their essential transcendent character is in no way affected by these processes, their association with *Prakriti* must be admitted for a rational explanation of this cosmic order. Though ever-changing non-self-luminous *Prakriti* and the changeless self-luminous Spirits (*Purushas*) have eternally and essentially separate and independent real existence of their own, *Prakriti* may be said to be eternally in the *service* of the *Purushas*, for otherwise this cosmic order would be purposeless and meaningless. Ignorance of this essential transcendent character of the *spirits* is the cause of our experience of bondage and imperfection and sorrow, since we falsely identify our souls or spirits with the operations of *Prakriti* and its evolutes. When the *soul* is known to be essentially and eternally transcendent and free from all bondage and imperfection and sorrow, there is the experience of *Moksha* or *Kaivalya*. Thus a man can attain *Moksha* only and solely through the discrimination of his soul from

Prakriti (Viveka-khyāti). This implies that true self-knowledge is the direct means to the realisation of the Supreme Ideal of life, and not any pious and noble action.

Ignorance and knowledge, bondage and liberation, sorrow and joy, sense of individuality and its limitations and imperfections, sense of virtue and vice, *karma* and its fruits, desires and their fulfilments and frustrations, states of waking and dream and deep sleep, etc. etc.,—all these are phenomena of empirical consciousness and belong to the phenomenal cosmic system evolved from *Prakriti*. But they can not be rationally explained without the assumption of the existence of a *plurality* of permanent transcendent self-luminous consciousnesses or souls or spirits (*purushas* or *ātmans*) behind the empirical consciousnesses, through which they are revealed and with which they are falsely identified. Every individual consciousness, every phenomenal ego, every individual mind and intellect, every individual living body, every organised *pañcabhautika* object, must have an individual spirit (*Purusha*) as the ground of its unity and individuality,—as the changeless permanent background of its identity and continuity amidst constant changes and modifications and transformations.

Thus Kapila maintains that there must be a *numberless plurality of individual purushas*, eternally transcendent in their essential character, but eternally associated with *Prakriti* and its course of evolution and involution, and that in this cosmic order a particular *purusha* is apparently related to a particular phenomenal egoistic consciousness and a particular phenomenal body (gross or subtle), evolved from *Prakriti*. The permanent "I" in every individual consciousness essentially refers to the *Purusha* related to it, but it is usually unconscious of the eternally transcendent character of this *Purusha*. This is the reason for the *apparent* bondage and worldliness and sorrow of the "I" or Purusha. When in course of evolution any phenomenal individual consciousness is illumined with the knowledge of the essentially pure and self-luminous transcendent character of the *Purusha*, that particular *Purusha* is liberated from its association with *Prakriti* and the cosmic system and becomes thus free from all phenomenal qualifications and limitations, free from all apparent bondages and sorrows, free from the sense of individuality and relativity and causality. The entire world-order becomes as good as non-existent to that liberated *Purusha*, though to the innumerable unliberated *Purushas* the world-order goes on uninterruptedly. For this liberation of a *Purusha* the illumination of the individual phenomenal consciousness to which it is related is necessary, and this can finally be attained through *Jñāna* and *Yoga*, and not as the effect of any *Karma*, however noble and virtuous.

The *Sānkhya Darśana* of Kapila gave a powerful and permanent lead to the philosophical approach to the Ultimate Truth and the rational conception of the world-order in India and immensely strengthened the cult of *Jñāna* and *Yoga* and *Sannyāsa* and *Nivritti-Mārga* in preference to the cult of *Karma* and *Yajña* and *Gārhasthya* and *Pravritti-Mārga*. The *Yogis* in general adopted the method of metaphysical reflection of *Sānkhya*, though they laid greater emphasis upon the actual practice of austerity and privation, mastery over the body and the senses and the vital forces and the mind, and the progressive purification and refinement and illumination of the whole empirical being (born of *Prakriti*), as the effective means to the realisation of the true transcendent Self or Spirit *(Ātmā* or *Purusha)* in dissociation from *Prakriti* and the attainment of *Moksha*.

The *Upanishads* also accepted the view that *Brahman* or *Ātman* was realisable in the path discovered by *Sānkhya* and *Yoga*, and not in the *Pravritti Mārga*,—the path of *Karma* and *Yajña*. The *Upanishads* however did not accept the *Sānkhya* metaphysical theory of the *ultimate plurality* of the Spirits or *Purushas* or *Ātmans* in the transcendent plane and of the *ultimate independent existence* of *Prakriti*. They held on the authority of the Vedic Revelation that ultimately there is only One *Purusha* or *Ātman* or *Brahman* in the transcendent plane, Who appears as many *Purushas* or *Ātmans* in the realm of *Prakriti*, i. e. the phenomenal plane, and that *Prakriti*, the Mother of all phenomenal existences, is nothing but the inscrutable *Power* of *Brahman*, through which the non-dual Absolute Spirit *(Brahman)* reveals Himself in the phenomenal plane as diverse orders of phenomenal existences and phenomenal consciousnesses. When all phenomenal existences and consciousnesses are in the totally unmanifested state, *Prakriti* can not be said to have any actual existence apart from and distinguishable from that of the Absolute Spirit, Who then shines alone in His transcendent self-luminosity, with of course the *possibility* of phenomenal diversified self-manifestation. *Prakriti* in its absolutely unmanifested state is nothing but this *possibility* of phenomenal diversities and as such should reasonably be conceived as the *Śakti* (Power) of *Brahman*, existing in and by and for *Brahman* and hence essentially non-different from Him. It is also rationally meaningless to speak of the *plurality* of *Purushas* or self-shining spirits in the transcendent plane, wherein there is no sense of individuality or self-distinguishing consciousness. Individuality lies only in the phenomenal plane, and the One Absolute Spirit is ultimately the true Self of all individuals. *Moksha* is attainable through the realisation of this ultimate Truth.

Thus the *Upanishads*, claiming to unveil the final and essential truths of the *Vedas*, though differing from *Sānkhya* in respect of some important metaphysical concepts, agreed with the latter in holding *Nivritti-Mārga* and the practice of *Yoga* and *Jñāna* as the true and direct means to the attainment of *Moksha* or perfect liberation from all kinds of bondage and sorrow, which is the supreme ideal of life. The *Brahma-Sutras* of *Bādarāyana*, known as *Vedānta-Darśana*, gave an authoritative philosophical form to the teachings of the *Upanishads*, and this was widely accepted as the true and final philosophy of the *Vedas* by a very large circle of truth-seekers. It had the authority of the *Vedas* behind it, and at the same time it was strongly argumentative. It very ably maintained that the Ultimate Transcendent Truth was not ascertainable purely by the strength of intellectual metaphysical arguments, but that It was to be taken on faith from the *Revealed Texts* and then deeply reflected upon and directly experienced through the deepest meditation and self-absorption in It.

Sānkhya and *Vedānta* constructed permanently the philosophical foundation of *Nivritti-Mārga* and stimulated in all ages the cultivation of *Vairāgya* and *Jñāna* and *Yoga* as the means to the ultimate fulfilment of life. The philosophical literature based on *Sānkhya* and *Vedānta* developed wonderfully during all these thousands of years, and they had their influence upon the general life of the people and their arts and common literature. Neither *Sānkhya* nor *Vedānta,* it should be noted, denied altogether the relative values of domestic and social duties and the various kinds of practices enjoined in the *Pravritti-Mārga* as well as the relative importance of *Dharma, Artha* and *Kāma,* in the gradual development and elevation and refinement of the human life. They emphasised the essential importance of renunciation and exclusive self-devotion to *Yoga* and *Jñāna* in the higher stages of life's spiritual progress, when the body and the mind and the intellect would be sufficiently purified and qualified for this higher course of spiritual self-discipline through the due discharge of worldly duties and the faithful performance of noble deeds in accordance with the laws of *Dharma-Śāstras* and social traditions.

X. Development of Bhakti Cult

The view-point of *Upāsanā-Mārga* (the path of devotional worship) also continued to develop since that early age and to expand its sphere of influence upon the minds and hearts and modes of conduct of the people. In the earlier stages the plurality of Gods glorified in the revealed Vedic Texts were worshipped ceremoniously in the prescribed forms with an earnest devotional spirit, and each of the Gods was conceived by his devoted admirers as possessed of all the superhuman Divine powers and qualities. Gradually emphasis was laid more and more upon the One Supreme Spirit, of Whom all these Gods were described even in the *Vedas* themselves as special powerful and majestic self-manifestations in the cosmic order. The school of worshippers of the Supreme Spirit gradually assimilated the groups of devotees of all the special Gods. While recognising that all the different groups of worshippers earnestly devoted to the worship of the particular Gods were indirectly and often without true knowledge worshipping the same Supreme Spirit, these devotees who claimed to be direct worshippers of the Supreme Spirit also *conceived* Him in different ways and applied various significant Holy Names (not always Vedic) to Him and adopted different modes of worship. The spirit of devotion was however common to them all, and the aim of all was to be in direct emotional touch with the Absolute Spirit through different Names and Forms.

Accordingly, even in a very early age, the school of spiritual aspirants, maintaining that devotional worship to the One Supreme Spirit was the principal means to liberation from all actual and possible bondages and sorrows and enjoyment of eternal spiritual bliss, was divided into a number of sub-sects. Thus there arose in that ancient period a good many *Upāsaka Sampradāyas,* devoted to the worship of *Śiva, Rudra, Paśupati, Maheśwara, Vishnu, Nārāyana, Bhagawan, Śakti, Surya* and others. Each of these *Sampradāyas* had its distinctive features, a religious philosophy of its own and a complete code of moral and spiritual self-discipline for the fulfilment of life and the attainment of *Moksha.* Each of them, however, claimed to be devoted to the Absolute Spirit, the Supreme Source of all phenomenal existences, the Ultimate Lord of the universe, and each bowed down to the authority of the *Vedas.* One point to be specially noted is that in the development of these devotional sects the Supreme Spirit was gradually more and more *personalised* and *humanised,* and of all the Divine powers and attributes Love and Mercy were more and more emphasised. Truth-realisation and Liberation also were believed to be gifts of Divine Mercy. Each developed a religious literature of its own, and the original authoritative literature of each is known as *Āgama.* These devotional schools steadily developed into the wide-spread *Bhakti*-schools of later centuries. In course of time the devotees of Śiva, Krishna, Rāma and Śakti (in the forms of Kālī and Durgā) became the most popular and wide-spread devotional *sampradāyas* in the country. They all conceived and worshipped the Supreme Spirit in these Divine Names and Forms.

CHAPTER XIX

THE EVOLUTION OF HINDU SPIRITUAL CULTURE (II).

I. Sri Krishna's Grand Synthesis of All Cults

As the Aryan Society developed and expanded and gradually spread over all the parts of this great sub-continent, its culture naturally became more and more variegated and poly-morphous; but all its aspects continued to be pervaded by the three (or four) aforesaid idealistic and spiritualistic thought-currents, flowing down from the Vedic Revelations. The exponents of these view-points were sometimes engaged in heated controversies with one another, but they generally cooperated with one another for the peace and unity and steady progress of the society and the race. Faith in the *Vedas* was the strongest bond of union among all the sections of the ever-growing community. Saints and sages with extraordinary intellectual powers and spiritual intuitions flourished in all ages among the advocates of all these view-points and spread their influence upon the minds and hearts of the people at large, including the people of the alien races who were culturally conquered by the Aryans and gradually absorbed in the Aryan Society. As the result of friendly controversies and also as the inevitable result of co-existence and cooperation, the followers of each path of self-discipline appreciated more and more deeply the practical values of the other paths and adapted many of their modes of moral and spiritual and social discipline to their own. Each cult was thus more and more liberalised and assimilative in course of its development and expansion.

A psychological, social, moral and spiritual necessity was always felt in the inner consciousness of impartial and earnest truth-seekers for a perfect synthesis and harmony of *Karma, Jñāna, Yoga* and *Bhakti,*—of *Pravritti-Mārga, Nivritti-Mārga, Vicāra-Mārga, Dhyāna-Mārga,* and *Upāsanā-Mārga,*—of domestic and social duties and responsibilities as demanded by our Moral Consciousness, detachment from worldly affairs and concentration of the whole energy upon the realisation of the Ultimate Truth as demanded by our spiritual consciousness, and cultivation of emotional love and reverence for the beautiful and magnificent Divine Source of the cosmic order and the Soul of all souls as demanded by our enlightened emotional and aesthetic consciousness.

Early post-Vedic religious, philosophical, social, moral and poetical literature of the illustrious saints and sages definitely indicates that various admirable attempts were made even in those ancient times for a rational reconciliation of the various modes of interpretations of the *Vedas*, for a real satisfaction of all the fundamental demands of the human consciousness and for a synthesis of the view-points of the different schools of thought. But the most successful attempt in this direction was made by Lord Śri Krishna in the small Divine Song,—*Bhagavad-Gītā*. Śri Krishna was the truest representative of the *Spirit of the Vedic Revelations*. His extraordinarily eventful life, his super-human dynamic personality, his profound spiritual insight, and his most comprehensive and practical philosophy and religion, gave him a unique place in the history of the evolution of the spiritual culture of Bhāratavarsha. Even in his own life-time he was acclaimed and adored as a veritable Incarnation of God in human form. He was the greatest statesman and strategist, the greatest hero and man of action, and all the same the greatest philosopher and sage and *Yogi* of his age.

The *Bhagavad-Gītā*, believed to have been spoken by him to Arjuna on the battle-field of Kurukshetra just before the commencement of the horrible all-out battle, gives within the shortest possible compass the most rational and most practicable synthesis of all forms of moral and social and emotional and spiritual discipline based upon the spiritual outlook on human life and human society and all physical environments, as taught by the *Vedas*. Krishna Dwaipāyana Vyāsa, who gave the widest publicity to the life and teachings of Śri Krishna and put his *Gītā* at the centre of his most celebrated national Epic, *Mahā-Bhārata*, described it as *Brahma-Vidyā*, *Yoga-Śāstra*, *Bhakti-Śāstra* and *Karma-Śāstra* at the same time and as having exposed the true essence of the *Vedas* without dishonouring or doing injustice to any aspect of their teachings or any school of thought. The *Gītā* raised our ordinary domestic and social duties to a high spiritual level, taught us to perform our duties efficiently for duty's sake with the spiritual end of life in view, gave enlightened conceptions of *Yajña, Yoga, Jñāna, Karma, Tyāga, Sannyāsa, Upāsanā,* and *Moksha* from the true spiritual point of view, brought the Supreme Source and Lord of all existences very near to the hearts of all classes of men and the Supreme Spiritual Ideal of life within the scope of the practical realisation of common people of all strata of the society, and showed the people the most practicable way to the spiritualisation of the entire human life.

Śri Krishna taught the Art of the thorough spiritualisation of the entire life of a man and preached this as the Ideal immanent in all the teachings of the *Vedas*. He protested against all the one-sided and narrow interpretations of the Vedic Revelations. He preached that every man,—

whatever may be his social status or intellectual attainments or domestic and social obligations or environmental and economic conditions,—should become a *Yogi* in his practical life. *Yoga* should be the regulative principle of everybody's life, and not only of the lives of those exceptional few who renounce all worldly connections and devote themselves exclusively to certain forms of physical and psychical and religious discipline and practise deep meditation in solitude. *Yoga* essentially consists in living a God-centric life,—a life governed by a Spiritual Outlook on all the affairs of the world of normal experience, a Spiritual Ideal of all human activities (domestic and social and religious and intellectual), and an attitude of whole-hearted Devotion and Love and Self-offering to the Supreme Spirit (God) Who is eternally revealing Himself in all the phenomenal existences and wonderfully regulating and harmonising all the affairs of His self-manifestations in this cosmic system.

Every man ought to remember that he is a particular self-manifestation of God for serving God's purpose in God's world, that he is endowed with particular capacities and placed in a particular situation for the faithful discharge of particular Divinely allotted duties *for His sake*, that he should devotionally play the part allotted to him, without any attachment to the works or any egoistic desire for their fruits, in a spirit of loving worship to Him, and that the ultimate aim of all his works and all his physical and mental and intellectual endeavours should be the realisation of perfect Spiritual Union with Him. Some men may be fit for the performance of ordinary domestic and social duties ; some may be fit for more brilliant works of public utility ; some may be fit for making valuable contributions to the literary or artistic or scientific or philosophical culture of Humanity ; some may be fit for retirement from outer worldly concerns and exclusive self-application to esoteric *yogic* practices ; and so on. According to different kinds of fitness, different men may have different *Swadharma* and God may have different purposes to be accomplished through the lives of different men. But *Yoga* can and should be the regulative principle in the lives of all men of all orders of fitness and of all strata of the society, and all people disciplining their life according to this universal principle of *Yoga* become worthy of realising the Supreme Spiritual Ideal.

Yogeśwara Śri Krishna, with his enlightened conception of all-comprehensive *Yoga*, put an end to the age-long quarrel between *Pravritti-Mārga* and *Nivriiti-Mārga,* by bringing out the inner significance and the underlying spiritual unity of the two forms of discipline. *Pravritti-Mārga* is based on the undeniable fact that man is by nature an active self-conscious and self-determining being and that without carefully regulated voluntary actions even the continuity of his physical existence is impossible. Hence every man must perform actions as a matter of necessity for his existence. But no man ought to be contented with the performance of duties imperative upon him for the mere sustenance of his physical life, which is sure to terminate sooner or later. He has indefinite potentialities for higher and higher development of his life through the performance of nobler and nobler actions of more and more permanent and intrinsic values. The Vedic *Pravritti-Mārga* prescribes various orders of such noble and valuable actions for men of different orders of physical and mental and intellectual capacities for their progressive self-development and self-elevation to higher and higher *planes* of self-conscious existence. Such actions always contribute to the multiform welfare of the society along with the moral and spiritual development of the individual who performs them. The ultimate aim of all such actions should be *the moral and spiritual perfection of the individuals* who should faithfully perform them. This is the Ideal of *Nivritti-Mārga* as well.

Now, the *Vedic Pravritti-Mārga* exhorts all men to perform such noble and useful and elevating actions with pure bodies and pure hearts and a purely religious attitude in a spirit of *Yajña* or Sacrifice. *Yajña*, as Śri Krishna interprets it, does not consist merely or even mainly in the scrupulous performance of certain ritualistic ceremonies and the correct pronunciation of certain *Mantra* in connection with those ceremonies, though the special values and efficacies of these rituals and *Mantras* for special purposes on special occasions are undeniable. *Yajña* essentially consists in the cultivation of the spirit of *sacrifice* and *selfless service*,—the sacrifice of a man's personal earthly possessions for common good with an attitude of worship to the Supreme Spirit, the Soul and Lord of all beings of the universe. The highest forms of *Yajña* is the absolute sacrifice of the ego and all egoistic desires and ambitions and feelings and all senses of possessions, with the awakened idea that everything belongs to God. The True spirit of *Yajña* makes a man a *Yogi*.

Whatever is God's should be humbly offered to God. *Yajña* accordingly is resolved into pure worship of God with the materials (rich or poor) which God Himself in His mercy supplies to the worshipper, and the worshipper should inwardly try to be free from the sense of ownership and all egoistic feelings with regard to them. All actions should be performed in this spirit of worship and in this spirit of offering to God what is God's. The outer forms of the actions will involve apparent sacrifice, and they will also be of substantial service to the human society. The materials with which *Yajña* or worship is performed may not always be earthly materials or outer possessions; all *Japa, Dhyāna, Tapasyā*,

Brahmacaryya, Vidyā-dāna, Prāṇāyāma, Samāja-Seva, Rāstra-Sevā, Dharma-Yuddha, Prāna-dāna for the good of others, etc. etc., should be practised in a spirit of *Yajña* or offering to God what is God's, in as much as all our internal powers and possessions also really belong to God and are obtained from the Divine Mercy; and these should be used as materials for the worship of God.

Śri Krishna points out that when apparently other Deities are worshipped with offerings of outer or inner materials, all these also go to the Supreme Spirit, though in an indirect way on account of the prevailing sense of difference in the minds of the worshippers. Truly the One Supreme Spirit is the Soul of the plurality of Deities who are only His *glorified Self-manifestations* in diversified names and forms. He receives worship through all these holy Names and Forms. Every intelligent worshipper ought to see the One God in all Gods and concentrate his attention upon this God of all Gods. But there must not be any condemnation of the diverse modes of worship of the Supreme Spirit through all these varieties of Divine Names and Forms.

If the whole consciousness of a man is permeated by the spirit of *Yajña*, i.e. the spirit of self-offering and all-offering worship to God, then the actions, whether performed as prescribed religious rites or as ordinary domestic and social duties, do not become sources of bondage and do not stand in the way of Self-realisation or God-realisation. Rather they may become as efficacious as the practices of *Jñāna* and *Yoga* for emancipation from bondage and realisation of union with God. Thus enlightened *Pravritti-Mārga* may lead to the same spiritual goal as enlightened *Nivritti-Mārga*. Both may be practised as true *Yoga* i.e. as the means to the spiritualisation of the whole being of a man and the union of the individual with the Universal Soul.

Śri Krishna proclaimed in the Divine voice that if a householder or an active member of the society, while enthusiastically discharging his multifarious domestic and social responsibilities and performing various kinds of noble and pious and useful actions in different spheres of life, can adequately train his mind and heart to remain free from pride and vanity, free from selfish desires and ambitions, free from cares and anxieties about the consequences of his actions, and can form the habit of calmly and delightfully playing the parts allotted to him by the Lord of his soul in His cosmic play as His humble servant or as an instrument in His hands, in a spirit of self-offering devotional service to the Lord, then he is to be regarded as a true *Yogi* and a true *Bhakta*, a true *Tyāgi* and *Sannyāsi*, a true *sādhaka* of the *Nivritti-Mārga*. On the other hand, if a cave-dwelling or wandering ascetic, who having abandoned all domestic and social responsibilities lives an austere life of hardship and privation or a life of pure contemplation or metaphysical speculation or devotional intoxication or esoteric *yogic* practices, cannot free himself from the sense of ego, selfish desires and ambitions, from pride and prejudice, hatred and fear, attachments and aversions, cares and anxieties and other weaknesses of his psychical nature, he is not worthy of being regarded as a true *Yogi* or a true *Bhakta* or a true *Jñāni* or a true *Tyāgi* or *Sannyāsi*.

Śri Krishna taught people to judge the true spiritual advancement of a person, not by the outer modes of his life, not by his outer action or inaction, not by his outer *bhoga* or *tyāga*, not by his home-dwelling or forest-dwelling, but by his genuine internal transformation, by the true spiritual illumination of his mind and heart, by the degree of his emancipation from the sense of *Me* and *Mine* and his realisation of the Supreme Spirit in himself and in the world of his experience. Śri Krishna taught the spiritual aspirants to see *Karma* in *Akarma* and *Akarma* in *Karma, Pravritti* in *Nivritti* and *Nivritti* in *Pravritti,* by deep consideration of inner attitude and realisation of the *sādhakas* concerned. When *Akarma* or *Nivritti* is attended with egoistic vanity or selfish desires or hatred of active life, it is as good as actions born of egoism and selfish desires and becomes a source of bondage. *Karma* in a spirit of selfless devotional service to the Supreme Spirit is to be conceived as *akarma*, since it cuts asunder the bondage of the world.

According to Śri Krishna's interpretation of the true Vedic way of life, the faithful discharge of domestic and social obligations, the performance of sacrificial deeds and other religious rites in accordance with the injunction of the *Dharma-Śāstras*, the cultivation of devotional sentiments and the various modes of ceremonial worship, the systematic practice of the various methods of self-discipline and self-control and self-concentration and self-illumination as prescribed in the *Yoga-Śāstras*, deep reflection *(vicāra)* and contemplation *(Dhyāna)* upon the true character of the Absolute Spirit or God in pursuance of the philosophical method *(Jñāna-Mārga)*, the practice of renunciation of or detachment from all worldly concerns and voluntary submission to all kinds of privations and hardships for the sake of Truth-realisation, etc.,—all these are diverse ways, suited to persons of diverse tastes and capacities and temperaments and aptitudes, for the attainment of the same spiritual Ideal of human life. The *Vedas* give approval to all these ways. All of them are particular modes of self-discipline and self-refinement and self-elevation, with a view to the progressive self-emancipation of man from the bondages and limitations and sorrows of the earthly life.

But, Śri Krishna points out emphatically, for the purpose of deriving the best, the highest and the most desirable and valuable benefits from these apparently diverse modes of spiritual self-culture, attention must be freed as practicable from their *outer forms* and directed to their *inner spirit.* The *outer forms* of the various kinds of injunctions of the *Vedas* may appear to be different from and often conflicting with one another, but the inner intention of all of them is the same. Undue emphases upon the differences of *outer forms* among the various modes of spiritual discipline gave rise to unwholesome controversies and different schools of thought and different religious and social sects and subsects. The innermost spirit of all these forms of discipline enjoined by the *Vedas* is what Śri Krishna called the spirit of *Yoga.* It is intended that each of the modes of discipline should be pursued with the spirit of *Yoga* at heart. According to Śri Krishna, if even the most ordinary domestic duties are performed consciously with the genuine spirit of *Yoga* at heart without any selfish feelings and desires and without any attachment or aversion, this can lead to the same spiritual good as the systematic practice of meditation and renunciation.

Śri Krishna exhorted every human being to live the life of a *Yogi,* i. e. to live a thoroughly God-centric life, in whatever situation he might be placed and for whatever form of works or practices he might be fit by his temperament and his physical and mental capacities. He interpreted *Yoga* in such a universal way as to be practicable to every man and woman, to the humblest *Śudra* or labourer as much as to the most learned *Brāhmana* or the most warlike *Kshatriya* or the most commercialist *Vaiśya,* to a person born in the lowest cadre of the society as much as to an illustrious person occupying the highest position in the society, to an ordinary householder as much as to an all-renouncing *Sannyāsi.* He brought down God, the Universal Soul and the Absolute Lord of the universe, very near to the mind and heart of every man and woman of the world. He presented the Ultimate Reality of philosophy in such a popular and attractive form that even a person without any book-learning might feel His vivid presence within himself and in all around him,—in his home and society, in his natural and social surroundings, in all physical and historical events, in all forces of nature, in all mountains and rivers, in Earth and Water and Fire and Air and Ether, and where not? God is everywhere, within and without.

Śri Krishna exhorted all men and women to cultivate this Divine outlook on everything and to feel the Divine presence in all the concerns of life. Every person should be inspired by the constant remembrance that he lives in God, he lives for God, he has to play his role in God's world for God's sake out of love and reverence for God without any care or anxiety for the fruits of his endeavours which belong to and are determined by God. Every person should cherish the most cordial personal love for God and look upon Him as eternal Father and Mother and Brother and Friend and Lord, nay, as the Soul of his soul, as the eternal Beloved of his heart, as the absolute Ruler of his destiny and the unerring Guide in all his actions. Everybody should always hope for absolute and perfect Union with God, in which the final success and fulfilment of his self-conscious and self-disciplined life in the human body lies. In this system of popular and universal *Yoga* preached by Śri Krishna, *Bhakti* or whole-hearted self-offering love for God obviously plays the most predominant part, in as much as it supplies the motor force to all the noblest human endeavours, makes all these endeavours pleasant and joyful and is also a universal factor in the nature of man. This *Bhakti* has of course to be purified and enlightened by the cultivation of true knowledge and moral goodness and fully concentrated on God, Who is the Truth and Ideal of life.

In his philosophical view Śri Krishna assimilated the *Prakriti-Purusha-Vāda, Kshetra-Kshetrajña-Vāda, Kshara-Akshara-Vāda*, of the earlier Sānkhya philosophers, with the *Brahma-Vāda* of the *Upanishads*, and highly enriched the conception of *Brahma* by the wonderful amalgamation with it of the conceptions of *Paramātmā, Iśwara, Maheśwara, Mahā-Yogīśwara, Bhagawān, Nārāyana, Purushottama*, etc., as conceived and interpreted by the schools of *Yogis* and *Bhaktas* and others. He preached an all-comprehensive conception of God (the Supreme Spirit) which could equally satisfy the rational demand of the intellect and the emotional demand of the heart of all classes of truth-seekers and spiritual aspirants.

The Supreme Spirit he preached is personal as well as impersonal, active as well as inactive, transcendent as well as immanent, *nirguna* as well as *saguna*, infinite and eternal and also revealing Himself in a variety of finite and transitory forms, eternally unmoved by feelings and emotions and all the same infinitely loving and merciful. He is the absolute Cause—material, efficient, final as well as formal,—of this phenomenal cosmic order in time and space, but He is eternally above time and space and never in any way affected by the spatio-temporal changes and diversities. He is eternally possessed of infinite wisdom and knowledge, infinite goodness and beauty, infinite strength and power, infinite love and mercy, infinite justice and benevolence, infinite creative will and activity, and the phenomenal universe consists of finite and variegated self-expressions of these Divine qualities.

Everywhere it is God Who manifests Himself. Whatever specially attracts our notice is His *Vibhūti* or special self-manifestation. We have to see God everywhere in His world.

Thus in stead of cursing the world as an ugly and dreadful place of bondage and sorrow, Śri Krishna gives a glorified account of the world, emphasising that it is really a Divine world full of Divine self-expressions and it should be adored as such. Bondages and sorrows arise from our egoistic outlook and our selfish desires to convert this world into an object of our sensuous enjoyment. When we do not see God in His world of phenomenal self-manifestation and try to look upon it as our possession and to exploit it for our enjoyments in the lower planes of our conscious life, it amounts to a revolt against God, and sufferings are the inevitable results. Śri Krishna intends that we should see God face to face in His world, love and adore Him in all the forms of His manifestations, serve Him with all the outer and inner materials He has placed at our disposal, absolutely surrender ourselves to His love and mercy and be free from *me* and *mine*. This would lead to deliverance from all bondage and sorrow and participation in His infinite joy and freedom and beauty and peace.

Śri Krishna conveyed to Humanity another great message of hope and strength, viz. Incarnation of God *(Avatāra-Vāda)*. He announced emphatically and unambiguously that in whatever age unrighteousness appears to become the prevailing order in the human society and righteousness appears to be depressed or suppressed,—whenever there happens to be the predominance of materialism and militarism and dishonesty and hypocrisy and arrogance in the human society and the moral and spiritual idealism inherent in the inner nature of man becomes weakened and loses its controlling force and is domineered over by the *Āsuric* powers,—the Supreme Spirit incarnates Himself in special embodied forms and exercises extraordinary Divine powers in those forms, for subduing the forces of unrighteousness, strengthening the forces of righteousness, reinterpreting the eternal Truth and Law immanent in the Divine Cosmic order in appropriate forms suited to the age and restoring a proper atmosphere for the normal development and invigoration of the moral and spiritual outlook of the people.

It is quite in conformity to the Divine plan of the Cosmic Order that there is practically a continuous tug-of-war among the Divine and Satanic,—pro-spiritual and anti-spiritual,—centripetal and centrifugal,—forces in this constantly moving and changing world, and there are alternate victories and defeats of these apparently antagonistic forces. In reality both kinds of forces are self-manifestations of the inscrutable

Divine Power in His Cosmic Play, and they are by the Divine Will arrayed into rival parties as instruments for the maintenance of the magnificent Play, each in its own way immensely adding to the grandeur and beauty of the Play. It is also in accordance with the Divine Design that on certain occasions peace and harmony and orderly progress of the Play appears to be endangered by the heated excitements of the rival parties and the blurring of the moral and spiritual outlook, and that on such occasions there are special Divine interventions for putting things in order. In the mundane lives of these *Avatāras* men get special opportunities to witness directly not only God's superhuman wisdom and power in a variety of forms, but also various evidences of His love and mercy and beauty and sweetness. Through the study of the conduct of the *Avatāras* men can get a very good training for cultivating various forms of sweet personal relationship with God. The Infinite comes down to us in a finite form, the Birthless takes birth, the Blissful participates in our joys and sorrows, the Transcendent One becomes our kith and kin, for our sake,—for the sake of elevating us to His plane. How merciful and loving He is to us!

II. Vyasa, Valmiki, Epics, Puranas

Śri Krishna Dwaipāyana Vyāsa, who was a senior contemporary of Bhagawān Śri Krishṇa and who also lived long after him to continue his cultural work, played a unique role in the consolidation of the spiritual thoughts of Bhāratvarsha and in popularising them throughout the length and breadth of this great country. He was a *Mahāyogi, Mahā-Jñāni, Mahā-Bhakta, Mahā-Premī,* as well as a great intellectualist, a great philosopher, a great poet, a great preacher and organiser. He made a wonderful compilation and synthesis of all the earlier Intellectual, moral and spiritual achievements of the Aryan society, assimilated all the important cultural developments of the Non-Vedic and even the Non-Aryan people with those of the Vedic society, brought about a reconciliation among the exponents of *Pravritti-Mārga* and *Nivritti-Mārga* in the light of the inspiration obtained from the life and teachings of Śri Krishna, laid down a solid *philosophical* foundation of the all-assimilating views he preached through the exposition of his *Brahma-Sutras*, composed the encyclopaedic work, the *Mahābhārata*, in the form of a great epic in popular Sanskrit for bringing all the loftiest thoughts of all the greatest saints and sages of all the religio-philosophical schools of the country within the scope of the understanding and appreciation of the common people, and initiated the composition and recitation of the various *Purānas* for giving the widest publicity to the noblest moral and spiritual and social ideas and ideals in the most popular forms in every corner of the country.

All his works were of permanent values. He may be said to have given a definite and ever-lasting shape to Hindu spiritual culture. All the subsequent developments were on the basis of his works. He became immortal with his immortal bequests. He is still adored as the immortal *Guru* by all sections of the Hindu community. His authority with regard to the interpretation of the Vedic revelations and his judgments upon the various religious and moral and social and other practical problems of life are generally regarded as unchallengeable. After the wholesale destruction of all the ruling military powers of the country in the great civil war depicted in the *Mahābhārata*, Vyāsa and his followers (for a good many generations) appear to have admirably done the gigantic work of the cultural reconstruction of the country and accomplished the lasting union of the whole country on the basis of spiritual idealism.

Śri Krishna Dwaipāyana's first immortal work was the most comprehensive compilation of all the *Vedic Mantras* with their early commentaries and the authoritative treatises dealing with their practical applications and the arrangement and classification of them in the most scientific method. In this compilation he laid the most solid foundation of the ever-growing ever-expanding Hindu culture and guaranteed the unity of the Hindu community amidst its ever-increasing diversities and complexities for all times to come. In this compilation he inseparably linked together the Upanishadic Brahma-centred spiritual thoughts and the cults of *Sannyāsa* and *Yoga* and *Jñāna* and *Bhakti* with the *Mantras* addressed to the (apparent) plurality of Deities and the various kinds of injunctions and prohibitions for ennobling and spiritually elevating the practical life of all sections of people. He wanted to live no room for any serious antagonism between *Pravritti-Mārga* and *Nivritti-Mārga* or among the different systems of moral and spiritual self-discipline. It was specially on account of his accomplishing this super-human work of most far-reaching importance that he was honoured with the title of *Vyāsa.* Further, he trained several batches of most highly intelligent and scholarly disciples for specialising in different branches of the Vedic literature and for propagating them among the rank and file of the society. The Vedic studies thereafter passed on and on through successions of preceptors and disciples generations after generations and kept up the basic spiritual outlook of Hinduism throughout the chequered history of its expansion and complication and its periods of brilliance and darkness.

Secondly, he did the great work of founding the school of *Vedānta-Darśana*, which has since then occupied the exalted position of the central and most popular philosophical school of the Hindus. This *Darśana* established the spiritual outlook of the *Vedas* on a rational basis. It showed that the *Upanishads* and the *Bhagavad-Gītā* of Śri Krishna clearly unveiled the innermost essence of the Revelations. It supplemented the deepest spiritual experiences of the *Rishis* and *Mahā-Yogis* by sound intellectual arguments to demonstrate that *Brahma* or the Supreme Spirit is the Absolute Reality, the sole self-existent self-shining effortless changeless Ground and Cause and Soul and Lord of the amazingly diversified and harmonised Cosmic System. It accordingly proved that Truth-realisation means the experience of *Brahma* as the Ultimate Truth of all actual and possible existences and of the essential non-difference of the world and all individuals within it from *Brahma.* It showed that the Supreme Ideal of human life lies in this Truth-realisation.

It is obvious that, according to this *Darśana,* from the view-point of the Supreme Ideal of human life *Nivritti-Mārga* is superior to *Pravritti-Mārga, Yoga* and *Tattwa-Vicāra* are superior to *Karma, Tyāga* and *Sannyāsa* is superior to *Bhoga.* This superiority of *Nivritti* to *Pravritti* has been universally recognised theoretically as well as practically by all sections of Hindus, and this idea cherished for so many generations has given a special mould to their minds and hearts as well as their customs and habits. But *Vedānta Darśana* never ignored the fact that only morally and spiritually advanced *individuals* could renounce all worldly concerns and devote themselves exclusively to *Yoga* and *Tattwa-Jñāna* for the realisation of the Ultimate Ideal. For the generality of people *Pravritti-Mārga,* i.e., the path of well-planned and well-regulated actions, was essentially necessary, and it was indispensably necessary also for the *Abhyudaya* (all-round progress) of the human society, which alone could provide the specially gifted spiritual aspirants with adequate favourable conditions for their undisturbed devotion to deeper intellectual and spiritual self-discipline.

Vedānta Darśana accordingly exhorted the people in general to advance in the path of well-planned and well-regulated active life in conformity to their *Swa-Dharma,* but with the supreme spiritual ideal of life in view. In this path the people of all levels of moral and intellectual attainments and of all strata of the society could on the one hand be truly serviceable to the *Abhyudaya* of the society and on the other hand prepare themselves for higher and higher stages of spiritual self-discipline and finally for renunciation and exclusive devotion to *Yoga* and *Jñāna* for the attainment of *Moksha.* Those who would not be able to acquire the fitness for the higher spiritual discipline of *Nivritti-Mārga* in this life must not on that account feel depressed or be misled to think that they would be absolutely deprived of the opportunity for the attainment of *Moksha,* since they would, as the result of their faithful pursuit of *Swa Dharma* in this life, be born with higher capacities and under better conditions in the future births and get better opportunities for the realisation of the supreme spiritual ideal. Thus *Vedānta* gave a well-planned programme of life based on the spiritual outlook on the life and the world to all classes of people. This has moulded the Hindu life since then.

Śri Krishna Dwaipayana's third encyclopaedic work was the composition of *Mahābhārata,* which has since then been regarded not only as the greatest national Epic of Bhāratavarsha, but also as the most authoritative interpretation in a popular style of all the various aspects of Hindu culture. Bhagawān Śri Krishna is the central figure of this great epic and His *Gītā* occupies the central position in its discussion of all problems. There is scarcely any important domestic, social, political, economic, ethical, religious and metaphysical problem, which is not introduced for discussion in this gigantic book, and the final solutions of all these problems are arrived at in the light of the spiritual outlook as taught in the *Vedas* (including the *Upanishads*) and the *Bhagavad-Gītā*. It also contains the resume of the views of all the important philosophical and religious schools, which by that time grew in the country, whether within the Vedic society or outside.

Discussions on *Karma-Mīmāmsā* and *Ātma-Mīmāmsā* and *Brahma-Mīmāmsā*, on *Sānkhya* and *Yoga* and *Nyāya,* on the cults of the *Pāncarātra* and *Bhāgavata* and *Nārāyanīya* schools as well as those of the *Śaiva* and *Pāsupata* schools, on the materialistic views of the *Cārvākas* and the semi-materialistic views of some other sects, on *Varnāśrama-Dharma* and *Sannyāsa-Dharma* and *Bhakti-Dharma*, on *Ahimsā* and *Satya* and *.tapasyā* and *Asteya* and *Dāna* and *Yajña* and *Jiva-Sevā* and service and sacrifice and other ethical principles, etc.,—all these found their places in this great national Epic. All classes of people in all situations of life in all ages could obtain inspiration and practical guidance from the study or the hearing of this immortal literary work. There are innumerable didactic stories in the book, which at once appeal to the conscience of the people and create lasting impressions upon their minds and hearts. Really the *Mahābhārata* has rendered an unparalleled service during all these centuries in moulding the intellects and minds and hearts and the practical lives of all classes of men and women of Bhāratavarsha and inspiring them with a spiritual outlook on all affairs. The stories of the *Mahābhārata* have supplied the poets and dramatists and artists and musicians of all generations with the themes for their productions, which also exercised their influence upon the people and consolidated their spiritual outlook. Even now an intensive study of the *Mahābhārata* can impart an all-round education (excepting of course scientific and technological education of the present age) to earnest scholars and thoroughly acquaint them with what Bhāratavarsha stands for.

fourth important work of Śri Krishna Dwaipayana was the initiation of the composition and dissemination of a number of *Purānas* for the edification of the masses of people in all parts of the great land. The *Purānas* brought the Spirit of the *Vedas*, the *Upanishadeṣ*, the *Gītā* and the *Vedānta-Darśana* very near to the doors of every section of people in various Names and Forms and presented Him as accessible to everybody. In the opinion of a renowned western scholar the *Purānas* are "a popular encyclopaedia of ancient and mediaeval Hinduism, religious, philosophical, historical, personal, social and political". Along with various stories illustrating God's infinite mercy and love for His human children, the *Purānas* describe various anecdotes about the lives of *Mahāyogis, Mahājñānis, Mahābhaktas* and *Mahākarmis,* about the lives of a good many national saints and national heroes, about the sacredness of various places of historical and geographical importance, about the efficacies of various religious rites and ceremonies, about the instructive character of various historical events, about the sources of strength and weakness in the social and political lives of the people, and so on. All the descriptions and discussions have a common aim in view,—viz., to make all people religious-minded and pure-hearted and God-centred in all affairs of their individual and collective lives under all possible circumstances. All the loftiest problems of philosophy and religion are discussed in the most popular forms from the most liberal point of view, so as be intelligible and appealing to all classes of people.

Though a leaning towards *Bhakti* or devotion to the Supreme Spirit is predominant in all the *Purānas,* they seek to harmonise *Pravritti* with *Nivritti, Karma* with *Jñāna* and *Yoga, Bhoga* with *Tyāga*, energetic active life with the calmness and tranquillity of the mind, the faithful discharge of domestic and social obligation with the Supreme Spiritual Ideal of life. Due homage is paid to all the religious sects and subsects seeking to realise the ultimate ideal through different methods of moral and spiritual discipline and cultivating devotion and love for the same Supreme Spirit through such different Divine Names and Forms, as *Vishnu, Nārāyana, Hari, Vāsudeva, Śiva, Rudra, Pasupati, Kālī, Durgā, Krishna, Rāma, Skanda, Ganapati, Suryya, Agni, Vāyu,* etc. etc. Thus all the outwardly diverse religious groups with their different creeds and rituals and formalities are nicely assimilated within the bosom of Hinduism. The unity of Hinduism has never been lost in these differences. The *Purānas* contributed greatly to the maintenance of the unity of Hinduism without disturbing the specific features of the sects.

Besides the *Mahābhārata* and *Purānas,* the *Rāmāyana* of *Mahākavi* Vālmiki played a very important role in the evolution of the ethical and spiritual idealism of the Hindus. The *Rāmāyana* was the first national

Epic of Bhāratvarsha, the *Mahābhārata* being the second in point of time. It was as popular and inspiring, though not so encyclopaedic and philosophical, as the latter. In the composition of this great Epic Maharishi Vālmiki was inspired with the idea of presenting to the human society the life of an ideal man, in whom there should be a combination of Humanity with Divinity, in whom Humanity should be elevated to the level of Divinity and Divinity should be revealed to man as the perfection of all human excellences. He found such a God-Man in Śri Rāma, who, besides being an ideal son, an ideal brother, an ideal friend, an ideal husband, an ideal king, an ideal hero, a man of universal sympathy and compassion, a man of truth and love and purity and sacrifice, an ideal man of action with the spirit of a *Yogi* and a veritable embodiment of goodness and greatness,—carried the banners of the Aryan ethico-spiritual culture upto the southern-most extremity of this vast continent after having vanquished the materialistic self-aggrandising military powers by his wonderful heroism and having won over the hearts of the people at large by his moral and spiritual excellences.

Taking Śri Rāma as the Human-Divine Hero of his Epic, the immortal saint-poet depicted a good many ideal characters, narrated great varieties of situations, dealt with varieties of domestic and social and political and racial and moral and spiritual problems and in and through all these presented the ethico-spiritual culture of the Aryans at its best. Everywhere the Mahākavi demonstrated the all-conquering power of the Spirit, the supremacy of *Dharma* and *Moksha* over *Artha* and *Kāma,* the superiority of love to hatred, of benevolence to selfishness, of sacrifice to possession, of the dictates of duty and virture to the demands of the natural desires and propensities. The *Rāmāyana* exercised a tremendous influence upon the minds and hearts and the practical conducts of all sections of people in the country and also abroad. The *Rāmāyana* inspired a great many poets and thinkers of later times to write charming poems on the life-story of Rāma and the other noble characters of the Epic and on the topics dealt with therein, Rāma has since then occupied in the hearts of the people the position of one of the greatest Incarnations of God and some sections of the people have been and are still devoted to the worship of Rāma as the Supreme Spirit.

The *Rāmāyana,* the *Mahābhārata* and the *Purānas* did not belong to any particular school of religious or philosophical thought, and did not want to destroy any of the thought-currents which flowed on in the Aryan society through different interpretations of the *Vedic* and the *Āgamic* Revelations and the diverse spiritual experiences of saints, or any of the systems of moral and religious philosophy which developed in the society through the intellectual efforts of great sages. They rather wanted to link them together and to reconcile and unify them by discovering the deeper spiritual significance and practical utility of each and illustrating each with inspiring examples. As the result of their wide-spread propaganda-work, *Pravritti-Mārga* and *Nivritti-Mārga* and *Upāsanā-Mārga, Karma* and *Jñāna* and *Yoga* and *Vairāgya* and *Bhakti,*—all these continued to develop in the ever-expanding Hindu society. They preached in the most attractive forms the spiritual ideal of life and universal moral principles of conduct to the farthest corners of the land and aryanised all the non-aryan peoples in course of a few centuries.

Ahimsā (harmlessness) *Satya* (truthfulness), *Asteya* (non-stealing), *Brahmacaryya* (control) of the sexual and sensual propensities), *Aparigraha* (control of the tendencies to hoard money), *Śauca* (self-purification), *Santosha* (contentment), *Tapah* (austerity), *Swādhyāya* (search for true knowledge) and *Iśwara-Pranidhāna* (devotion to God in any Name and Form),—which were the bases of *Yoga* and were known as *Yama* and *Niyama* in the *Yoga-Śāstras,*—were taught to all people by the Epics and the *Purānas* as the universal principles of good and noble conduct (*sārva--bhauma mahāvrata*), Sympathy and compassion for and selfless service to all fellow-beings (men as well as all other living creatures) was taught as a highly noble form of worship of God. Spiritual advancement (*Dharma* and *Moksha*) was preached as superior, even in worldly life, to political authority and economic prosperity and materialistic grandeur. The stratification of the society into *Varnas* and *Āśramas* was made on the basis of spiritual culture, and the *Brāhmanas* and the *Sannyāsis* were given the most honourable positions. Before the time of Buddha and Mahāvīra the Hindu society-building and nation-building on the moral and spiritual basis was (at least theoretically) almost complete. The bond of unity of all the diversities in Hinduism was supplied by their faith in the authority of the *Vedas* and their spiritual outlook on all the affairs of individual and collective life.

III. Buddha and Mahavira

Lord Buddha, the illustrious founder of Buddhism, and Lord Mahāvīra, the illustrious founder of Jainism, who led two powerful ethico-religious movements, more than a thousand years after Śree Krishna and Vyāsa, were both of them *Mahāyogis*, and in all their fundamental teachings they followed the line of the ancient *Yogi* school and the *Nivṛtti-mārga* of the *Vedas*. Like the old enlightened *Siddha-Yogis* these two great teachers regarded a life of renunciation, the systematic practice of internal and external self-control, self-purification, self-refinement and self-concentration, the abandonment of all selfish desires and ambitions for and attachments to the transitory things of this world as well as of the other worlds, as assential for the attainment of perfect liberation from all actual and possible sorrows and bondages. Like those ancient *Yogis* they were little interested in subtle metaphysical speculations with regard to the ultimate Source and constitution of the cosmic order or with regard to the existence of any eternal transcendent Reality bchind this ever-changing and ever-continuous phenomenal universe of our normal experience or with regard to the essential character of the individual soul; like them they were chiefly interested in the practical problem of the discovery of the most suitable and effective means of liberation from all kinds of *sorrows* in this life or in any form of life hereafter. Like those ancient *Yogis* these two illustrious teachers were convinced of the inefficacy of these Vedic *Karma-Kānda* and the various kinds of complicated ritualistic sacrifices and ceremonial forms of worship offered to the Deities, as well as of the subtle metaphysical reasonings practised by different schools of philosophers, for liberating the people permanently from all possible *sorrows.*

Moreover, they were convinced that Vedic ceremonial *Karma-Kānda* as well as metaphysical *Jñāna-Kānda* and even complex forms of *Upāsanā-Kānda* were not practicable for the common people who were the worst sufferers in this world. They accepted the view of the all-renouncing *Yogis* and *Jñānis* that all the objects of this phenomenal world-order are transitory or momentary and that desires for and attachments to such transitory objects of the world are the real causes of all sorrows and also that ignorance of the inevitably transitory character of all things of the world is the root-cause of all desires and attachments and hence of all sorrows. Accordingly the universal remedy for all sorrows is to root out all desires and attachments from the mind. For this purpose the normal nature of the mind has to be sufficiently purified and transformed. The consciousness of the transitoriness of worldly things has to be fully awakened and dynamic. For this the earnest practice of *Yoga* and *Jñāna* is necessary, but *Yoga* must not be confused with excessive self-mortification and asceticism, nor should *Jñāna* be confused with hair-splitting metaphysical argumentation and logical warfare. They expounded *Yoga* and *Jñāna* in a way, which made them practicable to common people.

The rules of ethical conduct and the modes of spiritual discipline practised and preached by Buddha and Mahāvīra were essentially the same as those prescribed by the *Āgamas* and the old *Yogi Sampradāya,* though they formulated them in some cases in different languages. *Ahimsā,* to which both of them attached great importance, was the first item of *Yama* of the *Yogi* school. The latter, however, had not raised any strong voice of protest against the killing of animals in Vedic sacrifices and other religious ceremonies prescribed in the *Dharma Śāstras* of *Pravritti-Mārga*, though they did not approve it. Both Buddha and Mahāvīra raised a standard of rebellion against the killing of living creatures in all cases and consequently against all forms of Vedic sacrifices and religious ceremonies involving *Himsā* in any shape. They refused to recognise the distinction between *Vaidha* and *Avaidha* (approved and disapproved) *Himsā* and openly revolted against the infallible authority of the Vedas. This revolt against the Vedas was the main cause of the separation of Buddhism and Jainism from Hinduism. Hinduism, while allowing unrestricted freedom to all sections of people to hold any philosophical views and to follow any course of religious practices according to their wisdom and choice, could not tolerate the open rebellion by any community within its fold against the authority of the revealed *Vedas*, which constituted the strongest bond of union for a good many centuries among the large variety of Hindu peoples holding diverse kinds of philosophical and religious views and living under diverse political and military powers in diverse economic and physical conditions in different parts of the vast country. Revolt against the *Vedas* meant to the Hindus revolt against the cultural and spiritual unity of Bhāratavarsha.

Both the illustrious *Mahāyogi* teachers, Buddha and Mahāvīra, seem to have had conceived the idea of propagating a non-dogmatic non-ritualistic non-metaphysical non-communal system of ethico-religious discipline for the common people based on purely moral and spiritual principles and appealing to the common-sense of these people. This was quite consistent with the traditions of the ancient *Yogi* school. This seems to have impelled them in their practical teachings to make adverse criticisms against all current ritualistic practices, all prevailing popular beliefs (including belief in the infallibility of the *Vedas* and the unverifiable miraculous effects of the Vedic rites and ceremonies), all widely respected but mutually contradicting metaphysical theories, all social institutions based on the birthright of certain privileged classes, all injustices and cruelties in the name of religion and all kinds of narrowness and exclusiveness and violence and untruth. They of course harboured no ill feeling against any school of thought or any form of religious discipline sincerely pursued for emancipation from this sorrow-ridden world by any class of people, and they considered it irreligious to hurt the feelings of other people. Still they fought with their *Yogic* calmness and tranquillity against the prevailing traditions for the propagation of their independent views.

Each of the two Master-Yogis founded a monastic organisation (not far off from populous localities) for the systematic training of all-renouncing spiritual aspirants in the art of *yogic* self-discipline and self-enlightenment and in living the life of perfect purity and desirelessness, perfect tranquillity and harmlessness, perfect chastity and universal friendliness, perfect peace and bliss and freedom from the touch of all sorrows and cares. They hoped that through these specially trained *sannyāsi-yogis* the true ideal of sorrowless and blissful life should be effectively propagated to all classes of people in all grades of the human society. There must be contact between the *sannyāsis* and the *grihasthas*, since the former would have to depend upon the latter for their food and the barest necessaries of their physical existence and the latter must humbly approach the former for learning the art of getting rid of sorrows and anxieties from which they all suffered. Though *renunciation* had been quite familiar to Hindu spiritual culture, such *organised monasticism* was rather new.

The two great Masters did not naturally claim any absolute originality for their modes of *sādhanā* and their teachings. Each of them referred to the long line of their spiritual forefathers,—the long line of *Mahāyogis* (*Buddhas* and *Tirthankaras*) from whom they obtained the light. They however used different languages, different techniques, different terminology and nomenclature, in expounding their views and spiritual experiences. They often differed from each other in their emphasis upon particular details of the *yogic* discipline they taught and with regard to the outer modes of conduct. Hence these two contemporary religious movements grew separately and in competition with each other, but both of them greatly popularised the *yogic* ideal of life. The sphere of influence of Buddhism vastly expanded, when Emperor Asoka of immortal fame made it his state-religion and sent missionaries to all parts of this vast country and even to many foreign countries for preaching the noble message of Buddha. Asoka's contribution to the propagation of Buddha's Gospel of Non-violence and Universal Love and Friendliness and Compassion for all distressed and neglected men and animals is unparalleled. Gradually selfless service to helpless men and animals became a prominent feature in the religion of the Buddhist *Sangha*, and active compassion for the sorrows of others came to be regarded as the most effective method for emancipation from one's own sorrows.

In spite of the intention of Buddha and Mahāvīra to keep their systems of ethical and spiritual discipline free from metaphysical controversies and ritualistic complications, several philosophical schools developed in Buddhism and Jainism within the framework of their teachings and a number of *tāntric* rituals and modes of worship gradually appeared in them. Buddha's utterances about the impermanence and ever-changeableness of all objects of our experience, his non-committal attitude towards all questions, regarding any permanent transcendent Reality like *Brahma* or *Ātmā* or any Ultimate Material or Efficient Cause of this ever-changing phenomenal world, his discreet silence about the true nature of the illumined experience attainable in the deepest *Samādhi* and about the real significance of *Nirvāna* or *Moksha*, were construed by his intellectualist followers into the philosophical doctrines of the momentariness (*kshanikatwa*) of all existences, the non-existence of any eternal supra-phenomenal Reality like *Branma* or *Ātmā*, the absolute annihilation of the individual soul in *Nirvāna*, the Absolute Void or the Absolute Negation of all existences (*Śunya*) being the ultimate Truth of all existences, and logical corollaries were drawn from these conclusions.

The development of such philosophical views, not only widened the gulf of difference between Buddhism and Hinduism, but also created schisms within the Buddhist church. The Budhhists were divided into *Sarvāstitwa-Vādi*, *Vijñāna-Vādi*, *Śunya-Vādi* and other minor schools, and each school was further subdivided on different grounds. Some schools, while denying God or the Supreme Spirit, put Buddha in His place and offered prayer and worship to Him as the eternal Divine Personality with the devotion of their hearts and also with ritualistic ceremonies. *Dharma* was personified by some as the Supreme Goddess and ceremoniously worshipped. Some put the whole emphasis upon Renunciation and some upon Compassion and Service. Thus Buddhism was divided into too many schools. *Mahā-Yāna*, *Hina-Yāna*, *Vajra-Yāna* and *Sahaja-Yāna* became prominent for some time in different parts of India. But they were all gradually weakened in this country for various reasons, particularly on account of their internal conflicts and conflicts with Hinduism. But it cannot be doubted that the ideal life and the universally appealing teachings of Mahāyogi Gautama Buddha and the highly noble educational and cultural and philanthropic activities of the Buddhist organisations exercised a great liberalising influence upon Hindu philosophical schools, Hindu social institutions, Hindu religious systems and Hindu codes of morality as a whole to a considerable extent.

Philosophical doctrines as well as ceremonial modes of worship developed also within the Jainism of Mahāvīra, and different subsects arose within his monastic organisation. The *Anekānta-Vāda*, *Syād-Vāda* and *Saptabhangi-Nyāya* of *Jaina* philosophers made rich contributions to philosophical studies in the country. Their interpretation of the *Law of Karma* also had its special features. Jainism however had no opportunity like Buddhism to spread beyond the borders of India.

In spite of the original ways of the Buddhist and the Jaina philosophers and religious teachers in formulating and logically supporting their doctrines, the spiritual and ethical ideas which they preached were neither foreign to Hinduism nor new to the enlightened *Yogis* and *Jñānis* and *Bhaktas* of the ancient times or of the time of Buddha and Mahāvīra. *Sunya-Vāda, Catuskoti-vinirmukta-Vāda, Syād-Vāda, Anekānta-Vāda,* etc., were all of them only different philosophical formulations of the deepest spiritual experiences of *Mahā-Yogis, Mahā-Bhaktas* and *Mahā-Jñānis* (including Buddha and Mahāvīra) of all times in their super-conscious *Samādhi* state as well of the revelations of the *Vedas*, viz., that the Absolute Transcendent Reality is beyond the range of thought and speech, beyond the comprehension of our phenomenal mind and intellect, incapable of being described in terms of any of the categories of our phenomenal understanding and of being proved by any logical arguments, incapable even of being characterised either as existent or as non-existent or as both existent and non-existent or as neither-existent-nor-non-existent (in the sense in which we commonly understand these predicates). The ever-changing ever-unstable character of all objects of our phenomenal experience and knowledge and of our subjective phenomenal consciousness itself is also obvious to all enlightened as well as deep-thinking persons. Amidst all changes the continuity of the phenomenal world-order is also quite palpable to all. When attempts are made by the phenomenal intellect to go beyond its range and to phenomenally conceive and describe the Inconceivable and Indescribable Transcendent Absolute Reality, differences of views naturally arise. Truth reveals Itself differently to different viewpoints of different phenomenal intellects. Hence philosophers differ. Spiritually enlightened persons do not mind these differences, because they see the Ultimate Truth behind all philosophical views. The transcendent experiences of these spiritually enlightened saints and sages are the real foundations of Hindu outlook, and it is on this account that the Hindus have the capacity and tendency to assimilate all differences and to tolerate all kinds of views.

For several centuries, while Buddhism and Jainism and some other minor systems were developing as *Non-Vedic* (and hence Non-Hindu) ethico-religious and philosophical *sampradāyas,* the progress of the *Veda*-believing Hindu philosophical schools, devotional sects, socio-domestic ritualistic practices and *yogi-sannyāsi sampradāyas,* was not retarded, but rather accelerated in healthy competition with the opposite camps. The religious and philosophical literature of each system was greatly enriched, in the intellectual attempts of the thinkers and scholars of every system to meet the criticisms of those of the other systems and to justify and strengthen their own views. The stories of the *Epics* and the *Purānas* were widely spread and the ethical and spiritual significance of these stories was clearly and artistically explained in suitable forms so as to be intelligible and inspiring to the common people of all grades of the society; the Buddhist missionaries also similarly preached the stories of the present life and of many other previous lives of Buddha with their moral and spiritual meanings for the edification of the common people. Different groups of people were attracted towards the devotional and ceremonial worship of the Deities glorified in the *Purānas* for the fulfilment of their particular desires and aspirations; but their views were enlightened by the idea that all these Deities were the same Supreme Spirit appearing in apparently different Names and Forms. The worship of the *Avatāras* (special Divine Incarnations), particularly of Krishna and Rāma, became popular. *Mahā-Yogiśwara Śiva* also was worshipped by all classes as a most popular God accessible to all. Buddha was ceremonially worshipped as God Incarnate by many devotees of the (apparently atheistic) Buddhist church. He was accepted as a great *Avatāra* by large sections of Hindus as well and worshipped as such. The faith in the spiritual efficacy of devotional worship deeply permeated the hearts of large sections of Buddhist spiritual aspirants. Vedic *Yajñas* continued to prevail in the Hindu society, and they were celebrated by the people in accordance with the prescribed rules and regulations as far as their resources and circumstances allowed. The belief in the religious and moral values of these practices was never lost in the Hindu society. Many *Yajñas* entered into the ceremonial forms of devotional worship and became their essential parts. The common people all over the country were not much affected by the ideological differences among the higher circles. They followed their customs in practical life and cherished the feelings of admiration and reverence for the saints and sages of all communities and sects and subsects. To them a *Buddhist Bhikshu* or a *Jaina Muni* was as much adorable as a *Hindu Sannyāsi or Yogi.* However the philosophers and the orthodox advocates of the different systems might on the intellectual plane fight against each other, it was in course of time more and more widely appreciated that there were not much differences on fundamental moral and spiritual principles among Hinduism and Buddhism and Jainism, and hence the viewpoint of each was more and more liberalised.

IV. Kumārila, Śankara and Gorakshanatha.

A few centuries later some exceptionally talented super-human saintly personalities appeared as exponents of all the currents of Vedic spiritual culture and marvellously revivified them throughout the length and breadth of this vast country. Kumārila Bhatta appeared as the great exponent of Vedic *Pravritti-Mārga* or *Karma-Mārga.* He infused new life into *Mimāmsa-Darśana* and *Smriti-Śāstra.* He refuted with irresistible force all adverse criticisms against the authority of the *Vedas* and the efficacy of the Vedic sacrificial ceremonies as well as against the *Varna* and *Āśrama* organisation of the society based upon the differences of spiritual aptitude of men and the spiritual importance of the due discharge of domestic and social obligations. He strongly counteracted the belief, which was being created by the preachings of the monastic schools, that the renunciation of domestic and social life of service and sacrifice and the adoption of *sannyāsa* or *Bhikshutwa* or *Munitwa* in the very early stages of life were the only way to *Moksha* or *Nirvāna* or spiritual self-fulfilment. He and his school restored the shaking faith of many people in the dignity and nobility of the life of *Dharma* within the society and its necessity for spiritual advancement towards *Moksha*, the ultimate ideal of human life. The Vedic *Pravritti-Mārga* got a new vigorous life from the preachings of Kumārila and his school.

Ācārya Śankara appeared as the greatest exponent of the Vedic or Vedantic *Nivritti-Mārga* and *Jñāna-Mārga*. He was a born philosopher, endowed with superhuman intelligence. He based his philosophy on the authority of the *Upanisnads*, the *Geetā* and the *Brahma-sutras*, and established with irresistible logical arguments that they all reveal the existence of One Infinite Eternal Changeless Differenceless Actionless Attributeless Self-luminous Transcendent Spirit (or *Brahman*) as the Absolute Reality and that they all teach us to look upon all phenomenal relative contingent realities of our normal experience (i.e. the cosmic system with all its diversified orders of existences, subjective as well as objective) as illusory appearances of *Brahman* through the instrumentality of some inexplicable mysterious Power or Entity, called *Māyā*. This *Māyā* is of the nature of Root-Ignorance (*Mula-Avidyā*), and all diversities of subjects and objects constituting this universe are products of this Ignorance, which is not explicable either as existent or as non-existent. All individual souls also illusorily appear as individual and finite and under bondage on account of this Ignorance. They are really no other than Brahman.

This is the famous *Adwaita-Vāda* of Śankara. It established on the authority of the recognised Scriptures as well as by cogent logical arguments of the Spiritual Oneness of all phenomenal existences. It sought to awaken in man the enlightened consciousness of the essential unity of mankind, irrespective of caste or creed or race or sex, the essential unity of men and all other living creatures on account of the same Supreme Spirit being embodied in all of them, and also the real spiritual character of all conscious beings as well as of all unconscious material objects. It proclaimed that all differences are illusory and the underlying unity is truly real,—that all differences are merely in *names* and *forms*, which are changeable and unsubstantial, while the Substance upon Which these *names* and *forms* are superimposed is the same infinite eternal Absolute Spirit. It disclosed that every *Jeeva* is *in reality Śiva* or *Brahman*, though it in its embodied state *illusorily appears* as an individual being, limited in time and space and capacity, passing through births and deaths and developments and degradations, and suffering from bondages and sorrows. By its metaphysical conclusion Śankara's *Adwaita-Vāda* aimed at thoroughly spiritualising the outlook of man on himself and the whole world of phenomenal experience.

Śankara did not, however, deny the practical values of the philosophical conceptions of the other schools of thought or of the diverse forms of religious discipline or different modes of devotional worship or even of the various kinds of domestic and social duties and ritualistic practices and ceremonies of *Pravritti-Mārga*. Though the Ultimate Truth of all existences is, according to Śankara, One Changeless Differenceless Actionless Uncharacterisable Impersonal Spirit or Brahman, this Brahman as qualified by the inexplicable (*anirvacaniya*) *Māyā* appears as One Personal God or *Iśwara* endowed with infinite power and wisdom, capable of self-manifestation in infinite ways and forms in the spatio-temporal cosmic system and eternally creating and destroying and ruling over this diversified world of Māyā. This Personal God has undoubtedly a glorious *phenomenal* existence like the existence of the cosmic order of which He is the Supreme Lord, though from the highest metaphysical point of view He is to be characterised as neither-real-nor-unreal or as the *Māyika* appearance of Impersonal *Nirguna Brahma*. *Saguna Brahma* may be worshipped in diverse holy Names and Forms and He has love and mercy for His devotees and fulfils the desires and aspirations of the devotees through all Names and Forms. Śankara himself worshipped *Saguna Brahma* in all Names and Forms. *Moksha*, however, consists in transcending *Saguna Brahma* and realising the absolute non-dual reality of *Nirguna Brahma*.

Śunya-tattwa of the Buddhists could be easily equated with the *Nirguna-Brahma-tattwa* of Śankara. *Nirguna-Brahma* is as much beyond the range of intelleetual phenomenal knowledge and uncharacterisable in terms of the categories of phenomenal understanding as *Śunya*. By Existence (*sattā*) Buddha in his common discourses meant phenomenal existence possessing practical efficiency (*artha-kriyā-kāritwa*) and hence he preferred to give a negative term (implying non-existence) to what is beyond this phenomenal cosmic order. On the other hand, Śankara in his philosophical discourses used the term Existence to mean eternal infinite noumenal existence (the non-existence of which at any time is inconceivable) and hence he described the Eternal Infinite Background of all phenomenal spatio-temporal existences as Absolute Existence, and the phenomenal existences as false or illusory or non-existent (*Asat*). Both Buddha and Śankara pointed to the same Ultimate Reality behind and beyond all apparent phenomenal existences which are orginated and destroyed in the temporal order. According to both Buddha and Śankara, *Avidyā* is the beginning of the causal chain giving birth to this phenomenal world, and *Nirvāna* or *Moksha* consists in liberation from this *Avidyā*. This ever-flowing cyclic world-order being ultimately a product of *Avidyā* (Ignorance) may reasonably be conceived as of the nature of an illusory appearance.

Buddha is ordinarily silent about the Substratum (*adhisthāna*) and Support (*āśraya*) of this Cosmic Illusion or speaks of It as *Śunya* (Absolute Void); Śankara speaks of It as *Brahma,*—as of the nature of Absolute Existence (*Sat*), Absolute Consciousness (*Cit*), Absolute Bliss (*Ānanda*). Buddha is silent about whether there is any *permanent being* that suffers from *Avidyā* and consequent desires, sorrows, etc., undergoes the system of discipline necessary for the attainment of liberation from them and finally attains *Nirvāna* or *Moksha;* and he does not definitely disclose whether *Nirvāna* means total self-annihilation or infinite eternal supra-phenomenal absolute existence. Śankara delivers a positive message of hope and aspiration. He says that the individual soul illusorily suffering from *Avidyā* and its consequents and seeking for liberation is not only a *permanent being,* but is essentially no other than *Brahman,* the Transcendent Soul and Substratum and Support of this illusory cosmic order, and in *Nirvāna* or *Moksha* this individual soul realises its essential infinite eternal blissful transcendent character and its absolute identity with *Brahman*. An enlightened *Yogi* feels even in his embodied state that he is eternally free from all bodily bondages and sorrows and limitations, that he is eternally free from all births and deaths and diseases and worldly connections, and also that all the diversities of the world are essentially nothing but his own apparent self-manifestations or appearances.

Thus Śankara's *Adwaita-Vāda* assimilated *Śunya-Vāda* of Buddhism, supplied positive spiritual significance to the Buddhist conceptions of *Śunya* and *Nirvāna,* and added an inspiring message of hope for mankind. It assimilated *Jaina Anekānta-Vāda* as well, in as much as the Ultimate Reality, *Adwaya Brahman* may reasonably be regarded as having many-faced appearances, when viewed from different phenomenal stand-points. It assimilated all the mutually conflicting *Dwaita* schools of philosophy, in so far as it brought to the forefront the Ultimate Spiritual Ground of Unity of all Dualistic Intellectual Conceptions, and sought to put an end to all quarrels among the various sects of worshippers, each of whom claimed that the Deity it worshipped was the highest God or the Supreme Spirit. *Adwaita-Vāda* pointed out that all the Gods worshipped by all sects of devotees are the same Absolute Spirit, *Brahma,* differing only in *Names* and in the phenomenal attributes and activities and glories ascribed to them. While recognising the spiritual value of *Bhakti-sādhanā* (devotional worship), he regarded it as subsidiary to *Jñāna,* since the former is based upon the conception of phenomenal *Saguna-Brahma,* i.e. the Absolute Spirit as conditioned by *Māyā* and hence possessing illusory phenomenal attributes and powers, and therefore necessarily involving difference between Him and the individual soul; *Jñāna,* on the other hand, seeks directly to transcend the dualistic phenomenal plane, to rise above the apparent difference between the soul and *Brahma* and to realise the ultimate noumenal non-difference of *Brahma* and the soul. *Bhakti* finds its fulfilment in *Jñāna,* i.e. the realisation of the identity of the soul with the Absolute Spirit.

Similarly Śankara appreciated the social, moral and spiritual values of *Pravritti-Mārga* and *Karma-sādhanā* and preached them as useful and necessary for all householders and all classes of common people living in the domain of Ignorance (*Avidyā*). Through the due discharge of domestic and social obligations and the performance of sacred sacrificial works they have to purify and ennoble and elevate their minds and hearts, so as to acquire the capacity of cultivating *Yoga* and *Jñāna* for the attainment of *Moksha.* Thus Śankara made a marvellous attempt to link together and harmonise and unify on the basis of his *Vedāntic Adwaita* philosophy all the currents of *Vedic* ethico-spiritual discipline and even the systems which revolted against the authority of the *Vedas.* He founded a powerful monastic organisation with branches in all parts of this vast country for the intensive cultivation of *Vedāntic Jñāna-sādhanā* and for the extensive propagation of his views. He discovered and revived many old sacred places and many shrines and many centres of pilgrimage throughout India. He exercised a great influence upon the reorganisation of Hinduism after the Buddhistic revolt.

Near about the same time Mahāyogi Gorakshanātha (commonly spoken of as Gorakhnath) appeared as a great teacher of *Yoga* and popularised the *Yogic* culture throughout the length and breadth of India and even beyond its borders. As a true *Mahāyogi* he was not much interested in metaphysical controversies. He principally expounded and practically taught the *yoga* system of moral and spiritual self-discipline and demonstrated by the example of his own extraordinary life the miraculous effects of the practice of *yoga.* He placed before all classes of truthseekers

Mahā-Yogīśwara Śiva or Ādinātha as the eternal and supreme *Ideal* of human life as well as the Ultimate Truth of the universe. Śiva, by virtue of His eternal self-luminous (*cinmaya*) self-concentrated (*samādhimaya*) self-enjoying (*ānandamaya*) self-perfect (*swayampurna*) character eternally transcends this phenomenal cosmic system, and also by virtue of the infinite Power (with infinite wisdom) inherent in His nature eternally manifests Himself without any effort or motive in infinite ways as an infinitely diversified and changeful variety of spatio-temporal phenomenal existences constituting one magnificent and beautiful and harmonious Cosmic Order, and also as an infinite number of finite individual spirits or souls playing distinctive parts in various forms under various conditions within this phenomenal Cosmic Order and capable of transcending it and consciously participating in the blissful transcendent character of Śiva. Thus Śiva has eternally a supra-cosmic supra-phenomenal supra-personal transcendent character as well as a freely and delightfully self-revealing self-diversifying playful dynamic character, and similarly every individual soul also has a transcendent as well as a conditioned character. An individual soul has to realise its transcendent character, i.e. its essential *Śiva*-hood, through the systematic practice of *Yoga* and the attainment of the perfectly illumined state of *Samādhi*.

Gorakhnath regarded the controversy among the advocates of Dualism (*Dwaita*) and Non-Dualism (*Adwaita*) and all other *'isms'* (*Vādas*) as useless from the spiritual point of view, in as much as the Absolute Reality, the Ultimate Ground and Source of all phenomenal existences, is beyond all intellectual conceptions, though realisable in supra-intellectual subject-object-less Absolute Experience in the perfectly illumined *samādhi-state* of the individual phenomenal consciousness. Philosophically his doctrine was described as *Dwaita-Adwaita-Vilakshana*. While fully subscribing to the *Adwaita-view* of the Absolute Spirit, he did not look down upon *Dwaita* as illusory or false caused by any such mysterious entity as *Māyā* or *Avidyā* essentially unrelated to the *Adwaita-tattwa*. In the place of *Māyā-Vāda* of Śankara, Gorakhnath and his *Sampradāya* preached *Śakti-Vāda*, *Śakti* being the real *Absolute Power* of the *Absolute Spirit* for His diversified self-manifestation.

V. Medieval Hinduism

The advocacy of Kumārila and the *Mīmāmsā* school founded by him for the *Pravritti-Mārga* of the *Vedas* made a substantial contribution to the re-establishment of the Hindu Society in all the parts of Bhāratavarsha on the basis of the principle of *Catur-Varna* (stratification of the society into four *Varnas*, viz. *Brāhmana*, *Kṣatriya*, *Vaiśya* and *Śudra*, and regulation of their religious and social duties in accordance with the

Swa-Dharma of each) and *Catur-Āśrama* (division of each individual life into four stages, viz. *Brahmacaryya, Gārhasthya, Vānaprastha* and *Sannyāsa,* with special kinds of duties and forms of self-discipline allotted to each). The most dignified position in the society was given to the *Brāhmana-Varna* on the principle that those who were devoted to the advancement of Learning and the enrichment of higher culture in the society should be voluntarily recognised as superior and worthy of homage by those who had political and executive power and authority in their hands as well as those who had economic resources and prestiges in the society, not to speak of the various grades of skilled and unskilled labourers. There must of course be mutual dependence upon and hearty cooperation between each other among the four *Varnas,* without which the society would be disintegrated and there would be constant rivalry and warfare among the different classes. It may be noted that the division of each *Varna* of the society into hundreds of *castes* artificially created by the varieties of professions and means of livelihood as well as geographical distances had no spiritual significance, and that such *casteism* was no essential factor in Hinduism. It may further be noted that Hinduism with its fundamental spiritual outlook, though admitting *adhikāra-bheda* in respect of duties and rights, does not and can not look down upon any section of people as *untouchable* or unworthy of offering worship to God, Who is the Indwelling Spirit of every man and every living being. However, the social structure of Hinduism throughout this vast country, which is principally based on *Pravritti-Mārga* together with the spiritual outlook of the *Vedas,* has in its fundamental features continued to uphold itself in spite of repeated attacks upon it for several thousand years.

Along with the invigoration of the long-standing frame-work of the Hindu society based on the cultural leadership of the *Brāhmanas* and the spiritual leadership of the *Sannyāsis* and *Yogis* all over Bhāratavarsha, faith in the authority of the Vedas was also strengthened and the Vedic ritualism was also revivified particularly among the upper sections of the society. But for the masses of Hindus (including those who were *Brāhmanas* by birth, but without any proficiency in Vedic culture) the Vedic *Yajña* generally took the forms of *Sevā* and *Pujā* and pilgrimage to the sacred places. For the people in general the ritualistic Vedic Sacrifices *(Śrauta-Yajña)* were in most cases found inconvenient, if not impracticable; works of social and public utility involving personal sacrifice and performed in a spirit of worship became more popular forms of *Yajña* and they were known as *Smārta-Yajña.* The spiritual significance of these forms of *Yajña* was highly appreciated by all sections of the society. Elaborate ceremonial worship *(Pujā)* of a variety of Gods and Goddesses (or rather of the One Supreme Spirit in a variety of glorified Names and Forms) became widely popular throughout the country. In such *Pujā* there was a splendid amalgamation of *Karma* and *Bhakti,* of ritualism and devotion, of *Yajña* and *Upāsanā,* of the Vedic principle of *Sacrifice* and the *Pauranic* form of the loving worship of Personal God conceived as very near and dear to the worshipper. Many *Yogic* practices also are involved in the prescribed methods of worship, and the *Mantras* uttered in eulogising the Deities imply in every case the conception of One Supreme Spirit as the Soul of all the apparently different Deities and as the true ultimate Object of worship. *Image-worship* became a part and parcel of Hinduism. This had a great spiritual significance, in as much as it awakened in the hearts of all grades of men and women the feeling that the infinite and eternal Supreme Spirit,—the Supreme Source of all existences,—was vividly present before their eyes in finite forms to receive their humble offerings and to bestow all kinds of blessings upon them. The Divine Images, even though products of imagination, are of immense help in making the people heartily feel the presence of God in their midst. The practice of pilgrimage, which was enjoined upon all Hindus, kept alive the consciousness of the unity of all Hindus in all parts of this vast country (however different their outer manners and customs and garments and dialects might be) and the consciousness that they were worshippers of the same God Who might be met with everywhere and in amazingly various forms.

While the social system and the practical life of the Hindus all over the vast country were principally governed by the *Smritis* or *Śāstras* based upon the *Pravritti-Mārga* of the *Vedas* amalgamated with the spiritual ideology and devotional attitude of the *Upāsanā-Mārga,* the thought-atmosphere became gradually more and more saturated with the thorough-going spiritual outlook of the *Nivritti-Mārga* under the influence of the *Vedānta-Darśana* as most elaborately and philosophically expounded by Ācāryya Śankara and his school and widely preached in every corner of the country by the great monastic organisation founded by him. Śankara's contribution to the reorientation of Hindu religious thought was unparalleled. Since his time the *Vedānta* became the prevailing philosophy of Bhāratavarsha and Hinduism became essentially the *Religion of the Vedānta.* Within his short life-time he is said to have personally met most of the leading philosophers and religious heads of his time (not only of the diverse sects of Hindus, but also of the Buddhist and the Jaina churches) and convinced them with irresistible arguments of the Vedāntic view-point. Kumārila's chief disciple, Mandana Misra, who was then the greatest exponent of *Pravritti-Mārga* and *Mīmāmsā-Darśana,* had after a stiff intellectual fight to admit the superiority of *Nivritti-Mārga* and *Vedānta-Darśana* and to embrace the monastic order. Many Buddhist leaders also with their followers were won over by Śankara.

Śankara travelled in all parts of this vast country, gave new life to many old centres of Hindu Learning and converted them into centres of Vedāntic culture, created many such centres in different provinces under the supervision of competent spiritual guides, revived many old holy places of pilgrimage and turned them into living centres of spiritual inspiration, and made efficient provisions for close contact between world-renouncing *Sannyāsis* and world-bound house-holders so that there might be continual flow of Vedantic spiritual ideas into every stratum of the society. His *Vedanta* did not in any way disturb the social order and the practical life of the worldly people, as they were regulated by the *Śāstras* of *Karma-Kānda* and *Upāsanā-Kānda,* but sought to keep all the people of the society awake to the Ultimate Truth of the universe and the Ultimate Ideal of human life, to save them from excessive attachment to the transitory things of the world and the relative ideals of worldly life, to teach them *Tyāga* and *Vairāgya* even in the midst of their *Karma* and *Bhoga* and to show them the path for remaining free from cares and anxieties and enjoying peace and tranquillity even when bearing the burden of domestic and social responsibilities.

The fundamental contentions of Śankara and his school were that the *Vedas* must be accepted as the supreme authority with regard to the super-sensuous super-mental super-intellectual ultimate Truths and Principles upon which true Religion in its higher aspects is and ought to be based and that the *Upanishads,* the *Bhagavad-Gītā* and the *Brahma-Sutras* unveiled the true spirit and essence of the *Vedas.* These three were regarded as *Śruti-Prasthāna, Smriti-Prasthāna* and *Nyāya-Prasthāna* respectively of the *Vedānta* (i.e. the ultimate truths revealed in the *Vedas*), and it was contended that the whole of the *Vedas* should be studied in the light of these three. Śankara wrote elaborate commentaries on each of them and philosophically established on the basis of them his famous *Adwaita-Vāda* which he preached as the true essence of Hinduism, i. e. the Religion of the *Vedas.* He strongly criticised all other conceptions about the Ultimate Reality and the Ultimate ideal of human life, which were propounded by other religio-philosophical *sampradāyas* on the basis of their intellectual thought or the religious experiences of particular individual saints. He sought to prove that what he established as the Religion of the *Vedas* (i.e. the *Vedānta*) was the only genuine Religion for all Humanity.

Now, the fundamental contentions of Śankara and his school were generally accepted by all the philosophical schools and all religious sects among the Hindus all over India. They admitted the authority of the *Vedas* and also admitted the *Upanishads* and the *Gītā* and the *Brahma-Sutras* as expounding the innermost spirit of the *Vedas.* Thus all sections of Hindus were united under the banner of the *Vedānta*. It was almost universally agreed that a *sampradāya* whose creed was not based upon or demonstrably consistent with the *Upanishads*, the *Gītā* and the *Brahma-Sutras* should not have recognition as a genuine *Hindu sampradāya*. Hence the illustrious *Ācāryyas* of the various *Upāsaka Sampradāyas*, devoted to the worship of the Supreme Spirit in various *Names* and *Forms* and holding the view that *Bhakti* (emotional love and reverence for the Supreme Spirit) was the most effective means to the realisation of the Supreme Ideal of life, applied their intelligence and energy to the interpretation of the *Upanishads* and the *Gītā* and the *Brahma-Sutras* from their own respective view-points in order to demonstrate that their *sampradāyas* also were *Vedāntic Sampradāyas*, that the particular modes of religious discipline they preached were truly based on the *Vedānta* and that they had their legitimate rights to be recognised as truly *Hindu*.

In the centuries that followed the age of Kumārila, Śankara and Gorakhnath, both *Pravritti-Mārga* and *Nivritti-Mārga,—Karma-Mārga* and *Jñāna-Marga* and *Yoga-Mārga,*—were considerably influenced by each other and were developing side by side in the society throughout the country;—the ritualistic ceremonies as well as the domestic and social duties emphasised in *Pravritti-Mārga* were suitably modified and enlightened by the philosophy and the spirit of renunciation of *Nivritti-Mārga*, and the *Sannyāsis* and *Yogis* of *Nivritti-Mārga* established more and more *Maths* and *Mandirs* and *Āśramas* amidst social surroundings for the propagation of their higher spiritual ideals and participated more and more in practical works of social welfare as parts of their spiritual self-discipline. This close contact between *Yogis* and *Sannyāsis* and *Grihasthas* sustained and developed the spiritual outlook of *Veda* and *Vedānta* among all sections of the Indian Humanity in the midst of their normal works and enjoyments and sufferings.

But in these centuries *Upāsanā-Mārga* and the *Bhakti-cult* got a great impetus by the birth of a pretty large number of extraordinary *Bhakta-saints* with high spiritual attainments in different provinces of the country. We may name a few of them, such as, Ramanuja, Nimbarka, Madhwa, *Vallabha,* Caitanya, Jñānadeva, Nanak, Kabir, Ramananda, Tulsidas, Mirabai, etc. They and their disciples and followers exercised a a great spiritual influence upon the minds and hearts of all classes of people and practically moulded the character of mediaeval Hinduism. Mainly due to their influence *Bhakti* became the predominant note of popular Hinduism in this age. They preached the Religion of Divine Love and Devotion and also emphasised the importance of love and sympathy and compassion for and active service to God's creatures (particularly poor and distressed human beings) as a practical expression of Divine Love. All men and all creatures ought to be adored as living Temples of the Supreme Spirit, because He resides in the hearts of all as the Soul of their souls. Life should everywhere be respected and loved and served and nowhere should it be trampled down upon or injured in any way. This is part and parcel of *Bhakti* to God. These saints also popularised the worship of God in the forms of His special Incarnations, such as Krishna, Rama, etc. and also in the forms of Holy Images. It was due to their teachings that *Purānas* acquired great prominence in Hinduism in this age, and *Bhāgavata* acquired a foremost position. The inspiring anecdotes of the lives of Krishna and Rama and other Divine Incarnations as well as of the lives of remarkable Mahā-Bhaktas, Mahā-Yogis, Mahā-Jñānis, Mahā-Karmis, all orders of saints and sages, reached every corner of India, and became perpetual fountains of spiritual inspiration to all classes of people.

Among these influential teachers of the *Bhakti* schools, Ramanuja, Nimbarka, Madhwa, *Vallabha* and Baladeva Vidyabhushan (Chaitanya's follower) wrote independent commentaries on the *Vedanta* and thus founded distinct *Vedāntic Bhakti-sampradāyas.* In distinction from Śankara's *Adwaita Vāda,* their interpretations of the *Vedānta* came to be known respectively as *Viśista-adwaita-vāda, Dwaita-adwaita-vāda, Dwaita-vāda, Suddha-adwaita vāda* and *Acintya-bheda-abheda-vāda.* Each of them attempted to establish that its own interpretation truly represented the spirit of the *Vedānta* and therefore of the *Vedas.* Their fundamental difference from Śankara's view lay in this that they did not regard the Creation and the Creative Power of Brahma as *illusory* nor did they regard the individual souls as absolutely identical with Brahma. Instead of the *Māyā-vāda* of Śankara, they preferred to accept the *Śakti-vāda* of Gorakhnath, though neither Gorakhnath nor any of his direct *yogi-*followers wrote any commentary on the *Vedānta.* They all accepted the Vedāntic Brahma as the sole ultimate absolute self-existent Reality and as the sole Ground and Cause of this phenomenal Cosmic Order, and they looked upon the *Śakti* (Power) of Brahma manifested in this Cosmic Order as a real Power eternally inherent in His nature. They however interpreted the relation of this *Śakti* to Brahma *logically* in various ways, which created differences among them. The plurality of individual souls or finite spirits were also conceived by them as having eternal spiritual individuality, though eternally existing in and by and for the Absolute Spirit, Brahma, and holding inalienable spiritual relationship with Him.

For the purpose of religious discipline and devotional worship, different *Ācāryyas* and their *sampradāyas* generally designated Brahma by different Divine Names, such as, *Hari, Vishnu, Nārāyana, Vāsudeva, Krishna, Rāma,* etc. They all revived the old *Vaishnava* or *Bhāgavata* cult. The old *Śaiva* cult also was revived by a large number of saints and philosophers flourishing in various parts of the country and exerting their influence far and wide. The *Śaiva-Siddhānta,* the *Vīra-Śaiva,* and the *Kashmiri-Śaiva Sampradāyas* deserve special mention. *Śaiva* philosopher, Śri-Kantha, wrote a valuable commentary on the *Vedānta* from the Śaiva point of view. Abhinava Gupta wrote a huge number of learned treatises to expound the *Śaiva* philosophy and religion. There was a great revival of the *Tāntric* system of religious discipline and the worship of *Śakti* in the names of Kālī, Durgā, etc. In many places Buddhism also was greatly *tāntricised.* Thus the *Upāsanā-Mārga* or the *Bhakti-Mārga* was widely popularised in various forms in this age in all parts of the country. As the result of all these revivalist movements Buddhism and Jainism were almost wholly assimilated with Hinduism.

The *Śiva-Śākti-Vāda* or *Brahma-Śakti-Vāda,* as preached by Gorakhnath and his *Yogi-Sampradāya* and the *Tāntric Sampradāya,* appears to have had far-reaching influence, not only upon the philosophical thought-current of the age, but also upon the popular mode of devotional worship of most of the *Bhakti*-schools since that time. The Supreme Spirit was conceived and represented in the form of a Divine Couple (*Yugala*) eternally and inalienably associated by a bond of *conjugal union* as it were. The Supreme Spirit and His Infinite Power (essentially immanent in His nature) were imagined and adored as eternally wedded to and in loving embrace with each other. Brahma is eternally non-dual and also eternally reveals Himself in the duality of forms. He is one in two and two in one. The Dynamic Aspect of the Absolute Spirit is represented by His *Śakti* through Whom He manifests Himself in this phenomenal Cosmic Order. His *Śakti* is the Divine Mother of the universe, and He is the Divine Father. The Absolute Spirit reveals Himself in this dual form.

Almost every *Upāsaka Sampradāya* adopted this conception in its mode of worship. The *Vaishnava Upāsaka Sampradāyas* worshipped the Absolute Spirit in the names and forms of *Nārāyana* in union with *Lakshmi, Krishna* in union with *Rādhā, Rāma* in union with *Sitā,* and so on. In the *Saiva Sampradāyas,* the *Mahā-Śakti* was represented as *Sati, Umā, Gaurī, Kālī, Tārā, Tripura-Sundarī, Bhairavī, Chinna-mastā, Shoḍaśī, Bhuvaneśwarī, Dhumāvatī, Bagalā, Chandi,* Mātangī, Kamalā, Kāmākhyā, etc. The Mahā-Śakti, the eternal Divine Consort of Śiva, is worshipped in various Names and Forms as the Mother-God in all parts of the country. Śiva, however, is usually worshipped, not in any *image-form,* but *Linga-form,* which perhaps stands for a flame of light representing the transcendent spiritual character of Śiva.

Image-worship in a wonderful variety of forms became in this period the most popular and universal mode of religious discipline among all sections of Hindus and it was considered to be an essential feature of Hinduism. It was really one of the most glorious factors of Hindu spiritual outlook that the mind was trained to feel the shining presence of the Infinite Eternal Absolute Spirit in the finite transitory relative and conditioned material objects of normal sensuous experience (natural as well as artificial). *Image worship* played an important part in this spiritual training of the Hindu mind. It was therefore encouraged by the greatest Hindu philosophers, and the saints of the highest spiritual attainments. The Hindu mind was also trained in the conception of the Divinity of Man through the worship of the Human Incarnations of God and of the Holy Personalities,—of extraordinary *Mahā-Yogis*, *Mahā-Jñānis*, *Mahā-Bhaktas* and *Mahā-Karmis*. The Divinity of Nature also was brought home to the Hindu mind through the worship of sacred rivers, sacred mountains, sacred forests and other places of sacred associations and through insistence on pilgrimage to sacred places scattered over all parts of the vast country. Bhāratavarsha as a whole was specially *Divinised* in the conception of the Hindus and was worshipped as a glorious self-manifestation of the Divine *Mahā-Śakti*. Many so-called rationalist thinkers, lacking in spiritual insight and blinded by various secular and materialistic superstitions, looked down upon many of these religious conceptions and modes of spiritual training as blind superstitions of the Hindus.

It was during this period that *Islam* entered into Bhārata as an inveterate enemy of *Image-worship*, of the worship of God in the forms of a plurality of Gods and Goddesses, of the worship of the Infinite and Eternal in finite and destructible human or superhuman or subhuman forms, of the One in the variety of Names and Forms. *Islam* in its deeper spiritual aspects is essentially a religion of unflinching faith in and absolute devotion and self-surrender to One Omnipotent and Omniscient and Merciful God (the Supreme Spirit) and a religion of Unity, Peace, Harmony, Cooperation, Universal Brotherhood, Social Equality of men as men, Active Sympathy for and Compassion upon all the distressed and depressed sections of God's creatures. But unfortunately the message of *Islam* was carried to India as well as to other countries, *not* by Moslem saints and sages, *but* by invading and conquering warriors, plundering hordes and builders of kingdoms and empires, who exploited religion for purposes of their military and political and economic adventures. Hence

Islam fell upon Hinduism as a fanatical iconoclastic religion and a religion of forcible conversion. It converted large sections of Hindus, but had little to contribute to the spiritual culture of the Hindus.

VI. Modern Hinduism

Hinduism, as it took shape and form in the middle age, continues without much substantial change in the present age, though it had occasionally to adjust itself with newer and newer situations. During several centuries of the political sovereignty of Afghans and Moghals, Hinduism was to some extent rather terror-stricken on account of the aggressive iconoclastic and proselytizing attitude of the fanatical Moslems under the patronage of the short-sighted rulers. But Hinduism never lost its vitality and vigour. Innumerable Images were broken, Temples were demolished, Maths and Monasteries were destroyed, the sanctity of religious institutions was violated and thousands and thousands of Hindus were forcibly converted. But the spiritual faith as well as the social structure of Hinduism were immortal. Hinduism survived all these crises. By the Divine Grace it was during these critical periods that *Mahā-Yogis, Mahā-Jñānis, Mahā-Bhaktas* and *Mahā-Karmis* flourished in different parts of the country in large numbers and they revived the spiritual glories of *Sanātana Dharma* even under unfavourable outer circumstances. The social leaders had to make the rules of social discipline more stringent for the sake of moral defence of the society and the religious leaders had to interpret the religious concepts and the methods of spiritual discipline in more liberal ways.

The illustrious religious teachers of the age formulated the spiritual doctrines of Hinduism in such a way as to assimilate the essential spiritual truths of Islam with them and to be appealing to the inner hearts of those Moslems who were sincere and earnest seekers of Truth. Among the upholders of Islam also there appeared on the scene a good many saints with deeper spiritual experiences and liberality of outlook, who represented in their life and teachings the inner spirit of Islam. They, having come in close contact with the Hindu saints and philosophers, discovered that Islam in its deeper spiritual aspects had more in common with the teachings of the *Vedānta* and the *Yoga* and the *Bhakti* of the Hindus than with the professions and practices of the political and the fanatical Moslems. Thus closer and closer contact between Hindu saints and Moslem saints brought Hinduism and Islam very near to each other and contributed substantially to the establishment of brotherly relationship among Hindus and Moslems. In many places there were Hindu saints with Moslem disciples and Moslem saints with Hindu disciples, without interfering with each other's social duties and responsibilities.

Sufism was one of the products of the spiritual union of Hinduism and Islam, and in it Hindus and Moslems jointly try for spiritual elevation.

In the modern times Hinduism with its spiritual outlook on human life and all its worldly concerns had to face a tremendous challenge, when the adventurous peoples of Western Europe with their materialistic outlook and scientific and technological achievements made commercial and political and military inroads into India and finally the British people acquired the absolute sovereign power over the whole country. These enterprising Western nations professed Christianity as their religion and paid lip homage to Christ and the Bible. Each of these nations had their church-organisations, through which they preached the outward features of the Christian faith wherever they would go with their commercial and political motives. But in their outlook on the human life and the worldly concerns, they were far from being truly Christian,—far from being guided by the exemplary life and the spiritual teachings of Christ.

Christianity, it may be noted, had made its way into India long before it went to Western Europe and established itself as the sole religious faith there, and also before the rise of the Islamic faith. But as in those early stages Christianity was preached by saintly persons and men who sincerely and earnestly believed in the religious path shown by the life and the teachings of Christ, it accommodated itself quite easily and naturally with Hinduism, the essential moral and spiritual principles of Christianity and Hinduism being almost the same. Jesus Christ was a true *Yogi* with emphasis on *Bhakti*, and there is a strong tradition that for a certain period of his life he had been in India and learnt the spiritual principles and practices of *Yoga* from the Himalayan *Yogis* and also from other Hindu and Buddhist saints. Those spiritual aspirants who wanted to pursue the path of *Yoga* and *Bhakti* as expounded by Christ found a more congenial social climate in India amidst Hindu environments than even in the country of Christ's birth, where for several generations Christianity could not even be openly professed.

But in the modern times the situation was quite different. This time it was not the ethico-spiritual religion of Christ that came to be gently and lovingly preached by genuine followers of Christ ; it was the Christianity of the Western type as developed by the Churches organised under the patronage of political authorities of particular countries, that came to be aggressively pushed into this land of Hinduism as a secondary force for popularising the Western domination in the country. This Christianity was identified with what was called Western civilization, which was associated with the glamorous scientific and technological advancements as well as the military and political organisations of the modern western nations.

Enamoured by the onward march in secular life of the modern Western nations, many over-enthusiastic intellectualist Hindus felt deeply inclined to have their countrymen initiated, not only into the scientific and politico-economic culture of the West, but also into the religion and the social customs of the western people. The Christian missionaries also did their utmost to carry on a systematic crusade against Hinduism in all its various aspects. The more sober and far-sighted and religious-minded Hindu thought-leaders, however, while keenly desirous of introducing the scientific and secular culture of the West into the country for its material progress, wanted to keep the ancient Hindu Religion and Spiritual Outlook free from the influence of the Western Christianity. They wanted to modernise Hinduism on the basis of the lofty spiritual Ideals and philosophical concepts preached in the ancient Hindu Scriptures. The orthodox Hindu religious teachers as well as the masses of Hindus tried their best to keep in tact all their holy traditions and ideologies and practices on the strength of their profound faith in the *Śastras* and the infallible spiritual wisdom of seers and saints. The British Ruling Powers, unlike most of the Moslem Rulers, tried to maintain, at least outwardly, an attitude of non-interference and impartiality in matters of religion and social customs of the people.

In the meantime a pretty good number of western scholars and truth-seekers took to a serious critical study of the Sanskrit language and the ancient Hindu Scriptures, such as the *Vedas*, the *Upanishads*, the *Gītā* and the *Mahābhārata*, the *Purānas*, the *Tantras*, etc., and also the Hindu philosophical systems. They were enamoured with the vast treasure-house of knowledge contained in this ancient language, hitherto unknown to the western world. It was a great discovery to them. Many of these ancient Hindu Scriptures were translated into European languages. The western truth-seekers saw new light in these old Scriptures. The appreciation of Hinduism by the scientific and rational modern minds reawakened the consciousness of the glories of Hindu culture in the minds of the western-educated Hindus, who had lost faith in themselves and wanted to be thoroughly westernised. The Theosophical Society, founded by Madame Blavatsky and Col. Olcott and developed by Dr. Annie Besant made substantial contributions to the deeper scientific study of several aspects of Hinduism and Buddhism. The *Brāhma Samāj*, founded by Raja Ram Mohan Ray, and the *Ārya Samāj*, founded by Swami Dayānanda Saraswati, made attempts to give some new shape and form to Hinduism to suit the requirements of the present age, on the basis of the

Upanishads and the *Vedas*. But Hinduism as a whole was little affected by these socio-religious organisations, though much socially liberalised on their accounts.

While the West was thus engaged in the political and economic as well as cultural and spiritual conquest of the East and Bhāratavarsha was making various attempts to save her national religion and culture and long-standing sacred traditions and social customs from being swept away by the flood of western materialistic ideas, a pretty good number of *Mahā-Yogis, Mahā-Jñānis, Mahā-Bhaktas, Mahā-Premis* and *Mahā-Karmis* with exceptionally brilliant spiritual attainments and social influence flourished by Divine Grace in various parts of this country and re-established the intrinsic supremacy of spirit over matter, of *Dharma* and *Moksha* over earthly power and prosperity, of Sacrifice and Renunciation over enjoyment of worldly splendours and economic exploitation of others, of spiritual self-realisation over scientific and technical knowledge. Their lives and teachings together with their unostentatious occult powers exercised an irresistible influence upon the minds and hearts of the intellectualists as well as the common people and drew back their respectful attention to the inherent glories of Hinduism. They demonstrated that the old ideals of *Yoga* and *Jñāna* and *Bhakti* and *Prema*, the old religious rites and ceremonies and the old social customs and habits, and the old concepts of performing domestic and social duties in a spirit of worship of God, have as much value and efficacy under the present conditions of life as in the past. The saints, however, did not dissuade the worldly people of the present age, but rather encouraged them, to learn the sciences and arts and technologies which, by the Divine Design, were rapidly developing in this age in the western countries and whose values from the standpoint of *Abhyudaya* (individual and collective) were undeniable. But, these great saints warned, it would be most unfortunate, not only for the Hindus, but also for the entire human race, if in course of acquiring knowledge in these new sciences and arts and technologies the Hindus lose their ancient spiritual heritage and accept the materialistic view-point of the present western nations. They foresaw that if the Humanity was to ascend to a higher stage of civilization the modern western people must have to be initiated into the spiritual idealism of the Hindus and apply it to their practical life; scientific and technological knowledge must be enlightened and regulated by the supreme spiritual ideal of human life and the supreme realisation (or at least a dynamic faith) of the spiritual unity of mankind and all existences; power and wealth must be placed in the voluntary and loving service of the living self-manifestations of the Supreme Spirit.

Due to the spiritual influence of the modern saints and sages and the exigencies of the present age, a tendency towards a comprehensive synthesis of *Karma, Jñāna, Yoga* and *Bhakti,* as expounded in the *Bhagavad-Gītā* of Śri Krishna, appears to be the most remarkable feature of modern Hinduism. This synthesis involves the cultivation of the spiritual outlook on Humanity and the world and of the spirit of renunciation and sacrifice and worshipful service and mental tranquillity in the normal practical life. It exhorts the house-holders to perform their domestic and social duties faithfully and conscientiously without any selfish desires and ambitions and in a spirit of loving worship to the Universal Soul and to cultivate the spirit of *Yoga* and *Sannyāsa* in their inner life ; it seeks to create in the minds of the all-renouncing *Sannyāsis* and *Yogis* also a tendency to live as practically useful members of the society and to engage themselves in humanitarian works and to set before common men noble examples of living in a higher spiritual domain even in the midst of the complexities and troubles of the modern social life. Though ritualistic traditions continue to have their sway upon the popular minds, *Pravritti-Mārga* is gradually taking the form of private and public charities and works of social utility according to the needs of the present age, with the inspiring idea that these would contribute to the spiritual welfare of those who perform them with the right attitude of the mind. The *Varna-Dharma* has greatly lost its healthy spiritual influence upon the character and conduct of the members of the different *Varnas* and it has been practically degraded into a secular caste-system. Moreover, the rise of a pretty good number of saints and sages with exemplary moral lives and inspiring spiritual excellences from among the people of the lower castes seem to have laid an axe at the sacredness of the *Varna-based* structure of the Hindu Society. The society is being steadily liberalised to meet the needs of the age.

Another most remarkable feature of modern Hinduism is its emphasis upon the Harmony of all Religious Faiths and the spiritual efficacy of all modes of religious discipline preached by all the religious systems of the world. Modern Hinduism has discovered the underlying unity of all the religious orders founded by great saints and messengers of God at different times in different parts of the world and is preaching the message that all religious paths lead ultimately to the same spiritual goal,—the realisation of union with the same Supreme Spirit. This is a message, not only of universal tolerance, but of universal acceptance and respect and love. Pursue your own *Swa-Dharma* in the right spirit to the end, and you will realise the Supreme Ideal of human life, which is the same for all. This truth was most brilliantly demonstrated in the life of Sri Ramakrishna and most forcefully preached to the East as well as to the West by Swami Vivekananda.

The spirit of modern Hinduism has found the finest expression in the comprehensive *Sādhanā* and in the simple, but inspiring, teachings of Sri Ramakrishna Paramahamsa. He practised *Sādhanā* in accordance with prescribed forms of *Bhakti* and *Yoga* and *Jñāna*, of *Śāktism* and *Śaivism* and *Vaishnavism* and *Rāmāyatism*, of *Buddhism* and *Jainism* and *Christianity* and *Mahomedanism*, and in various other forms, and attained *Siddhi* or perfect enlightenment in and through each of them. He demonstrated in his life the spiritual unity of all the religious paths. He saw the same Supreme Spirit in all the Gods and Goddesses worshipped in different ceremonial forms by the different religious sects and saw the same infinite and eternal Spirit embodied in all the finite and artificial material *Images* of Gods and Goddesses. He bowed down to all of them and was often immersed in *Samādhi* at the sight of the One Absolute Spirit in the plurality of holy Names and Forms. He taught the truth-seekers that the sectarian modes of religious discipline, if sincerely and earnestly pursued with a real spiritual hankering in the heart, were all good and useful for spiritual self-fulfilment; but sectarian bigotry and narrowness and fanaticism was horribly bad, being born of sheer ignorance and being a stumbling block in the path of spiritual advancement. He realised and taught the unity of all men and made no distinction between eastern and western people or between Hindus and Moslems and Christians or between Brahmanas and Śudras and Pariahs, in as much as the same Brahma was embodied in all of them. He brought down the *Vedānta* and the *Gitā* to the plane of our practical life and taught us how to follow them in our domestic and social affairs.

His chief disciple Swami Vivekananda was the most brilliant interpreter of the spirit of modern Hinduism in the light of the life and teachings of his Master. He carried the message of *Vedānta* and *Gītā* to the West and expounded it in the most forceful language in a form which was intelligible and acceptable to the modern-minded people. He also gave institutional and organisational forms to the message, by establishing the *Ramakrishna Math and Mission* and a good many humanitarian and educational and socio-religious institutions in this country as well as in several countries in the West. He gave a solemn warning that the western civilization was rapidly heading towards a catastrophe, from which the teachings of *Vedānta* (i.e. true Hinduism) could alone save the Humanity. Other illustrious saints and sages, like Sri Aurobindo, Rama Tirtha, Rabindranath, Gandhi, Yogananda and others, have interpreted the spiritual outlook of Hinduism to the modern world in the same line. Hinduism is thus going ahead towards bringing about a real transformation in the outlook of the modern people and elevating their minds to a higher spiritual plane of unity and peace and harmony amidst the diversities of the modern age.

CHAPTER XX.

CONCLUSION

From the foregoing discourses it is evident that ever since the pre-historic age the whole course of development of Hindu culture has been based on the great discovery that all the diverse orders of phenomenal realities of the universe of our ever-expanding experience and knowledge are wonderfully variegated self-manifestations of One self-existent self-conscious self perfect and self-enjoying Absolute Spirit—One Dynamic *Sat-Cid-Ānanda*—and that the Supreme Ideal of human life is to realise this One Spirit in every individual body, in every phenomenal existence, in every animate and inanimate, conscious and unconscious object of experience, as well as in the entire Cosmic Order. Not only the Hindu religious life, but also the Hindu domestic life, social life, political life, economic life, artistic life—all the manifold aspects of Hindu individual and collective life—have been sought to be organised and expanded and elevated and refined in the light of the same spiritual outlook on all existences and with the inner motive of the realisation of the same spiritual unity of all existences as the true final end of life in and through all human institutions.

Hence in every affair of the individual as well as the collective life of the Hindus, spiritual values have been held superior to economic and hedonistic values, spiritual self elevation superior to earthly self-aggrandisement, renunciation of wealth and power and other transitory things of the world superior to ambition for and attachment to them, inward self expansion and realisation of unity with all superior to outward self-expansion through domination over others and enhancement of the sense of difference. But with the progress of worldly civilization and culture the human life inevitably becomes more and more complicated and the differences among men and men and the differences among the various orders of self-manifestations of the Supreme Spirit come more and more to the forefront. Difficulties in the way of the realisation of the spiritual unity in all of them become more and more formidable. Material differences over cloud the spiritual oneness. Hindu *Yogis* and *Jñānis* and *Bhaktas*, saints and seers and philosophers, have in different epochs formulated various ways and means for the realisation of the spiritual Oneness in the midst of of all such differences and for keeping the Supreme Ideal of life brilliantly before the minds of all classes of people in the society.

Thus the greatest message of Hinduism to all humanity in all ages has been the message of One Self-shining, Self-revealing, Supreme Spirit pervading and transcending all orders of diversities in the cosmic system and consciously or unconsciously sought after and adored by all men in various Holy Names and Forms and through various modes of discipline; secondly the message of One beginningless and endless Cosmic Order pervaded aud enlivened and illumined by One Divine Life and governed and unified by One Divine Law; thirdly the message of the identity of every individual soul with the Supreme Spirit—the Soul of the universe—of Whom every soul is an individualised finite self-expression; fourthly the message of the sacredness of all individual living bodies, in all of which the same Supreme Spirit shines as the Soul; fifthly the message of the direct realisation of the Supreme Spirit in the individual consciousness and the actual experience of the spirituality and unity of all orders of existences as the Supreme Ideal of all human endeavours; sixthly the message of devotion to and sacrifice for the *common good* with love for all and in a spirit of worship to the Supreme Spirit dwelling in all as the most effective pathway to the attainment of the true good of every individual; seventhly the message that all religious and social and economic and political and educational and other human institutions and all codes of discipline in human life ought to be based upon this spiritual outlook on all phenomenal existences and the spiritual ideal of human life.

This message of Spirit in Matter, Unity in Diversities, Tranquillity in Action, Renunciation in Loving Service, is the message of the Heart of Bharatavarsha to the Human World, and all the illustrious Truth seers and Religious Teachers of this Holy Land have in all ages given expression to it from various points of view in various forms of language and taught various practical methods and processes in individual as well as collective life for the realisation of the same Truth and Ideal, in accordance with the need of the times and the social conditions. This message has gone forth from the Heart of Bharatavarsha to all the directions of the Earth and shown the path of Unity and Spirituality to all races and classes of people in all the epochs of history.

Yogiguru Gorakhnath, a veritable Incarnation of the eternal Mahāyogīśwara Ādinath Śiva, a general outline of whose philosophy has been sought to be expounded in the preceding chapters, was one of the most illustrious and powerful exponents of this glorious message that Mother Bhārata ever produced. His teachings are as fresh and as appealing and effective in the present age and under the present conditions of life as they were more than a thousand years back, when he is believed to have moved among the people in his holy physical body and personally inspired them. He founded a monastic organisation of all-renouncing *Yogis,* known as

Siddha-Yogi—or *Nātha-Yogi*—or *Avadhuta-Yogi—Sampradāya,* which is one of the most wide-spread and most alive monastic orders of Bhāratavarsha even to-day. There is no province or region in this vast country where living centres of this *Sampradāya* are not to be found. The *Sampradāya* has produced the most perfectly illumined truth-seers *(Mahā-Siddha Yogis)* with exceptional spiritual powers almost in every generation since the time of the great founder.

Gorakhnath and many of his disciples are believed to be immortal (conquerors of death) even in their physical bodies and to be living even now and showering mercies upon sincere and earnest truth-seekers and upon distressed people fervently praying to them for help, though they ordinarily keep themselves hidden from the views of the men of the world. This possibility of immortalising and spiritualising the physical body and making it permanently invulnerable to all the forces of nature through the systematic practice of some esoteric *yogic* processes is one of the special teachings of Gorakhnath and the Siddha-Yogi school. This is known as *Kāya-siddhi.* But they never speak of it as the highest ideal of the life of a Yogi. Gorakhnath and his enlightened followers always attached greater value to the universal principles of *Yoga,* which can be and ought to be scrupulously practised by all seekers of self fulfilment and perfect peace and bliss in this phenomenal life, whatever philosophical views or religious creeds they may adopt, to whatever country or society or religious community they may belong, whether they live as householders or as *sannyāsins* in cities or villages or hills or forests. Gorakhnath and his enlightened followers initiated into the path of *Yoga* earnest spiritual aspirants from all classes of people irrespective of their social strata or religious creeds.

Gorakhnath and his direct followers are popularly known as the most expert teachers of various forms of esoteric *yogic* discipline and as the most powerful preachers of the *Śiva-Śakti* cult; his conception of *Yoga,* it is to be noted, is most universal and perfectly spiritual and his philosophy of *Śiva-Śakti* is absolutely non-dogmatic and thoroughly rational. The *Yoga-Vidyā* and the *Śiva-Śakti* cult represent the whole spiritual message of the heart of Humanity, the heart of Bharatvarsha. It is the same spiritual outlook on the world of our experience and the same spiritual ideal of life, as has been variously known in Bharatvarsha as *Adhyātma-Vidyā, Brahma-Vidyā, Parā-Vidyā, Ātma-Vidyā Nihśreyasa-Vidyā,* etc. It is the *Vidyā,* which alone can lead to self-fulfilment and perfect freedom and peace and bliss in individual life, to unity and liberty and happiness and the reign of love and mutual service in mankind, to perfect adjustment and friendly relations between man and man, between man and nature, between man and all creatures. It is the panacea for all the evils of the world and the way to the attainment of the Highest Good.

Gorakhnath, as a representative of the Soul of *Bhāratiya* culture, placed before mankind the ideal of *Yoga* as the end as well as the means in human life. He gave a most inspiring and universally applicable definition of *Yoga,* viz. *Samarasakaraṇa,* This deeply and widely significant Sanskrit term may be superficially translated as *perfect assimilation.* It means that all the various kinds of objects of our internal and external experience, all the changing diversities of our life and the world, have to be thoroughly transformed in our experience into the unity of the spiritual substance of our essential being by the power of our enlightened spiritual consciousness, so that we may fully realise and enjoy the play of Unity in all diversities, the play of Spirit in matter, the play of the Changeless in all changes, the play of the Transcendent One in all the phenomena of the world. This is *Yoga.* This is not mere thorough adjustment of ourselves with the world of changing diversities or mere attempt to adjust the world with ourselves, but it is perfect assimilation of the world within ourselves and thereby attainment of perfect freedom from slavery to all the forces of the world and from all sorrows resulting from this slavery. By such assimilation the Yogi sees himself in the world and the world within himself, and thus perfect love and friendliness is established between a *yogi* and the world,—between man and nature.

Yogiguru Gorakhnath refers to the Ultimate Truth of all existences and experiences as *Sama-Tattwa* or *Para-Tattwa* or *Parā-Samvit* or *Para-Brahma* or *Parama-Pada* or *Parama-Śunya* or *Para-Śiva,* and he says that the Absolute Truth is the Nameless and Formless and Subject-Objectless Perfect Unity of *Existence* and *Experience,* free from all Contradiction and Relativity, all Qualification and Limitation and Negation. But, he says, the same *Sama-Tattwa* or *Sarva-Tattwātīta-Tattwa,* by virtue of His *Nijā-Śakti* or Infinite Eternal Dynamic Aspect, eternally and freely manifests Himself in all kinds of Names and Forms, all orders of phenomenal existences and experiences, all sorts of dualities and relativities, and harmonises and unifies them all in His perfectly calm and tranquil all-comprehending all-unifying Self-Consciousness.

Gorakhnath does not enter into any controversy with any philosophical school or any religious community; he assimilates all views with his *yogic* insight into the Truth manifested in all forms of intellectual speculations and religious disciplines. He says that some are advocates of *Non-dualism,* some are advocates of *Dualism,* different schools advocate different *isms* (*vādas*) by force of logical arguments and attempt to demolish the views of other schools in a partisan spirit; they fail to realise the *Sama-Tattwa* which is above any conflict among *Adwaita* and *Dwaita* and other intellectual *isms* and which assimilates as well as transcends them all. Every intellectual concept about the Ultimate *Tattwa,* which as a matter of course involves negation or refutation of other rival concepts, is according to Gorakhnath inadequate to fully represent the *Tattwa,* but is a more or less reasonable approach to It. The Ultimate Truth is realisable in the Ultimate Experience to be attained through the culture of *Yoga* culminated in the perfect spiritual illumination of the phenomenal consciousness, in which all *isms* will vanish and absolute assimilation (*Sāmarasya*) will be established. Gorakhnath accordingly exhorts all truth-seekers and spiritual aspirants not to divide themselves into narrow groups on the ground of their philosophical ideas and religious beliefs and thereby to further accentuate their differences (*bheda* and *vaishamya*), but to emphasize the common universal essential spiritual principles involved in all sound philosophical approaches and religious disciplines and to adopt the path of *Samarasakarana* in knowledge and action and feeling in all stages of life with a view to the realisation of absolute *Sāmarasya.*

The Ideal of *Sāmarasya,* as preached by Gorakhnath and the Siddha-Yogi School, i.e. the Ideal of the sweetest and most perfect adjustment and harmony and unification in our entire life and experience, has far-reaching practical importance in all the stages and conditions of our phenomenal existence. We have to realise *Sāmarasya* in our physical life, in our psychical life, in our intellectual life, in our moral and religious life, in our domestic and social life, in our relations to our fellowmen, in our relations to all creatures, in our relations to the whole world. Whatever may be the diversities and divergences in the midst of which we may happen to live, we have to experience and enjoy unity and beauty in them by dint of voluntary regulation and enlightenment of the instruments of our action and knowledge and feeling, we have to realise them all as beautifully interrelated self-expressions of *One Dynamic Saccidānanda,* we have to acquire the power to maintain perfect equanimity and tranquillity within our hearts and to behave with all with the utmost cordiality and love, we have to play our parts in relation to all these differences joyfully with the consciousness that we and they all belong to the Cosmic Body of One Universal Soul.

For the actual realisation of this Ideal of *Sāmarasa,* the body and the senses and the vital forces and the mental.functions have to be brought under control and thoroughly systematised and the intellect has to be refined and enlightened. The consciousness has to be elevated to higher and higher planes. The Yogi school asserts and practically demonstrates that man has got in his inner nature the capacity to exercise perfect control not only over his own physical and vital and sensuous and psychical nature but also over the forces of outer nature. It is also demonstrated that control over one's own nature is the surest and most effective way to the development of power to control the forces of outer nature. Through self-control the will-power of a man is extraordinarily developed and this development has practically no limit. A man with perfect self-control can develop such will power in himself as to conquer all the forces of the world. But his nature becomes so calm and tranquil and so perfectly adjusted and harmonised and all-assimilative, his individual nature becomes so wonderfully attuned to the life of Cosmic Nature, that he usually enjoys the magnificent unity and beauty of all the diversified self-manifestations of *Saccidānanda* in the world and seldom finds any occasion for exercising his personal will for bringing about any revolutionary change in this world-order. It is to be remembered that the human individuality and the cosmic process are evolved from and regulated by the same Supreme Power of the same Supreme Spirit.

The Yoga-system, which is as old as the spiritual culture of Bhāratavarsha and which has been greatly expatiated and widely popularised by Gorakhnath and the monastic organisation founded by him, is not conditioned by any metaphysical theory or any particular religious belief or creed. It is quite compatible with every philosophical and religious system. It is open to all those who earnestly seek for the fulfilment of their life and the attainment of peace and bliss and perfect adjustment and harmony and unity of all internal and external relations. It is the most scientific and comprehensive method of self-discipline for the attainment of perfect mastery over the body and the senses and the vital functions and the mental tendencies as well as the forces of external nature and for the progressive purification and enlightenment and universalisation and harmonisation of the human consciousness till the highest plane of absolute *Sāmarasya* is reached. The system never becomes too old and antiquated for any modern age and in any modern circumstances. One may be a man of action and an advocate of *Karma-mārga*, or a man of emotional temperament and an advocate of *Bhakti-mārga*, or a man of philosophic temperament and an advocate of *Jñāna-mārga*, the *Yoga* system of self-discipline is suitable for all and it strengthens the character and develops and refines the mental and intellectual and spiritual powers of everybody to march forward more easily and quickly in the path he chooses.

The Yoga-system is generally known to have eight principal steps or limbs (*ashta-anga*). The first two are known as *Yama* and *Niyama*, which are universal ethical principles for the proper regulation and refinement of a man's character and conduct and the perfect adjustment of his individual and social life. Gorakhnath and his school formulated ten rules of *Yama* and ten rules of *Niyama* which every man aspiring for higher life must conform to, to whatever religious sect or to whatever society or country or age he may belong. Through the practice of *Yama* and *Niyama* a man can develop in himself immense moral powers and strength of will, can bring all his natural passions and propensities under his control, can establish calmness and equanimity in his body and mind and the most healthy and noble relationship with all fellowmen and fellow creatures, and also refine and liberalise his outlook on all objects of experience and elevate his consciousness to higher planes. When *Yama* and *Niyama* become habitual in the character of a man, not only does he become a man of extraordinary personal magnetism, but the world becomes a land of beauty and harmony to him.

The second two limbs of the Yoga-system are called *Āsana* and *Prāṇāyāma*. In a general way these two consist in steadying the body and subduing its habitual restlessness and in regulating the breathing process and thereby harmonising the vital functions. These are necessary for all cultured people, as well as for all moral and spiritual aspirants, whatever religious cult or social institution they may be attached to. Gorakhnath and his followers have however immensely developed and elaborated these two limbs of Yoga. They have formulated various forms of *Mudrā*, *Bandha*, *Vedha*, etc., through the intensive practice of which all the bodily and vital functions can be brought under the control of rational will and a man can become a perfect master of his physiological organism and acquire various kinds of miraculous powers. These esoteric processes have of course to be practised under competent guidance—under the guidance of some *Guru* who is an adept in them. But nobody is debarred from practising them by reason of his birth or social strata or religious creed or nationality.

The developments made by Gorakhnath and his school in these aspects of the Yoga-system are so valuable for the attainment of complete mastery over the entire psycho-physical organism and the elevation of the phenomenal consciousness to the higher spiritual planes of enlightenment, that they have got special recognition as a distinctive branch of Yoga known as *Hatha-Yoga* and this school has come to be famous as the *Hatha-Yogi* school par excellence. The enlightened members of this school, it may be noted, never attach primary importance to the miraculous or supernatural physical or psychical or intellectual powers attained through such esoteric practices. No doubt these achievements show what ordinarily inconceivable powers are present in a sleeping state in the nature of man and how they can be awakened and what wonders they can accomplish. But they are not meant for display. It is to be realised that all such powers are only partial manifestations of One Supreme Divine Power, Which is the Source and Sustainer and Harmoniser of the universe, but Which at the same time is present in the nature of every individual and the direct enlightened experience of Which within himself is the goal of all voluntary efforts of every individual human being. According to Gorakhnath and his school, *Hatha-Yoga* should on the one hand make man conscious of what infinite potency remains hidden in him and on the other enlighten his whole being so as to make him perfectly fit for the realisation of the Supreme Spirit Sīva with the Supreme Spiritual Power (*Mahā-Śakti*) immanent in Him as his own soul and as the Soul of the universe.

The third two limbs of Yoga are called *Pratyāhāra* and *Dhāranā*. They essentially consist in the practice of checking the restlessness and outward movements of the mind and concentrating it upon some chosen object or ideal, so that the mind may be purified and refined and elevated and strengthened and opened to the self-revelation of the Truth. Through the practice of these two, attention has to be withdrawn from the finite and transitory diversities of sense-experience and to be fixed more and more steadily upon the relatively infinite and permanent unities behind sense-experience, to be withdrawn from the lower planes of experience and to be concentrated in the higher planes, to be withdrawn from the pettier and grosser interests of outer life and to be devoted to wider and subtler interests of inner life, to be withdrawn from the superficial hedonistic and materialistic values of sensuous animal life and to be directed towards the deeper moral and spiritual values for fulfilment of the fundamental demands of man's essential spiritual nature, to be withdrawn from egoistic desires and ambitions and sentiments and to be concentrated upon the Universal Good and perfect self fulfilment, which lies in the realisation of absolute *Sāmarasya*.

Gorakhnath and other enlightened *Mahāyogis* have taught various processes of *Pratyāhāra* and *Dhāranā* for the self-discipline of the novitiates, all with the same end in view. One most important form of *Pratyāhāra* and *Dhāranā*, which Gorakhnath emphasized, is that a spiritual aspirant should see one infinite and eternal self-shining and self revealing *Ātmā* (Self or Spirit) in all objects of experience and all finite changing diversities, should withdraw his attention from their non-essential differentiating outer characteristics and should concentrate his attention upon the one *Ātmā*, which is the Soul of them all and which is revealed in and through them. A *Yogi* should learn to realise the spiritual unity of all existences and to be absorbed in the thought of this unity.

The last two limbs of *Yoga* are *Dhyāna* and *Samādhi*. *Dhyāna* means a continuous stream of calm and tranquil consciousness with only one objective content or concept in it without any distraction or agitation, and *Samādhi* means absolute unity of consciousness, in which the container and the content, the subject and the object, are completely identified, in which even the process of consciousness is stopped and the consciousness reveals itself as One Infinite External Transcendent Existence-Consciousness-Bliss.

Pratyāhāra, Dhāranā, Dhyāna and even *Samādhi* may be efficiently practised in every plane of experience and on the basis of every metaphysical theory and every religious creed, and in every case they are useful forms of self-discipline for the development of man's internal powers, for the acquisition of temporary self mastery and tranquillity and for the elevation of the consciousness to higher spiritual planes. A man may with sincerity and earnestness choose any particular object or concept or ideal for the practice of the concentration of his mind, withdraw his attention from all other objects and concepts and ideals, fix his mind with firm determination upon the chosen object or concept or ideal and progressively increase the duration of concentration and deepen its intensity, so that the entire consciousness occupied with that *one content* may flow on in a still peaceful luminous current and may ultimately be perfectly identified with it with no trace of difference between the consciousness and its content. Such identification is possible, because in every plane the consciousness and its content are of the same spiritual essence. In natural course the mind is again drawn down to the state of fickleness and attracted by the varieties of objects of normal sense-experience and habituated desires and passions. Hence the effort for concentration has to be repeated strenuously again and again.

But a *Yogi* with the highest spiritual aspiration is not to be satisfied with the attainment of *Samādhi* in any but the highest spiritual plane of transcendent experience or with the acquisition of supernatural powers in the lower planes. The Yoga system has to be taken as a whole. The consciousness has to be adequately purified and refined and liberalised through the practice of the subsidiary processes like *Yama* and *Niyama*, a refined idea of the supreme Ideal of human life has to be formed through the thoughtful study of the most sacred Scriptures and the deepest experiences of the highest order of *Mahāyogis, Mahājñānis* and *Mahābhaktas*, and inspiration and guidance have to be obtained from personal contact with saints and sages having no sectarian bias or prejudice. *Yogīswara* Gorakhnath has given the most suggestive, most comprehensive, most illuminative and most universal expression to the Supreme Spiritual Ideal of human life in his doctrine of *Sāmarasya,* which ought to be sought after by all spiritual aspirants of all religious communities and all philosophical schools in all times and places, and the processes of *Pratyāhāra, Dhāraṇā, Dhyāna* and *Samādhi* should be so practised that the phenomenal consciousness may transcend all phenomenal limitations and may be permanently established in the state of *Sāmarasya.*

Thus *Yoga-Sādhana,* as popularised by Gorakhnath and his school, is a form of universal physical and psychical and moral and spiritual self-discipline, capable of being appropriately practised by all people of all times and places and of all religious denominations and leading them all to perfect peace and harmony and tranquillity and bliss in inner as well as in outer life. It seeks to lead humanity from darkness to pure Light, from ignorance to self-shining Truth, from struggle for existence to perfect all-comprehensive Existence, from limited and conditioned egoistic consciousness to infinite and unconditioned Universal Self-Consciousness, from the region of cares and fears and death to the realm of calmness and fearlessness and immortality, from the plane of differences and rivalries and hostilities to the plane of unity and harmony and love. It wants to show to every human being the path of identifying himself with the Humanity and the whole universe,—vividly experiencing the mankind and the whole cosmic system within himself and himself as pervading the mankind and the whole cosmic system. It seeks to lead every truth-seeker to the realisation that the whole universe with all its complexities and diversities and changes and evolutions and involutions is essentially one magnificent and beautiful spiritual Entity, being the phenomenal Cosmic Body of One Supreme Spirit *(ŚIVA)*, with Whom his own individual Soul is identical.

Through the popularisation of the devotional worship of *Śiva* and *Śakti,* Gorakhnath and the enlightened Yogis of his school have brought down the Supreme Ideal of Yoga vividly before the eyes of all classes of people. *Śiva* is *Samarasa-Tattwa* personified. He is eternal *Mahā-Yogīśwara.* He eternally transcends the world and inwardly enjoys the absolute bliss of his transcendent non-dual existence, and all the same He eternally reveals and enjoys the infinite glories of His all-perfect nature in the forms of diverse orders of phenomenal existences by virtue of His immanent Power *(Śakti).* His *Śakti* is represented as His eternally wedded Divine Consort, Who is in constant union with Him and always in His service for giving Him delight in an endless variety of ways, though He is totally indifferent to and disinterested in all Her affiairs. Thus His *Śakti* is the eternally active Mother and He is the eternally indifferent Father of all phenomenal beings, though there is never any separation between Them.

Śiva is thus an eternal *Sannyāsi* and *Mahāyogi* as well as an eternal Householder. This ideal *Sannyasi-Yogi* in an ideal worldly life is presented to all as the Supreme Deity for devotional worship, and the worshipper is instructed to seek inspiration and blessing from Him for the advancement of his life in the *yogic* path,—the path of *Sāmarasya.*

Again, though Śiva is the Supreme God,—the God of all Gods,—eternally transcending and eternally manifested in this Cosmic Order,—He is conceived as the most cosmopolitan and most easily accessible and lovable Deity. Men and women and children, Brāhmanas and Śudras and Chandālas, Devas and Asuras and Rākshasas,—all have equal unrestricted access to Śiva, and He receives direct worship from and showers blessings upon all devotees without consideration of their social or racial or sexual differences or differences of religious or philosophical views. There is no untouchability or unapproachability in the domain of Śiva. He is the indwelling Soul in every individual body and in every body it is His own *Śakti* that is manfested in a particular form. Every body is in constant touch with Him. How can any body be untouchable to Him or He unapproachable to any body? He is most easily pleased with every body that may take refuge in Him. No correctly pronounced sanskrit *Mantra* is necessary for offering worship to Him, nor any mediation of a Brahmana priest, nor any elaborate ritual. A sincere and devoted heart with purity of character is enough to please Him. He is conceived as a never-failing friend in life as well as in death. He is spoken of as *Viśwa-Nāth, Loka-Nātha, Maheśwara, Mahā-Deva,* and also *Bhuta-Nāth, Preta-Nāth, Paśu-Pati*, etc. All such appellations indicate His perfect Divinity. absolute lordliness, supreme transcendence, as well as His love and sympathy and compassion for all orders of creatures in life and death. He can be worshipped in all the planes of human experience and by the highest and the lowest alike. An enlightened *Yogi* deeply meditates on the transcendent character of Śiva and aims at realising Śiva-consciousness or Śivahood in himself. A common man worships Him as the most loving and merciful and easily-pleased Divine Father and prays to Him for relief from distress and fulfilment of his heart's craving. The symbols for Śiva are the simplest and at the same time most significant. A burning lamp. a lump of clay, a piece of stone, etc. may be enough, for He shines as the Soul of everything,—He is the ever-self-shining Light in the universe. He may be worshipped in artistic images also according to the aesthetic tastes of the devotees.

Thus Gorakhnath and the enlightened Yogis of his school, as religious teachers, have placed before mankind a pattern of Universal Religion which can solve all the problems of religious differences in the modern world and which can inspire mankind with the spiritual Ideal of *Sāmarasya* in the midst of all kinds of differences that outwardly prevail in the world. The yogic ideal of life is the panacea for all the evils of the world and this is the message of Bhāratavarsha to mankind in all ages and particularly in the present age.

ओम्

गोरक्ष-वचन-संग्रहः ।

द्वैताद्वैतविलक्षणम् परमतत्वम् ।

अद्वैतं केचिदिच्छन्ति द्वैतमिच्छन्ति चापरे ।
समं तत्वं न विन्दन्ति द्वैताद्वैतविलक्षणम् ॥१॥
यदि सर्वगतो देवः स्थिरः पूर्णो निरन्तरः ।
अहो माया महामोहो द्वैताद्वैत विकल्पना ॥२॥
भावाभावविनिर्मुक्तं नाशोत्पत्तिविवर्जितम् ।
सर्वसंकल्पनातीतं परब्रह्म तदुच्युते ॥३॥
हेतुदृष्टान्तनिर्मुक्तं मनोबुद्ध्याद्यगोचरम् ।
व्योमविज्ञानमानन्दं तत्वं तत्वविदो विदुः ॥४॥

अभिन्न शिवशक्तितत्त्वम्

शिवस्याभ्यन्तरे शक्तिः शक्तेरभ्यन्तरे शिवः ।
अन्तरं नैव जानीयात् चन्द्रचन्द्रिकयोरिव ॥५॥
शिवोऽपि शक्तिरहितः शक्तः कर्तुं न किञ्चन ।
स्वशक्त्या सहितः सोऽपि सर्वस्याभासको भवेत् ॥६॥
अलुप्तशक्तिमान्नित्यं सर्वाकारतया स्फुरन् ।
पुनः स्वेनैव रूपेण एक एवावशिष्यते ॥७॥
अकुलं कुलमाधत्ते कुलं चाकुलमिच्छति ।
जल वुद्वुद्वद् न्यायात् एकाकारः परः शिवः ॥८॥
प्रसरं भासयेत् शक्तिः संकोचं भासयेत् शिवः ।
तयोर्योगस्य कर्ता यः स भवेत् सिद्धयोगिराट् ॥९॥
तथा तथा दृश्यमानानां शक्ति सहस्राणां एकसंघट्टः ।
निजहृद्योद्यमरूपो भवति शिवो नाम परम स्वच्छन्दः ॥१०॥
स एव विश्वमेषितुं ज्ञातुं कर्तुं चोन्मुखो भवन् ।
शक्ति स्वभावः कथितो हृदयत्रिकोण मधुमांसलोल्लासः ॥११॥

शक्तिपरिणामक्रमेण समष्टि-व्यष्टि-पिण्डोत्पत्तिः ।

नास्ति सत्यविचारेऽस्मिन्नुत्पत्तिश्चाण्डपिण्डयोः ।

तथापि लोकवृत्त्यर्थं वक्ष्ये सत्संप्रदायतः ॥१२॥
यदा नास्ति स्वयं कर्त्ता कारणं न कुलाकुलम् ।
अव्यक्तं च परंब्रह्म अनामा विद्यते तदा ॥१३॥
निजा पराऽपरा सूक्ष्मा कुण्डलिन्यासु पंचधा ।
शक्तिचक्रक्रमेणोत्थो जातः पिण्डः परः शिवः ॥१४॥
सृष्टिः कुण्डलिनी ख्याता द्विधा भागवती तु सा ।
एकधा स्थूलरूपा च लोकानां प्रत्यगात्मिका ॥१५॥
अपरा सर्वगा सूक्ष्मा व्याप्तिव्यापक वर्जिता ।
तस्या भेदं न जानाति मोहिता प्रत्ययेन तु ॥१६॥

परा संवित्

सत्वे सत्वे सकलरचना राजते संविदेका,
तत्वे तत्वे परममहिमा संविदेवावभाति ।
भावे भावे बहुलतरला लम्पटा संविदेषा,
भासे भासे भजनचतुरा बृंहिता संविदेव ॥१७॥

सर्वात्मकम् आत्मतत्वम् ।

आत्मा खलु विश्वमूलं तत्र प्रमाणं न कोऽप्यर्थयते ।
कस्य वा भवति पिपासा गंगास्रोतसि निमग्नस्य ॥१८॥
अमेध्यमथवा मेध्यं यत् यत् पश्यति चक्षुषा ।
तत्तदात्मेति विज्ञाय प्रत्याहरति योगवित् ॥१९॥
यत् यत् शृणोति कर्णाभ्यामप्रियमथवा प्रियम् ।
तत्तदात्मेति विज्ञाय प्रत्याहरति योगवित् ॥२०॥
अमिष्टमथवा मिष्टम् यत् यत् स्पृशति जिह्वया ।
तत्तदात्मेति विज्ञाय प्रत्याहरति योगवित् ॥२१॥
सुगन्धमथ दुर्गन्धं यत् यत् जिघ्रति नासया ।
तत्तदात्मेति विज्ञाय प्रत्याहरति योगवित् ॥२२॥
कर्कशं कोमलं वापि यत् यत् स्पृशति च त्वचा ।
तत्तदात्मेति विज्ञाय प्रत्याहरति योगवित् ॥२३॥

जीवात्म परमात्मनोरभेदः ।

आत्मेति परमात्मेति जीवात्मेति विचारणे ।
त्रयाणामैक्य संभूतिः आदेश इति कीर्तितः ॥२४॥
आदेश इति सद्वाणीं सर्वद्वन्द्वक्षयावहाम् ।
योगिनं प्रति वदेत् स वेत्यात्मानमीश्वरम् ॥२५॥

आत्मज्ञानान्मुक्तिः ।

निर्मलं गगनाकारं मरीचिजलसन्निभम् ।
आत्मानं सर्वगं ध्यात्वा योगी मुक्तिमवाप्नुयात् ॥२६॥
समस्तोपधिविध्वंसात् सदाभ्यासेन योगिनः ।
मुक्तिकृत् शक्तिभेदेन स्वयमात्मा प्रकाशते ॥२७॥
विरजाः परमाकाशात् आत्माकाशो महत्तरः ।
सर्वदेत्थं भावनया तत्वं योगिजना विदुः ॥२८॥
एतद् ब्रह्मात्मकं तेजः शिव ज्योतिरनुत्तमम् ।
ध्यात्वा ज्ञात्वा विमुक्तः स्यादिति गोरक्षभाषितम् ॥२९॥

ओंकार-रहस्यम् ।

भूर्भुवः स्वरिमे लोकाश्चन्द्र सूर्याग्निदेवताः ।
प्रतिष्ठिताः सदा यत्र तत्परं ज्योतिरोमिति ॥३०॥
त्रयः कालास्त्रयो वेदास्त्रयो लोकास्त्रयोऽग्नयः ।
त्रयः स्वराः स्थिता यत्र तत्परं ज्योतिरोमिति ॥३१॥
सत्त्वं रजस्तमश्चैव ब्रह्म-विष्णु-महेश्वराः ।
सर्वे देवाः स्थिता यत्र तत्परं ज्योतिरोमिति ॥३२॥
कृतिरिच्छा तथा ज्ञानं ब्राह्मी रौद्री च वैष्णवी ।
त्रिधा शक्तिः स्थिता यत्र तत्परं ज्योतिरोमिति ॥३३॥
शुचिर्वाप्यशुचिर्वापि यो जपे त्प्रणवं सदा ।
न स लिप्यति पापेन पद्मपत्रमिवाम्भसा ॥३४॥
पद्मासनं समारुह्य समकायशिरोधरः ।
नासाग्रदृष्टिरेकाकी जपेदोङ्कारमव्ययम् ॥३५॥

देहरहस्यम् ।

बिन्दुमूलं शरीरस्य शिरास्तत्र प्रतिष्ठिताः ।
भावयन्ति शरीराणि चापादतलमस्तकम् ॥३६॥
सपुनर्द्विविधो बिन्दुः पाण्डुरो लोहितस्तथा ।
पाण्डुरं शुक्रमित्याहु र्लोहित ञ्च महारजः ॥३७॥
बिन्दुः शिवो रजः शक्ति र्बिन्दुरिन्दू रजो रविः ।
उभयोः संगमादेव प्राप्यते परमं पदम् ॥३८॥
शुक्रं चन्द्रेण संयुक्तं रजः सूर्येण संगतम् ।
तयोः समरसैकत्वं यो जानाति स योगवित् ॥३९॥
यावद्बिन्दुः स्थितो देहे तावन्मृत्युभयं कुतः ।

मरणं विन्दुपातेन जीवनं विन्दुधारणात् ॥४०॥
एक स्तम्भं नवद्वारं गृहं पंचाधिदैवतम् ।
स्वदेहं ये न जानन्ति नते सिध्यन्ति योगिनः ॥४१॥
षट्चक्रं षोडशाधारं त्रिलक्ष्यं व्योम पंचकम् ।
स्वदेहे चेन्न जानन्ति कथं सिध्यन्ति योगिनः ॥४२॥

व्यष्टिपिण्डे समष्टि पिण्डदर्शनम् ।

पिण्डमध्ये चराचरं यो जानाति, स योगी
पिण्ड-संवित्तिर्भवति । यथा च शिवसंहितायाम्,—
देहेऽस्मिन्वर्तते मेरुः सप्तद्वीप समन्वितः ।
सरितः सागराः शैलाः क्षेत्राणि क्षेत्रपालकाः ॥४३॥
ऋषयो मुनयः सर्वे नक्षत्राणि ग्रहास्तथा ।
पुण्यतीर्थानि पीठानि वर्तन्ते पीठ देवताः ॥४४॥
सृष्टिसंहारकर्तारौ भ्रमन्तौ शशिभास्करौ ।
नभो वायुश्च वह्निश्च जलं पृथ्वी तथैव च ॥४५॥
त्रैलोक्ये यानिभूतानि तानि सर्वाणि देहतः ।
मेरुं संवेष्ट्य सर्वत्र व्यवहारः प्रवर्तते ॥४६॥
जानाति यः सर्वमिदं स योगी नात्र संशयः ॥४७॥

श्वास-रहस्यम् (अजपा)

हं-कारेण वहिर्याति स-कारेण विशेत्पुनः ।
हंस-हंसेत्यमुं मन्त्रं जीवो जपति सर्वदा ॥४८॥
षट् शतानि दिवारात्रौ सहस्राण्येक विंशतिः ।
एतत्संख्यान्वितं मन्त्रं जीवो जपति सर्वदा ॥४९॥
अजपा नाम गायत्री योगिनां मोक्षदायिनी ।
तस्याः संकल्पमात्रेण नरः पापै र्विमुच्यते ॥५०॥
अनया सदृशी विद्या त्वनया सदृशो जपः ।
अनया सदृशं ज्ञानं न भूतं न भविष्यति ॥५१॥

परमपदस्य स्वसंवेद्यता ।

यत्र बुद्धिर्मनो नास्ति तत्वविन्नापरा कला ।
ऊहापोहौ न कर्तव्यौ वाचा तत्र करोति किम् ॥५२॥
वाग्मिना गुरुणा सम्यक् कथं तत्पदमीर्य्यते ।
तस्मादुक्तं शिवेनैव स्वसंवेद्यं परं पदम् ॥५३॥

समाधि स्वरूपम् ।

यत्समत्वं द्वयोरत्र जीवात्मपरमात्मनोः ।
समस्त नष्ट संकल्पः समाधिः सोऽभिधीयते ॥५४॥
अम्बु-सैन्धवयोरैक्यं यथा भवति योगतः ।
तथात्ममनसोरैक्यं समाधिरभिधीयते ॥५५॥
यदा संलीयते जीवो मानसं च विलीयते ।
तदा समरसत्वं हि समाधिरभिधीयते ॥५६॥
इन्द्रियेषु मनोवृत्तिरपरा प्रक्रिया हि सा ।
ऊर्ध्वमेव गते जीवे न मनो नेन्द्रियाणि च ॥५७॥
नाभिजानाति शीतोष्णं न दुःखं न सुखं तथा ।
न मानं नापमानं च योगी युक्तः समाधिना ॥५८॥
अभेद्यः सर्वशस्त्राणामवध्यः सर्वदेहिनाम् ।
अग्राह्यो मन्त्रसंघानां योगी युक्तः समाधिना ॥५९
निरालम्बे निराधारे निराकारे निरामये ।
योगी योगविधानेन परब्रह्मणि लीयते ॥६०॥
यथा घृते घृतं क्षिप्तं घृतमेव हि जायते ।
क्षीरे क्षीरं तथा योगी तत्वमेव हि जायते ॥६१॥

षडङ्ग-योगः ।

आसनं प्राणसंरोधः प्रत्याहारश्च धारणा ।
ध्यानं समाधिरेतानि योगांगानि वदन्ति षट् ॥६२॥
आसनेन रुजं हन्ति प्राणायामेन पातकम् ।
विकारंमानसं योगी प्रत्याहारेण मुंचति ॥६३॥
मनोधैर्यं धारणया ध्यानाच्चैतन्यमद्भुतम् ।
समाधेर्मोक्षमाप्नोति त्यक्त्वा कर्म शुभाशुभम् ॥६४॥
आसनानि च तावन्ति यावन्त्यो जीवजातयः ।
एतेषामखिलान् भेदान् विजानाति महेश्वरः ॥६५॥
आसनेभ्यः समस्तेभ्यो द्वयमेव प्रशस्यते ।
एकं सिद्धासनं प्रोक्तं द्वितीयं कमलासनम् ॥६६॥
बद्ध पद्मासनो योगी नमस्कृत्य गुरुं शिवम् ।
नासाग्रदृष्टिरेकाकी प्राणायामं समभ्यसेत् ॥६६॥
ऊर्ध्वमाकृष्य चापानं वायुं प्राणे नियुज्य च ।
ऊर्ध्वमानीय तं शक्त्या सर्व पापैः प्रमुच्यते ॥६८॥
प्राणायामे महान् धर्मो योगिनां मोक्षदायकः ।

प्राणायामे दिवारात्रौ दोषजालं परित्यजेत् ॥६९॥
प्राणायामेन युक्तेन सर्वरोगक्षयो भवेत् ।
अयुक्ताभ्यासयोगेन सर्वरोगस्य सम्भवः ॥७०॥
युक्तं-युक्तं त्यजेत् वायुं युक्तं युक्तं च पूरयेत् ।
युक्तं-युक्तं च बध्नीयादेवं सिद्धिमवाप्नुयात् ॥७१॥
चरतां चक्षुरादीनां विषयेषु यथाक्रमम् ।
यत्प्रत्याहरणं तेषां प्रत्याहारः स उच्यते ॥७२॥
अंगमध्ये यथांगानि कूर्मः संकोचयेद्ध्रुवम् ।
योगी प्रत्याहरेदेवं स्वेन्द्रियाणि तथात्मनि ॥७३॥
आसनेन समायुक्तः प्राणायामेन संयुतः ।
प्रत्याहारेण सम्पन्नो धारणां च समभ्यसेत् ॥७४॥
हृदये पंचभूतानां धारणं च पृथक्-पृथक् ।
मनसो निश्चलत्वेन धारणा साऽभिधीयते ॥७५॥
सर्वं चिन्तासमावर्त्ति योगिनो हृदि वर्तते ।
या तत्वे निश्चला चिन्ता तद्धि ध्यानं प्रचक्षते ॥७६॥
द्विधा भवति तद्ध्यानं सगुणं निर्गुणं तथा ।
सगुणं वर्णभेदेन निर्गुणं केवलं विदुः ॥७७॥

दशविधयमास्तथा दशविधनियमाः ।

अहिंसा सत्यमस्तेयं ब्रह्मचर्यं दयार्जवम् ।
क्षमा धृतिर्मिताहारः शौचं चेति यमा दश ॥७८॥
तपः सन्तोष आस्तिक्यं दानमीश्वर पूजनम् ।
सिद्धान्त श्रवणं चैव ह्रीर्मतिश्च जपो हुतिः ।
दशैते नियमाः प्रोक्ता योगशास्त्रविशारदैः ॥७९॥
अत्याहारः प्रयासश्च प्रजल्पोऽनियमग्रहः ।
जनसंगश्च लौल्यं च षड्भिर्योगो विनश्यति ॥८०॥
उत्साहान्निश्चयाद् धैर्यात् तत्वज्ञानार्थदर्शनात् ।
जनसंगपरित्यागात् षड्भिर्योगो प्रसिद्ध्यति ॥८१॥
सुस्निग्धं मधुराहारं चतुर्थांशविवर्जितम् ।
भुक्ते य ईश्वर प्रीत्यै मिताहारी स उच्यते ॥८२॥
ब्रह्मचारी मिताहारी त्यागी योग परायणः ।
अब्दादूर्ध्वं भवेत्सिद्धो नात्र कार्या विचारणा ॥८३॥
सत्यमेकमजं नित्यमनन्तं चाक्षयं ध्रुवम् ।
ज्ञात्वा यस्तु वदेद्धीरः सत्यवादी स उच्यते ॥८४॥

शुद्धं शान्तं निराकारं परानन्दं सदोदितम् ।
तं शिवं यो विजानाति शुद्धशैवो भवेत्तु सः ॥८५॥

देहमध्यस्थचक्राणि ।

आधारं प्रथमं चक्रं स्वाधिष्ठानं द्वितीयकम् ।
तृतीयं मणिपूराख्यं चतुर्थं स्यादनाहतम् ॥८६॥
पंचमन्तु विशुद्धाख्यं आज्ञाचक्रन्तु षष्ठकम् ;
सप्तमन्तु महाचक्रं ब्रह्मरन्ध्रे महापथे ॥८७॥
चतुर्दलं स्यादाधारे स्वाधिष्ठाने तु षड्दलम् ।
नाभौ दशदलं पद्मं सूर्यसंख्यादलं हृदि ॥८८॥
कण्ठे स्यात् षोडशदलं भ्रूमध्ये द्विदल न्तथा ।
सहस्रदलमाख्यातं ब्रह्मरध्रे महापथे ॥८९॥
आधारं प्रथमं चक्रं स्वाधिष्ठानं द्वितीयकम् ।
योनिस्थानं तयोर्मध्ये कामरूपं निगद्यते ॥९०॥
आधाराख्ये गुदस्थाने पंकजं यच्चतुर्दलम् ।
तन्मध्ये प्रोच्यते योनिः कामाख्या सिद्धवन्दिता ॥९१॥
योनिमध्ये महालिंगं पश्चिमाभिमुखं स्थितम् ।
मस्तके मणिवद्बिम्बं यो जानाति स योगवित् ॥९२॥

देहमध्ये आत्मध्यानस्थानानि ।

आधारे प्रथमे चक्रे स्वर्णाभे चतुरंगुले ।
नासाग्रदृष्टिरात्मानं ध्यात्वा योगी सुखी भवेत् ॥९३॥
स्वाधिष्ठाने शुभे चक्रे सन्माणिक्य समप्रभे ।
नासाग्रदृष्टिरात्मानं ध्यात्वा ब्रह्मसमो भवेत् ॥९४॥
तरुणादित्यसंकाशे चक्रे तु मणिपूरके ।
नासाग्रदृष्टिरात्मानं ध्यात्वा संक्षोभयेत् जगत् ॥९५॥
अनाहते महाचक्रे द्वादशारे च पंकजे ।
नासाग्रदृष्टिरात्मानं ध्यात्वा ध्याताऽमरो भवेत् ॥९६॥
सततं घण्टिकामध्ये विशुद्धे दीपकप्रभे ।
नासाग्रदृष्टिरात्मानं ध्यात्वा दुःखं विमुञ्चति ॥९७॥
स्रवत्पीयूष सम्पूर्णे लम्बिका चन्द्रमण्डले ।
नासाग्रदृष्टिरात्मानं ध्यात्वा मृत्युं विमुञ्चति ॥९८॥
ध्यायेन्नीलनिभं नित्यं भ्रूमध्ये परमेश्वरम् ।
आत्मवान् विजित प्राणो योगी योगमवाप्नुयात् ॥९९॥
ब्रह्मरन्ध्रे महाचक्रे सहस्रारे च पंकजे ।

नासाग्रदृष्टिरात्मानं ध्यात्वा सिद्धो भवेत्स्वयम् ॥१००॥
गुदं मेढ्रश्च नाभिश्च हृदयं कण्ठ ऊर्ध्वगः ।
घण्टिका लम्बिका स्थानं भ्रू मध्यं च नभोविलम् ।
कथितानि नबैतानि ध्यानस्थानानि योगिनाम् ॥१०१॥
उपाधितत्त्वयुक्तानां कुर्वन्त्यष्टगुणोदयम् ।
उपाधिश्च तथा तत्त्वं द्वयमेतदुदाहृतम् ।
उपाधिः प्रोच्यते वर्णं स्तत्त्वमात्माऽभिधीयते ॥१०२॥
उपाधिरन्यथा ज्ञानं तत्त्वसंस्थितिरन्यथा ।
अन्यथा वर्णयोगेन दृश्यते स्फटिकोपमम् ॥१०३॥
समस्तोपाधिविध्वंसात् सदाभ्यासेन योगिनः ।
मुक्तिकृच्छक्तिभेदेन स्वयमात्मा प्रकाशते ॥१०४॥

कुण्डलिनी प्रबोधः ।

कुटिलांगी कुण्डलिनी भुजंगी शक्तिरीश्वरी ।
कुण्डल्यरुन्धती चैते शब्दाः पर्यायवाचका ॥१०५॥
येन मार्गेण गन्तव्यं ब्रह्मस्थानं निरामयम् ।
मुखेनाच्छाद्य तद्द्वारं प्रसुप्ता परमेश्वरी ॥१०६॥
कन्दोर्ध्वं कुण्डली शक्तिः सुप्ता मोक्षाय योगिनाम् ।
बन्धनाय च मूढानां यस्तां वेत्ति स योगवित् ॥१०७॥
कुण्डली कुटिलाकारा सर्पवत्परिकीर्तिता ।
सा शक्तिश्चालिता येन समुक्तो नात्र संशयः ॥१०८॥
गंगायमुनयोर्मध्ये बालरण्डां तपस्विनीम् ।
बलात्कारेण गृह्णीयात् तच्छंभोः परमं पदम् ॥१०९॥
इडा भगवती गंगा पिंगला यमुना नदी ।
इडा-पिंगलयोर्मध्ये बाल रण्डा च कुण्डली ॥११०॥
पुच्छे प्रगृह्य भुजगीं सुप्तामुद्बोधयेच्च ताम् ।
निद्रां विहाय सा शक्तिः उर्ध्वमुत्तिष्ठते हठात् ॥१११॥
सुप्ता गुरु प्रसादेन यदा जागर्ति कुण्डली ।
तदा सर्वाणि पद्मानि भिद्यन्ते ग्रन्थयोऽपिच ॥११२॥
प्राणस्य शून्यपदवीं तदा राजपथायते ।
तदा चित्तं निरालम्बं तदा कालस्य वंचनम् ॥११३॥

दशविध-मुद्राः ।

महामुद्रा महाबन्धो महावेधश्च खेचरी ।
उड्डानं मूलबन्धश्च बन्धो जालन्धराभिधः ॥११४॥

करणी विपरीताख्या वज्रोली शक्तिचालनम् ।
इदं दि मुद्रादशमं जरामरणनाशनम् ॥११५॥
आदिनाथोदितं दिव्यमष्टैश्वर्यं प्रदायकम् ।
वल्लभं सर्वसिद्धानां दुर्लभं मरुतामपि ॥११६॥
गोपनीयं प्रयत्नेन यथा रत्नकरण्डकम् ।
कस्यचिन्नैव वक्तव्यं कुलस्त्री सूरतं यथा ॥११७॥
मुद्मोदे तु रा दाने जीवात्म परमात्मनोः ।
उभयोरेक संवित्तिमुद्रेति परिकीर्तिता ॥११८॥
मोदन्ते देवसंघाश्च द्रवन्तेऽसुरराशयः ।
मुद्रेति कथिता साक्षात्सदा भद्रार्थदायिनी ॥११९॥

शाम्भवी मुद्रा ।

अन्तर्लक्ष्यं बहिर्दृष्टि र्निमेषोन्मेषवर्जिता ।
एषा वै शाम्भवी मुद्रा वेदशास्त्रेषु गोपिता ॥१२०॥
अन्तश्चेता बहिश्चक्षु रधिष्ठाय सुखासनम् ।
समत्वं च शरीरस्य ध्यानमुद्रा च कीर्तिता ॥१२१॥
अन्तर्लक्ष्यविलीनचित्तपवनो योगी सदा वर्तते ।
दृष्ट्या निश्चलतारया बहिरधः पश्यन्नपश्यन्नपि॥१२२॥
मुद्रेयं खलु शाम्भवी भवति सा लब्धा प्रसादाद्गुरोः ।
शून्याशून्यविलक्षणं स्फुरतितत् तत्त्वं
परं शाम्भवम् ॥१२३॥

प्राणायाम भेदाः ।

प्राणायामस्त्रिधा प्रोक्तो रेच-पूरक-कुम्भकैः ।
सहितः केवलश्चेति कुम्भको द्विविधो मतः ॥१२४॥
यावत्केवल सिद्धिः स्यात् सहितं तावदभ्यसेत् ॥१२५॥
रेचकं पूरकं मुक्त्वा सुखं यत्प्राणधारणम् ।
प्राणायामोऽयमित्युक्तः स वै केवल कुम्भकः ॥१२६॥
कुम्भके केवले सिद्धे रेच-पूरक-वर्जिते ।
न तस्य दुर्लभं किंचित् त्रिपु लोकेपु विद्यते ॥१२७॥
शक्तः केवलकुम्भेन यथेष्टं वायुधारणात् ।
राजयोगपदं चापि लभते नात्र संशयः ॥१२८॥
कुम्भकात् कुण्डलीबोधः कुण्डलीबोधतो भवेत् ।
अनर्गला सुषुम्ना च हठसिद्धिश्च जायते ॥१२९॥

हठं विना राजयोगो राज योगं विना हठः ।
न सिध्यति ततो युग्मम् आनिष्पत्तेः समभ्यसेत् ॥१३०॥
दृष्टिः स्थिरा यस्य विनापि दृश्याद्,
वायुः स्थिरो यस्य विना प्रयत्नात् ।
मनः स्थिरं यस्य विनावलम्बात्,
स एव योगी स गुरुः स सेव्यः ॥१३१॥

मनो लयः !

मनः स्थैर्ये स्थिरो वायुस्ततो विन्दुः स्थिरो भवेत् ।
विन्दु स्थैर्यात्सदा सत्वं पिण्डस्थैर्यं प्रजायते ॥१३२॥
इन्द्रियाणां मनो नाथो मनोनाथश्च मारुतः ।
मारुतस्य लयो नाथः स लयो नादमाश्रितः ॥१३३॥
प्रणष्टृश्वासनिश्वासः प्रध्वस्त विषय ग्रहः ।
निश्चेष्टो निर्विकारश्च लयो जयति योगिनाम् ॥१३४॥
उच्छिन्न सर्व संकल्पो निःशेषाशेष चेष्ठितः ।
स्वावगम्यो लयः कोऽपि जायते वागगोचरः ॥१३५॥
भ्रुवोर्मध्ये शिवस्थानं मनस्तत्र विलीयते ।
ज्ञातव्यं तत्पदं तूर्यं तत्र कालो न विद्यते ॥१३६॥
स्वमध्ये कुरु चात्मान मात्ममध्ये च स्वं कुरु ।
सर्वं च तन्मयं कृत्वा न किञ्चिदपि चिन्तयेत् ॥१३७॥
वाह्यचिन्ता न कर्तव्या तथैवान्तर चिन्तनम् ।
सर्वचिन्तां परित्यज्य न किञ्चिदपि चिन्तयेत् ॥१३८॥
मनोदृश्यमिदं सर्वं यत् किञ्चित् सचरा चरम् ।
मनसो ह्युन्मनीभावात् द्वैतं नैवोपलभ्यते ॥१३९॥
ज्ञेयवस्तु परित्यागाद् विलयं याति मानसम् ।
मनसो विलये याते कैवल्यमव शिष्यते ॥१४०॥

नादानुसंधानम् ।

मुक्तासने स्थितो योगी मुद्रां सन्धाय शाम्भवीम् ।
शृणुयाद्दक्षिणे कर्णे नादमन्तः स्थमेकधीः ॥१४१॥
यत्र कुत्रापि वा नादे लगति प्रथमं मनः ।
तत्रैव सुस्थिरीभूय तेन सार्धं विलीयते ॥१४२॥
कर्णौ पिधाय हस्ताभ्यां यं शृणोति ध्वनिं मुनिः ।
तत्र चित्तं स्थिरी कुर्यात् यावत् स्थिरपदं व्रजेत् ॥१४३॥

श्रूयते प्रथमाभ्यासे नादो नानाविधो महान् ।
ततोऽभ्यासे वर्धमाने श्रूयते सूक्ष्म सूक्ष्मकम् ॥१४४॥
आदौ जलधि जीमूत भेरी झर्झर सम्भवाः ।
मध्ये मर्दल शंखोत्था घण्टा काहलजास्तथा ॥१४५॥
अन्ते तु किंकिणी-वंश-वीणा-भ्रमर-निःस्वनाः ।
इति नानाविधा नादाः श्रूयन्ते देहमध्यगाः ॥१४६॥
महति श्रूयमाणेऽपि मेघभेर्यादिके ध्वनौ ।
तत्र सूक्ष्मात्सूक्ष्मतरं नादमेव परामृशेत् ॥१४७॥
अनाहतस्य शब्दस्य ध्वनिर्य उपलभ्यते ।
ध्वनेरन्तर्गतं ज्ञेयं ज्ञेयस्यान्तर्गतं मनः ।
मनस्तत्र लयं याति तच्छंभोः परमं पदम् ॥१४८॥
यत्किंचिन्नाद रूपेण श्रूयते शक्तिरेव सा ।
यस्तत्त्वान्तो निराकारः स एव परमेश्वरः ॥१४९॥

अवधूत-योगि-लक्षणानि ।

क्लेश पाशतरंगाणां कृन्तनेन विमुण्डनम् ।
सर्वावस्था विनिर्मुक्तः सोऽवधूतोऽभिधीयते ॥१५०॥
लोकमध्ये स्थिरासीनः समस्त कलनोज्झितः ।
कौपीनं खर्परोऽदैन्यं सोऽवधूतोऽभिधीयते ॥१५१॥
पादुका पदसंवित्ति मृगत्वक् स्यादनाहता ।
शेली यस्य परा संवित् सोऽवधूतोऽभिधीयते ॥१५१॥
मेखला निर्वृतिर्नित्यं स्वस्वरूपं कटासनम् ।
निर्वृत्तिः षट्विकारेभ्यः सोऽवधूतोऽभिधीयते ॥१५२॥
चित्प्रकाश परानन्दौ यस्य वै कुण्डलद्वयम ।
जपमालाक्ष विश्रान्तिः सोऽवधूतोऽभिधीयते ॥१५३॥
यस्य धैर्यमयो दण्डः पराकाशं च खर्परम् ।
योगपट्टो निजाशक्तिः सोऽवधूतोऽभिधीयते ॥१५४॥
भेदाभेदौ स्वयं भिक्षां कृत्वा स्वास्वादने रतः ।
जारणी तन्मयीभावः सोऽवधूतोऽभिधीयते ॥१५५॥
आवर्तयति यः सम्यक् स्वस्वमध्ये स्वयं सदा ।
समत्वेन जगद् वेत्ति सोऽवधूतोऽभिधीयते ॥१५६॥
स्वात्मानमव गच्छेद् यः स्वात्मन्येवावतिष्ठते ।
अनुत्थानमयः सम्यक् सोऽवधूतोऽभिधीयते ॥१५७॥
अवभासात्मको भासः प्रकाशे सुख संस्थितः ।

लीलया रमते लोके सोऽवधूतोऽभिधीयते ॥१५८॥
क्वचिद् भोगी क्वचित्यागी क्वचिन्नग्नः पिशाचवत् ।
क्वचिद् राजा क्वचाचारी सोऽवधूतोऽभिधीयते ॥१५९॥
विश्वातीतं यथाविश्वं एकमेव विराजते ।
संयोगेन सदा यस्तु सिद्धयोगी भवेत्तु सः ॥१६०॥
उदासीनः सदा शान्तः स्वस्थोऽन्तर्निजभासकः ।
महानन्दमयो धीरः स भवेत् सिद्धयोगिराट् ॥१६१॥
परिपूर्णं प्रसन्नात्मा सर्वासर्वं पदोदितः ।
विशुद्धो निर्भरानन्दः स भवेत् सिद्ध योगिराट् ॥१६२॥
प्रसरं भासते शक्तिः संकोचं भासते शिवः ।
तयो र्योगस्य कर्ता यः स भवेत् सिद्धयोगिराट् ॥१६३॥
गते न शोकं विभवेन वाञ्छा, प्राप्ते न हर्षं च करोति योगी ।
आनन्दपूर्णो निजबोधलीनो, न बाध्यते कालपथेन नित्यम् ॥१६४॥

सद्‌गुरु-महिमा

सहजं स्वात्मसंवित्तिः संयमः स्वस्वनिग्रहः ।
स्वोपायं स्वस्वविश्रान्तिः अद्वैतं परमं पदम् ।
तज्ज्ञेयं सद्‌गुरोर्वक्त्रान्नान्यथा शास्त्रकोटिभिः ॥१६५॥
असाध्याः सिद्धयः सर्वाः सद्‌गुरोः करुणां विना ।
अतः सद्‌गुरुः संसेव्यः सत्यमीश्वर भाषितम् ॥१६६॥
अनुबुभूषति यो निजविश्रमम्,
स गुरुपाद सरोरुहमाश्रयेत् ।
तदनुसंसरणात् परमं पदम्,
समरसीकरणं च न दूरतः ॥१६७॥
कथनात् शक्ति पाताद्वा यद्वा पादावलोकनात् ।
प्रसादात्सद्‌गुरोः सम्यक् प्राप्यते परमं पदम् ॥१६८॥
वाङ्मात्राद्वाथ दृक् पातात् यः करोति च तत् क्षणात् ।
प्रस्फुटं शाम्भवं वेद्यं स्वसंवेद्यं परं पदम् ॥१६९॥
करुणाखण्ड पातेन छित्वा पाशाष्टकं शिशोः ।
सम्यगानन्द जनकः सद्‌गुरुः सोऽभिधीयते ॥१७०॥
किमत्र बहुनोक्तेन शास्त्रकोटि शतेन च ।
दुर्लभा चित्तविश्रान्ति र्विना गुरुकृपां पराम् ॥१७१॥
दुर्लभो विषयत्यागो दुर्लभं तत्वदर्शनम् ।
दुर्लभा सहजावस्था सद्‌गुरोः करुणां विना ॥१७२॥

Glossary of Philosophical Terms

Absolute	परम । चरम । केवल । निरपेक्ष । अनवच्छिन्न । अद्वैत । निरुपाधिक । देश-काल-सम्बन्धातीत ।
Absolute Reality Absolute Truth	परम या चरम या केवल या निरपेक्ष या अनवच्छिन्न या निरुपाधिक या अद्वय तत्व या सत्य । पारमार्थिक तत्व या सत्य । ब्रह्म । परमात्मा । शिव ।
Absolute Existence Absolute Being	परम या चरम या केवल या निरपेक्ष या निरुपाधिक या अद्वय तत्व या सत्य । पारमार्थिक तत्व या सत्य । ब्रह्म । परमात्मा । शिव । परम सत्ता या सत्स्वरूप । स्वतंत्र-सत्ता ।
Absolute Consciousness Absolute Spirit	परमचैतन्य । परा-सम्वित् । केवल या स्वतंत्र या अद्वय या निरुपाधिक चित्-तत्व या ज्ञान-तत्व । देश-कालानवच्छिन्न विषय-विषयिभेद-रहित परम चैतन्य-तत्व । परमात्मा । ब्रह्म । शिव । परमेश्वर ।
Absolute Bliss	परम आनन्द-तत्व या आनन्द-स्वरूप । भोक्तृ-भोग्य-भेद-विरहित विषय-निरपेक्ष निरुपाधिक आनन्द । भूमानन्द । ब्रह्मानन्द । निरवच्छिन्न अद्वय आनन्द ।
Absolute Cause	परम निरपेक्ष अद्वय कारण । सर्व-कारण-कारण । मूल कारण ।
Consciousness (in the metaphysical or noumenal sense)	चित् । चैतन्य । सम्वित् । ज्ञान-तत्व । बोध-तत्व । सम्बोध मात्र । वृत्ति-रहित नाशोत्पत्ति-रहित चैतन्य या ज्ञान या बोध । स्वप्रकाश, स्वय-ज्योति चेतन-तत्व । पारमार्थिक चैतन्य । विषय-विषयि-भेद-रहित चिन्मात्र ।
Consciousness (in the phenomenal or empirical sense)	वृत्ति-चैतन्य । चेतन-वृत्ति या ज्ञान-वृत्ति या बोध-वृत्ति या अनुभव-वृत्ति । परिणामशील चेतना । देश-कालावस्थापरिछिन्न विषय-विषयि-भेद-युक्त चेतन-वृत्ति या अनुभूति । व्यावहारिक चेतना । चित्तवृत्ति या मनोवृत्ति या बुद्धि-वृत्ति । अन्तःकरण-वृत्त्यवछिन्न-चैतन्य ।

Consciousness-individual	व्यष्टि-चैतन्य। जीव-चैतन्य। अन्तःकरण-विशेषोपहित-चैतन्य।
Consciousness-intellectual	बुद्धि-चैतन्य। विचारात्मिका या अध्यवसायात्मिका चैतन्य-वृत्ति। युक्ति-तर्क-सिद्धान्तादि-रूपा अन्तःकरण-वृत्ति।
Consciousness-mental	मानस-चैतन्य। संकल्प-विकल्पाद्यात्मिका विचित्रवासनानुरंजिता-जाग्रत-स्वप्नाद्यवस्थाधीना चैतन्य-वृत्ति।
Consciousness-supramental, Super-Consciousness	अतिमानस चेतना या अनुभव। समाधि-चेतना। उन्मनी-भाव। तुरीय-चेतना। तुर्यातीत चेतना। ब्रह्माकाराकारित चेतना।
Consciousness- sensuous	इन्द्रियाधीना चेतना-वृत्ति। विषयेन्द्रिय-संस्पर्श-जन्य ज्ञानेच्छासुखदुःख काम लोभादि अन्तः करण वृत्ति।
Consciousness-momentary	क्षणिक चैतन्य-वृत्ति। क्षणिक विज्ञान। क्षणभंगुर चेतना।
Consciousness-transcendental or transcendent	देश-कालातीत विषय-सम्बन्ध रहित चित्तेन्द्रियवृत्ति निरपेक्ष चैतन्य या अनुभव या सम्वित्। समाधि-चेतना। ब्रह्मचैतन्य। शिव-चैतन्य।
Witness-Consciousness	साक्षि चैतन्य। निर्विकार-चैतन्य। सर्वावभासक-चैतन्य। वृत्तिरहित सर्वार्थप्रकाशक चैतन्य।
Self-Consciousness I—consciousness	आत्मचेतना या आत्मानुभव। अहं प्रत्यय या अहं बोध। अहंता। सर्व-शारीर-मानस-परिणामानुस्यूता अहंवृत्ति।
Moral consciousness	नैतिक चेतना। धर्माधर्म बोध। औचित्यानौचित्य बोध। श्रेयः-प्रेयो-विवेक। नैतिक मूल्यबोध। धार्मिक-आदर्शानुप्राणना।
Aesthetic Consciousness	रसचेतना या रस-बोध। सौन्दर्य-बोध। रसास्वादनात्मिका चैतन्य वृत्ति।
Spiritual Consciousness	अध्यात्म चेतना। आत्मानुसन्धानात्मिका या ब्रह्म-सन्धानात्मिका या परमपुरुषार्थ-सन्धानात्मिका चैतन्य-वृत्ति या चित्तवृत्ति। मोक्षानुकूला अंतःकरणवृत्ति। मुमुक्षा। ब्रह्मज्योतिर्दीप्तचेतना। अद्वैत-वासना। योगवासना।

Cosmic Consciousness Universal Consciousness	विश्वचैतन्य। समष्टिचैतन्य। विश्वात्मा। सर्वभूतात्मभाव। विश्वात्मभाव। विराट्-चेतना। हिरण्यगर्भ-चेतना।
Non-dual Consciousness Non-dual Spirit	अद्वैत चैतन्य। सजातीय-विजातीय-स्वगत-भेदशून्य चैतन्य। देश-काल-वस्तु-परिच्छेद-रहित केवल चैतन्य। अखण्ड चैतन्य। चिन्मात्र।
Divine Consciousness	दिव्य-चेतना। भागवत चेतना। ब्रह्म-चैतन्य। शिव-चैतन्य। ईश्वर-चैतन्य।
Dynamic Consciouness	शक्तियुक्त चित् या चैतन्य। शक्तिगर्भ चैतन्य। स्वयंक्रिय चैतन्य।
Manifested Consciousness	व्यक्त चैतन्य। स्फुरित-चैतन्य।
Unmanifested Consci. ousness	अव्यक्त चैतन्य। अनभिव्यक्त चैतन्य।
Pure Consciousness	चिन्मात्र। शुद्ध या निरुपाधिक चैतन्य।
Selfluminous Consci-ousness	स्वप्रकाश या स्वयंज्योति चैतन्य।
Existence (in the abstract sense)	सत्ता। अस्तिता। सद्भाव। स्थिति।
Existence (in the concrete sense	सद्वस्तु। भाव-पदार्थ। सत्व।
Pure Existence Pure Being	सन्मात्र। सत्ता-मात्र। भाव-मात्र। शुद्ध-सत्। निरुपाधि सत्ता
Phenomenal Existence ,, Being ,, Reality	परिणामी सत् या सत्ता। व्यावहारिक सत् या सत्ता। देश-कालावच्छिन्न उत्पत्ति-स्थिति-ध्वंश-शील पदार्थ या सत्ता। दृश्य या प्रत्यक्षादि-प्रमाण गोचर पदार्थ या सत्ता
Transcendental Existence ,, Being ,, Reality	देश-कालानवच्छिन्न उत्पति-विनाश-रहित प्रत्यक्षादि-लौकिक प्रमाण-गोचर सत् या सत्ता। अतीन्द्रिय अतिमानस योगानुभूति-गम्य तथा श्रुति विचारादिगम्य तत्व।
Derivative Existence	उत्पत्तिशील कारणोद्भव सत्ता या कार्य पदार्थ।

Conditional Existence	सोपाधिक सत्ता। कारणादि सापेक्ष सत्ता।
Unconditional Existence	निरुपाधिक कारणादिनिरपेक्ष स्वतन्त्र सत्ता।
Relative Existence	सापेक्ष सत्ता। वस्त्वन्तर-सम्बन्ध-सापेक्ष सत्ता। विषय-विषयिसंबंधाधीन सत्ता।
Contingent Existence	व्यावहारिक सत्ता। दृश्यसत्ता। अनवश्यम्भावी सत्ता। अनित्य अस्वतन्त्र सत्ता।
Eternal Existence	नित्य सत्ता। कालातीतनित्य सत्ता। सर्वकालव्यापी नित्यसत्ता।
Temporal Existence	कालिक सत्ता। कालावच्छिन्न परिणामी सत्ता।
Spatial Existence	दैशिक सत्ता। देशावच्छिन्न सत्ता।
Infinite Existence	अपरिच्छिन्न सत्ता। सर्व देशव्यापी सत्ता।
Supra-temporal Existence	कालातीत या कालानवच्छिन्न सत्ता। नित्य अपरिणामी सत्ता।
Supra-Spatial Existence	देशातीत या देशानवच्छिन्न सत्ता।
Illusory Existence	प्रातिभासिक या प्रातीतिक सत्ता
Apparent ,,	
False ,,	आध्यासिक सत्ता। मिथ्या या अवस्तु सत्ता।
Imaginary Existence	कल्पित सत्ता।
Self-Existence	स्वयंसिद्ध निरपेक्ष सत्ता।
Existence-Consciousness-Bliss	सच्चिदानन्द।
Planes of Existence	विभिन्न सत्ता-भूमि या सत्ता-स्तर। विभिन्न कोटिक सत्ता। विभिन्न लोक।
Higher plane of Existence	उच्च कोटिक सत्ता। उच्चतर लोक।
Lower plane of Existence	निम्नकोटिक सत्ता। निम्नतर लोक।
Cause	कारण। कार्यजनन सामर्थ्य।
Material Cause	उपादान कारण।
Efficient Cause	निमित्त कारण। कर्त्ता।
Auxilliary Cause	सहकारी कारण।

Phenomenal Cause	परिणामी कारण। विकारी कारण। नियत-पूर्वभावित्व-रूप कारण। समसत्ताक कार्योत्पादक कारण।
Metaphysical cause	अविकारी कारण। कालिक-पौर्वापर्य-सम्बन्ध-विहीन तात्त्विक कारण। पारमार्थिक कारण। निम्नकोटि सत्ता। कार्योत्पादक उच्चकोटिक सत्ता युक्त कारण।
Efficient-cum-Material Cause	अभिन्न-निमित्तोपादान कारण।
Root Cause first Cause	मूल कारण। आदि कारण।
Illusory Cause	प्रातीतिक कारण। आध्यासिक कारण।
Cause-effect relation	कार्य कारण सम्बन्ध।
Law of Causation Law of Causality	कार्यकारण-विधान। कार्यकारण-शृंखला।
Cousa Sui	स्वतःविद्य कारण। कारणान्तर निरपेक्ष कारण। स्वयंभूकारण।
Experience	अनुभूति। ज्ञान। अभिज्ञान।
Phenomenal Experience " Knowledge	व्यावहारिक या जागतिक ज्ञान। प्रत्यक्षानुमानादिजन्य ज्ञान।
Transcendental Experience " Knowledge	अतीन्द्रिय अतिमानस अनुभुति। समाधि-प्रसूत ज्ञान। तत्त्व-साक्षात्कार।
Intuitive Experience	अन्तर्दृष्टि-प्रसूत ज्ञान। इन्द्रियनिरपेक्ष अनुभव। सहज ज्ञान।
" Knowledge	ध्यानलब्ध आन्तरिक अनुभव।
Supersensuous Experience	अतीन्द्रिय अनुभूति।
Supramental Experience	अतिमानस अनुभूति। समाधिज अनुभूति।
Normal Experience	प्राकृत या लौकिक व्यवहारिक ज्ञान।
Super-normal-Experience	अप्राकृत या अलौकिक या असाधारण ज्ञान। योगज ज्ञान या अनुभव।

Mind (in the general sense)	अन्तःकरण । मन । चित्त । वृत्ति-चैतन्य ।
Mind (in a restricted sense)	मनस् । संकल्प-विकल्पाद्यात्मिका अन्तःकरण वृत्ति ।
Mind in the waking state	जाग्रदवस्थायुक्त मन । व्युत्थानावस्थायुक्त मन ।
Mind in the dream state	स्वप्नावस्थायुक्त मन ।
Mind in the sleeping state	सुषुप्ति या निद्रावस्थायुक्त मन
Mind in the swoon state	मूर्च्छावस्थायुक्त मन ।
Mind in the subconscious state	अनुद्बुद्ध वृत्ति युक्त या संस्कारात्मक वृत्ति युक्त अन्तःकरण । अन्तर्लीन-चेतन चित्तवृत्ति । सूक्ष्मवृत्ति युक्त मन ।
Mind in the unconscious state	अव्यक्त-चेतन मन । प्रसुप्त मन । संस्कारबीजात्मक मन ।
Mind in the superconscious state Supermind	उन्मनीभावात्मक मन । समाधि-चेतन मन । तुरीयावस्थानिष्ठ मन । अवस्थात्रय मुक्त मन । मल-विक्षेपावरणमुक्त मन ।
The Supreme Mind-the same as the Supreme Spirit	परमात्मा । परमेश्वर । विश्वनियन्तृ मन ।
The Cosmic Mind	विश्वान्तर्यामी या विश्वाधिष्ठाता मन । समष्टि मन ।
Individual Mind	व्यष्टि मन । व्यष्टि अन्तःकरण । व्यष्टि देहावच्छिन्न मन ।
Enlightened Mind Illumined Mind	तत्वज्ञानालोकित मन । ज्ञानदीप्त मन । प्रबुद्ध चित्त । योगि-चित्त, अविद्यामुक्त मन ।
Pure Mind	विशुद्ध चित्त । शुद्ध सत्त्व । मलादि-दोष-मुक्त चित्त ।
Body	शरीर । देह । पिण्ड ।
Gross Body Physical Body	स्थूल शरीर । भूत-पिण्ड या भौतिक-पिण्ड ।
Subtle body	सूक्ष्म देह । लिंग देह । भूत सूक्ष्ममय देह । प्राणेन्द्रियान्तःकरणात्मक शरीर ।
Causal Body	कारण-शरीर । अव्यक्त शक्त्यात्मक शरीर । मूल

	प्रकृत्यात्मक शरीर । संस्कार-मात्रात्मक शरीर ।
Individual body	व्यष्टि-शरीर । जीव देह ।
Cosmic Body	विश्वरूप देह । विराट् शरीर । ब्रह्माण्ड । समष्टिदेह । महा साकार पिण्ड ।
Power	शक्ति । क्रिया-करण-सामर्थ्य । कार्योत्पादन-सामर्थ्य ।
Supreme Power	पराशक्ति । ब्रह्म-शक्ति । शिव-शक्ति । शिवाभिन्ना शक्ति । आद्याशक्ति । महाशक्ति ।
Subtle Power	सूक्ष्माशक्ति ।
Unique power (of Siva)	निजाशक्ति । अनन्यसाधारणी शक्ति ।
Will-Power	इच्छाशक्ति । संकल्प-शक्ति ।
Free Power	स्वतन्त्रा-शक्ति ।
Consciousness-Power	चित्-शक्ति । चतन्यमयशक्ति । चैतन्याभिन्नाशक्ति । चिद्रूपाशक्ति । दृक् शक्ति ।
Inscrutable Power	अनिवर्चनीया शक्ति । अघटन घटनपटीयसी शक्ति । अचिन्त्या शक्ति ।
Moral Power	नैतिक शक्ति । धर्म शक्ति । विधिनिषेधात्मिका शक्ति ।
Spiritual Power	आत्मिक या आध्यात्मिक शक्ति । चिति-शक्ति । दिव्य-शक्ति । भगवती शक्ति । ऐशी शक्ति । योग शक्ति ।
Sleeping Power	सुप्ता शक्ति । अनभिव्यक्ता शक्ति । कुण्डलिनी शक्ति ।
Awakened Power	प्रबुद्धा शक्ति । व्यक्ता शक्ति । योगोन्मुखी शक्ति ।
Power of selfmanifestation Power of selfexpression	आत्मप्रकाशिनी शक्ति । आत्मविलासिनी शक्ति । आत्माभिव्यक्ति शक्ति । विमर्श शक्ति ।
Power of selfenjoyment	आत्मास्वादिनी शक्ति । आत्म-विनोदिनी शक्ति । ह्लादिनी शक्ति ।
Power of selfilluminattion	स्वप्रकाश शक्ति ।
Power of self-diversification	आत्म-बहुत्व-बिधायिनी शक्ति । आत्मवैचित्र्य-प्रसविनी नानाकार विलासिनी शक्ति ।

Power of creation	सृष्टि शक्ति।
Power of Preservation ,, ,, Sustenance	स्थिति-शक्ति। पालिनी-शक्ति। रक्षा विधायिनी शक्ति।
Power of Destruction	संहारिणी शक्ति। ध्वंसकारिणी शक्ति।
Power of Dissolution	प्रलयकारिणी शक्ति। शोषिणी शक्ति।
Power of Annihilation	विलोपकारिणी शक्ति।
Power of Harmonisation ,, of Unification	समरसकरण-शक्ति। एकीकरण-शक्ति। एकत्व-विधायिनी शक्ति।
Power of Assimilation	आत्मसातकारिणी-शक्ति। ग्रासिनी-शक्ति। पाचिनी शक्ति। अंगीकरण शक्ति।
Power of Spiritualisation	चिन्मयत्व-संपादिनी शक्ति।
Power of materialisation	जड़त्व-संपादिनी शक्ति। स्थूलत्व-संपादिनी शक्ति।
Power of Self-expansion	आत्मप्रसारण-शक्ति।
Power of Self unfoldment	आत्म-विकाश-शक्ति।
Power of Self-contraction	आत्म संकोचन-शक्ति।
Power of Self-veiling	आत्मावरण-शक्ति।
Reality	सद् वस्तु। सत्ता। वास्तव वस्तु। भाव-वस्तु। तत्व।
Objective Reality	प्रमाण-गोचर वस्तु या तत्व। प्रमेय या ज्ञेय वस्तु। व्यावहारिक सत्ता विशिष्ट ज्ञेय विषय। दृश्य सत्ता।
Phenomenal Reality	See Phenomenal Existence.
Subjective Reality	भावनामय या विज्ञानमय सत्व। दृक्-सत्ता। आन्तर सत्ता।
Imaginary Reality	कल्पित सत्व।
Externel Reality	बाह्य सत्व।
Internal Reality	आन्तर सत्व।

Transcendental Reality The same as Transcendental Existence.

Absolute Reality-See adove.

Realities of the same order	समसत्ताक पदार्थ।
Realities of different orders	विषमसत्ताक पदार्थ।

Planes of Realities-The same as Planes of existence,	
Inexplicable Reality	अनिर्वचनीय भाव-पदार्थ । अनिर्वाच्य तत्व ।
Both-real-and-unrcal	सदसत् तत्व ।
Neither-real-nor-unreal	सदसद्भ्याम् अनिर्वचनीय । न सत् न असत् । निःसदसत् तत्व ।
Unreal	मिथ्या । असत् । तुच्छ । अलीक ।
Illusory Reality	प्रातीतिक या प्रातिभासिक सत्व ।
Self-Perfect-Reality	स्वयं पूर्ण तत्व ।
Void	शून्य । असदभाव । व्यावहारिक-सत्ता-भाव । असत् । व्यावहारिक तथा प्रातिभासिक सत्तातीत पारमार्थिक तत्व ।
Fulness	पूर्णता ।
Action	कर्म ।
Fruits of actions Effects of actions	कर्म फल ।
Visible effects of actions Perceptible ,, ,, Physical ,, ,,	दृष्ट-फल । प्रत्यक्ष गोचर फल ।
Invisible or imperceptible effects of actions Moral effects of actions	अदृष्ट फल । पुण्य पापात्मक फल । अपूर्व फल । धर्मविधानानुसारी फल । भाविप्रसू-सुख दुःख स्वर्ग नरकादि-जनक फल । प्रत्यक्षागोचर फल ।
Psychological effects of actions.	प्रवृत्ति-संस्कारादि जनकत्व रूप फल । शुभाशुभ-चित्तवृत्ति-जनकत्व रूप फल ।
Matured actions Fructifying actions	प्रारब्ध कर्म । वर्तमान-जन्म-विधायक तथा जात्यायु-र्भोगादि नियामक प्राक्तन कर्म ।
Accumulated actions	संचित कर्म ।
Current actions	क्रियमाण ।
Virtuous or pious actions.	पुण्य कर्म । शुक्ल कर्म । शुभफलदायी कर्म ।
Vicious or sinful actions.	पापकर्म । कृष्ण कर्म । अशुभफलदायी कर्म ।

Neither-virtuous-nor vicious actions	अशुक्लाकृष्ण कर्म। मुक्त कर्म । जीवन्मुक्त कर्म। अपुण्यपापात्मक कर्म । शुभाशुभफलदायित्य विहीन कर्म।
Partly virtuous and partly vicious actions	मिश्र कर्म। पूण्य पापात्मक कर्म। शुभाशुभ-उभय-विधिफलदायी कर्म।
Desireless actians	निष्काम कर्म।
Actions enjoined or approved by scriptures.	विहित कर्म।
Actions prohibited or disapproved by scriptures	निषिद्ध कर्म। अविहित कर्म।
Daily duties Duties of perfect oblgation	नित्य कर्म। नियत कर्म।
Occasional duties.	नैमित्तिक कर्म।
Actions tor the fulfilment of desires.	काम्य कर्म ।
Actions for the fulfil-ment of worldly desires.	ऐहिक कर्म ।
Actions for the fulfil ment of other-wordly desires.	पारत्रिक या पारलौकिक कर्म।
Actions fcr the sake of God, Actions for pleasing God.	ईश्वरार्थ कर्म। ईश्वरप्रीत्यर्थ कर्म।
Sacrificial actions	याज्ञिक कर्म।
Substance	द्रव्य। वस्तु।
Attribute	गुण। विशेषण।
Attributeless	निर्गुण।
Space	देश। दिक्।
Time	काल।
Coexistence	सहवर्तित्व। सहावस्थान। समकालवर्तित्व। साहचर्य। सहभावित्व।

Succession	पर्वापरभावित्य । पौर्वापर्य ।
Invariable coexistence	नियतसहभावित्व ।
Invariable succession.	नियतपूर्वापरभावित्व ।
Dualism	द्वैतवाद Pluralism बहुत्ववाद ।
Materialism	जडवाद । लोकायतवाद ।
Non-dualism	अद्वैतवाद । निर्गुण ब्रह्मवाद ।
Qualified Non-dualism	विशिष्टाद्वैतवाद ।
Dualism-cum-non-dualism	द्वैताद्वैतवाद ।
Pure Non-dualism	विशुद्धाद्वैतवाद
Theism	ईश्वरवाद । सगुण ब्रह्मवाद ।